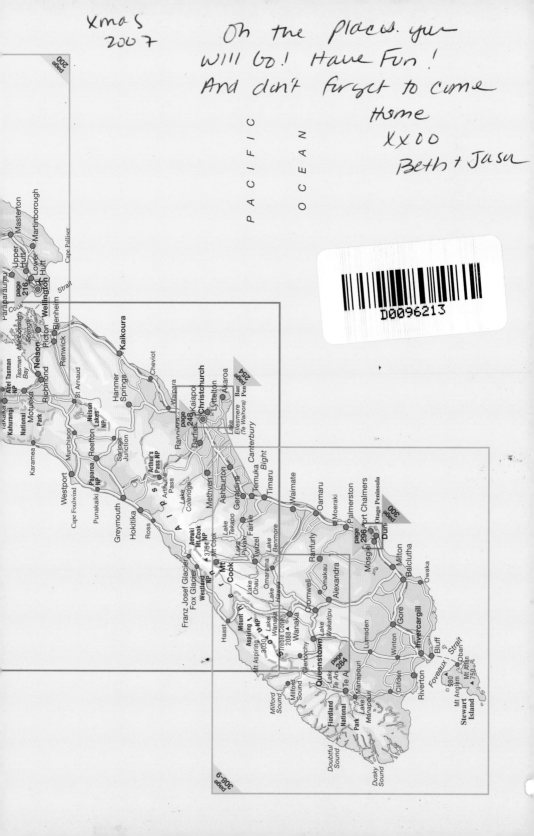

Xmas
2007

Oh the places you
will Go! Have Fun!
And don't forget to come
Home
XXOO
Beth + Jasa

PACIFIC

OCEAN

D0096213

INSIGHT GUIDES

New Zealand

APA PUBLICATIONS

Part of the Langenscheidt Publishing Group

INSIGHT GUIDE

New Zealand

Editorial

Project Editor
Francis Dorai
Editorial Director
Brian Bell

Distribution

UK & Ireland
GeoCenter International Ltd
Meridian House, Churchill Way West
Basingstoke, Hampshire RG21 6YR
Fax: (44) 1256-817988

United States
Langenscheidt Publishers, Inc.
36–36 33rd Street, 4th Floor
Long Island City, NY 11106
Fax: (1) 718 784-0640

Australia
Universal Publishers
1 Waterloo Road
Macquarie Park, NSW 2113
Fax: (61) 2 9888 9074

New Zealand
Hema Maps New Zealand Ltd (HNZ)
Unit D, 24 Ra ORA Drive
East Tamaki, Auckland
Fax: (64) 9 273 6479

Worldwide
**Apa Publications GmbH & Co.
Verlag KG (Singapore branch)**
38 Joo Koon Road, Singapore 628990
Tel: (65) 6865-1600. Fax: (65) 6861-6438

Printing

Insight Print Services (Pte) Ltd
38 Joo Koon Road, Singapore 628990
Tel: (65) 6865-1600. Fax: (65) 6861-6438

©2007 Apa Publications GmbH & Co.
Verlag KG (Singapore branch)
All Rights Reserved
First Edition 1984
Seventh Edition 2004
Updated 2007

CONTACTING THE EDITORS

We would appreciate it if readers
would alert us to errors or out-
dated information by writing to:
**Insight Guides, P.O. Box 7910,
London SE1 1WE, England.
Fax: (44) 20 7403-0290.
insight@apaguide.co.uk**

www.insightguides.com
In North America:
www.insighttravelguides.com

ABOUT THIS BOOK

The first Insight Guide pioneered the use of creative full-colour photography in travel guides in 1970. Since then, we have expanded our range to cater for our readers' need not only for reliable information about their chosen destination but also for a real understanding of that destination. Now, when the Internet can supply inexhaustible – but not always reliable – facts, our books marry text and pictures to provide those much more elusive qualities: knowledge and discernment. To achieve this, they rely heavily on the authority of locally-based writers and photographers.

Insight Guide New Zealand has been carefully structured to convey the startling beauty of the country, provide a keen insight into its culture and people, and guide readers to its various sights and activities.

◆ The **Features** section, indicated by a yellow bar at the top of each page, covers the history and culture of the country in a series of authoritative essays written by specialists.

◆ The main **Places** section, indicated by a blue bar, provides a full run-down of all the attractions worth seeing. The principal places of interest are cross-referenced by number to maps.

◆ The **Travel Tips** section, with an orange bar, provides a handy point of reference for information on getting around, hotels, restaurants, outdoor activities and more.

The contributors

This fully revised and updated edition was produced by **Francis Dorai**, Insight Guides' Singapore-based managing editor. It builds on the best-selling earlier edition produced by **Craig Dowling** in 1998. Existing chapters were expanded and updated, and several new features were commissioned to reflect the vibrancy of New Zealand in the 21st century.

Striking new photography – from picture agencies **Photo New Zealand** and **Fotopress** – was also added.

Anchoring this edition was Auckland-native **Paul Little**, a veteran writer of print, radio and TV, and former editor of *Metro* and *The New Zealand Listener* magazines. He revised a substantial part of the book (including Travel Tips) and assembled an accomplished team of local writers to update the existing text as well as write several new chapters.

Denis Welch, the former arts and books editor of *The New Zealand Listener*, was the ideal choice for the chapter on Contemporary Art and Literature. The feature on Performing Arts, Music and Film was written by **Philip Matthews**, also a former arts editor with *The New Zealand Listener*. Lending her expertise to the info panel on Contemporary Maori Art was **Ngarino Ellis**, a Maori lecturer on art history at the University of Auckland.

Cuisine is a subject close to the heart of ex-restaurateur **Lois Daish**. Complementing it is the feature on Wines by **Keith Stewart**, an art and wine critic, and writer of the book *Taste of the Earth: Creating New Zealand's Fine Wine*.

The chapter on Outdoor Activities was the work of **Angie Belcher**, a writer who also happens to be an adventure sports enthusiast.

The chapters on Auckland and Auckland's Surroundings were by **Peter Calder**. Nelson-based writer **Gerard Hindmarsh** revised the chapters on Nelson and Marlborough, West Coast and Southland. Finally, New Zealand wildlife expert **Brian Parkinson** wrote Stewart Island and the info panel on Flora and Fauna.

Past contributors whose work remains in this edition include **David McGill** (Wellington); **Graeme Stevens** (Natural History); **Michael King** (Arrival of the Maori, Modern Maori); **Gordon McLauchlan** (Voyages of Discovery, Settlement and Colonisation, Antarctica); **Terence Barrow** (Maori Art); **Janet Leggett** (Waikato); **John Harvey** (Taranaki, Wanganui and Manawatu); **Geoff Conly** (Poverty Bay and Hawke's Bay); **John Goulter** (Christchurch); **Robin Charteris** (Dunedin); **Les Bloxham** (Canterbury, West Coast); **Anne Stark** (Queenstown and Central Otago); **Clive Lind** (Southland); **Joseph Frahm** (Coromandel and Bay of Plenty); **William Hobbs** (Nelson and Marlborough); **Colin Taylor** (Rotorua); **Jack Adlington** (Northland) and **Jane Wynyard** (Travel Tips).

In 2007 the guide was updated by **Helen West**, who also wrote the People feature. The update was supervised by **Low Jat Leng** at Insight Guides' Singapore office.

Map Legend

● – – –	National Park/ Nature Reserve
– – – –	Ferry Route
✈	Airport
🚌	Bus Station
P	Parking
❶	Tourist Information
✉	Post Office
✝	Church/Ruins
	Mosque
✡	Synagogue
	Castle/Ruins
∴	Archaeological Site
∩	Cave
★	Place of Interest

The main places of interest in the Places section are coordinated by number with a full-colour map (e.g. ❶), and a symbol at the top of every right-hand page tells you where to find the map.

CONTENTS

Maps

North Island **130**
Auckland **134**
Auckland and
Surroundings **149**
Northland **158**
Central North
Island **172**
Rotorua **184**
Southern North
Island **200**
Wellington **216**
South Island **230**
Northern South
Island **234**
Christchurch **248**
Banks Peninsula **254**
Queenstown and
Surroundings **284**
Dunedin **296**
Otago Peninsula **300**
Southern South
Island **308**

New Zealand
inside front cover

Auckland
inside back cover

Introduction

The Best of New Zealand **6**
Aotearoa **13**

History

Chronology **16**
Arrival of the Maori.................**19**
Voyages of Discovery **25**
Settlement and Colonisation....**31**
A New Nation........................**39**

Features

Natural History **49**
People **61**
The Modern Maori **69**
Ancient Maori Art and Society ..**75**
Contemporary Art and
Literature **85**
Performing Arts, Music
and Film **91**
Cuisine.................................**99**
Wines **107**
Outdoor Activities **113**

Information panels

Unique Flora and Fauna...........**55**
What Makes a New Zealander..**67**
Contemporary Maori Art..........**81**
Lord of the Rings Locations.....**95**
The Farming Life....................**104**
Trendsetting Kiwi Fashion......**145**
South Island Tracks..............**243**
Antarctica...........................**258**

Insight on....

National Parks.......................**46**
Maori Handicrafts..................**82**
Thrillseekers' Paradise..........**120**
Rotorua's Thermal Activity.....**196**

Travel Tips

Getting Acquainted **324**

Planning the Trip **325**

Practical Tips **328**

Getting Around **330**

Where to Stay **332**

What to Eat **333**

Culture **334**

Festivals **335**

Shopping **338**

Outdoor Activities **339**

Further Reading **342**

North Island **343**

South Island **369**

◆Full Travel Tips index
is on page 323

Places

Introduction **129**

North Island

Introduction **131**
Auckland...............................**133**
Auckland's Surroundings **147**
Northland **157**
Waikato **165**
Coromandel and the
    Bay of Plenty **171**
Rotorua and the
    Volcanic Plateau...............**183**
Poverty Bay and Hawke's Bay..**199**
Taranaki, Wanganui and
    Manawatu **209**
Wellington............................**215**

South Island

Introduction **231**
Nelson and Marlborough **233**
Christchurch **247**
Canterbury **261**
The West Coast **271**
Queenstown and Otago **283**
Dunedin **295**
Southland **307**
Stewart Island......................**316**

THE BEST OF NEW ZEALAND

The unique attractions of New Zealand, absorbing museums, dynamic culture, breathtaking landscapes, exciting adventure activities... here, at a glance, are our recommendations, plus some tips that even New Zealanders won't always know

ABOVE: the flightless kakapo parrot, found on Ulva Island.

NEW ZEALAND FOR FAMILIES

● **Kelly Tarlton's Antarctic Encounter and Underwater World, Auckland.** Get up close and personal with sharks, rays, piranhas, turtles, crayfish, moray eels and brightly coloured fish. *Page 143*

● **Rainbow's End, Manukau, South Auckland.** Go crazy with the kids in New Zealand's premier theme park. *Page 150*
● **Wellington Cable Car.** Jump on for the 5-minute ride up the hill from Lambton Quay to the Botanic Gardens entrance. There are great views and an excellent children's playground in the gardens. *Page 220*

ABOVE: wacky Puzzling World.
RIGHT: the Champagne Pool at Wai-O-Tapu Thermal Wonderland.

● **Canterbury Museum & Christchurch Botanic Gardens, Christchurch.** Kids will love **Discovery**, the Museum's natural history centre for children, brimming with weird and wonderful exhibits. Outdoors in the gardens, there are trees to climb and lakes to explore, plus a playground and a children's outdoor pool in summer. *Pages 251–2*
● **Puzzling World, Wanaka.** Be amazed, dumbfounded and totally disorientated in this zany park of optical illusions. *Page 292*

ONLY IN NEW ZEALAND

● **Rotorua.** The Maori cultural hot spot and geothermal wonderland – don't leave town without experiencing a **Maori cultural performance and *hangi* meal**. *Pages 183–7, 196–7*
● **Napier.** Visit this architecturally unique town rebuilt entirely in the style of the times – art deco – after a devastating earthquake in 1931. *Pages 203–5*

● **TranzAlpine Express.** Hop on one of the world's greatest rail journeys connecting New Zealand's east and west coasts via mountain passes, tunnels and the impressive Otira viaduct. *Page 263*
● **Ulva Island.** Take a guided walk to spot kiwis and even the exceedingly rare flightless parrot, the kakapo. *Pages 55, 317–8*

TOP HISTORICAL SIGHTS

● **Waitangi National Trust Treaty House and Grounds, Northland.** The scene of one of the most significant events in New Zealand's early history. *Page 158*
● **Waipoua Kauri Forest, Northland.** Awe-inspiring natural history; this is the home of ancient kauri trees. The oldest giants, Te Matua Ngahere and Tane Mahuta, are millennia old. *Page 163*
● **Arrowtown, Otago.** Journey back in time along the streets and in the museums of this picturesque former gold-mining town. It's prettiest in autumn when gold adorns the trees. *Pages 288–9*
● **Dunedin.** Amble around this town and enjoy its unique Victorian, Edwardian and art deco architectural heritage. Don't miss the **Dunedin Railway Station**, the country's most photographed building. *Pages 295–300*
● **Taieri Gorge Railway, Otago.** Vintage rail at its best, traversing one of the country's greatest rail journeys through stunning Southland. *Page 303*

ABOVE: the Dunedin Railway Station.

BEST ARTS AND CULTURE EXPERIENCES

ABOVE: Te Papa Tongarewa Museum.

● **Auckland War Memorial Museum.** Newly revamped and home to the world's finest collection of Maori and Polynesian artefacts, Maori cultural performances and so much more. *Page 142*
● **Whakarewarewa Thermal Valley, Rotorua.** See culture in action at the geothermally powered Maori village and the nearby **Te Puia Maori Arts and Crafts Institute**. *Pages 186–7*
● **Te Papa Tongarewa – Museum of New Zealand, Wellington.** Art, artefacts, natural history and hands-on interactive fun for kids (don't miss the earthquake house) – this state-of-the-art museum has it all. *Pages 217–8*
● **Court Threatre, Christchurch Arts Centre.** World-class theatre down under. *See page 251*
● **Dunedin Public Art Gallery.** Home to one of the country's finest collections of national and international art. *Page 297*

BEST NATURAL ATTRACTIONS

● **Tongariro National Park, North Island.** Hike the **Tongariro Crossing**, ski the slopes, mountain bike or simply drive along the volcanic loop to take in the three volcanoes of Ruapehu, Ngauruhoe and Tongariro. *Pages 194–5*
● **Coastal Kaikoura.** Go whale watching, swim with the rare Hector's dolphins, watch the antics of Dusky dolphins, spot albatross and more – the choices are yours. *Pages 236–7, 371*
● **Abel Tasman National Park.** Paradise on earth for campers, kayakers and hikers. Its Coastal Track offers exceptional views. *Pages 239–40, 243*
● **Arthur's Pass National Park.** A skiing and hiking mountain playground with awesome alpine scenery. *Page 263*
● **Punakaiki, West Coast.** Spectacular petrified pancake rocks and blowholes complemented by stunning coastal views. *Pages 278–9*
● **Stewart Island.** A birdwatcher's heaven with unique ecology; a wonderland of rainforests, high granite peaks, white sandy shores and deep inlets. *Pages 316–9*

BELOW: Kaikoura is the world's whale-watching capital.

BEST WINING AND DINING

ABOVE: New Zealand wines are among the world's best.

● **Bluff Oyster and Southland Seafood Festival, Bluff.** An annual celebration of Southland's most sought-after delicacy. *Pages 310, 336*
● **Dine by Peter Gordon, Auckland.** At celebrity chef Peter Gordon's restaurant at Sky City Grand Hotel, superbly crafted fare with a hint of Kiwiana is presented. *Page 344*

● **The French Café, Auckland.** Winner of the 2006 *Cuisine* magazine's Restaurant of the Year Award. Enjoy an authentic taste of France in downtown Auckland. *Page 345*
● **Nelson.** A must for lovers of good food and seafood; enjoy the catch of the day at any of the excellent eateries in this town. *Page 372*
● **Winery eateries** throughout the land offer the best of both worlds. Check out **Amisfield Bistro, Queenstown**, an award-winning winery bistro serving great food and wine with views to match. Nearby is the equally stunning **Gibbston Valley Wines**, where you can also go on a tour of its 76-metre (250-ft)-long wine cave. *Page 383*

BEST FESTIVALS AND EVENTS

● **World of Wearable Art Awards, Wellington.** An international fashion extravaganza of wild, weird and wonderfully wacky wearable art See it at the Queens Wharf Events Centre. *Pages 238–9, 337*
● **Hokitiki's Wild Foods Festival.** Fancy some possum pie or huhu grub sushi? Shock your taste buds with some of the wildest local fare around. *Pages 276, 335*
● **Pasifika Festival, Auckland.** The world's largest Pacific Island festival, a fabulously vibrant one-day celebration of all things Pasifika – food, art, theatre and more. *Page 335*
● **Queenstown Winter Festival.** Enjoy winter

ABOVE: wild foods – not for the faint-hearted.

sports and one of the southern hemisphere's biggest winter parties. *Page 336, 381*
● **Ellerslie Flower Show**, Auckland. The southern hemisphere's largest floral exhibition combines floral art with great food, wine and entertainment. *Page 337*

BELOW: the famous Hole in the Rock in the Bay of Islands.

MOST BREATHTAKING VIEWS

● **Bay of Islands, Northland.** A 800-km (500-mile) rugged coastline embracing 150 islands and steeped in history, where beauty knows no bounds. *Pages 157–63*
● **Waitomo Caves.** A magical subterranean world of stunning natural sculptures, stalactites and stalagmites lit by thousands of glowworms. *Page 169*
● **Fiordland National Park.** Scenery at its

most stunning with jewels such as the spectacular **Mitre Peak**, **Milford Sound**, and **Doubtful Sound**. *Pages 243, 313–31*
● **South Westland.** Travel along the spectacular **Haast Pass** Heritage Highway, the only crossing between Otago and Westland, and take in the magnificent **Fox** and **Franz Josef glaciers**. *Pages 273–76*

BEST SHOPPING EXPERIENCES

● **Queen Street, Auckland.** For things antique, boutique and unique, from something to wear or wares of all sorts, Queen Street offers some of the best shopping in New Zealand. *Pages 138–9*

● **Victoria Park Market, Auckland.** Open daily for the real outdoor market experience; offers everything from antiques, clothing and crafts to fruit and vegetables. *Page 143*

● **Arts Centre Galleria and Weekend Market, Christchurch.** Showcases a great array of New Zealand crafts and art; a great browsing experience even if you're not buying. *Page 251*

● **The Cabbage Tree, Paihia, Bay of Islands.** Bring home some Kiwiana from these fantastic shops. Take your pick from handcrafted glassware, greenstone jewellery and more. *Page 351*

ABOVE: work up an adrenaline rush – try tandem skydiving.

BELOW: Victoria Park Market.

BEST ADVENTURE ACTIVITIES

● **Dive off the Poor Knights Islands.** Discover a microcosm of underwater diversity amid dense kelp forests, drop-offs and massive sea caves, notably Riko Riko, the world's largest. *Page 117*

● **Tandem Skydiving.** Free-fall attached to a parachute and a skydiving professional who pulls the cord just in time for the perfect touchdown. *Pages 120–1*

● **Base Jumping, Auckland.** For a view with a difference, leap off Auckland's highest structure, the Sky Tower – suitably restrained, of course. *Pages 139, 346*

● **Bungy Jumping, Queenstown.** Take the plunge off where it first began – the Kawarau Bridge, home of the bungy, or have a go at the Nevis Highwire or the Ledge. *Pages 119, 286, 288, 381*

● **Jet Boating, Queenstown.** Jump in and hold on tight – jet boat-powered thrills and spills on the Shotover River. *Page 288*

MONEY-SAVING TIPS

● Pick up free maps and accommodation guides at **Automobile Association outlets** and **i-Site Visitor Centres** throughout the country.

● **Kids' holiday specials.** During New Zealand school holidays (April and December to early February), **Real Journeys** (www.realjourneys.

co.nz), one of the largest operators in the South Island, offers free travel for children under 18 years (maximum two kids free per paying adult) on many of their excursions.

● **Museums and botanic gardens.** Hours of pleasure to be had for free exploring the country's museums and botanic gardens, all of which have

great play areas for children. In summer kids can enjoy splashing around in the open-air pool at the Christchurch Botanic Gardens.

● **Camping and walking.** Immerse yourself in the great outdoors – the fabulous walks and beaches and breathtaking views throughout Godzone are free for all.

AOTEAROA

*How did New Zealand become home to so many natural
marvels? An ancient myth may hold the answer*

New Zealand – called Aotearoa, "land of the long white cloud",
by the Maori – is breathtakingly beautiful, a land of majestic
snow-capped peaks and unexplored rainforests, of pristine
lakes swarming with trout and turquoise ocean bays speckled with
wooded isles, of glaciers and fiords, geysers and volcanoes. And you
don't have to travel enormous distances to experience the many
aspects of its spectacular landscapes – an alpine peak can be just a
short drive from a barren desert, a primeval beach minutes from a
busy city. There are kauri forests and kiwi fruit plantations, modern
cosmopolitan cities and back-country sheep stations, and a range of
wildlife that is quite unique, including the flightless kiwi – the symbol of New Zealand – and the prehistoric tuatara.

There are two main islands, North and South, plus little Stewart
Island off the southern tip, and a number of uninhabited islands,
some of which have been made into nature reserves. The North
Island has the largest population, though there are still vast expanses
of empty landscapes; the South Island is wilder and more spectacular – the "Middle Earth" of the film version of the *Lord of the Rings*
trilogy. It is a combination of a land that time forgot, completely
uninhabited until relatively recent times, and a land that is impossible to forget. But first, it was the land of the Maori.

Anthropologists tell of a remarkable migration as the Polynesian
ancestors of the Maori moved through the Pacific, arriving on these
islands by outrigger canoe from about AD 800. Maori legend tells a
much more evocative story, about the birth of all life in the stillness
of a long dark night, Te Po, from the primordial parents – Rangi, the
sky father, and Papa, the earth mother. Tane, their eldest son and god
of the forests, pulled himself free of his parents in the darkness and
struggled to push them apart, but Rangi's sorrow at parting from his
mate caused his tears to flow, filling Papa's (that is, the land's) surface with oceans and lakes.

Its natural wonders have made New Zealand a recreational wonderland, and New Zealanders love the outdoors – from the rugby
fields to the ski fields, from barbecues to bungy-jumping. While
preserving their natural gifts, they have used them not only as a spectacular backdrop for thrilling adventures (and films), but also to
produce some of the world's finest food and wine, to create great art
and to make leisure and recreation part of daily life. They are an active
people, but they are reflective too, taking pride in what they have and
what they do. Above all, they are eager to share their marvellous
country and its bounty with all visitors. *Haere mai*. Welcome. ❏

PRECEDING PAGES: various Kiwi transports of delight – by jeep on Northland's Ninety
Mile Beach; and by Shotover Jet around the very ragged rocks of Shotover River.
LEFT: Pohutu Geyser at Rotorua.

Decisive Dates

Prehistoric times

130 million years ago The most isolated land mass on earth that will eventually contain New Zealand breaks away from New Caledonia, eastern Australia, Tasmania and Antarctica.

80 million years ago New Zealand becomes physically independent, splitting from Gondwana as the Tasman Sea begins to take shape.

60 million years ago New Zealand reaches its present distance from Australia of more than 1,500 km (930 miles).

Traders and explorers

AD 800 About now the first Polynesians arrive, according to tradition, with the voyager Kupe, who names the country Aotearoa, or Land of The Long White Cloud, and later returns to his native Hawaiiki.

1300s A wave of immigrants arrive, it is said, from Hawaiiki, in 12 outrigger canoes. They bring taro, yam, kumara (sweet potato), the rat and the dog.

1642 Abel Tasman, of Dutch East India Co., is first European to sight the land; names it Nieuw Zeeland.

1769 Englishman Captain James Cook is the first European to land and explore New Zealand.

1791–2 Deep-sea whaling begins.

1814 Church Missionary Society (Anglican) begins at Rangihoua, Bay of Islands.

1815 First Pakeha (white European) child, Thomas King, born.

1818 "Musket Wars" begin as Maori appropriate muskets from Europeans. About 20,000 people killed in 12 years of inter-tribal conflict.

1839 Captain W.B. Rhodes establishes first cattle station on the South Island, at Akaroa.

Colonisation

1840 New Zealand Company colonists reach Port Nicholson, Wellington, and establish settlements there. Some 50 Maori chiefs sign the Treaty of Waitangi, ceding sovereignty to Queen Victoria. In return the queen guarantees Maori possession of the lands, forests, fisheries and other property. Lieutenant-Governor William Hobson chooses Auckland as the capital.

1844 Hone Heke, the first Maori to sign the Treaty of Waitangi, cuts down its symbol, the flagstaff at Kororareka, three times, and sacks and burns the town, in protest over land disputes. About 1,000 Maori take arms against the British.

1848 Otago on the South Island is settled by a community of Scottish farmers.

1850 Canterbury is settled.

1852 The colonisation of Taranaki is begun by the Plymouth Company.

1853 The Maori King movement takes off, centred in the Waikato-Maniapoto tribes, designed to protect tribal land.

1856 New Zealand becomes a self-governing British colony. Gold rush and land struggles.

1860 Wiremu Kingi's claim to the Waitara starts the Maori Land Wars; vast tracts of land are confiscated from rebel tribes.

1861 Otago gold rush begins when Gabriel Read makes discovery at Blue Spur, Tuapeka.

1865 Wellington becomes the capital.

1866 Cook Strait submarine telegraph cable is laid.

1867 Maoris are given the vote.

1868 Raids from Maori leaders Titokowaru and Te Kooti throw the colony into crisis.

1869 Te Kooti defeated at Ngatapa. Otago University, New Zealand's first, established.

1870 First rugby match is played.

1877 Treaty of Waitangi ruled "a simple nullity" by Chief Justice Prendergast. Free compulsory education introduced.

1881 Parihaka Maori religious community broken up by troops.

1882 The first refrigerated agricultural produce cargo is dispatched to England.

1886 Mount Tarawera erupts, resulting in the loss of some 153 lives.

Social reforms and world wars
1893 Women are given the vote, 25 years before this happens in Britain and the USA.
1896 Maori population down to 42,000 (from 100,000 in 1769) due to disease.
1898 World's first old-age pension for men introduced by Liberal Richard Seddon. First cars imported.
1899–1902 New Zealand troops fight in Boer War.
1901 Cook Islands are annexed.
1904 Richard Pearse believed to have achieved first artificially powered flight, near Timaru.
1907 New Zealand is elevated from a colony to dominion.
1908 Ernest Rutherford awarded Nobel Prize for Chemistry. Population exceeds 1 million.
1914 The first New Zealand feature film, *Hinemoa*, is released.
1915 New Zealand suffers heavy losses during the Gallipoli campaign of World War I.
1918–19 Influenza epidemic kills 6,700.
1926 National public broadcasting begins.
1938 Health care and social security are introduced.
1939 World War II breaks out. New Zealand again suffers heavy losses.

An independent nation
1947 New Zealand becomes fully independent.
1951 Anzus defence alliance with Australia and the United States signed.
1953 New Zealander Edmund Hillary and Nepal's Tenzing Norgay become the first to reach the summit of Mount Everest.
1956 Colin Murdoch invents the disposable syringe.
1958 Hillary reaches the South Pole by land.
1959 Auckland Harbour Bridge opens.
1961 Capital punishment is abolished.
1962 Maurice Wilkins shares Nobel Prize in physiology and medicine for discovery of DNA.
1963 William Lilley performs the first blood transfusion on a foetus with blood incompatible with the mother's.
1965 Troops sent to Vietnam.
1967 Sir Arthur Porritt becomes first New Zealand-born Governor-General.
1968 The ferry *Wahine* is wrecked on a reef near Wellington Harbour in a storm which kills 51 people.
1971 New Zealand joins South Pacific Forum. A period of economic trouble and strife begins.
1973 Britain joins Common Market, depriving New Zealand of its traditional market for primary produce.

LEFT: a Maori girl of yesteryear.
RIGHT: NZ's defence forces on parade at Wellington.

1975 Parliament passes the Treaty of Waitangi Act, establishing a tribunal to investigate claims.
1977 *Sleeping Dogs*, starring Sam Neill, marks rebirth of New Zealand film-making.
1981 Anti-apartheid protests during a tour by a South African rugby team see unprecedented civil unrest.
1983 Closer Economic Relations Agreement is signed with Australia.
1985 Greenpeace nuclear-protest vessel *Rainbow Warrior* is bombed by French secret agents in Auckland. Sir Paul Reeves becomes first Maori Governor-General. Welfare state dismembered in drastic programme of economic reform. Government bans visits by ships carrying nuclear weapons.

1987 Maori becomes an official language by law.
1993 Proportional representation election system, MMP (Mixed Member Proportional) introduced.
1994 *The Piano* wins three Academy Awards.
1995 New Zealand wins the America's Cup.
1997 Resignation of Jim Bolger. National Party's Jenny Shipley appointed as New Zealand's first woman Prime Minister.
1999 Labour Party's Helen Clark is New Zealand's first elected woman Prime Minister.
2001 World premiere of the first part of *Lord of the Rings* by New Zealand director Peter Jackson.
2003 Population hits the 4 million mark.
2005 Civil Union Act passed, giving same sex couples the equivalent legal rights as married couples. ❏

ARRIVAL OF THE MAORI

In around AD 800, Polynesian settlers arrived in New Zealand

and evolved a sophisticated and highly organised culture

Apart from Antarctica, New Zealand was the last major land mass to be explored by people. These earliest Pacific navigators preceded those from Europe by some 800 years. They were "Vikings of the Sunrise" and their descendants came to be called Maori.

Few subjects have been the source of more controversy than the origins of the Maori. Nineteenth-century scholars devised bizarre theories. Some asserted Maori were wandering Aryans, others believed that they were originally Hindu, and some thought that they were indisputably a lost tribe of Israel. Interpretations of evidence in the 20th century were more cautious, and the current consensus among scholars is that Maori were descendants of Austronesian people who originated in Southeast Asia. A few authorities still dispute this. Minority opinions have suggested they came from Egypt, Mesopotamia or South America.

Factual evidence

Linguistic and archaeological evidence establishes, however, that New Zealand Maori are Polynesian people; and that the ancestors of the Polynesians sailed into the South China Sea from the Asian mainland some 2,000 to 3,000 years ago. Some went southwest, ultimately to Madagascar; others southeast along the Malaysian, Indonesian and Philippine island chains. What appears to have inspired these vast journeys was the introduction of the sail to Southeast Asia and the invention of the outrigger. In the Austronesian languages shared by the people of the Pacific and the Southeast Asian archipelagos, the words for sail, mast, outrigger float and outrigger boom are among the most widespread and therefore among the oldest.

The Pacific Austronesians who made their way along the Melanesian chain of islands, reaching Fiji by about 1300 BC and Tonga before 1100 BC, left behind fragments of pottery with distinctive decorations. This pottery has been called Lapita, and the same name has been applied by archaeologists to the people who made it. With their pottery they also carried pigs, dogs, rats, fowl and cultivated plants. All of these originated on the mainland of Southeast Asia, except the yellow-fleshed kumara, a

sweet potato originally from South America.

Polynesian culture as recognised today evolved among the Lapita people in Tonga and Samoa. It was from East Polynesia, possibly from the Society Islands or Marquesas Islands, that a migration was eventually launched to New Zealand. The East Polynesian characteristics of early Maori remains, the earliest carbon dates and, the rate of growth and spread of the Maori population all indicate that a landfall was made in New Zealand around AD 800.

The land was unlike anything that Polynesians had encountered elsewhere in the Pacific. It was far larger – more than 1,500 km (over 900 miles) from north to south – and more var-

LEFT: a Maori chief as depicted by Sydney Parkinson, an artist on one of Captain James Cook's expeditions.

RIGHT: Maori feather box.

ied than islands they had colonised previously. Mountains were higher, rivers wider. It was temperate rather than tropical and sufficiently cold in much of the South Island to prevent the growing of traditional crops. They had to adapt to a range of climatic conditions they had never previously experienced. Other than bats, there were no mammals ashore until the ancestors of the Maori released the rats (*kiore*) and dogs (*kuri*) they had brought with them. They probably also brought pigs and fowl. These animals did not survive, but the ancestors of the Maori did, showing great fortitude and adaptability.

The lack of meat was compensated for by an abundance of seafood and aquatic mammals: whales, dolphins and seals, plus edible seaweed. Inland waterways contained additional resources: waterfowl, eel, fish and more shellfish and there were nearly 200 species of bird, many of them palatable. In addition, meat was temporarily available from the limited supply of dogs and rats they brought with them.

The land provided fern root that offered a staple food (though it had to be heavily pounded). To all these the immigrants added the cultivated vegetables they had imported: taro, kumara, yam, gourds and the paper mulberry.

Perhaps the most spectacular of the new

The New Zealand forests contained larger trees than Polynesians would previously have seen. This enabled them to build bigger dugout canoes, and also resulted in a fine tradition of woodcarving. Later, they used wooden beams in their houses. Materials such as *raupo* and *nikau* made excellent walls and roofs. Flax plaited into cords provided fine fibre for garments and baskets. There was stone for adzes and drill points, bone for fishhooks and ornaments, and obsidian for flake knives. With these materials, the New Zealand Polynesians developed one of the world's most sophisticated neolithic cultures.

country's resources was the huge flightless bird, the moa. There were several species, ranging from the turkey-sized *anomalopteryx* to the gigantic *dinornis maximus*, several times the size of an ostrich or emu. They offered a food supply on a scale never before encountered in Polynesia, other than when whales were cast ashore. Some early groups of Maori based their economy around moas in areas where the birds were relatively plentiful, until over-hunting led to their extinction *(see page 54)*.

The history of the first colonists, from the time of their arrival until the advent of Europeans, is a history of their adaptation to the environment – the matching of their skills and cultural resources to it, and the evolution of new features in their culture in response to the conditions that the environment imposed.

Maori culture

Ethnologists recognise two distinguishable but related phases in Maori civilisation. The first is New Zealand East Polynesian, or Archaic Maori, revealed by the archaeological remains of the earliest settlers and their immediate descendants. The second, known as Classic Maori, is the culture encountered and recorded by the earliest European navigators to reach the country. The process by which the first phase

and traditions of the culture, the most important features were practised throughout the country.

Competitive tribalism, for example, was the basis of Maori life. The family and *hapu* (sub-tribe) were the unit of society that determined who married whom, where people lived, where and when they fought other people and why. Tribal ancestors were venerated, as were gods representing the natural elements (the earth, the sky, the wind, the sea, and so on). The whole of life was bound up in a unified vision in which every aspect of living was related to every other. And the universal acceptance of concepts such as *tapu* (sacredness), *mana* (spiritual

evolved into the second is quite complex.

What is certain, however, is that by the time James Cook observed New Zealand in 1769, New Zealand Polynesians had settled the land from the far north to Foveaux Strait in the south. The language these inhabitants shared was similar enough for a speaker to be understood anywhere in the country, although dialectal differences were pronounced, particularly between the North and South Islands. While regional variations were apparent in the details

authority), *mauri* (life force), *utu* (satisfaction) and a belief in *makutu* (sorcery) regulated all aspects of life.

Maori hierarchy

Maori society was stratified. People were born into *rangatira* or chiefly families, or they were *tutua* (commoners). They became slaves if they were captured as a consequence of warfare. Immediate authority was exercised by the *kaumatua*, the elders who were family heads. Whole communities, sharing a common ancestor, were under the jurisdiction of the *rangatira* families whose authority was in part hereditary and in part based on past achievement. Occa-

---

LEFT: idealised view of Maori by Sydney Parkinson.
ABOVE: early depiction of the traditional Maori greeting, the *hongi.*

sionally federations of *hapu* and tribes would come together and join forces under an *ariki* (paramount chief) for joint ventures such as waging war against foreign elements, trading or foraging for resources. The most common relationship among even closely related *hapu*, however, was fierce competition.

Communities ranging from a handful of households to more than 500 lived in *kainga* (villages). These were usually based on membership of a single *hapu*. The *kainga* would be close to water, food

COPING WITH SCARCITY

When items of food became scarce in a *kainga* (village) or *pa* (fortified settlement), they had a *rahui*, or prohibition, laid on them to conserve precious supplies.

growing and (in areas where fighting was common) warfare. Cultivation and foraging were carried out by large parties of workers, seasonally.

Warfare was an important feature of Maori life in most parts of the country. It was sometimes conducted to obtain territory that was abundant in food or other natural resources (for example, stone for toolmaking); sometimes its purpose was to avenge insults, sometimes to obtain satisfaction from *hapu* whose members had allegedly transgressed the social code; and

sources and crops. Some settlements, called *pa*, were fortified. More often the *kainga* were adjacent to hilltop *pa*, to which communities could retreat when under attack.

Defensive settlements

Maori *pa* were elaborately constructed with an interior stronghold, ditches, banks and palisades. Some proved impregnable; others were taken and lost several times in the course of a lifetime. Some scholars speculate that the primary function of hilltop *pa* was to protect kumara tubers from marauders.

Communal patterns of life in Maori settlements were organised around food gathering, food

sometimes as a result of serious disagreements over control or authority.

Prior to the introduction of the musket, however, most warfare was not totally destructive. It often involved only individuals or small raiding parties, and ambush or short, sporadic attacks. Even when larger groups met in head-on confrontation or siege, the dead rarely amounted to more than a few score. Most battles occurred in summer and, except when a migration was under way, fighting was rarely carried on far from a tribe's home territory.

For individual men, as for tribes, the concept of *mana* (spiritual authority) was paramount. An individual's *mana* was intensified by victory, and diminished by defeat. Courage and combat skills were also essential ingredients in initiation, and in acceptance by male peers, especially in the case of chiefs. Favourite weapons were *taiaha* (long wooden-bladed swords) and short clubs known as *patu* and *mere*.

Non-combatants were able to achieve high standing in the arts, or in the exercise of esoteric powers as *tohunga* (priests or experts). With no written language, the indigenous Maori relied on sophisticated oral traditions. Considerable *mana* was bestowed on the best orators. An ability to carve was also highly regarded and the working of wood, bone and stone reached heights of intricacy and delicacy in New Zealand seldom seen elsewhere. The best woodcarving was seen on door lintels, house gables and canoe prows, and in stone and bone in personal ornaments such as *hei-tiki* (a pendant representing a human figure). The most prized material for carving was *pounamu* (New Zealand jade or greenstone), the search for which led Maori on expeditions to some of the most inhospitable parts of the South Island. *Pounamu* was valued for its hardness and the sharpness of the edges which could be fashioned from it. More than just a resource, it holds mystical associations. Like the other Polynesians, the Maori had no access to metals. With animal skins also unavailable, Maori weavers fashioned intricate ceremonial clothing from feathers, flax and other materials.

Personal decoration in the form of *moko* (tattooing) was also a feature of Maori art. Men were marked primarily on the face or buttocks, women largely on the face and breasts. The Maori usually used a straight rather than a serrated blade. This left a grooved scar which looked more like carving than tattooing.

In spite of competition, warfare and tribal demarcations among Maori, trading was also extensive. South Islanders exported greenstone to other parts of the country for use in chisels and ornaments. Bay of Plenty settlers distributed high-quality obsidian from Mayor Island. Nelson and D'Urville Island inhabitants quarried and distributed argillite. Food that was readily available in some districts but not in others, such as mutton birds, was also preserved and bartered. People travelled long distances for materials and food delicacies. Although ocean-going vessels disappeared from New Zealand by the 18th century, canoes were still widely used for river, lake and coastal transport.

Land of the Long White Cloud

Medical examination of pre-European remains reveals that few Maori lived beyond the age of 30. From their late 20s, most people would have suffered considerably as a consequence of arthritis, and from infected gums and loss of teeth brought about by the staple fern-root diet. Many of the healthy-looking "elderly" men, on whose condition Captain James Cook com-

mented favourably in 1770, may have been, at the most, around 40 years of age.

This was the Maori life that Cook and other navigators encountered in the late 18th century. The population, probably 100,000 to 120,000, had been so long separated from other cultures that they had no concept of nationhood. But they were fiercely assertive of the identity that they took from their ancestry and *hapu* membership. To that extent they led a tribal existence, but one thing they did share strongly, no matter which tribe they were born to, was a deep and profound affinity with the land and its bounty. They called the land Aotearoa: "the land of the long white cloud". ❑

LEFT: a Maori fort or *pa*.
RIGHT: Sydney Parkinson's portrait of a Maori warrior.

VOYAGES OF DISCOVERY

A Dutchman searching for a "Great Southern Continent" first stumbled upon
New Zealand in 1642, but it was another 130 years before any European returned

The southern Pacific was the last habitable part of the world to be reached by Europeans. It was then only gradually explored at the end of long-haul routes down the coast of South America on one side and Africa on the other. Once inside the rim of the world's largest ocean, seafarers faced vast areas to be crossed, always hundreds or thousands of miles away from any familiar territory. So it required not only steady courage to venture into this region but a high degree of navigational skill.

The countries of the South Pacific – tucked away near the bottom of the globe – were left to the Polynesians for nearly 150 years after the Europeans first burst into the Western Pacific. And then New Zealand was left alone for another 130 years after the Dutchman Abel Janszoon Tasman first sighted its coast in 1642.

It was left to the Englishman James Cook to put the South Pacific firmly on the world map. A famous New Zealand historian and biographer of Cook, Dr J.C. Beaglehole, wrote of the three great Cook voyages: "...his career is one of which the justification lies not so much in the underlining of its detail as in the comparison of the map of the Pacific before his first voyage with that at the end of the century. For his was a life consistent and integrated; to a passion for scientific precision he added the inexhaustible effort of the dedicated discoverer..."

The Dutch traders

European knowledge of the Pacific Ocean had gradually expanded during the 16th and 17th centuries following the first view of it by Vasco Nuñez de Balboa from the Isthmus of Panama in 1513. Spanish and Portuguese seafarers such as Magellan and Quiros, and England's Francis Drake, made their epic expeditions. The Spanish were motivated by their zeal to claim converts for the Catholic Church as well as the search for rare and precious metals and spices.

But towards the end of the 16th century, the Dutch emerged as the great seafaring and trading nation of the central and western Pacific. They set up a major administrative and trading centre at Batavia (now Jakarta) in Java early in the 17th century, an operation dominated by the Dutch East India Company. For 200 years the

Dutch were a power in the region, though for most of that period, voyages of exploration were incidental to the activities of trade.

The Dutch ships eventually found that by staying south after rounding the tip of Africa at the Cape of Good Hope and catching the consistent westerlies almost as far as the western coast of Australia, they could make the journey to Java more quickly than by adopting the traditional route – sailing up the east coast of Africa and then catching seasonal winds for the journey eastwards. And so islands off the west coast of Australia and stretches of the coast itself began to be noted on charts but were not yet recognised as the western side of a huge continent.

LEFT: Captain James Cook arrives at Golden Bay, New Zealand, in 1769.
RIGHT: 18th-century sketch of Cook's ship *Endeavour.*

Then, an ambitious governor of Batavia, Anthony van Diemen, showed a more imaginative interest in discovering new lands for trade than most of his predecessors.

Tasman's visit

In 1642 Abel Tasman was chosen by van Diemen to lead an expedition south, to be accompanied by a highly competent specialist navigator, Frans Visscher. The proposed voyage would take them first to Mauritius, then southwest to between 50° and 55°S in search of the great southern continent, Terra Australis Incognita. The expedition, aboard the vessels

Heemskerck and *Zeehaen*, was then to travel eastwards if no land had been found to impede their progress and to sail across to investigate a shorter route to Chile, a rich trading area and the monopoly of the Spanish. The expedition went only as far as 49°S before turning eastwards, whereupon it made two great South Pacific discoveries – Tasmania (or Van Diemen's Land, as he named it at the time) and New Zealand (which he called Staten Landt).

On 13 December 1642, Tasman and his men saw what was described as "land uplifted high" – the Southern Alps of the South Island – and, in strong winds and heavy seas, sailed northwards up the coast of Westland, before rounding Cape Farewell and entering what is now known as Golden Bay. Tasman's voyage was not immediately regarded as a major success *(see box below)*, but ultimately he was given his due for a gallant and well-recorded exploration.

Cook's exploration

Within a year or two, other navigators had discovered that New Zealand could not be attached to a huge continent which ran across to South America. The name was therefore changed from Staten Landt (the Dutch name for South America) to New Zealand, after the Dutch province of Zeeland.

But it was left to James Cook to open up the South Pacific like a huge oyster and reveal its contents. It was primarily to observe the transit of Venus over the disc of the sun in June 1769 that he was dispatched to the South Seas in the 373-tonne Whitby-built barque, *Endeavour*. He was instructed to sail to Otaheite (Tahiti) for the transit and then to sail southwards as far as 50°S latitude on another search for the great southern continent, charting the positions of any islands he might incidentally discover.

Cook rounded Cape Horn and entered the Pacific Ocean for the first time on 27 January 1769. After observing the transit of Venus and investigating other islands (which he named the Society Islands), he sailed south and then west. On 6 October, a ship's boy, Nicholas Young, sighted the east coast of the North Island where it is today called Young Nick's Head.

Two days after this first sighting of what he knew to be the east coast of New Zealand, the land reported by Tasman, the *Endeavour* sailed into a bay where smoke could be seen – a clear sign that there were inhabitants. Their first visit

TASMAN'S NEAR MISS

Tasman's first and only encounter with the Maori was nothing short of disastrous. When a canoe rammed a small boat that was travelling between the *Zeehaen* and the *Heemskerck*, fighting broke out and there was loss of life on both sides. Tasman called the place Massacre Bay and continued his journey northwards. He did not land again. What Tasman failed to realise was that he had actually been inside the western entrance to the stretch of water separating North and South islands, now known as Cook Strait. A voyage eastwards of only a few kilometres would have revealed this to him, and perhaps it might be known today as the Tasman Strait.

ashore ended with violence when a band of Maori attacked four boys left guarding the ship's boat; one of the attackers was shot dead.

It was discovered that a Tahitian chief on board the *Endeavour*, Tupaea, could converse with the Maori and he was taken ashore with Cook the next morning. But the Maori were in a threatening mood and Cook ordered one of them shot to make them retreat. That afternoon, the firing of a musket over a canoe (merely to attract attention) brought an attack on the boat from

MAPPING MISTAKES

James Cook made two major cartographical errors: attaching Stewart Island to the mainland as a peninsula, and mapping Banks Peninsula as an island.

the planet Mercury was made there. In Mercury Bay, for the first time, the explorers made friends with the local Maori and traded trinkets for supplies of fish, birds and clean water. They were shown over the Maori settlement and inspected a nearby fortified *pa* which greatly impressed Cook.

The expedition circumnavigated New Zealand and with brilliant accuracy made a chart of the coastline which proved basically reliable for more than 150 years. Cook and his crew spent weeks in Ship Cove, in a long inlet which

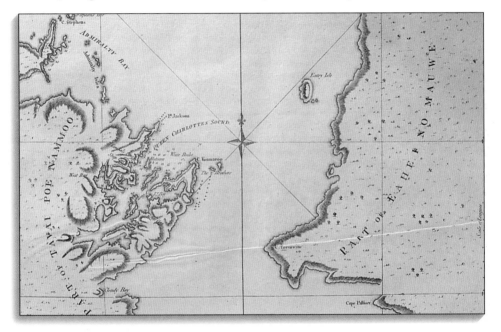

which the shot had been fired; a few more Maori were shot. Cook had quickly learnt that the native population were powerful, aggressive and brave. He called the place Poverty Bay because he didn't find the supplies he wanted.

First friendly encounter

The *Endeavour* sailed south into Hawke's Bay, and then north again around the top of East Cape. It spent 10 days in Mercury Bay, so called because an observation of the transit of

he called Queen Charlotte Sound, on the northern coast of the South Island, refurbishing the ship and gathering supplies. The stay gave the two botanists aboard, Joseph Banks and Daniel Solander, a wonderful opportunity to study closely the flora and fauna of the area. While the ship was being cleaned, the boats did detailed survey work.

The *Endeavour* left for home at the end of March 1770, sailing up the east coast of Australia, through the Dutch East Indies and then rounding the Cape of Good Hope to complete a circumnavigation of the world. The expedition was an extraordinary feat of seamanship, putting New Zealand firmly on the map and

LEFT: Abel Tasman.
ABOVE: map showing the yet-to-be-named Cook Strait, used by Captain Cook on one of his early expeditions.

gathering a huge amount of data. Cook seemed to personify the Great Discoverer as defined by his biographer, Beaglehole: "In every great discoverer there is a dual passion – the passion to see, the passion to report; and in the greatest this duality is fused into one – a passion to see and to report truly." Cook's first voyage was one of the most expert and detailed expeditions of exploration in all history.

Return visits

Cook twice again led expeditions into the Pacific – from 1772 to 1775 and from 1776 to 1780. During the second of these, he twice took his ship south of the Antarctic Circle where no vessel was known to have gone before, but he was unlucky, in that he did not become the first person ever to see the Antarctic continent.

It was to Dusky Sound in New Zealand that Cook repaired for rest and recovery after the extreme hardships faced by his crew in the southern ocean. During the seven weeks his expedition was there, the crew set up a workshop and an observatory, and restored their health with spruce beer (to defeat scurvy) and the plenitude of fish and birds. They made contact with a single family of Maori in an area which was never thickly populated, then or now.

They planted seeds on the shore of the sound, and then sailed for their favourite anchorage in Ship Cove at the other end of the South Island.

On Cook's way home from New Zealand during his second voyage a few years later, he gave pigs, fowl and vegetable seeds to a Maori community near Hawke's Bay before he again sailed for Ship Cove to a rendezvous with another vessel of the expedition, *Adventure*.

On his third voyage, Cook went again to New Zealand, and to his home from home at Ship Cove. By now he had a friendship with some of the local Maori that had lasted nearly 10 years. In his journals, he referred to the Maori as "manly and mild" and wrote that "they have some arts among them which they execute with great judgement and unwearied patience."

By then he had done such a thorough job of charting the coasts of New Zealand that there was little else for explorers to discover without going inland. But a number of navigators followed during the remaining years of the 18th century – Frenchmen Dumont d'Urville (who arrived only two months after Cook first set foot in New Zealand) and later Marion du Fresne; an Italian, Don Alessandra Malaspina, who commanded

COOK'S DEMISE

Captain Cook was killed in January 1778 in Kealakekua Bay, Hawaii, after a series of thefts from his expedition led to a skirmish with locals.

of the South Island in 1792. There was a brief boom in the early years of the 19th century but it wasn't long before the seals were in short supply and the ships had to venture further south to the sub-Antarctic islands.

Next, at the turn of the 19th century, came the whalers – some of them driven from the Pacific coast of South America because of the dangers brought about by the war between Spain and Britain. Ships from Britain, Australia and the United States hunted the sperm whale in this region and

a Spanish expedition; and George Vancouver, who had served with Cook.

In 10 years, within the decade of the 1770s, Cook and his contemporaries had opened up the Pacific entirely and, in 1788, Sydney, in Australia, was established as a British convict settlement. Traders were soon based there, ready to extract whatever valuable goods they could get their hands on.

The first Europeans to make an impact on New Zealand, however, were the sealers, with the first gang put ashore on the southwest coast

visits brought their crew-members into frequent contact with the Maori of Northland at Kororareka (later renamed Russell). At first, relations between Europeans and Maori were friendly. But visits were infrequent for a few years after the burning of a vessel called the *Boyd* in 1809 and the massacre of its crew. This was a reprisal against previous punishment of high-born Maori seamen by Pakeha (European) skippers.

The inland exploration of New Zealand took place mostly during the early to mid-19th century, mainly those parts that were fairly accessible from the coast. Vast areas of the South Island, however, were not successfully explored by Europeans until the 20th century. ❏

LEFT: a 1990s replica of Cook's ship *Endeavour*.
ABOVE: an English visitor is greeted by native Maori.

HARRIETT
HEKI'S WIFE   HEKI   KAWITI

THE WARRIOR CHIEFTAINS

of

NEW ZEALAND

own by Jos.ᵉ J. Merrett   Drawn on Stone by W Nichol

SETTLEMENT AND COLONISATION

The colonisation of New Zealand was debated and fought over by
Maori, missionaries, politicians, settlers and land speculators

The bleak experiences of Abel Tasman – and the much more successful endeavours of James Cook nearly 130 years later – had no immediate impact on the future of the two main islands. The Dutch were preoccupied with getting all they could out of the Indonesian archipelago; the British were concerned with consolidating and expanding their trading territories in India. New Zealand, it seemed, had little to offer a colonial power.

Australia's Botany Bay, not so far across the Tasman Sea, was established as a penal settlement in 1788 as a direct result of America's victory in the War of Independence (convicts had previously been sent to America) and as a by-product of Cook's voyages, but the Land of the Long White Cloud was mostly ignored.

Sealskins and whale oil

As the 19th century began, with Europe engulfed in the Napoleonic Wars, demand increased for commodities such as sealskins and whale oil. Seals and whales were plentiful in New Zealand waters, and skippers from Port Jackson (Sydney's harbour) and the newer settlement of Hobart, in Van Diemen's Land (Tasmania), wasted no time in putting to sea.

Many skippers found a convenient watering hole at Kororareka (now Russell) in the Bay of Islands. The anchorage there was calm and well-protected and there was a ready supply of kauri wood for spars and masts.

Kororareka, with its new European arrivals, rapidly became a lusty, brawling town; the missionaries who arrived there damned it as the "hell-hole of the Southwest Pacific". The newcomers carried dangerous baggage which in time completely eradicated some of the Maori tribes and *hapu*, and seriously affected others: muskets, hard liquor or "grog", prostitutes, and a host of infectious diseases – many of which

proved fatal – to which the Maori had never previously been exposed and therefore had no natural resistance.

Isolated hostilities occurred in the early decades of the 19th century, such as the burning of the brig *Boyd* and the killing and eating of its crew in Whangaroa Harbour in 1809.

Despite such ugly episodes, contacts between Maori and Europeans were essentially peaceful. A barter trade flourished, the Maori trading vegetables and flax for a variety of European trinkets, tools and weapons (including, of course, the musket). The Maori helped cut down giant kauri trees and drag the trunks from bush to beach; they crewed on European sealing and whaling vessels; they were physically strong and vigorous but they were also proud – the latter fact overlooked by most Europeans.

In 1817, mainly in response to lawlessness in the Bay of Islands, the laws of the Colony of New South Wales were extended to also include New Zealand.

LEFT: Maori chief Hone Heke with his wife, Harriet, on his right, and Chief Kawiti on his left.
RIGHT: Samuel Marsden is credited with introducing Christianity to New Zealand.

Around this time, the Reverend Samuel Marsden arrived from New South Wales, Australia. Marsden is still reviled in Australia as the "flogging parson", a result of his tenure as a magistrate at Port Jackson. Kiwis however see him in a different light, as the man who introduced Christianity to New Zealand.

A dedicated evangelist, he believed that missionary tradesmen should not only encourage the conversion of Maori to Christianity but also develop their expertise in carpentry, farming and European technology.

By 1830, Maori were involved in export trading. In that year 28 ships (averaging 110 tonnes) made 56 cross-Tasman voyages, carrying substantial cargoes, including tonnes of Maori-grown potatoes, mainly to Sydney.

The inclusion of New Zealand within the framework of the laws of New South Wales had still not made New Zealand a British colony, nor did the legislation prove very effective. The governors had no way of proving charges nor of enforcing their authority while a ship was in New Zealand waters,

Kororarika Bay of Islands N.Z. 1836

But the missionary-tradesmen-teachers in whom Marsden had placed his faith were in fact an ill-assorted bunch who could hardly be regarded as a civilising, evangelising force by the people they had come to convert. With so many of them involved in gun-running, adultery and drunkenness, it is not surprising that 10 years passed before the first Maori baptism. Not until the 1820s did the Maori begin to find Christianity an attractive proposition.

The missionaries did accomplish some good. Thomas Kendall was instrumental in compiling the first grammar and dictionary of the Maori language, and in 1820 accompanied two famous chiefs, Hongi and Waikato, to Britain.

and they had no authority over foreign vessels and their crews.

The early missionaries did not want to see New Zealand colonised. They hoped to be allowed to spread what they saw as the benefits of Christian civilisation among the Maori, leaving them uncorrupted by the depravity introduced to earlier colonies by European settlers and adventurers.

But many British people believed that organised and responsible settlement would be able to avoid the disasters inflicted by Europeans upon indigenous peoples of other countries. The most influential proponent of this view was Edward Gibbon Wakefield.

On a less idealistic level, there was also pressure among Britons for new colonies with land for settlement, and the notion that if Britain did not take sovereignty over New Zealand and populate it with European immigrants, some other colonial power – most probably France – would do so. In retrospect, however, it seems doubtful that the French had any specific designs upon New Zealand.

The "home government" remained steadfastly irresolute, and the issue of colonisation was allowed to drift. By the 1830s, the scramble for land was in full swing – a scramble that was to produce tragic results within 20 years.

The Maori had no concept of permanent, private ownership of land. Their land was held by tribes who traditionally inherited it. A chief's authority was generally strong enough to have a sale accepted by most members of the tribe – but even this could be complicated by conflicting claims of ownership among tribes or subtribes, and such claims could involve very large areas. Many land transfers between Pakeha and Maori led to conflicts in the 1860s; some of them are still being legally contested today.

There was also the problem of what was being bought. The settlers, and the rapacious speculators in Britain, thought they were buying outright freehold land; in many cases, the Maori believed they were merely leasing their lands for a fee.

The missionaries were not skilled in matters of British law, and certainly not in the area of land conveyancing. Nor were they renowned as administrators, and they did not want to get involved because of their professed anti-settlement beliefs. The time had finally come for government intervention, however reluctant.

In 1833, with the arrival in the Bay of Islands of James Busby as British Resident, the move was made. The notion of "Resident" was vague. A Resident, in most cases, had the full backing of His or Her Majesty's Government as a diplomat representing British interests in a territory that had not yet been annexed by the Crown. He could advise local chieftains, he could cajole – but he had no real power.

Busby did what he could. He attempted to create some unity and overall sovereignty

among the disparate Maori by formally establishing a confederation of Maori chiefs, and then in 1835 he proposed that Britain and the United Tribes of New Zealand should agree to an arrangement under which the confederation would represent the Maori people and gradually expand their influence as a government while the British government, in the meantime, administered the country in trust.

Busby won personal respect from the Maori. Even so, he keenly felt his own impotence and was well aware that he could never be able to achieve law and order here without the backing of some adequate force.

The Wakefield Scheme

In the course of the 1830s it had become obvious that land buying was going to cause serious trouble. Speculators were gambling on Britain taking over and settling the country, while Busby, the British Resident, was powerless to prevent such "deals" from taking place. Colonisation, in fact, was developing a kind of inevitability. In 1836, Edward Gibbon Wakefield told a committee of the House of Commons that Britain was colonising New Zealand already, but "in a most slovenly and scrambling and disgraceful manner".

In 1837, at the behest of the government of New South Wales, Captain William Hobson,

LEFT: *Kororarika Bay of Islands*, a painting by Charles Heaphy in 1841.
RIGHT: Edward Gibbon Wakefield.

commanding HMS *Rattlesnake*, sailed from Sydney to the Bay of Islands to report on the situation. Hobson suggested a treaty with the Maori chiefs (which Busby thought he had already achieved) and the placing of all British subjects in New Zealand under British rule. Hobson's report provoked a response, but without Wakefield's influence there might not have been such an outcome.

Wakefield disliked the results of colonisation in the United States, Canada, New South Wales and Tasmania. He believed that if land was sold at what he called "a sufficient price" to "capitalist" settlers, labourers among the immigrants

would not disperse thinly but would stay in the new communities working for landowners – at least for a few years until they could save enough to buy land for themselves at the "sufficient price" and employ more recently arrived immigrant labour.

Land prices were crucial to Wakefield's system, and New Zealand his testing ground. Unfortunately he underestimated the aspirations of immigrant labourers who were prepared to suffer extreme isolation in order to farm their own land, and he did not foresee the readiness with which "capitalists" would move out of the centralised settlements to areas they considered more profitable.

During the late 1830s and early 1840s Wakefield helped establish the New Zealand Company. This became a joint stock company so that the people involved would bear the costs of establishing the settlements they planned.

The Treaty of Waitangi

Around this time the British government at last responded to the anti-colonial feelings of the missionary groups. Britain decided that the Maori should be consulted on their own future, and that their consent should be given to the annexation of their country. The result was the Treaty of Waitangi, signed at the Bay of Islands on 6 February 1840 by Hobson (now appointed Lieutenant-Governor) on behalf of the British government. The treaty was later taken to other parts of the country for signing by most of the Maori chiefs.

Ironically, the treaty was never ratified. Within a decade the Chief Justice, Sir William Martin, ruled that it had no legal validity because it was not incorporated in New Zealand's statutory law. The second irony is that the date of the original signing of the treaty is now said to be the "founding day" of New Zealand as a British colony, the opposite of what the missionaries had hoped to achieve.

The treaty itself remains a bone of contention. The text of the document was written in English, apparently amended by Hobson after it was first explained to the assembled Maori leaders. A rather loosely translated version in Maori was signed by most of the Maori leaders. The Maori had put much faith in advice from the missionaries, being told that they were signing a solemn pact, under which New Zealand sovereignty was being vested in the British Crown in return for guarantees of certain Maori rights. Many Europeans (and also Maori) genuinely believed this, and for some years the British government upheld the agreement.

It is almost impossible now to regard the treaty objectively. In the context of its time it was an example of enlightened respect for the rights of an indigenous population. But because it was never ratified, and never truly honoured by the land-hungry white settlers, it is easily construed these days as an expedient fraud and is the focus of some civil dissent.

The formal British annexation of New Zealand implicit in the 1840 Treaty of Waitangi was quickly followed by the arrival of the first ships carrying immigrants organised by Wakefield's New Zealand Company. The *Tory*, despatched from England before the treaty had been signed and arriving early in 1840, carried a batch of immigrants who were to settle in Wellington. The Wanganui district received its first settlers shortly afterwards, and in 1841 a subsidiary of the Company, based in Plymouth, England, and drawing emigrants from Devon and Cornwall, established New Plymouth.

The South Island was not ignored. Captain Arthur Wakefield, one of Edward's many brothers, arrived at Nelson in 1841 and was followed by 3,000 settlers in 1842.

royal authority) on three occasions, and once sacked the entire town as Pakeha scampered off into the woods or took to boats.

George Grey, who arrived as Governor in 1845, called in the army to suppress Hone Heke. With the help of Maori dissidents who refused to support Heke, Grey won the day.

Such open conflict did nothing to encourage emigration, and the New Zealand Company went into a terminal decline. It eventually became almost bankrupt in the late 1840s, surrendered its charter, and handed over to the government some 400,000 hectares (about 1 million acres) of land for which about $500,000

In the Bay of Islands, the events in the south were having their repercussions. Hone Heke, a prominent Maori leader and signatory to the Treaty of Waitangi, had become more than disenchanted with the treaty's implications. Although Kororareka (Russell) had been the de facto "capital" of New Zealand before the signing of the treaty, Lieutenant-Governor Hobson decided that Auckland should be the site of the new country's capital. Trade from Russell declined and Hone Heke got fractious. He and his warriors demolished the flagpole (symbol of

LEFT: Tomika Te Mutu, chief of Motuhoa Island.
ABOVE: stagecoach fording a North Island stream.

THE WAIRAU MASSACRE

Despite (or perhaps because of) the Treaty of Waitangi, land claims soon became a matter of bitter dispute. In 1843, Arthur Wakefield (brother of Edward Wakefield) led a party of armed Nelson settlers into the fertile Wairau Valley. It was his contention that the land had been bought by the New Zealand Company from the widow of a European trader, who had previously given the Maori a cannon in exchange for it. The local chief, Te Rauparaha, and his nephew, Rangihaeata, thought otherwise, and when the two sides met violence inevitably broke out. Te Rauparaha's wife was shot and the Maori killed 22 of the Pakeha, including Wakefield himself.

were due; the New Zealand Company was finally dissolved in 1858.

Even with the writing on the wall, in its last decade of operation the New Zealand Company remained active, lending its organisational support to members of the Scottish Free Church who established Dunedin in 1848, and to the Anglicans who founded Christchurch in 1850 and quickly opened up the excellent pasturelands of the Canterbury Plains. More and more settlers imported sheep, mostly merinos, from Australia. What was to become New Zealand's principal economic asset was soon underway: sheep-farming on a large scale.

Edward Wakefield, architect-in-absence of the planned settlement, eventually arrived in New Zealand for the first time in 1852, the year in which the colony was granted self-government by Britain. He achieved much, but at the same time lived long enough (he died in 1862) to see that his ideal of cohesive but expanding communities, complete with "capitalists" and "labourers", was not viable. The immigrants didn't necessarily make the choice for "town life", and many left the fledgeling settlements to establish – or, at least, attempt to establish – agricultural or pastoral properties well beyond the confines of the towns. However, thanks largely to Wakefield's efforts, the settlement

and colonisation of New Zealand were achieved in a more orderly manner than had been the case, several decades earlier, in Canada and Australia.

The New Zealand Wars

The new colony, however, was facing problems. There had been a great deal of speculation in land sales, and many Maori were beginning to realise this: land was being sold for as much as 20 times what they had been paid for it.

A direct result of this injustice was the election in 1858 of a Maori "King" (later called the Kingitanga or Maori King Movement, *see page 69*) by tribes in the North Island near Waikato. There had never been such a title among the Maori, who owed their allegiance to a tribe or sub-tribe, but it was hoped that the *mana* (spiritual authority) of a king, uniting many tribes, would help protect their land against purchase by the Pakeha. However, it didn't work out that way.

In Taranaki, another group of tribes rose up against the government in June 1860 following a blatantly fraudulent land purchase by the colonial administration, the Waitara Land Deal. British regular troops, hastily assembled, were virtually annihilated south of Waitara.

For the next few days, the North Island was ablaze with clashes between Maori and Pakeha. The New Zealand Wars were marked by extraordinary courage on both sides. The conflicts were frequently indecisive, but bloody. On the Pakeha side, the brunt of the early fighting, until 1865, was borne by British regular troops, 14 of whom received Britain's highest battle honour, the Victoria Cross.

Between 1865 and 1872 (which was the "official" end of the war, although sporadic fighting continued until the formal surrender of the Maori King in 1881), locally raised militia and constabulary forces played an important role – assisted by some Maori tribes who had decided not to join the Maori King's confederation.

Despite war, the country's prospects continued to improve. The discovery of gold in the South Island led to a fresh influx of migrants in the early 1860s; the capital was moved from Auckland to Wellington in 1865; and the pursuit of pasture was opening up vast tracts of the country. ❏

LEFT: gold was what attracted the early settlers.
RIGHT: the NZ Wars were marked by bloody clashes.

A NEW NATION

The 20th century saw a series of unprecedented economic, social and political challenges for the people of New Zealand

Progress towards full independence from Britain began almost as soon as the Maori-Pakeha land wars began to settle down. An economic boom in the 1870s was sparked by Sir Julius Vogel, who as colonial treasurer borrowed heavily overseas for public works construction, notably railways. A flood of immigrants followed, mainly from Britain but also from Scandinavia and Germany.

But Vogel miscalculated the negative impact of his borrow-to-boom credo. In 1880, New Zealand narrowly averted bankruptcy. Within a few years, wool and grain prices dropped so hard that depression set in and unemployment spread rapidly. In 1888, more than 9,000 settlers left the colony, most of them for Australia, which had remained relatively prosperous.

The years of hardship may have had something to do with the emergence of New Zealand as one of the most socially progressive communities in the world. Free, compulsory and secular education was created by law in 1877; two years later, every adult man – Maori as well as Pakeha – won the right to vote.

Lamb for the world's tables

There were some other signs of hope, too, with a new industry emerging that was to help the country make its way in the world for years to come. In 1882, the refrigerated vessel *Dunedin* was loaded up with sheep carcasses and made the voyage to England, where it arrived three months later. The trip was an arduous one, but the meat arrived safely and profits in England were much higher than they would have been back in New Zealand. Farmers then began to breed sheep for meat as well as wool, and the frozen meat industry became an economic staple.

In the waning years of the 19th century, a barrage of social reforms was fired by a new Liberal Party government headed by John Ballance. Sweeping land reforms were introduced,

breaking down the large inland estates and providing money for first mortgages to put people on the land. Industrial legislation provided improved conditions for workers as well as the world's first compulsory system of industrial arbitration. The aged poor were awarded a pension. And for the first time anywhere (with the

exceptions of tiny Pitcairn Island and the American state of Wyoming), women were granted the right to vote on an equal basis with men.

The principal minds behind these great social reforms were William Pember Reeves, a New Zealand-born socialist, and Richard John Seddon, who became prime minister when Ballance died in 1893. Seddon's legendary toughness and political judgement gave him enormous power within the party and in the country.

The burgeoning frozen meat industry and the expansion of dairy exports in the early 20th century saw the affluence and influence of farmers grow. New Zealand politely refused an invitation to become a part of the new

LEFT: the united colours of modern New Zealand.
RIGHT: Richard John Seddon, a much admired prime minister from 1893 until his death in 1906.

Commonwealth of Australia and was subsequently upgraded by the British Empire from "colony" to "dominion". The new Reform Party squeezed into power in 1911. The new prime minister, William Massey, a dairy farmer, helped consolidate New Zealand's position as an offshore farm for Britain.

World wars and depression

War brought a new sense of nationalism to New Zealand while at the same time reinforcing the country's ties to Britain. Between 1914 and 1918, 100,000 men joined the Australia-New Zealand Army Corps (ANZAC) forces fighting

Africa, Italy and Crete. More than 10,000 died. American writer James A. Michener once claimed that the bravest soldier in each of the world wars was a New Zealander – Bernard Freyberg in the first and, in the second, Charles Upham, "a stumpy square-jawed chap" whose "behaviour under fire seems incredible". Upham is only the third member of the armed forces to have won the Victoria Cross twice.

Back home, a successful economic stabilisation policy and full employment made the 1940s a decade of relative prosperity, and the country emerged from the war with a developed sense of nationhood. It was an appropriate

with the Allies in Africa and Europe.

The Great Depression of the 1930s hit New Zealand hard. Curtailed British demand for meat, wool and dairy products led to severe unemployment and several bloody riots. The new Labour Party swept into power in 1935 and utilised the resurgent world economy to pull the nation out of the doldrums. Under Prime Minister Michael Savage, New Zealand again moved to the forefront of world social change, establishing a full social security system. Savage led the country into World War II. This time, nearly 200,000 Kiwis were called to battle, many of them under MacArthur in the nearby Pacific campaign, others in North

WORLD WAR I

By the time World War I had ended, almost 17,000 New Zealanders had lost their lives. Indeed, the casualties were out of all proportion to the country's population, then about a million. The futility was underscored by the debacle on Turkey's Gallipoli Peninsula, from 25 April 1915 (a day now marked in memoriam every year as "ANZAC Day") until British naval evacuation some eight months later; the affair cost the lives of 8,587 servicemen from Australia and New Zealand. Somehow this heroic tragedy, dramatised some years later in Peter Weir's film Gallipoli, gave New Zealand a new identity within the British Empire.

time, in 1947, for the government to adopt the Statute of Westminster and formally achieve full independence from Britain.

The Labour Party, however, had by then lost its vigour and its defeat in 1949 ended an era. The victors were the National Party, who ran on a platform extolling private enterprise.

The 1950s began with a political tremor as a new National Party government abolished the Legislative Council, the upper house of the national Parliament. New Zealand became one of the few democratic nations with a unicameral legislature. This gave inordinate power to the executive – a Cabinet made up from mem-

End of isolation

The first post-war revolution, however, came with the end of isolation. Before mass travel became a possibility, hotels shut at 6pm, restaurants were forbidden to sell liquor and a rigid 40-hour, five-day working week meant shop hours were strictly controlled and most families spent weekends at home. Society remained in that time warp until the 1950s, when passenger ships began their trade again. Thousands of young Kiwis went away for their "OE" (overseas experience), almost always to London, and for the first time could compare their society with that of the old world.

bers of the ruling party. The power to change the law dramatically and within hours enabled the Labour Party to transform the nation's economy – and its whole social structure – when it swept into power from 1984–90.

One of the first actions taken by the unicameral House was the ratification of the ANZUS (Australia-New Zealand-United States) security pact in 1951. This was a clear indication by New Zealand and Australia that they had to look away from Britain to meet their defence requirements.

Air travel and advances in telecommunications in the 1960s and '70s led to radical changes in this narrow, closed, highly controlled society. By the 1980s, shops were staying open to offer extended services into the evenings and weekends, most restrictions were lifted from hotels and taverns, New Zealand wines began to rank with the world's best, and restaurants and cafés made eating out part of the national culture. On the back of such sophistication, tourism boomed.

The transition has not always been smooth. In the early 1970s New Zealand began grappling with the problem of diversifying both its production away from bulk commodities and its

Left: the Cook Islands (seen here marking ANZAC Day) aided New Zealand in its war effort in Europe.
Above: a 1970s visit by Britain's Queen Elizabeth II.

markets away from Britain. When oil prices soared, debt began to pile up as both Labour and National administrations borrowed and hoped primary production prices would pick up. It was a matter of marketing. But marketing was something New Zealanders had never needed to do. They had lived well for so long, by the relatively simple process of farming well, that the British transition into the European Economic Community (EEC) in 1973 left them in confusion.

Tumultous times

During the 1970s, sheep numbers rose past 70 million for the first time as farmers received

strongly (up to 17 percent) that farm costs skyrocketed and the Muldoon ministry humiliatingly had to bolster subsidies to New Zealand farmers. All the regulation and readjustment caused an agony of doubt about the short-term future of the economy. By 1984, unemployment had reached 130,000 and the national overseas debt stood at NZ$14.3 billion.

But when a new Labour government came to power towards the end of 1984, farm and other production subsidies were withdrawn virtually overnight, import licences abandoned, wage structures dismantled and a broad policy of economic laissez-faire put in place.

SHOULD AULD ACQUAINTANCE BE FORGOT?

state payments to boost stock numbers. Primary industry was widely subsidised and manufacturing tightly protected from 1975–84.

The trade barriers imposed on Britain by EEC membership, combined with rocketing oil prices, sent the cost of industrial goods sky high.

Led by Sir Robert Muldoon, the National government doubled the tight measures imposed by Labour on immigration, imports and the dollar. Muldoon, a pugnacious man, provoked the anger of trade unionists by imposing a wage freeze, but held his line in the face of numerous strikes and demonstrations.

By the end of the 1970s and the beginning of the 1980s, internal inflation was raging so

Another change came in the area of foreign affairs, with New Zealand ready at last to assert herself on the international stage. During the 1960s, as France began stepping up a campaign of nuclear testing in its Polynesian possessions, there were several mass demonstrations.

A strong anti-nuclear feeling reached its peak in New Zealand when the Labour government refused nuclear-armed or nuclear-powered US naval vessels entry to New Zealand ports. The Americans insisted on their right as allies under the ANZUS Pact and broke off all defence arrangements with New Zealand.

Labour, under Prime Minister David Lange, pledged to set up a 320-km (200-mile) nuclear-free zone around the shores of New Zealand, and to renegotiate the 33-year-old ANZUS security pact to force the US to keep nuclear armaments out of New Zealand ports. Division within the Labour government on other issues had grown so wide, however, that Lange resigned in 1989. The new prime minister, Jim Bolger of the National Party, quickly made it clear that his government would stay with economic deregulation.

In the mid-1990s the economy began to recover and the government eased up slightly

NO NUKES

In 1990, overwhelming public opinion forced the new National government to maintain the Lange government's anti-nuclear stance.

beginning of the 1990s, free trade was virtually in place across the Tasman Sea, with only some services still not completely liberated.

Both New Zealand and Australia have also turned their economic attention northwards to the burgeoning economies of Asia. Japan is now New Zealand's second biggest market (behind Australia). More than one-third of exports go to Asian markets – more than to North America and Europe combined – and almost one-third of imports come from Asia. Japan and Singapore have long been

on its expenditure and its tight monetary policy.

Early in the post-war period, New Zealand had realised that its best economic hope for the future was some sort of pact with Australia. In 1965, the New Zealand Australia Free Trade Agreement (NAFTA) was signed. The plan was gradually to dismantle trade barriers between the two countries, but progress was slow and a better agreement was needed.

In 1983, the two governments signed the CER (Closer Economic Relations) pact, and by the

LEFT: Britain's entry into the EEC in 1973 dealt a serious blow to New Zealand's economy at the time.
ABOVE: campaigning for a nuclear-free state (late1960s).

trading partners but business is building up with Korea, Thailand, Malaysia, Indonesia, Taiwan, China, Brunei and Chile.

The Maori issue

During the 30 years of social and economic turbulence that began in the 1960s, New Zealand proved to be one of the most stable democracies in the world. But there remained a festering sore beneath the surface, caused by injustices to the Maori over a century ago.

The 1984–90 Labour government finally acknowledged the validity of Maori claims for land, fishing grounds and other assets that the Maori insist were illegally taken from them –

claims that were based on the 1840 Treaty of Waitangi. The Labour government set up the Waitangi Tribunal to consider specific Maori claims, and its work continued under the National government later. Many land claims were conceded, particularly where the land was held by the government, and a major fishing concession was awarded to the Maori.

Although there is a consensus that redress is due, a great deal of tension has prevailed over particular Waitangi claims. That tension has spilt over on several occasions. The landmark tree on One Tree Hill in Auckland *(see page 144)* was attacked in 1994 and again in 1996;

harder and compete more fiercely, both in the domestic market and overseas. This has brought about a growing division between rich and poor – and a new volatility in national politics. The old, narrow division between the two political groupings, neither of them far from the centre, no longer seems wide enough to contain national aspirations.

Electoral reform

Dissatisfaction with the rapid pace of change and with the performance of recent governments was expressed in a referendum on electoral reform. In 1993, the country voted to scrap

another activist attacked the America's Cup yachting trophy with a sledge-hammer, claiming it was a symbol of Pakeha elitism. Progress towards settlement of land claims continues and is high on the political agenda, but whatever progress is made is destined to fail to please everyone, and tensions are likely to continue. The difficulties, however, are seen by many as the growing pains of a new nation.

Cosmopolitan influences and the modern economic infrastructure have dramatically re-oriented social attitudes. Whereas for 150 years there was a national sense of egalitarianism, many now believe that to hold its place in the world the country and its people must work

traditional first-past-the-post elections in favour of a proportional system called the MMP (Mixed Member Proportional). Many worried that this would further fragment the structure of political parties – and to an extent it has.

In the 1996 elections, the National Party, led by Jim Bolger, won 44 seats in the 120-member house, while the Labour Party won 37. The New Zealand First Party, having won 17 seats, including four Maori seats off Labour, held the balance of power and emerged as the coalition partner in a new government with the National Party. The situation became volatile after 1996, with change becoming a constant theme in politics; in 1997 Prime Minister Bolger resigned.

In December 1997, Jenny Shipley became the country's first female prime minister, replacing Jim Bolger as leader of the National Party. However, weakened by the break-up of her coalition party and a floundering economy, Shipley lost the 1999 elections to a Labour Party-led coalition, helmed by another woman, Helen Clark. Clark's tough-as-nails approach, aided by a strong domestic economy and lower unemployment rate, clinched her and the Labour Party a second term at the 2002 elections. In the hard-fought 2005 elections, Clark and her Labour-led coalition won a third term, albeit by the narrowest of margins.

Clark's administrative pragmatism is accompanied by a populist knack for generating pride in their own country among New Zßealanders, an attitude that hitherto had been sporadic at best.

A new confidence

New Zealand was long dominated by a self-denigrating "cultural cringe" which saw it constantly measuring itself unfavourably against other countries. This accounts in part for the high number of people who leave for what are perceived as greener pastures. Many, from writer Katherine Mansfield to rock group The Datsuns, were only recognised in their own country after they had achieved overseas success.

But on 31 December 1999, New Zealanders made much of the fact that the position of the international date line meant their country was the first in the world to enter the new millennium. This reflected a growing awareness of the nation's uniqueness and individuality.

New Zealand had long ceased to be a smaller version of Australia or a pale reflection of the "mother country", England. But once New Zealanders had realised what it wasn't, they had to work out what it was. The process of defining this identity was facilitated by several factors, not least among them the institution of the MMP system in 1993, which established a truly representative government. In the elections immediately following its adoption, there were more Maori and women MPs, and the first Pacific Island, Asian and Muslim MPs were elected.

This in turn made it clear that New Zealand was no longer a bicultural, Maori-Pakeha society but a multicultural one. And this process was abetted by a generous immigration policy which saw a boom in the number of Asian immigrants, a side-effect of which has been an opportunity for demagogues to incite new racial tensions in the community.

New Zealand will find its own solutions to these difficulties. Its remoteness may have made its people parochial, but it has also forced them to develop the so-called No. 8 wire mentality – after the legend that a Kiwi can fix anything with a piece of No. 8 fencing wire – in which they take much pride. And they will increasingly appreciate who they are and what they have – something which has long been obvious to visitors. ❑

A WOMAN'S WORLD

New Zealand has always taken pride in the fact that in 1883 it became the first country in the world to give women the vote, and at the start of the 21st century the prominence of women in public life suggested a developed degree of equality. Arguably the three top positions in the country – Prime Minister, Governor-General and Chief Justice – have been held by women; the second, third and fifth biggest cities have had women mayors; and the chief executive officers of the two major telecommunications companies and biggest bank were women. However, statistics indicate that the median wage for women remains less than that enjoyed by men.

LEFT: Wellington's Civic Square; the city is capital of New Zealand. **RIGHT:** Prime Minister Helen Clark.

EXPLORING THE NATIONAL PARKS

Well-marked tracks with plenty of accommodation along the way make it easy to find your way around New Zealand's great outdoors

People come from all over the world to tramp New Zealand's famous tracks, such as the 3-day Coastal Track, along the north coast of the South Island; the Milford Track, which gets so crowded that booking ahead is necessary; and the Routeburn, in the south of the South Island. Yet there are some beautiful tracks where you can walk for hours without seeing a soul. A bonus is that there's often a hot spring around, just when you need to soothe those aching joints.

However, New Zealand's 14 national parks offer much more than walking. Department of Conservation (DOC) offices, in all cities and in many towns, provide information on wildlife, flora and fauna in the parks, and on walking the trails. Visitor Centres generally provide DOC leaflets and information, too.

UNIQUE ECOLOGY

The country's many flightless birds reflect the absence of predators, yet many of its trees are not so fortunate. Possums, imported in 1837 from Australia to start a fur trade, are highly destructive to New Zealand's native forests. In Australia the trees have a built-in protection against being stripped bare by the creatures; New Zealand's trees do not: one reason why the country often seems to be engaged in a running battle to preserve the natural ecological balance. The life forms found in this country are so distinctive that scientists have likened studying New Zealand's native species to studying life on another planet.

△ **SOUTHERN ALPS**
Mt Cook is the crowning glory of the magnificent Southern Alps range. The training ground for Everest conqueror Sir Edmund Hillary, it's a terrain that is not to be taken lightly. Heli-skiing and glacier skiing are popular here.

▽ **LAKE ROTOROA**
A fishing paradise, Lake Rotoroa is one of two glacial lakes which give Nelson Lakes National Park its name – the other one is Lake Rotoiti.

▷ **THE YAKAS TREE**
Waipoua Kauri Forest, Northland, is a protected nature reserve with trails that lead to the Yakas, the eighth-largest kauri in New Zealand. Trails also lead to Tane Mahuta, at 52 metres (171 ft) the country's tallest tree, and probably 1,200 years old.

SAFETY IN THE NATIONAL PARKS

◁ **GO WEST**
Lake Matheson with mounts Tasman and Cook, Westland National Park. This park also contains the glaciers Fox and Franz Josef and has some great walks, like the Copland Track. Weather conditions here are very unpredictable.

△ **MOUNT NGAURUHOE**
The youngest of the three volcanoes in Tongariro National Park is a great tramping (hiking) location. The park is also renowned for the ski slopes on recently active Ruapehu, as well as wildlife, game and fishing.

△ **MOUNT TARANAKI/EGMONT**
Despite being one of New Zealand's wettest places, it's the country's most frequently climbed mountain and a popular winter skiing venue.

▷ **EMERALD LAKES**
Minerals give these mountain lakes their brilliant hues. The Tongariro Northern Circuit passes close by these and other brightly coloured lakes and volcanic formations.

A few simple precautions will help you enjoy some of the most beautiful scenery in the world. Always check with the local DOC office or Visitor Centre before you go tramping, as weather conditions can change very rapidly. Even in the height of summer, be prepared for very adverse weather conditions. Some DOC offices will also be able to advise you on the availability of accommodation, time and food supplies required, and even volcanic activity. You may get more out of some walks and climbs with the assistance of a guide who knows the area well – guided group walks are available in some areas too.

Do not set out on a tramp – long or short – without suitable thermal clothing and footwear. Bring a map, compass, torch, matches and a first-aid kit. Sunblock, sunglasses and a good raincoat are also essential. If required, there are plenty of shops where you can purchase or hire decent gear, and some hostels and hotels can supply clothes, gloves and hats. Always inform someone else where you're going before you depart and on your return. All movements should be logged at DOC offices and the huts.

Once you step off the main road, if you set out in the wrong direction it could become a much longer walk than you'd planned.

NATURAL HISTORY

New Zealand has an exciting geological history and intriguing wildlife, from the lingering memory of the extinct moa to the tenuous hold of the symbolic kiwi

Of all the land masses on earth the islands of New Zealand take the prize for being the most isolated, surrounded on all sides by great expanses of ocean, and located thousands of miles away from Asia and the Americas, and a half a world away from Europe. But that has not always been the case.

The actual birth of a physically independent New Zealand occurred some 80 million years ago during the heyday of the dinosaurs. It was then, though over an extremely long period of time, that New Zealand split away from the prehistoric continent of Gondwana as the Tasman Sea began to form. By 60 million years ago New Zealand had reached its present distance from Australia of more than 1,500 km (930 miles). But even by then, the country's rocks had recorded an incredibly complex history.

In the beginning it is thought that a massive continent spanned the region where New Zealand was eventually going to appear. What is now the east of Australia was joined with another continent – and in one of the more interesting developments of geological investigation this has been suggested to have been North America. It was only when these two landmasses moved apart, over 500 million years ago, that an arc of volcanic islands was able to develop in between. These rocks, which are preserved in the mountains of Fiordland and the northwest of the South Island, record the start of New Zealand's history. In places they preserve fossils such as trilobites and brachiopods, the oldest signs of life in New Zealand.

Leaving Gondwana

For several hundred million years, New Zealand lay along a "convergent" edge of the supercontinent of Gondwana. Along this margin, oceanic crust, which is continually moving outwards from a mid-oceanic ridge, was pushed under the continent in a process known

as plate tectonics. Various types of rock and sediment from the sea floor move along on the oceanic crust like a giant, albeit very slow, conveyor belt until they reach a convergent margin and are "plastered" on top of each other like layers of spread on a piece of toast. For many millions of years, New Zealand grew in this

way, as a rather chaotic collection of rock from various places was brought together.

Finally, a huge sliver of land broke away from Gondwana and headed out into the Pacific. Almost immediately it began to sink and the sea washed further and further inland. Mountains eroded to low hills and waves ate them away. The New Zealand of today is just the tiny emergent part of a huge drowned continent, "Tasmantis", which can be seen on charts of the sea floor, stretching all the way to New Caledonia in the north, and to Campbell Island in the south. In fact, 30 million years ago New Zealand was so subdued and had sunk so much that there is very little evidence of any emergent land at all.

LEFT: the great spotted kiwi in its habitat, South Island.
RIGHT: beech forest in Fiordland National Park, South Island.

Most of what is now New Zealand was a shallow undersea shelf rich in sea life.

It was only at the "last minute" – geologically speaking – that compressive movements came to the rescue, pushing the country up and back out of the sea. As these forces continued, hills grew to become jagged mountains, volcanoes erupted, and were then carved by water and ice to form the landscape of today.

New Zealand currently sits right on the boundary of two of the huge moving "plates"

NIGHT BIRD

The kiwi, New Zealand's national bird, takes its name from the cry of the male. This nocturnal bird eats fruit, insects, worms and grubs.

Australian Plate, while the Alps, from the base up, are on the oceanic Pacific Plate which is being thrust upwards.

The effect of the Alps is enormous. Besides creating alpine environments from a land that had for millions of years been flat, they present a major barrier to the westerly circulation flow. At this latitude only the Southern Alps and the southern tip of South America prevent free circulation of these moisture-laden winds *(see box below)*.

At the time that the Alps were growing,

which cover the surface of the earth. In the south the Indo-Australian plate pushes under the Pacific one, while in the north the oceanic Pacific plate pushes the other way, under the Australian plate. In between, with little other option, the land rises and rises. The terrific wrenching forces that result can hardly help but produce a land of earthquakes and volcanoes.

The mighty Southern Alps in the South Island are almost entirely the result of the last 2 million years – a mere blink in geological time. They rose, and continue to rise by several centimetres a year. The plate boundary forming them is plain to see while travelling through Westland. The lowlands are on the Indo-

RAIN AND THE RAINFOREST

When air currents are forced to rise over the Southern Alps of New Zealand, their moisture is dropped, causing the enormous levels of rainfall – sometimes over 5,000 mm (200 inches) a year – that occur on the West Coast. On the other side of the mountains, though, there's a corresponding rainfall shadow, so that only a few kilometres from the wettest parts of New Zealand, the annual rainfall can be as low as 300 mm (12 inches). Odd as it may sound, high rainfall can actually be totally incompatible with the survival of the rainforests, as the soil is rapidly leached of the nutrients it needs to sustain them, resulting in stunted vegetation.

worldwide cooling became extreme and the Ice Age ensued. In reality this was a whole succession of cold periods, separated by warmer ones. In the colder intervals huge glaciers appeared in New Zealand and flowed down valleys. This period had an enormous effect on the present landscape – where young mountains and glaciers have combined, the scenery is some of the most spectacular to be found on earth. In Fiordland, the rock walls of ancient glacial valleys drop vertically thousands of feet directly into the sea. This kind of extreme environment has ensured a minimum of human impact on the land.

which has been broken and pushed up by the later mountain-building events. Much of the surface is probably a wave-cut platform, dating from the time when most, if not all, of New Zealand was below the waves. In regions that combine alpine weather with gentle topography, cross-country skiing has become popular.

Closely tied to the history of the Southern Alps are New Zealand's most precious materials. What the Maori call *pounamu* (greenstone) was formed from thin slivers of the exotic rock which exists deep below the earth's crust. Altered by heat and pressure during mountain-forming processes, these rocks were pushed to

Much of the country remains in near pristine state and travellers who wish to experience a true "wilderness" are easily satisfied here. On the other side of the Alps, the South Island lakes, like Wanaka and Wakatipu, are the direct result of glacial "bulldozing". Lying in the rain-shadow, the sunny climate combines to make an ideal holiday environment. Swimming, water-skiing and fishing are the key activities.

Away from the Alps, one curious feature of much of the uplands is their flattened tops. These are fragments of the old land surface

LEFT: land still in the making at White Island.
ABOVE: the tuatara, a prehistoric relic, still exists.

the surface in only a few isolated spots in the west of the South Island. Its rareness, intrinsic beauty and material properties in a culture where metal was unknown gave *pounamu* a value like gold to the Europeans. Here too was gold itself weathered from quartz veins within "schist", the rock which forms most of the Alps. As the mountains grew, they too eroded, and while the lighter and softer minerals of the schist washed away, gold, by virtue of its high density, became concentrated in the quieter nooks and crannies of river beds.

Not all New Zealand's recent history has been one of uplift. In the north of the South Island, the Marlborough Sounds were produced by the drowning of an extensive river system. The sunny climate, endless bays and islands make it another good place for boating and walking. In the North Island the major geological story is of volcanoes, and in a complex situation a whole variety of volcanic types has been produced.

Auckland city is built amongst numerous small (extinct), perfectly formed volcanic cones. These were formed by gentle outpourings of lava and ash. As naturally defensive positions, most of them have since been terraced and palisaded by Maori to form "pa" (forts). In the Central Plateau a different form

Dinosaurs and other fauna

The most striking aspect of New Zealand's fauna is its absence of large four-footed land animals, in particular of mammals (other than two species of bat that are found nowhere else), as well as its complete lack of snakes. This was originally attributed to the timing of New Zealand breaking-away from Gondwana, but recent discoveries suggest that carnivorous and herbivorous dinosaurs, as well as flying pterosaurs, were still living in New Zealand at that time. The only fossil evidence of land-based, four-footed animals since the dinosaurs is a single crocodile jawbone discovered near St

of lava produces a very dangerous, explosive type of volcano. About AD 130 one of the largest volcanic explosions in historical times formed Lake Taupo. This spread hot ash over a large part of the North Island, simultaneously annihilating huge areas of forest and everything in them. There's never been a period in New Zealand's history where volcanism has been entirely absent and there is every reason to expect it will continue. In the long run these events are blessings in disguise. Volcanic rocks rejuvenate the landscape. They weather to form New Zealand's richest soils, a fact well-recognised by the dairy industry. The volcanoes of the Central Plateau also form perfect ski-fields.

Bathans, in Central Otago. Crocodiles, however, are a species which do not exist in New Zealand today.

Mammals, too, may once have been part of a "native" fauna that developed before New Zealand broke away from Australia. The present absence of large land animals – other than birds – is almost certainly a result of extinction over the past 80 million years. With nothing to prey on them, birds proliferated and took over many niches which would elsewhere be occupied by mammals. Some of these birds, lacking the need, eventually lost the ability to fly, and perhaps the most famous is the extinct moa (see box below). Of the very distinct New Zealand animals, such as the moa, kiwi and tuatara (three-eyed centenarian lizards), we have no ancient fossil record.

The climate factor

For much of the time that New Zealand was a part of Gondwana, it lay poleward of 66°S, the polar circle, but fossil evidence indicates that there was no polar ice sheet, or even glaciers in the region. It certainly was not too cold for plant and animal life, but one inescapable fact of life at this latitude was the unusual light regime – permanent summer light, and long, dark winters. At Curio Bay, near the southern-

period when coral reefs grew around the coasts. Palm trees, once common throughout New Zealand, now have their southernmost limit in the area part-way down the South Island.

Some organisms didn't cope with the changes, and became extinct, while others managed to fly, swim, or were simply blown across the sea to New Zealand from elsewhere. The simple notion of New Zealand as an "ark" which drifted away and preserved ancient Gondwanan life is just not true – there may have been nearly complete replacement of the original biota – but what did evolve is unique to New Zealand. Around 80 percent of New

most point of the South Island, one of the best preserved "petrified forests" in the world is exposed on a tidal platform and dates from this early time. The lumps on the platform are the stumps of pine trees and tree ferns, and scattered around are long, straight petrified logs.

After New Zealand broke away it drifted towards the warmer equator and experienced a variety of climate changes. For instance, about 20 million years ago, a worldwide burst of warmth created what was probably the hottest period New Zealand has known, the only

LEFT: kaka parrot on Kapiti Island in the North Island.
ABOVE: kea in the South Island.

THE MOA

The demise of the moa was a huge loss. The giant, flightless bird weighed up to 250 kg (550 lbs) and could be 3 metres (10 ft) tall. Its size, and lack of natural predators, made it easy prey for the early human settlers, and it was hunted to extinction by the early 16th century. Nevertheless, it became as big in myth as it was in stature, with stories of sightings including that of two gold prospectors in the 1860s who were locked up as a result, and an alleged sighting on the beach of Martins Bay in the early 20th century. In 1993 a pub owner was adamant that he'd photographed one. While the chance of moas surviving is remote, so are parts of New Zealand, so who knows?

Zealand's trees, ferns and flowering plants are found nowwhere else in the world. Gum trees *(Eucalyptus)*, wattles *(Acacia)* and she-oaks *(Casuarina)* – all typical Australian plants – do not occur in New Zealand (although fossil evidence proves they once did). Instead, the native bush is dominated by tall, evergreen trees.

One of the most characteristic trees here today is the southern beech *(Nothofagus)*, dominating large areas, just as it does in Tasmania, patches of the Australian mainland, New Guinea, New Caledonia in the Pacific, and Patagonia in South America, and once did in Antarctica.

The human factor

There is some debate as to when the ancestors of the Maori arrived *(see page 19)*. In any case, on a global scale, it was very recently and New Zealand was the last large landmass (Antarctica excepted) to be colonised. One immediate result of human settlement was an increase in fire frequency. Whether this was accidental or by design is academic – the result was the permanent removal of large areas of forest.

Another result was rapid extinction of some of the bird life. Moa in any one area became extinct within a few hundred years, no doubt due to "overkill" by humans. Rats and dogs were also introduced and took their toll on

birdlife. Once the moa became scarce or disappeared altogether there was a corresponding and distinct change in human culture. Fish became more central in the diet and around the same time, cannibalism developed. One theory relates this early cannibalism amongst the Maori to a simple lack of animal protein.

The onslaught of Europeans from the late 18th century speeded up what the Polynesians had begun. A very large area of New Zealand's forest was milled, or simply burnt. Wholesale introduction of browsing mammals and farming have altered parts of the landscape to the point where today no native species remain. Possums, rabbits and deer browse plants so heavily they often kill them, and this destruction can take place on a huge scale. In very steep country which relies on forest to retain the soil, massive erosion has ensued. Introduced weasels, stoats, cats and rodents have wrought havoc on the native birdlife, which never had to cope with these predators before.

No period has seen such a dramatic metamorphosis of the New Zealand landscape as the last few hundred years. The pace of change has been so rapid that many of New Zealand's large forest trees are old enough to have once had moa browsing around them, while many native birds have had little time to develop a fear of humans. This theme of constant change will no doubt continue. The challenge is to ensure that, despite inevitable alteration, the land and its biota remain distinctly "New Zealand".

New Zealanders are well aware of this crisis. Tuatara, which have been around for 250 million years, are now being bred in captivity while sanctuaries are prepared for their safe return to the wild. Conservationists are also trying to restore lost nesting sites for birds and are campaigning vigorously against further coastal development.

A notable success story has been that of the Penguin Place project at Otago Peninsula in the South Island. This was set up to save the rare yellow-eyed penguin (of which only 5,000 survive in the wild), and has witnessed numbers rise from only 16 penguins in 1984 to 160 breeding pairs in 2000. Seals and the royal albatross have also been left to breed in healthy numbers on the Otago Peninsula *(see page 302).* ❑

LEFT: keep your eyes peeled – you might just spot a moa (along with Elvis and the yeti...).

New Zealand's Unique Flora and Fauna

Because of its evolutionary history, New Zealand has a suite of unique archaic and exotic elements. Nearly all of the country's insects and marine molluscs, 80 percent of the flora and 25 percent of birds are found nowhere else. As such New Zealand flora and fauna – and efforts to preserve them – are rapidly gaining importance worldwide.

It is relatively easy to see animals such as albatrosses, penguins, whales, seals and dolphins. On boat trips from Kaikoura *(see page 236)* at the top of the South Island, sightings of half a dozen sperm whales and pods of several hundred dolphins are not uncommon. Back on shore, Kaikoura has a lively seal colony at the end of town.

New Zealand has a high percentage of the world's total number of endangered bird species and numerous projects are underway to preserve and increase their numbers. One such is the kakapo, the world's only flightless parrot, which historically inhabited all three islands but is now confined to areas of Fiordland and Stewart Island – two of the most remote spots in the country. Kakapo have also been transferred to predator-free islands. In 1974 it was unclear whether any existed at all, then, incongruously, a population of males was found in Fiordland followed by a population of males and females on Stewart Island. The Department of Conservation has 10 people working full-time on kakapo-related projects (www.kakaporecovery.org.nz) but the bird remains at great risk.

There was jubilation in 2002 when the first hand-reared kakapo did what all birds should do – laid an egg and managed to rear her chick.

A number of offshore islands have been cleared of predators, and a variety of other endangered birds, reptiles and insects introduced, which now flourish in these safer environments. Islands such as Tiritiri Matangi and Kapiti in the North Island, Motuara in the South Island and Ulva on Stewart Island are all easy to visit, and here, for example, you can see birds such as the takahe, the saddleback and the stitchbird and get some idea of what New Zealand must have been like before the Pakeha arrived.

There are at least 10,500 insect species in New Zealand, of which around 1,100 were introduced

from elsewhere – usually inadvertently – by humans.

Plantlife is equally as interesting as animal life. In particular, New Zealand boasts some of the most spectacular stands of forest in the world. There is not much that can beat the magnificent kauri forests of Northland, the splendid broadleaf-podocarp forests of Pureora or Whirinaki in the central North Island, or the great, ancient beech forests that you pass through when crossing over the Main Divide in the South Island.

It is also worth taking a bit of time to seek out the alpine vegetation, which includes some 600 species of plants, the vast majority of which are endemic. Although the best known is the Mount Cook lily,

which is actually a type of buttercup, there is a host of other striking and unusual plants, such as the vegetable sheep – a strange, decidedly woolly-looking plant which grows together in "flocks" – and the spaniards, to mention just a couple. Many of these plants have evolved in a peculiar way in order to cope with the sometimes harsh environment.

Professional biologists and amateur horticulture enthusiasts alike will find much to amaze and delight them in New Zealand. Birdwatchers wanting to tick off some of the magnificent seabirds on their list will find the best variety of these here. And visitors with a fascination for marine mammals will certainly not be disappointed by the magnificent creatures offshore. ❑

RIGHT: the flightless kakapo is a nocturnal ground parrot and only found in New Zealand.

PEOPLE

Maori, Pacific Islanders and Pakeha have been joined by diverse new people,
who are helping to shape the distinctive New Zealand character

New Zealanders, while numerically rare by global standards, are found the world over, with one million of them living overseas. The other 4.1 million live at home in Godzone, one of the least crowded and most stunning countries on the planet. Yet at the same time New Zealand is also one of the world's most urbanised and suburbanised countries, more so in fact than America and Japan. Eighty-seven percent of its residents live in the inner cities and suburbs of the four main centres – Auckland, Wellington, Hamilton and Christchurch. The rest are scattered in the relatively empty spaces in between. The population of Auckland alone exceeds that of the entire South Island while half the South Island population is to be found in Canterbury. And you're less likely to run into anyone in Westland, where it rains 180 days out of 365. Here, perhaps more than anywhere else, one can sense that New Zealand has been home to humans for only a very short time – in fact, less than 800 years. By any standards New Zealand is a very young country.

Rural and urban New Zealanders

Despite the overwhelming majority of urbanites, farming remains the backbone of the economy. It is a way of life valued by close-knit rural communities throughout the land. Voluntary activity runs everything, from the churches and the A&P (Agricultural & Pastoral) shows to fire and ambulance services. In the countryside you will also find the warmth, friendly neighbourhood security and community spirit that once set the tone for the nation as a whole. As for the legendary black-singletted, gumboot-clad Fred Dagg-like character (Fred Dagg was invented by the satirist John Clarke in the 1970s), the doyen of the family farm with a dog at his heel – he's increasingly rare. Chances are, today, the guy working in the cowshed hails from Mumbai or Tokyo.

PRECEDING PAGES: Maori dancers do the *haka* (war dance); a multicultural crew at the helm in Auckland Harbour. **LEFT:** traditional dances survive in local celebrations. **RIGHT:** young couple from Auckland.

Many an urban office worker may be only one or few generations away from the farm. Until the 1950s, the rural–urban split was roughly 50/50, but that changed with the post-war drift of jobseekers to the cities where they laid claim to their own slice of the "Half-Gallon, Quarter-Acre Pavlova Paradise", the New Zealand

dream of home ownership in the suburbs as defined by the political scientist Austin Mitchell in the early 1970s. Although New Zealand is still paradise, growing crime – the main offenders being drunk and drug-fuelled youth – renders Godzone less so today. Meanwhile, the standard quarter-acre (about 1,000 sq. metres) suburban section has shrunk to a mere eighth of an acre, and the traditional vegetable plot, a former essential in most Kiwi families, is history.

A little Britain in Aotearoa

Migration to New Zealand began in the 13th century with the Maori, who are known as *tangata whenua*, the people of the land (*see* pages 19–23). The Maori impact on the landscape was minimal, compared to what was to follow. The next arrivals, some six centuries later, were the English, Scottish, Irish and Welsh settlers, who were responsible for New Zealand's pioneering culture. The original plan, mooted by the New Zealand Company, was to establish a "Better Britain" or "Britain of the South". Although it is the brainchild of a former convict, Edward Gibbon Wakefield, unlike the other British settlement in Australia, a criminal record was not a pre-requisite for a one-way ticket to "Better Britain". Instead, industrious immigrants, respectable, hardworking rural

labourers and cultured men of capital were determinedly sought. Where class was lacking, prosperity and respectability were promised in exchange for hard work. The idea of owning one's own land, deeply entrenched in the Kiwi psyche, arrived with the settlers, whose minds were set on acquiring their own piece of land, largely an impossibility back home. With the dawn of the 21st century, soaring property prices due in part to foreign investments are seriously threatening this hard-won Kiwi tradition.

Land issues were a constant source of conflict between the Maori and the Europeans in the early days. The Europeans' land-grabbing ways, and later wars between the two groups, did nothing to endear many of the new arrivals to the native population. The greatest conflicts arose over the mutual misunderstanding of what constituted land ownership. Even today, land issues surrounding the 1840 Treaty of Waitangi (*see page 34*) remain some of the most contentious.

For the first 50 years of European settlement, almost half the newcomers were English while some were Welsh (the original statistics lumped both together). Nowhere in New Zealand does this English heritage survive better than in the city of Christchurch, whose founders transplanted here a complete section of English Episcopalian society, with an earl and a bishop (both of whom soon fled the privation of the pioneering scene) at the top and the labouring classes at the bottom. The utopian Episcopalian dream might have foundered, but Christchurch has prospered and remains about as close to England as it gets in New Zealand.

The Scots made up the second-largest immigrant group at 24 percent. Their pioneers,

NOTEWORTHY NEW ZEALANDERS

In 1991 the Reserve Bank of New Zealand announced that new banknotes were required and suggested that portrait of the Queen on some of the banknotes be replaced by those of notable New Zealanders. The nation was called upon to nominate worthy candidates. The illustrious Nobel Prize-winning scientist Sir Ernest Rutherford topped the bill. The first to split the atom, he looks pensively from the $100 note that bills him as Lord Rutherford of Nelson.

National hero Sir Edmund Hillary polled a close second. Voted the country's most trusted citizen in a nationwide poll, Sir Ed is respected as much for his conquest of Mount Everest, as for his humanitarian and conservation

causes. He looks towards the mountains in the distance on the $5 bill.

Kate Sheppard graces the $10 bill. An intelligent Christian socialist, Sheppard led the women's movement whose efforts made New Zealand the world's first sovereign state to give women the vote.

Maori leader, Apirana Ngata, adorns the $50 note. The first Maori to obtain a degree, Ngata graduated with a Bachelor of Arts in 1893, and in 1905 entered parliament as member for Eastern Maori, a seat he held for 38 years. To appease the royalists, the Queen's visage was retained on the $20 note.

a stiff-backed band of Free Kirk (Church) Presbyterians, arrived in 1848, driven by the urge to escape economic depression and the split between their church and the Church of Scotland. This clannish but brave little community possessed the determination and toughness to endure the notoriously bleak winters and the rugged terrain of Otago, where they created their "Scotland of the South". Their main city, Dunedin (the old Gaelic name for Edinburgh), became the nation's most populous town in the 19th century.

The Irish, many of whom were diggers who followed the gold trail down from California

The gold rushes also brought a host of fortune seekers from many nations, flooding into the country through Dunedin, the nearest port to the Otago goldfields. Among the newcomers were Germans, Scandinavians, Poles, French, Italians and Chinese. Yet, despite the influx of these new immigrants, as the 19th century progressed the distinctly British character of New Zealand continued strongly, bolstered by the arrival of another 100,000 Europeans in the 1870s.

Old prejudices also arrived, plus a few new ones. In many a Protestant mind, there was a distinctive "us" and "them" mentality – "them"

and Australia, reached their population peak of in the wake of the gold rushes of the 1860s.

The pioneers brought with them their northern traditions, language, festivals, faith and food, many of which have passed unchanged into 21st-century Kiwi culture. With their menus intact, Pakeha (New Zealanders of European descent) continue to enjoy haggis on Burns Night and Hogmanay, and eggs on Easter, as well as roast, fruit mince pies and steamed fruit pudding – traditional winter fare – at Christmas, eaten in the heat of summer.

being the Catholic Irish. This prejudice persisted well into the 1950s. For some others, their prejudice extended to the Maori.

Not all Europeans who came found what they were looking for. Alfred Domett (1811–87), poet, sometime politician and champion of the early New Zealand Company migrants, settled in Nelson in 1842. On retirement he returned to the more civilised life of a poet in London. He summed up the experience of the more artistic pioneers like himself in this excerpt from his epic poem, *Ranolf and Amohia*, subtitled *South Sea Day Dream*:

Ambition – progress – all the hope and pride
Of true existence seem to him denied.

LEFT: Dunedin still has strong Scottish links.
ABOVE: Chinese lantern festival in Auckland.

*The land so rich in beauty's sensual smile
Seemed for the soul only a desert Isle.*

The new New Zealanders

Up to the 1960s, there was little to challenge the original plan of a distinctly British New Zealand. Most immigrants were British, and those who were not, like the 30,000-strong Dutch community who arrived in the 1950s, were expected to adopt the local ways and get on with it. But with the 1960s came television and cheap air travel, which opened New Zealand to the world and the world to New Zealand like never before. The 1970s saw a severing of traditional ties with Britain joining the European Economic Community and an end to assisted British immigration. A new wave of immigrants, from Asia and the Pacific, followed. Add to the mix a growing number of refugees and asylum seekers, attracted by New Zealand's progressive humanitarian stance, liberal politics, and world-leading social welfare. Today they continue to arrive from various hot spots – Afganistan, Iran, Somalia, South Africa and Zimbabwe. Overall, about 20 percent of New Zealand's residents today were born overseas, with more living in Auckland than anywhere else in the country.

KIWI INGENUITY

It is popularly said that a New Zealander can fix anything with a length of No. 8 (4mm/0.2 inch) fencing wire. New Zealanders' inventiveness and do-it-yourself mentality arrived with the early European settlers, who found themselves in an untamed land, devoid of the trappings (and spare parts) of civilisation. Machinery had to be fixed or redesigned with whatever was available. Necessity has endowed New Zealand with more inventors per capita than anywhere else. Among them are two South Island farmers – Sir William Hamilton, who invented the Hamilton jet boat, and Richard "Mad" Pearse, who designed his own planes and reputedly flew before the Wright brothers.

While certain Kiwi characteristics prevail (*see text box on left and page 67*), the 21st-century New Zealander is becoming increasingly difficult to define. Statistically speaking, if one were to gather together 100 randomly selected New Zealanders, one would be in the company of roughly 79 Pakeha, 15 Maori, seven Pacific Islanders and seven Asians. The median age would be 35 years, 12 would be over 65 years old, and 31 would be from Auckland.

Pacific Islanders

Auckland's distinctly multicultural character contrasts markedly with the rest of the country. South Auckland, in particular, is home to the largest Pacific Island population in the world. The first Pacific Islanders were brought by missionaries to New Zealand for training; after World War II, they came to fill labour shortages.

The majority of the Pacific Islanders today are New Zealand born. Their contributions to New Zealand culture are considerable, particularly in the fields of sport and music. Former All Blacks Tana Umaga and Jonah Lomu, shot put champion Beatrice Faumina, Silver Fern netballer Bernice Mene, and hip-hop artists Che Fu and Scribe are all Kiwi heroes. The largest group among the Pacific Islanders are the

While traditional fish and chips remains the favourite for the rest of New Zealand, Asian foods are the takeaway of choice in Auckland, home to the country's largest Asian population. Today, Chinese from China, Taiwan and Hong Kong form the largest Asian immigrant group, followed by Indians. Within these groups are families who have been in the country for several generations. The rest of the Asian community come mainly from Korea, Sri Lanka and Japan. Their reasons for coming vary; some came for education, others to invest or transfer their skills, and many to establish their families in a less crowded, cleaner and healthier environment.

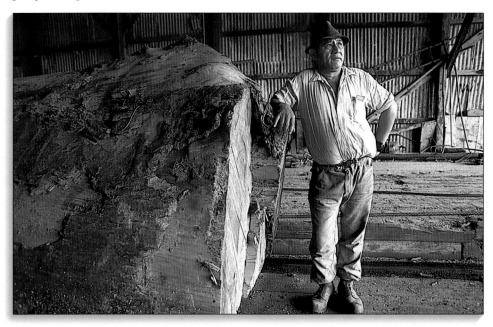

Samoans, whose payments to relatives back home provide half of Samoa's foreign exchange. Cook Islands Maori and Tongans make up the next largest groups, followed by Niueans, Fijians and Tokelauans. Indeed, many more Niueans, Cook Islands Maori and Tokelauans are found in New Zealand than in the islands themselves. Of the many tongues spoken in New Zealand, the most common after the official English and Maori is Samoan, followed by Tongan, Cantonese and Mandarin.

LEFT: a couple from Cook Islands in the South Pacific.
ABOVE: a Pacific Island immigrant from Tonga working at a timber mill.

The big OE

For all who come to New Zealand, many also leave, whether permanently, indefinitely or merely for the short term to visit relatives in other countries. New Zealanders have long been ranked among the world's most travelled citizens. Just why one million New Zealanders live overseas has everything to do with New Zealand's geographical remoteness and the national rite of passage known as the big OE – Overseas Experience. Lasting anything from a few years to decades, OE was originally a sea journey home to Britain and Europe for the early settlers. It then became an essential cultural escape for New Zealand artists and writers of the 1920s and 1930s, stifled by the insular, tight-lipped narrow-mindedness of home. From the 1960s onwards, cheaper air travel brought the rest of the world within the reach of more Kiwis who chose to escape and explore their past and the world at large, and pursue lives around the globe.

The main meccas of Kiwi pilgrimage remain Britain, London being the city of choice, and Australia. Between 1976 and 1982, 103,000 New Zealanders moved to Australia and settled there permanently. According to

> **FAIR EXCHANGE**
>
> Given the large number of Kiwis who leave for their OE, it is not unexpected that New Zealand employs the world's second-highest proportion of immigrants.

The next generation

Migrants and their children, regardless of origin, share a common story, one perfectly portrayed by the lonely Dalmatian immigrant Nick in Kiwi writer Frank Sargeson's *The Making of a New Zealander*: "Nick and I were sitting on the hillside and Nick was saying he was a New Zealander, but he knew he wasn't a New Zealander. And he knew he wasn't a Dalmatian any more."

The first generation, born in a new country, live between two cultures, that of the land of

New Zealand's then-prime minister, Robert Muldoon, "New Zealanders who leave for Australia raise the IQ of both countries". Today an estimated half a million New Zealanders call Australia home, attracted by higher wages, lower taxes, warmer climate and proximity to home. Another 50,000 Kiwis are overseas in countries other than Australia and Britain. Most, having satisfied their curiosity, return home eventually, to bring up their children or to retire. Settling back in has its challenges though; the more travelled finds it less easy to adjust to the limits of their homeland's insular shores, particularly if they are not fans of rugby or the great outdoors.

their birth, and that of their parents' homeland. While some stay in touch with their parents' culture and speak their mother tongue at home, others struggle with identity issues. Many first-generation Pacific Island New Zealanders regard the loss of language as the main reason for their generation's lack of confidence and equate fluency in their parents' language as the key to preserving their culture. Yet with each passing generation, cultural anxiety may lessen. The multicultural Kiwi melting pot bubbles on with the healthy addition of increasing mixed parentage and new immigrants. ❏

ABOVE: the All Blacks doing the *haka* warrior dance.

What Makes a New Zealander

New Zealanders are as homogeneous – or as diverse – as the people of any other nation in this age of globalism, the Internet and international air travel. That said, the isolation and insularity of this country have bred some distinct qualities and characteristics that are more noticeable here than elsewhere.

One that is likely to be noticed early on by visitors is known as the "cultural cringe", the belief that, because New Zealand is so small and remote, anything from another country is automatically seen as superior to the local version. This characteristic indicates a desperate need for approval from foreigners. The first question visitors are likely to be asked is: "How do you like New Zealand?" (The correct answer is : "It's wonderful, I'm thinking of moving here.")

As a consequence of this dependence on overseas approval, the New Zealanders who have succeeded overseas are the ones who are most respected at home – the likes of Sir Edmund Hillary, Sam Neill and Kiri Te Kanawa. There is a suspicion that those people who choose to remain here to climb mountains or act or sing opera do so because "they couldn't make it overseas".

Don't be a "tall poppy"

Another corollary of New Zealand's smallness is that it is quite easy for an individual to shine. Anyone engaged in any form of endeavour is likely to be among the top five in his or her field simply because there won't be many more than five people engaged in it. This is directly connected to the so-called "tall poppy" syndrome, meaning that anyone who rises above the crowd will be cut down in a frenzy of negative criticism generated by envy. This is much-quoted but simply not true, and the syndrome may well be the invention of an over-sensitive elite who cannot abide any suggestion that they fall short of perfection.

The notion of a tall poppy springs from the fact that, despite the wide gap between rich and poor, New Zealand is still at heart an egalitarian society, the legacy of the utopians who colonised it. There is a class system but it is far less rigid and

confining than in most other Western democracies.

New Zealanders are a relatively laconic race, so it's paradoxical that when they do speak, they talk very quickly, packing a greater number of words into a breath than most other native English-speakers. At the same time, their conversation labours under a conspicuous drawl. Those who recoil at the length of time it takes a New Zealander to meander through a vowel should be warned that many linguists theorise that the English-speaking world is undergoing a Great Vowel Shift which will eventually see everyone talking like "thus".

A highly active sense of humour is a strong part of the national make-up, though it often goes unno-

ticed because it is so dry. If a New Zealander says something that sounds absurd, he probably means it to be, but he won't drive it home with series of hearty guffaws and thigh-slapping.

Though overwhelmingly urbanite in number, New Zealanders' heritage has given them many rural values which persist beyond the farm gate – diligence, support for others, strong community spirit, practicality (with a concomitant distrust of intellectuals) and a can-do attitude. The phrase "No. 8-wire spirit" holds that a New Zealander can solve any practical problem with a piece of No. 8 fencing wire. New Zealanders are certainly ingenious; they are also diverse, imaginative and entertaining hosts. ❑

RIGHT: Maori woman proudly displays her heritage with traditional bone jewellery.

THE MODERN MAORI

Gradually, Maori are gaining a higher profile in all aspects of New Zealand life, and non-Maori are showing increasing respect for traditional Maori beliefs

If one person has been more responsible than any other for the survival of Maori culture into modern times, it must be the great parliamentarian from the east coast of the North Island, Sir Apirana Ngata (1874–1950). The extent of his contributions to Maoridom make him a figure of enormous significance. By the late 1920s, knighted and made Minister of Native Affairs, Ngata had devised legislation to develop Maori land, established a caring school at Rotorua and initiated a work programme for the building of Maori community facilities.

Working with Ngata to implement national policy at a local level was a group of community leaders including Princess Te Puea Herangi of Waikato (1883–1952).

Maori King Movement

Te Puea was for 40 years the reinvigorating force behind the Kingitanga, or Maori King Movement, which was formed in 1858 to unite and strengthen the Maori community and to halt the loss of Maori land to the colonial settlers. The British tried to crush the Kingitanga by invading Waikato in 1863–4 and confiscating 500,000 hectares (1.2 million acres) of Waikato land. It was Te Puea who began the quest for compensation for confiscated Maori land. She raised the morale of her people, revived their cultural activities, built a model village at Ngaruawahia *(see page 166)* which became the nerve centre of the King Movement, and established thousands of Waikato Maori back on farm land. She also won a wide degree of Maori and Pakeha acceptance for the institution of the Maori kingship, which had previously been regarded with suspicion outside Waikato.

Te Puea's great-niece, Te Arikinui Dame Te Atairangikaahu, led the Kingitanga for the next 40 years, during which it grew in stature. It is today seen as Maoridom's single most important leadership. The five-day *tangi* (funeral service) following Te Ata's death in August

LEFT: the late Sir James Henare, noted Maori leader.
RIGHT: modern Maori mum and child.

2006 brought Maori together on an unprecedented scale. Her eldest son, Tuheitia Paki, has succeeded as king.

Rise in living standards

A Labour government was elected towards the end of the Great Depression in the 1930s. Its

welfare programme did more to lift Maori standards of living than any previous measures and ensured the physical survival of the Maori race, which had been threatened by diseases introduced by European settlers. The Maori electorate acknowledged this by returning only Labour Members of Parliament until New Zealand First gave them another option in the 1996 election. The formation of the Maori Party in 2004 has provided Maori with yet another option for the 2005 election.

Following World War II, however, there was a major shift in Maori society. A decline in rural employment and a rapid expansion of secondary industry in urban areas brought Maori into the cities in increasing numbers. By the 1980s less than 10 percent of Maori lived in rural settlements. For the first time, Maori (who comprise 15 percent of the total population) and Pakeha (who make up 75 percent) had to live alongside one another.

This new relationship brought difficulties. With no ready access or encouragement to further their education, many new urban Maori became trapped in low-paying jobs. Housing conditions were also poor. That led to stereotyping that further hindered their prospects. It was a harsh and different world, lacking the support network offered by the extended family in the rural environment. Many born in the new environment reacted in a strongly anti-social manner. The Maori crime rate increased, adding further to a negative Maori stereotype.

The problems, however, have been recognised, and progress has been made in the past few decades. The education system in New Zealand has gradually adapted to the new demands. *Kohanga Reo* (language nests) have been set up to expose pre-school Maori to their language and customs. The school curriculum better reflects the importance of Maori culture to the New Zealand way of life. Programmes have been established to encourage Maori to

THE HUI, A TRADITIONAL MAORI GATHERING

At the start of a *hui*, visitors are called on to the *marae*, the area in front of the meeting house, with a *karanga* – a long, wailing call, performed only by women, that beckons the living and commemorates the dead. Answering the call, the visitors enter the *marae* led by their own women, usually dressed in black. Then follows a pause and a *tangi* (ritual weeping) for the dead. This is succeeded by the *mihi* (speeches) of welcome and reply, made by male elders.

At the end of each speech, the orator's companions get to their feet and join him for a *waiata* (song), usually a lament. Once these formalities are over, the visitors come forward and *hongi* (press noses) with the locals, thereby being absorbed into the ranks of *tangata whenua* (host tribe) for the remainder of the function.

The food served on such occasions is special: meat and vegetables are cooked in a *hangi* or earth oven. There will be a preponderance of seafood, with delicacies such as shellfish, *kina* (sea egg), eel and dried shark. Fermented corn is a speciality, as is *titi* (muttonbird). The bread offered is likely to be *rewena* (a scone-like loaf) or another variety similar to fried doughnuts. Far more than in Pakeha society, eating together is a ritual means of communicating goodwill. Acceptance of such hospitality is often considered as important as offering it.

carry their education through to university, and several laws ban discrimination in the workplace. Legal aid and translation facilities are now available in the courts, and Maori is now the country's second official language.

Yet poverty remains a problem for Maori in many areas, and they still make up a disproportionate part of the prison population. Some commentators have suggested the social problems are deep-rooted, perhaps going back as far as to European colonisation.

The institution devised to help Maori is the Waitangi Tribunal, established in 1975. This allows Maori to claim compensation in the form

profile is increasing and a more positive stereotype is replacing the old negative image.

The *hui (see box opposite)* offers the most revealing and moving glimpse of Maori culture. It will usually be held on a *marae* (a courtyard in front of a meeting house) under the supervision of the *tangata whenua* or host tribe. After the opening formalities, the *hui* will be taken up with public and private discussion of matters of local, tribal and national Maori interest. It will also include community eating, singing and religious services. The participants sleep in the large meeting house or hall, where discussions often go on until the early hours of the morning.

of land, cash or fishing quotas for resources unfairly taken. Based on the 1840 Treaty of Waitangi, the tribunal has done more than any other measure to address Maori grievances.

Bicultural conflicts continue to arise periodically. In the mid-1990s a movement for Maori sovereignty – *Tino Rangatiratanga* – blossomed briefly, and in 2003 the nation became obsessed with Maori claims to the foreshore, roughly the damp sand between high and low tides. This highly contentious issue is still not laid to rest.

In all aspects of New Zealand life, the Maori

Maori weddings, christenings and funeral ceremonies are also quite different from Pakeha ones. They will include speeches, songs and proverbs in Maori, and an impressively open display of feelings. Maori values, too, pulsate beneath the cloak of Western appearances. Concepts such as *tapu* (sacredness), its opposite, *noa*, *wairua* (things of the spirit) and *mana* (spirtual authority), all persist in modern Maori life.

Non-Maori are now pressured to show increasing respect for Maori rituals and for places that are *tapu* (sites of sacred objects, historic events or burials). Maori ceremonials are increasingly honoured by Pakeha. The hope is that the benefits are seen to be there for both races. ❏

LEFT: the *hongi*, a formal Maori greeting.
ABOVE: war canoes are still used for ceremonies today.

Names of Tatus

V Shape centre

Bands on fore[head] and temples

Where thes[e] in side the eyelids

ornament on of Tiwhana corner of ey[e]

ornament o[n] between the K

double spira[l] upper par[t]

notching d[own] nose. Wh[ere]

double spiral nostrils Po[n]

pattern ove[r] lip

Both Lips ta Ngutu pu Pattern on [the] Ka[u]

8 Bands from to chin patt[ern] RER

stab on the outer centre of the

SPIRAL on the upper cheeks
KOWIRI —
lines of above, just under the eyes

ANCIENT MAORI ART AND SOCIETY

Maori works of art are not only beautiful to look at, but also reveal a great deal about their society's beliefs, history and social structure

The classic art of New Zealand Maori is an unsurpassed Pacific tribal art. Many creative styles and much skilled craftsmanship yielded, and continue to yield, objects of great beauty. To appreciate the achievements of Maori arts and crafts, it is invaluable to have an understanding of the materials used, the techniques of crafts, design and symbolism, and the economic, social and religious requirements that inspired the making of artefacts.

The working of wood, stone, bone, fibre, feathers, clay pigments, and other natural materials by skilled craftspeople is at the heart of Maori art and craft. The carving of wood is perhaps the most important craft of all, since canoes, storehouses, dwellings, village fortifications, weapons, domestic bowls and working equipment were made of wood.

Cultural connections

Maori artefacts fell into three distinctive categories. The first was communally owned objects, such as war canoes. The second category consisted of personal items, such as garments, greenstone ornaments, combs, musical instruments and indelible skin tattoos. The tools of the carver, lines and fishhooks of the fisherman, implements of the field worker, and snares and spears of a fowler were usually made by the users and should be included in this category. The last category encompassed artefacts of ritual magic kept under the guardianship of priests *(tohunga)* – godsticks, crop gods and anything else used in ceremonial communication with gods and ancestral spirits. Such things were often elaborate versions of utilitarian objects; an ordinary digging stick, for example, would be ornately carved in its ritual form.

Periods of Maori art merge, yet there are four distinctive eras: Archaic, Classic, Historic and Modern. The Archaic Maori were the immediate descendants of the Polynesians who first

settled the land, surviving by hunting, fishing and foraging. Their art work, including carvings and bone and stone work, is characterised by austere forms that, as pure sculpture, can surpass much of the later work.

In time, the cultivation of the sweet potato or kumara and other crops, along with an

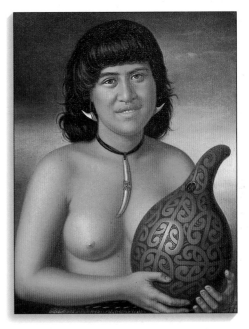

advanced ability to exploit all natural resources of forest and ocean, allowed a settled way of village life. With this came food surpluses, a tightly organised tribal system and territorial boundaries. These were the Classic Maori, and their altered society supported dedicated craftspeople within each community.

The Historic period of Maori art underwent rapid changes due to the adoption of metal tools, Christianity, Western fabrics, newly introduced crops, muskets and cannon. After 1800, warfare became particularly brutal as the first tribes to possess muskets descended on traditional enemies still armed with clubs and spears. Fortified villages *(pa)* could no longer

---

PRECEDING PAGES: Maori meeting house in Waitangi.
LEFT: sketch of a traditional *moko* (facial tatoo).
RIGHT: Maori woman with a decorated gourd.

be defended and were abandoned, and the great war canoes became useless as gunpowder weapons changed the strategy of battle.

The fourth period of Maori art, the Modern, was underway before 1900, and remains with us. The great rise in interest in Maori culture (*Maoritanga*) in recent decades is in step with a renaissance of Maori culture. The roots of this Maori art resurgence reach well back into the 19th century, yet it was the early 20th-century leaders, notably Sir Apirana Ngata and Sir Peter Buck (Te Rangi Hiroa), who advocated the study and renewal of Maori art. The meeting house proved an ideal, practical medium.

Traditional Maori society

Society and the arts have always been associated with fighting chiefs who had an hereditary right to control tribal affairs. They were the best dressed, ornamented and accoutred; and tribal prestige (*mana*) depended on these leaders.

A well-appointed warrior was not fully dressed without his weapons: a short club thrust into his belt and a long club held in his hand. Weapons were always kept near, mostly for defence – a stealthy, sudden attack on an unsuspecting foe was much admired. Warriors were also well versed in the practice of oratory as they took pains to stress the points of a speech.

Society as a whole was an autocratic hierarchy. Individuals belonged to extended families (*whanau*) which in turn clustered to form sub-tribes (*hapu*) allied as tribes through blood ties. Family trees led back to ancestral canoes (*waka*), the names of which provided tribal names.

Society was divided into two classes, which overlapped to some degree. The upper class was composed of the nobles (*ariki*) and the generals or chiefs (*rangatira*). The majority lower class was made up of the commoners (*tutua*). There were also slaves (*taurekareka*) who held no rights and did menial work and sometimes died as sacrificial victims or when special events required human flesh.

People dressed according to rank, yet when engaged in daily routine work both high and low classes used any old garments. Men and women wore a waist wrap, plus a shoulder cloak when weather or ceremony required. Pre-pubescent children usually went about naked. On attaining adulthood, it was considered indecent to uncover the sexual organs.

MAORI MEETING HOUSES

In the Classic period, large storehouses (*pataka*) were built to house the foreign goods that ushered in a new economy, and some of these are preserved in museums, including the Auckland War Memorial Museum (*see page 142*).

During the Historic era, the meeting house (*whare runanga*) increasingly became the focus of Maori social life and of a Maori art revolution. They played a vital role throughout the 19th century, when meetings were held to discuss issues affecting the tribe – including the ravages of foreign diseases and losses caused by fighting with settlers. Many of these ornate meeting houses can still be seen throughout the North Island.

Important Maori buildings were named after an ancestor and the construction symbolised the actual person; the ridge pole represented the spine, the rafters were his ribs, and the façade boards, which at times terminated in fingers, were his arms. At the gable peak was the face mask. Some tribe members still believe that when they enter a particular house they are entering the protective body of their ancestor. Many communal houses can be visited, and a fine example is Tama-te-Kapua at Ohinemutu, Rotorua, built in 1878. While Maori meeting houses are often on private property, visitors are welcome as long as they get permission beforehand.

Tattoo art

The special indication of rank was the facial tattoo. Tattooists were well paid, proportionate to their skill, in goods and hospitality. Men were tattooed over the whole face in painful, deep-grooved cuts made by birdbone chisels dipped in a sooty pigment, which looked blue under the skin. Northern warriors often had additional tattoos over buttocks and thighs. Women were deeply tattooed on their lips and chin, but the lips were made blue by the use of comb-type "needles".

The remarkable art of the tattooist can still be seen on Maori mummified heads. Tradi-

Tattooists and other craft specialists were generally drawn from the higher ranks and were respected priests. Skill in craft work was honoured by chiefs and commoners alike, and even the nobles turned their hands to creative art work. High-ranking women enjoyed making fine garments and chiefs often filled in leisure hours with carving chisel in hand, working on a box or some other small item.

Art for the gods

Religious inspiration in Maori art was based on the prevailing beliefs about gods and ancestral spirits. In pre-Christian times supernatural

tionally, the heads of enemies were taken home to be reviled, but those of kinsfolk were preserved to be mourned over. Mummification was carried out by a process involving steaming, smoking and oiling, and heads so treated remained intact and retained hair, skin and teeth. Out of respect for Maori beliefs, such heads are rarely shown as exhibits in museums, and there is currently strong pressure by Maori for the return of mummified heads held by overseas museums.

LEFT: a Maori rooftop carving.
ABOVE AND RIGHT: elaborate facial tattoo *(moko)*, then and now.

beings were believed to inhabit natural objects. Rituals and chants were thus necessary to ensure the successful pursuit of any task.

People, hand-made items and natural objects were all thought to have an inner psychic force called *mana*. This key idea is essential to the understanding of Maori art and behaviour. *Mana* has many shades of meaning, such as prestige, influence, authority, and most significantly, psychic power. *Mana*'s presence was traditionally manifested in efficiency or effectiveness, such as a warrior's success in a battle or a fishhook's fish-catching ability. *Mana* increased with success or decreased through improper contact or pollution. If a chief or his possessions were touched by a person of lower rank, then there was pollution and *mana* was diminished.

In traditional Maori society the sexes were kept apart in all their craft activities. While men worked the hard materials of wood, bone and stone, women followed crafts using soft materials *(see page 82)* or they prepared flax fibres used in making garments and decorative *taniko* borders. It was believed women were created from the earth by Tane. The first man was a direct spiritual creation of the god Tu. Thus it was said that women were *noa* – non-sacred – and the male, conversely, a *tapu* (sacred or holy) being. This, of course, put females in a

subservient position which precluded them from high religious practices and from crafts and activities in which high gods and ancestral spirits were directly involved. Women were not allowed to approach men working at their crafts. This was the law and severe punishment followed any infringement.

Chiefs and priests had the highest status; they attained their positions only after a long apprenticeship with training in religious rites.

Wooden stickgods *(tiki wananga)*, bound with sacred cords and dressed in red feathers, were used by priests when communicating with gods and ancestral spirits to protect the welfare of the tribe. Stone crop gods *(taumata atua)* were placed in or near gardens to promote fertility in growing crops.

Remarkable wooden burial chests, hollowed out and backed with a slab door, were used to contain the bones of the deceased. Maori burial practice, at least for persons of rank, required an initial burial, then a recovery of the bones a year or two later when a final, ceremonial burial would take place. The spirit of the deceased was thought to journey to Cape Reinga, at the North Island's northern tip, where it plunged into the sea, en route to the ancient homeland of Hawaiki. Burial chests often have a canoe-like form; some even possess a central keel ridge. These magnificent chests, concealed in caves or in other hidden places, were found in the Auckland districts and many have been preserved in museums.

Monuments and cenotaphs of various forms were erected in memory of the dead. Some were posts with carvings of stylised humans called *tiki* while others took the form of canoes buried in the earth deeply enough to stand vertically. Posts were also erected to mark tribal boundaries and to commemorate momentous events.

Maori art motifs

Maori art can appear as a disordered jumble. However, an understanding of the small number of symbols and motifs used reveals orderliness. The human form, dominant in most compositions, is generally referred to as a *tiki* and represents the first created man of Maori mythology. *Tiki* represent ancestors and gods in the sculptural arts, and may be carved in wood, bone or stone. The nephrite (greenstone) *hei-tiki* pendant is the best known of ornaments. In ceremonial meeting-house architecture, ancestral *tiki* were carved on panels supporting the rafters or on other parts of the structure. They were highly stylised with large heads to fill in areas of posts or panels. This design also stressed the importance of the head in Maori belief – along with the sexual organs, it was the most sacred part of the body.

Sexual organs were often exaggerated in both male and female carved figures; both penis and vulva were regarded as centres of potent magic in promoting fertility and protection. Small

CARVING STYLES

Local styles of carving differ in many respects. The figures of the east coast Bay of Plenty region in North Island are square, while those of the Taranaki and Auckland districts are more sinuous.

world. *Tiki* figures often have slanted, staring eyes, clawed hands with a spur thumb, a beaked mouth and other bird-like features. These bird-like motifs were superimposed on the basic human form to create a hybrid – a bird-man. The practice probably stemmed from the belief that the souls of the dead and the gods used birds as spirit vehicles.

The *manaia*, another major symbol, is a beaked figure rendered in profile with a body that has arms and legs. When it is placed near *tiki* it appears to

birth figures were often placed between the legs or on the bodies of *tiki* representing descending generations. The bodies of panel figures were often placed in the contorted postures of the war dance. The out-thrust tongue was an expression of defiance and of protective magic.

The Maori *tiki* carver provided material objects to serve as the vehicles of gods and ancestral spirits. Some post figures are portraits depicting an individual's tattoo, though most are stylisations of beings not of the mortal

---

LEFT: a Maori *tiki* woodcarving with eyes made of iridescent *paua* shell.

ABOVE: Maori woodcarver Keri Wilson at work.

bite at them about the head and body. Sometimes *manaia* form part of the *tiki* themselves and often alternate with *tiki* on door lintels. They may represent the psychic power of the *tiki*. In form, it is a bird-man or lizard-man. Lizards made rare appearances in Maori woodcarving and other sculptural arts.

Whales *(pakake)* and whale-like creatures appeared on the slanting façades of storehouses. The head part terminates at the lower end in large, interlocking spirals representing the mouth. Some fish, dogs and other creatures occurred in carvings, but on the whole they are rare; there was no attempt to depict nature in a naturalistic way.

Marakihau, fascinating mermen monsters of the *taniwha* class (mythical creatures that lurked in river pools and caves), appeared on panels and as greenstone ornaments. *Marakihau* were probably ancestral spirits that took to the sea and are depicted on 19th-century house panels with sinuous bodies terminating in curled tails. Their heads have horns, large round eyes and tube tongues, and were occasionally depicted sucking in a fish. *Marakihau* were supposedly able to swallow canoes and their entire crews.

CHANGE IN METHOD

When Europeans introduced metals, the old stone tools were cast aside in favour of iron blades, which altered carving techniques.

Painted patterns can be seen on rafter paintings and are based on a curved stalk and bulb motif called a *koru*. Air New Zealand uses a *koru* as the company logo.

Tools and materials

The tools and materials of the Maori craft work were limited to woods, stone, fibres and shells; metal tools did not exist. Adzes, the principal tools of woodcarvers, were made of stone blades lashed to wooden helves. Adzing art was basic to all traditional Maori wood sculpture. Forms were first adzed, then chisels were used to give surface decoration. Greenstone was the most valued blade material. Chisels had either a straight-edged or gouge-type blade which was lashed to a short wooden handle. Stone-pointed rotary drills and various wooden wedges and mallets completed the Maori stone-age tool kit.

The introduction of oil-based paints quickly ousted the old red ochre pigment *(kokowai)*, which can be seen today only in traces on older carvings. The later practice of overpainting old carvings with European red paint was unfortunate in that it obliterated much patination and often the older ochres, resulting in the loss of the polychrome-painted work of the Historic period.

The relatively soft yet durable totara and kauri trees, the latter only found in the warm, northern parts of the North Islands, were favoured by the carvers. Hardwoods were also abundant. *Pounamu*, the nephritic jade also known as greenstone, was valued as a sacred material. Found only in the river beds of the Arahura and Taramakau on the West Coast of South Island, this rare commodity was widely traded. Greenstone is of such a hard texture that it cannot be scratched by a steel point. To work it in the days before the diamond cutters of the lapidary was laborious. The worker rubbed away with sandstone cutters to abrade a greenstone piece into the form of a pendant, *hei-tiki*, weapon or some other object.

Bone was used in many ways. Whalebone was especially favoured for weapons, while sperm-whale teeth made fine ornaments and dog hair decorated weapons and cloaks. The brilliant feathers of New Zealand birds were placed on cloaks in varied patterns. The iridescent *paua* (abalone) shell was used as inlay in woodcarving, and textile dyes were made from barks. A deep black dye was obtained by soaking fibres in swamp mud.

Flax plants were used by Maori in many ways. Green leaf strips could quickly be made into field baskets or platters, or could be water-soaked, pounded and bleached to produce a strong fibre for warm garments, cords and ropes. Maori war canoes, houses and foodstores were assembled using flax cord, as metal nails did not exist and the Maori did not use pegs as wooden nails. ❑

LEFT: the Maori *koru* motif has been adopted by Air New Zealand as its official logo.

The Art of the Modern Maori

There are hundreds of Maori artists working in New Zealand today, and their work spans many media, from the newest technologies tò the arts of their Maori forefathers.

During the 20th century Maori art formed into two main streams. The first were those arts based in the *whare whakairo* (carved meeting house), such as *whakairo* (carving), *kowhaiwhai* (painting) and *tukutuku* (woven panels). Many Maori artists welcomed new artistic movements introduced into New Zealand, such as modernism and postmodernism, and have interacted within these styles in their own particular way, fusing the indigenous with the global.

By the 1960s, Maori were showing their works within galleries, both individually and collectively. There have been successive generations of artists, starting with the *kaumatua* generation of men and women, who are now in their 60s and 70s, such as Ralph Hotere, Paratene Matchitt, Arnold Manaaki Wilson, Sandy Adsett, Fred Graham and others. Their work showed New Zealand that Maori art deserved to be exhibited in a gallery setting rather than be seen merely as anthropological specimens.

During the 1970s and 1980s a new group emerged, including artists such as Emare Karaka, Robyn Kahukiwa, Kura Te Waru-Rewiri and Shona Rapira-Davies. Much of their work was overtly political, including symbols of protest, bright colours and expressive paint styles. Since then, a further wave of artists has emerged, such as Brett Graham, Michael Parekowhai, Natalie Robertson, Areta Wilkinson and Lisa Reihana, many of whom have been trained in universities. Their work ventures into new territories in terms of media, such as digital/video installation, and in so doing challenges the stereotypes of what Maori art is in form.

The traditional Maori house is still an important centre for contemporary arts. Many contemporary *whare whakairo* maintain aspects of the traditional in terms of the basic architectural structure and choice of design elements (carving, painting and woven panels), yet innovate with the range of materials and imagery used. Master carvers, such as Pakaariki Harrison, are highly sought after, and travel the country and globe to talk about their work.

The number of publications about Maori art and artists has increased, and they examine both the tribal arts and the modern. Most notable is the fact that all of these publications are written by Maori, for Maori. Galleries are now opening dedicated solely to Maori art, such as the Mataora Gallery in Parnell Street and Te Taumata Gallery in Upper Symonds Street, both in Auckland.

The face of the Maori is also changing, and *moko* (tattooing) is a visible expression of the culture. Traditional sites on the body to *ta moko* (tattoo) are still used, especially the face (full facial for men, lips and chins for women) and thighs and legs of both men and women. *Tohunga ta moko* (tattoo

specialists), both men and women, practise around the country and are highly sought after. Since the mid-1970s there has been a renaissance of *moko* and it is not uncommon to see wearers sipping lattes in upmarket cafés. Experts such as Te Rangikaihoro Nicholas, Derek Lardelli, Rangi and Julie Skipper and Gordon Hadfield all use modern gun machines yet there is an exciting shift to learning more about traditional tools, such as the *uhi* (chisel), a technique which sets *moko* apart from all other tattoo styles, in that it is carved into the skin.

Contemporary Maori art is as diverse as the Maori people themselves, and wherever you travel to in New Zealand, you will easily find exhibitions and galleries that reward exploration. ❑

RIGHT: contemporary Maori artists actively challenge stereotypes of traditional work.

MAORI HANDICRAFTS: FOR LIFE AND LEGEND

The Stone-Age culture of the Maori developed extraordinary skills using the simplest of resources, and traditional crafts are flourishing once again

When the Maori migrated to New Zealand from Polynesia, much of what they found was unfamiliar, but they soon learned to make the best use of the available resources. For example, they used stone adzes to make long, graceful canoes from giant kauri trees, or from totara, whose wood was ideally suited to carving. To ensure durablity, they preserved their sculptures by painting them with a mixture of red clay and shark oil.

PRACTICAL OBJECTS

Everyday items such as eating utensils, tools and weapons were obviously important to the Maori, but so were the fine arts, which were inextricably linked with the drama of Maori mythology. The *marae*, or traditional meeting-place, is still dominated by imposing wooden figures of important ancestors. A *tiki* is a good luck charm of a stylised human figure and made from greenstone or bone, and a *hei-tiki* is a pendant worn round the neck. Traditionally, women wove flax leaves into mats and baskets, or turned the fibres into decorative clothing for special occasions.

A RENAISSANCE

As the Maori have grown increasingly aware of their heritage, so traditional crafts have enjoyed a rebirth. The main place where young people learn to carve wood, bone and greenstone is the Maori Arts and Crafts Institute in Rotorua.
Recently, there has been increased demand from New Zealanders of European origin for traditional Polynesian crafts. Greenstone carving in particular has become an extraordinarily intricate art, which has nothing in common with the mass-produced items for sale in souvenir shops.

▷ **TRAINING CENTRE**
The NZ Maori Arts and Crafts Institute in Rotorua is where most traditional Maori woodcarvers are trained in their craft. Located in Whakarewarewa, it is open to visitors *(see page 186)*.

▽ **TRADITIONAL WEAVING**
Flax is softened in thermal springs before its fibres are woven into elegant dresses by Maori women. Maori men also wore cloaks made from flax and bordered with geometric patterns.

▷ **GRAPHIC STORYTELLING**
As the Maori had no written language, their myths and legends were passed on verbally from generation to generation. Here a grandmother skilfully creates string figures to illustrate her story of the Tongahiro and Ruapehu volcanoes, which are believed to personify temperamental nature gods.

◁ **BONE *TIKI***
Centuries ago, these richly ornamented carvings were made from moa bones, using sharp stone tools. Now that the huge flightless birds have become extinct, *tiki* are made from the bones of other animals.

◁ FRIGHTENING FACE

Sculptures of monstrous skulls and grimacing faces are typical of Maori art, which had a strong spiritual dimension. Originally, such carvings would have been placed on the protecting palisades of a *pa* (fortified village) to frighten off attackers.

▽ RITUAL ADZE

Maori used stone tools for woodcarving, but greenstone adzes, or *toki*, like this one were too precious to use for that purpose. Ornate adzes were made to be carried in ceremonies by tribal chieftains and other high-ranking figures, to symbolise their status and authority.

▽ SPECIAL PROTECTION

Wooden figures of important ancestors were used to protect a tribe against the wrath of the gods and to intercede on the tribe's behalf.

COMMUNAL WAR CANOES

War canoes, ornately decorated with both sculpture and painting, were objects of great prestige in a Maori community. Most were painted red, with black and white detailing, and festooned with feathers. The magnificent 35-metre (115-ft) war canoe *(above)* in Waitangi was skilfully carved from the trunks of two huge kauri trees from the Puketi Forest. It took 27 months to build, and was launched in 1940 to mark the centenary of the Waitangi Treaty.

The streamlined hull is at no point more than 2 metres (7 ft) wide, but the canoe was big enough for 160 warriors to sit without treading on one another's feet. Propelled by 80 paddles, the canoe reached an impressive speed in the sheltered waters of the Bay of Islands, and the seafaring skills of this Polynesian people were brought vividly to life for the spectators.

In their quest for a new homeland, the Maori crossed the vast and often turbulent Pacific in handbuilt boats; not slender war canoes like this one, but more stable outriggers with greater space for food and personal belongings. In 1985, a 21-metre (69-ft) replica of one of these traditional boats sailed from Rarotonga in the Cook Islands to New Zealand. The 5,000-km (3,107-mile) journey took just over five weeks, with the crew steering by the stars, moon and tides, just as the Maori had once done.

CONTEMPORARY ART AND LITERATURE

Behind much of New Zealand's art and literature lies a degree of tension
between the landscape and the people who inhabit it

Many New Zealanders have always had something of an ambivalent attitude towards the arts. Grants to artists and writers announced by Creative New Zealand – the state funding agency – regularly arouse derision, as if wastrels and idlers were getting money for nothing. Philistinism is never far from the surface of public life. But in spite of this – or perhaps precisely because of it – a robust indigenous culture has flourished. The very isolation of artists has forced them to forge their own way, without too much reliance on overseas models or local encouragement.

The practical do-it-yourself tradition of New Zealanders in other fields – notably farming and home renovation – shows through in the work of artists as diverse as the funkily inventive Michael Parekowhai and the masterful Ralph Hotere, whose paintings frequently incorporate items like corrugated iron and old timber. New Zealand's contribution to the 2003 Venice Biennale, an installation by Michael Stevenson, featured a Trekka (the country's only locally designed production vehicle) alongside a Moniac (a water-driven computer that, not surprisingly, never went into production anywhere). Robert Leonard, co-curator of the admirable Te Papa Tongarewa museum in Wellington *(see page 217)*, saw this as a clever subversion of the "Kiwi can-do attitude".

It remains a scandal that there is no national art gallery in New Zealand. The remains of what used to be one have been squeezed into an upstairs space at Te Papa, and although this museum is a must, don't expect to find a truly representative display of New Zealand art. Instead you should trawl the fine range of city and provincial galleries – notably the superb Christchurch Art Gallery *(see page 250)*, which finally opened in 2003. The long wavy line of its glass-and-metal exterior hints at the shape of the *koru*, a stylised fern that also decorates the tails of Air New Zealand planes. Wellington's City Gallery *(page 219)*, the Auckland Art Gallery *(page 140)*, the Dunedin Public Art Gallery *(page 297)* and the adventurous Govett-Brewster Gallery *(page 209)* in New Plymouth, not to mention the more multicultural Pataka in Porirua, are all stimulating, accessible places.

MOVING PICTURES

Outside the mainstream of New Zealand art – and outside the country for much of his life – is Len Lye (1901–1980). Lye worked in numerous media but is mainly remembered as a kinetic sculptor and pioneer of direct film, in which he scratched and otherwise worked directly on film to create magnificent abstract images. These were set to music in a way that has resulted in them being described as proto-music videos. The Govett-Brewster Gallery in New Plymouth *(see page 209)* holds the Len Lye collection and archive, and regularly exhibits his work. His arresting sculpture *Wind Wand* has been installed on the New Plymouth foreshore.

LEFT: hewing art out of solid rock at the Wellington Sculpture Festival. **RIGHT:** Len Lye's soaring *Wind Wand* takes pride of place at New Plymouth's foreshore.

Fine art

Significantly, one of the first artists to be exhibited at the new Christchurch Art Gallery was W.A. (Bill) Sutton, the long-lived region painter (1917–2002) whose spare semi-abstract landscapes seem to symbolise the artist's relationship with the land – often perceived in New Zealand art as empty, brooding, even hostile to humans.

The hugely popular realist landscapes of Grahame Sydney, though softer in style, catch some of this mood. Sydney's work has been likened, with good reason, to that of Andrew Wyeth. The godfather of New Zealand art, as it were, is Colin McCahon, whose work moved

Sculpture and pottery

Sculpture has always laboured to find its feet in New Zealand. The size of the country and a perception that money spent on art is not money well spent has meant that public commissions are rare and grudging. Sculptors tend to work on a small scale but there are two who merit particular attention. Terry Stringer's work often playfully exploits the tension between the firmness of bronze, one of his favourite media, and the softness of his subject matter. Something of a traditionalist, though often with a postmodern edge, Stringer is also an accomplished portrait painter.

beyond simple landscapes with religious connotations to vast, dark, mystical incantations whose brooding power lay as much in the prayers that were inscribed upon them as in their massive cubist forms.

But contemporary New Zealand art is not all gloom and doom. McCahon's less tormented successors have been more inclined toward playfulness and post-modern irony in their work, particularly artists like Joanna Braithwaite, Shane Cotton, Dick Frizzell, Don Driver, Richard Killeen, Seraphine Pick, Peter Robinson and the quirky Bill Hammond, of whose surrealist paintings it has been said: "Everything about them is odd."

Experimentation with light is regarded as the province of the painter, but Neil Dawson creates sculptures in which the shadows cast by the work can be as equally important as the shapes he has moulded out of such favoured materials as aluminium and steel. His dramatic *Ferns* hover above the Civic Square in Wellington, and he has created the monumental *Chalice* to adorn Cathedral Square in his home town Christchurch.

It's not entirely clear why pottery has been such a popular creative endeavour in New Zealand. Perhaps it's the equivalent of the persistence of baking as a feature of local cuisine. There are two representative currents in New Zealand pottery. The first is the rough-hewn, hands-on, earth-connecting style. One iconic name in this field is Barry Brickell. The other strand is a more "fine art" approach represented by John Parker, who has worked for years producing pottery solely in white and where an elegant severity of form and line is a major concern.

Literature

The first New Zealand writer to attract any attention outside her own country was Katherine Mansfield, whose delicate short stories have – despite her own gloomy prediction – survived numerous changes of fashion and can be read with as much pleasure today as when they were

wide. A difference between the two writers that summarises the development of New Zealand literature is that Mansfield's work, with its lightness of touch, was only marginally concerned with New Zealand issues, while Hulme's monumental work was almost aggressively focused on issues of national identity and biculturalism alongside more universal themes.

Incredibly, it was only as recently as 1972 that the first book by a Maori writer was published in New Zealand – Witi Ihimaera's short-story collection *Pounamu Pounamu*. Ihimaera went on to become one of the country's leading novelists: his 1987 novel *The Whale Rider* was

written, mostly in the 15 years or so before her death in 1923 at the age of 34. New Zealand in the early 20th century was too constricting for the young writer and in 1908 Mansfield left her country, with some eagerness, in pursuit of a career, first in London and later in Switzerland and the south of France. She never returned.

Not until 1985 was another New Zealander so widely read, when the Booker Prize was awarded to Keri Hulme for *The Bone People*. The book has been translated into some 40 languages and has sold millions of copies world-

LEFT: Christchurch Art Gallery is a huge draw.
ABOVE: a ramshackle potter's workshop.

SURE TO SELL

The best-selling book in New Zealand history is not a volume of verse by one of the country's many fine poets, nor an internationally esteemed novel such as Keri Hulme's Booker-prize winning *The Bone People*. It is the *Edmonds Cookery Book*, initially published to promote the use of Edmonds Baking Powder ("Sure to Rise") and first published in 1907. It is determinedly old-fashioned and slow to keep pace with changing tastes in food, though this may have been part of its appeal to traditionalists in New Zealand. In 2003, in its 51st edition, it had sold some 4 million copies in a country whose population had only just reached that figure.

a hit film in 2003. Another work that was successfully adapted for the big screen was *Once Were Warriors* by Alan Duff, a sensational book – "the first New Zealand novel," according to the *Oxford Companion to New Zealand Literature*, "to deal full on with the actualities of modern urban Maori life" – that took the country by storm in the 1990s.

Novelists to have made their mark since then include Elizabeth Knox, who broke into the international market with *The Vintner's Luck*, a fantasy about a 19th-century Frenchman's encounters with an angel, and the protean Lloyd Jones, who followed *The Book of Fame* – a

remarkable riff on the 1905 All Blacks' rugby tour of Britain – with the completely different *Here at the End of the World We Learn to Dance*.

The field of history and biography has been dominated for many years by the late Michael King, who moved on from pioneering biographies of Maori woman leaders (Te Puea, Whina Cooper) to the lives of two of the country's greatest writers: Frank Sargeson and the late Janet Frame. Historians such as Miles Fairburn, James Belich, Anne Salmond and Philip Temple have helped to move the writing of history away from the recording of purely political and economic matters to more finely shaded explorations of society, culture and Maori-Pakeha relations.

Children's literature is spearheaded by such international successes as Lynley Dodd, famous for the *Hairy McLary* series for younger children, and Joy Cowley, whose novel *The Silent One* was memorably filmed and whose reading texts are widely used in the field of education the world over. And then of course there is Margaret Mahy, who was the 2006 winner of the Hans Christian Andersen Author Award, the world's premier prize for children's literature. Through her books and through readings and public appearances, she has virtually become a national treasure.

Writer-illustrators such as Gavin Bishop have also done lively work for younger children, but it is perhaps in the writing of books for young adults that the most exciting developments have taken place. Novels by Paula Boock, David Hill, Bernard Beckett, Tessa Duder and in particular Kate de Goldi (whose *Closed, Stranger* is a real *tour de force*) have tackled challenging themes such as adolescence and emerging sexuality.

Poetry

Poetry does surprisingly well in New Zealand. Though the average volume of verse sells no more than a few hundred copies, dozens are published every year while poetry workshops and creative writing courses are booming. When the American poet Billy Collins visited New Zealand, he was virtually mobbed like a rock star. Most major cities have poetry cafés, bars or venues where open readings are regularly held; and a remarkable number of literary festivals have sprung up around the country, some as adjuncts to arts festivals. The biennial Auckland Writers Festival and the Writers & Readers Week of Wellington's biennial International Arts Festival are probably the pick of these.

New Zealand does have an unofficial poet laureate, but it is not a position that is widely recognised. Only one poet has achieved the kind of stature that might be called legendary: the passionately nationalistic James K. Baxter, who was famous for wandering through the country barefoot with long hair and a Jesus-like beard in the last years before his death in 1972 at the age of 46. "For us," wrote Baxter in *Poem in the Matukituki Valley*, "the land is both matrix and destroyer" – concisely and memorably sum-

LEFT: the acclaimed Maori writer Witi Ihimaera.
RIGHT: Frederic Hundertwasser's whimsical toilet art at Kawakawa has its residents flushing with pride.

marising the conflicted relationship with the land that characterises the work of so many artists.

Since Baxter's death the favoured style has been cooler, more distanced and ironic, less given to big-picture stuff – less given, in fact, to ideas. Bill Manhire would be the leading exponent of this school. The old pre-occupation with forging a "New Zealand identity" has long been discarded because New Zealand writers are surer of their place in the world now. Even Allen Curnow, the country's senior poet till his death in 2002, moved a long way from the romantic nationalism of his youth to what one commentator described as a more "vividly colloquial"

style: both dry and abbreviated and razor-sharp.

Younger poets to have firmly established their names include Jenny Bornholdt, James Brown, Kate Camp, Glenn Colquhoun, Anna Jackson, Andrew Johnston and Robert Sullivan – who, along with the effervescent Hone Tuwhare, is the best of the poets claiming Maori ancestry.

Most Maori poets and novelists write in English, but there is a great deal of crossover between the languages. Read the self-deprecating poems of Colquhoun, for instance, and you'd be hard pressed to know if he was Pakeha or Maori. It is more than likely you would conclude that it really doesn't matter much anyway. ❏

ARCHITECTURE: STYLE OR KITSCH?

While Maori themes have sometimes been incorporated into the design of European-style public buildings, notably Te Papa in Wellington and the Christchurch Art Gallery, they have not influenced architectural thinking to any great degree. Examples of English gothic may still be seen here and there – in Wellington's splendid Old St Paul's Cathedral for instance – built not with stone but with timber.

With the possible exception of Napier – rebuilt largely in art deco style after an earthquake flattened the town in 1931 – no major town or city has achieved architectural unity. Dunedin retains a certain pre-war charm, while Oamaru is distinctive for its use of the local white stone. John Scott's

Futuna chapel in suburban Wellington is a highly regarded modernist work; but perhaps the capital's most impressive public building is the post-modernist Wellington Central Library, whose designer, Ian Athfield, pillared the front face with metallic versions of the nikau palm-tree. The adjacent Athfield-designed Civic Square is equally striking.

For architectural impact – in terms of just being noticed – the country's two best-known buildings run the gamut from the sublime to the ridiculous. You work out which is which. One is Auckland's Sky City Tower poking out like a giant ice-lolly stick and the other is Frederick Hundertwasser's public toilet in Kawakawa, Northland.

PERFORMING ARTS, MUSIC AND FILM

Music, theatre and their sister arts have struggled to survive as meagre resourcing stifled creativity, but recently have become more confident and secure

Given New Zealanders' reputation as a laconic, almost self-effacing people, it may seem remarkable that they can be persuaded to engage in any of the performing arts at all. Many New Zealanders have found it necessary to go overseas to find work which is commensurate with their talent, notably Kiri Te Kanawa, Russell Crowe and Jane Campion.

While there is pride in their success, it is the New Zealanders who have remained and continued to strive with, work for and speak to their own people, who are most admired. Peter Jackson's insistence that Hollywood had to come to him to make his movies inspired a confidence in the "local product" that resulted in a tremendous upsurge of all kinds of creative activity in the first years of the 21st century.

Classical music

The New Zealand Symphony Orchestra, based in Wellington, was formed in 1946 amid a postwar optimism in which the nation's few intellectuals, composers, painters and actors conspired to invent a national culture (such groups as the Royal New Zealand Ballet and the New Zealand Players were born in the same era). The world-class NZSO works hard for a national orchestra – performing more than 100 concerts per year. Standards are equally high in the Auckland Philharmonia.

Concurrent with the formation of the National Orchestra were these words from New Zealand's first modern composer, Douglas Lilburn: "Music has been written here and is being written here, but I feel that all of it is only the most tentative of beginnings towards solving that problem – the discovery of our own identity." Many composers have followed in his wake, creating a rich and diverse repertoire, some of it drawing on Maori and Polynesian styles. They include Jack Body, Hirini Melbourne, Gareth Farr and Philip Dadson.

But New Zealand's most famous practitioner of classical music remains the soprano Kiri Te Kanawa. A true diva, she seldom performs at home and, worse, according to New Zealanders, appears to have little affection for it. Still, New Zealand is a prolific producer of good singers, including the soprano Malvina Major

LEFT: Peter Jackson is regarded as a cultural icon in New Zealand for his *Lord of the Rings* trilogy.
RIGHT: soprano Kiri Te Kanawa found her fame overseas.

MAORI MUSIC AND DANCE

Music has always played a major role in Maori life, and as far back as the Classic era, instruments were fashioned from wood, whalebone and even stone. Traditional chants and songs *(waiata)* are an important feature of ceremonies such as funerals *(tangi)* and weddings. So too is Maori dance, which is both rhythmic and physical, with the beat added by the slapping of chest and thighs with the hand, foot-stamping or sometimes the hitting of sticks. Drums were unknown. "Concert Parties" now take part in competitions each year to find the best performers, and some groups travel the world to share their impressive and entertaining cultural arts.

and the up-and-coming bass Jonathan Lemalu; a performance by New Zealand Opera (usually at The St James in Wellington or Aotea Centre in Auckland) is a fairly safe bet. The company is often accused of making safe choices, but productions are frequently first-rate. However, anyone hoping to see an opera written by a New Zealander should plan to be in Wellington for its biennial New Zealand Festival, a highlight of the performing arts calendar.

Ballet and modern dance

The history of dance in New Zealand is one of struggle and perseverance, writ large. Dance is costly to develop and tour, and it was something of a miracle that the Royal New Zealand Ballet celebrated 50 years in 2003. It has a reputation for hard work and commitment, but the tutu-and-fairy-dust expectations of audiences often keep it from more groundbreaking work.

New Zealand's two leading modern choreographers, Douglas Wright and Michael Parmenter, emerged from the trail blazed by the influential modern dance troupe Limbs, formed in the 1970s and dissolved in the 1980s. Both have produced stunning, moving and important work, but have found it increasingly difficult to create works with scant financial resources.

CONTEMPORARY MUSIC SCENE

Thankfully, New Zealand's once-thriving pub rock scene hasn't been entirely decimated by the onslaught of dance music in the 1990s. If anything, the international success of such rock bands as The Datsuns (once seen as something of an embarrassment for ploughing the musical furrow of retro hard rock when it was far from fashionable) and The D4 have created a pro-rock backlash at home.

The "alternative" tradition of the country's legendary Flying Nun Records – which during the 1980s produced such cult groups as The Clean, The Chills and Straitjacket Fits – is also maintained in pubs and bars in the major cities. Other names to look out for are the Polynesian hip-hop success stories Nesian Mystik and Che Fu, and the singer-songwriter Bic Runga.

If jazz is more your style, be sure to catch the annual Waiheke Island Jazz Festival over the Easter weekend in Auckland, with international names on the bill, or Wellington's smaller jazz festival every October/November.

The popular world-music festival Womad has appeared sporadically in New Zealand, but is now tentatively pinned down to every second year, within New Plymouth's Taranaki Arts Festival. Along with an international line-up, Womad usually includes the very best of Maori and Polynesian groups and it's a big, friendly event.

Black Grace, an Auckland-based all-male troupe who combine the physicality of rugby players and the grace of ballet dancers, is renowned for its energetic blend of modern dance and Maori and Polynesian forms. Catch them if you happen to be in Auckland.

Theatre

Richard and Edith Campion didn't just produce film director Jane Campion, they also inaugurated professional theatre in New Zealand when they formed the New Zealand Players in 1953.

> ### VERY THEATRICAL
>
> Auckland's Civic Theatre is an architectural folly built in 1929 featuring Buddhas, elephants, panthers and a replica of the southern hemisphere sky.

its position as the top theatre in the country's unofficial "theatre capital" was lost to the rival Circa some years ago. Circa has a reliable company of actors who perform international work and local plays, notably those written by Roger Hall.

No history of New Zealand theatre is possible without mentioning Hall, a British emigrant with a style of middle-class, middle-aged and middle-brow comedy that both connects with the audience's fears, desires and interests and reminds them of British TV comedies. More

Before this, theatre-lovers only had sporadic visits by condescending British companies or community repertory groups. Summarising the suspicion visited upon all arts in those years, playwright Bruce Mason remembers such repertory groups being "ignored, sometimes actively abhorred by the average Kiwi".

The New Zealand Players folded in 1960 but inspired a whole new generation of actors and professional companies. The first was Wellington's Downstage, which survives even though

challenging playwrights have emerged since, including Ken Duncum, Duncan Sarkies, Jo Randerson, Hone Kouka and Briar Grace Smith; the latter two have written about New Zealand history from a Maori perspective.

Professional theatre in New Zealand exists on a diet of the latest intelligent British or American blockbuster, revivals of the classics and, when they're feeling adventurous, new local works. Beyond Downstage and Circa, these theatres are Palmerston North's Centrepoint, Christchurch's Court Theatre and Dunedin's Fortune. The Auckland Theatre Company does not have its own theatre, but usually performs at the Aotea Centre's Herald Theatre or Auckland

LEFT: local boys made good, The Datsuns.
ABOVE: Auckland's all-male dance troupe Black Grace combines rugged athleticism with elegant ballet.

University's Maidment. ATC's productions have been criticised as being conservative, but more and more local plays are being staged as the company grows, and it has a large pool of capable actors, most of whom are pleased to get a break from less challenging TV work.

New Zealand's avant-garde theatre scene is less visible, but Auckland's Silo and Wellington's Bats can both feel like tiny pockets of anti-establishment resistance. The work can be patchy but sometimes daring and inspired; one of the few reliable practitioners is the Christchurch multimedia group called The Clinic. Stylistically, the avant-garde theatre scene is pitched somewhere

between lively stand-up comedy and the more traditional dramatic fare on offer at places like Silo and Bats. In the 1990s, comedy found a permanent venue at Auckland's Classic, and there's a big comedy festival in March every year.

Festivals provide opportunities for new works to debut and existing works to tour. The biggest is Wellington's biennial (on even years) New Zealand Festival. Christchurch, New Plymouth, Taupo, Tauranga, Nelson and the Bay of Islands also have their own arts festivals.

Film

New Zealand directors produced the occasional film prior to the 1970s, the most notable being by John O' Shea who specialised in bicultural themes (his interracial melodrama *Broken Barrier*; *Don't Let It Get You*, a kitsch musical masterpiece featuring a young Kiri Te Kanawa).

It wasn't till Roger Donaldson's 1977 thriller *Sleeping Dogs* that a wave of commercial filmmaking was launched – and which continues to this day. Donaldson moved on to Hollywood, where his biggest commercial hit was the 1988 Tom Cruise vehicle *Cocktail*. Others to emerge around this time were the art-house favourite Vincent Ward (*Vigil* and *The Navigator*), Geoff Murphy, whose "Maori western", *Utu*, was vastly under-rated, and Gaylene Preston, whose *Mr Wrong* was a slyly subversive feminist thriller. One of the most successful exports was Jane Campion, who followed the distinctively New Zealand *The Piano* (1993) with the equally accomplished *The Portrait of a Lady* (1996).

Niki Caro followed her dazzling debut *Memory and Desire* with the international hit *Whale Rider*, based on a Maori legend as told by one of the country's foremost Maori writers, Witi Ihimaera. Peter Jackson did the impossible by making a *Lord of the Rings* trilogy *(see page 95)* that won 11 Oscars, pleased critics, Tolkien fans and audiences who had never heard of the book. He became that rarest of creatures, a New Zealand cultural hero. Although his remake of *King Kong* (2005) lacked the same magic, it still had its following.

Another New Zealander director, Andrew Adamson, has made his mark with *Shrek I* (2001)*, Shrek II* (2004) and *The Chronicles of Narnia, the Lion, the Witch and the Wardrobe* (2005). The latter, filmed in New Zealand, had superb graphics produced by Weta Workshop, which also animated Jackson's *Rings* trilogy. Adamson is set to dazzle the world once more with *Prince Caspian*, the second in the Narnia series, in 2008.

For its size, New Zealand seems to have given the world a disproportionate number of international film stars, notably Sam Neill (who started out in the aforementioned *Sleeping Dogs*), and the Oscar winners Anna Paquin and Russell Crowe. Among the contemporary generation of film actors, Danielle Cormack and Joel Tobbeck are two stand-out performers. ❏

● *See Travel Tips for contact details of theatre and performing arts venues.*

LEFT: NZ actor Sam Neill found his fame in Hollywood.

The Bonanza of the Rings

The *Lord of the Rings* trilogy of movies were shot at locations that ranged almost the entire length of New Zealand, and, while some computer enhancements were inevitably employed, many of the sites are natural, unique and almost unbelievably spectacular. The movies have sparked enormous outside interest in the country and its pristine landscapes, and also ignited a boom in commercial tours taking fans – quite literally millions of them since the first movie was screened – to many of the sites.

While some of the places featured in the movie trilogy are relatively inaccessible or on private land, and can only be visited under the aegis of a tour operator, others are easy to reach by individuals. Anyone can get a glimpse, for instance, of large tracts of "Mordor" or the "Misty Mountains". But don't expect to find actual movie sets – due to the environmental considerations so dear to New Zealanders' hearts, all but one of them has since been demolished.

The only movie set that has been left in place is the one for **Hobbiton**, the home of Bag End itself, or at least the front door – the interior was a set in Wellington. It stands on private land at Matamata but can be visited for a fee. Much of this verdant, intensely farmed area will suggest the peaceful Shire to visitors.

Further south is **Mordor**, otherwise known as Tongariro National Park. Much computer wizardry was used to create the movie landscapes, but the vast bleakness and volcanic devastation of much of this barren area makes it clear why it was a suitable site for Sauron's realm. And in the form of Mt Ngauruhoe, one of the three peaks that dominate the park, you have **Mt Doom** itself.

Kaitoke Regional Park, north of Wellington, where the productions were based, was a location for **Rivendell**, home of Elrond, and for the **River Anduin**. The Hutt River, which runs alongside the motorway out of Wellington, and Lake Manapouri in the South Island were also drafted into service to play part of the river.

Perhaps the easiest of the *Rings* locations to access is the centre of Wellington, where Mt Vic-

toria was used for numerous scenes, including Frodo and Sam's departure from the **Shire** and the Ringwraiths' pursuit of the hobbits.

The journey to Mordor involves a detour to the South Island, where the **Dead Marshes** in which Frodo, Sam and Gollum fought over the ring were filmed at a swamp called Kepler Mire on the Kepler Track near Te Anau. On a brighter note, also near Te Anau, on Takaro Road, is **Fangorn Forest**, home of the Ents, where Merry and Pippin haggled with Treebeard to persuade him to join the battle for Helms Deep.

Outside Queenstown, near Arrowtown, lies Skippers Canyon, and this is where Arwen, while res-

cuing the wounded Frodo, confronted the Ringwraiths before they were swept away in a mighty torrent.

From many points in the South Island you can enjoy views of the **Misty Mountains**, along which the Fellowship trudged before being broken. Of course, hereabouts (and on all the maps) they are known as the Southern Alps.

New Zealanders, who have something of a weakness for praise from other parts of the world, are immensely proud of the success of the *Lord of the Rings* trilogy. Forgive them, though, if they appear to be just a little blasé about the movie's locations. For them, this is simply home, and it has always looked like this. ❏

RIGHT: you're not likely to come across nasty guys like this one at LOTR sights, just eye-popping scenery.

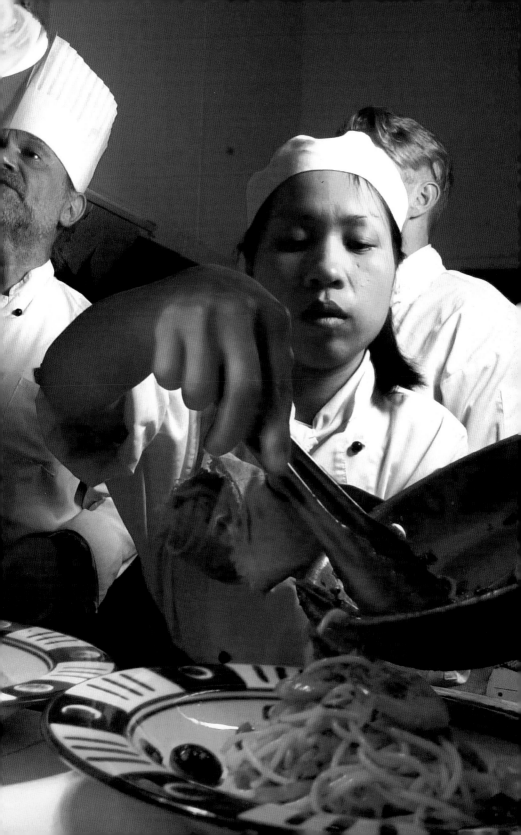

CUISINE

Kiwi cooking is distinguished by ingredients that are fresh and flavourful, and a style that fuses a medley of influences, reflecting the country's cultural diversity

At the heart of New Zealand's exuberant cuisine is the pristine freshness of its fruit and vegetables, meat, seafood and dairy products. Most often, the principal ingredients on your plate will have been grown within 100 kilometres of your table. But what New Zealand cooks do with those ingredients has none of the simplicity of a traditional peasant cuisine. Indeed, there are very few indigenous foods eaten at all. Except for the wealth of seafood, the raw materials are descended from those brought here from many parts of the world, each one finding a suitable environment, whether in the year-round warmth of the north or the climatic extremes of the south.

Cosmopolitan cuisine

When it comes to culinary styles, New Zealand cooks have a lot in common with their counterparts in Australia and California. Although all are located on the rim of the Pacific Ocean, they are less influenced by their place on the map than by a common mood of buoyant confidence, a love of vibrant flavours and a willingness to sample whatever food they fancy. Peppers, aubergines, olives, asparagus and garlic are easily grown, giving a boost to Mediterranean cuisine. Pesto and hummus are as popular here as anywhere in the world. Not far behind are the foods of Asia. Curries, stir-fries, sushi and miso soup are commonplace.

New Zealanders also bring ideas from their travels abroad and keep up with international trends through books, magazines and television. In addition, each smaller cultural group living in the country – Pacific, Indian, Chinese, Greek, Cambodian, Croatian, Dutch, Thai, German, and many others – has added their own colour and flavourful ingredients to the culinary melting pot, through importing speciality foods, opening restaurants and continuing to cook their traditional food at home.

PRECEDING PAGES: frenetic behind-the-scenes work at Nicollini's restaurant in Wellington.
LEFT: freshly caught crayfish, also known as rock lobster.
RIGHT: exotic food from the Pacific Islands add colour.

Colonial roots

The cooking styles of England, Scotland and Ireland, the homelands of the largest number of immigrants since colonial times, remain a powerful element, particularly in home cooking. When families gather, even grown-up children ask Mum to roast a leg of lamb, with crisp

golden potatoes, pumpkin, parsnip and kumara (sweet potato) baked in the same pan and served with gravy, mint sauce, peas and silver beet (Swiss chard). In summer, the traditionally high status of meat is reflected in barbecues with a variety of steaks, lamb chops and sausages, or an array of seafood served with bread and salads. Despite the influence of other cuisines, many main courses in restaurants still take the traditional form of a fine piece of meat or fish accompanied by vegetables. Many women, and more than a few men, are a dab hand when it comes to home-baked scones, pikelets and muffins, as well as cakes and biscuits plus jams, marmalade, chutney and pickles, too.

Maori cooking

Many of the country's indigenous foods – birds, berries and fern root – were laborious to gather, prepare and preserve. Such traditional Maori delicaries include mutton birds (the distinctly fishy-flavoured young of the sooty petrel), freshwater eels, and seafood such as paua (abalone), pipi and tuatua (shellfish) and kina (prickly sea urchins). While the kumara, a sweet potato brought from Polynesia, enhanced the range of nourishing foods that could be grown in warmer regions, Maori cuisine benefited from the arrival of pigs and other farm animals, vegetables, fruit and grains from Europe and America.

Seafood has always been a vital part of the cuisine, and its continuing importance is recognised in the customary rights extended to Maori to allow the gathering of otherwise controlled species. The traditional Maori meal most likely to be offered to visitors is the *hangi* (earth oven), a tender and flavourful feast in which meat and vegetables are packed into baskets and steamed over hot rocks in a covered pit. A hearty broth ("boil-up") includes pork or beef, potatoes, onions, carrots and watercress, *rauraki* or *puha* (sow thistle) and sometimes dumplings ("doughboys"). *Paraoa rewana* is a large wheaten loaf made with potato leaven.

POTATO HEADS

The purple-skinned, yellow-fleshed kumara, a staple in most New Zealand homes and many restaurants, is just one of more than 20 varieties of potato – *taewa* – that are unique to the Maori. Not widely eaten, and unfamiliar to many except specialists, several of these other varieties are in danger of becoming extinct, and efforts are being made to conserve them, possibly for commercial exploitation. One of the principal – and most unusual – potatoes is the highly nutritious *urenikai*, which has not only purple skin like the kumara but also a vivid purple flesh. This exotic potato found great success at the Slow Food 2000 awards in Milan, Italy.

Fresh fruit

Each season brings with it an amazing range of fresh fruit, none of which is native to New Zealand. However, over the past two centuries each has become a much-loved part of the local cuisine, and several are now important exports. Fruit and vegetable shops and supermarkets stock a good range, although some fruit is barely ripe when sold and needs to be kept for a few days. Delicious tree-ripened fruit can be bought direct from roadside stalls near where they are grown throughout the country. Weekend farmers' markets in the cities and growing regions are an increasing phenomenon, and a significant number of supermarkets, stalls and speciality shops offers organic produce.

Autumn is perhaps the most exciting season of all, when sub-tropical fruit, grown in the warmer parts of the country, is widely available. First in the season is the feijoa, a scented, oval green fruit with a smooth skin and flavour reminiscent of pineapple and strawberries. The wrinkled purple passionfruit holds a spoonful of black seeds in an aromatic golden juice. Kiwifruit, with tart green flesh or the more mellow, golden-fleshed types, marketed under the Zespri label, have been

A CHRISTMAS DESSERT

After Christmas dinner, dessert often consists of bowlfuls of mixed fresh berries with icing sugar and lightly whipped cream.

and red currants. By Christmas, cherries, the first of the stone fruits, will also be ripe; small boxes of top quality fruit are a popular gift.

As summer progresses, other stone fruits rush by – plums, peaches (locally-bred Golden Queens, white fleshed early in the season and with deep golden flesh later), nectarines, peaches and apricots – and in their primary growing regions of Hawke's Bay and Central Otago can often be bought from roadside stalls. Autumn brings apples, including the flavoursome Braeburn, pears,

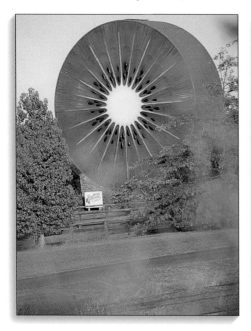

joined by a cherry-sized, smooth-skinned variety. The deep red, or sometimes golden flesh of glossy-skinned tamarillos is spicy and tart – an acquired taste for many visitors. Some citrus fruit also ripen in the winter – easy-to-peel mandarins, navel oranges and the New Zealand grapefruit, an unusual variety with golden peel and sweet-sour golden-hued flesh.

Strawberries start to ripen in spring, and by December they will be joined by raspberries, blackberries, loganberries, boysenberries, black

notably the luscious Doyenne du Comice, nashi – an apple-shaped type of pear with crisp juicy white flesh – and glossy orange non-astringent persimmons, which should be eaten while they still feel hard in the hand. Varietal honey and locally grown chestnuts, walnuts, hazelnuts and macadamia nuts are other treats.

From the seas

In every season of the year commercial fishing boats bring in a wonderful variety of species, from the delicate hoki, gurnard and flounder, to the local favourites, the flavoursome tarakihi and snapper, flakey blue cod and firm John Dory, as well as the meaty hapuka and bluenose. All year

LEFT: purple-skinned kumara is almost a staple.
ABOVE: glorifying the kiwi – the national fruit.
RIGHT: juicy vine-ripened cherry tomatoes.

round, excellent farmed Pacific salmon is available. Salmon and other species are often enjoyed skilfully smoked. While winter is the season for highly regarded Bluff oysters, the closely related Nelson variety is a delectable alternative. Farmed Pacific oysters are also often available. Large and succulent greenshell mussels, which are farmed in the Marlborough Sounds, can be bought live from most supermarkets. Smaller shellfish collected from sandy beaches include pipi, tuatua and little neck clams, known locally as cockles. Abalone *(paua)*, cling to the rocks along many shores and can be collected in controlled numbers. Whitebait are eaten whole,

often bound with egg in a delicate fritter. Another springtime treat is dredged scallops, while eels are particularly delicious when smoked. Salted muttonbirds are also sometimes available from seafood providers. These are the chicks of titi (sooty shearwaters), which are collected from a few tiny islands near Stewart Island. Their rich meaty flavour is relished by aficionados. Crayfish, also known as rock lobster, was once commonplace, but is now a luxury.

Meat and dairy produce

Wide grassy pastures are the year-round home of many millions of lambs and sheep, raised

SWEET RIVALS

If New Zealand has a national dessert, it is the pavlova. And if Australia has a national dessert, it is also the pavlova. The two countries maintain a rivalry over where this giant egg white meringue, smothered in whipped cream and topped with fresh fruit, was first concocted.

An equally contested side issue is the best way of preparing the confection. Two things are incontestable, however: firstly that this delicious dessert was originally made in honour of Russian ballerina Anna Pavlova, who visited both countries more than a century ago; and secondly that it is an unbeatable way to consume a large amount of sugar in one sitting.

for wool as well as meat, cattle for beef and milk, and also smaller numbers of deer. The pastures, known locally as paddocks, are licked by salty sea breezes, which give the meat a delicious and distinctive flavour. All meats are available all year round. A rack of lamb, seared on the outside and still pink inside, is always delicious, or for old-fashioned comfort, look for braised lamb shanks. Lamb's liver, known as lamb's fry, is also good. For steak lovers, fillet is the most tender, while sirloin, porterhouse, rump or Scotch fillet have a richer flavour. Tender farm-raised venison, which is often marketed as Cervena, is best when cooked quickly and served medium rare.

Milk, butter and cheese have long been an important part of the cuisine. Thick cream and tangy yoghurt are of excellent quality. More than 60 varieties of cheese are produced in New Zealand – look out for aorangi, kirima, blue supreme and Dutch-style cheeses made by several small producers – but cheddar remains the most popular and is widely available, from creamy mild to richly aged. Sheep and goat milk cheeses are a new but growing part of the scene.

There are plenty of feral deer, pigs and goats in the bush for hunters, although you don't often find wild meat on a restaurant menu. If you do, you can rest assured knowing that it has been processed in a licensed abattoir and will be safe to eat. Trout, found in many rivers and streams, are reserved exclusively for licensed anglers and are never sold. Big game fishing – and eating the catch – is another attraction.

Picnic supplies

One takeaway meal that has a long local history is the meat pie. These are sold in convenience stores, bakeries and petrol stations, where they are heated to order. The single serve pies are oval, round or square and most contain ground or diced beef in gravy. A layer of cheese is a popular addition and some pies are topped with mashed potato instead of pastry. Also at the bakeries you will find sweet goodies that will often be the same distinctively New Zealand specialities that are traditionally baked in the home – Anzac biscuits, afghans with chocolate icing and walnut on top, peanut brownies, ginger crunch, bran or cheese muffins, and banana cake. The coffee is almost always espresso and often made with beans roasted by small speciality businesses. A range of teas and herbal teas is always available as well as local mineral water and fruit juices.

Despite the presence of the usual international franchises, owner-operated fish-and-chip shops still provide the most popular takeaway meal, comprising thick golden chips (french fries) and fish deep-fried in batter or crumbs, as well as seasonal oysters, scallops, sausages and other items. Wait while your meal is cooked to order, wrapped in absorbent paper or piled on a cardboard tray. Then take it to eat at a pretty spot by the sea. The seagulls will help out with the leftovers.

LEFT: outdoor dining at an Auckland eatery.
RIGHT: table with a view.

Fine dining

New Zealand has a large number of world-class fine dining restaurants, even in more remote locations where it flourishes in the guise of luxury lodges and vineyards. Even under the fine dining rubric, the variety of food is dazzling. It can range from a reinvention of that controversial classic, tripe, to the finest of freshly caught game and seafood. Inspiration is eclectic – drawing from the world's great cuisines – and creativity seemingly boundless as chefs strive to find a balance between respect for their ingredients and the true artist's desire to improve on nature.

The relatively small size of the market means that competition is intense – chefs are likely to be poached as quickly as fish if they make a name for themselves– which in turn helps keep standards high. But top-end restaurants in Auckland, Wellington and other big cities are vulnerable to a domestic tendency to faddishness. It is not unusual for a new restaurant to be booked solid for its first three months, then find itself almost empty as the locals' attention is caught by the next shiny new establishment to open. However, plenty of fine restaurants have survived changing times and tastes to assure an unsurpassed dining experience. ❑

● *See Travel Tips for restaurant recommendations.*

The Farming Life

Although New Zealand was built on its farm produce, changing times have made life tough for farmers – yet most of them would not swap their jobs for the world.

It's early morning, high summer in the heart of the South Island. Daniel Jamieson, second-generation farmer, father of two and sometime recreational cricket player, has breakfast with his wife, Colleen, then heads outdoors to start work on the land where he was born and raised. More than 600 dairy cows await him and his staff in a high-tech

has been one of the biggest trends, but is certainly not the only shift to alter the look of the land.

Thousands of hectares of pine trees now cloak hills too steep to support profitable livestock farming, particularly in parts of the North Island. Horticulture, including apples, stone fruit and kiwifruit, remains a mainstay in the Bay of Plenty, Gisborne, Hawke's Bay, Nelson and Otago. But new crops, particularly large-scale vegetable production, have made inroads into other fertile coastal areas. Grapes now flourish on many hillsides. Olives, deer, ostriches, emus, alpacas, lavender and goats are all in commercial production. The expansion of dairy farming and forestry is predicted to continue for some time.

milking parlour not far from where the woolshed once stood. Daniel remembers the heat, sweat and dust of summer shearing back when he used to be a sheep farmer. Four years ago he and Colleen were among the first on the plains of North Canterbury to switch from sheep to dairy. Now their herd is one of many grazing where sheep had been raised for nearly a century.

Fields of change

Such changes are sweeping the rural heartland of New Zealand. The rapid spread of dairy farming from traditional North Island regions like Waikato, Taranaki and Manawatu to former sheep farming strongholds in Canterbury, Otago and Southland

The humble sheep, it seems, is under siege. For decades a cornerstone of New Zealand agriculture, and indeed of the nation's export-driven economy, pastoral sheep production and its supporting industries have arguably borne the brunt of radical political and market changes. The loss of secure markets in the UK when Britain joined the EC was the first blow. This was followed from 1984 by systematic dismantling of extensive farm subsidies. New Zealand's rural industries are now among the least subsidised in the world.

New growth

Farmers met these challenges head-on. They've scoured the world for fresh opportunities and continued as guardians of New Zealand's largest industry, responsible for producing more than half of the country's merchandise exports, with dairying currently the biggest single export earner of all.

Traditional commodity sales to Europe may have withered, but sophisticated new products have found buyers elsewhere, most notably throughout Asia and in Australia. The same spirit of innovation that allowed New Zealand to begin refrigerated shipment of frozen sheep carcasses way back in 1882 has led to rapid advances in food processing technology and farm production systems, not to mention a whole new attitude down on the farm.

The sheer diversity of New Zealand's land-based exports, from powdered deer antler and fresh flowers to chilled gourmet meat cuts and hand-made boutique cheeses, reflects only part of the transformation that has taken place. Equally important, though less apparent, has been the farmers' willingness to adapt to new market trends. For the thousands who remain committed to the nation's sheep industry, this has meant increasingly specialised production of specific types of meat and wool, many of which are now brand-marked. For others, it has meant branching out into different types of agriculture or horticulture altogether.

Pressures and possibilities

New Zealand's farmers have been quick to respond to the increasing worldwide consumer concern about chemical residues, animal welfare and food safety. Gifted with a sparse population, relatively clean air and water, and a productive, temperate climate, the country's exports of organic products have shown tremendous growth, and strict animal welfare codes and quality assurance programmes have now been implemented in many of New Zealand's rural industries.

Contrary to the doomsayers of the mid-1980s, who predicted the industry would barely survive without subsidies, farms owned and operated by rural families have remained the backbone of New Zealand agriculture. Admittedly, these properties now tend to be bigger than they used to be and with fewer staff. One or other of the spouses is likely to have a job off-farm to help supplement income; and the tradition of passing land down to the children is by no means as secure as it used to be. In addition, there is a growing number of "mega-farms" owned by large corporations.

Left: Waikato's verdant dairy pastures.
Right: a logging contest participant shows his mettle.

Possession of the land itself remains a source of contention in several regions, as many Maori tribes seek redress for the grievances of the past *(see pages 34, 43 and 71)*, including the confiscation of large tracts of land.

The tortuous process of Government compensation for these losses has largely centred on cash settlements with some return of public land to Maori ownership. While today's farmers face little risk of being themselves dispossessed after 150 years of European settlement, indigenous land claims have nonetheless heightened tensions in many small rural communities, especially in Taranaki and Northland.

Protecting the future

Beyond these domestic issues, and beyond its borders, insect pests and animal and plant diseases from other countries continue to pose enormous potential threats to New Zealand. Border control is among the strictest in the world, implemented with more than a little obsession as the country strives to protect itself from tiny invaders which could tank multi-million dollar export markets.

Having survived these changes and challenges, it's hardly surprising that farmers like Daniel and Colleen Jamieson have much on their minds these days. But the interesting thing is that they, and thousands of others earning a livelihood from the land, wouldn't dream of doing anything else. ❏

WINES

New Zealand, a latecomer to the world of wine-making, now
produces outstanding vintages that are sold worldwide

New Zealand was the last place on earth inhabited by humans, so it is no surprise that it is also the last place on earth to make wine. Still, it has made an impressive run, especially in the realm of small, individual wine-making of truly high standard.

It all began at the top of the country in the Bay of Islands, with James Busby, official British Resident, horticulturist extraordinaire, pioneer viticulturist (he also founded the wine industry in New South Wales, Australia) and author of the Treaty of Waitangi. He planted the first vineyard on his property at Waitangi *(see page 158)* in the Bay of Islands in 1834, and a couple of years later the very first New Zealand wine was produced. It was sampled by French admiral Dumont d'Urville, who pronounced it to be light, sparkling, white and delicious.

Matakana, just north of Auckland, and associated vineyards in the Kaipara region were the first to attempt serious commercial wine-making – in the last quarter of the 18th century – but suffered from the scourge of prohibition politics that effectively destroyed the wine industry between 1900 and 1920. Now enjoying an optimistic revival, this pretty rural area produces some of New Zealand's classiest wines and most visitor-friendly wineries, notably Heron's Flight (www.heronsflight.co.nz), with its garden dining and delightfully casual attitude.

International standing

If New Zealand has a "signature wine", it is sauvignon blanc, produced here with as much – and often greater – success as anywhere in the world. Saint Clair Estate Wines (www.saint clair.co.nz) in Marlborough was named the maker of the best sauvignon blanc in the world at the 2006 San Francisco International Wine Competition, America's largest and most prestigious competition. The award-winning wine was its Vicar's Choice Sauvignon Blanc 2006.

Also in the running as the country's signature wine is pinot noir. The Black Poplar Block Pinot Noir 2003 from Central Otago's Pisa Range Estate (www.pisarangeestate.co.nz) won a gold medal (best in class) in the 37th International Wine and Spirit Competition in London. Even more noteworthy is that the label

WINES OF CHARACTER

New Zealand wine has a character, a crystalline purity of fruit flavour, that no one has yet been able to explain. It is certainly not the climate, mostly maritime, and like the landscape tremendously varied, though everywhere could be classified in wine-growing terms as cool and similar to the world's great wine-growing regions. It may be the soil, which is uniquely young by geological standards, or it may have something to do with how bright daylight is here, a similar phenomenon to that of Cognac in France, where locals say it contributes to the finesse and concentrated flavour of that region's famous brandy. Most likely it is a combination of all these things.

LEFT: winemaker samples a pinot noir – one of the varietals that NZ is well known for – from a barrel.
RIGHT: a vineyard in Hawke's Bay.

was only launched in 2002. One expert has also predicted a syrah (known in Australia and New Zealand as shiraz) revolution. Needless to say, New Zealand wines are the only complement to the local cuisine that visitors should consider during their stay.

With an eye to the export market, New Zealand wine-makers have become enthusiastic participants in international wine competitions, and many have returned home bearing medals. To give just one example, at the Vinexpo gathering in Bordeaux in

efforts of immigrants from the Croatian province of Dalmatia. Many of the wineries, including Babich (www.babichwines.co.nz) at the original site in Henderson, are still run by descendants of the Dalmatian founders.

Wineries in this area have a strong sense of old-time hospitality. At Collards (tel: 09-838 8341), on Lincoln Road, you can sample some of the classiest white wines made anywhere in the country, along with a little across-the-counter conversation. Kumeu Valley, northwest of the city, is home to

> **LABEL LORE**
>
> It is fashionable these days for wineries to commission leading artists to design labels which, occasionally, are more satisfying than the bottle's contents.

2003, Te Mata Estate's Coleraine Cabernet Merlot 2000 was voted a top-ten wine. The same wine was voted the second-best red wine at the show, and the sixth best wine overall. Thus inspired, enthusiasm has equally been applied to marketing: exports – mainly to Australia, the UK and the US – grew five-fold between 1990 and 2001.

North Island wineries

Wines produced close to Auckland are among the finest you will find anywhere in the country, and the winery restaurants are more serious. This is what Aucklanders call "Dally country", because the wine culture is based on the sterling

the fabulous Kumeu River vineyard (www.kumeuriver.co.nz), as sophisticated as anything in Burgundy, and with chardonnay to match. Down the road, Matua Valley (www.matua.co.nz) could be in California, with its restaurant and visitors centre, while both Westbrook (www.westbrook.co.nz) and Soljans (www.soljans.com) are more like restaurants with wineries attached – but the wine is equally as good as the food.

Also close to Auckland is exotic Waiheke Island, fast becoming Auckland's answer to Martha's Vineyard, but with better wine. The Goldwater Estate (www.goldwaterwine.com) provides the ultimate Pacific idyll, while the road south offers Rongopai's (www.rongopai

wines.co.nz) lavish sweet wines, still holding out in the hills of Te Kauwhata.

Hawke's Bay and Wairarapa

Down the lumpy eastern coast of the North Island is Hawke's Bay, where wine-making is big. But there is no disputing the quality. One certainty is the aforementioned Te Mata Estate (www.temata.co.nz), the oldest winery in New Zealand with some fine architecture and wines that are among the world's best.

There are many other award-winning wineries here *(see box)*, but unusual among them is Stonecroft (www.stonecroft.co.nz) on the Ngaruroro River. It has its share of proprietorial individuality – a sign at the gate states: no buses, no tours, no sherry – but the wines are world-class gewürztraminer, chardonnay and shiraz.

Wairarapa is another exciting wine region, the centre of pinot noir excellence. And because the wineries are so close to each other, you can see everything on foot. Don't miss places like Ata Rangi (www.atarangi.co.nz), Martinborough Vineyard (www.martinborough-vineyard.co.nz) and Te Kairanga (www.tkwine.co.nz); the wines are very popular and sell fast, so don't expect everything to be available.

South Island wineries

Marlborough is the only place that actually feels like a totally dedicated wine community – not unlike Burgundy, with winery visitor centres crying out for your attention. Two crucial ones are Cloudy Bay (www.cloudybay.co.nz) and Fromm (www.frommwineries.com). Also well worth a visit is Villa Maria's (www.villamaria.co.nz) impressive modern winery, built confidently to allow for expansion.

Nelson is different altogether, ravishingly bucolic, sun-baked, both maritime and mountain-lined and full of potters and artists. Wineries here include Neudorf (www.neudorf.co.nz), which is one of the country's best producers.

Wineries at Waipara in North Canterbury produce some top pinot noirs, but for the greatest wine-and-landscape spectacle, go south to Central Otago, where the mountains soar over clinging vineyards, the lakes are deep blue-green, rivers rush down craggy valleys with chilly enthusiasm, and you can sit outside, sip some wine and watch the mountains against a crisp sky. Pinot noir is king here, but there are some scintillating Rieslings too. Almost every winery that is open to the public is worth a visit, notably Gibbston Valley (www.gvwines.co.nz) and Chard Farm (www.chardfarm.co.nz), which are both good for their food as well as their wine.

For that final memory of New Zealand wine, meander down to Black Ridge (www.blackridge.co.nz) in Alexandra to experience wine craft at its mythical best – challenging, fiercely individual and triumphantly satisfying. ❑

● *See Travel Tips for more wineries and contact details of vineyard tour operators.*

HAWKE'S BAY WINE TRAIL

Hawke's Bay wineries *(see page 206)* open to visitors are thick on the ground, and the local tourism office has mapped out a Wine Trail that includes no less than 36 of them. There are many famous names and award-winners here, but if you are selective, you will miss neither the best wines nor the best venues. A few recommendations include: Clearview Estate; Mission Estate; emphatically rural Alpha Domus; Ngatarawa, which reflects Hawke's Bay's old landed gentry; contemporay Te Awa Farm; Selini; Trinity Hill; the corporate-slick Montana; and Church Road, where a collection of old wine-making tools from various countries adds to its interest.

LEFT: checking fruit for damage at a Kumeu vineyard.
RIGHT: tasting a recent vintage.

OUTDOOR ACTIVITIES

With wide open spaces and a relatively healthy lifestyle, New Zealanders
are passionate about sport and adventure – and are keen to share it with others

New Zealanders embrace the great outdoors, and easy access to the oceans and wilderness areas is just one explanation for the great Kiwi sporting passion. In fact, it would be difficult to grow up in this country without spending a significant amount of time hiking in the mountains, fishing the rivers or riding the surf. Many of the country's most adored heroes are those who have achieved great things on the world's outdoor stage: Sir Edmund Hillary, the late Sir Peter Blake, the All Blacks.

From the moment children start school, sport and physical activity are a big part of the educational curriculum. More than 90 percent of the country's young people are actively engaged in sport through clubs or schools. This has helped make New Zealand a breeding ground for sportsmen and women, and a playground for adrenalin-hungry adventurers.

Team sports

Rugby union is the main national sport. More than 140,000 people play club rugby, and the national team, the All Blacks, is among the most successful in the world. February marks the start of the season with the regionally based Super 12 Competition and ends in late October with the National Provincial Championships.

A good season for the All Blacks guarantees celebratory status for players whose names and personal details will dominate nearly every tabloid and magazine in the country for months. The nation's obsession with the sport can be felt most strongly during international matches, when tens of thousands of fans decorate themselves in supporting colours. Failure to win results in collective mourning and a general post mortem of each player's performance.

Cricket is the main summer game and New Zealand takes part in the Test Match series and other international competitions. Cricketing heroes include the legendary Sir Richard

Hadlee, a Christchurch man who had a record-breaking career between the early 1970s and 1990 and was knighted for his services to the game. The excitement of one-day matches, with players dressed in brightly coloured uniforms complete with names across the back for easy identification, has raised the profile of what

some people considered a rather dull and tedious pastime.

The women's winter sport of netball also has a high profile, partly due to television coverage of all major international events and the feisty competitiveness between New Zealand and its greatest rival, Australia. Volleyball has moved outdoors onto New Zealand's most beautiful beaches. Beach volleyball for two- or four-person teams has become a popular spectator sport and is sufficiently casual for teams to be thrown together at the last minute.

Other team sports – hockey, soccer and basketball – all have healthy numbers of followers with the games' codes taught in schools

PRECEDING PAGES: kayaking in Marlborough Sounds.
LEFT: a snowboarder at Whakapapa, Mt Ruapehu.
RIGHT: an All Blacks' rugby player in action.

throughout the country. On any winter Saturday, nearly every sports field in the country will be busy with children participating in one or more sporting events. Large numbers of parents gather along the sidelines, cheering, calling and sometimes offering unnecessary instructions to their protégés.

Hunting, fishing and skiing

Many sports considered elite in other parts of the world are readily accessible in New Zealand. Very few towns are without a carefully manicured golf course and fast growing club memberships. No longer the domain of the

between the two islands. Both start in October, but in the North Island it finishes at the end of June, while in South Island at the end of April. Licences can be obtained from any sports shop in one of the 22 fishing districts.

Game fishing is equally popular in New Zealand. Ever since writer Zane Grey alerted the world to the game fishing opportunities in the Bay of Islands, fishermen have dreamed of reeling in a giant marlin or swordfish. Although many like to take their catch home, others prefer to tag and release the giant specimens caught off the East Coast, Northland and Bay of Plenty. Game fishing is possible throughout the

retired population, golf has a growing popularity among younger people.

There are ample opportunities for hunters to bag deer, chamois, wild pigs, thar and goat. In an effort to diversify, farmers in more remote areas actively encourage hunters onto their properties. The Southern Alps hold some of the world's finest wild game species for trophy hunting. The main hunting period is from March to September during the "rut", when the big males are looking for mates. Hunting here can be challenging and with harsh conditions; a high level of fitness is therefore necessary.

Trout fishing became popular after its introduction by British immigrants.The seasons vary

year, but the period from mid-January until the end of May is considered the prime time.

Clear blue skies, lofty mountains and dazzling snow slopes guarantee the popularity of skiing and snowboarding here, with commercial ski fields, Nordic cross-country and heli-ski areas. The North Island has three fields on Mount Ruapehu and another on Mount Taranaki. The South Island fields are spread throughout the Southern Alps, with Coronet Peak at Queenstown being the southernmost and possibly the country's best. These fields are a favourite training venue for northern hemisphere ski teams. Heli-ski and glacier skiing operators offer an extensive range of off-piste skiing from July to October.

Take a hike

New Zealand has some of the greatest walks in the world. From remote Fiordland forests to the wilderness of the Whirinaki Forest, from crossing the volcanic plains of Tongariro National Park or heli-hiking on the Franz Josef Glacier, there is no disputing the diversity and beauty of the walks available.

If you are particularly energetic, you can walk the length of the country on marked trails *(see pages 46–7)*. Details of most walks, regardless of duration or recommended

> **CITY OF SAILS**
>
> On the last Monday of January, the Auckland Anniversary Regatta takes place. With more than 1,000 entries it is the world's biggest one-day yachting event.

tored to ensure preservation of the special nature and wildlife of these pristine areas.

On the water

On any fine weekend the waters which embrace Auckland ripple with the wakes of thousands of watercraft. From Westhaven to Buckland's Beach, from the East Coast Bays to Murray's Bay, they fly in the prevailing southwesterly breeze, skimming like tiny white butterflies over the water with barely a gap between them. Then, as the

fitness level, are available from information centres and Department of Conservation (DOC) offices. New Zealand walks are safe. There is no dangerous wildlife and tracks are well signposted and maintained. However, be aware that the weather is extremely changeable and walkers of every level must always go well prepared.

Bookings with the DOC are required for some of the most popular and world-renowned tracks, such as the Milford, Heaphy and Routbourn. The number of visitors is closely moni-

shore is left behind, they spread out, revealing themselves as a mix of yachts, launches, fizz boats, windsurfers and jet skiers. The scenario is repeated around the country's coastal waters.

Is it any wonder that yachting is another of the nation's great passions? Winning the America's Cup, the world's oldest sporting trophy, in 1995 highlighted the sport, which reached a climax in 2000 when *Black Magic* defended, and won the America's Cup for a second time.

Adrenaline action

Early in the 19th century, "adventure" meant people pushed to the edge of human endurance. There were things to be discovered, unexplored

LEFT: fisherman snagging a brown trout at Nelson Lakes National Park.
ABOVE: yacht race at Auckland Habour.

territories to be conquered, land to chart. Those were the days before double-edged harnesses, poly-prop garments and satellite navigation. Adventure, real adventure, meant facing hardships, discomfort and often death. Today's adventurers need only the spirit of adventure, some cash and a slight dose of insanity.

New Zealand's capacity for inventing and commercialising adventures is legendary *(see pages 120–121)*. Leaping from aeroplanes, mountains and bridges, pounding down untamed rivers and over terrifying waterfalls, sinking beneath surging seas in search of wrecks or swimming with sharks are all readily available.

or nearby. For many, completing a tandem sky-dive is high on their list of "must-do" adventure activities. Taupo, Christchurch, Wanaka and Queenstown are notably popular areas for skydiving. After leaving the plane, jumpers will spend the first 30 seconds in freefall, plummeting to the ground at 200 kph (124 mph) before enjoying the leisurely drift down to earth. Others might prefer a hot air balloon ride over the Canterbury Plains or aerobatics in a bi-plane near Rotorua. For those wanting a more sedate aerial adventure, gliding is a calming option. Wairarapa, Matamata and Oamaru are renowned for their superb gliding conditions.

Fly by Wire is indicative of Kiwi ingenuity. Invented and patented worldwide by Neil Harrap, the adventure is the world's first flight offering full pilot control of a high-speed, tethered plane. Based at Queenstown, the planes are suspended from an overhead suspension point 55 metres (180 ft) high. Speeds of up to 125 kph (77 mph) have been recorded.

Parasailing, paragliding and parachuting are other great ways to obtain an adrenalin fix while also getting a superb aerial sightseeing tour. During the summer months, commercial parasailers operate on most of the major lakes. Small airfields near main tourist destinations will generally have gliding or skydiving centres on site

Surfing and diving

For many thrillseekers, the waters of New Zealand are the biggest, wildest and most exciting playgrounds of them all. Big wave surfing, windsurfing, traction kiting and scuba diving pit the participant's human-sized strength and courage against one of nature's most powerful and untamable elements.

Kite surfing is one of the country's fastest-growing new watersports. Surfers use the power of both the waves and the wind to propel themselves as high as 30 metres (100 ft) into the air and can cover some long distances across the water. Riders are strapped by their feet to "surfboards" and connected to a billowing kite by a harness similar to that used by windsurfers. Kite surfing has been described as a combination of aerobatics, windsurfing and skysurfing.

New Zealand's coastline and offshore islands have some of the best temperate water diving in the world. From the rocky headlands of the far north to the fiords of the deep south, you can explore wrecks, swim under ice, enter dark caves, meander through forests of black coral trees, frolic with fish and confront camera-shy sharks. The coastal waters reflect the diversity of the land, providing a huge range of diving experiences within a very small area.

The Poor Knights Islands, off the coast from Tutukaka are undoubtedly the jewel of New Zealand diving. Affectionately referred to as "The Diver's Knights", the labyrinth of caves, archways, air bubble caves, caves and drop offs, combined with the prolific fish life which thrives due to the island's Marine Reserve status, ensure the diving is nothing less than spectacular. Experienced divers could never be disappointed with dive sites like Taravana Cave, Kamakazi Drop Off, Northern Arch and Wild Beast Point. For the less experienced and meandering photographers, Maomao Arch, Middle Arch and the Cream Garden offer colour and action at shallower depths. A short distance away from the Poor Knights lie two scuttled frigates, the *Tui* and the *Waikato*. Both make great wreck dives as does the *Rainbow Warrior*, which lies further north. Dive operators at Tutukaka offer a variety of trips and cater for divers at all levels. Gear and guides are provided for those who require it.

South Island diving is colder but no less exciting. The Russian cruise liner *Mikhail Lermontov* lying in 36 metres (120 ft) of water near Port Gore in the Marlborough Sounds excites wreck divers, the cave system of the Riwaka Source in the Takaka Valley challenges cave divers, and Fiordland intrigues budding marine biologists. The heavy rainfall in Fiordland makes it one of the wettest places on earth and is also responsible for creating unique diving conditions. A permanent layer of fresh water up to 10 metres (32 ft) deep sits above the seawater. The result is a great sunblocking filter, which tricks deep-dwelling creatures into the shallow depths. The

14 fiords support the world's biggest population of black coral trees, about seven million colonies, some up to 200 years old and in depths only accessible to sport divers.

White-water thrills

Every year thousands of adrenalin-hungry thrill seekers climb into kayaks or bouncy orange inflatable rafts and attempt to navigate some of the most scenic, dramatic and dangerous rivers imaginable. Undaunted by nature's obstacles, they plummet over waterfalls and career through sharp-rocked rapids in a frenzy of foam and madness. Then when the waters are quiet,

RAFTING RULES

In addition to a sense of adventure, inexperienced rafters need two other things in order to take part in this exhilarating experience – the ability to listen and a well developed sense of humour. It is vital that you listen to all the instructions handed out before you set off, and take note of how to front paddle and back paddle, how to swap sides without smacking someone in the head with your paddle, how to hold on very tight when you get right into deep white-knuckle territory. And, after you've confused everyone by mixing left with right, been hit over the head by someone who didn't listen, and been washed overboard, you really need to be able to smile.

LEFT: a parachutist obviously happy with her successful descent.

RIGHT: surfer riding a wave at a Christchurch beach.

they let their crafts and their minds drift in aimless contentment. There are more than 80 commercial white-water rafting operations in New Zealand, carrying a total of 130,000 clients annually on 57 rivers. Between Christmas and the end of February each year about 13,000 people will pour down the Shotover River alone. The rapids encountered range from grade one to five, so you can choose your level of excitement. Participants are provided with wetsuits, life jackets and helmets.

Kayaking is a more sedate pursuit, and trips on fresh or coastal waters are available everywhere. Fiordland is high on the list of most spec-

and decorated with stalactites and stalagmites, before surfacing to warm up with hot soup and crumpets. Be prepared to get wet, cold and scared. The same company can also introduce you to wilder adventures. Another reliable operator, Waitomo Adventures (which measures its adventure danger level at "Rambo Rating"), will have you abseiling down waterfalls or dropping 100 metres (330 ft) down into a gaping hole in the earth known as The Lost World. The South Island's answer to Waitomo is found on the West Coast, where The Wild West Adventure Company provides a similar range of heart-stopping activities.

tacular kayaking sites, with towering mountains rising sheer from the mostly navigable fiords. Abel Tasman National Park is also memorable for day, overnight or longer adventures. The pristine coastline is speckled with safe overnight campsites, and the chance of being accompanied by dolphins or an inquisitive seal is high.

Deep down and dirty

Cavers Dave Ash and Peter Chandler took the underground experience into the commercial realm when they established The Legendary Black Water Rafting Company at Waitomo in 1987. Cavers float on inner tubes through underground flooded caves lit with glowworms

Canyoning is the exploration and descent of steep-sided, confined river gorges using specialised ropes, abseiling skills, and sometimes the less specialised arts of jumping and swimming. It was introduced to New Zealand by The Deep Canyoning Company when they began exploring the spectacular gorges carved out of the schist rock around Wanaka. The thrill comes from abseiling down, in and behind huge cascades and witnessing the artistic grandeur of rock sculptures formed by the water action.

Off the edge

New Zealanders seem to have this obsession with throwing themselves off things, and the higher the better. None is higher than Auckland's Sky Tower, the tallest tower in the southern hemisphere. It protrudes 192 metres (630 ft) above the Sky City casino in central Auckland. This is the site of Skyjump, best described as base-jumping without the parachute. Jumpers are escorted to a lift, which takes them to the 53rd floor. After donning a harness and having equipment checked, they make their way to the edge of a platform where, after summoning together their last reserves of courage (or madness), they leap off the building towards the city below.

There are various bungy jumping sites throughout New Zealand with one of the most

A similar thrill is on offer at the Shotover Canyon Swing where you jump in a harness from 109 metres (358 ft) and freefall 60 metres (197 ft) into the canyon before a twin rope system pendulums you in a smooth 200-metre (656-ft) arc at 150 kph (90 mph).

A more recent attraction is the Skywire, located just 10 minutes from Nelson town. You are strapped into a four-seat carriage, after which you are launched 1.6 km (1 mile) on an endless cable across a valley at a speed of 100 kph (62 mph). ❏

● *See also pages 339–42 of Travel Tips and its regional listings for contact details of operators.*

notable being on the Auckland Harbour Bridge. The Bridge Walk to the jump site is equally exciting for spectators. Jumpers who opt for the South Island have the choice of three Queenstown jumps. They can leap 43 metres (141 ft) off the original bungy site at Kawarau Bridge, drop 47 metres (154 ft) off the Ledge Bungy in Central Queenstown, or brave the Nevis Highwire Bungy, the ultimate high-wire jump of 134 metres (440 ft) from a gondola that overlooks the meeting of the Nevis and Kawarau rivers.

LEFT: white-water action on the Rangitata River in Canterbury.
ABOVE: plunging off Kawarau Bridge, Queenstown.

A BRIEF HISTORY OF BUNGY

Life was easy for adolescent males in ancient Vanuatu in the Pacific. To prove their manhood, all they had to do was climb a bamboo tower, tie some fine ropes around their legs and jump. Finding an appropriate rite of passage today is less simple, but bungy jumping still rates as one of the biggest challenges for people who want to prove their courage, test themselves, or are just too chicken to resist peer pressure. Modern-day bungy jumping was started in England by the Oxford Dangerous Sports Club, but was commercialised in New Zealand by A.J. Hackett and Henry Van Asch, who brought it into the international spotlight in 1987 with a spectacular jump from the Eiffel Tower.

THRILLSEEKERS' PARADISE

There's no end to the variety of adventure sports in New Zealand. Just as your heartbeat slows to normal speed, a new crazy activity comes along

New Zealanders have become famous for their willingness to jump off bridges, speed down shallow rivers, or roll down hills inside inflatable balls. They're happy to help others do the same, too, and have introduced new heart-pumping sports to the world – but they do it safely. Every week thousands of visitors experience the heady euphoric feeling of an adrenaline rush.

New Zealanders seem to be addicted to adrenaline. It's the best legal drug you can get, but like any drug you have to get more of it in different forms. So adventure addicts now consider bungy-jumping "boring" – rap jumping is currently their way to get a high. Another favourite thrill is jet-boat rides down river gorges, travelling at breakneck speeds perilously close to the rocky banks *(above)*.

TALKING UP THE RISKS

The industry is now strongly regulated and the operators highly trained. They've all been to the same charm school and so delight in making any activity seem more dangerous than it really is. They reason that the higher you think the risk is, the higher the adrenaline rush when you "miraculously" survive the experience.

Should you ask your partner for a parachute jump how long he's been doing tandem jumps, he'll tell you that today is his first time with a paying customer. Stand on a bridge and ask how many jumps a bungy rope is used for before it's retired, and you'll be told "100, and yours is the 99th".

Such tricks are simple but extremely effective. In fact, the adventure sports industry in New Zealand has a remarkably good safety record.

Nobody has ever satisfactorily explained why New Zealanders are so successful at dreaming up new adventure activities – from cave-rafting to parapenting. It must be a combination of the beautiful outdoors and their isolation from the rest of the world. They have to get their kicks at home and they'll try anything once. If it works, they'll develop it for their visitors' fun and enjoyment.

△ **TANDEM SKY DIVE**
This is a 30-second, 200 kph (120 mph) freefall with a professional attached to your back. The 4-minute final descent by parachute is the perfect way to calm down.

▽ **RAP JUMPING**
Face-forward abseiling was invented by the SAS. It allows you to safely see the city from a new angle.

ZORBING YOUR WAY DOWN THE HILL

Zorbing is the epitome of New Zealanders' love of the bizarre. An NZ Air Force pilot described zorbing as "the same sensation as spinning loops and barrel rolls and then crashing to the ground in a jet. Only in a zorb it doesn't hurt." Lesser mortals say it's like "being inside a tumble drier".

The zorb is actually two spheres, one suspended inside the inflated outer one. The view from inside is a tumbling blur of blue sky and green grass which eventually seems to blend into one as you bounce and fall and roll down a hillside. Aficionados throw a bucket of water in first just to remove any chance that they can cling to the sides. There are also plans to take it onto the country's fast-flowing rivers and over waterfalls.

Like many adventure sports, it's almost as much fun to watch as to participate. It starts with mirth as a vacuum cleaner working in reverse is used to pump up the zorb, and finishes with hilarity as the dizzy participant tries to climb out of the sphere.

Zorbing is probably the safest of all the adventure sports. Like all of them there is no logical reason to do it. New Zealand's first and foremost adventure sportsman was Sir Edmund Hillary, who probably climbed Everest in 1953 for the same reason as today's adrenaline seekers: because it's there.

△ AEROBATICS

The plane looks tiny and the pilot looks crazy. They don't even give you a sick bag, although you can tell the pilot to stop. Loops and rolls, upside-down flying, inverted turns and more all conspire to twist your stomach into unbelievable shapes. Miles better than any fun-fair ride – just remember not to have a meal first.

△ TANDEM HANG-GLIDING

This is probably one of the safer activities, even though the aluminium and fabric wing looks fragile. If you're lucky, you can fly yourself during part of the 15 minutes you're aloft.

▽ GLACIER WALKING

Walking on what appears to be a living, moving, creaking, mountain of ice is awe-inspiring. You may be roped up to your guide in case you slip and fall down a crevasse.

△ HELI-BUNGY

To jump out of a helicopter attached to a rubber band is the ultimate dinner party story – if leaping off a bridge isn't enough for you.

PLACES

A detailed guide to the entire country, with principal sites
clearly cross-referenced by number to the maps

People aside – albeit friendly, heartwarming people – it's the places in New Zealand that arouse your sense of wonder and make you catch your breath. The pristine beauty of Milford Sound, the silver dazzle of the Southern Lakes, the bush-wrapped solitude of Lake Waikaremoana, the boiling surprises of the thermal regions … these have inspired even the most travelled of visitors to wax lyrical.

The Maori story of creation explains that land and human beings are all one – flesh and clay from the same source material. The indigenous Maori emotional attachment to place is profound and has influenced Pakeha (European) culture, contributing to the national belief that "clean and green" is a philosophy, not just a tourism marketing tool.

The first Europeans, transplanted 20,000 km (12,400 miles) from the tailored communities of Europe they still called home, tried initially to remake the face of the New Zealand countryside into a Britain look-alike. They cut and burned the forest and sowed grass, but when they had the leisure to look around, they soon realised how special their new home was.

The North Island's spas and hot pools earned an early reputation for their curative powers. As early as 1901, the government hired an official balneologist and formed a tourist department, the first government-sponsored tourism promotion organisation in the world.

The thermal regions still draw enormous attention from travellers today. But nowadays – in a world packed with ever-increasing numbers of people in dense and clogged cities – it's mainly the unsullied, uncluttered landscape, and the sense of space and timelessness that bring thousands of visitors to its shores. Some come just to soak in the scenery, while an ever-increasing number want to walk in the wilderness; for them a tramp through New Zealand's outposts of scenic beauty becomes a sort of purification rite.

New Zealand's remoteness from the rest of the world has served both to limit the number of visitors and preserve the land from over-exploitation. Those who did come were delighted by what they found packed into a country whose length can be driven in a couple of days, and whose width can be crossed in a few hours. And what was known to a small number of enthusiasts became known to millions of people all around the world in 2001, with the release of the movie *The Lord of the Rings: The Fellowship of the Ring*, directed by native son Peter Jackson. Cast in the role of Middle Earth, the unique and exotic variety of the country's landscapes was clear for all to see. Suddenly, New Zealand has become travel's worst-kept secret. ❏

PRECEDING PAGES: Milford Sound in a sombre mood; pastures and peaks of the West Coast area in perspective; a sea of sheep in the hills of Canterbury.
LEFT: the mighty Remarkables mountain range in Queenstown with Lake Wakatipu in the foreground.

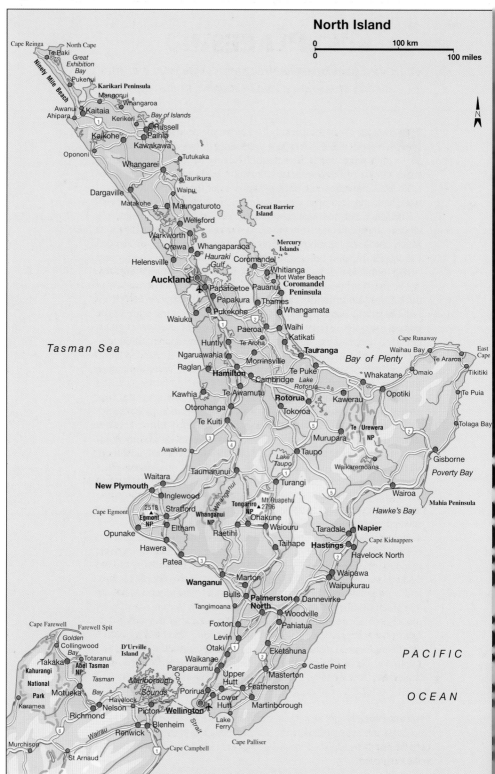

North Island

NORTH ISLAND

This is New Zealand's hub, where frenetic activity is a feature
of business, leisure and even the earth itself

The North Island, according to Polynesian legend, is the fish pulled from the sea by Maui. What a catch it is. The more populous of the two main islands of New Zealand, the North Island will hook visitors, too, with its range of sights to see and things to do.

Three of New Zealand's largest cities – Auckland, Wellington and Hamilton – are here. While many of the North Island's features are little different from those elsewhere or are duplicated in other parts of the country, attention should be drawn to three in particular which are in a class of their own: the Bay of Islands, Rotorua and – much less accessible or visited – Te Urewera National Park.

Northland, at the top of the island, has a strong Maori heritage and was also one of the first areas settled by Europeans. Visit the Bay of Islands townships of Paihia and Russell and it's easy to understand why. Activities here centre on the sea: sailing, big game fishing, pleasure cruising. There are also numerous sites of historical interest, from the house where the Treaty of Waitangi was signed to the oldest stone building in the country. The pace of life in the Far North is slow, but the same can't be said of its brash neighbour Auckland, home to more than a million of New Zealand's 4.1 million population. It's also the largest Polynesian city in the world, and its wide range of shops, restaurants and activities make it truly cosmopolitan.

In common with the rest of New Zealand, you don't have to go far for a change of scenery. An hour's drive and you travel through fertile market gardening and dairy country and into Waikato – its name borrowed from New Zealand's longest waterway, the Waikato River, which winds its way through the region. The gold rush drew the first European settlers to Coromandel, and its beautiful beaches in secluded bays tempt modern-day explorers to put down roots. For sustenance, the Bay of Plenty lives up to its name while the East Cape and its remoteness offers a special charm of its own.

Inland things heat up considerably. Hot mineral springs, boiling mud, geysers and volcanoes have led to Rotorua being aptly called a "thermal wonderland". Further south is New Zealand's largest lake, Lake Taupo, where fishing is the activity of choice for many. The fertile grounds of Taranaki, Wanganui and Manawatu are some of the most intensely farmed regions in New Zealand, with the dairy industry to the fore. The numerous small towns that service local farms also offer friendly stopover points for travellers. Though situated at the bottom of the North Island, Wellington is at the centre of New Zealand life. It is the nation's capital and within its harbour-fringed confines are the head offices of many of the country's major companies. ❑

AUCKLAND

*It's one of the world's most sprawling cities, yet you can easily walk
across it in less than 20 minutes. Volcanoes and the sea define
its landscape, but its people are still defining themselves*

Map on page 134

Auckland North Island
Wellington
Christchurch
South Island

Auckland is built on an isthmus located between two stunning harbours and has, from the beginning, been defined by the water that surrounds it. The harbour that laps at the foot of what would become Auckland's main street was called Waitemata – sparkling water – by the pre-European Maori and from every vantage point, ancient and modern, man-made and natural, the aptness of the name may be seen today.

Even when the sun is not shining – and Aucklanders like to think of their city as a sunkissed gem of the South Pacific – the water glistens, silver under overcast skies, and becomes positively diamantine when the clouds part.

So insistent is the sea – nosing up creeks and estuaries and lapping on the shores of a hundred bays – that less than a mile of *terra firma* stops it from cutting Auckland completely adrift. The 19th-century townships that have linked up to make the 21st-century city were sprinkled along an S-shaped isthmus which at its narrowest point is barely 1.3 km (0.8 mile) wide. Across it runs Portage Road whose name recalls that it was the crossing point between two harbours. Here, Maori would beach and haul their canoes across the only break in an aquatic highway leading from the sheltered eastern bays of the far north and joining up with the Waikato, the country's longest river, which punches deep into the heart of the North Island. There are not many countries one may walk across, coast to coast, in less than 20 minutes.

The City of Sails

The Waitemata is the gateway to the island-studded boating paradise of the Hauraki Gulf – Aucklanders are keen boaties. Ownership of recreational boats – from ostentatious gin palaces and deep-sea fishing craft to aluminium "tinnies", battered rowboats and kayaks – is reputedly the world's highest per capita.

Not for nothing has Auckland branded itself "The City of Sails". Its anniversary day, the last Monday in January, is marked by a regatta – first staged in 1840, it's as old as the city itself – which crowds the harbour with as many as 1,000 sailing craft of all sizes in an organised mayhem of spectacle and competition.

A nation of boat owners produced a team of world-beating sailors, of course. Team New Zealand was operating on a budget a fraction the size of its competitors' when it snatched the coveted yachting trophy the America's Cup in 1995 and successfully defended it in 2000. The pain of losing the cup to the Swiss-based Alinghi syndicate in 2003 was somewhat eased by the knowledge that the victor boat's key crew members were all New Zealanders.

Technically, the Auckland region is made up of four cities. Auckland City itself is bordered by Manukau (the country's most populous) to the south; Waitakere to the

LEFT: Auckland skyline and harbour.
BELOW: a city of keen boat owners.

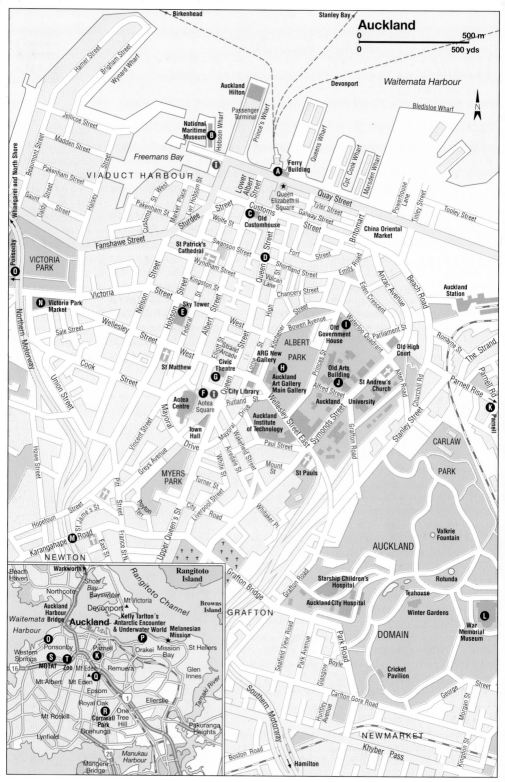

Auckland

| 0 | | 500 m |
| 0 | | 500 yds |

Map on page 134

west; and North Shore city across the Waitemata. But Auckland City – which has 30 percent of the region's and 10 percent of the nation's population – is undeniably the country's economic powerhouse. Population increased by almost 25 percent in the decade from 1991, and Aucklanders produce and consume a disproportionate share of the national wealth. This fact engenders a fair degree of hostility and resentment from the less well-off who live in smaller cities and provincial centres.

Turbulent history

A geological newborn, Auckland came to life with a bang. Some 60 volcanoes were created by eruptions which began only 50,000 years ago. The youngest – the bush-clad Rangitoto Island, whose blue-green hulk dominates the downtown waterfront view – last erupted only six centuries ago, burying a Maori settlement on the adjoining Motutapu Island.

The city's human history is no less turbulent than its geological past. The ancestors of the Maori are believed to have arrived from eastern Polynesia around AD 800. Traditional lore tells of incessant bloody inter-tribal warfare which gave Auckland its early Maori name, Tamaki Makaurau, meaning "battle of a hundred lovers": the poetic description alluded not to a love story but to the conflict, which was as fierce as a suitor's rivalry.

Contact between Maori and the white people they would come to call Pakeha had been occurring haphazardly for half a century as traders and whale-hunters, whose venereal hygiene was seldom commensurate with their sexual appetites, sought shelter along the coast. But British settlement of Auckland officially began with the visit of the enterprising Samuel Marsden in 1820 *(see box below)*.

The British wit and raconteur Clement Freud famously remarked in 1978 (of

A popular nickname for an Aucklander is JAFA – three of the four initials stand for "just another Aucklander" (no prizes for guessing what the third initial stands for). Part of this animosity stems from a resentment of the Aucklander's perceived wealth and status.

BELOW: Queen Street in yesteryears.

A BARGAIN BUY

The British settlement of Auckland officially began with the visit of the enterprising Reverend Samuel Marsden in 1820. The Sydney-based missionary named the fledgeling capital after the Earl of Auckland, George Eden, the Viceroy of India. This intrepid preacher crossed the Auckland isthmus on board the sailing ship *Coromandel* in November, the first European to do so, and his arrival heralded a process of land purchase which remains deeply problematic till this day.

It is more than probable that the Maori – whose traditional relationship with the land rendered the concept of ownership as meaningless – did not realise they were selling their real estate but rather accepting gifts in return for letting the new settlers live on their land.

Certainly the newcomers got a snip for what they paid: they purchased the area that now comprises the heart of Auckland for 50 blankets, 20 pairs of trousers, 20 shirts and other assorted sundries plus £50 cash, with another £6 paid the following year. The 1,200 hectares (3,000 acres) that the British settlers purchased covered the area from today's Freemans Bay to Parnell and inland as far as Mount Eden. Today, just one acre of downtown land in the city is worth at least NZ$12 million.

New Zealand as a whole) that he found it hard to say what he thought of it "because when I was there it seemed to be shut". The comment was doubtlessly apt at the time, but in the following decades the city transformed itself into an exciting locale with much to offer the visitor.

Auckland's growth was in part fuelled by an immigration boom in the 1990s, with an influx of Asians – wealthy immigrants in the southeastern areas of Howick (unaffectionately dubbed "Chowick") and legions of students seeking a Western education. The change has caused palpable unease among long-established Kiwis who feel the ethnic composition of the city is changing too fast, but, no one can deny that it has made the city a vibrant Pacific-Asian metropolis.

An early arrival described Auckland as "a few tents and huts and a sea of fern stretching as far as the eye could see". Today, the gaze of the modern visitor ranges over a sea of suburbs. Fittingly, sprawling Auckland is a sister city of Los Angeles: at 1,016 sq km (392 sq miles) it's far larger than London and in proportion to its population of barely 1.3 million, Greater Auckland is one of the world's largest metro areas. The sea on the east and the regional parkland of the Waitakere Ranges in the west have provided barriers to the sideways sprawl. Planning restrictions have halted the remorseless march north and south: the four cities now stretch 80 km (50 miles) from Whangaparaoa in the north to Drury in the south. Today, residential construction goes up not out.

Generally, Aucklanders live, work and shop in the suburban hinterland, which is dotted with busy shopping malls, and venture into the city only for special events. From the mid-1980s the inner city area developed rapidly, with the building of office towers and (often shoddily constructed) apartment blocks. In aesthetic and heritage terms it has been something of a disaster. More than perhaps

Auckland's 1.3-km (0.8-mile) width at its narrowest can be comfortably walked in minutes, making New Zealand one of the few large cities in the world where the average person can walk across with ease.

BELOW:
the Auckland skyline pierced by the needle-sharp Sky Tower in the middle.

any other city outside the former communist world, Auckland has butchered its past and replaced elegant Victorian buildings with cheap, characterless high-density apartments. Remarkable or even interesting modern architecture is lamentably rare, although some exciting new developments have taken place in the Viaduct Harbour *(see overleaf)*, the site of the America's Cup Village.

Map on page 134

Auckland Harbour

Urban sprawl makes getting round greater Auckland something of a challenge. Taxis are expensive by world standards (although there is an efficient system of buses and ferries), but the city centre's historic highlights are easily reached by what older locals refer to as Shanks' Pony – which is to say on foot.

The sturdy red-brick **Ferry Building** Ⓐ on Quay Street at the foot of Queen Street is a good place to start an exploratory ramble. The 1912 building, which once housed the offices of harbour officials, now contains two of downtown's better restaurants, and behind it you can board the ferries to the North Shore and the islands of the Hauraki Gulf.

If you stand on the street front with your back to the building, the Viaduct Harbour precinct, including the excellent **New Zealand National Maritime Museum** Ⓑ (daily 9am–5pm; entrance fee; tel: 09-3730 8003; www.nzmaritime.org), is barely 3 minutes walk to your right. Its collection covers maritime history from the earliest Polynesian explorers to the present day. Vessels on display include the *Rapaki* floating steam crane and *KZI*, the yacht that launched New Zealand's America's Cup obsession when it sailed and lost in San Diego in 1988.

New Zealand's defence of the America's Cup prompted the redevelopment of the **Viaduct Harbour**. Site of the southern hemisphere's largest super-yacht

The KZI, which took part in New Zealand's first ever America's Cup race in 1988, is on display at the NZ National Maritime Museum.

BELOW: the historic Ferry Building.

TIP

Auckland i-SITE Visitor Centres are found at the following locations: Viaduct Harbour at the corner of Quay and Hobson streets (daily 9am–5pm winter, daily 8.30am–6pm summer) and Atrium Sky City, corner Victoria and Federal streets (Sun–Wed 8am–8pm, Thur–Sat 8am–10pm). Inquiries at tel: 09-979 2333; www.aucklandnz.com.

BELOW: alfresco restaurants line the Viaduct Harbour.

marina, the Viaduct is also a fashionable, if overpriced, restaurant and bar precinct allowing for that conjunction of fine food and water views which so many find irresistible. When the super-yachts are in port, particularly at the height of summer, these sometimes gaudy floating palaces are a major attraction in themselves. At the northeast end of Viaduct Harbour is the **Auckland Hilton**, on the water's edge at Prince's Wharf, cleverly designed to suggest a cruise liner and one of Auckland's better examples of post-modern architecture. You may want to return in the evening for dinner at one of the Viaduct's waterfront restaurants.

Just across **Quay Street** is **Queen Elizabeth Square**, dominated by the city's main transport hub, **Britomart**. Housed in the former Chief Post Office, the neo-classical building dates back to 1910. As you leave the square to cross **Customs Street**, look again to your right (west). A block away, on the corner of **Albert Street** is the **Old Customhouse** ◉ now occupied by DSS Galleria, which was the financial heart of Auckland for more than 80 years. Designed in French Renaissance style, the building was completed in 1889 and is one of the last remaining examples of monumental Victorian architecture to be found in a central business district where the wrecker's ball has been far too busy.

Queen Street central

The aforementioned Clement Freud would not recognise downtown Auckland these days. Shops seeking the tourist dollar stay open till late on weekdays and through the weekends. But **Queen Street** ◉ – the city's main drag, traditionally been known as the "Golden Mile" – does not glitter as it once did. Cheap noodle houses and Internet cafés cater to the huge number of Asian students, and convenience stores serve inner-city apartment dwellers, though there is a healthy

sprinkling of upmarket boutiques and fashion brand stores. Much of corporate New Zealand headquarters itself in the Queen Street valley, which can be gloomy and sparsely peopled outside business hours. Some excellent restaurants do good business in the streets that radiate out from Freyberg Place but it's the inner suburbs – particularly Parnell to the east and Ponsonby to the west – where some of the city's best eateries are to be found. If you're so inclined, check out the tourist stores in the lower part of Queen Street: the prices, while not cheap, will not be extortionate, though some of the more chintzy merchandise may be made in Taiwan – check the label.

As you walk south up the main street, pause at the intersection of Queen and Fort streets. Waves lapped the shore at this spot less than 150 years ago and Shortland Street, a block further up, was the main street; Queen Street was a bush-covered gully along which ran a canal serving as an open sewer.

You will have hardly avoided noticing, some 500 metres (1,600 ft) to the southwest, the cloud-piercing **Sky Tower** (daily 8.30am–11pm, till midnight on Fri and Sat; entrance fee; tel: 09-363 6000; www.skycity.co.nz) on Hobson Street, the western ridge of the valley. The tallest structure, at 328 metres (1,076 ft), in the southern hemisphere and the eighth highest in the world, it was the butt of many jokes when it was built; critics saw its giant syringe shape as an apt symbol of the gambling addiction being generated by the casino at its foot. But it has rapidly become a familiar and dramatic feature of the city skyline – best seen from the harbour or while driving over the harbour bridge. Visitors are whisked in high-speed lifts to the top for a view, which, on a clear day, can stretch more than 80 km (50 miles). Those less prone to vertigo might like to consider a 2-hour guided tour up the inside of the Sky Tower (tel: 09-368 1917; www.4vertigo.com), or the 192-metre (630-ft)-high base jump off the tower (contact Skyjump, tel: 09-368 1835; www.skyjump.co.nz).

Civic pride

Back down to earth on Queen Street, and some 400 metres (1,300 ft) to the south on the left is **Aotea Square** , dominated by the monolithic **Auckland City Council** administration building, and, on the western side of the square, the city's main cultural complex, the **Aotea Centre**. Built over the howls of those who could not understand why the city's pre-eminent public building was not being sited on the waterfront, the Aotea Centre is an impersonal and unwelcoming space. Its 2,300-seat multi-purpose theatre is acoustically problematic to say the least – most classical music performances take place in the beautifully restored and acoustically warm **Town Hall** on the square's southeastern boundary – but it is popular as a convention centre. The Aotea Centre, The Civic, Auckland Town Hall and Aotea Square all come under the collective administrative umbrella, The Edge (tel: 09-309 2677). For programme details, check www.the-edge.co.nz.

Just down the road to the north at the corner with Wellesley Street is the opulent **Civic Theatre**  (daily 10am–4pm; free; tours by arrangement; tel: 09-309 2677). Built in 1929, it was one of the world's finest atmospheric picture palaces, though now mostly used for touring musicals and shows. Its ornate

Map on page 134

Sky Tower, which soars 328 metres (1,076 ft) into the sky, is an impressive sight on any day.

BELOW: the old Civic Theatre has been sensitively restored.

construction was a sign of the times – it employed many hundreds of tradesmen during the Great Depression – and the labyrinthine stairways are watched over by hundreds of plaster elephants. From 1997 to 1999 it underwent a multi-million-dollar refurbishment for the millennium retained a mock sky, complete with twinkling stars, which makes it one of the city's finest sights.

Aotea Square and the Civic Theatre are separated by the city's major cinema centre. A block away in **Lorne Street** is the **Central City Library** (Mon–Fri 9.30am–8pm, Sat 10am–4pm, Sun noon–4pm; tel: 09-377 0209). Its reading room is popular with homesick travellers and immigrants devouring the foreign press.

One block east on the corner of Kitchener and Wellesley streets is one half of the **Auckland Art Gallery ❺** (daily 10am–5pm; free; tel: 09-307 7700; www.aucklandartgallery.govt.nz), called the **Main Gallery** since it was joined by the equally unimaginatively christened **New Gallery** in 1995 across the street. The former holds historical collections while the latter has fine exhibitions of contemporary art from New Zealand and overseas. Visitors are likely to be intrigued by the idealised 19th-century portraits of Maori by Gottfried Lindauer and Charles Goldie in the Main Gallery.

After visiting the gallery, head northeast about 600 metres (2,000 ft) uphill – there is a path to the left of the Main Gallery's main entrance – through **Albert Park**, which combines Edwardian public garden design features with some mildly incongruous contemporary sculpture, before entering the leafy grounds of the **University of Auckland**. At the corner of Princes Street and Waterloo Quadrant and part of the university grounds is the **Old Government House ❶**, built in 1856 as the home of the Governor. The building appears to be made of stone, though in fact its exterior cladding is all kauri, the wood of the tall conif-

Auckland's pre-eminent private art gallery is the Gow Langsford Gallery opposite the Auckland Art Gallery in Kitchener Street. Many of New Zealand's leading contemporary artists and a selection of international artists are represented here. Mon–Fri 10am–6pm, Sat 11am–3pm. Tel: 09-303 4290; www.gowlangsford gallery.com.

BELOW: cutting-edge New Gallery houses mainly contemporary art.

erous tree which once dominated the New Zealand bush and was the building material of choice until well into the 19th century.

The university's central attraction, however, a few metres south on Princes Street, is the **Old Arts Building** with its intricate clock tower. It was completed in 1926 in Gothic style and immediately dubbed The Wedding Cake by locals because of its decorative pinnacled white-stone construction.

Note the refurbished **High Court**, some 250 metres (820 ft) to the northeast, where grinning griffins and gargoyles adorn the exterior walls. It stands on the corner of Anzac Avenue and Parliament Street, whose name is another vestige of Auckland's former glory as New Zealand's capital. It was only pressure from the gold-rich South Island and new settlements further south in the North Island that resulted in the movement of the capital from Auckland to Wellington in 1865.

East of the city centre

Continue east through the park known as **Constitution Hill**, named after the fact that businessmen took a "constitutional" walk up its steep slope from their Parnell homes to their city offices. Follow Parnell Rise for 2 km (1 mile) up through **Parnell** . It's an oddity of the city's history – some say it's because the upper classes didn't like the sun in their eyes on the way to and from work in the city – that the suburbs east of Queen Street have always been the city's more affluent. So it's no accident that Parnell oozes a refined style. It's also the gateway to **Newmarket**, a busy shopping strip which is home to some of fashion's big-name outlets, and **Remuera**, where the serious, old money lives. Parnell largely overcame the unfortunate faux heritage refurbishment of the 1970s which hideously attempted to re-imagine it as a pioneer village in low maintenance materials.

Map on page 134

TIP

If feeling peckish while at the Auckland Domain, drop in for a bite at its charming Wintergarden Teahouse (daily 10am–3pm). The delightful three-tiered tea stand laden with sinful goodies is recommended.

BELOW: leafy Auckland Domain at sunrise.

TIP

The impressive
Manaia Maori cultural
performance takes
place at the Auckland
War Memorial
Museum (3 times
daily, Apr–Dec 11am,
noon and 1.30pm;
4 times daily Jan–
Mar 11am, 12am,
1.30pm and 2.30pm).
Admission to the
30-minute show is
by ticket only (NZ$15
adult and NZ$7.50
child). Tel: 09-306
7048, 0800-256 873.

BELOW: stately
Auckland War
Memorial Museum.

At the end of Parnell Road, past the Anglican Cathedral, enter the **Auckland Domain** by turning right on Maunsell Street. This 75-hectare (185-acre) park is the city's oldest, with duck ponds, playing fields, traditional statuary and the Wintergardens, two large glasshouses displaying temperate and tropical plants. This route provides easy access to the **Auckland War Memorial Museum ❶** (daily 10am–5pm; entrance fee; tel: 09-306 7067; www.aucklandmuseum.com) which presides over the rambling grounds of the Domain.

The recently renovated museum is not devoted to war artefacts but in fact is a particularly fine museum on subjects as diverse as natural history, ethnology and archaeology spread over its three floors. The building was erected in 1929 as a memorial to soldiers who died in World War I. It houses one of the world's finest displays of Maori and Polynesian culture, with some artefacts dating back to as far as AD 1200. A highlight is the 35-metre (115-ft) war canoe, *Te-Toki-A-Tapiri* (The Axe of Tapiri), carved in 1836 from a single giant totara tree and designed to seat 100 warriors at one go.

South and west of the city centre

Auckland is the world's biggest Polynesian city. Almost 250,000 New Zealanders – about one in 16 – are of Pacific Island ethnicity, with more than 60 percent of them in the Auckland region. In some cases, Auckland's Polynesian population outnumbers those at home (nine out of 10 Niueans live here) and in most cases, more than half are New Zealand-born. Most of the Pacific peoples settled in the central city in the mid-20th century, particularly in Ponsonby and adjoining Grey Lynn, until soaring property prices and the accompanying gentrification of those suburbs saw the islanders migrate again, to Manukau City *(see page 149)*.

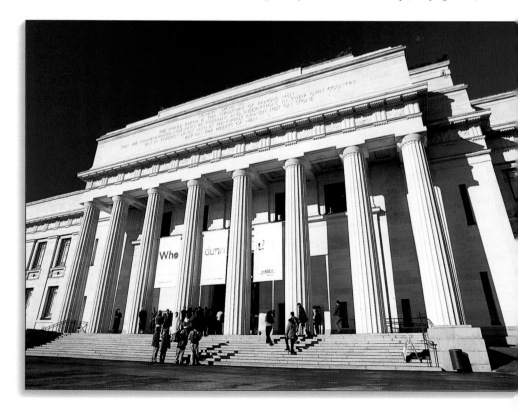

Heading west from the Domain for some 1½ km (1 mile) brings you to **Karangahape Road** — known to locals as K Road — which runs west from Grafton Bridge, and where traces of the city's Pacific connections linger. Shops display brilliantly coloured cloth, taro, yams, papaya, mangoes, green bananas, coconut products and other tropical foods. K Road is the raffish but undeniably charming side of the central city. Its western end was once home to much of the city's sex industry, which now lurks in downtown's Fort Street. Renewal and development have given the area a facelift, which is not an unalloyed improvement for those who enjoy urban diversity (it will take some years for the blandness to become completely entrenched).

About 1 km (½ mile) north of K Road is the **Victoria Park Market** (daily 9am–6pm; free, www.victoriaparkmarket.co.nz), built on the site (and under the tall brick chimney) of what was the city's rubbish destructor until the 1970s. The market is a seven-day tourist lure and the quality of most merchandise is high although the prices can be too. Retail fruit and vegetable stalls operate here, though this is no atmospheric farmers' market.

Old-world Ponsonby Town Hall.

Further west still – a 10-minute walk or a short bus ride up the hill – is **Ponsonby**. This ribbon of road, festooned with the best selection of restaurants in town, is the sister of Parnell, about the same distance from Queen Street. Once home to hirsute students and whole streets of Pacific Island immigrant families, Ponsonby is today the refurbished turn-of-the-19th-century-villas on pocket-handkerchief sections fetch ludicrous prices at auctions, and the streets are full of the elegant and the self-regarding. It's not exactly Rodeo Drive, and many of the city's more creative types live down the narrow streets, but in the 21st century it's definitely Auckland's Golden Mile.

BELOW: Victoria Park Market.

Along Tamaki Drive

A return to the Ferry Building is as good a place as any to start Auckland's waterfront drive. The ribbon of tarmac that runs east from the port around the harbourside is the city's scenic gem. Quay Street becomes **Tamaki Drive**, which winds some 8 km (5 miles) along the seafront. The safe beaches are good for swimming at high tide and excellent for picnics. Rangitoto Island looms ahead, seemingly close enough to touch. The footpath is busy with cyclists and walkers on sunny weekends, and bicycle, boat and windsurfer hire businesses ply a roaring trade.

En route **Kelly Tarlton's Antarctic Encounter and Underwater World** (daily 9am–6pm; entrance fee; tel: 09-528 0603, 0800-805 050; www.kellytarl tons.co.nz) is a virtually compulsory stop. This world-class facility is constructed in what was a sewage pumping station before Auckland stopped pouring its effluent into the harbour in the 1960s. Dozens of varieties of fish and sharks can be viewed from a moving walkway passing through a huge transparent tunnel. At the new Stingray Bay, where one can view an array of magnificent rays, the 41-year-old 250-kg (550-lb) stingray with a metre-wide wingspan, named Phoebe, is the star attraction. The Antarctic section features a Snow Cat ride to view the colony of King and Gentoo penguins in their own world of snow and ice.

Map
on page
134

The obelisk at One Tree Hill – minus the tree that once stood beside it.

BELOW: sea lion at the Auckland Zoo.

Mount Eden and Cornwall Park

Just 3 km (2 miles) south of the city centre is the 196-metre (643-ft) extinct volcanic cone of **Mount Eden Ｑ**, Auckland's highest point. It offers a dramatic 360-degree panorama of the region almost as good as the view from the Sky Tower. In an old lava pit on the eastern side, at 24 Omana Avenue, is **Eden Garden** (daily 9am–4.30pm; entrance fee; tel: 09-638 8395; www.eden garden.co.nz), which provides a heady display of many blooms, notably the largest collection of camellias in the southern hemisphere. It was created in 1964 on the site of an abandoned quarry and is entirely manned by volunteers.

Another 3 km (2 miles) southeast, in **Cornwall Park Ｒ** (daily 7am–sunset; free; tel: 09-630 8485; www.cornwallpark.co.nz) is the landmark cone of **One Tree Hill** and the obelisk which crowns the tomb of the "Father of Auckland", Sir John Logan Campbell. He set up a tent as Auckland's first store at the bottom of Shortland Street on 21 December 1840, and was the city's most prominent businessman until his death in 1912 at the age of 95. The 135-hectare (334-acre) estate encompassing One Tree Hill, which Campbell donated to the people of Auckland when he became mayor, was given its name in 1901 when he hosted Britain's Duke and Duchess of Cornwall. Campbell also built **Acacia Cottage** in 1841. Now Auckland's oldest building, the restored cottage is preserved in Cornwall Park at the base of One Tree Hill.

The Maori name for One Tree Hill is Te Totara-i-ahua, in deference to the sacred totara tree that stood here until 1852 when it was replaced by a pine tree by the early settlers. Today, the "One Tree" sobriquet is in fact something of a misnomer: the lone pine tree that used to stand on the summit was cut down in 2002, after failing to recover from an attack by a chainsaw-wielding Maori activist who was seeking to draw attention to political grievances.

Cars and kiwis

Close to the city, just off the northwestern motorway at Western Springs, is the **Museum of Transport and Technology Ｓ** (MOTAT; daily 10am–5pm; entrance fee; tel: 09-815 5800; www.motat.org.nz). It has over 300,000 items in its collection, including working vintage vehicles, aircraft and machinery and excellent hands-on applied science displays. The museum also has an aircraft built by New Zealander Richard Pearse, who, some devotees claim, flew in March 1903, several months before the Wright Brothers. Volunteer enthusiasts operate many exhibits at the weekends.

A brief ride from MOTAT in an old tram or a pleasant walk eastward around the lake at Western Springs Park leads to **Auckland Zoo Ｔ** (daily 9.30am–5.30pm; entrance fee; tel: 09-360 3800; www.aucklandzoo. co.nz), where you can see the kiwi, New Zealand's unique flightless bird and the tuatara, a "living fossil" which has not changed since the age of the dinosaurs.

Auckland is unquestionably the gateway to New Zealand, and the wise visitor should linger at the country's biggest city before travelling on to the more well-worn tourist attractions to the north and south. There is much to see within easy reach of the city centre. Any Aucklander will tell you: you've got to get out of town or you'll go mad.   ❑

Trendsetting Kiwi Fashion

New Zealand fashion may not quite have come of age yet, but somewhere around the turn of the 21st century it developed the ability to walk. At that time, New Zealand designers – like others in an industry where, if imitation is the sincerest form of flattery, everyone is constantly paying compliments to everyone else – began developing a distinctive style of their own.

In 1997, four homegrown labels– Moontide, World, Wallace Rose and Zambesi – took part in the Australian Fashion Week. Two years later, Kiwi designers took part in the London Fashion Week. "There seems to be a remarkable difference between Australia and New Zealand. New Zealanders have a darker outlook. Less show-offy. More intellectual," observed French *Vogue*. In March 2005, the labels Sabatini, NOM*D, WORLD and NG were showcased at the prestigious Tranoi show during Paris Fashion Week for the first time. All, plus Zambesi, made a return visit in 2006, launching New Zealand fashion further into new global markets.

Overseas fashion writers and opinion shapers are no longer the novelty at major New Zealand fashion events that they once were. Whatever the truth of *Vogue*'s pronouncement, the New Zealand style is less individualistic than it is a brilliant assimilation of a variety of influences. As in so many other areas, the country's isolation has forced the locals to come up with their own solutions – in fashion no less than in agriculture. While still heavily influenced by northern hemisphere designs, many designers draw on Polynesian styles, while others amass a globally eclectic mix and turn it into a coherent whole. (Much contemporary young Polynesian fashion, in turn, is strongly influenced by US hip-hop culture.)

Often those who do best in the fashion industry are those who market themselves as their brand – Karen Walker, Trelise Cooper and Sharon Ng are notable examples. Many of the prominent designers (and labels) who are matching local popularity with some overseas success – Walker, Cooper, Kate Sylvester, Scotties, Zambesi and WORLD are based in Auckland. But New Zealand's biggest city doesn't have the field entirely to itself.

While Wellington has stores representing the better-known local labels, local names to look out for include Andrea Moore, Madcat, Ricochet and Voon. Leading labels NOM*D, Carlson, Mild Red and Dot Com all call Dunedin home, and the student influence gives a lot of the city's fashion a slightly funkier air than the fashion favoured in other centres.

Some of the more invigorating fashion is occurring on the fringes, produced by names who may well be big one day, or fashion being fashion, disappear altogether. Away from Auckland's High Street and Chancery you'll find the odd gem on the city's somewhat louche Karangahape Road. Elsewhere, cutting-edge design is likely to be found in various small studios dotted around Dunedin.

As for men's fashion, for a Kiwi male to care about his appearance is still, except in certain circumstances, regarded as anomalous. ❏

RIGHT: designer Trelise Cooper at her workshop in the trendy Parnell district.

AUCKLAND'S SURROUNDINGS

Auckland is a conglomeration of many cities, and it has different flavours depending on whether you travel west, north, south – or even east, to the 47 islands of the Hauraki Gulf

Map on page 149

Aucklanders, like the inhabitants of their sister city Los Angeles, are passionately, obsessively, blindly devoted to the motor car, as the rush-hour snarl on the motorways quickly reveals. Decades of political prevarication have prevented the development of a respectable rail system and the buses have to tangle with the traffic. Outside peak hours, the buses get around smartly enough and there is no shortage of organised tours which take in the most important sights. But the discerning explorer who doesn't want to run up an eye-watering taxi bill will want to rent a car to make the most of a short stay by exploring beyond the city limits.

To the west

Auckland's frontier, like the New World's, is out west. **Waitakere City ❶**, 15 km (9 miles) west of downtown Auckland on State Highway (SH) 16, burst into life in the mid-1950s when a causeway road was laid across part of the upper harbour, bringing the west much closer to the city. For all that, it still maintains a distinctive wildness. Its inhabitants are collectively nicknamed Westies but any generalisation masks the city's variety. Artists, craftspeople, back-to-nature bush-lovers and substantial Maori and Polynesian populations as well as communities of new immigrants are all part of Waitakere's mix.

Travelling from downtown Auckland, the visitor's first taste of Waitakere City will be at **Henderson Valley ❷**, west of SH16 at the Lincoln Road turnoff. The valley was settled early by Dalmatian and Croatian wine-growers. Today, their dynasties are commemorated in many of the street names, and the roads of modern Waitakere are studded with vineyards, some world-class, others old family operations whose rough reds are still sold in half-gallon flagons.

Beyond the city limits – stay on SH16, bypassing Henderson and you'll come to **Kumeu ❸**, 20 km (12 miles) past the Henderson turnoff, where weekend farmers run horses on their small lifestyle blocks. These are small farming properties whose owners work in a nearby town but indulge in some hobby farming at weekends. Here are to be found some of the more substantial vineyards, like **Kumeu River** (www.kumeuriver.co.nz), **Nobilo** (www.nobilo.co.nz) and **Matua Valley** (www.matua.co.nz).

These days much of suburban west Auckland is shopping-mall country. The wide roads are lined with bland commercial and light industrial ribbon development but it's also the gateway to the thickly forested **Waitakere Ranges**, which commence just 20 km (12 miles) from downtown Auckland. Here tall kauri trees, giant ferns and nikau palms create paradise for bush-walkers – known locally as trampers – and for film-makers. The popular TV series *Xena* and *Hercules*

LEFT: abseiling in the Waitakere Ranges west of Auckland.
BELOW: budding Kumeu farmer.

were filmed here in the **Waitakeve Ranges Regional Park**. The ranges are easily explored by following the aptly named **Scenic Drive** (SH24) which runs for 28 km (17 miles) along their spine from Titirangi to Swanson. Some 5 km (3 miles) from the **Titirangi ❹** end of the drive, the **Arataki Visitors Centre** (daily 9am–5pm summer, 10am–4pm winter; tel: 09-817 4941), is the place to plan detailed explorations which include walks of varying degrees of difficulty and suggestions for camping out overnight.

Breeding season from September to March is the best time to vist Muriwai's gannet colony.

West coast beaches

Beyond the ranges, the west gets truly wild: the edge of the land is stitched by a line of black sand surf beaches and lashed by the prevailing winds and waves off the Tasman Sea. The northernmost beach, 32-km (20-mile) long **Muriwai ❺**, is actually designated a public road (though only the foolhardy would venture on it with a two-wheel drive vehicle) and at the end of the southernmost **Whatipu**, 24 km (15 miles) away, the sea seems to boil as it pours into the tidal Manukau Harbour. At the southern end of Muriwai is a gannet colony which, seen up close from viewing platforms, is one of the region's great sights. Muriwai was one of the most important visual inspirations for the late Colin McCahon *(see page 86)*, who is this country's pre-eminent artist.

In between, the line of beaches raked by the sea includes **Piha**, the surfers' paradise and a favourite of holidaymakers, and **Karekare ❻**, where the spectacular opening sequence of Jane Campion's *The Piano* was filmed. All the West Coast beaches are very dangerous for swimming and their death tolls include many unwary tourists. Although patrolled in summer, always swim between the flags and beware the rogue wave that can pluck a beachcomber or fisher off a rock.

BELOW:
surfing action
at Piha beach.

Further south, **Manukau Harbour**, one coast of which marks the Manukau City's western border, lacks the scenic charm of the Waitemata. It's mostly mudflats at low tide but the roads drop down off the ranges to placid tree-fringed beaches. Fisherfolk swear by it as a fishing ground and it's uncrowded too: many Aucklanders ignore it since it used to be polluted with industrial and domestic run off but its clean-up has been a triumph of conservation planning.

Map on
page 149
or Map
below

South Auckland

The words "South Auckland" are loaded for Aucklanders. The suburbs strung on each side of the southern motorway beyond Otahuhu unquestionably include the region's most economically depressed – although there are parts of **Manukau City**, the region's southern city, that are extremely affluent. Here is to be found the social and physical landscape depicted in *Once Were Warriors*, which showed the cost of drinking, domestic violence and gang warfare on Maori families.

Manukau's faces are disproportionately brown, though many Pakeha New Zealanders would like to think it isn't so – the correlation between Maori and Polynesian ethnicity and poor social status are strong. **Otahuhu ❼**, 14 km (9 miles) south of Auckland on SH1, gives a good glimpse of Manukau City's cultural diversity: wander down the main street, where Asian and Pacific traders jostle cheek-by-jowl and clamour for the attention of passers-by.

But the city has success stories to tell as well, and its happy face is plainly to be seen 3 km (2 miles) further south at the colourful and noisy **Otara Market** (Sat only 6am–noon) on Newbury Street in the Otara Shopping Centre (take the East Tamaki Road/Otara turn-off on SH1). Here is where the sensible tourist will shop for souvenirs, not just because they are better value for money than the

The landmark Kiwi film "Once Were Warriors", based on a novel by Alan Duff and directed by Lee Tamahori was released in 1994 to rave reviews. Set in south Auckland, it takes a painful look at the problems that plague working-class Maori families.

BELOW:
a Manukau rap
artiste in action.

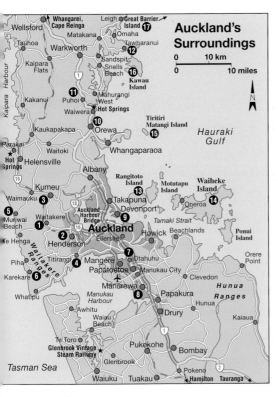

*For those with
enough derring-do,
take a 2-hour climb
up the Auckland
Harbour Bridge
(tel: 09-361 2000).*

shops in the tourist traps but because of the obvious authenticity. Standing in the midst of this multi-cultural community is **Mangere Mount**, which rises 100 metres (328 ft) and overlooks Manukau Harbour.

Travel another 5 km (3 miles) south to **Rainbow's End** (daily 10am–5pm; entrance fee; tel: 09-262 2030; www.rainbowsend.co.nz), the country's premier theme park with crazy rides you won't find anywhere else in the country. The park's newest attraction, Power Surge, offers the closest thing to a spin and tumble in a washing machine.

Elsewhere in Manukau, about 5 km (3 miles) south of Rainbow's End, is the **Auckland Regional Botanic Gardens** (daily 8am–6pm; free; tel: 09-267 1457; www.aucklandbotanicgardens.co.nz) near **Manurewa ❽**, with a dazzling variety of species, both native and exotic. The gardens are now the permanent home of the Ellerslie Flower Show, held over five days every November.

North Auckland

The opening of the **Auckland Harbour Bridge** in 1959 turned Auckland's status from country into city almost overnight. What had been a string of sleepy seaside settlements backed by rolling pastureland became – potentially at least – part of Auckland, thanks to this 1,020-metre (3,350-ft) "coathanger" stretching from the north end of the city centre at Fanshawe Street to Northcote across the water. These days the bridge carries an average of 136,000 vehicles a day.

The bridge leads to a vast northern hinterland of apparently endless suburbia and industrial development which is a city in itself (many North Shore citizens avoid coming into Auckland and many Aucklanders would say that's a very good thing). An enterprising operator, **Auckland Bridge Climb** (tel: 09-361

BELOW: Auckland
Harbour Bridge.

2000; www.aucklandbridgeclimb.co.nz) offers a 1½-hour guided climb over the bridge, giving those immune to vertigo a bird's eye view of the city and inner harbour. Alternatively, try the **Auckland Bridge Bungy**. Two things you can't do on the bridge are, strangely, walk and ride a bicycle.

Ferries departing from the Quay Street Ferry Building *(see page 137)* offer a regular service throughout the day between downtown Auckland and Devonport just across the harbour. **Devonport ❾** – at least 20 minutes from downtown by road but only 3 km (2 miles) north by ferry – is an affluent area with many grànd Victorian houses, arts and craft galleries and a plethora of bars and cafés. Nearby, the volcanic promontories of Mount Victoria and North Head, 1 km (½ mile) northeast of the wharf, give unobstructed views of downtown Auckland and across the harbour to the eastern bays. The two hills were honeycombed with fortified tunnels during a Russian invasion scare in the 1870s and were inhabited by Maori communities over a 700-year period through to 1863.

North from Devonport the coastline is an endless procession of sheltered coves and white-sand beaches which start out as suburban and become steadily more spectacular all the way to the tip of the North Island. **Takapuna** offers good shopping and has a popular beach overlooking Rangitoto Island.

But it's further north, beyond **North Shore City**, that the day tripper begins to reap rewards. **Orewa ❿**, at the foot of the Whangaparaoa Peninsula, 40 km (25 miles) from the centre of town, was mostly rolling pastureland and beach cottages barely a generation ago, but has now become Auckland's northern-most dormitory suburb. As a result it has lost much of its former charm, though the suburban neighbourhoods run down to safe swimming beaches and a well-manicured regional park at the eastern end is a nice picnic spot.

Map on page 149

TIP

The Riverhead Ferry's riverway and inner harbour chartered cruises provide a unique view of Auckland's sights and suburbs. They depart from Hobson West Marina, Viaduct Basin (tel: 09-376 0819; www.riverhead ferry.co.nz).

BELOW: Devonport viewed across the harbour.

TIP

If you have time, drop by the Puhoi Bohemian Museum (daily 1–4pm summer, 1–4pm weekends; www.puhoihistorical society.org.nz) on Puhoi Road. The museum recounts stories associated with the area's settlement in the 19th century by migrants from Bohemia.

Beyond Orewa, the countryside begins to open up. Make a note to visit **Waiwera Thermal Resort** (daily 9am–10pm; entrance fee; tel: 09-427 8800; www.waiwera.co.nz). Tucked under the brow of the hill 6 km (4 miles) north of Orewa, the pools (whose Maori name means "hot water") are one of only two thermal areas in the Auckland region (the other is at **Parakai**, near Helensville, 55 km (34 miles) northwest of the city on SH16).

Just 6 km (4 miles) north of Waiwera is **Puhoi** ⓫, which was the country's earliest Catholic Bohemian settlement. If you're passing by, be sure to stop for a drink at the **Puhoi Tavern**, full of old world charm and pictures of the early Bohemian migrants and farming paraphernalia on display.

Driving north, watch out for the **Honey Centre** (daily 9am–5pm; free; tel: 09-425 8003; www.honeycentre.co.nz), 4 km (2 miles) south of Warkworth, where you can buy varieties of New Zealand's excellent honey and watch the bees making it behind the glass walls of working hives. **Warkworth** itself is a pretty riverside country town which marks the northern boundary of the Auckland region. It's also the leaping off point for some of the region's real gems. Turn east on the Matakana-Leigh Road for a drive through the new wine-growing country near Matakana and take in **Tawharanui** ⓬, 25 km (16 miles) from Warkworth, the northernmost of the regional parks where – on a weekday at least – you stand a pretty good chance of having an endless white-sand beach to yourself.

Hauraki Gulf islands

No sensible visitor should leave without venturing onto the waters of the beautiful island-dotted **Hauraki Gulf**, or at least the inner harbour. All the islands mentioned here are easily accessible by fast ferry from Auckland's Ferry Building along Quay Street *(see page 137)*.

BELOW:
Waiheke Island.

In many ways the most striking island visit is to **Rangitoto Island** ⓭ – 8 km (5 miles) northeast of Auckland – the 600-year-old dormant volcano which dominates the downtown views. The summit is a bracing, though not hugely demanding, walk and there is a buggy trip for those who don't fancy the exertion. Take stout shoes; the volcanic stone path can butcher fancy leather. From the 260-metre (850-ft) summit there are spectacular 360-degree views of the city, the northern bays and the Hauraki Gulf. A causeway joins Rangitoto with **Motutapu Island**, which is farmed.

Barely 19 km (12 miles) from downtown Auckland is **Waiheke Island** ⓮, the most populated of the gulf islands. A generation ago it was a retreat for the impecunious and the artistic who had to brave the hour-long bouncy ferry ride into town. These days a high-speed catamaran makes the commute shorter, and as a result the island's population and profile have changed beyond recognition. Much of the work of local craftspeople is now world-class rather than hippie-cottage. The steep slopes overlooking the many beautiful bays are now sprinkled with architect-designed houses where once only simple cottages stood. Chic cafés line the streets of the main settlement, **Oneroa**. The island's bus service is infrequent – it's tied to the ferry timetable – but the taxis and rental cars are cheap and the walking is pleasant.

Waiheke has a burgeoning wine industry too. And

while it can be comfortably sampled in a day trip, if you decide to stay a while, you'll find accommodation to suit even the most extravagant of tastes.

Tiritiri Matangi Island ⓯, 25 km (16 miles) north of Auckland, makes for a lovely day trip (guided tours are an option) and is one of the world's biggest conservation success stories. Reclaimed from weeds and feral predators which several centuries of settlement had introduced, it has been restored to a superb open wildlife sanctuary featuring many species of endangered New Zealand birdlife, including the kiwi and takahe.

Further to the north again, **Kawau Island** ⓰, 46 km (29 miles) from the city is a sleepy retreat with a sheltered harbour popular with yachties. The stately **Mansion House** (daily 9.30am–3.30pm; entrance fee; tel: 09-422 8882) in the bay of the same name, was the country home of one of the early governors, Sir George Grey. It was he who introduced the wallaby, more commonly associated with Australia, which are now an excessively numerous intrusion.

Those with more time to spend might set aside a couple of days to explore **Great Barrier Island** ⓱, the gulf's most remote at 90 km (56 miles) northeast of Auckland. This is truly another country, where the small permanent population lives without mains power; electricity is supplied by private generators or alternative sources. The 700 or so islanders, who refer to their home as "the Barrier" are renowned as among the country's most reclusive and hardy souls. The beaches are stunningly unspoiled, much of the native forest is virgin and the island is home to several unique plant and bird species. There are good day walks and the island is also a popular destination for diving, fishing, surfing and camping. Ferries and flights connect to Auckland, but to drop in for an hour is rather to miss the point. The Barrier deserves a definite lingering over. ❑

Map on page 149

TIP

For more information on what to do on Great Barrier Island, visit its visitor centre (daily 9am–4pm; tel: 09-429 0033) at the Claris Postal Centre or check www.greatbarrier.co.nz.

BELOW: historic Mansion House on Kawau Island.

NORTHLAND

Northland's picturesque charm makes it an ideal holiday and retirement spot, while concealing a dramatic past of debauchery, excess, wars, rebellion, conquest and, finally, settlement

Tribal warfare, bloody clashes between Maori and Pakeha, debauchery, insurrection, missionary zeal, a treaty of peace and promises – all are part of Northland's turbulent historical backdrop. But Northland has more to offer than the past. It is a place where you can relax and enjoy the sun, food, sights and distinctive way of life. It is famed for its scenery – its pastoral, productive south and the wilder, remoter and legendary far north. Northland is also noted for its fine game fishing, unspoiled beaches, pleasant climate, thermal pools, kauri forests – and its friendliness. This irregular peninsula juts upwards some 450 km (280 miles) north from Auckland to the rocky headlands of North Cape and Cape Reinga, New Zealand's northernmost accessible point. It is labelled the winterless north because of its mild, damp winters and warm and humid summers. A distinctive feature of this region are its pohutukawa trees, which in early summer rim the coast and decorate the hinterland with their bright red blossoms.

PRECEDING PAGES: Bay of Islands. **LEFT:** toe toe plants on the sand dunes at Ninety Mile Beach. **BELOW:** Kawakawa's art in a toilet.

Bay of Islands

For those wanting to explore the region freely, Paihia, a Bay of Islands township on the far northeast coast, is a good base to work from. It's a smooth and scenic 3½-hour drive up State Highway (SH) 1 from Auckland. The route from Auckland begins across the Harbour Bridge, proceeds along the **Hibiscus Coast** with its beachfront resorts, then continues through the small farming towns of Warkworth and Wellsford and around Whangarei city, gateway to the north. Drivers leave the main highway at **Kawakawa** – where New Zealand's most famous public toilets, a baroque confection designed by Austrian artist emigrant Frederick Hundertwasser is found – and snake down to the harbourside resort of **Paihia ❶**, 240 km (150 miles) north of Auckland.

This is the **Bay of Islands**, the cradle of New Zealand. Its irregular 800-km (500-mile) coastline, embracing some 150 islands, is steeped in historical association as the site of the country's earliest settlement.

Polynesian explorer Kupe is said to have visited here in the 10th century, followed by another canoe voyager, Toi, 200 years later. Captain James Cook discovered the harbour for Europeans in 1769. Impressed, he gave the sheltered waters of the bay their current name. In the scattered group are eight larger islands and numerous islets – a total of 144 in all. The largest measures 22 hectares (54 acres). Many are uninhabited; some are privately owned; others are Maori reserves. The region's small permanent population is multiplied during the traditional New Zealand summer holiday period, from Christmas to late January, when many thousands more head north to camp, boat, swim, fish and relax. As most Northland visi-

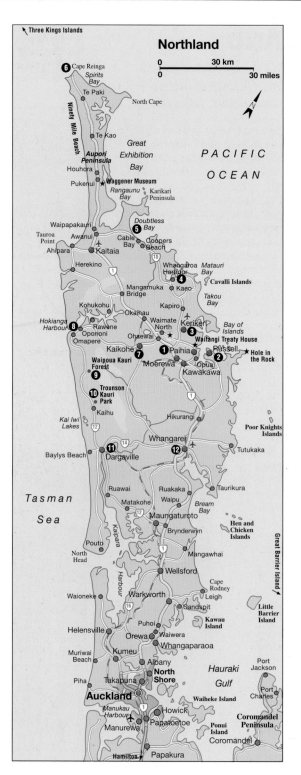

Northland

0	30 km
0	30 miles

Three Kings Islands

6 Cape Reinga
Spirits Bay
Te Paki
North Cape

Ninety Mile Beach

Te Kao

Great Exhibition Bay

Aupori Peninsula
Houhora
Pukenui ★ Waggener Museum
Rangaunu Bay Karikari Peninsula

PACIFIC OCEAN

Waipapakauri
Tauroa Point
Awanui
Ahipara Kaitaia
Cable Bay
5 *Doubtless Bay*
Coopers Beach
10

Herekino
1

Whangaroa Harbour *Matauri Bay*
4
Kaeo ❀ *Cavalli Islands*

Mangamuka Bridge
Kapiro
Takou Bay

Kohukohu
Okaihau
Waimate North
Kerikeri
3
Bay of Islands
★ Waitangi Treaty House

Hokianga Harbour
8 Rawene
Opononi
Omapere
Ohaewai ★
1 Paihia
2
Russell
★ Hole in the Rock

Kaikohe
7
Opua
Kawakawa

Waipoua Kauri Forest
9
Moerewa

10 **Trounson Kauri Park**

Kaihu

Kai Iwi Lakes
8
12
Hikurangi
Poor Knights Islands

Whangarei
12
Tutukaka

Baylys Beach
11
Dargaville
14

Ruawai
Matakohe
12
Ruakaka
Waipu
Bream Bay
Taurikura

Tasman Sea
Maungaturoto
Hen and Chicken Islands
Brynderwyn

Pouto
North Head
1
Mangawhai

Kaipara Harbour
Wellsford
Cape Rodney
Leigh
Little Barrier Island
Sandspit
Kawau Island

Waioneke
Warkworth
16

Puhoi
Helensville
Orewa Waiwera
Kumeu Whangaparaoa
Muriwai Beach
Albany
North Shore
Port Jackson
Hauraki Gulf
Piha
Takapuna
Auckland
Waiheke Island
Port Charles
Manukau Harbour
1
Howick
Papatoetoe
Coromandel Peninsula
Manurewa
Ponui Island
Hamilton
Papakura
Coromandel

Great Barrier Island

tors go to the bay, a visit during this period requires accommodation reservations well in advance.

Since the 1950s, Paihia has been revamped to meet the challenge of tourism. Modern hotels have sprung up alongside a neat, expanded shopping centre. A variety of eating places and modest nightlife make it a worthy hub of Northland. The wharf, its focal point, caters for island cruises and fishing trips. Paihia has marked its places of historical note with bronze plaques along the red-sand seafront. It is also a town of many firsts: New Zealand's oldest Norfolk pine stands here; a mission station was created on the town site in 1823; missionaries built and launched the country's first ship, the *Herald* here in 1826; from the first printing press, brought from England in 1834, was published the first Bible in Maori. Colonial history is very obviously etched in Paihia's graveyard.

The Waitangi Treaty

The most significant act in New Zealand's early history took place on the lawn of the **Waitangi Treaty House**, about 2 km (1¼ miles) north of Paihia over a one-way bridge that also leads to the Waitangi Reserve and a golf course. The house is now part of the **Waitangi National Trust Treaty Grounds** (daily 9am–5pm; entrance fee; tel: 09-402 7437; www.waitangi.net.nz).

On 6 February 1840, with Governor William Hobson signing on behalf of Queen Victoria, Maori chiefs and English gentlemen inked a pact to end Maori-Pakeha conflict, guarantee the Maori land rights, give them and the colonists Crown protection and admit New Zealand to the British Empire. At the time of the signing, the house was the home of James Busby, British Resident in New Zealand from 1832 to 1840.

The gracious colonial dwelling, with its commanding views of the bay, later fell into disrepair. It has since been restored and today the Treaty House is a national museum. Also worth visiting is the adjacent Maori meeting house or *whare runanga* where one of the world's largest war canoes, the impressive 35-metre (115-ft) long *Ngatoki Matawhaorua* is proudly displayed.

Russell – former Sin City

Runaway sailors, escaped convicts, lusty whalers, promiscuous women, brawling and drunkenness: **Russell ❷**, 15 km (9 miles) northeast of Paihia, formerly known as Kororareka and dubbed "hell hole of the Pacific", has known them all. Russell is easy to get to as it's linked by a regular passenger ferry service to Paihia and Waitangi. A vehicular ferry also serves the small peninsula from Okiato Point at the deep-sea port of **Opua**, 9 km (6 miles) south of Russell.

Colonists first arrived in 1809, making it New Zealand's first white settlement. Today it's small, quiet and peaceful. There's an aura of stored history, of romance, of skeletons jangling in those Victorian cupboards. But things liven up at Christmas and New Year when celebrating boaties and other visitors get the place rocking again. Like several other locations around the country, this was briefly New Zealand's capital. In the early 1830s lust and lawlessness prevailed, with up to 30 grog shops operating on Russell's tiny waterfront. Shocked early settlers responded by building **Christ Church**, at the corner of Robertson and Beresford streets, two blocks east of the harbour, in 1835. It is New Zealand's oldest surviving church; its bullet-holed walls grim reminders of a siege in 1845.

Maori chief Hone Heke, who reluctantly signed the Treaty of Waitangi in 1840, later became discontented over government land dealings when the promised financial rewards did not materialise. In 1845, he defiantly chopped down the British flagstaff, symbol of the new regime, on Maiki Hill behind Russell. Meanwhile, Chief Kawiti, an ally of Heke, burned and sacked church

Maori-carved figure at Waitangi's Maori meeting house.

BELOW: Waitangi Treaty House.

property. A showdown came in 1846 near Kawakawa, at Kawiti's *pa*, Ruapekapeka. A strong Redcoat force captured this formidable fortress, somewhat unfairly on a Sunday when the converted Maori were busy worshipping their new Christian god. Heke was eventually pardoned and his men freed.

Pompallier (daily 10am–5pm; May–Nov: 5 guided tours daily; entrance fee; tel: 09-403 9015; www.pompallier.co.nz) is housed in a charming sole-surviving building of the French Catholic missionaries, who built it in 1842 to serve as their printing press. Today, extensively restored as a working museum, its original printing press, bookbindery and tanning pits reproduce the Roman Catholic books in the Maori language, which were printed here in the 1840s. **Russell Museum** (daily 10am–4pm, till 5pm January; entrance fee; tel: 09-403 7701), one block east on York Street, has a seagoing model of Cook's *Endeavour*, one-fifth the size of the original, and numerous colonial curios. The **Duke of Marlborough Hotel** (tel: 09-403 7829), one of the country's oldest, is a pub of great character.

Trips on the Bay

The true beauty of the islands in the bay can best be appreciated on one of the daily Cream Trips operated by **Fullers** (www.fboi.co.nz) from both Paihia (Marsden Road; tel: 09-402 7422) and Russell (Cass Street; tel: 09-403 7866). These 6-hour boat trips retrace the voyages of bygone days when cream was regularly collected from island farms. Mail and provisions are still handled this way today. The Fullers cruise covers about 96 km (60 miles), and passengers can see the island where Captain Cook first anchored on his 1769 voyage; the cove where French explorer Marion du Fresne, along with his 25 crew members, were slain by Maori in 1772; and bays where the earliest missionaries landed.

BELOW: angler Jerry Garrett sets a record with his 369-kg (814-lb) broadbill swordfish catch in May 2003 at Bay of Islands.

FISHING AT BAY OF ISLANDS

Deep-sea fishing for some of the world's biggest gamefish is a major lure in the Bay of Islands. The main fishing season is from December through June, when the huge marlin are running. Many world records for marlin, shark and tuna have been set here. Yellowtail kingfish, running on till September, provide good sport on light rods. Snapper, one of New Zealand's favourite table fish, is also plentiful.

Fighting fish up to 400 kg (880 pounds) are caught in the bay, and weigh-ins attract appreciative crowds. Competitions for line-fishing and surf-casting are frequently held; the foremost are in January. Despite the "seasons", fishing is a year-round sport here. Charter boats are available at Paihia or Russell for half- or full-day hire, and on a share basis. But a more laid-back fishing experience is also possible. The towns' numerous small wharves are seldom without at least one small-scale angler hopefully dangling a line in the water.

The Bay is also popular as a sea kayaking destination with its numerous sandy coves within short reach of each other. In the summer months the waters become crowded with yachts, many sailed by their owners up from Auckland for a holiday on the water.

Map on page 158

Fullers also offers a shorter 4-hour cruise to the Cape Brett lighthouse and Piercy Island and, weather permitting, passes right through the famous **Hole in the Rock**. For a bit more thrill, try the Mack Attack, operated by **Kings** (tel: 09-402 8288; www.kings-tours.co.nz), a 90-minute blast to the Hole in the Rock and back in a powerful catamaran with a top speed of 90 kph (56 mph).

With its myriad islands and remarkably clear waters, the Bay of Islands is also a diving paradise. By world standards, top quality diving is incredibly cheap and accessible with numerous reliable commercial operators *(see Travel Tips)*.

Kerikeri and surroundings

The next major stop in Northland is **Kerikeri ❸**. Located 23 km (14 miles) north of Paihia, beside a pretty inlet, it is a township of unusual interest and character which has a rich backdrop of early Maori and European colonial history. Here, missionary Samuel Marsden planted the country's first vineyard in 1819. Today, much of New Zealand's finest citrus and subtropical fruits, including kiwifruit, are grown on Kerikeri's fertile land.

The bright red flowers of the pohutukawa or "Christmas tree".

The township and its immediate environs, with a population of nearly 5,000, is a thriving centre for handicrafts and cottage industries. The climate and relaxed lifestyle have attracted many creative residents, along with wealthy retirees from other New Zealand centres. Two vineyards and a plethora of quality restaurants do nothing to discourage new residents.

The oldest surviving European building in the country, **Mission House**, formerly **Kemp House** (daily 10am–5pm; entrance fee; tel: 09-407 9236), on Kerikeri Road, was built in 1822 of pit-sawn kauri and totara as a mission house. The **Stone Store** (daily 10am–4pm; free; tel: 09-407 9236) next door, built in 1836 to house New Zealand mission supplies, is the country's oldest standing European stone building. It still serves as a shop and has a museum upstairs. Just to the northeast the site of **Kororipa Pa** should not be overlooked. This was celebrated warrior chief Hongi Hika's forward army base between 1780 and 1826. Warriors were assembled here before launching raids on southern tribes as far south as Cook Strait.

BELOW: passing through the famous Hole in the Rock.

At nearby **Rewa's Village** (daily 9am–5pm, donation; tel: 09-407 6454) further north on Landing Road is a replica 18th-century Maori fishing village built by traditional methods and using only materials that would have been available at the time.

Not far from Kerikeri, 15 km (9 miles) southwest is **Waimate North**, the first inland settlement for white people. Built in 1831–32, the **Te Waimate Mission** (Mon–Wed and Sat–Sun 10am–5pm, winter Sat–Sun only; entrance fee; tel: 09-405 9734) in Waimate North was the home of Bishop George Augustus Selwyn, New Zealand's first Anglican bishop, in 1842.

Cape Reinga and Ninety Mile Beach

In Maori mythology, Cape Reinga is where the spirits of the dead depart on their homeward journey to the ancestral land of Hawaiki. Coach tours now make their way up this legendary flight path, along the Aupori Peninsula to its northernmost point, and return via Ninety Mile Beach. As cars frequently get trapped

*Cape Reinga's lone
lighthouse guards
the coast off this
isolated spit of land.*

BELOW: sunset at
Opononi beach.

on the sands of Ninety Mile Beach, coaches and four-wheel drive vehicles which leave Paihia, Kerikeri and other Northland towns daily are the best option. The east-coast route traverses the worked-out gum fields north of Kerikeri, a relic of the huge kauri forests that once covered this region. The dead trees left pockets of gum in the soil, which early settlers found to be a valuable export for fine varnish. In fact, it triggered a "gum rush". By the 1880s, more than 2,000 men were digging up a fortune there.

In **Whangaroa Harbour** ❹, 25 km (16 miles) north of Kerikeri, a deep-sea fishing base, lies the wreck of the *Boyd*. The ship called in for kauri spars in 1809 and sent a party of 11 ashore. However, the group was murdered by the local Maori inhabitants, who donned the victims' clothes, rowed back to the vessel and massacred the rest of the crew, then set fire to the ship. Reliably serene now, Whangaroa is another popular destination for cruising yachts and sea kayaking.

About 24 km (15 miles) further is **Doubtless Bay** ❺, named by Cook, with its string of gently sloping sandy beaches. **Coopers Beach**, lined with pohutukawa trees, is just as attractive, as is **Cable Bay** with its golden sand and colourful shells. There is a limited choice of accommodation and places to eat at both beaches. At **Awanui**, the road forks north, passing through **Te Kao**, the largest settlement in the far north, to Cape Reinga with its lighthouse.

The whole district is rich in Maori folklore. At **Cape Reinga** ❻ itself, 130 km (80 miles) north of Doubtless Bay, at the tip of **Aupori Peninsula**, a gnarled pohutukawa, at least 800 years old, grows out of the rocks at the foot of the cape. Spirits are said to slide down its roots into the sea to begin their journey in the underworld. Less disputable is that nearby **Spirits Bay** is the last landfall for migratory godwits flying across the planet to the Arctic. Views from the cape,

Map on page 158

where the lone lighthouse stands guard, are impressive. You with see the turbulent merging line of the Pacific Ocean and Tasman Sea, the **Three Kings Islands**, 57 km (35 miles) offshore and neighbouring capes and secluded beaches.

Ninety Mile Beach, south of Cape Reinga and running along the western side of the peninsula, is actually 60 miles (96 km) long, and lined with tall dunes and hillocks of shell. It is noted for its shellfish, particularly the succulent but protected toheroa. The route back to Paihia is via **Kaitaia**, New Zealand's northernmost town, and a place of little interest.

The west coast

A more interesting west-coast route leads back to Auckland. **Kaikohe** ➐, 150 km (93 miles) south of Cape Reinga, has a hilltop monument to Chief Hone Heke, with spectacular views of both coasts. Nearby are **Ngawha Hot Mineral Springs** (daily 9am–7.30pm; entrance fee), with tempting mineral-rich mercury and sulphur waters for a refreshing soak.

Some 40 km (25 miles) west of Kaikohe is **Hokianga Harbour** ➑, a long sheltered harbour with a score of ragged inlets that keep the place quiet, serene and rural. Kupe is said to have left from here in AD 900 to return to Hawaiki. The tiny seaside resort of **Opononi** at the harbour mouth briefly became world famous in the summer of 1955–56, when a young dolphin began frolicking with swimmers at the beach. When "Opo" the dolphin died in somewhat mysterious circumstances, the nation mourned. She is remembered in a song and a monument.

The road then heads south through the **Waipoua Kauri Forest** ➒ with its 2,500 hectares (6,200 acres) of mature kauri trees, the largest pocket of kauri left in the land. Two giants, close to the road tower above them all: Te Matua Ngahere (Father of the Forest), about 2,000 years old, and Tane Mahuta (Lord of the Forest), 1,200 years old with a girth of 14 metres (46 ft). Further south at **Trounson Kauri Park** ➓ are more fine kauri, including one with four stems. **Dargaville** ⓫, 90 km (56 miles) south of Hokianga Harbour, was founded on the timber and kauri gum trade. **Dargaville Museum** (daily 9am–4pm; entrance fee; tel: 09-439 7555; www.welcome.to/maritime) in Harding Park, is built of clay bricks brought in from China as ship's ballast. It has fine gum samples and a display of the environmental vessel *Rainbow Warrior*, which was bombed by French agents in Auckland Harbour in 1985. It was scuttled near Kerikeri in 1987 and is now an artificial reef, teeming with marine life and popular with divers.

The highway turns east, for 58 km (36 miles) to **Whangarei** ⓬. This lightly industrialised city of 48,000 is a deep-sea port with a harbour, glassworks, cement plant and an oil refinery. Mount Parahaki gives panoramic views of city and harbour. There are plenty of hotels and restaurants in the city. A major attraction is **Claphams Clocks – The National Clock Museum** (daily 9am–5pm; entrance fee; tel: 09-438 3993; www.claphamsclocks.co.nz) on Whangarei Quayside. It has 1,500 clocks and clockwork items dating back to the 17th century. Safe swimming beaches and the deep-sea fishing base of Tutukaka are two more good reasons to linger in Whangarei. ❑

Ancient kauri is the oldest timber on earth, retrieved from swamps and dating back 30,000–50,000 years. At the Ancient Kauri Kingdom (tel: 09-406 7172; www.ancientkauri.co.nz) on Far North Road at Awanui, 8 km (5 miles) north of Kaitaia, it is turned into beautiful craft pieces.

BELOW: ancient kauri tree in Waipoua Kauri Forest.

WAIKATO

Dairy production and agriculture flourish in these rich, fertile lands south of Auckland, lands which also have a wealth of historical artefacts and cultural traditions

Map on page 172

Dawn birdsong in the central and western region of the North Island has an unusual accompaniment – the chugalug-chugalug of electric milking machines. Grass grows more quickly here through the year than anywhere else in the world and the cows that crop it daily have brought prosperity to generations. Dairy herds free-graze on Waikato pastures along fertile river valleys. The grass is fed by a mild, wet climate (rainfall averages 1,120 mm or 44 inches). On the flats and rolling country, farm diversification has expanded the production of fruit and vegetables. The Waikato is also premium thoroughbred horse breeding country, and dairy cattle studs abound.

Much of the now-green pastures were the spoils of land wars between Maori and Pakeha in the 1860s. The Waikato was once relatively highly populated by Maori tribes and its land communally owned, according to ancestry. It was a landscape of dense bush on the hills, peat swamp and kahikatea (white pine) forests on flat land, and the low hills of the Waikato and Waipa river systems.

The New Zealand Wars changed everything; it took nearly 20 years for the British and colonial forces to subdue Maori tribes who were intent on keeping what was left of their land. What land was not confiscated by the government was effectively taken through the 1862 legislation which forced the traditional Maori group ownership to be individualised. Single owners were easy prey for land agents and the way was opened for the gradual development, during the 20th century, of the natural wilderness into the intensively farmed land it is today.

LEFT: Marokopa Falls, Waitomo.
BELOW: dairy herds abound on the Waikato pastures.

Capital of the Waikato

Hamilton ❶, New Zealand's fourth-largest city, is 136 km (85 miles) south of Auckland. It straddles the **Waikato River**, the country's longest, some 50 km (30 miles) inland in the heart of farmland. Parklands and footpaths cover most of the city's riverbanks, and these provide popular walking and jogging routes for locals. Known to the Maori as Kirikiriroa, the city was renamed by Europeans after Captain Fane Charles Hamilton of the *HMS Esk*, who was killed at the Battle of Gate Pa, near Tauranga, in 1864.

It was the Waikato River, long a vital Maori transport and trading link to the coast, that first brought the Europeans to the area and led to the establishment of Hamilton in the 1860s. The first businesses grew on the riverbank and today the commercial hub of the city runs parallel to it on the west bank.

The central city's most notable riverbank amenity is the **Waikato Museum** (daily 10am–4.30pm; free; tel: 07-838 6606; www.waikatomuseum.org.nz). It is sited at the southern end of the main thoroughfare, on the corner of Victoria and Grantham streets. Of particular

note in its collection of fine arts, ethnography and Waikato history are 15,000 Tainui (Waikato's Maori tribe) artefacts, including wood and stone carvings, woven flax garments and tribal items. National and international touring exhibitions are a regular feature but permanent displays worth noting are a magnificent war canoe and a contemporary Tainui carving and weaving commissioned for the museum's opening in 1987. Located within the complex is **Exscite Centre** (entrance fee; www.exscite.org.nz), an interactive science and technology centre which boasts among its delights an earthquake simulator.

Another local favourite, the paddle steamer *MV Waipa Delta* (tel: 0800-472 3353; www.waipadelta.co.nz), is found on the banks of the Waikato River by Memorial Park. Its lunch, dinner and afternoon-coffee cruises up the river are something of an institution, offering different, more scenic views of the city.

Just south of the city centre on State Highway (SH) 1 is the 58-hectare (143-acre) **Hamilton Gardens** (daily 7.30am–sunset; free; tel: 07-856 3200; www.hamiltongardens.co.nz). Organised by various themes, the gardens were created in the 1950s and are now the city's most popular attraction.

The Waikato River is now a recreational asset for the region but it is also of primary importance for the power stations, which harness the river's waters to provide one-third of the nation's hydro-electric power. Behind each dam there are artificial lakes which are very popular spots for fishing, boating and rowing.

Maori stronghold

On the Waikato River north of Hamilton is **Ngaruawahia ❷**, capital of the Maori King Movement *(see pages 36 and 69)* and an important Maori cultural centre. On the east riverbank is the **Turangawaewae Marae**, its name meaning "a place

The Chinese Scholar's Garden is among the themed gardens found at the Hamilton Gardens.

BELOW: a kaleidoscope of colourful balloons at Hamilton.

Map on page 172

to put one's feet". It contains traditionally carved meeting houses and a modern concert hall, and is open to the public on special occasions. The *marae* can be seen from the river bridge on the main road a little downstream. The famous **Waingaro Hot Springs** (daily 9am–10pm; entrance fee; tel: 07-825 4761; www.waingaro hotsprings.co.nz) are found 24 km (15 miles) west of Ngaruawahia.

Mount Taupiri, 6 km (4 miles) downstream, is the sacred burial ground of the Waikato tribes, with graves sprawling over the hill alongside the motorway. Nearby, the Waikato's waters are used to cool a massive coal-and-gas-fired power station at **Huntly**. Its two 150-metre (500-ft) chimneys tower over the town, which stands at the centre of New Zealand's largest coalfields.

In technicolour contrast is Taupiri's **Candyland** (daily 10am–5pm; fee for shows; tel: 07-824 6818; www.candyland.co.nz). This garish temple to confectionery is New Zealand's largest candy store. There are candy-making demonstrations and you can even make you own lollipop. Kids will love this place.

Racehorses and spas

The bucolic town of **Cambridge** ❸ also sits on the Waikato River, 24 km (15 miles) southeast of Hamilton. The town's charming **St Andrew's Anglican Church**, tree-lined streets and village green give it a very English atmosphere. Despite its serene aspect, Cambridge is the birthplace of the internationally successful rock act The Datsuns *(see page 92)*, who honed their craft in obscurity – and occasionally in the face of hostility – here before finding fame overseas.

Cambridge is a major centre for the horse-breeding industry. It is the location of **New Zealand Horse Magic** (daily; entrance fee; tel: 07-827 8118; www.cambridgethoroughbredlodge.co.nz), 6 km (4 miles) south of Cambridge on SH1.

Raglan, 48 km (30 miles) west of Hamilton, attracts surfers from around the world. The waves are so reliable that the local school has a Surfing Academy where students can earn qualifications in the sport.

BELOW: lush farmland typifies much of Waikato.

Performances here showcase a variety of horse breeds from a Lippizaner stallion (the only one in New Zealand) to the New Zealand wild horse, the Kaimaniwa, plus Arabian and Hackney specimens (check website or call for dates; entrance fee; bookings essential). Visitors can ride a horse at the conclusion of a show.

Provincial towns

Matamata was the setting for Hobbiton in the film "Lord of the Rings". Local tourism is cashing in on its claim to celluloid fame.

To the east of the river are the Waikato towns of Morrinsville, Te Aroha and Matamata. **Matamata ❹** is well known for its thoroughbred racehorse stables. A three-storey blockhouse built by an early landowner, Josiah Clifton Firth, in 1881, stands as a reminder of the settlers' insecurity after the wars. It's now part of the **Firth Tower Historical Museum** (Thur–Mon 10am–4pm; entrance fee; tel: 07-888 8369). The family homestead built in 1902 on the site contains many items belonging to the Firth family and it is administered with the intention of making it look lived in rather than as a museum piece. Several walking tracks lead into and over the nearby **Kaimai-Mamaku Forest Park**, including one to the picturesque **Wairere Falls**. Matamata's recent claim to fame was its transformation into Hobbiton in the movie trilogy *Lord of the Rings*.

Morrinsville is itself a centre for the surrounding dairy land, with its own large processing factory. **Te Aroha ❺**, on the Waihou River farther east, was once a gold town and fashionable Victorian spa sitting at the foot of 952-metre (3,123-ft) bush-clad **Mount Te Aroha**. The world's only known hot soda-water fountain, the **Mokena Geyser**, is here in the **Hot Springs Domain**, the 18-hectare (44-acre) thermal reserve that is the heart of the town's spa fame. The geyser performs every 40 minutes, gushing to a modest 4 metres (13 ft) while an elaborate piece of plumbing allows visitors to sample its allegedly health-

BELOW:
Kaimai-Mamaku
Forest Park.

giving waters at the source. The **Te Aroha Mineral Pools** (daily 10am–10pm; entrance fee; tel: 07-884 8717; www.tearohapools.co.nz) feature public and private pools – some in original 19th-century bathhouses – whose mineral waters are reputed to be good for numerous aches and pains.

Southwest of Hamilton, heading towards Waitomo, is **Te Awamutu ❻**, which has been dubbed "the rose town" for its gardens and rose shows. One of the country's oldest and finest churches, **St John's Anglican Church**, built in 1854, stands in the main street. Another, St Paul's, built in 1856, lies to the east in Hairini.

The **Te Awamutu Museum** (Mon–Fri, 10am–4pm; Sat–Sun 10am–1pm; entrance fee; tel: 07-871 4326; www.tamuseum.org.nz) houses, alongside numerous important Maori treasures, a permanent exhibition, "True Colours", dedicated to the history of local boys made good, the Finn brothers of Split Enz fame.

Waitomo Caves

In the northern King Country, so named because it was the centre of the Maori King Movement *(see pages 36 and 69)*, is the little village of **Waitomo**, famous for its caves and glowworm grottoes. The **Waitomo Caves ❼** (daily 9am–5pm winter, daily 9am–5.30pm summer, plus an 8pm trip; entrance fee; tel: 07-878 8227; www.waitomocaves.co.nz) are sublime. As you glide through black subterranean waters, look up at a starry sky provided by thousands of glowworms attached to the cave roofs. The caves also feature stunning stalactites and stalagmites, formed by the action of water on limestone over thousands of years. Three caves in all are open to the public – Glowworm Cave, Ruakuri and Aranui. The caves were long known to Maori, who kept the fact of their existence to themselves when the Europeans came. The first Pakeha to visit them was surveyor Fred Mace in 1887, who heard of their existence and persuaded a local Maori, Tane Tinorau, to guide him.

Waitomo is also a hotbed of the so-called blackwater rafting, which duplicates the thrills of the whitewater variety except underground and in the dark. One of the most reliable operators is **Waitomo Adventures** (tel: 07-878 7788; www.waitomo.co.nz), which offers a 2-hour blackwater journey as well as various permutations of abseiling down underground holes and waterfalls, and a 7-hour Lost World adventure where participants abseil in and walk, swim and climb out. The same company also leads tours through the spectacular St Benedicts Caverns, only discovered in 1962 and long inaccessible to all but speleological specialists.

Before embarking on a visit to the caves, however, be sure to stop by the **Waitomo Museum of Caves** (Dec–Mar daily 8am–8pm, Apr–Nov daily 8am–5pm; entrance fee; tel: 07-878 7640; www.waitomo-museum.co.nz), just beside Waitomo village's visitor centre. It has informative displays on the fascinating geography and history of these underground labyrinths.

At **Te Kuiti**, 19 km (12 miles) south, charismatic Maori leader Te Kooti Rikirangi took refuge and built a carved meeting house, later given to the local Maniapoto people as a gesture of thanks for their protection. Some 32 km (20 miles) to the west of Waitomo is the thundering **Marokopa Falls**, located a 10-minute walk from the main Te Anga Road. ❑

Map on page 172

A glowworm is actually the larvae of the fungus gnat (related to the mosquito) which attaches itself to the cave roof. The blueish-green glow the larvae emits comes from the sticky silk threads on its body, which it uses to trap flying insects for food.

BELOW: Waitomo Caves.

COROMANDEL AND THE BAY OF PLENTY

Map on page 172

This is where the great outdoors come to life – camping, tramping, fishing and boating. The less energetic can pick from any number of glorious beaches to laze at

T he popular phrase "Coromandel: Mine Today, Gone Tomorrow!" reflects the strong feelings of its inhabitants that the region's greatest asset is not its abundant mineral wealth but its natural attractions. The region once yielded abundant treasures, and early European settlers who flocked here were gold seekers and bushmen. Reminders of these earlier bonanzas abound, with colonial buildings, old gold-mine shafts and kauri relics. Today, people flock to the area for a less material and much more accessible treasure: the outdoors. "Outdoor" is the Coromandel's lodestone, offering opportunities for driving, diving, fishing, boating, swimming, camping, tramping, or fossicking for gemstones.

Thames and environs

At the base of the peninsula, **Thames ❽** was officially declared a goldfield in August 1867. The ensuing gold rush swelled the town's population to 18,000 at its peak. In its heyday, Thames had more than 100 hotels. Today there are just four, the oldest (1868) being the atmostpheric **Brian Boru Hotel** on the corner of Pollen and Richmond streets, a block from the waterfront at the southern end of town. To appreciate the town's past, one should head further north to the **Mineralogical Museum** and adjacent **School of Mines** (Sat–Sun 11am–3pm; entrance fee; tel: 07-868 6227) on Cochrane Street. This was one of 30 schools of mines around the country that used to provide practical instruction to a burgeoning population of miners.

Nearby, 500 metres (1,640 ft) to the northeast on Tararu Road, is **Goldmine Experience** (daily 10am–4pm; entrance fee; tel: 07-868 8514; www.goldmine-experience.co.nz), an old gold mine now turned into a tourist attraction, where members of the Hauraki Prospectors' Association demonstrate the technology used to retrieve gold.

Kauaeranga Valley is the site of the **Department of Conservation Visitor's Centre** (tel: 07-867 9080), 10 km (6 miles) northeast of the town. The first kauri spars were logged here in 1795, mainly for the Royal Navy – by 1830, kauri trees were being cut in greater numbers. This logging lasted for a century. Late in the 1800s, huge kauri timber dams were built across creeks on the peninsula to bank up water and then float the logs to sea. About 300 such dams were constructed, more than 60 of them in the Kauaeranga Valley. Many are still there, slowly disintegrating. Today the valley is a favourite spot for camping and tramping. Visitors have plenty of access to the wilderness along its more than 50 km (30 miles) of tracks.

LEFT: farmland meets the beach on the Coromandel Peninsula.
BELOW: Brian Boru Hotel in Thames.

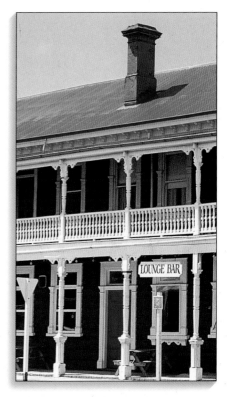

Coromandel and surroundings

North of Thames towards the town of Coromandel, up along the west coast of the peninsula, with the Hauraki Gulf on the left, one soon experiences a winding road and spectacularly changing views. The road hugs the coast for much of the way, passing bays where holiday homes huddle on the shore. At this point, the southern suburbs of Auckland are just a few kilometres across the water, and on clear days Coromandel can be seen from the city.

Tapu, 19 km (12 miles) north of Thames, is the junction for the **Tapu-Coroglen Road**, a scenic route climbing to 448 metres (1,470 ft) above sea level. The **Rapaura Watergardens** (daily 9am–5pm; entrance fee; tel: 07-868 4821; www.rapaurawatergardens.co.nz) are 7 km (4 miles) down this road. A 26-hectare (64-acre) private property, the garden features gentle walks, abundant native flora, lily ponds, bridges, streams, a waterfall and sculptures of ponga (a native fern), and the delightful **Café Koru** (tel: 07-868 4821). The road continues over the peninsula to the east coast but is rough and, in winter, dangerous. Most travellers to the east coast prefer to make the journey across at **Kopu**, just south of Thames.

Coromandel ❾ township, 55 km (35 miles) north of Thames, near the northern end of the peninsula, offers a quiet, alternative life for painters who farm, potters who garden, and weavers who rear their own sheep for wool. The town and peninsula were named after the Royal Navy ship HMS *Coromandel*, which called into the harbour there for kauri spars early in 1820. The township was less peaceful when it became the site of New Zealand's first gold find, by Charles Ring in 1852. More than 2,000 people dashed across the gulf from Auckland at the news, but on arrival they found that the gold was deeply embedded in quartz rock and expensive to extract. It wasn't until 15 years later that a gold-bearing reef rich

TIP

Coromandel's i-SITE information centre (Mon–Fri 9am–5pm, Sat–Sun 10am–1pm; tel: 07-866 8598; www.coromandel town.co.nz) is located at 355 Kapanga Road.

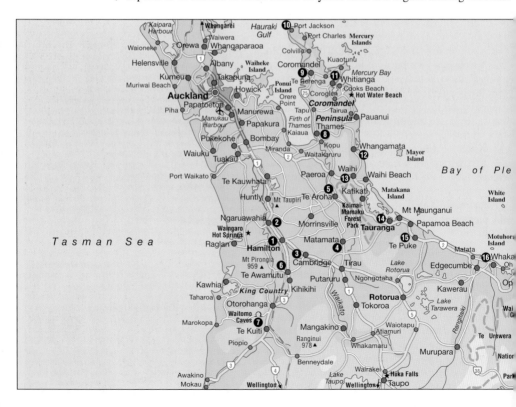

enough to warrant expensive extraction machinery was discovered. You can see the machine extraction process in action at the **Coromandel Battery Stamper** (tel: 07-866 7933), 3 km (2 miles) north of the township at 410 Buffalo Road. Over 100 years old and fully operational, this huge machine, used for processing gold from rock, is powered by New Zealand's largest working water wheel.

Coromandel has an air of the past about it and, even at the peak of the summer holiday season, the pace is slow and the lifestyle relaxed. Its sleepy history is recorded in the **Coromandel Historical Museum** (daily 10am–4pm, Sat and Sun 1–4pm in winter; entrance fee) at 841 Rings Road, which offers a glimpse of life in the gold rush days. There is even a jailhouse at the back.

One of New Zealand's most idiosyncratic attractions is located some 3 km (1 ¾ miles) north of town on Driving Creek Road. The **Driving Creek Railway and Potteries** (daily 10am–5pm; entrance fee; tel: 07-866 8703; www.driving creekrailway.co.nz), the creation of potter, conservationist and engineer Barry Brickell, is noted as much for its surreal train service as for the quality of its crafts. Brickell himself designed the train, built originally for carting clay from the hills for his pottery work. The miniature train takes passengers on a 1-hour return trip into the hills, and up to the mountain-top terminus, Eyefull Tower, for great views.

Beyond Coromandel, 28 km (17 miles) north, is **Colville**, with the last store before Cape Colville and the northernmost tip of the peninsula. Enthusiasts insist that visitors cannot experience the full spirit of the peninsula unless they travel to the end of this road. En route, the road skirts the **Moehau Range** whose 891-metre (2,923-ft) peak is the highest point on the peninsula.

Today's visitors might, however, sight the small, rare, native frog (Leiopeima archeyi). A refugee from the remote past, it lives only on the Coromandel Penin-

Map on page 172

narrow-gauge mountain railway runs on tracks only 388 mm wide (15 inches). Trips run at 10.15am and 2pm daily, with more frequent departures in summer (bookings recommended).

BELOW: rural idyll.

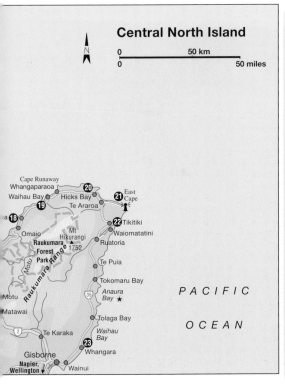

Central North Island

N

| 0 | 50 km |
| 0 | 50 miles |

Cape Runaway
Whangaparaoa
Waihau Bay • ⑳
⑲ Hicks Bay • ㉑ East Cape
Te Araroa
ⓐ ⑱
Omaio ㉒ Tikitiki
Mt Hikurangi Waiomatatini
Raukumara ▲1752 Ruatoria
Forest
Park Te Puia
Motu
Matawai Tokomaru Bay
Anaura Bay ★
Te Karaka Tolaga Bay
Waihau Bay
Gisborne ㉓ Whangara
Napier, Wellington Wainui

PACIFIC

OCEAN

sula. The unspoilt beauty and isolation of **Port Jackson** and Fletcher Bay draw people to enjoy some peace and solitude. **Fletcher Bay**, at the end of the road, is also the starting point for the **Coromandel Walkway**, a 3-hour walk to **Stony Bay**. If you prefer less energetic pursuits, visit Stony Bay by taking the road just north of Colville, across the peninsula to Port Charles and returning via Kennedy Bay on the east coast to Coromandel.

Whitianga and nearby beaches

Two roads lead from Coromandel town to Whitianga, situated on the opposite coast of the peninsula. The first, SH25, leads to the holiday resort of Matarangi and Kuaotunu Beach. (Here make a point of travelling the Black Jack Road, renowned as the most hair-raising route in the region.) Another 17 km (11 miles) southwest of Kuaotunu is Whitianga. The second route, 15 km (9 miles) shorter, is the 309 Road, which climbs to 300 metres (1,000 ft) before descending to approach the town from the south along the Whitianga Harbour edge.

Whitianga ⓫ is said to have been occupied for more than 1,000 years by the descendants of the Polynesian explorer Kupe. Kauri gum was shipped from Whitianga from 1844, peaking in 1899 with the shipment of 1,100 tonnes. Today's visitors enjoy fishing, swimming or rock-hunting. The latter draws those in search of the area's semi-precious gemstones: jasper, amethyst, quartz, chalcedony, agate and carnelian.

The town of Whitianga is actually on the shores of **Mercury Bay**, with the mouth of **Whitianga Harbour** at its southern end. Follow Whitianga Harbour south again from the town to **Coroglen** (formerly Gumtown). About 8 km (5 miles) east is the access road to two essential stopping points. The first of these

TIP

Be sure to stop by the Waiau Waterworks (tel: 07-866 7191; www.waiauwaterworks. co.nz) if taking the 309 Road from Coromandel to Whitianga. The entire family will enjoy this unique theme park with its assortment of water sculptures and swimming holes.

BELOW: rugged coastline near Whitianga.

is **Cook's Beach**, where Captain Cook first hoisted the British flag in New Zealand in November 1769 to claim the territory in the name of King George III. While here, he also observed the transit of Mercury; the occasion is marked by a cairn and plaque at the top of Shakespeare Cliffs.

Next in the peninsula's catalogue of exquisite beaches is **Hahei**, a beguiling stretch of white sand and a popular location for any number of water activities thanks to its clear waters. A track at the northern end of Hahei leads to **Cathedral Cove**, which is notable for its majestic eponymous rock formations. Also accessible by sea, it is a popular kayaking location.

The second essential site on the peninsula is the unique **Hot Water Beach**, 9 km (6 miles) south of Hahei, where thermal activity causes steam to rise from the sand in places and the visitor can dig a thermal hot pool on the beach, using "sand-castle" walls to keep the sea out or let it in to regulate the temperature. It is a great way to relax travel-weary bodies from the bumps and bends of the roads.

The next centre southward is **Tairua**, on the harbour of the same name. The area is dominated by 178-metre (584-ft) **Mount Paku**, whose summit offers views of nearby Shoe and Slipper islands. Across the harbour is the affluent resort of **Pauanui**, billed as a Park by the Sea but described by some as almost too tidy to be true. **Whangamata Beach** ⑫, 40 km (25 miles) further south, is a popular family holiday spot and the prime surfing beach of the peninsula.

Swimmers beware: Hot Water Beach is notorious for rips and sudden changes in tides.

Inland from Whangamata

The road winds inland from here; 30 km (19 miles) south is **Waihi** ⑬, where a rich gold- and silver-bearing lode was discovered in 1878. **Martha Hill Mine** was the greatest source of these minerals. Shafts were sunk to a depth of more than 500 metres (1,640 ft) and in a period of over 60 years, more than NZ$50 million worth of gold and silver was retrieved. Fascinating relics from the mining past are on display at **Waihi Arts Centre and Museum** (tel: 07-8638 386; www.waihimuseum.co.nz). Today, gold is still being won from a mining venture which has laid bare the original mine shafts on Martha Hill.

BELOW: kayakers at Cathedral Cove.

The bullion trail led through the Karangahake Gorge to **Paeroa**, 20 km (12 miles) from Waihi, from where the ore was shipped to Auckland. A walkway through part of the Waikino and Karangahake has been developed. Paeroa's pride and joy is a large concrete representation of a bottle. The mineral waters of Paeroa were used to make Lemon and Paeroa, an indigenous soft drink and national icon. L&P, as it is now known, has long been mass-produced commercially, and the bottle, which used to stand beside the main road, was moved back several metres in 2002 because photographers angling for a good view were creating a traffic hazard.

A road through the Athenree Gorge south of Waihi leads to **Katikati** on State Highway (SH) 2, promoted as "The Gateway to the Bay of Plenty". In 1991, the town, fearful that its small size and nondescript status was seeing it bypassed by travellers, decided to rebrand itself as a mural town. Within five years more than 20 outdoor murals adorned its buildings. Since then, as the number of murals depicting a variety of subjects connected to

TIP

For more down-to-earth thrills, try blokarting at Tauranga's Blokart Heaven (summer daily 10am–6pm, winter daily noon–5pm; tel: 07-572 4256; www.blokart.com) on Parton Road. A wind-powered Kiwi invention of 2002 vintage, the blokart is a cross between a go-kart and a land-sailer, with a top recorded speed of 90 kph (56 mph).

BELOW: lifesavers in training at Mt Maunganui's popular beach.

town life has increased, other art forms have also lent their weight to the "outdoor art gallery" including a number of sculptures and other installations.

Tauranga and the Bay of Plenty

After Katikati another 30 km (19 miles) to the southeast is the coastal city of **Tauranga ⓮**, which is both a tourist focal point and an important commercial centre served by the country's busiest export port at nearby Mount Maunganui. Located at the western end of the **Bay of Plenty**, Tauranga (meaning "safe anchorage") has a relaxed pace despite the obviously high level of commercial activity connected with the port. Its chief attractions are a benevolent climate and access to numerous beaches not far from the centre of town.

Tauranga has an interesting history. Flax trading began here about 150 years ago, missionaries arrived in 1838, and in 1864, during the New Zealand Wars, Tauranga was the site of fierce fighting during the Battle of Gate Pa. That battlefield was the scene of heroic compassion when Maori warrior Hene Te Kirikamu heard fatally wounded British officers calling for water and risked death during the battle to take water to his enemies.

The site of the original military camp, the **Monmouth Redoubt** and the mission cemetery, holds not only the remains of the British troops killed at Gate Pa but also the body of the defender of Gate Pa, Rawhiri Puhirake, killed during the subsequent Battle of Te Ranga. **The Elms Mission House** (Wed, Sat, Sun and public holidays 2–4pm; entrance fee; tel: 07-577 9772; www.theelms.org.nz) in Mission Street, was built in 1847 by Reverend A.N. Brown (who treated the wounded from both sides at the Battle of Gate Pa) and inhabited by members of the Brown family until 1991. Its library, finished in 1839, is the oldest free-standing library in the country.

Across the harbour from Tauranga is the **Mount Maunganui** resort area. Built around the 231-metre (758-ft) "Mount", it affords views of Tauranga and the surrounding area. Near the foot of the hill are fine beaches and saltwater pools.

The Bay of Plenty was named by Cook, and his description proved prophetic. Perhaps the greatest evidence of plenitude was the phenomenal growth of the furry kiwifruit, which has made the township of **Te Puke** ⓫, 28 km (17 miles) southeast of Tauranga, the "Kiwifruit Capital of the World". Just beyond Te Puke is **Kiwi 360** (daily 9am–5pm; entrance fee; tel 07-573 6340; www. kiwi360.co.nz), an orchard park, information centre and restaurant, with "kiwi karts" to take visitors for trips around the park.

Te Puke's subtropical horticulture has brought much prosperity. The kiwifruit, originally known as the Chinese gooseberry, was introduced to New Zealand from China in 1906, and thrived best in the Bay of Plenty. In the 1970s and early 1980s, fuelled by strong demand and high prices, many of Te Puke's farmers became millionaires from a harvest of only a few hectares. Over the years, acreage expanded swiftly through other New Zealand regions and gradually to other countries. These days, kiwifruit is just another orchard crop.

Along the coastal road to Whakatane

About 100 km (60 miles) southeast of Tauranga and 85 km (53 miles) east of Rotorua is **Whakatane** ⓰ at the mouth of the Whakatane River and the edge of the fertile Rangitaiki Plains. Until it was drained 70 years ago, the area was a 40,000-hectare (100,000-acre) tract of swampland.

Whakatane takes its name from the arrival of the Mataatua canoe from Hawaiki at the local river mouth. Legend records that the men went ashore,

Map on page 172

Get ready for a kiwi overdose at Te Puke's Kiwifruit Country – jams, honey, wine and even chocolates.

BELOW: beach beauty contest, Mt Maunganui.

TIP

There are several companies at Whakatane that organise tours of White Island. An excellent boat trip is offered by White Island Tours (tel: 07-308 9588; www.whiteisland.co.nz). More expensive are helicopter trips by Vulcan (tel: 07-308 4188; www. vulcanheli.co.nz).

BELOW: White Island's seething, fuming volcano.

leaving the women in the canoe, which began to drift away. Though it was *tapu* (forbidden) for women to touch paddles, the captain's daughter, Wairaka, seized one and shouted: *Kia whakatane au i ahau!* ("I will act as a man!"). Others followed suit and the canoe was saved. And thus the settlement was named Whakatane – to be manly. A bronze statue of Wairaka now stands on a rock at the river mouth. Above the area known as The Heads is Kapu-te Rangi ("Ridge of the Heavens"), reputedly the oldest Maori *pa* (fortified village) site in New Zealand, established by the Polynesian explorer Toi.

Whakatane is an eco-tourism centre, and in this respect one of its major attractions is **White Island**. Clearly visible from the town, the island is an active volcano only 50 km (30 miles) from Whakatane. Scenic flights pass over the steaming cone, which was mined for sulphur ore between 1885 and the mid-1930s. In 1914, 12 men lost their lives on the island during a violent eruption.

There are daily boat trips from Whakatane to White Island that include guided tours on the sulphuric moonscape. The island is also remarkable for its thriving birdlife despite the apparently inimical conditions. As well as numerous fishing charters which can be taken from the town, Whakatane is a good base for excursions that take you to swim with the dolphins who thrive in its warm waters.

Just over the hill, 7 km (4 miles) from Whakatane, is the popular **Ohope Beach**, described, with some justification, by former New Zealand Governor-General Lord Cobbam as "the most beautiful beach in New Zealand".

The last centre of note between Whakatane and the eastern boundary of the Bay of Plenty at Cape Runaway is the rural centre of **Opotiki** ⓱. Here in 1865, missionary Reverend Carl Volkner was murdered by a Maori rebel leader, Kereopa of the Hau Hau sect, in a gruesome episode which saw Volkner's head cut off and placed on the church pulpit, with the communion chalice used to catch his blood. Eight km (5 miles) southwest of Opotiki is the **Hukutaia Domain** with some beautiful walks through native vegetation. Many of the plants here are rare and one of them is in a class of its own – a puriri burial tree, Taketakerau, estimated to be more than 2,000 years old. It was discovered in 1913 when a storm broke off one of its branches to reveal numerous human bones that had been interred by Maori. The bones were later re-interred and the *tapu* (sacred or taboo) status lifted from the tree.

Towards East Cape

From Opotiki there are two routes to the east coast: across or around. The route across is the more straightforward and follows SH2, which runs through the spectacular Waioeka Gorge. The gorge narrows and becomes steeper before crossing into the deep rolling hills that line the descent into Gisborne. The alternative route, which follows SH35 around East Cape, provides some of the most beautiful coastal driving the country can offer. The road winds along the coast for 115 km (71 miles) to Cape Runaway. En route it crosses the Motu River and through the small settlement of **Te Kaha** ⓲, with its pretty crescent-shaped beach. As you drive around the coast from Te Kaha you will notice the distinctive **Raukokore Church**, an Anglican church built in 1894, jutting out

from the road almost into the sea. Nearby is **Waihau Bay** , a popular camping area and spot for divers to hire a boat and explore the rich seabed just metres from the shore. Several beautiful bays are passed on the way to **Whangaparaoa**.

Rounding the cape, the next stop is **Hicks Bay** ⑳, which offers glowworm caves for the adventurous night-time hill climber. **Te Araroa** is 10 km (6 miles) further along. There's a turn-off here that leads 21 km (13 miles) to **East Cape** ㉑ and its lighthouse. It is North Island's most easterly point and one of the first parts of the world to see the new day. On the foreshore stands a 600-year-old pohutukawa tree with nine trunks, believed to be the largest in the country

Heading south from Te Araroa, SH35 is largely barren and inland passes through **Tikitiki** ㉒ with its **St Mary's Church**, built in 1924 to honour Maori servicemen killed in World War I. The Maori design is one of the most ornate in the country. Just off the highway is **Ruatoria**, centre of the Ngati Porou tribe. Don't be surprised to see locals riding into town on horseback; some have taken on Rastafarian colours and beliefs. **Te Puia**, 25 km (16 miles) further south is pleasant with nearby hot springs, and a short drive further on is **Tokomaru Bay** where it is a delight to see the coast again. This entire stretch of coast, down to **Gisborne** *(see page 199)*, is popular with surfers and holidaymakers for its unhurried pace and wide expanses of beach. Do take any roads off the main highway because you will be rewarded with gems. Notable is **Anaura Bay** where there is a campsite, and **Tolaga Bay**, the site of New Zealand's longest wharf.

Closer to Gisborne is **Whangara** ㉓, another beautiful white-sand beach and the location for the 2002 film *Whale Rider*. As you approach Gisborne from Whangara, stop at **Wainui Beach** where there are several motels. It is close to the town and provides a convenient beach location while you visit the city. ❑

Map on page 172

TIP

Be sure to stop at Te Kaha Pub (tel: 07-325 2830) along the town's main road on a cliff. The pub was the setting for Taiki Waititi's Oscar-nominated short film *Two Cars, One Night*. It's a great place to meet the locals, especially if there is a rugby game on to kick-start the conversation.

BELOW: Te Kaha beach.

ROTORUA AND THE VOLCANIC PLATEAU

Maps:
Rotorua 184
Area 200

On the surface it's quiet and even genteel, but Rotorua's tranquillity is punctuated by intense hot and steamy thermal activity that has attracted tourists and healthseekers since Victorian times

O f his visit to Rotorua in 1934, playwright George Bernard Shaw declared: "I was pleased to get so close to Hades and be able to return." Shaw was not the first to draw an analogy between Rotorua and the devil's eternal dwelling of fire and brimstone. To pious Anglican pioneers the region must have had all the hallmarks of Dante's Inferno – a barren wasteland of stunted vegetation, cratered with scalding cauldrons, bubbling mud pools and roaring geysers hurling super-heated water into a sulphur-laden atmosphere.

Today, Rotorua represents pleasure and not torment, and the unusual resort has become one of the two jewels of New Zealand tourism (along with Queenstown in the South Island) – a place of thermal wonders, lush forests, green pastures and (usually) crystal clear lakes abounding with fighting trout. No fewer than 10 lakes are now the playground of anglers, campers, swimmers, water-skiers, yachtsmen, pleasure boaters, trampers and hunters.

The Rotorua region is situated on a volcanic rift which stretches in a 200-km (120-mile) line from White Island off the coast of the Bay of Plenty to Lake Taupo and the volcanoes of the Tongariro National Park in the Central Plateau of the North Island. About 68,000 people, around 35 percent of whom are Maori, reside in the Rotorua urban area and nearby smaller towns. Tourism is not the only major industry in the region. Bordering the city is Kaiangaroa, one of the world's largest man-made forests. Most of the exotic trees here are radiata pine, a renewable resource which is regularly cropped for timber pulp and paper. The region is also extensively farmed.

PRECEDING PAGES: the boiling mineral lakes of Rotorua. **LEFT:** Maori rooftop detail, Rotorua. **BELOW:** welcoming smile.

Cultural hotspot

Rotorua was settled by descendants of voyagers from the legendary Maori homeland of Hawaiki. Among the arrivals in the Te Arawa canoe around AD 1350 was the discoverer of Lake Rotorua, named in Maori tradition as Ihenga, who travelled inland from the settlement of Maketu and came across a lake he called Rotoiti, "little lake". He journeyed on to see a much larger lake which he appropriately called Rotorua, the "second lake". The city still has the greatest concentration of Maori residents of any New Zealand centre. Much of its allure to tourists is derived from the fact that it is the national "hot spot" of Maori culture.

The city is today a paradoxical mixture of the dishevelled and dilapidated alongside the upmarket and sophisticated. Visitors will not fail to notice the strong smell of sulphur, all part of the geothermal activity, which pervades the entire area. Most people, fortunately, become accustomed to it in a matter of minutes.

City centre attractions

Rotorua ❶ is 234 km (145 miles) south of Auckland, following State Highway (SH) 1 through Hamilton to Tirau and turning southeast on SH5. The majority of the town's biggest hotels and a large number of motels are located on or just off **Fenton Street**, running north-south across the city. It is only a short drive to the popular tourist attractions but some form of transport is essential. Rotorua's **i-SITE Visitor Centre** (tel: 07-348 5179; www.rotoruanz.com) in Fenton Street will provide assistance with hire cars, coach excursions and sightseeing.

At least some of a visitor's time in Rotorua will be spent soaking in hot mineral water, an activity which can be enjoyed in an apparently infinite variety of ways. The building of Rotorua's first sanatorium began in 1880 and, although the sulphurous waters of the baths are still regarded by some as useful in the treatment of arthritis and rheumatism, most people enjoy them as a pleasant form of relaxation.

East of the northern end of Fenton Street in the lovely grounds of the **Government Gardens** is the magnificent Tudor-style Bath House, built in 1908 as a spa centre. Known as the **Rotorua Museum** ❹ (daily 9.30am–5pm winter, till 8pm in summer; entrance fee; tel: 07-349 4350; www.rotoruanz.com/rotorua_museum) it contains, alongside art exhibitions, fascinating displays of slightly sinister-looking apparatus used for various forms of hydro-therapy more than a century ago. Permanent exhibitions tell the story of the local Te Arawa people and the devastating eruption of Mount Tarawera *(see page 190)* in 1886.

A one-minute walk away from the museum are the historic **Blue Baths** (daily 10am–7pm; entrance fee; tel: 07-350 2119; www.bluebaths.co.nz), which occupy a Spanish Mission building, first opened in 1933. Closed in 1982, they were beautifully restored in 1999 and re-opened, this time for public use.

In 1874, former New Zealand Premier Sir William Fox urged the government to "secure the whole of the Lake Country as a sanatorium owing to the ascertained healing properties of the water". This immediately sparked off the development of Rotorua into a spa town.

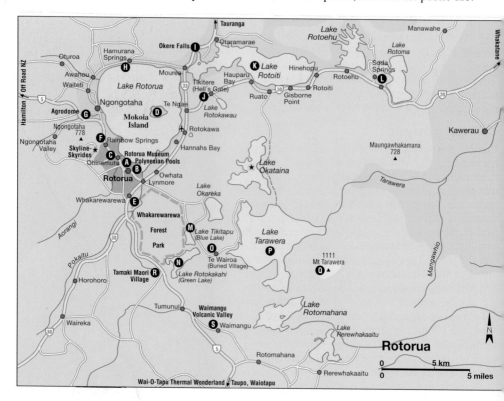

Rotorua

0   5 km
0   5 miles

A short stroll south of the museum is the **Polynesian Spa ❸** (daily 6.30am–11pm; entrance fee; tel: 07-348 1328; www.polynesianspa.co.nz). Choose from the 35 thermal pools, each having its own special mineral content and varying temperatures. The Priest Pool was named after a Father Mahoney, who pitched his tent alongside a hot spring on the site in 1878 and bathed in the warm water until he reportedly obtained complete relief for his rheumatism. The heat in some of the pools cannot be controlled and these are off-limits to children. Private pools and a range of spa treatments are also available.

Legends of the pools

Further along the lakefront is the historic Maori village of **Ohinemutu ❸**, once the main settlement on the lake. Its Tudor-style Maori **St Faith's Church**, built in 1910, is notable for its rich carvings, a window depicting a Maori Christ figure who looks as though he is walking on the waters of Lake Rotorua, and a bust of Queen Victoria. The church was presented to the Maori people of Rotorua in appreciation of their loyalty to the Crown and is an impressive expression of how the Maori adopted Christianity into their traditional culture.

The adjacent 19th-century **Tamatekapua Meeting House** took 12 years to carve and is named after the captain of the Arawa canoe, Tama Te Kapua. It is said that Hine-te-Kakara, the daughter of Ihenga, Rotorua's discoverer, was murdered and her body thrown into a boiling mud pool. Ihenga subsequently set up a memorial stone, calling it Ohinemutu, or "the place where the young woman was killed".

Sightseeing cruises on the newly refurbished *Lakeland Queen* (tel: 07-348 0265; www.lakelandqueen.com), a 32-metre (105-ft) paddle steamer, depart from the lakeside jetty four times daily. On its popular breakfast cruise, you

Maps:
Rotorua 184
Area 200

TIP

To appreciate fully the exhibits at the Rotorua Museum, take one of the daily free guided tours at 9.30am, 11am, 1pm, 2.30pm and 4pm. Enquire at the information desk.

BELOW: Rotorua Museum of Art and History.

can view the sunrise over **Lake Rotorua** while enjoying a hearty breakfast. If you're not an early riser, opt for a lunch or dinner cruise.

If you wish to explore **Mokoia Island ⑩** in the middle of Lake Rotorua and visit **Hinemoa's Pool**, contact Mokoia Island Cruises (tel: 07-348 6634, 0800-862 784; www.mokoiaisland.com). The Hinemoa is the legendary figure in a famous Maori love story. A young chieftain, Tutanekai, who lived on Mokoia Island, fell in love with the maiden Hinemoa, who lived in a village on the mainland. But their marriage was forbidden by family opposition. Hinemoa secretly planned to follow the sound of Tutanekai's bone flute over the water during the night and join her lover. The plot was foiled when her people beached all the canoes, forcing Hinemoa to tie gourds to her body and swim across the chilling lake, following the sounds of Tutanekai's flute. She recovered from her ordeal by warming herself in the hot pool that bears her name, before being reunited with Tutanekai.

Due to Rotorua's thermal activity, any construction or digging has to be carefully controlled. Houses do not have basements, and graves have built-in vaults that sit above the ground.

Mud and geysers

At the southern end of Fenton Street is the **Whakarewarewa ⑭** thermal area at **Te Puia** (www.tepuia.com), home to two major attractions. First is the impressive **Te Puia New Zealand Maori Arts and Crafts Institute** (daily 8am–6pm, till 5pm in winter; entrance fee; tel: 07-348 9047) where skilled Maori carvers and flax weavers can be observed at work. The intricately carved archway to the area depicts Hinemoa and Tutanekai embracing.

The other attraction at Te Puia is **Pohutu** ("Big Splash"), the greatest geyser in New Zealand, thundering to a height of more than 30 metres (100 ft) up to 20 times a day. In the evening there are concert performances, and a *hangi* (traditional earth oven meal) is served.

BELOW: craftsman at the Te Puia New Zealand Maori Arts and Crafts Institute.

Bordering the institute is **Whakarewarewa Thermal Village** (daily 8.30am–5pm; entrance fee; tel: 07-349 3463, 0800-924 426; www.whakarewarewa.com), whose residents inhabit an other-worldly terrain of bubbling mud pools and hot thermal springs. Tribal people have, for generations, used thermal waters for cooking, washing and heating. Opposite the entrance to the village, colonial-style shops sell sheepskins, furs and handicrafts, including *pounamu* or greenstone artefacts.

Departing via Froude Street, take a look at the **Arikapakapa Golf Course**, the only one in the world with boiling mud pool "traps" and hot pool "hazards".

Rainbow country

About 4 km (2 miles) northwest of Rotorua off SH5 on Fairy Springs Road is the delightful **Rainbow Springs Nature Park** ❼ (daily 8am till late; entrance fee; tel: 07-350 0440; www.rainbowsprings.co.nz). Its natural pools, set amid 12 hectares (30 acres) of lush surroundings, teem with thousands of brown, brook, rainbow and tiger trout. Huge trout, which swim here from Lake Rotorua to spawn, can be hand-fed and also viewed through an underwater window.

Lush Rainbow Springs Nature Park.

Adjacent to the nature park is **Kiwi Encounter** (daily 10am–4pm; entrance fee; tel: 07-350 0440; www.kiwiencounter.co.nz), a unique incubation facility, hatchery and nursery, the only one of its kind open to the public in the world. On your 45-minute guided tour, you can view kiwis, native geckos and skinks, plus adult and juvenile tuataras, New Zealand's living "dinosaurs", in a nocturnal house. There are also New Zealand native and exotic birds, and "Captain Cooker" wild pigs, introduced by the famous explorer himself.

BELOW:
sheep-shearing
performance at
Agrodome.

Close by the springs is the terminus for **Skyline Skyrides** (daily 9am–8pm; tel: 07-347 0027, 0800-865 843; www.skylineskyrides.co.nz), one of Rotorua's main adventure attractions, but with plenty on offer for the more timorous as well. Ride a gondola midway up **Mount Ngongotaha** for a breathtaking view of the city, lake and surrounding countryside. The more adventurous can plunge downhill again in a high-speed luge cart. The speed of the carts can be controlled and there are three tracks totalling 5 km (3 miles), including a relatively leisurely "scenic" one with bays where riders can stop to take photographs. The Sky Swing takes the children's playground favourite a few notches higher, reaching a height of 50 metres (164 ft) and speeds of 120 kph (75 mph).

About 10 km (6 miles) northwest of Rotorua, on Western Road near Ngongotaha, is the spacious **Agrodome** ❼ (daily 8.30am–5pm; entrance fee; tel: 07-357 1050; www.agrodome.co.nz) located on 160 hectares (395 acres) of pasture. Three times a day (9.30am, 11am and 2.30pm), 19 trained rams are put through their paces for an hour in "sheep shows". It's an educational and entertaining performance, and visitors receive handfuls of freshly shorn wool. Children love the chance to bottle-feed a lamb, though they're often less enthusiastic about the genuinely rural accompanying odours. While the sheep display – showcasing New Zealand's 19 major breeds put through their paces by almost unbelievably clever sheepdogs – is still the heart of the Agrodome experience, the enterprise now includes a huge number of other activities.

TIP

DON'T step off the designated path when visiting thermal attractions in Rotorua! That apparently firm surface may be the thin crust of a hot steaming pool. Accidents are rare but not unknown.

Visitors can take a tractor tour of the Agrodome farm and feed sheep, deer, alpacas and emus by hand. At the adjacent **Agrodome Adventure Park**, many thrill rides are on offer, perhaps the most unusual of which is Freefall Xtreme, which re-creates the sensation of skydiving with a column of wind that holds the adventurer 5 metres (16 ft) in the air. Also available are bungy-jumping, jet boat racing, zorbing *(see page 121)*, and the Swoop, which is an exhilarating combination of bungy jumping and flying that sees visitors being whisked 100 metres (330 ft) through the air at 130 kph (80 mph).

There are more trout at **Paradise Valley Springs** (daily 9am–5pm; entrance fee; tel: 07-348 9667; www.paradisev.co.nz), 11 km (7 miles) northwest of Rotorua, and at **Hamurana Springs** ➊ 17 km (11 miles) on the northern shore of Lake Rotorua. To protect sports fisheries, it has been made illegal to buy or sell trout in New Zealand. But many visitors can still enjoy a fresh trout dinner, as the fish is an easy catch with guides claiming a 97 percent daily "strike" rate. In fact, no trip to Rotorua or Taupo is complete without a fishing expedition on the lakes. Guides supply all tackle and will meet clients outside hotels, with trailer boats ready for action, or at the boat harbour. **Clearwater Cruises** (tel: 07-362 8590; www.clearwater.co.nz) and **Mana Adventures** (tel: 07-348 4186; www.manaadventures.co.nz) both provide a variety of trout-fishing excursions.

Rainbow trout on most lakes around Rotorua and on Lake Taupo average 1.4 kg (3 pounds) and on Lake Tarawera *(see page 190)*, where they are tougher to catch, fish of 3.5–5.5 kg (8–12 pounds) are not uncommon. The icing on the cake after a day of fishing is having a hotel or restaurant chef prepare the catch – a service speciality which they are well used to providing.

Some 8 km (5 miles) north of the Agrodome on SH5 is **Off Road NZ** (daily

BELOW: a trout fisherman with his prize catch.

Map on page 184

9am–5pm; entrance fee; tel: 07-332 5748; www.offroadnz.co.nz). This is for those who like to go very fast and make a lot of noise, especially in self-drive four-wheel-drive vehicles or Off Road's monster truck, over rough and challenging terrain. Adjacent is the **Mamaku Blue Winery** (daily 9am–5pm; free; tel: 07-332 5840; www.mamakublue.co.nz), New Zealand's largest blueberry winery. Winery and orchard tours are available if you are interested.

Along Central Road, past Ngongotaha township at Sunnex Road, the **Farm House** (daily 10am–3pm; tel: 07-332 3771) hires out ponies and horses for riding over 245 hectares (605 acres) of bush-edged farmland. Carrying on clockwise around Lake Rotorua, the scenic road continues to **Okere Falls ①** where, after a short walk through native forest and down a cliffside, the **Kaituna River** can be viewed thundering through a narrow chasm into the swirling pool below.

Knocking on Hell's Gate

Crossing the Ohau Channel outlet, from northeastern Lake Rotorua into Lake Rotoiti, an eastbound turn on to SH30, towards Whakatane, takes you to the very door of **Hell's Gate ②** (daily 9am–8.30pm; entrance fee; tel: 07-345 3151; www.hellsgate.co.nz), reputedly the most active thermal reserve in Rotorua. The Maori name, Tikitere, recalls the legend of Hurutini, who threw herself into a boiling pool because her husband treated her with contempt. Tikitere is a contraction of *Taku tiki i tere nei* ("my daughter has floated away"), bestowed by George Bernard Shaw. The volcanic activity here covers 4 hectares (10 acres), highlighted by the hot-water **Kakahi Falls**, the largest of its kind in the southern hemisphere. Hell's Gate is home to the **Wai Ora Spa**, the only place in New Zealand where you can experience the singular cosmetic benefits of a mud bath. Follow this with a bath in the sulphur waters of the **Hurutini Pool**.

On the shores of **Lake Rotoiti ③** is the family-run **Rotoiti Tours World of Maori** (nightly in summer, winter by arrangement; entrance fee; tel: 07-348 8969; www.worldofmaori.co.nz). Visitors are transported to the Rakeiao *marae* (meeting area) for a very traditional experience, which includes a concert performance and *hangi* plus the opportunity to sleep over communally in the *wharenui* (meeting house).

Farther down SH30 along the shores of **Lake Rotoehu** and **Lake Rotoma**, a side road between the lakes goes to **Soda Springs ④**. Here hot water percolates into a clear stream, where you can take a dip. Heading south of Lake Rotoiti is unspoiled **Lake Okataina**, where there is a walking track to Lake Tarawera *(see page 190)*.

The eruption of Tarawera

Southeast of Rotorua, heading in the direction of the airport, is the turn-off to the forest-clad **Lake Tikitapu ⑤** (Blue Lake) and **Lake Rotokakahi ⑥** (Green Lake), a favourite stomping ground for joggers and a retreat for those who enjoy walking or riding along the well-marked and graded trails through exotic pines and native bush. Horses and ponies are available for hire. On a fine day, follow the signs to the lookout points between the lakes to observe that, although they are side by side, one is blue and the other green.

BELOW: fiery hot mud at Hell's Gate.

Te Wairoa's breath-taking waterfall is worth the 20-minute walk it takes from the Buried Village.

BELOW: the volcanic crater atop Mt Tarawera.

The road continues to the larger Lake Tarawera via the **Buried Village** ⦿ (daily 8.30am–5.30pm summer, daily 9am–4.30pm winter; entrance fee; tel: 07-362 8287; www.buriedvillage.co.nz), destroyed on 10 June 1886 when a devastating eruption of Mount Tarawera blasted rock, lava and ash into the air over a 15,500-sq km (6,000-sq mile) area and buried the villages of Te Wairoa, Te Ariki and Moura, killing 147 Maori and six Europeans. The buried village contains items excavated from Te Wairoa, including the *whare* (hut) of a *tohunga* (priest) who fore-told the disaster *(see text box below)* and was unearthed alive four days after the eruption. There is an inescapable eerie feeling here as you walk past the remnants of Maori buildings frozen in time at the moment a community was extinguished.

Well worth the extra 20 minutes it takes at the end of your circuit of the vil-lage is the charming, if steep, **Te Wairoa Waterfalls Track**, a stroll through native bush to a 30-metre (100-ft) waterfall.

From the Buried Village, it's a short drive further east to **Lake Tarawera** ⦿, with **Mount Tarawera** ⦿ ("burnt spear") looming in the distance. From Te Wairoa, before the eruption, many Victorian tourists were rowed across Lake Tarawera to the fabulous Pink and White Terraces, which were two huge silica formations which rose 250 metres (820 ft) from the shores of **Lake Rotomahana** and were billed as one of "the eight wonders of the world". Today, you can retrace the route to the former site with **Lake Tarawera Launch Cruises** (tel: 07-362 8595; www.purerotorua.com/reremoana.htm), when you take the Erup-tion Trail Cruise aboard the classic, kauri-hulled *MV Reremoana*. The return journey cruises past the thermal activity at **Hot Water Beach** and across Lake Tarawera to Kariki Point. **The Landing Café** (tel: 07-362 8595), located within the cruise centre, is famous for its mussel chowder and should not be missed.

TARAWERA'S GHOSTLY SIGHTINGS

Adding to the area's mysterious aura is the tale of a ghostly war canoe full of mourning, flax-robed Maori seen by two separate boatloads of visitors on Lake Tarawera on the misty morning of 31 May 1886. Earlier that morning, the visitors had ventured out by boat from Te Wairoa, the launch point for boat trips on Lake Tarawera, to view the the famous Pink and White Terraces rising from the shores of nearby Lake Rotomahana.

When this sighting was reported back at Te Wairoa, it filled the local Maori villagers with terror, for the ceremonial war canoe that had been described to them had ceased to exist in the region for over 50 years. Tuhuto, the *tohunga* (priest) of Te Wairoa prophesied that the apparition was "an omen that all this region will be overwhelmed".

On a chilly moonlit night 11 days later, Mount Tarawera fulfilled his prophecy to the letter, blasting the Pink and White Terraces off the world tourist map forever, though not from Rotorua's memory. The eruption lasted some 5 hours and an area measuring some 15,540 sq km (6,000 sq miles) – including the village of Te Wairoa – was covered with ash, lava and mud. Rotorua never seems to have come to terms with the loss of the terraces and you may be surprised how often you are reminded of them during your stay.

If you fancy a bird's eye view, flights over the crater and thermal lakes depart from Te Puia, Agrodome Park as well as Skyline Skyrides. The flights are operated by **HELiPRO** (tel: 07-357 2512; www.helipro.co.nz), which has exclusive landing concessions on both Mount Tarawera and Mokoia Island. A thrilling landing on the mountain's slopes allows close inspection of the 6-km (4-mile) long, 250-metre (820-ft) deep chasm caused by the volcanic explosion.

Map on page 184

Heat and light

On SH5, some 14 km (9 miles) south of Rotorua is the **Tamaki Maori Village Ⓡ** (evenings; entrance fee; tel: 07-349 2999; www.maoriculture.co.nz). The brainchild of two enterprising brothers, Doug and Mike Tamaki, who started small by selling a Harley to buy a mini-bus, Tamaki's features a living pre-European Maori village, a tribal market where traditional crafts, made on site, are sold and cultural performances shown.

Twenty km (12 miles) south of Rotorua, still on SH5 going towards Taupo, is the turn-off to **Waimangu Volcanic Valley Ⓢ** (daily 8.30am–4.45pm summer, 8.30am–3.45pm winter; entrance fee; tel: 07-366 6137; www.waimangu.com). This unspoilt thermal area contains the **Waimangu Cauldron**, the world's largest boiling lake. An easy walk downhill from a tearoom leads past bubbling crater lakes, hot creeks and algae-covered silica terraces to the shores of Lake Rotomahana, where a launch can be taken to the intensively active **Steaming Cliffs** and the former site of the lost Pink and White Terraces.

Waimangu is one of the more colourful thermal attractions, presenting a vivid palette of hues that only adds to the other-worldly impression it creates. Surface activity began here on 10 June 1886, creating one of the newest eco-systems in the

BELOW: Waimangu Volcanic Valley.

Silica terraces like these at Wai-O-Tapu are a result of decades of mineral build-up.

world, with endangered plants and thermal-adapted flora existing side by side in the midst of intense thermal activity. The Waimangu Geyser was once the biggest in the world, reaching dizzy heights of 500 metres (1,640 ft). Today. it has less force and is dwarfed by Pohutu *(see page 186)* New Zealand's biggest geyser.

About 10 km (6 miles) further along SH5, a loop road leads to another thermal area, **Wai-O-Tapu Thermal Wonderland** ❷ (daily 8.30am–5pm; entrance fee; tel: 07-366 6333; www.geyserland.co.nz). *Wai-O-Tapu*, Maori for "Sacred Waters", is the home of **Lady Knox Geyser**, which erupts daily at 10.15am — with a little encouragement from a staff member who adds some soap powder into the vent to create tension and cause the spectacular spurt of super-heated water and steam. Other attractions include the bubbly **Champagne Pool**, tinted silica terraces and **Bridal Veil Falls**.

About 70 km (43 miles) south of Rotorua and 37 km (23 miles) north of Taupo is the "Hidden Valley" of **Orakei Korako** ❸ (daily 8am–4.30pm; entrance fee; tel: 07-378 3131; www.orakeikorako.co.nz), which is a cave and thermal park comprising geysers, hots springs, mud volcanoes, underground caves and some of the largest silica terraces in the world. The geothermal area is accessible only by boat across **Lake Ohakuri**. Maori chiefs painted themselves in the mirror pools here, hence the name, Orakei Korako — "adorning place".

The route to Taupo

If you've somehow emerged from Rotorua without being exposed to its geothermal wonders, you can rectify the omission on the way to Taupo. Some 7 km (4 miles) before Taupo, just below the junction of SH1 and SH5, visitors will encounter the **Wairakei** ❹ geothermal area. At **Wairakei Terraces** (daily 9am–5pm in summer, till 4.30pm in winter; entrance fee; tel: 07-378 0913; www.wairakeiterraces.co.nz) natural silica terraces wiped out for the construction of a power station in the area have been recreated artificially and left to develop their brilliant colours of blue, pink and white over time. Whether they will eventually provide an adequate substitute for the much-missed Pink and White Terraces, only time will tell. There is also the **Maori Cultural Experience** with evening performances, *hangi* meals and craft displays (bookings essential). Tours of the power station are also available. Super-heated water is drawn from the ground through a series of bores, enabling dry steam to be piped to electricity turbines in a nearby powerhouse.

Also located between Wairakei and Taupo, on a gravel road, is the **Craters of the Moon** (daily 9am–5pm; free; tel: 0274-965 131), another wild thermal area worth stopping at. Visitors can gaze into a frightening abyss of furiously boiling mud and walk around a track to see steam rising from natural fumaroles in the hillside. From here, the resort town of Taupo is only about 5 km (3 miles) away.

Before reaching Taupo, you will encounter the world's only geothermal **Prawn Farm** (daily 11am–4pm; entrance fee; tel: 07-374 8474; www.prawnpark.com). Visitors can observe, hand feed, catch and eat prawns here. Another interesting stop is the **Volcanic Activity Centre** (Mon–Fri 9am–5pm, Sat–

Sun 10am–4pm; entrance fee; tel: 07-374 8375; www.volcanoes.co.nz) which explains all you need to know about geothermal and volcanic activity in the region — one of the most active areas on earth. Just 200 metres (656 ft) down the road is the **Honey Hive** (daily 9am–5pm; free; tel: 07-374 8553; www. honey.co.nz), where you can learn all about bees and honey production. Be sure to buy a bottle of New Zealand's famous manuka honey to take home.

A nearby loop road leads to the spectacular **Huka Falls**, where the full force of the Waikato River hurtles from a narrow gorge over a 11-metre (36-ft) ledge. Enough water goes over the falls every second to fill two Olympic-sized pools. When lit by sunshine, the ice-cold water takes on a brilliant turquoise-blue colour before crashing into a foaming basin below. The falls are best observed across the footbridge from the opposite side of the river. For water-level views, book a white-knuckle ride on the Huka Jet boats which skim across the water near the base of the falls. A short distance along the loop road on the banks of the Waikato River is the renowned **Huka Lodge** (tel: 07-378 5791; www. hukalodge.com), an exclusive retreat for the well-heeled (and often famous).

Lake Taupo

Taupo is an abbreviation of Taupo-nui-Tia ("the great shoulder cloak of Tia"), which takes its name from the Arawa canoe explorer who discovered **Lake Taupo ❺**, New Zealand's largest. The lake covers some 619 sq km (240 sq miles) and was formed by volcanic explosions over thousands of years. It is now the most famous trout-fishing lake in the world, yielding in excess of 500 tonnes of rainbow trout annually. The rivers flowing into the lake are equally well stocked, so that fishermen frequently stand shoulder-to-shoulder at the mouth of

TIP

Magnificent Huka Falls is best experienced on the Huka Jet, which roars along Huka River and brings you to close proximity of Huka Falls. The 30-minute trip runs all day (tel: 07-374 8572; www.hukajet.co.nz).

BELOW: white-knuckle jet-boat ride with thundering Huka Falls behind.

the Waitahanui River, forming what has come to be known as the picket fence.

Apart from its trout fishing fame, Taupo offers a full range of activites, from sedate boat and kayak trips on its lake to skydiving, bungy-jumping and other adrenalin-pumping sports. Both accommodation and restaurants are aplenty at this family-style resort. For more information, drop by the **Taupo** i-SITE **Visitor Centre** at 30 Tongariro Street (tel: 07-376 0027; www.laketauponz.com).

Three mountains

At the southern head of Lake Taupo is the breathtaking 7,600-sq. km (2,930-sq. mile) **Tongariro National Park** ❻, containing the three active volcanic peaks of **Mount Tongariro** (1,968 metres/6,457 ft), **Mount Ruapehu** (2,796 metres/ 9,173 ft) as well as **Mount Ngauruhoe** (2,290 metres/7,513 ft), which starred as the scary Mount Doom in the film trilogy *Lord of the Rings*.

The most scenic route from Taupo leaves SH1 at **Turangi** heading for Tokaanu, not far from the Tongariro Power Station, and winds up through bush-covered mountains and around the shore of Lake Rotoaira. The alternative route is to turn off the main highway at Rangipo on to SH47.

According to Maori legend, when the priest and explorer Ngatoro-i-rangi was in danger of freezing to death on the mountains his fervent prayers for assistance were answered by the fire demons of Hawaiki, who sent fire via White Island and Rotorua to burst out through the mountain-tops. To appease the gods, Ngatoro cast his female slave into the Ngauruhoe volcano – called Auruhoe, by the local Maori. Mount Ngauruhoe, with its typical volcanic cone, is the youngest and most active of the three volcanoes and still bubbles and spits lava and ash occasionally. A major eruption in 1954–5 continued intermittently for nine months.

BELOW: Lake Taupo is a hot spot for some mind-blowing adventure sports.

Mount Ruapehu is a perpetually snow-capped volcano with a flattened summit stretching 3 km (2 miles) and incorporating an acidic, bubbling Crater Lake and six small glaciers. Ruapehu has blown out clouds of steam and ash a number of times in the past 100 years, raining dust over a 90-km (56-mile) radius in 1945, and closing the nearby Whakapapa and Turoa ski fields in 1996. On 24 December 1953, 151 people died in a tragic train disaster when a lahar, or violent discharge of water and mud, roared down the Whangaehu River from Crater Lake.

Top-class skiing

Mount Ruapehu is the major ski area of the North Island, with the action taking place at two locations, comprising in total 1,800 hectares (4,450 acres) of slopes. **Whakapapa** on the mountain's northwestern face has excellent beginner slopes as well as more challenging areas. **Turoa** is on the southwestern slopes, with magnificent views of Mount Taranaki. Accommodation abounds in the area, with Turoa skiers tending to base themselves at **Ohakune**, while those skiing at Whakapapa stay at **Whakapapa Village**, where the historic **Grand Chateau** (tel: 07-892 3809; www.chateau.co.nz) built in 1929 is found, or at the **National Park**, about 15 km (9 miles) away. Apart from skiing, adventure tour operators also offer white-water rafting down the Tongariro and Rangitikei rivers.

Outside of the ski season, Tongariro National Park has many fine walks, including the famous 16-km (10-mile) **Tongariro Crossing**, which covers spectacular scenery in a matter of 7–8 hours. Rangers at the **Whakapapa Visitors Centre** (tel: 07-892 3729) have details on walking tracks and huts. The walk can be done in one day if you push it; two days allow more diversions. The Grand Chateau (*see above*) also organises a Tongariro Crossing package. ❑

Map on page 200

TIP

There are several useful websites on skiing in New Zealand but skiers heading to Mount Ruapehu should check out www.mtruapehu.com. It has information on skiing at both Whakapapa and Turoa.

BELOW: trampers descending into a crater at Mt Tongariro.

HEALING WATERS OF ROTORUA

This strange, steamy landscape of bubbling springs and mud pools, saturated in Maori lore and history, has been attracting tourists for more than a century

Rotorua has been a top tourist resort for decades. A century ago genteel folk came to the spa from all over the world to promenade and take the waters. So it's a little surprising to learn that the town has been described as "Stink-ville" and "Rotten Egg Town". All becomes clear when you take your first breath of the sulphur-laden mist. You soon forget the sulphuric odour as you explore the surreal steamy surroundings. Every geyser, every spring, it seems, has a curious name with a story attached, like the Lobster Pool in Kuirau Park, so named because of the shade its acidic waters tinted fair European skins. And a concentrically ringed mud pool, charmingly named "Gramophone Record Pool".

LUNAR REBIRTH

One of these stories relates to the moon. Rotorua's healing waters have been described as "Wai-ora-a-Tane" (Living Water of Tane), where according to Maori legend the dying moon bathes each month in the great mythical lake of Aewa. Here, she receives the gift of life to sustain her on her journey through the heavens.

It's very important to obey the signposts and keep to the paths in this region, where the earth is a bit less stable than most of us are used to. The thermal pools may look tempting, but some of them are boiling hot. If your vision gets blocked with the steam, be sure to take a rest until it clears – don't stagger on blindly.

▷ **WAI-O-TAPU**
The name means "sacred waters", and Wai-O-Tapu is often justly billed as a "thermal wonderland". Star attractions are the Artist's Palette *(shown here)*, Lady Knox Geyser and Champagne Pool, the Wai-O-Tapu Terraces and Bridal Veil Falls – plus boiling mud pools galore. The Rainbow Crater is an underground thermal spring grotto which was formed by a violent hydrothermal explosion about 850 years ago.

◁ **CHAMPAGNE POOL**

Dinner parties and concerts are sometimes held in the misty, ethereal atmosphere of the Champagne Pool at Wai-O-Tapu Thermal Wonderland, just south of Rotorua. The pool is actually quite blue and steamy, and doesn't really look like champagne at all, but if a handful of sand is thrown into it, the water fizzes enthusiastically, just like a large glass of bubbly.

▽ **LADY KNOX GEYSER**

It's definitely not a good idea to peer into the throat of a geyser, even if it is guaranteed to go off just once a day promptly at 10.15am. Geysers tend to be rather unpredictable – Lady Knox Geyser's efficient timekeeping is kept to the minute with regular helpings of soap, as well as a few rags to help the pressure build up.

CROQUET AT THE BATH HOUSE

How very English! Splendid buildings like this one, the town's most frequently photographed edifice and superb backdrop to a croquet match, gives Rotorua its genteel charm.

Now known as Tudor Towers, the elegant building which graces Government Gardens was originally constructed as a bathhouse in 1908, complete with ancient sculptures in the foyer. To the left and right of the entrance foyer, double doors led to men's and women's bathhouses, where treatment could be obtained for rheumatism. The baths had facilities for Aix massage, steam baths and mud baths.

The building is no longer a bathhouse – if you want a dip in a thermal pool, the nearby Polynesian Pools, built in 1886 and the site of Rotorua's first building and bathhouse, is open daily.

Today, Tudor Towers houses the Rotorua Museum of Art and History (see page 184), with a number of collections tracing the development of painting and printmaking in New Zealand, as well as contemporary paintings. There is also a kauri gum collection and a wildlife display, plus exhibitions about the Te Arawa Maori people who first settled the area. A video on the 1886 Mount Tarawera eruption shows how the magnificent Pink and White Terraces, formed of silica deposits, were annihilated.

◁ **WHAKAREWAREWA**

This famous thermal area's full name is Whakarewarewa-anga-o-te-a-Wahiao, which means, "the uprising of a war party of Wahiao". New Zealand's highest geyser, Pohutu, bursts forth several times a day for up to 40 minutes at a time, reaching heights of 20–30 metres (65–100 ft). The nearby Prince of Wales Feathers Geyser generally goes off just before Pohutu.

POVERTY BAY AND HAWKE'S BAY

Map on page 200

Hawke's Bay and its neighbour, inappropriately named Poverty Bay, have a wealth of agriculture, bountiful vineyards, history, interesting architecture – and New Zealand's most easterly city

There are several reasons why Gisborne and the area around it are special to New Zealanders. Situated on 178 degrees longitude, Gisborne is noted for being the first city in the world to greet the rising sun each day, a fortunate accident of geography made much of at midnight on 31 December 1999, when it led worldwide television coverage of the turn of the new millennium. It is also an historic coast: Young Nick's Head, a promontory across the bay from the city of Gisborne, was the first piece of land that British explorer Captain James Cook and the crew of his ship *Endeavour* saw in 1769. Cook's landing site is at the foot of Kaiti Hill, a great viewing platform for Gisborne and the surrounds. Over the Turanganui River stands an impressive statue of Captain Cook, and further around the beachfront is a statue of Nicholas Young, the cabin boy on the *Endeavour*, who is credited with being the first on board to sight land.

LEFT: Lake Waikaremoana with the Urewera Range in the background. **BELOW:** the good life at Gisborne.

Gisborne

Cook, who got most things right, erred badly, however, in calling the region **Poverty Bay** because "it did not afford a single article we wanted, except a little firewood". Poverty Bay retains the name grudgingly. It is now sheep and cattle country and rich in citrus and kiwifruit orchards, vineyards, vegetable gardens and a variety of food crops which all support a large processing industry. With 15 wineries in the area (www.gisborne.co.nz/wine) it's no surprise that its wines – particularly chardonnay and gewürztraminer – are among the best in the country and should be tried on a visit to one of the many vineyards open to the public.

Poverty Bay offers spectacular coastal vistas of white sands and sparkling blue waters, accompanied by the scarlet blossom of the pohutukawa, often known as the New Zealand Christmas tree because it is at its best and brightest in late December. Some of this colour rubs off on **Gisborne** ❼ (with an urban area population of 35,000), a city of sun and water, parks, bridges and beaches. Watersports are a recreational way of life. Gisborne is a magnet for surfers, with reliable conditions at the nearby beaches of Wainui, Okitu and Makaorori.

Gisborne is also called the "City of Bridges" and is situated on the banks of the Taruheru and Waimata rivers and Waikanae Creek, all joining to form the Turanganui River. On Stout Street, adjacent to the town centre, **Tairawhiti Museum** (Mon–Fri 10am–4pm, Sat 11am–4pm, Sun 1.30–4pm; free; tel: 06-867 3832; www.tairawhitimuseum.org.nz) recounts the region's history. A section of the main building is a maritime

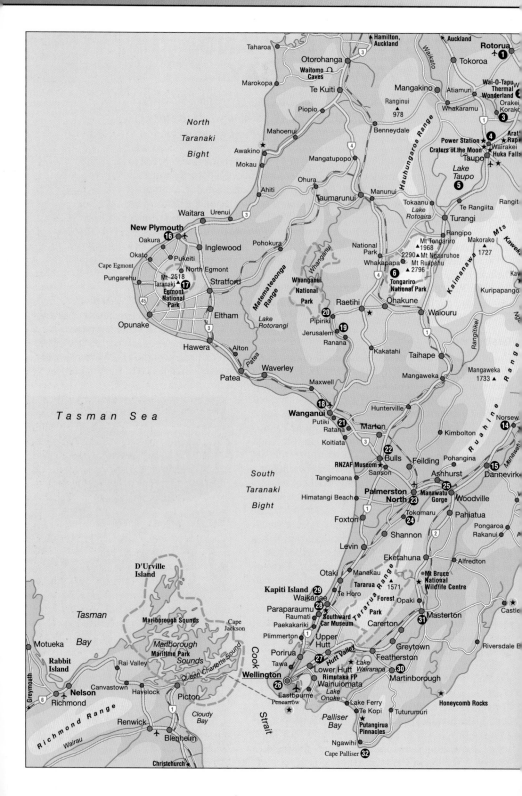

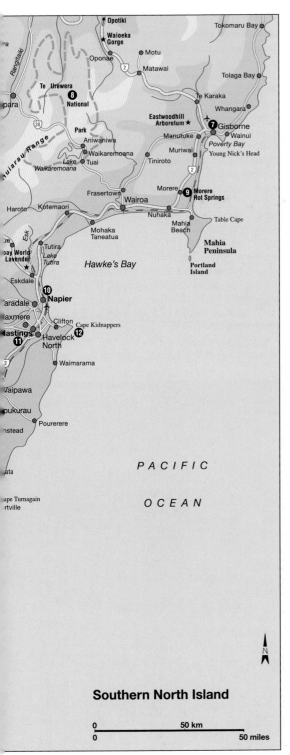

Southern North Island

0   50 km

0   50 miles

museum, made up from parts of the steamship *Star of Canada*, which was wrecked on Kaiti beach in 1912.

Gisborne lingers over its association with Cook, but the area's historic wealth pre-dates his visit. Maori land-holdings – some of them leased to Europeans – are extensive. Meeting houses are numerous and can be seen at many of the Maori settlements along the coast. Most feature carved lintels, panels and beams done in traditional style, embellished with the unorthodox painting of patterned foliage, birds and mythical human figures. One of the largest meeting houses in the country is **Te Poho-o-Rawiri** (visits by arrangement only; tel: 06-867 2103), at the base of **Kaiti Hill** on Queens Drive. Built in 1925, it did not use the traditional ridge-pole structure because of its size. However, it still contains some impressive *tukutuku* (woven reed) panels and magnificent carvings. Almost every Maori settlement on the coast has its treasured meeting house.

As a major forestry centre, it's quite appropriate that Gisborne is the location of New Zealand's largest tree collection, at **Eastwoodhill Arboretum** (daily 9am–5pm; entrance fee; tel: 06-863 9003; www.eastwoodhill.org.nz). Located just 30 minutes west of Gisborne via Patutahi, it was founded by Gallipoli veteran soldier W. Douglas Cook. His lifetime's work sprawls over some 70 hectares (173 acres).

Legendary Te Kooiti

While Poverty Bay is tranquil today, there were many tribal battles in the past. One of the most interesting stories concerns the Maori prophet Te Kooti, who in the 19th century led a rebellion against settlers. He was exiled to the Chatham Islands, hundreds of kilometres off the east coast of the North Island, along with dozens of other Maori arrested in the 1860s – but that wasn't to be the end of him. He masterminded a daring escape back to the mainland and, believing God had appeared to him and promised he would save the Maori as he had saved the Jews, founded a religious movement which still exists, called Ringatu ("The Upraised Hand"). The government sent an army in pursuit, but Te Kooti proved a formidable enemy in the wild bush of the **Urewera Range**, striking back with guerrilla attacks that kept him free and the government harassed. He was eventually pardoned in his old age and allowed to live with his followers in the far away King Country.

Many of Te Kooti's old haunts have been preserved in **Te Urewera National Park ❽**, 212,000 hectares (524,000 acres) of rugged mountains, forests and lakes, much of it still inaccessible to all but the toughest trampers. Located some 164 km (102 miles) northwest of Gisborne via Wairoa, the park's highlight is **Lake Waikaremoana** ("Lake of the Rippling Waters"), rich in trout and with bush thick to the water's edge on all but the eastern side, where it is hemmed in by steep cliffs. Chalet, motel and motor camp accommodation is available at Waikaremoana, and there are tramping huts throughout the park.

A unique feature of Te Urewera National Park is Lake Waikareiti, home of a lake within a lake. It contains tiny Ranui Island, which itself contains a lake called Te Tamaiti o Waikaremoana ("The Child of Waikaremoana").

Into Hawke's Bay

Poverty Bay runs southward to the **Mahia Peninsula** where it merges into the **Hawke's Bay** region. Sitting near the neck of the peninsula separating the two bays is **Morere ❾**, 60 km (37 miles) south of Gisborne and an attractive centre that is worth visiting for its hot springs, or for bush walks in the surrounding native forest. Past the town of **Wairoa** some 40 km (25 miles) away, a turn-off leads northwest to Te Urewera National Park *(see above)*. Continue west for another 104 km (65 miles) where 5 km (3 miles) up State Highway (SH) 5 from the turn off to Eskdale is **Whitebay World of Lavender** (daily 10am–4pm; entrance fee; tel: 06-836 6553; www.whitebay.co.nz). Apparently, wherever grapes grow well, conditions are right for lavender, so Hawke's Bay is ideal. Although the centre is open all year, harvesting at Whitebay is in January, so the time prior

BELOW: Whitebay's lavender fields are a great photo subject.

to that affords the best chance to soak up the spectacular sight of a sea of vivid purple lavender blooms. There are tours, a shop selling lavender products and a café – probably your best chance to sample lavender ice cream and lavender tea.

Map on page 200

Art deco Napier

Another 21 km (13 miles) south is **Napier** ❿, which together with **Hastings**, further south, form the two cities that make up Hawke's Bay. Napier and Hastings may be twin cities but both are strongly independent and even competitive. Napier is a seafront city with a population of 55,000, while Hastings is an agricultural marketing centre of some 67,000. The cities are bounded to the east by the Pacific Ocean, and to their west plains sweep away to the Kaweka and Ruahine ranges, rugged areas for hunters and trampers. Both are thriving cities today and there is little indication of the massive destruction they suffered in the tragic earthquake that rocked Hawke's Bay in 1931 (see below).

Ironically, the 1931 earthquake gave Napier a chance to reinvent itself. A new city arose from the ashes, with a distinctive art deco façade chosen by the architects to reflect both the era and the attitude of the new city. Napier's collection of art deco buildings in the inner city, with their bold lines, elaborate motifs and pretty pastel colours, is recognised internationally as extraordinary. Recognition of the quality of the architecture – and its popularity – has come only in the past few years, and with a vengeance. Napier's people are fiercely proud of the city's heritage. Building owners are encouraged to restore and preserve the façades, and civic leaders have done their bit too, developing the main street in a sympathetic fashion.

While New Zealand is well known for the effort it puts into preserving its many natural assets, it does not have a good record for preserving its architectural

Napier's art deco buildings are among the finest in the world.

BELOW: Napier, after it was devastated by the 1931 earthquake.

RISING FROM THE ASHES

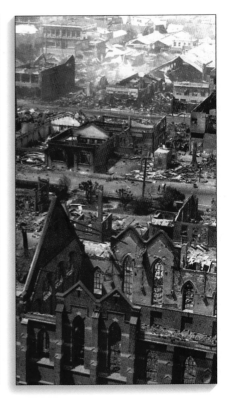

Hawke's Bay was where New Zealand's worst earthquake tragedy took place on 3 February 1931. Buildings crumpled under the impact of a 7.9 Richter scale earthquake. What the shock did not destroy in Napier and Hastings, fire finished off. The death toll of 258 included a number of people killed by falling parapets. Napier was closest to the epicentre and heroic deeds were performed by rescuers and by naval personnel from the HMS *Veronica*, which happened to be in harbour (along Napier's seafront today is a colonnade named after the naval sloop).

It was a time of economic depression, but a passionate government and a sympathetic world came to Hawke's Bay's post-quake aid with funds for a massive relief and rebuilding campaign. The opportunity was taken to widen streets, install new underground telephone lines, and a strict earthquake-proof building code was enforced, giving rise to a brand new city with architecture inspired by the art deco movement of the time.

It could be said that the whole of Napier today is a kind of memorial to the earthquake. Much of its suburban area, stretching out to the once-independent borough of Taradale in the southwest, is built on the 4,000 hectares (10,000 acres) of former marshland the earthquake pushed up.

BELOW: Daily Telegraph building – a fine example of Napier's art deco architecture.

heritage. To this end, Napier's **Art Deco Trust** (www.artdeconapier.com) was formed in 1985 by a visionary group. Without their efforts it is entirely possible the construction-crazy 1980s would have seen "progress" do as much damage to the buildings of the 1930s as the earthquake did to their predecessors. The trust organises a number of activities, including walks, for visitors as well as spearheading the annual Art Deco Weekends held in February, when the whole town seems to step back in time to the 1930s. The Trust also runs the **Art Deco Shop** at Desco Centre, 163 Tennyson Street (tel: 06-835 0022), which carries a wide selection of gifts and souvenirs relating to Napier's art deco heritage.

One exception to art deco's stranglehold on Napier's claims to architectural merit is the magnificent **County Hotel** (tel: 06-835 7800, 0800-843 468; www.countyhotel.co.nz) on Browning Street. Previously the County Council Chambers, it is in the Victorian-Edwardian classical revival style. And it is not just the design that harks back to those times. Quaintly, if not rashly, a complimentary decanter of port is always available in its library.

Another highlight of Napier is the city's 2-km (1-mile) long **Marine Parade**. A large recreational collection of gardens, sculptures, fountains, earthquake memorials and varied visitor attractions, the seaside promenade is dominated by towering rows of Norfolk pines. Look out for the **Statue of Pania**, a maiden of local Maori legend who fell in love with a young chief but later lost her life and that of their child to the sea. Marine Parade is also where you will find **Marineland** (daily 10am–4.30pm; entrance fee; tel: 06-834 4027; www.marine land.co.nz). Here, you can pat, feed and even swim with the dolphins as well as view fur seals, otters, sealions and other marine life.

At No. 65 Marine Parade is **Hawke's Bay Museum** (daily 10am–4.40pm,

9am–6pm summer; entrance fee; tel: 06-835 7781; www.hawkesbaymuseum. co.nz), which details events surrounding the earthquake and the city's rebuilding in addition to exhibits on Maori art and culture. Also on Marine Parade, is the **National Aquarium of New Zealand** (daily 9am–5pm, till 7pm in summer; entrance fee; tel: 06-834 1404; www.nationalaquarium.co.nz), which opened in 2002. Housed in a distinctive stingray-shaped building are more species than in any similar establishment in New Zealand. A moving footpath carries viewers under the "oceanarium", while sharks, stingrays and many other varieties of fish glide by. Land-based fauna are also featured: kiwi, tuatara and glowworms among them. It's a hands-on, interactive experience centre in the manner that is now *de rigueur* for museums around the world.

Residential **Napier Hill** overlooks the city centre. This was one of the earliest parts of the city to be developed by Europeans. Evidence of this remains in some of the fine Victorian and Edwardian homes and in the maze of twisting, narrow streets, designed before motor cars were anticipated. On the north side of the hill, next to the bustling port, is another historic locale, **Ahuriri**, the cradle of Napier and the site of the first European settlement in the area. A scenic road winds up **Bluff Hill** to a lookout for views over the city, harbour and bay.

Fruitful Hastings

Some 21 km (13 miles) south, architectural treasures from the post-earthquake period dot **Hastings ⑪** too, in the art deco and Spanish mission style. Despite their physical proximity, Hastings is rather a different city from Napier, laid out in a flat and formal fashion, and surrounded by a rich alluvial plain which hosts a huge range of horticultural crops. Hastings' main role is, as it is proudly

The Statue of Pania of the Reef on Marine Parade in Napier pays tribute to an ancient Maori legend.

BELOW: Hastings fruit vendor.

called by locals, "The Fruit Bowl of New Zealand". A Mediterranean-type climate, pure water from an underground aquifer, and innovative growers have made this one of the most important apple-growing regions in the world. Apricots, grapes, peaches, nectarines, plums, kiwifruit, pears, berries and cherries also grow profusely here and are on offer from roadside stalls during the harvesting season, along with tomatoes, sweet corn, asparagus and peas.

Despite the horticultural bounty, the twin cities rely heavily on farming, which has generated the region's historic wealth. Only pine forests are challenging the supremacy of sheep and cattle in the rolling hinterland. The pastoral farms are the legacy of Victorian settlers who laid claim to huge tracts of Hawke's Bay, and made their fortunes from wool and, later, sheep-meat, beef and hides.

All this may be lost on younger visitors more likely to be awed by Hastings **Splash Planet** (daily 10am–6pm summer; entrance fee; tel: 06-873 8033, 0508-775 274; www.splashplanet.co.nz), a family-friendly water theme park with more than 15 attractions and motorised rides, and a hit with toddlers, teens and the young at heart.

A short distance of 3 km (2 miles) across the plain from Hastings is "The Village", as the pretty, genteel town of **Havelock North** is known locally. It sits in the shadow of **Te Mata Peak**, a limestone mountain with a summit accessible by car. From the top you can enjoy the sweeping views or, if you are daring enough, you may go hang-gliding or paragliding from the steep cliff on one side. Havelock North is the also the home of **Arataki Honey** (Mon–Sat 8.30am–5pm; Sun and public holidays 9am–4pm; entrance fee; tel: 06-877 7300, 0800-272 825; www.aratakihoneyhb.co.nz) with over 17,000 hives, and a major honey producer. At the "Bee Wall" you can see an entire colony at work, from the queen to the drones.

Gannets and wineries

Hastings and Napier may enjoy distinctive identities but they share some significant attractions – the Cape Kidnappers gannet colony, for example, and the local wine industry. **Cape Kidnappers** ⓬ is 18 km (11 miles) from Hastings and a 20- to 30-minute drive from either city, followed by a ride along the beach in one of the tractor-towed trailer vehicles to what is thought to be the largest mainland gannet colony in the world. During the breeding season from June to October the cape is closed to visitors for scientific study. The Cape's name harks back to an incident in which local Maori attempted to abduct a Tahitian youth from the serving staff of Captain Cook's *Endeavour* while it lay at anchor nearby.

Over forty wineries are established around Napier and Hastings. Hawke's Bay is the oldest of the country's wine-growing regions and sees itself as the finest. Certainly it enjoys ever-increasing recognition for the quality of its chardonnays, sauvignon blancs and cabernet sauvignons. Wine enthusiasts often wax lyrical over wineries like **Trinity Hill** (www.trinityhill.co.nz), **Te Mata Estate** (www.temata.co.nz) and **Church Road** (www.churchroad.co.nz). Church Road is one of New Zealand's leading producers and one of its oldest, having been founded in 1897. This was

Map
on page
200

where pioneer wine-maker Tom McDonald earned the title of father of quality red wine-making in New Zealand. Church Road has the country's only wine museum, with some wine artefacts dating back to the Iron Age. There are numerous wineries in the region all open to visitors. Many offer free wine tastings and have a restaurant on site. If you cannot find a willing designated driver, book a winery tour with one of the many operators in Napier or Hastings.

South of Hastings

Fifty km (31 miles) south of Hastings, pastoral farming is the reason for the existence of another set of Hawke's Bay twin towns, Waipukurau and Waipawa. Near **Waipukurau** ⓭ is a hill with one of the longest names of any place in the world: Taumatawhakatangihangakoauauotamateapokaiwhenuakitanatahu. The 57 letters translate into "The hill where the great husband of heaven, Tamatea, caused plaintive music from his nose flute to ascend to his beloved".

Further south again, another culture has left its mark. In the 19th century, hardy Norwegian and Danish settlers cleared the rainforest in southern Hawke's Bay, which was so dense it had discouraged all others. They established such towns as Norsewood, 85 km (53 miles) south of Hastings, and Dannevirke ("Dane's Work"), another 20 km (12 miles) further south. The Scandinavian flavour is still evident at **Norsewood** ⓮. Although a tiny town, it has a well-known woollen mill producing a range of knitted goods bearing the settlement's name. **Dannevirke** ⓯ actively promotes its historic links with Scandinavia, though it once, probably wisely, rejected a plan to erect a giant statue of a Viking. It is a farm service town and a convenient staging post on the busy highway between Manawatu to the south and Hawke's Bay to the north. ❏

HAWKE'S BAY
WINE COUNTRY

Hawke's Bay is the oldest wine region, some say the finest as well, in New Zealand.

BELOW: enjoying a picnic in Hawke's Bay wine country.

TARANAKI, WANGANUI AND MANAWATU

Map on page 200

These predominantly rural regions encompass scenic splendour peppered with quiet, pleasant townships and crowned with the majestic peak of volcanic Mount Taranaki

The 169-km (105-mile) Te Kuiti to New Plymouth road along the North Island's western coast leads the southbound traveller through rugged farmed hill country, the Awakino River gorge and beautiful coast with cliffs and placid sandy bays. After a climb up the road over Mount Messenger, **Mount Taranaki** – also known as Mount Egmont – is in full view on a clear day. The road passes by a striking memorial to the famous Polynesian anthropologist Sir Peter Buck just north of Urenui, his birthplace. Near New Plymouth, Taranaki's main centre, the land flattens to fertile dairy plains which encircle the dormant volcano of Mount Taranaki, a near-perfect cone, 2,518 metres (8,261 ft) high.

New Plymouth and environs

With Mount Taranaki as its backdrop, the town of **New Plymouth** ⑯, home to 48,000 people, spreads down the coast. Its location, soils and climate were immediately attractive to European arrivals in the 1840s. Early missionaries and settlers found a Maori population depleted by inter-tribal wars, yet land troubles between the Maori and newcomers still beset the settlement. War broke out in 1860 and eventually placed New Plymouth under virtual siege.

Visitors should start at **Puke Ariki** (Mon–Tues and Thurs–Fri 9am–6pm, Wed 9am–9pm, Sat–Sun 9am–5pm; free; tel: 06-759 6060; www.pukeariki.com), on Ariki Street in the town centre, a museum, public library and visitor centre in one. Interesting exhibits and interactive displays will help you get acquainted with the history and culture of the Taranaki region. The museum also includes the historic **Richmond Cottage**, home of three of the first settler families.

East of here, at Queen Street, is the **Govett-Brewster Art Gallery** (daily 10.30am–5pm; free; tel: 06-759 6060; www.govettbrewster.com), home to an excellent contemporary art collection, including works by Len Lye, pioneer New Zealand artist and filmmaker *(see page 85).* **St Mary's Church** (tel: 06-758 3111; www.stmarys.org.nz) on Vivian Street, completed in 1846, is the oldest stone church in New Zealand.

New Plymouth is best known for its beautiful parks. At **Pukekura Park** (daily 7.30am–7pm, till 8pm in summer), a few blocks southeast of Govett-Brewster gallery, wasteland has been transformed into lovely lakes, gardens, a fernery, fountains and a waterfall, lit in rainbow colours by night. The **Brooklands Zoo** (daily 8.30am–5pm; free; tel: 06-759 6060) is also here.

A pleasant **Coastal Walkway** runs the length of the city for 7 km (4 miles) from the Waiwakaiho River mouth to Point Taranaki. At roughly the mid-point,

LEFT: Mt Taranaki, also known as Mt Egmont.
BELOW: Govett-Brewster Art Gallery in New Plymouth.

TIP

The best time to
explore Egmont
National Park is during
the flower season from
Dec–Mar, or Jul–Aug
(for snow). For guided
walks, contact
MacAlpine Guides, tel:
06-765 6234; 02-7441
7042; www.macalpine
guides.com, or Top
Guides, tel: 021-838
513, 0800-448 433;
www.topguides.co.nz.

BELOW: New
Plymouth hosts a
Rhododendron
Festival in late
Oct/early Nov.
RIGHT: Wanganui's
verdant landscape.

opposite Puke Ariki, is Len Lye's soaring 45-metre (148-ft) kinetic sculpture, *Wind Wand*, at first reviled, then fervently embraced by the locals.

Heading south from New Plymouth via Carrington Road, 8 km (5 miles) along, is **Hurworth Cottage** (Sat–Sun 11am–3pm; entrance fee; tel: 06-757 8409). One of the region's earliest homesteads, it was built in 1855 by Harry Atkinson, a young immigrant from England, who later became Premier of New Zealand.

Some 12 km (7 miles) further down the road is the **Pukeiti Rhododendron Trust** (daily 9am–5pm; entrance fee; tel: 06-752 4141; www.pukeiti.org.nz), a 320-hectare (791-acre) park, established in 1951, which showcases one of the world's best displays of rhododendrons and azaleas in a native bush setting.

Winter skiers and summer hikers will enjoy **Egmont National Park** ⑰ on Mount Taranaki, with its more than 300 km (180 miles) of bush walks. Climbing the summit is not supremely difficult, but weather conditions can change quickly so arm yourself with adequate information or take a guided hike *(see margin note)*. The easiest access to the park is via **Egmont Village**, 20 km (12 miles) southeast of New Plymouth. The **North Egmont Visitor Centre** (daily 9am–4.30pm; tel: 06-756 0990) here can help with more information on what to do in the area.

Wanganui

State Highway (SH) 3 from New Plymouth passes through the agricultural towns of Stratford (whose town clock is the only one in New Zealand boasting a glockenspiel), Hawera and Patea for about 160 km (100 miles) on the way to **Wanganui** ⑱, a city most famous for its river, which takes an extra "h". The Whanganui is New Zealand's longest navigable river, much loved by canoeists and jet-boaters, and runs through the town for part of its course. In the superb

Whanganui Regional Museum (daily 10.30am–4.30pm; entrance fee; tel: 06-349 1110; www.wanganui-museum.org.nz) on Watt Street is a store of Maori artefacts, a war canoe, Te Mata-o-Hoturoa, and a remarkable collection of paintings by well-known New Zealand artist Gottfried Lindauer. Built in the form of a Greek cross, the elegant **Sarjeant Gallery** (daily 10.30am–4.30pm; free; tel: 06-349 0506; www.sarjeant.org.nz) graces the hill above the museum.

Map on page 200

Before further exploring Wanganui, take the lift up to the **Memorial Tower** on **Durie Hill**. The elevator (daily 8am–6pm), built in 1918, climbs 66 metres (216 ft) inside the hill. But the 176 tower steps are worth the trouble on a fine day, and you'll be rewarded with a magnificent view of the city and river.

About 2 km (1 mile) south along Putiki Drive is **Putiki Church** (St Paul's Memorial Church). The building has a plain white exterior, but its interior is adorned with magnificent Maori carving and *tukutuku* (weaving) wall panels. Access enquiries are best directed to **Wanganui i-SITE Visitor Centre** (tel: 06-349 0509).

Chief attractions west on SH3 from the city are the **Bason Botanical Reserve** and **Bushy Park** scenic reserve, both easily reached via short detours. SH4 north through the Paraparas, is justly noted for its scenic beauty. To the east of Wanganui and north of Palmerston North *(see page 212)*, the **Rangitikei River** – excellent in its upper reaches for whitewater rafting – links with SH1 near Managaweka. Enquire there or in Wanganui or Palmerston North about rafting.

One highlight of Wanganui is the 79-km (49-mile) **Whanganui River Road**, which runs alongside the river from Wanganui to Pipiriki. Driving the route takes 2 hours. About 30 km (19 miles) of the road between Matahiwi and Pipiriki remains unsealed and could be hazardous for inexperienced off-road drivers, so a far better option is to book a bus tour (contact Whanganui River Road Tours, tel: 06-345 8488; www.whanganuiriver road.co.nz) to enjoy the stunning river views.

As you approach the village of **Jerusalem** ⑲ (Hiruharama), you will understand why French Catholic missionaries established themselves along this bend in the river in 1854, and why New Zealand poet, James K. Baxter chose the serenity of this site for a commune in the late 1960s. The mission remains today, but the commune disintegrated after Baxter's death in 1972.

Top of the route is **Pipiriki** ⑳, a popular base for tramping the many listed walks, and a gateway to the **Whanganui National Park**. From here you can get to the **Bridge to Nowhere**, more accurately a bridge in the middle of nowhere, built to service a new settlement for soldiers after World War I but abandoned when they were forced out by the depression and farming difficulties by 1942. It can be accessed by a 40-minute walk from the Mangapurua landing, a two-day tramp from the Whakahoro Hut via the Kaiwhakauka and Mangapurua Valleys, or by canoe or jet boat (contact Bridge to Nowhere Lodge, tel: 06-348 7122; www.bridgetonowhere-lodge.co.nz). For other points of interest and accommodation options in the park, contact the Wanganui i-SITE Visitor Centre *(see above)*.

Taranaki is the Maori name for the volcano that Captain Cook named Mount Egmont. After decades of dispute over the name, in 1986 the New Zealand government ruled that both names would be official.

BELOW: colonial-style house in Pipiriki.

South of Wanganui

SH3 proceeds southeast from Wanganui to Palmerston North, 74 km (46 miles) away. If you have time, stop by

Ratana ㉑, a small township named after a famous Maori prophet and faith healer. A temple was built there in 1927 to honour its founder. The largest township en route to Palmerston North is **Bulls ㉒**. Further your agricultural education by branching off here towards the coast and **Flock House**, an agricultural training institute. Built in 1895, it was purchased in 1923 by the New Zealand Sheep-growers, who ran a scheme to train the sons of British seamen's widows as farmers. Between Bulls and Sanson is the **Royal New Zealand Air Force Base** at **Ohakea**, home to the No. 75 Squadron of the RNZAF and its **Airforce Museum** (daily 9.30am–4.30pm; entrance fee; tel: 06-351 5020).

Palmerston North

On the approach to Palmerston North is **Mount Stewart**, with fine views of the rich Manawatu pastures. A memorial near the road commemorates early settlers. It's a short hop from here to the historic homestead and gardens at **Mount Lees Reserve**. **Palmerston North ㉓** itself is the flourishing centre (and capital) of agricultural Manawatu, with **The Square** as the city's focal point. Named in Maori as Te Marae o Hine or "Courtyard of the Daughter of Peace", it commemorates a female chieftain named Te Rongorito who sought an end to inter-tribal warfare during the early days of European settlement.

West of The Square, at 396 Main Street, is **Te Manawa** (daily 10am–5pm; entrance fee; tel: 06-355 5000; www.temanawa.co.nz), an institution combining history, art and science in its museum, art gallery and interactive science centre. Northwest of The Square, at 87 Cuba Street, is the **New Zealand Rugby Museum** (Mon–Sat 10am–noon and 1.30–4pm, Sun 1.30–4pm; entrance fee; tel: 06-358 6947; www.rugbymuseum.co.nz). This shrine to the national sport

BELOW: enjoying the national sport in Palmerston North.

displays items from blazers to historically significant whistles as well as a special section devoted to the country's famous All Blacks team.

Roads radiate outwards from the centre of "Palmy". **Fitzherbert Avenue** leads to the city's other major focal point, the **Manawatu River**. The river is crossed by only one bridge, used by thousands of cars and bicycles each day en route to **Massey University** and a number of science research stations. Also over the bridge is the **International Pacific College**, and New Zealand's largest army base, at Linton. Given the number of educational institutions in Palmerston North, it's not surprising it calls itself the Knowledge Centre of New Zealand.

On the city side of the Manawatu River is the city's much-loved **Victoria Esplanade** (open daily in daylight hours, free; www.pncc.govt.nz), an enchanting reserve featuring botanical gardens, a miniature train (www.esplanaderail.org.nz), a children's playground, an aviary and an education centre and conservatory. Don't miss the **Dugald Mackenzie Rose Garden** at the Esplanade, which has an international record for developing new varieties.

A stone's throw away, also on Park Road, is the **Lido Aquatic Centre** (Mon–Thur 6am–8pm, Fri 6am–9pm, Sat–Sun 8am–8pm; entrance fee, tel: 06-357 2684; www.lidoaquaticcentre.co.nz). Children especially will enjoy the exciting slides and chutes at this water park. A walkway girdles Palmerston North and native bush reserves are close by. Palmerston North is a popular national sporting venue because of its first-rate facilities.

Exploring Manawatu

A short drive south of Palmerston North on SH57 is **Tokomaru ㉔** and its creative **Tokomaru Steam Engine Museum** (Mon–Sat 9am–3.30pm, Sun 10.30am–3.30pm; entrance fee, tel: 06-329 8867; www.tokomarusteam.com).

SH56 heads west to beaches at Tangimoana, Himatangi and Foxton. They may not be the best beaches in New Zealand, but they are well-patronised by locals and have interesting coastal walks from one beach settlement to another. **Feilding**, 20 minutes northeast on SH54, is a large town which boasts two squares, a motor-racing track and racecourse, and a stock sale on Friday mornings. The region is perhaps the best place for a stud-farm tour, which is certainly a worthwhile experience in Manawatu.

But perhaps the most dramatic route in or out of Palmerston North and the Manawatu region is via the rugged Manawatu Gorge fi. SH3 first passes through the country town of Ashhurst. From here you'll get a good view of the **Tararua Wind Farm** (www.wind energy.org.nz), a surreal array of 40-metre (130-ft) high 660kw turbines, looking like free-standing aeroplane propellors, used to generate electricity.

Travellers can detour here to **Pohangina** and **Totara** reserves, an area of virgin native bush favoured for picnics. The road then narrows, and clinging to the southern side of the Manawatu Gorge it links the region to Hawke's Bay. Drive with care here. On the opposite bank of the river is the Hastings and Napier railway line, opened in 1891. But try not to be distracted by it: this road demands your constant attention. ❏

Map on page 200

BELOW: Tararua Wind Farm in Manawatu.

WELLINGTON

Vibrant Wellington, the seat of government as well as
the unofficial cultural centre of the country, has a
cosmopolitan buzz that is readily discernible

Maps:
Area 200
City 216

Auckland
North Island

Wellington

Christchurch

South Island

LEFT: Wellington
architecture
mingles the old
with the new.
BELOW: bar sign
in Wellington's
Courtenay Place.

T awhiri-ma-tea, the Polynesian god of wind and storm, fought many fierce battles with his earthbound brother gods in Wellington and the Wairarapa. No wonder Cook Strait, the stretch of water separating this end of the North Island from the South Island, had an early start as one of the most treacherous short stretches of open water in the world. The early Maori saw the North Island as a great fish, rich with food for their Polynesian families. Today the mouth of the fish is as pretty a capital city as any in the world. Wellington's great blue bowl of harbour is only mildly scarred by its port reclamations and the high-rise offices set below green hills dotted with white wooden houses.

The citizens of Wellington have shown scant respect for their Pakeha founding father, Edward Gibbon Wakefield. There is no memorial to Wakefield in Wellington other than his gravesite, partly due to lingering disapproval over a prison term he served for allegedly abducting an heiress; she was willing, but her father was not, and he brought a successful court case against the young Wakefield. It was in Newgate Prison that Wakefield witnessed first-hand the miserable lot of England's poor and devised a scheme to attract investment from the well-off in projects that offered a chance to those with nothing.

In practice it was a mess. Idealists were thin on the ground, speculators as thick as shovels in a gold rush. Wakefield's brother, William, was in charge of acquiring land for the new emigrants, but he had only four months to do so. His quick deals with the Maori included buying Wellington for 100 muskets, 100 blankets, 60 red nightcaps, a dozen umbrellas and such goods as nails and axes. Wakefield claimed to have bought for £9,000 the "head of the fish and much of its body", a total of about 8 million hectares (20 million acres).

San Francisco's twin city

Wellington ㉖ has long been compared to San Francisco, and accurately so. In addition to a susceptibility to earthquakes and a punishingly hilly topography, both cities have their share of "painted ladies", old wooden houses done up in rainbow colours. Like San Francisco, Wellington has a cable car, zooming out of its city belly on Lambton Quay to a fine view of the harbour, beside an ivy-clad, red-brick Victoria University.

Wind is the other handicap with which nature has afflicted Wellington. A cartoon image of residents permanently bent over, as they struggle to make way against a chilly southerly bringing icy blasts borne down from the Southern Alps, is not too remote from the truth. The city's dwellers have compensated by making their home the most architecturally attractive in New Zealand. That it is also the seat of government has not seen it go short when it comes to funding public buildings.

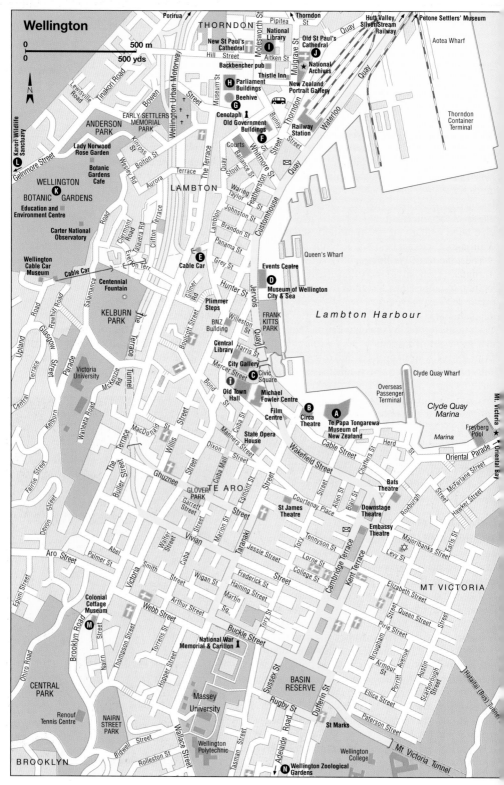

Wellington

0 _____ 500 m
0 _____ 500 yds

In the second half of the 1970s the city was shaken by man-made quakes, as a downtown area of quaint Victorian wedding-cake two- and three-storey premises was demolished on the grounds of earthquake risk. The skyscrapers of steel and glass that replaced them, however, look equally vulnerable.

After the decade of demolition, Wellington tarted up the few old buildings left, like Victoria University, downtown relics like the baroque St James Theatre on Courtenay Place and the government buildings centred around The Terrace, which are built of native woods in the masonry style of European architecture.

Despite moving its port operations a mile or so north to a new container complex around this time, Wellington continues to rate as the busiest of the country's 13 main ports. This is largely due to the all-weather sailing of the Cook Strait rail ferries and foreign fishing vessels that call here for registration and provisioning.

New Zealand's finest museum

The buildings left behind when port operations moved north are a major part of Wellington's reinvention of itself after the public service, a major employer, was decimated in the 1980s. Physically confined by the sea on one side and the Rimutaka range on the other, the capital went about the job with gusto, culminating in the construction of the country's most assertive museum. Any exploration of the city should start on Cable Street at **Te Papa Tongarewa – Museum of New Zealand** Ⓐ (daily 10am–6pm; till 9pm Thur; free; tel: 04-381 7000; www.tepapa.govt.nz) which is regarded as one of the finest in the country and houses some of the most important *taonga* (treasures) of New Zealand. There is no better introduction to the country to be found under one roof, and its aggressively post-modernist approach guarantees mental stimulation of a kind

Map on page 216

TIP

Before deciding what to do in Wellington, drop by the city's i-SITE Visitor Centre at Civic Square, corner of Wakefield and Victoria streets. Tel: 04-802 4860, www.wellington nz.com.

BELOW: Te Papa Tongarewa is New Zealand's finest museum.

Signature metal palm trees dot Wellington's Civic Square. The city's leading architect, Ian Athfield, designed Civic Square and the Wellington Central Library just adjacent.

BELOW: Civic Square – the hub of Wellington.

not always found in New Zealand museums. It features a wide range of exhibits and presents uniquely New Zealand experiences from Te Marae, a contemporary Maori gathering place, to Awesome Forces, where you get to experience the powerful geological forces that shape New Zealand's landscape. Don't miss the earthquake house. There are also discovery and state-of-the-art time travel and virtual reality centres, cafés, a souvenir shop and a bar. Visitors should reserve at least one full day at this landmark museum.

Leaving the museum and turning right, out on the old wharf area, you will see a building with a wedding-cake façade, which was rescued from the demolished Westport Chambers to make a home for one of the city's liveliest and most innovative professional theatres, **Circa Theatre ❸** (tel: 04-801 7992; www.circa.co.nz). The Circa Theatre building is a perfect example of the born-again look that has transformed the original port area.

If you turn left after leaving Te Papa, you'll find the city's two other major theatres. **Bats Theatre** (tel: 04-802 4175; www.bats.co.nz), found by turning right from Cable Street onto Kent Terrace, is an intimate venue, home of the fringe, that presents diverse and challenging theatre. Turn right again on Marjoribanks Street to encounter the skew-whiff concrete, iron and wood pyramid of **Downstage Theatre** (tel: 04-801 6946; www.downstage.co.nz) offers total entertainment, great shows, licensed bar and accommodation. The country's first professional theatre, established in 1964, Downstage marks the southern tip of **Courtenay Place**, the city's hip bar and restaurant centre.

But to discover the commercial, retail and historic centre of Wellington, follow the wharf north from Circa Theatre to where a lagoon has been carved out beside the rehousing of two traditional city rowing clubs. Here, intricately

Map
on page
216

carved arches lead across the main road to **Civic Square ⓒ**. In between the remnants of Wellington's Victoriana, colourful and architecturally impressive buildings and malls, and a craze for cafés selling latté and espresso brighten the city. Nowhere is this more apparent than in the generous pink and beige piazza of Civic Square. On one side of Civic Square is **Michael Fowler Centre** – the trendy steel colander housing the city's municipal chambers – and the rectangular **Old Town Hall**. The Old Town Hall was saved after testimonials from visiting conductors, such as the late Leonard Bernstein, rated it one of the best symphonic halls in the world, a fitting venue for the home-base of the New Zealand Symphony Orchestra. In even-numbered years, the Michael Fowler Centre and Old Town Hall are the focus of the New Zealand Festival, reinforcing Wellington's status as the capital of the performing arts in New Zealand.

On the other side of Civic Square is the **Wellington City Library** (Mon–Thur 9.30am–8.30pm, till 9pm Fri, till 5pm Sat, 1–4pm Sun; tel: 04-801 4040; www.wcl.govt.nz). The library's interior is like an industrial plant of exposed metal and awash with natural light; outside, its gorgeous plaster curve is decorated with metal palms. In between is the **City Gallery** (daily 10am–5pm; free; tel: 04-801 3021; www.city-gallery.org.nz) which hosts a collection of contemporary local and international artworks in its 1930s art deco style building.

Wellington's wharves

The streets between Wellington's skyscrapers are narrow and windswept with few parks, but the city's office workers are never more than a stone's throw from the wharves with views of wide open skies and invigorating sea breezes. Turn right from the Civic Square towards the water and follow the wharves

A much-loved Wellington heritage building (opposite the Embassy Theatre), known locally as the Taj, built in 1928 as public toilets, is now occupied by a much frequented and more savoury watering hole, The Welsh Dragon Bar & Scorpios Restaurant (tel: 04-385 6566; e-mail: scorpiojos@ xtra.co.nz).

BELOW: Wellington harbour scene.

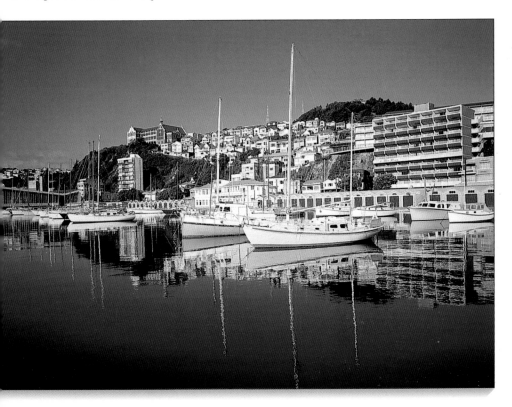

north again. These are among the few wharves in the world open to the public; politicians and civil servants are among the lunchtime joggers who zip past puzzled Russian and Korean fishing crews. New restaurants in converted stores offer haute fish cuisine, but if you're not hungry you can still see what the sea has to offer at the **Museum of Wellington City and Sea** Ⓓ (daily 10am–5pm; free; tel: 04-472 8904; www.museumofwellington.co.nz) at Queens Wharf. The museum houses a captivating collection of maritime memorabilia.

Part of the museum is **Plimmer's Ark Gallery** which contains the excavated remains of the 150-year-old sailing ship, *Inconstant*, later known as Plimmer's Ark. Wakefield's controversial part in the struggles of the early settlers may explain why the title "Father of Wellington" was conferred on John Plimmer instead, a merchant settler who displayed less idealism. Plimmer complained that a place represented to him as "a veritable Eden" had proved "a wild and stern reality". Plimmer in fact had little cause for complaint – he had converted the wreck of the *Inconstant,* the fallout from a bad day, into a flourishing trading enterprise on the beach. Like many of his fellow entrepreneurs, Plimmer added his own wharf, eventually becoming one of the solid citizens of the town, and his wreck ended up as the boardroom chair in the country's Bank of New Zealand.

Lambton Quay and the Parliamentary District

Follow Grey Street opposite the museum until you reach Lambton Quay, turn right and you'll find **Wellington Cable Car** Ⓔ (Mon–Fri 7am–10pm, Sun and public holidays 9am–10pm; tel: 04-472 2199). Given Wellington's precipitous downtown topography, the cable car, which terminates at the Botanic Gardens (*see page 222*), is a popular route between the shopping precinct to the numerous offices uphill.

Now a major shopping strip, **Lambton Quay** was once the beachfront where Plimmer and his fellow traders set up shops, its narrowness prompting reclamations ever since. The enforced shift across the harbour to the narrow Wellington foreshore ensured a continuous struggle to turn back the tide. The result today is that Lambton Quay has moved back several blocks from the harbour.

If you make a return trip on the cable car, you can continue north on Lambton Quay for 600 metres (2,000 ft) to the **Old Government Buildings** ⓕ, the second largest wooden building in the world. Constructed in 1876, the building comprises 9,300 sq metres (100,000 sq ft) of timber. The tides lapped at this site before land was reclaimed in 1840. Directly opposite, politicians and top public officials and business folk buzz around the capital's unique circular Cabinet offices, known as **The Beehive** ⓖ. A large amount of the administrative and financial clout of the country is centred here.

Built in the late 1970s, the copper-domed Beehive is a soft contrast with the square marble angles of the adjacent **Parliament Buildings** ⓗ (daily 10am–4pm; till 3pm Sat; free; tel: 04-471 9503; www.ps.parliament.govt.nz) finished in 1922, and the Gothic turrets of the **General Assembly Library**, dating back to 1897. To one side of the Beehive is the historic, red-brick **Turnbull House**, tucked below the pristine skyscraper Number One The Terrace, office for the Treasury, with the Reserve Bank across the road. North of the Beehive and Parliament are the new **St Paul's Cathedral** with its pink concrete façade and the **National Library** ⓘ (Mon–Fri 9am–5pm, Sat 9am–4.30pm, Sun 1–4.30pm free; tel: 04-474 3000; www.natlib.govt.nz), within which is the **Alexander Turnbull Library** with its remarkable collection of New Zealand and Pacific history.

Map on page 216

TIP

If you fancy rubbing shoulders with Kiwi politicians, have a drink at their traditional watering hole, appropriately called Backbencher Pub and Café. It's found at No. 34 Molesworth Street (tel: 04-472 3065).

LEFT: Beehive is where the power brokers sit.
BELOW: Old St Paul's Cathedral.

Leave the National Library via Aitken Street, turn left on Mulgrave Street and note the pohutukawa trees that surround **Old St Paul's** (daily 10am–5pm; free; tel: 04-473 6722), a small but impressive Gothic Revival-style cathedral made entirely of native timbers, even down to the nails. Consecrated in 1866, this is the jewel in a city of 30 churches, many of them built in the wooden adaptation of the soaring stone Gothic style that was a unique colonial feature.

About 10 minutes north is the district of **Thorndon**, location of **Katherine Mansfield's Birthplace** (Tue–Sun 10am–4pm; entrance fee; tel: 04-473 7268) at 25 Tinakori Road. The two-storey family home where the writer was born in 1888 has been beautifully restored and features an authentic Victorian town garden.

Wellington's suburbs

On the fringes of the city centre lie some of Wellington's premier attractions. Just over 1 km (½ mile) southwest of Old St Paul's are the luxuriant grounds belonging to the **Botanic Gardens** (daily sunrise–sunset; free; tel: 04-499 1400; www.wbg.co.nz), notable for the formal glory of the **Lady Norwood Rose Garden**. The gardens are ideal for a stroll, and in the summer months, the colourful blooms are spectacular. There is also a good children's adventure playground here.

Another 1 km (½ mile) southwest of the Botanic Gardens is the remarkable **Karori Wildlife Sanctuary** (daily 10am–5pm, last entry 4pm; entrance fee; tel: 04-920 9213; www.sanctuary.org.nz) on Waiapu Road. This oasis has 35 km (22 miles) of tracks covering 252 hectares (623 acres) of regenerating forest. This is a chance to see – or at least hear – birds such as kiwi, weka and morepork in their natural environment. Night guided tours are also available (booking is essential, tel: 04-920 9213).

Wellingtonians flourish on urban environmental battles. From the late 1960s, citizens of gentrified Thorndon cut their conservation teeth on opposition to a motorway and saved some of the threatened suburb. Even more successful were residents on the other side of the city, in the raffish community of the Aro Valley below the Victoria University. Students and old-timers successfully repelled council plans to demolish their wooden cottages in favour of concrete.

Heading east, back towards the city centre, from the Karori Wildlife Sanctuary, is a good site to view the result of one such battle. At 68 Nairn Street, near the corner of Willis Street, which runs south from the city is the **Colonial Cottage Museum** ⓜ (daily 10am–4pm summer, Sat–Sun and public holidays noon–4pm winter; entrance fee; tel: 04-384 9122; www.colonialcottagemuseum.co.nz). The museum is located in Central Wellington's oldest building, a four-bedroom house built in 1858. The house was to be demolished in the 1970s, but the tenacity of its occupant, a granddaughter of the original builders, inspired local support and it was saved. From Aro Valley, head southeast through Mount Cook towards the **Basin Reserve** cricket ground, which was a lake before an earthquake drained it.

To the southeast of the basin is the suburb of **Newtown**, its narrow streets teeming with new migrants from the Pacific, Asia and Europe. At the local school, you can hear 20 different languages spoken, while shops that look like clapboard façades of a Hollywood wild west set sell exotic foods from a dozen lands. Newtown is also the site of **Wellington Zoological Gardens** ⓝ (daily 9.30am–5pm; entrance fee; tel: 04-381 6755; www.wellingtonzoo.com). This is New Zealand's oldest zoo, built in 1906 and now run on the natural-habitat conservation model favoured by zoos worldwide.

Wellington's suburban housing.

BELOW: bikers taking in views of the Hutt Valley.

Valley of the Hutt

To enjoy the rest of what Wellington has to offer, head north again, leaving the city via the Hutt Road and heading for the topographically blander environment of the **Hutt Valley** ㉗ *(see map page 200)*, the cities of **Lower Hutt** and **Upper Hutt** and their satellite suburbs. The first settlers had little to thank Wakefield for when they were dumped on a beach at the swampy bottom of the Lower Hutt Valley. After their tents flooded, the settlement moved to the narrow but dry site of the present city. The abandoned Lower Hutt area, today's **Petone**, meaning the End of the Sand, evolved into a working-class town of heavy and light industry. The flat shoreline is now a popular recreational area, the workers' cottages are being gentrified and the **Petone Settlers' Museum** (Tues–Fri noon–4pm, Sat–Sun 1–5pm; tel: 04-568 8373; www. petonesettlers.org.nz) commemorates the early struggles. The museum is notable for its close involvement with the local community and is as much about the present as the past.

Further up the valley at Silver Stream, with its red-brick exclusive Catholic boys school of St Patrick's College, is a chance to ride on a hillside steam train at **Silver Stream Railway Museum** (Sun only 11am–4pm; entrance fee; tel: 04-971 5747; www.silverstream rail way.org.nz). It is operated by a group of "enthusiastic volunteers" and has one of the largest collections of working vintage steam trains in New Zealand.

Also in Lower Hutt Valley, at Guthrie Street, is one of Wellington's essential attractions, **Maori Treasures** (Mon–Sat 10am–4pm; entrance fee; tel: 04-939 9630; www.maoritreasures.com). These are the private studios of the Hetet family, Maori artists of great distinction who work in ancient traditions of craft. Maori Treasures also houses temporary exhibitions of Maori artwork and gives visitors the opportunity to practise some of the traditional techniques themselves. One of the guiding principles of the enterprise is the importance of sharing knowledge in traditional Maori society.

Head back south towards Wellington and take the eastern turn-off to explore some of the small communities tucked into the steep eastern bays. **Wainuiomata**, famous for its rugby league club, is the gateway to the **Rimutaka Forest Park**. At the Hutt base of the hill is are government science research institutes and the petrol storage wharf complex, leading to pristine bushy bays.

A hill road away is another valley centre, **Eastbourne**. It can also be reached by ferry or a drive around the bays from the city centre, and is worth a visit for its craft shops and quiet contrast. It is an easy 8-km (5-mile) hike around this coast to view the **Pencarrow Lighthouse**, the country's first permanent lighthouse. This 1859 cast-iron structure at Pencarrow was "manned" at the time by one Mary Jane Bennett, New Zealand's only woman lighthouse keeper.

The Kapiti Coast

At weekends many Wellingtonians head northwest to the **Kapiti Coast**. One of the many good beaches in the area is at **Paraparaumu** ㉘ where there are water slides and watersport facilities, and a variety of accommodation to spend the night. It is possible to arrange trips out to the unspoiled native bird sanctuary of **Kapiti Island** ㉙, which was the capital of the warrior chief Te Rauparaha, who ruled the Wellington region when the Pakeha arrived. Cats, goats and dogs blighted the native fauna here until the Department of Conservation embarked on an eradication programme. The island is now a secure home for native birds such as the kakariki, takahe, kea and kiwi. **Kapiti Tours Ltd** (tel: 04-237 7965; www.kapititours.co.nz), which is based at Paraparaumu, can take you there.

A few kilometres further up the "Gold Coast", as it is known, you can enjoy locally made gourmet cheeses, watch the sheep shearing and milking of cows at the **Lindale Centre** (daily 9am–5pm; free; tel: 04-297 0916) or visit the vintage car collection in the **Southward Car Museum** (daily 9am–4.30pm; entrance fee; tel: 04-297 1221; www.southward.org.nz), the largest and most diverse in the Southern hemisphere.

Wairarapa region

Yet another world awaits northeast of Wellington. The city's central position has maintained its importance as a port for shipping products from the adjacent farming lands of the **Wairarapa**. It takes an hour to drive northeast over the 300-metre (1,000-ft) Rimutaka range; cars sometimes need chains to negotiate the road during winter. In the old days, a Fell locomotive hauled people and goods up the mountain's almost vertical incline.

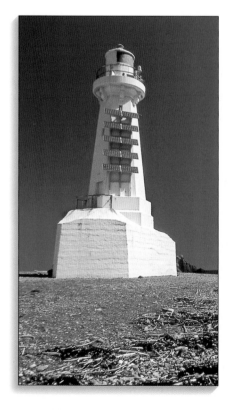

BELOW: Pencarrow Lighthouse.

The vast plain north of Lake Wairarapa hosts towns of marked contrast to the rowdy capital. **Greytown** is associated with a former governor, while **Featherston** played a grim part in history as a POW camp for Japanese. Today, these are places to buy antique furniture that has been carved with the Maori adze. The **Fell Locomotive Museum** (daily 10am–4pm; tel: 06-308 9379) in the town centre houses the only Fell locomotive left in the world. **Martinborough ㉚**, 18 km (11 miles) southwest of Featherston, has burst onto the map as a producer of boutique wines, particularly pinot noir. A good way to experience the area is to join one of the vineyard tours that leave from Wellington. The **Martinborough Wine Centre** at 6 Kitchener Street (tel: 06-306 9040; www.martinboroughwine-centre.co.nz) is a fine place to learn all about the wineries in the region.

The town of **Masterton ㉛**, 51 km (32 miles) north of Martinborough, still fits the traditional image of the area as host town of the **Golden Shears** sheep-shearing competition (www.goldenshears.co.nz) in March every year. Although New Zealand has long shed its image as one giant farm, the Golden Shears is still one of the few regular agricultural events in which the whole country takes an interest. In the duck shooting season the population rises as dramatically as the lake levels after heavy rain. The surrounding hills and rivers are popular with all who wish to get away from the more crowded and busier side of the Rimutaka range.

About 60 km (37 miles) southwest of Martinborough the rough windswept coast of **Cape Palliser ㉜** stretches north to Castle Point. From Lake Ferry, a scenic drive down the twisting Cape Palliser Road, followed by a walk along a dirt track, will lead to the strange **Putangirua Pinnacles**. Here, rain and floods have washed away the silt to expose a series of rock spires reaching up to 50 metres (164 ft) in height. ❑

Map on page 200

Masterton's hard-to-miss tribute to its annual Golden Shears sheep shearing competition.

BELOW:
Wairarapa's farmlands.

South Island

0	100 km
0	100 miles

Cape Farewell · Farewell Spit · D'Urville Island · Cape Jackson

Golden Bay · Collingwood · Totaranui · Marlborough Sounds · Cook Strait

Takaka · Abel Tasman NP · Tasman · Wellington

Kahurangi · Tasman Bay · Havelock · Picton

Motueka · Nelson · Blenheim

Richmond · Renwick

Karamea · Wairau · Cape Campbell

National · St Arnaud · Lake Rotoiti · Inland Kaikoura Range

Park · Westport · Buller Gorge · Murchison · Lake Rotoroa · Clarence · Kaikoura

Cape Foulwind · Reefton · Nelson Lakes NP · Mauria Springs

Paparoa NP · Punakaiki · Springs Junction · Lewis Pass · Hanmer Springs

Pancake Rocks & Blow Holes · Cheviot

Tasman Sea

Greymouth · Hurunui

Hokitika · Waipara

Ross · 924 · Arthur's Pass NP · Rangiora

Arthur's Pass · Kaiapoi

Lake Coleridge · Darfield · Christchurch · Lyttelton

Okarito Lagoon · Methven · Akaroa

Franz Josef Glacier · Aoraki Mt Cook NP · Rangitata · Canterbury Plains · Banks Peninsula

Fox Glacier · 3754 Mt Cook · Lake Ellesmere (Te Waihora)

Westland NP · Mt Cook · Ashburton

Haast · Lake Tekapo · Geraldine · Temuka · **Canterbury Bight**

Mount Aspiring NP · Twizel · Fairlie · Timaru

Lake Ohau · Lake Benmore · Waimate

Omarama · Lake Hawea · Waitaki · Oamaru

3030 Mt Aspiring · 971 Lindis Pass · Kurow

Treble Cone 2088 · Lake Wanaka · Wanaka · Ranfurly

Milford Sound · Glenorchy · Arrowtown · Omakau · Palmerston

Homer Tunnel · **Queenstown** · Cromwell · Alexandra · Port Chalmers

Fiordland · Lake Wakatipu · Roxburgh · Mosgiel · Otago Peninsula · **PACIFIC**

National · Te Anau Downs · Clutha · **Dunedin** · **OCEAN**

Lake Te Anau · Te Anau · Lawrence

Park · Mossburn · Riversdale · Milton

Doubtful Sound · Manapouri · Lumsden · Balclutha

Lake Manapouri · Winton · Gore · Catlins Forest Park · Owaka

Dusky Sound · Clifden · **Invercargill** · Tuatapere · Riverton · Bluff · Waipapa Point

Foveaux Strait

980 Mt Anglem · Oban · Paterson Inlet

Stewart Island · Mt Allen 750

Southwest Cape

SOUTH ISLAND

*An island of unparalleled scenic variety, where you can sit on
a beach and look at nearby snow-capped mountains*

Towering snow-capped peaks preside over flat, broad sun-
parched plains. In dense, almost impenetrable rainforests, spectacular waterfalls wash into deep fiords. Add to this the rich
farmlands, glaciers of immense grandeur and lakes of serene beauty.
Variety is the catch-cry of the South Island: the boat from which
Maui fished the North Island out of the sea, according to the ancient
Polynesian legend, seems to have captured much of nature's bounty.

Economic pressures, however, have seen steady migration north in
search of jobs and financial security for decades. The beneficial side-
effect, for visitors, is that the South Island is remarkably uncrowded.

The two main points of entry are Christchurch, the very English
"garden city" of New Zealand, or Picton in the picturesque Marlborough Sounds. In Marlborough, at the top of the island, a region of
secluded bays, there are also plains that soak up some of the highest
sunshine hours in the whole country, much to the pleasure of grape
growers who turn out vintage after vintage of fine wine.

Hit the West Coast and things start to get wild; beaches pounded
by the turbulent Tasman Sea meet with the immensity of the Southern Alps. The West Coast is a region that's taken time out from the
glory days of the gold rush era, but has reinvented itself as a tourist
destination where the real treasure is its raw natural beauty. Through
the winding mountain passes the landscape opens up to one of wide
braided rivers and high country sheep farms. Hot mineral springs
seep from the ground where the giant moa once roamed.

Christchurch, on the opposite coast, adds its touch of colour with
parks and gardens, pedestrian malls and cafés all lining the meandering Avon River. Queenstown is the jewel in the tourist crown, its lakes,
forests and mountains combining to make a setting of extraordinary
beauty with a range of adventure activities guaranteed to get the adrenaline pumping. East and on the coast is Dunedin, a university city
where the influence of the early Scottish settlers is plain to see.

Southland forms the base of the island, a region of rich farmland
where the people shine, perhaps in place of the sun. The Bluff oyster, a national culinary treasure, is dredged from the seabed of
Foveaux Strait. And if all the above is not enough, there is Fiordland.
Hardly an afterthought, Fiordland is 10 percent of New Zealand's
land area but has a minuscule .075 percent of its population. Found
here are the renowned Milford Track, Milford Sound, Mitre Peak
and Doubtful Sound.

Stewart Island is the anchor of the South Island. Little known to
many New Zealanders themselves, some aficionados regard it as the
most remarkable place in a remarkable country. ❑

PRECEDING PAGES: lofty snow-covered peaks of the Southern Alps; windswept
waters along the West Coast of the South Island.

NELSON AND MARLBOROUGH

The South Island's northern tip is a magnet for wildlife and offers rest, relaxation and a slow pace, which many travellers will welcome after a bumpy journey across the Cook Strait

Map on page 234

N elson and Marlborough provinces in the South Island lie due west from Wellington and can be reached from the North Island by flying to Blenheim or Nelson, or by catching the inter-island ferry for the 3-hour trip to Picton in the Marlborough Sounds. Either way, you enter a region of contrasts, mostly dry in the east and dripping rainforest in the west. Collectively, the provinces enjoy the highest number of sunshine hours in the country (2,000–2,400 a year).

New Zealanders holiday here in droves. Nelson's usual 50,000 population is said to double at Christmas and New Year. Its Tahunanui Motor Camp, empty much of the year, becomes a small city in its own right. At beach resorts like Kaiteriteri, numbers jump from several hundred to several thousand. Visitors pour into hotels, motels and motor camps in cars full of children, towing caravans or boats, with tents strapped to roof-racks.

Across Cook Strait to Picton

Cook Strait is a natural funnel for the strong northwesterly wind current known as the Roaring Forties. On a bad day, it can be one of the most unpleasant short stretches of water on earth. But squeezing through the narrows to enter Tory Channel in the **Marlborough Sounds ❶** is like entering another world, its sheltered coves and bays beckoning with blissful hues of greens and blues. This complex configuration of sunken valleys has more than 1,000 km (620 miles) of shoreline.

Derelict buildings from the last whaling station in the country can be seen just inside the entrance to **Tory Channel**. It closed in 1964, ending more than 50 years of speedboat pursuit of the migratory humpback whale by the Perano family. Even today, few Sounds residents enjoy the luxury of road access to their homes, with launches still the main mode of transport; even mail and doctor come by boat. The journey down Tory Channel and **Queen Charlotte Sound** aboard the ferries gives only a glimpse of the glorious scenery. The shores invite exploration and are dotted with isolated houses, many offering holiday accommodation.

The most famous of all Pacific explorers, Captain James Cook, spent more than 100 days in and around Ship Cove during his travels. It was on the highest point of Moutara Island in Queen Charlotte Sound that Cook claimed New Zealand for the King, and the Sound for his Queen. A monument erected near the entrance to Queen Charlotte Sound commemorates his visits.

The commercial centre for almost all activity in the Sounds is picturesque **Picton ❷**, near the head of Queen Charlotte Sound. Picton is the start (or finish) of the South Island section of both State Highway (SH) 1 and the main trunk railway. It is the terminal for the Cook Strait ferries to Wellington and the base

LEFT: whale spotting along the Kaikoura coast.
BELOW: idyllic Queen Charlotte Sound.

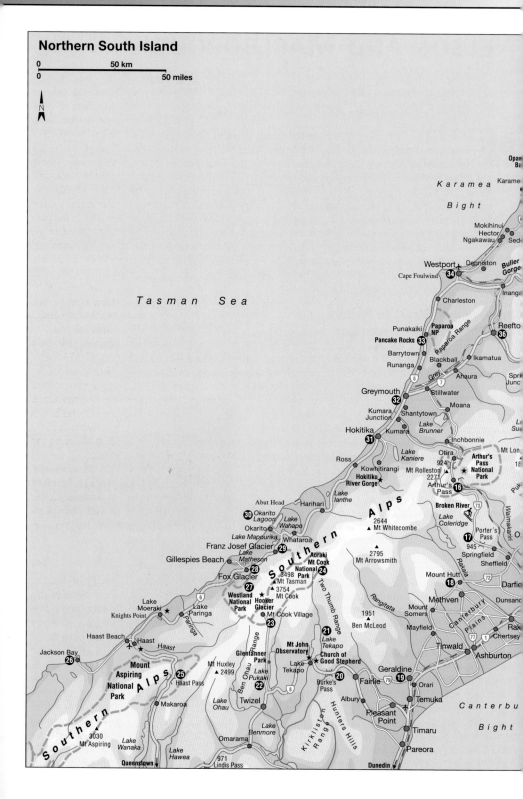

Northern South Island

0 _____ 50 km
0 _____ 50 miles

N

Tasman Sea

Opar
Ba

Karamea Karame

Bight

Mokihinui
Hector
Ngakawau Sed

Westport Denniston Buller
Gorge
Cape Foulwind **34**

Charleston Inanga

Punakaiki Paparoa Reefto
Pancake Rocks **33** NP **36**

Barrytown Blackball Ikamatua Spr
Runanga Grey Ahaura Junc

Greymouth Stillwater
32
Kumara Moana
Junction Shantytown L
Lake Su
Hokitika Kumara Brunner
31
Inchbonnie
Ross Lake
Kaniere Otira Mt Lon
924 Arthur's 18
Kowhitirangi Mt Rolleston Pass
Hokitiku 2271 National
River Gorge Arthur's Park
Lake Pass **16**
Ianthe
Abut Head Harihari Broken River **73**

Okarito Southern Lake
30 Lagoon Alps Coleridge Porter's
Okarito Lake 2644 Pass
Wahapo Mt Whitecombe **17**
Lake Mapourika Whataroa 945
Franz Josef Glacier **29** Springfield
Lake 2795 Sheffield
Gillespies Beach Matheson Aoraki Mt Arrowsmith
Mt Cook **72**
Fox Glacier **28** National Mount Hutt Darfie
3498 Park **24** **18**
27 Mt Tasman
Westland 3754 Two Methven Dunsan
National Hooker Mt Cook Thumb Mount
Lake Park Glacier Range Somers Canterbury
Moeraki Lake Mt Cook Village Rangitata Mayfield Plains Rak
Knights Point Paringa **23** 1951 Tinwald Chertsey
Ben McLeod **77** **1**
Haast Beach Haast **21** Lake Ashburton
26 Jackson Bay Haast Lake Tekapo Geraldine
Mt John **20** **19**
Glentanner Observatory Fairlie **79** Orari
Park Church of Temuka
Mount Mt Huxley Good Stepherd Burke's
Aspiring **25** 2499 Lake Pass Albury *Canterbu*
National Haast Pass Tekapo Pleasant
Park **22** Point *Bight*
Twizel Timaru
Makaroa Lake
3030 Ohau Pareora
Mt Aspiring Lake
Lake Benmore
Wanaka Omarama
Lake Kirkliston
971 Hawea Range
Queenstown Lindis Pass Dunedin

Southern Alps
Ben Ohau Range
Hunters Hills

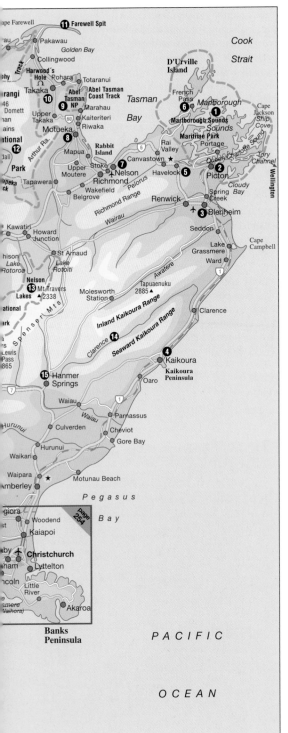

for the assorted launches, water taxis and charter boats on which locals and visitors rely for transport.

An old trading scow, the *Echo*, usually drawn up on the beach on one side of Picton's bay, was one of the last of New Zealand's old trading scows to remain in service, and is now a café bar (tel: 03-573 7498; closed in July). Its exploits during World War II, when it was commandeered by the US Navy, inspired the book and later film *The Wackiest Ship in the Navy*. A shipping relic of far greater antiquity, the teak hull of the *Edwin Fox*, lies in the purpose-built **Edwin Fox Maritime Centre** (daily 9am–3pm, till 5pm in summer; tel: 03-573 6868) at Dunbar Walk. Built as a Moulmein trader in India in 1853, the *Edwin Fox*, in her long and colourful history, carried cargo worldwide, troops in the Crimean War, convicts to Australia and immigrants to New Zealand.

For the more adventurous, Picton's **SkyDive the Sounds** (tel: 03-573 9101, 0800-373 264; www.skydivethesounds.com), located at Picton Airport, offers tandem skydives across the Sounds, Cook Strait and deep into the North and South islands. Its unforgettable tandem skydive from Wellington into Picton has to be the ultimate thrillseekers' arrival.

Picton has several museums, mostly devoted to its maritime heritage. Much of the activity here centres around scenic cruises and kayak trips as well as dolphin-watching expeditions to the labyrinthine waterways in the area.

Blenheim

Thirty km (19 miles) south of Picton, **Blenheim** ❸ is the administrative centre of sparsely populated Marlborough. Sitting on the Wairau Plain, this pleasant rural service town has truly blossomed since the establishment in 1973 of the original Montana vineyards, which are now known as **Pernod Ricard New Zealand** (www.pernod-ricard-nz.com). They are New Zealand's largest winemaker, producing a bewildering array of wines. One of its wineries, **Montana Brancott Winery** (tel: 03-578 2099), is located just south of Blenheim.

Marlborough is one of the country's most important wine-producing regions, with wineries at every turn, including the renowned **Cloudy Bay** (www.cloudy bay.co.nz), an abundance of fine restaurants and cafés, and a great selection of places to stay. The annual BMW **Marlborough Wine and Food Festival** (www.bmw-winemarlborough-festival.co.nz) in February celebrates the vital relationship between good food and wine and is now an important regional staple. The other regional staples – grapes, apples, cherries, sheep – all take advantage of Marlborough's warmth to grow fat and juicy. But nothing utilises the province's long, hot, dry days of summer more than the salt works at **Lake Grassmere**, 30 km (19 miles) southeast of Blenheim, where sea water is ponded in shallow lagoons and then allowed to evaporate until nothing is left but blinding white salt crystals.

Kaikoura's whales and dolphins

The coastline along the southern part of the province, leading down to Canterbury on the east coast, is exposed and rocky. Marlborough stretches all the way down to **Kaikoura** ❹ (population 3,200), 130 km (81 miles) south of Blenheim, nestled at the base of a small peninsula which provides shelter for the fishing boats that work out of here. The crayfish or rock lobster which they pursue on this rocky coast is sold freshly cooked from numerous roadside stalls.

But more important now to Kaikoura's economy are the visitors who come to see the sperm whales which congregate a few kilometres offshore. The sonar "clicks" from the submerged animals, in depths of a kilometre or more, chasing giant squid, are tracked by a sensitive hydrophone, so the boat can be positioned roughly where the whale will resurface to loll about for around 10 minutes, taking breaths before

Whales can be identified by their tails when they lift their flukes high into the air and slam them down on the water. This incredible manoeuvre can be witnessed regularly at Kaikoura.

BELOW:
a Blenheim vineyard.

Map on page 234

it "sounds" again. The best part is when the leviathan throws up its big flukes and disappears. The 2½-hour long tours, available throughout the year, are operated by **Whale Watch Kaikoura** (tel: 03-319 6767; www.whalewatch.co.nz).

It's ironic that this quaint seaside town, founded on the killing of whales over a century ago, should find new prosperity showing them off. Whale-watching trips can also be taken in a light plane (Wings Over Whales, tel: 03-319 6558; or Kaikoura Aero Club, tel: 03-319 6579), or helicopter (tel: 03-319 6609; www.world ofwhales.co.nz). The Maori-run whale watching business has provided a big boost for the town and it's now a worthy stopover activity on any journey in the area.

Another of Kaikoura's attractions is also found in its waters. Dolphin watching tours by **Dolphin Encounter** (tel: 03-319 6777; www.dolphin.co.nz) allows swimmers to frolic in the waters with these friendly creatures. These tours are hugely popular so make sure you book in advance during summer.

Inland from Kaikoura, two parallel mountain ranges thrust skywards, the highest peak **Mount Tapuaenuku**, towers 2,885 metres (9,465 ft). Beyond that is the **Awatere Valley** and **Molesworth Station**, New Zealand's largest sheep and cattle mountain ranch which stretches over 182,000 hectares (450,000 acres).

The dusky dolphin (Lagenorhynchus obscurus), found in Kaikoura's waters, belongs to a group known collectively as cetaceans; this comprises all whales, dolphins and porpoises.

Mussels and gold

The road northwest from Blenheim to Nelson, SH6, takes you 39 km (24 miles) down the attractive Kaituna Valley to **Havelock ❺**. This fishing and holiday settlement at the head of Pelorus Sound is like a smaller Picton without the bustle of the inter-island ferries, but with the same feeling that all the important businesses are waterborne. Pelorus and Kenepuru sounds are key to New Zealand's aquaculture industry, their uncrowded and sheltered waters being used for growing salmon in sea cages and green-lipped mussels on buoyed rope lines. Scallops and Pacific oysters are also harvested here but Havelock is best known for its juicy mussels.

Just beyond Havelock is **Canvastown**, named after the tent village which popped up when gold was discovered on the **Wakamarina River** in the 1860s. It was a short-lived rush, with most of the diggers going south to Otago. Canvastown remembers its brief heyday with a memorial of old mining tools and equipment set in concrete. Visitors can hire pans and still get a "show" of gold on the Wakamarina.

Rai Valley further north provides a rest stop for buses travelling the 115 km (71 miles) between Blenheim and Nelson. A road turning off here leads to **French Pass ❻** at the outermost western edge of the sounds. This narrow, reef-strewn waterway separates the mainland and **D'Urville Island**, resembles more a raging river as it tries to equalise the waters of Admiralty and Tasman Bays. New Zealand's fifth largest island was named after 19th-century French explorer Dumont d'Urville, who sailed through the pass in 1827, narrowly escaping from wrecking his corvette, the *Astrolabe*, when it got dragged over the reef.

BELOW: Kaikoura offers a chance to cavort with its dolphins.

Nelson and environs

Marlborough and **Nelson ❼** used to be one province, but the conservative sheep farmers of Marlborough ceded away Nelson, which was largely colonised by

TIP

A few hundred metres north on Trafalgar Street, at Montgomery Square, is Nelson Markets (Sat 8am–1pm; tel: 03-546 6454), a good opportunity to see and buy some of the region's best produce as well as a cross-section of local crafts.

progressive European artisans and craftspersons perceived as troublemakers. It set the tone for a city unlike any other in New Zealand, a hotbed of creative flair. The acquisition of city status in 1858 served to set Nelson apart from new and bigger cities. Geographically, it has never been linked with the country's railway network, increasing its isolation, although air services have helped to alleviate this.

The city owes more than its municipal status to Andrew Suter, Bishop of Nelson from 1867 to 1891. Suter bequeathed what is considered to be the country's finest collection of early colonial watercolours to the people of Nelson. The **Suter Gallery** (daily 10.30am–4.30pm; entrance fee; tel: 03-548 4699; www.the suter.org.nz) on Bridge Street, in which they are housed, is one of the centres of cultural life in the city, along with the **School of Music** (tel: 03-548 9477) two blocks south on Nile Street and the **Theatre Royal** (tel: 03-548 3840) to the west on Rutherford Street, the oldest theatre building in the country. One block east of Rutherford Street is Trafalgar Street with **Christ Church Cathedral** set imperiously at the head of a flight of steps at its southern end.

At the northern end of the city, on Atawhai Drive, is **Founder's Historic Park** (daily 10am–4.30pm; entrance fee; tel: 03-548 2649), a collection of historical buildings, including a windmill, a 3-D maze, an organic brewery and nautical exhibits in a garden setting. Further north are the **Miyazu Gardens** (daily 8am–sunset; free), a traditional Japanese strolling garden, and a better bet for garden lovers than **Botanical Hill** on Milton Street at the town's eastern border.

Art that you can wear

Nelson's image also draws on its sandy beaches and extensive apple orchards, not to mention its thriving arts and cultural community. Until 2004, Nelson hosted the

BELOW: the World of Wearable Art and Classic Cars Museum.

world-famous **World of Wearable Art Awards** (WOW), an annual theatrical extravaganza that attracts local and overseas competitors. Designers compete to create the most outlandish garment that encompasses it all – fashion, sculpture and art.

In 2005 the WOW awards show moved to the Queens Wharf Events Centre in Wellington, but the creations from previous competitions have a permanent home in Nelson at the **World of Wearable Art and Classic Cars Museum** (daily 10am–5pm; entrance fee; tel: 03-547 4573; www.wowcars.co.nz) at 95 Quarantine Road. Allow at least an hour to take in the wearable art and classic car galleries, audio-visual theatre and illumination room.

Some of the prettiest churches in the area are found in Waimea Plain, at **Richmond**, 12 km (7 miles) southwest of Nelson and **Wakefield**, 15 km (9 miles) southwest of Richmond, where the parish church of **St John's** was built in 1846, making it New Zealand's second oldest church and the oldest in the South Island. Halfway between Nelson and Richmond, at **Stoke**, is the pioneer homestead **Broadgreen Historic House** (daily 10.30am–4.30pm; tel: 03-547 0403; www. geocities.com/broadgreen_house) at 276 Nayland Road. Built circa 1855, this 11-room stately cob house provides a glimpse of an earlier and more genteel era.

Abel Tasman National Park

Nelson also contributes a large part of the nation's production of nashi pears, kiwifruit and berryfruit and the entire national crop of hops. Vineyards in Nelson are increasing in number, particularly in Waimea and the Moutere Hills. Hops to flavour the country's beer are grown near **Motueka ❽**, 35 km (22 miles) north of Richmond on SH60, where large fields of tobacco once filled every paddock. Forestry, fishing and ship servicing are other big local industries.

Map on page 234

Fruit orchards dot Nelson's landscape.

BELOW: Broadgreen House offers a slice of life from the mid-19th century.

The handicraft revival of the 1960s saw the Nelson region develop as an important pottery centre, largely due to the good local clay, nowhere more so than Motueka which is a thriving artistic community (with excellent trout fishing on the Motueka River). Potteries still abound but weaving, silver working, glass blowing and other crafts are also well represented.

Some 20 km (12 miles) north of Motueka is the **Abel Tasman National Park ❾**, with its emerald bays and orange, granite-fringed coastline. This is best savoured by walking the **Coastal Track** *(see page 243)* connecting **Marahau** at its southern end to **Totaranui** in the north. The full walk takes three or four days, but the less energetic can take coastal launch services from Kaiteriteri or Tarakohe to a selection of bays along the way. Kayak trips around the bays, both guided and unguided, have exploded in popularity in recent years. A memorial to Abel Tasman, the 17th-century Dutch navigator who discovered New Zealand for Europe, stands at Tarakohe on the road to the park which bears his name.

Golden Bay

The 791-metre (2,595-ft) high **Takaka Hill Road** section of SH60, which runs west of the park to **Golden Bay**, is not the country's highest mountain pass, but 25 km (16 miles) and 365 bends does make it the longest single hill road drivers in New Zealand will ever tackle. Rainwater has etched this marble mountain into a bizarre landscape of rifts, rills, runnels and flutings. A walk of 400 metres (1,300 ft) from the end of a road up the Riwaka Valley, on the Nelson side of Takaka Hill, will take you to the first visible part of the Riwaka River, where it emerges in full spate from its invisible source inside the hill.

Down a side road to Canaan, **Harwoods Hole** plunges an awesome 183

The availability of relatively cheap smallholdings and seasonal work made Nelson province something of a magnet for people seeking alternative lifestyles. House trucks abound and the valleys of the Motueka River and Golden Bay have attracted many people with ideas about holistic living.

BELOW: Abel Tasman National Park is fringed with stunning beaches.

Map on page 234

metres (600 ft), giving abseilers the ultimate test of plunging into the void. The first descent was in 1957, when one member of that original party was killed by a falling rock while he was being winched back up. After the summit is the hill's hairpin bend lookout, where Golden Bay unfolds before you.

Just 5 km (3 miles) west of **Takaka** ⑩, the town which serves as the gateway to Golden Bay, **Pupu Springs** (also known as Waikoropupu Springs) made world news in 1993 when scientists recorded that New Zealand's largest freshwater springs discharge the world's clearest water – giving near perfect underwater visibility for a stunning 62 metres (203 ft). The effect is spectacular. Aquatic plants grow madly, providing the glorious freshwater equivalent of a coral reef. Further up, at the head of the mist-clad valley, a car park marks the start of the **Pupu Walkway**. This 2-km (1 mile) section of curving, cliff-hugging water channels and aqueducts remains a tribute to the eight men who built it with picks and shovels in 1901 to provide enough water for the gold sluicers below.

The **Wholemal Café** (tel: 03-525 9471), established 1977 in Takaka as the Wholemeal Trading Company, was once the only eatery around. Now it competes with nearly a dozen cafés and restaurants around the bay. **Mussel Inn** (tel: 03-525 9241), about midway on the 30-km (19-mile) road north from Takaka to **Collingwood** (the last town near the end of the highway), is an institution. Owners Andrew and Jane Dixon believe small is beautiful when it comes to brewing beer (their micro-brewery is one of the smallest in the country).

Golden Bay takes its name from the precious metal that inspired the Aorere Goldrush in 1857. Today it is synonymous with the long, lazy swerve of sandy beaches that arch northwest up to **Farewell Spit** ⑪. Covered in huge sandhills and scrubby forest, this unique 35 km-long (22 miles) sandspit, declared a nature

TIP

Rather than mimic classic styles, the Mussel Inn microbrewery near Takaka invented a whole lot of new ones. Start off with a "goose" and finish with a "strong ox". In between, sink a "black sheep", "dark horse" and "pale whale", to mention a few.

BELOW:
Pupu Spring's pristine waters.

Map on page 234

reserve in 1938, is the longest in the world and curves out across Golden Bay like a scimitar, with turbulent waves on one side and vast tidal flats on the other. Built from schist sands washed north along the West Coast, the Spit is slowly growing, spreading, lengthening and widening as the action of the strong winds and currents bring their forces to bear on the constantly shifting sands of this dynamic environment. Farewell Spit is managed by the Department of Conservation (DOC), with strict limits on access. Walking is permitted from **Puponga**, 26 km (16 miles) from Collingwood. Four-wheel-drive sightseeing trips also regularly leave from Collingwood for the lighthouse and the gannet colony near the spit's end.

Facing the raging Tasman Sea, Golden Bay's wild western flank can be an inhospitable coastline, but is always inspiring. From Puponga, the 30-minute walk to **Wharariki Beach** is second to none, with bold cliff lines, arches, caves, and row upon row of massive dunes. The road over **Pakawau** saddle gets you to **Westhaven Inlet**. When it was gazetted as a marine reserve in 1994, disgruntled locals put up a sign: "Westhaven Human Reserve. No birds, DOC or bird brains".

The narrow, dusty road around the inlet affords excellent views. The best reflections are at high tide if it's not windy. **Echo Point** is worth a stop and a good scream for an eight-fold reverberation sound effect. Remnants of the once thriving town of **Mangarakau** give little hint of an industrious past based on coal, timber, flax and gold. Spare a thought as you drive on past the old school house, another closure. Just off to the right is the overgrown entrance to the town's coal mine, where an explosion of built-up gas killed four miners on 17 January 1958, their first day back after summer vacation. The town's fifth miner, who rushed in to help the others, was seriously gassed.

Farewell Spit also makes Golden Bay the world's deadliest whale trap. Pilot whales migrating past in summer get stranded in shallows, often hundreds at a time, when armies of residents and holiday makers can be relied upon to refloat them.

BELOW: aerial view of Farewell Spit.

Trout and trampers

South of Golden Bay, even four-wheel-drive vehicles are of no use. This is the area set aside for **Kahurangi National Park** ⓬, at 452,000 hectares (1 million acres), the country's second largest national park and home to more than half of New Zealand's 2,400 plant species, including 67 found nowhere else. Many people come here to hike over 550 km (342 miles) of trails, the most popular being the 85-km-long (53 mile) **Heaphy Track** *(see page 243)*. This is a tramp of four to five days which starts 30 km (19 miles) south of Collingwood and heads up through the mountains, then down the West Coast to Karamea. Overnight accommodation along the way is available, for a small charge, in DOC huts.

There are other oases, too, for people of softer feet and softer muscles. A restored 1920s fishing lodge called Lake Rotoroa Lodge on the shores of **Lake Rotoroa**, 90 km (56 miles) south of Nelson in the scenic **Nelson Lakes National Park** ⓭ area, boasts "blue-chip" fishing waters within a short walk of the front door, and 26 top-class fishing rivers within an hour's drive. **St Arnaud** village on the shores of nearby **Lake Rotoiti** also offers comfortable accommodation and (for winter visitors) two skifields nearby.

Another route from here, down the Wairau Valley, takes you back to Blenheim, if you don't want to head on to Christchurch or the West Coast. ❑

South Island Tracks

Seeking the great New Zealand outdoor experience can be as simple as a walk in the park. The **Department of Conservation** (www.doc.govt.nz) administers walking tracks, including its 10 best Great Walks, through national parks scattered throughout the length of the country. Behold New Zealand's very best scenery.

Perhaps the most famous is the **Milford Track** in Fiordland. It leads from an inland lake through a deep river valley and over an alpine pass to finish four days later by a fiord. The track follows the Clinton River from the head of Lake Te Anau up to the Mintaro Hut. From there it crosses the scenic MacKinnon Pass and descends to the Quintin Hut. Packs can be left here while walkers make a worthwhile return journey to Sutherland Falls, the highest waterfall in New Zealand. From the Quintin Hut the track leads out through rainforest to Milford Sound.

Due to its popularity you must book ahead if you want to walk the Milford Track. A permit can be obtained from the national park headquarters in Te Anau. The track can be completed either as part of a guided walk or independently as a "freedom walker". It attracts people of all ages, but a reasonable standard of fitness is required and all-weather clothing is essential.

Only slightly less well known, but equally spectacular, is the 3-day **Routeburn Track** that links the Fiordland National Park with the Mount Aspiring National Park. This track was part of an early Maori route to find greenstone (jade). It leads from the main divide on the Te Anau–Milford Highway over Key Summit to Lake Howden before dropping into the Mackenzie Basin. From there it crosses the Harris Saddle into the Routeburn Valley. The highlight is the view from Key Summit.

A very different experience is offered by the **Coastal Track** at Abel Tasman National Park. This 3- to 4-day track idles through bush and dips down into golden sand beaches. The exceptional beauty of the track has made it immensely popular in recent years and it can be difficult getting hut accommodation, so bring a tent. If the tide is in, you occasionally have to divert around the inlets: check tide times in the local paper or pinned up in the huts for details. Bring repellent for sandflies.

The **Heaphy Track**, from Collingwood to Karamea, takes 4–6 days. Most of the track is within the boundary of Kahurangi National Park. From Brown Hut the track rises through beech forest to Perry Saddle. One highlight is the view from the summit of Mount Perry (a 2-hour return walk from Perry Saddle Hut). The track then winds through the open spaces of the Gouland Downs and on to the Mackay Hut. Nikau palms are a feature of the section from Heaphy Hut along the spectacular coastal section, where the track drops down along the beach in parts. This is the most beautiful part of the walk, but again, be prepared for sandflies.

Detailed information on these and other tracks can be obtained from offices of the Department of Conservation. There is no charge for using the tracks and reasonable rates apply to accommodation. ❑

RIGHT: hiker on the Heaphy Track takes in views of Kahurangi National Park from a rocky bluff.

CHRISTCHURCH

The city has always prided itself on its Englishness – and, true to fine old British tradition, among the pleasantly cultivated gardens and elegant edifices you can generally find the odd eccentric

Map on page 248

Christchurch enjoys its traditional pleasures – punting on the Avon River, riding a tram through the inner-city streets, having coffee alfresco in the old university precinct. Such pastimes say much about the way Christchurch sees itself, as peculiarly English.

Yet of all New Zealand's main centres, Christchurch was the first to adopt some rather more aggressive tactics to entice tourists. So now it's possible to take an aerial gondola up the Port Hills, the city's volcanic backdrop. Or shop in one of the many multilingual souvenir shops that dot the inner city. Or gamble in a casino. Or ride a hot-air balloon over the city and plains at dawn. Or fly in a helicopter to sample the French charms of Akaroa, out on Banks Peninsula.

But first, the city itself. Start at Cathedral Square where a lofty neo-Gothic Church of England cathedral, whose spire once made it the city's tallest building, presides. From its base a grid of streets spreads across the plains. The central streets assume the names of English bishoprics – minor ones, because by the time the city was planned in the early 1850s, the best names had already been taken for other communities of the Canterbury province.

At the limits of the city centre run four broad avenues. They enclose a square mile that mirrors the City of London. Within their bounds are extensive parklands and tidy, tree-lined squares with names such as Cramner, Latimer and Victoria. Winding through the parklands and the city is the Avon River. On one 1849 Canterbury map, the river Avon appears as the "Shakespeare" and Christchurch, as "Stratford". Indeed, many locals mistakenly believe that the Avon is named after the river in Shakespeare's Stratford but, in fact, the name is taken from that of a stream, a little larger than the Avon, which burbled past the home of the city's pioneering Deans family. The Avon borders the **Riccarton House & Deans Bush** (tel: 03-341 1018; www.riccartonhouse.co.nz), the Deans' beautiful home at 16 Kahu Road. Guided tours are available (Sun–Fri 2pm; fee), and the 1-hectare (3-acre) property includes the sole remnant of native kahikatea forest in the Canterbury Plains.

PRECEDING PAGES: giant chessboard, Cathedral Square. **LEFT:** town crier at Victoria Square. **BELOW:** Botanic Gardens occupy part of Hagley Park.

Forever England

Christchurch did not happen by accident. A city does not become more English than England without putting its mind to it. Named after an Oxford college, it was a planned Anglican settlement, masterminded largely by a young English Tory with the delightfully apt name of John Robert Godley. Repelled by the egalitarianism and industrialisation of the 19th century, Godley aspired to a mediaeval notion of a harmoniously blended church and state, presided over by a benevolent gentry. He founded the Canterbury Association, with no fewer than two archbishops, seven bishops, 14 peers, four baronets and 16 Members of Parliament as backers. The idea was to raise money and find settlers for the new, perfect little corner of England in the South Pacific. Only the best sort of migrant needed apply. To qualify for an assisted passage to the other side of the world, a migrant had to furnish a certificate from his vicar vouching that "the applicant is sober, industrious and honest", and that "he and all his family are amongst the most respectable in the parish".

From such ideals came the Canterbury pilgrims, 800 of whom arrived on board four ships at the neighbouring port of Lyttelton in 1850. By 1855, a total of 3,549 migrants had made the journey. Inevitably, things went wrong. Dreams of an ecclesiastical utopia crumbled under the harsh realities of colonial life. It was as difficult to revitalise Anglicanism in the New World as it was anywhere else. Christchurch's growth from the mid-1850s became less ordered, less ideal. Yet dreams endure. To be of First Four Ships stock still brings some cachet, even today. You can find the names of those first official migrants engraved on plaques in a corner of Cathedral Square.

The Garden City

Christchurch holds its traditions dear. It has also recognised that its charms have more tangible values: Japanese newlyweds come to Christchurch to have their marriage vows blessed in the Gothic charm of churches such as **St Barnabas**, on Tui Street in the leafy suburb of Fendalton, to the west of Hagley Park. And there are gardens – acres and acres of them – both public and private. On Fendalton Road, the 6-hectare (13-acre) **Mona Vale** (daily daylight hours; free; tel: 03-941 7590; www.monavale.co.nz) with beautiful gardens is a real delight,

TIP

The Christchurch and Canterbury i-SITE Visitor Centre is located at Cathedral Square in the former Post Office (tel: 03-379 9629; www.christchurchnz.net). It is open daily 8.30am–5pm, till 7pm in summer.

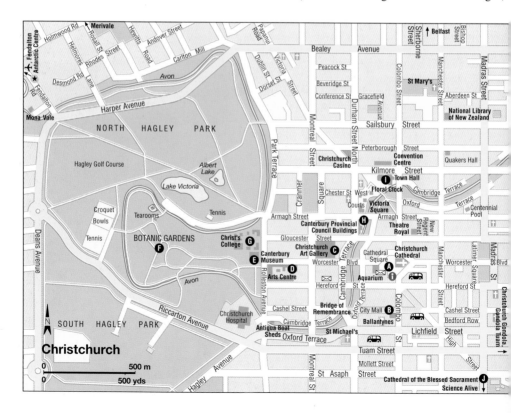

Christchurch

even more if you have time for a leisurely punt on the Avon, which flows through the grounds. The "Garden City" label became official in 1997, when Christchurch was named Garden City of the World. Come to Christchurch – especially in late summer – and you will truly see a city that knows how to garden.

Map on page 248

Cathedral Square and environs

Christchurch is an enjoyable city in which to walk, and where better to start than in the heart of the city at **Cathedral Square Ⓐ**. The square is officially countenanced, London's Hyde Park-style, as a public speaking area. Lunchtime on a sunny weekday is best. Star performer is The Wizard (www.wizard.gen.nz). An immigrant from Australia in the early 1970s, Ian Brackenbury Channell has been appearing at the Square (usually lunchtime in summer) to harangue bemused crowds ever since. Dressed in black robes he delivers an impassioned line on everything from Queen and country (for) through feminism (against) to his view of the causes of global warming.

During summer, the square is alive with festivals of fun and food and all manner of stalls selling art and crafts and ethnic foods. Lunchtime concerts run through December and January. Sadly, the square takes on a more sinister tone after dark, when it is not advisable to walk there alone.

Christchurch Cathedral (daily 9am–5pm, 8.30am–7pm summer; free; tel: 03-366 0046; www.christchurchcathedral.co.nz), on the east side of the square, is worth a visit. Dating back to the mid-19th century, it is one of the southern hemisphere's finest neo-Gothic churches. Building began in 1864 but was halted soon after due to a lack of funds. Some argued that the Church had better things to spend its money on – a recurring theme in New Zealand ecclesiastical building

The Wizard of Christchurch – catch him in action at the Cathedral Square.

BELOW: landmark Christchurch Cathedral.

BELOW: exterior of
Christchurch Art
Gallery.

history – and construction only began again when the bishop of the time promised to contribute some of his own salary. The cathedral was finally completed in 1904. A visitors centre was added 90 years later. For a small admission fee, climb the 134 steps up the tower past the belfry for a breathtaking view of the city.

West across the Square is the **Southern Encounter Aquarium** (daily 9am–5.30pm, last entry 4.30pm; entrance fee; tel: 03-359 0581; www.southern encounter.co.nz), a walk-through, hands-on-style aquarium and kiwi display. South down Colombo Street is **Ballantynes**, on the corner of the **City Mall B** pedestrian precinct. It is the establishment department store, Christchurch's Harrods if you like. The assistants dress in black and are notoriously helpful.

A walk down City Mall – prime Christchurch shopping territory– takes you to the **Bridge of Remembrance**, under which much water has flowed since it was opened on 11 November 1924. From here, just a short stroll along the river south of the bridge, on the corner of Oxford Terrace and Durham streets, stands the Anglican **St Michael and All Angels Church**. Completed in 1872, this historic church is built entirely of native wood and ranks among the largest timber Victorian Gothic churches in the world. The belfry, which stands apart from the church, houses the bell brought out from England with the first four ships.

The heart of Christchurch

North along the Avon up Cambridge Terrace, the city's old library, a small, architectural gem, is on the left. Like many others, the building has been carefully restored and now houses offices. A little further on is **Worcester Boulevard**, route of the restored trams. At the corner of Montreal Street stands the **Christchurch Art Gallery C** (daily 10am–5pm, Wed till 9pm; free; tel: 03-941 7300; www.christ

churchartgallery.org.nz), a stunning glass-and-steel building, designed by the Buchan Group, houses an impressive collection of New Zealand art.

Continue down Worcester Boulevard and you will come to the **Christchurch Arts Centre D** (daily 9.30am–5pm; free; tel: 03-366 0989; www.artscentre. org.nz). A mass of dreaming spires, turrets and cloisters, this was once the site of the University of Canterbury. When the university moved to more spacious grounds in the suburbs, the site was dedicated to arts and crafts studios, theatres, restaurants and apartments, all nestled within the granite Gothic shells. The centre is home to the **Court Theatre** (tel: 03-963 0870; www.courttheatre. org.nz), a professional company long established as one of New Zealand's best.

This is the heart of old Christchurch. Directly across Rolleston Avenue is another Gothic structure, designed by the country's most distinguished Victorian architect, Benjamin W. Mountfort (1825–98). Opened in 1878, this significant landmark was designed to house the **Canterbury Museum E** (daily 9am–5.30pm in summer, till 5pm in winter; free; tel: 03-366 5000; www.canterbury museum.com). Besides displays exploring Canterbury's pre-European and pioneer history and showcasing a fine collection of European decorative art and costume, the museum also devotes space to the discovery and exploration of Antarctica, and to **Discovery** (entrance fee), the museum's natural history centre for children.

Beyond, moving further into Hagley Park, the 30-hectare (74-acre) **Botanic Gardens F** (daily 7am–sunset; free; tel: 03-941 6840; www.ccc.govt.nz/parks) are a truly splendid celebration of the city's gardening heritage, from English herbaceous borders to native sections and glasshouses of subtropical and desert specimens. Considered one of the top botanic gardens in the world, the gardens are enclosed within a loop of the Avon River as it winds through the 161-

Juggler in drag at the Christchurch Arts Centre.

BELOW: Polynesian cultural performance at the the Christchurch Arts Centre.

TIP

The Christchurch
Trams (daily 9am–9pm
Nov–Mar, 9am–6pm
Apr–Oct; tel: 03-366
7830; www.tram.co.
nz), restored after a
43-year absence, have
been plying their 2.5-
km (1½-mile) circuit
since 1995. You can
get on and off at any
of the nine stops as
the trams loop around
the central city.

BELOW:
the Christchurch
Tramway.

hectare (500-acre) **Hagley Park**. The park, originally set aside to separate city and farmland, also includes a golf course, playing fields and tennis courts.

Immediately north along Rolleston Avenue is **Christ's College ❻**, a very Anglican, English public school for boys. The buildings, old and new, are marvellous. Guided tours are available from October to mid-April (Mon, Wed and Fri 10am; fee; book at the college office). Head back to town down Armagh Street and you'll pass **Cranmer Square**. On the far side is the former **Christchurch Normal School**, built in 1878 to provide trainee teachers with a "normal" school environment in which to observe experienced teachers in a classroom situation. Long since deserted by educationalists, the building is now known as **Cranmer Courts**, and houses luxury apartments.

Further along Armagh Street, on the Durham Street corner, stand the old **Canterbury Provincial Council Buildings ❼** (Mon–Sat 10.30am–3pm; donation requested), occupied in part by an establishment worthy of patronage, the **Belgian Beer Café Torenhof** (tel: 03-377 1007). Constructed between 1858 and 1865, these Gothic Revival-style buildings are the work of Benjamin Mountfort.

Architectural triumphs

Continue east along Armagh Street to **Victoria Square**. Once the city's market place, it is now a restful expanse of green anchored by the **Town Hall ❶**. Opened in 1972, after the city had dithered for 122 years over a civic centre, the Town Hall remains the pride of modern Christchurch. Designed by local architects Warren and Mahoney, it is restrained and elegant, with an auditorium, concert chamber, conference rooms and a restaurant overlooking the Avon River and square.

The Town Hall has been linked to one of the city's newer architectural features,

the **Crowne Plaza Hotel**, and via an overhead walkway to a new convention centre for the city. Just another block away on Victoria Street stands **Christchurch Casino** (tel: 0800-227 446; www.christchurchcasino.co.nz; dress code applies), the country's first, with its distinctive, stylised roulette-wheel façade.

Further down Armagh Street on the right is **New Regent Street** with its charming Spanish Mission-style façades painted in pastel blues and yellows. The street is closed to traffic (except the tram) and has cafés, restaurants and boutiques.

Map
on page
248

The other cathedral

If you're interested in ecclesiastical architecture, the city's other cathedral is worth seeking out. Two km (1 mile) south of Cathedral Square, on Barbadoes Street, is the Roman Catholic **Cathedral of the Blessed Sacrament** ❶ (daily 9am–4pm; tel: 03-377 5610). This high Renaissance Romanesque basilica, opened in 1905, replaced a wooden church that was moved to a new site on Ferry Road. George Bernard Shaw visited the city soon after the building opened and praised Christchurch's "splendid cathedral". The pride of local Anglicans turned to chagrin when they realised that he was not referring to Christchurch Cathedral, but to the Catholic basilica. The building's architect, Francis W. Petre, though born in New Zealand, was descended from England's foremost Catholic families.

Turn right from Barbadoes Street onto Moorhouse Avenue, where the old railway station has been converted into a hands-on science centre, **Science Alive** (daily 10am–5pm; entrance fee; tel: 03-365 5199; www.sciencealive.co. nz), an interactive temple to technology. Visitors can experience New Zealand's highest vertical slide, sample astronaut training on a human gyroscope and look into a Black Hole – all for the best scientific motives, of course.

Cathedral of the Blessed Sacrament at Barbadoes Street.

BELOW: the Town Hall fountain with the Avon River in the background.

Port Hills and the Banks Peninsula

Further from the city centre in the suburbs you can tour countless streets of fine homes. Christchurch's real estate is fiercely class-conscious, along lines that are somewhat inexplicable. **Fendalton** and **Merivale**, northwest of the city, are easily recognised, with their fine trees and secluded gardens, as havens of the wealthy. Yet cross the wrong street and values plummet.

To the south, **Port Hills** enjoy a clear geographical advantage over the rest of the city. Their elevation lifts them above the winter smog, which can be severe. The **Summit Road ❶**, along the tops of the hills, gives spectacular views of the city, the plains and the Southern Alps and, on the other side, the port of Lyttelton and the hills of Banks Peninsula. There are extensive walking tracks over the Port Hills and peninsula beyond. They range from 1- or 2-hour strolls to ambitious hikes, with shelters to rest in. Ask at an information centre for details. The hills can be tackled by the **Christchurch Gondola** (daily 10am–10pm; tel: 03-384 0700; www.gondola.co.nz) that has become one of the city's big attractions. A restaurant, bar and souvenir shops have been installed for diversions after the ride. The hardier can hire mountain bikes at the summit for an alternative route down, or an exploration of the hills.

There are many gardens in the hills. One of the most notable is **Gethsemane Gardens** (daily 9am–5pm; entrance fee; tel: 03-326 5848; www.gethsemane gardens.co.nz) on Revelation Drive, a private garden that has many unusual specimens of flora. Its little avenues and tiny trellised chapel are worth a visit, but the highlight, the Noah's Ark, is a new addition and a must-see.

It's also worth taking a drive or bus to **Lyttelton ❷**, 12 km (7 miles) to the southeast, the sleepy-looking port over the hill from Christchurch, with its charm-

Get an overview of Christchurch's countryside on a balloon flight. Contact Up Up and Away, tel: 03-381 4600; www.balloon ing.co.nz).

BELOW: Port Hills.

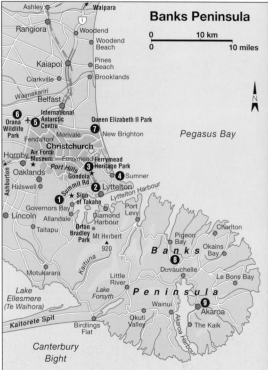

Banks Peninsula

ing cottages that cling to the slopes. You can return through the Lyttleton road tunnel or drive over the hill to the beachside suburbs of Ferrymead, Redcliffs and Sumner. **Ferrymead Heritage Park** ❸ (daily 10am–4.30pm; entrance fee; tel: 03-384 1970; www.ferrymead.org.nz) is a working re-creation of a pioneer village. Members of no fewer than 18 volunteer societies keep the village alive, and tram and train rides are available. A steam train runs the first Sunday of every month. **Sumner** ❹ has the air of an artists' retreat. It's also slightly bohemian and gets extra busy at weekends, when families come to enjoy its golden sand beach.

On the other side of the city, a short distance from the airport, is the fascinating **International Antarctic Centre** ❺ (daily 9am–5.30pm, till 7pm in summer; entrance fee; tel: 03-353 7798; www.iceberg.co.nz), which celebrates Christchurch's history as the stepping-off point for ice-bound expeditions *(see page 258)*. As part of the "Snow and Ice Experience" visitors are exposed to Antarctic temperatures at any time of the year and can explore a snow cave. Generally considered the next best thing to being in Antarctica – if not slightly better because it omits the privations that accompany the real thing – it's well worth a visit. The centre's newest attraction is the **New Zealand Little Blue Penguin Encounter**, featuring the world's smallest penguins.

Nearby is **Orana Wildlife Park** ❻ (daily 10am–5pm; entrance fee; tel: 03-359 7109; www.oranawildlifepark.co.nz), New Zealand's largest wildlife and conservation centre and open-range, safari-style zoo. Visitors can enjoy a hands-on experience with domestic animals in a farm enclosure, but the most attention is given to the rhinoceroses, cheetahs, giraffes, zebras and other exotic species. The park also has excellent displays of New Zealand wildlife, including the rare tuatara, and endangered birds such as the kiwi, kereru and kaka.

Map on page 254

TIP

An extra NZ$12 gets you a seat on the Hagglund at the International Antarctic Centre. The 15-minute ride on 16-seat all-terrain vehicle takes you along on a bumpy adventure course, including an exhilarating plunge into a pond.

BELOW: otters at Orana Wildlife Park.

If talk of Antarctic expeditions and wild animals seems a bit rugged, the rest of the family can take more refined pleasures at the many wineries that have dotted the rural outskirts of Christchurch since Canterbury became one of New Zealand's boutique wine-growing regions.

To the northeast, on Travis Road, is **Queen Elizabeth II Park** ❼ (Mon–Fri 6am–9pm, weekends 7am–8pm; entrance fee; tel: 03-941 8999; www.qeiipark. org.nz). Its stadium and swimming sports complex was built for the 1974 Commonwealth Games. City taxpayers didn't want to be landed with a white elephant, so it's been turned into an all-round family attraction, with wave machine, fountains and a pirate ship, among other diversions.

French-influenced Akaroa

If you have time before you head south to the mountains and lakes, you might want a change from the city lights. **Banks Peninsula** ❽, over the Port Hills to the east, is the best destination for a short trip. It is the scene of one of two blunders made by Captain James Cook when he circumnavigated New Zealand in the 18th century. He mapped the peninsula as an island. He would have been right if he had come several millennia earlier. The extinct volcanoes which formed the peninsula were once separated from the mainland. (Cook's other gaffe was Stewart Island, at the southern tip of the South Island, which he linked to the mainland.)

The once bush-covered hills of Banks Peninsula were long ago logged for timber. There are still some pocket remnants of bush, and plenty of delightful valleys and bays. Sheltered microclimates support many horticultural products and plants that cannot be cultivated anywhere else this far south, including kiwifruit. There are also some keen growers of exotic nuts and herbs in the area.

To experience the real charm of Canterbury, seek out Diamond Harbour, Okains Bay, Okuti Valley and Port Levy. They are fertile, inviting and unspoiled, and in many other parts of the world they would be bristling with condominiums.

But the real gem of the peninsula is **Akaroa** ❾, about 80 km (50 miles) from Christchurch. This little settlement began its European life in 1838 when a French whaler, Captain Jean-Francois Langlois, landed on its shores and bought – or so he thought – Banks Peninsula from the Maori. Sixty-three settlers set out from France on the *Comte de Paris* to create a South Seas outpost. But they arrived in 1840 to find the Union Jack flying. Pipped at the colonial post, the French settlers nevertheless stayed. They planted poplars from Normandy, named streets after places in their home country and grew grapes, but by 1843, they were outnumbered by the English.

The French dream lingers on though, and has been brushed up for visitors. Little streets, with names such as Rue Lavaud and Rue Jolie, wind up the hill from the harbourfront. A charming colonial style predominates, and has been protected by town planning rules. Of most note is the **Langlois-Eteveneaux House**, now fitted out as a display and part of the **Akaroa Museum** (daily 10.30am–4.30pm; tel: 03- 304 7614; entrance fee) at the corner of Rue Lavaud and Rue Balguerie. Churches are also among Akaroa's notable sights.

Christchurch is not without its share of interesting stories. In the 1950s the city was rocked by a scandal that became known as the Parker-Hulme murder – in which two teenage girls of good standing murdered the mother of one of the girls. The story was revived in a play and later a film in 1994 by director Peter Jackson, entitled "Heavenly Creatures".

BELOW: Langlois-Eteveneaux House, Akaroa.

The Roman Catholic **St Patrick's Church** on Rue Lavaud is the oldest in anything like original form. It was built in 1864 and was in fact the third in town to serve Akaroa's French and Irish (hence the name) Catholics. It is a charming and cluttered little building with a noteworthy Bavarian window on the east wall.

The nearby Anglican **St Peter's Church** at Rue Balguerie was built in 1863, and generously enlarged about 15 years later. Compared to St Patrick's this is a more austere building in the Protestant style. Most distinctive of all is the tiny **Kaik**, a Maori church some 6 km (4 miles) south of the township along the foreshore. It is a remnant of a once strong Maori presence around Akaroa Harbour, in a haunting and evocative setting.

In the town of Akaroa, a climb through the domain, called the **Garden of Tane**, is worthwhile on its own count, and will take you to the spectacularly sited graveyard. Its graves must have the best views in the country, and they make up a rich record of the region's history. The **Old French Cemetery** however, on the other side of town, is a disappointment. It was the resting place of Akaroa's earliest Europeans and after a hot slog up the hill it affords a good view of the harbour. But a benevolent government tidied the place up in 1925, in the process destroying most of the headstones for a mediocre memorial.

Akaroa Harbour, on the south coast of Banks Peninsula, is on the doorstep of the habitat of the rare Hector's dolphin. There are regular sea cruises to catch glimpses of the dolphin and other features of the region.

Many Christchurch people own holiday houses in Akaroa or nearby, and the town can become crowded in January and February. There are many bars, restaurants and cafés. Due to the isolation, restaurants tend to be pricey. Fresh catches of fish can instead be bought from the wharf. ❑

Map on page 254

TIP

If driving to Akaroa from Christchurch, take the south fork off the SH75 at Barry's Bay for the French Farm Winery and Restaurant (tel: 03-304 5784). It makes its own range of wines (the chardonnay is excellent) and runs a highly recommended restaurant.

BELOW: Akaroa's well-preserved St Patrick's Church.

Antarctica: Last Bastion For Heroes

Many adventurous travellers, like the brave explorers who blazed their trail, are succumbing to the lure of Antarctica, a continent with unusual beauty as well as unusual dangers. The coldest, windiest and most hostile continent, Antarctica has teased our curiosity for centuries and its short human history is populated by heroes. Those who have been there report awesome encounters with the raw forces of nature, but also times of ineffable, luminous peace and beauty.

Christchurch has long been a base for Antarctic expeditions. Polar hero Robert Falcon Scott spent three weeks there in 1901 preparing for his journey. Today, several commercial operators *(see Travel Tips)* sail from Christchurch to Antarctica and the sub-Antarctic islands of New Zealand. These far-flung islands teem with wildlife and have been described as the Galapagos of the South.

Last wilderness

Antarctica is the last great wilderness, with close to 90 percent of the world's ice sprawling over an area larger than the United States. If the ice melted, the continent would be about three-quarters of its present size and world sea levels would rise.

Antarctica's exploration has close associations with New Zealand. When Abel Tasman arrived off the west coast of New Zealand in 1642 he believed it might be the western edge of a continent that stretched across to South America. Accordingly, he called it Staten Landt, then the name for South America. A year later, when it was decided there was no huge landmass across the South Pacific, the name was changed to Zeelandia Nova.

The next European visitor to New Zealand, Captain James Cook, also showed an interest in a possible southern land mass. In one of the most daring voyages ever made, Cook sailed along 60 degrees latitude and then penetrated as far as 71 degrees south without sighting the legendary continent. He stayed south so long, his crew verged on mutiny. Fifty years later, the Russian navigator Fabian Gottlieb von Bellinghausen circumnavigated the world between 60 and 65 degrees south, dipping to 69 degrees on two occasions, and became the first man to see land inside the Antarctic Circle.

New Zealander Alexander von Tunzelmann, the 17-year-old nephew of a pioneer settler of Central Otago, is believed to have been the first person to step ashore on Antarctica, at Cape Adare, in January 1895. Exploration on the land began soon afterwards, and New Zealanders took part in the explorations by Englishmen Robert Falcon Scott and Ernest Shackleton between 1900 and 1917, and Australian Sir Douglas Mawson during the years before World War I. Scott and his party reached the South Pole in January 1912, only to learn that the Norwegians under Roald Amundsen had beaten them to it. Scott and his team died on their return journey.

In 1923, the territory south of latitude 60 degrees south and between longitudes 160 degrees east and 150 degrees west was claimed by the British, and placed under the administration of the Governor-General of New Zealand. In 1933 the New Zealand Antarctic Society was formed, but it was another 15

LEFT: snow-crusted Antarctica explorer.

years before the first New Zealand onshore base was established on the continent.

In 1957, Everest conqueror Sir Edmund Hillary led a group of five fellow countrymen on an overland dash by tractor to the South Pole. He was supposed to have acted solely as a support for Britain's transpolar expedition led by Sir Vivian Fuchs, laying down supply bases on the New Zealand side of Antarctica for Fuchs to use. But Hillary and his small group made such progress that they decided to push for the Pole themselves, becoming the first to make it overland since Scott 45 years before.

Since 1958, parties from New Zealand have wintered over, exploring and mapping huge areas and intensively researching the geology of the region. In 1964, New Zealand erected a new base of its own, named Scott Base after Captain Scott, at McMurdo Sound.

Care of resources

Five years earlier, the Antarctic Treaty designed to "ensure the use of Antarctica for peaceful purposes only and the continuance of international harmony" was signed by 12 nations, including New Zealand. This culminated in a Convention on the Regulation of Antarctic Mineral Resource Activities (CRAMRA) in Wellington in 1988. In 1991, the CRAMRA signatories signed a protocol that prohibits mining on the continent until 2041. It is probable that mineral-bearing rocks of the sort prevalent in Australia and South Africa are common on the Antarctic mainland. There are also known to be huge deposits of sub-bituminous coal and large deposits of low-grade iron ore. The CRAMRA agreement was an attempt to impose the strictest rules on any possible exploitation activities.

Tourism interest in Antarctica remains strong, but access is still extremely difficult, and likely to stay that way for many years. If it becomes easier, protection of this special environment may have to include stringent controls on tourism. For now, visitors who can't get to Antarctica can get a taste of the continent at Christchurch's International Antarctic Centre and Auckland's Kelly Tarlton's Antarctic Encounter and Underwater World. ❑

BELOW: icy sculpture.

CANTERBURY

This province's flat coastal and inland plains are bordered with mountain ranges of breathtaking beauty. There can be no finer place to be – when the wind's in the right direction

Map on page 234

Canterbury is a marriage of mountain and sea, linked by snow-fed rivers that cut braided courses across the plain. The Southern Alps, Pacific Ocean and two rivers (the Conway in the north and Waitaki in the south) form the boundaries of this eastern province, which surrounds Christchurch. The popular view of Canterbury as a patchwork plain where lambs frolic under a nor'west sky does exist in reality. The plain, 180 km (112 miles) long and an average of 40 km (25 miles) wide, is New Zealand's largest area of flat land. Canterbury lamb, bred for meat and wool, is regarded as the country's best. The Canterbury nor'wester is a notorious wind, a true *föhn* with its warm, dry, blustery weather whipping up dust from riverbeds and furrowed farmlands, blamed for the moodiness of Cantabrians.

The province also encompasses New Zealand's highest mountains and widest rivers, alongside pastoral and forested hills, fine beaches, extinct volcanoes and the sheltered bays of Banks Peninsula. Settlement is diverse, from cities to high-country sheep stations where genteel English traditions are vigorously upheld. To explore Canterbury's highlights, we must first head north of Christchurch, then work our way south.

LEFT: rock climbing at Aoraki Mount Cook National Park. **BELOW:** Canterbury's lamb, reputedly the country's finest.

North Canterbury

The isolated **Clarence Valley** ⑭ is worth exploring for its rugged tussocked beauty, especially upstream. Note, however, that the road, originally built to install and maintain the high-voltage transmission lines from the hydro schemes of Otago to Blenheim, Nelson and beyond, is an unsealed, often steep track, suitable only in good weather. It is not a through road and ends in locked gates at the Acheron River bridge (downstream from Jack's Pass) and at the Rainbow Station over the Main Divide. Hanmer Springs *(see page 262)*, therefore, remains very much a "dead-end" town. Travellers have little choice but to backtrack 13 km (8 miles) to the Waipara-Reefton road – State Highway (SH) 7.

Westwards this road climbs up the Waiau Valley to **Lewis Pass**. This all-weather route which opened in 1939 offers a comparatively gentle, picturesque crossing to the West Coast at an altitude of 865 metres (2,838 ft) through beech-covered mountains. The highway descends to Maruia Springs and then on to the Rahu Saddle, Reefton and Greymouth.

Southwards from the "Hanmer turn-off", as it is locally known, SH7 runs through the rolling hills of North Canterbury to join SH1 at **Waipara**. On the way, sample the fare at one of its award-winning wineries, including **Pegasus Bay** (www.pegasusbay.com) and **Canterbury House** (www.canterburyhouse.com). The road then continues through the small rural settlements of Culverden, Hurunui and Waikari. The road then passes

Choose your poison at Thrillseeker's Canyon (tel: 03-315 7046; www.thrill seeker.co.nz), a short drive from Hanmer – rafting, jet boating, go-karting or bungy jumping.

BELOW: autumn glory along Hanmer's Mount Isobel track.

through Waikari's limestone landscape, where the keen-eyed can detect naturally sculpted animal forms, Frog Rock and Seal Rock being two of the best-known.

A favourite retreat of Cantabrians is **Hanmer Springs ⓕ**, a little alpine village an easy 136-km (85-mile) drive north of Christchurch, nestled in a sheltered, forested valley. The **Hanmer Springs Thermal Pools and Spa** (daily 10am–9pm; entrance fee; tel: 03-315 7511, 0800-442 663; www.hanmer springs.co.nz), on Amuri Avenue, has hot mineral pools set in a garden of giant conifers. Few experiences are more pleasurable than relaxing in these open-air pools on a winter's night, watching the snowflakes dissolve silently in the steam.

A European settler stumbled upon the springs in 1859 and they were harnessed by the government in 1883. Since then their recuperative powers have been used at various times to help rehabilitate wounded soldiers, the mentally ill and alcoholics. The landscaped rock gardens include numerous thermal pools and a separate family area where children can enjoy waterfalls and slides. Several easy, well-defined paths meander through more species of exotic trees here than on any other plantation in New Zealand. This was the first exotic forest established by the government in the South Island.

More demanding walks to the summits of **Conical Hill** and **Mount Isobel** provide magnificent panoramas. The **Mount Isobel track**, which passes 200 different kinds of sub-alpine flowering plants and ferns, is a naturalist's delight.

Hanmer's 18-hole golf course is one of the highest in New Zealand, while fishing, hunting, jet boating, river rafting, bungy jumping, skiing and horse-trekking are also available. Although Hanmer provides accommodation in the form of small hotels and guesthouses, the main street has retained the low-key atmosphere of a typical rural township.

South Canterbury: a touch of Switzerland

Canterbury's finest scenery is inland, along the foothills and valleys of the **Southern Alps**. Three main roads provide easy access to passes to the mountains, beyond which lies Westland. Northernmost is the aforementioned Lewis Pass, central is spectacular Arthur's Pass and the surrounding national park of the same name; southernmost is Burke's Pass, which leads to the Mackenzie Country and the magnificent panorama of glacial lakes and alps of the Aoraki Mount Cook region.

The quickest route between Christchurch and Westland is the West Coast Road (SH73) through Arthur's Pass, which boasts New Zealand's version of a Swiss village. Although **Arthur's Pass** ⓰ township, in the heart of the Southern Alps 154 km (96 miles) west of Christchurch, lacks green pastures and tinkling cowbells, it does have a chalet-style restaurant and a railway station. The **TranzAlpine** train stops here twice daily on its journey between Christchurch and Greymouth *(see page 277)*. For information on walks and climbs in the area, and on weather conditions, call the information centre (tel: 03-318 9211; www.apinfo.co.nz).

Arthur's Pass marks the eastern portal of the **Otira Tunnel**, the only rail link through the mountains. The 8-km (5-mile) tunnel, completed in 1923 after 15 years of construction, was the first electrified stretch of line in what was then the British Empire – a necessary advance to save passengers from being choked to death by the steam locomotive's sulphurous smoke. Today the rail link between the West Coast and Canterbury remains a vital one.

Arthur's Pass is also the headquarters of **Arthur's Pass National Park**. Its proximity to Christchurch and access to numerous tracks of varying difficulty through inspiring scenery, mountain climbing and skiing make the 114,500-hectare (282,930-acre) park one of the most popular in the country. You can also enjoy night skiing on the floodlit slopes of Temple Basin (www.templebasin.co.nz) on the main divide of the Southern Alps. There are 16 peaks over 2,000 metres (6,500 ft) in the park; the highest is **Mount Murchison** at 2,400 metres (7,870 ft) while the most accessible is **Mount Rolleston** at 2,271 metres (7,451 ft).

The 924-metre (3,032-ft) pass, named after Arthur Dudley Dobson who rediscovered the former Maori route in 1864, marks the boundary between Canterbury and Westland, a boundary often reinforced by distinctive weather patterns. During a nor'wester, travellers leave a dry and warm day on the Canterbury side of the pass to descend into heavy rain in the West Coast's Otira Gorge. Conversely, during a southerly or easterly, West Coast-bound travellers leave the rain and cold behind in Canterbury for a landscape bathed in bright sunshine.

Storms are often as intense as they are sudden, dropping as much as 250 mm (10 inches) of rain in 24 hours. The annual rainfall here is 3,000 mm (120 inches). Bad weather in winter often forces the closure of the highway, which in the Otira Gorge is very steep, with a series of tight bends requiring special care in wet weather and in winter.

The road is not suitable for vehicles towing caravans, and in bad weather, it is advisable for camper vans to take the longer, but easier and safer, Lewis Pass route to Westland.

Map on page 234

TIP

One of New Zealand's most spectacular train journeys is the TranzAlpine from Christchurch to Greymouth, passing through farmland, mountains and valleys. The 233-km (145-mile) long journey takes 4½ hours. Contact Tranz Scenic at tel: 04-495 0775, 0800-872 462; www.tranzscenic.co.nz.

BELOW: snow-clad Mount Rolleston.

TIP

One way to get really
stunning views of
Canterbury is to drift
over it sipping
champagne in a hot-
air balloon, gazing at
the Southern Alps.
Aoraki Balloon Safaris
operate from Methven
(tel: 03-302 8172;
www.nzballooning.co.nz).

Porter's Pass and Mount Hutt

Arthur's Pass is actually not the highest point on the West Coast road. That distinction belongs to **Porter's Pass** ⓱, 88 km (55 miles) west of Christchurch, which traverses the foothills at 945 metres (3,100 ft). Porter's Pass is a popular winter destination for day-trippers from Christchurch who enjoy tobogganing and ice-skating at Lake Lyndon and skiing on the many skifields in the vicinity, such as the commercial field at **Porter Heights** (www.porterheights.co.nz) and the club fields at **Craigieburn** (www.craigieburn.co.nz), **Broken River** (www.brokenriver.co.nz) and **Mount Cheeseman** (www.mtcheeseman.com).

Canterbury's most popular and best developed skifield is **Mount Hutt** ⓲, 100 km (60 miles) west of Christchurch and serviced by the small town of **Methven**, 11 km (7 miles) away, which provides accommodation to suit all budgets. Ski aficionados regard Mount Hutt as one of the best skifields in New Zealand. It has a vertical rise of 672 metres (2,205 ft) and the longest run stretches for about 2 km (1 mile). The ski season is also one of the longest in the country, from June to late October, with conditions that are well-suited for both skiing and snowboarding.

To Aoraki Mount Cook via Burke Pass

Paradoxically, although New Zealand's highest peak, Aoraki Mount Cook, is almost directly due west from Christchurch, the journey by road is a circuitous 330 km (205 miles), heading first south, then west, then north again. Getting there, however, is half the fun.

The main route from Christchurch follows SH1 south for 121 km (75 miles), marching easily across plain and braided river alike, casually belying the mighty challenges this journey once posed for Maori and pioneer. The wide rivers

BELOW:
snowboarder
and skiier on
Mount Hutt.

proved major obstacles to travel and settlement in the 1850s and difficult river crossings caused numerous drownings in Canterbury. Throughout New Zealand 1,115 people lost their lives in river accidents between 1840 and 1870 and it was suggested in Parliament that drowning be classified a natural death! Nowadays motorists speed over the Rakaia, Ashburton and Rangitata rivers without a thought for the hazards that once confronted travellers.

Immediately past the Rangitata River, the road to the Mackenzie Country (SH79) branches westwards from the main highway. It leads to the foothills and the tiny inland country town of **Geraldine ⑲**, 138 km (86 miles) southwest of Christchurch. The town snuggles into the hills, offering detours to an historic pioneer homestead in the Orari Gorge and excellent picnic and fishing spots in the nearby Waihi and Te Moana gorges and Peel Forest.

The road to **Fairlie**, 42 km (26 miles) west of Geraldine, a country town with an historical museum, passes a Clydesdale stud farm and Barkers, the only elderberry wine cellars in New Zealand. The gentle countryside is left behind at Fairlie as the road, now SH8, rises with deceptive ease to **Burke Pass ⑳**. At this gap through the foothills a different world stretches beyond – the great tussocked basin known as the **Mackenzie Country**, named after a Scottish shepherd who in 1855 tried to hide stolen sheep in this isolated high-country area.

Long, straight stretches of road take you for about 100 km (62 miles) southwest, eventually to **Twizel** (www.twizel.com), a town built to provide accommodation for workers on the region's major dam projects, and thought likely to become a ghost town when the projects were completed. The town, however, has defied pundits, and is enjoying a mini boom as it is a good base for exploring the area.

But first, winding across the stark-bronzed landscape the road first reaches

Map
on page
234

A common sight in the mountains of Canterbury is the kea, a native parrot.

BELOW: Canterbury "sheep jam".

Lake Tekapo ㉑, 58 km (36 miles) from Twizel, a lovely turquoise glacial lake reflecting the surrounding mountains. By the lake's edge is the simple stone **Church of the Good Shepherd**. Nearby, the high-country sheepdog which has played an essential role in building New Zealand's prosperity is commemorated in a bronze statue erected by runholders from Mackenzie Country.

From Tekapo the road south continues across the tussocked quilt of the Mackenzie Basin. Winter sports are popular here, with skiing at Round Hill, Fox Peak, Dobson and Ohau, and ice-skating on the lake. In summer, fishing and boating take over. The road then passes **Irishman Creek**, the sheep station where Sir William Hamilton developed the propellerless jet boat to travel up, as well as down, the shallow rivers of the lonely back country. For much of the way, the road follows the course of the man-made canal that drains Tekapo's waters to the first of the Waitaki hydro-electric scheme's powerhouses on the northern shore of **Lake Pukaki ㉒**.

Pukaki today is twice the size it was in 1979, when its waters were allowed to flow unimpeded to Lake Benmore. Concrete dams now hold Pukaki in check, forcing it to rise to a new level for use in hydro-electric power generation. The dams have flooded the once convoluted maze of streams of the broad river that flows into it from the nearby Tasman and Hooker glaciers. About 2 km (1 mile) north of the turn-off to Aoraki Mount Cook is a lookout with spectacular views of the area.

Aoraki Mount Cook National Park

Travellers on the highway that skirts the southern slopes of the Pukaki valley and concludes at **Aoraki Mount Cook Village ㉓**, 99 km (62 miles) west of Tekapo, might catch glimpses of the old road undulating above and disappearing into the surface of the lake far below. But the new highway, sealed with an easy gradient,

Beautiful Lake Tekapo, about 710 metres (2,329 ft) above sea level, gets its name from the Maori words meaning sleeping mat and night. The lake's gorgeous turquoise colour is caused by "rock flour", finely ground rock particles suspended in glacial meltwater.

BELOW: Church of the Good Shepherd, Lake Tekapo.

has halved the driving time to the lodge with the million-dollar views, **The Hermitage** (tel: 03-435 1809; www.mount-cook.com), with rooms nearly as pricey.

The village is the gateway to the monarch of New Zealand's national parks, the **Aoraki Mount Cook National Park ㉔**, where the highest peaks in the land soar above the crest of the Southern Alps. Supreme is Aoraki Mount Cook itself, which until 1991 was 3,764 metres (12,349 ft) high. However, the famous mountain lost about 10 metres (33 ft) from its summit in that year in a massive avalanche. The re-surveyed official height today is 3,754 metres (12,316 ft) which allows it to still retain its standing as New Zealand's highest mountain.

The Aoraki Mount Cook alpine region was the training ground for Sir Edmund Hillary, the first person to scale Mount Everest. The narrow park extends only 80 km (50 miles) along the alpine spine, yet it contains 140 peaks over 2,134 metres (7,011 ft) high as well as 72 glaciers, including five of New Zealand's largest – the Godley, Murchison, Tasman, Hooker and Mueller. Of these, the **Tasman Glacier** is the largest and longest in the southern hemisphere at 27 km (17 miles) long and in places some 3 km (2 miles) wide. The ice in this glacier can reach over 600 metres (2,000 ft) in depth.

Due to its sacrosanct status within a national park, accommodation in the village has been limited. Nevertheless, in addition to The Hermitage hotel, there are also self-contained A-frame chalets, a camping ground, a well-equipped youth hostel and a new lodge. Well-defined tracks lead from the village up to the surrounding valleys. These eventually become "climbs" that are definitely not for novices and should only be tackled with the right equipment, and then only after consultation with the park rangers. Easier mountain ascents are provided by ski-equipped scenic aircraft which land on the high snowfields.

Skiing is available from July to September, the most exciting run being the descent of the Tasman Glacier. As the spectacular upper reaches of the glacier slopes can only be accessed via fixed wing skiplane, skiing the Tasman can be an expensive affair. The Aoraki Mount Cook-based **Alpine Guides** (tel: 03-435 1834; www.alpineguides.co.nz) operates ski trips to the Tasman during the season. The same company also organises guided climbs of Aoraki Mount Cook and mountaineering instruction courses in the summer.

On SH80 near Aoraki Mount Cook Village is a tiny airport from where **Aoraki Mount Cook Skiplanes** (tel: 03-435 1026; www.mtcookskiplanes.com) offer magnificent scenic flights to view the glaciers up close and, on some routes, land on them. The Grand Circle Option lasts nearly an hour and flies first to the west side of the alpine divide to land on either Franz Josef or Fox Glacier *(see page 274)* before returning via Tasman Glacier.

The spectacular views of Aoraki Mount Cook, especially when the last rays of the midsummer sun strike its blushing peak in late twilight, form the highlight of many a traveller's exploration of Canterbury. The mountain, named Aorangi (Cloud Piercer) by the Maori, frequently hides shyly in a cloak of cloud, depriving sightseers of its face. But come rain or shine, this alpine region is ever masterful, ever dramatic, and a corner of Canterbury where people are dwarfed into comparative insignificance. ❑

Map on page 234

The Aoraki Mount Cook National Park covers approximately 700 sq km (270 sq miles), and was formally gazetted as a National Park in 1953. Together with the Westland National Park, it forms a World Heritage Park.

BELOW: mighty Tasman Glacier.

THE WEST COAST

Wild and rugged, this area's inhospitable terrain makes many of its scenic spots difficult to reach: those who persevere will be rewarded with untamed nature at its best

Map on page 234

Most New Zealanders refer to their South Island's western flank as simply "the Coast", a rugged and primaeval region that plummets westwards from the South Island's Main Divide, through luxuriant rainforest hemmed in by a breathtaking coastline. Days can be spent exploring this region, which Rudyard Kipling referred to as "last, loneliest, loveliest, exquisite apart". No other area in the country is so stamped with identity or character. Hollywood may have immortalised North America's Wild West heritage, but equally riproaring is New Zealand's Wild West Coast. In the gold rush days of the 1860s men lit their cigars with £5 notes and dozens of towns with populations of thousands mushroomed around the promise of buried riches.

The hard-drinking, hard-fighting and hardworking men and women of those bygone days have left behind little more than a legend. The entire population along the 500-km (300-mile) Coast is almost back to what it was in 1867, when it peaked at 40,000 – 13 percent of New Zealand's total population. Today, West Coasters number 38,000 – a mere one percent of the country's 4 million people. Old buildings ramble into misty landscapes and rainforest relentlessly reclaims sites where towns such as Charleston (with 12,000 souls and 80 grog shops) once boomed.

Living here is still for the hardy. There are more "settlements" than towns and cities. Along with the mist and mountains, a pioneering spirit still hangs in the air. The Coasters who remain have developed a strong identity, with a reputation for being down-to-earth, rugged, independent and hospitable. For years, they made a habit of flouting liquor licensing laws, in particular that which forbade the sale of alcohol after 6 o'clock, which was regarded as some kind of joke originating from the city. Many West Coasters still harbour a deep suspicion of "Greenies", conservationists who want to preserve intact the area's native forests and birdlife. Many locals, struggling to scratch a living from coalmining and timber-milling, angrily oppose the environmentalist concerns of these outsiders.

Early explorers

The West Coast has never seduced its inhabitants with an easy life. It was settled late by the Maori, from about 1400, the main attraction being the much-coveted greenstone at Arahura, the hard and translucent jade traded up and down the country to make fine quality tools and weapons. Because of the sea conditions along this coastline, the stone had to be arduously carried out on backs, first through a route north to Nelson and later across alpine passes in the Main Divide to Canterbury.

Neither of the two great European discoverers, Abel Tasman and James Cook, was enamoured of what they saw when sailing past the West Coast in 1642

PRECEDING PAGES: climbing a steep incline on Fox Glacier. **LEFT AND BELOW:** different facets of Westland National Park.

and 1769, respectively. "An inhospitable shore" was Cook's description. "One long solitude with a forbidding sky and impenetrable forest" was the view, about 50 years later, of an officer in a French expedition.

So forbidding was the West Coast that European exploration inland did not begin in earnest until 1846. The opinion of one of the early first explorers, Thomas Brunner, who described it as "the very worst country I have seen in New Zealand", only served to discourage others. His distaste resulted from the great hardships suffered during his nightmarish 550-day journey, when he got so hungry he had to eat his dog. There must be something about this place and desperate eating; the last act of cannibalism reputedly took place here in the late 1800s.

It was only in 1860, after favourable reports of huge low-level glaciers in the south and possible routes through the Alps to Canterbury, that the central government purchased the West Coast from the Maori for 300 gold sovereigns. Discovery of gold in 1864 at Greenstone Creek, a tributary of the Taramakau River, would change everything here. Hordes of gold-hungry miners converged on the area from all over the world. New strikes followed up and down the Coast, in the river gorges and gravels, the precious metal even being found in the black sand of the beaches. These "diggers" brought a cheerful camaraderie that gave a distinctive character to the new province. The boom did not last long, but the surviving town sites, workings and rusty relics provide glimpses of that golden past.

A raw savagery pervades the West Coast today. Times of disappointment and hardship are given mute testimony in the tumbledown weatherboard farmhouses and moss-covered fences. Everywhere the sense of decline, not seedy but sad, is tangible. New Zealand's past is frozen here, an unheralded bonus for the traveller in this naturally primaeval and emotionally raw retreat.

Heavy rainfall in the West Coast – some 5 metres (200 inches) pours annually – accounts for its lush greenery and vibrant colours. In fact some Kiwis refer to it as the "Wet Coast".

BELOW: tidal fury on the jagged rocks that line the waters off the West Coast.

Travelling up the Coast

Driving access to the Coast is by one of three spectacular mountain passes or through the scenic Buller Gorge that winds back to Nelson in the north. Snaking up from the Southern Lakes and the dry brazen, tussocked scenery of Central Otago, State Highway (SH) 6 over the 563-metre (1,867-ft) high **Haast Pass** ㉕ was the last major arterial route to be pushed through in New Zealand. It was completed in 1965 and enables travellers to follow almost the entire length of the Coast as part of a South Island round trip. The **Haast Visitor Centre** DOC (daily 9am–6pm Nov–Mar, 9am–4.30pm Apr–Oct; tel: 03-750 0809; www. haastnz.com) near the Haast junction has useful information on attractions in the area. Try and catch the interesting *Edge of Wilderness* film (shown on request) for an excellent overview of the region.

Turn south at Haast township and encounter an especially lonely terrain, crossed by a road for 36 km (22 miles) to the fishing village of **Jackson Bay** ㉖, where it comes to an end. This small community swells during the spring, when whitebaiters descend en masse to the nearby river mouth, an annual occurrence which is repeated beside swift-flowing rivers all along the Coast. Fishing is a major preoccupation in this southern part of Westland. Haast in particular offers river fishing while 45 km (28 miles) north at the quiet holiday spot of **Lake Paringa**, anglers are enticed by the prospect of brown trout and quinnat salmon. Near Jackson Bay are several interesting walks: **Wharekai Te Kau Walk** (40 minutes), **Smoothwater Track** (3 hours) and **Stafford Bay Walk** (8–18 hours).

Eco-tourism is breathing new life into rural communities once entirely reliant on exploiting resources. Thirty km (19 miles) north of Haast, at **Wilderness Lodge Lake Moeraki** (tel: 03-750 0881; www.wildernesslodge.co.nz) in South

Fisherman with his catch at Lake Paringa.

BELOW: Jackson Bay is famous for its brown trout.

TIP

When the rain is
exhausted and the
cloud rolls back from
the mountain-tops, the
air fills with birdsong
and – the sole flaw in
this Eden – sandflies
with their craving
for human blood. Be
sure to slather
yourself with plenty
of insect repellent.

BELOW: Fox Glacier
RIGHT: an ice
princess at Franz
Josef Glacier.

Westland, guests are immersed in the nature experience while cosseted in luxury. For many, gazing up at the Southern Cross and hearing the screech of a kiwi are among the highlights of their stay. In the light of day, there is the Fiordland crested penguin colony near **Knights Point** to visit, or dolphins to be seen cavorting in the surf off **Ship Creek**.

Fox and Franz Josef glaciers

Most of the country's finest mountains lie in the geographical region of the West Coast, comprising that chain of spectacular cloud-piercing peaks called the **Southern Alps**. Aoraki Mount Cook is the highest and a serious challenge to the alpine climber. Dozens of other peaks over 3,000 metres (9,850 ft) are named after early navigators, including Tasman, Magellan, La Perouse, Dampier and Malaspina.

About 120 km (75 miles) north of Haast, an astonishing 15 metres (49 ft) of snow dumped annually at high altitudes gives rise to some 140 glaciers. Of these, only two, **Fox Glacier**, and further down the road, **Franz Josef Glacier** penetrate the lower forest. Few sights equal the spectacle of these giant tongues of ice grinding down through temperate rainforest to just 300 metres (984 ft) above sea level. Explorer and geologist Julius von Haast made the first recorded visit to the glaciers in 1865. His unbridled enthusiasm soon made them known as far away as Europe. Within two decades, guided glacier trips had become fashionable. One old photo of the period shows a party of 90 picnickers high in the jumbled ice. Venturing onto the ice alone has never been recommended, and a succession of mountain guides have made their living sharing their glacial passion.

Years of heavy snowfall high in the mountains caused both glaciers to begin a spectacular advance in 1982. Such was the progress of Franz Josef Glacier that

its sparkling white ice could be seen again for the first time in 40 years from the altar window of St James Anglican Church, which sits hidden in a superb setting of native bush near the centre of Franz Josef township. During the last decade it has advanced 1.6 km (1 mile) down the valley. Fox Glacier's advance has slowed, but it still extends 600 metres (2,000 ft) further down the valley now than it did in 1982, having advanced nearly 1 km (½ mile) in the same period.

Both glaciers are located, about 25 km (16 miles) apart, in the **Westland National Park ㉗**, with its 88,000 hectares (217,000 acres) of alpine peaks, snowfields, forests, lakes and rivers. The main highway which traverses the park's western edge passes close to both glaciers. As well as guided walks on both glaciers *(see below)*, narrow bush-clad roads provide easy access to good vantage points for postcard views of the southernmost Fox Glacier and the more picturesque Franz Josef Glacier from reasonably close vantage points. But take note that the glacier terminals are very fragile, and towering blocks of ice have been crashing down with increasing frequency. It's wise to keep within the boundary ropes. Helicopter and skiplane flights over both glaciers provide remarkable views of the greenish-blue tints and the apparently infinite crevasses.

Two small but buzzing townships, **Fox Glacier ㉘** and **Franz Josef ㉙**, each with a decent range of accommodation and restaurants on offer, cater to the needs of visitors to the glaciers. **Department of Conservation** offices in Fox Glacier (daily 8.30am–6pm in summer, till 4.30pm in winter; tel: 03-751 0807) and Franz Josef (daily 8.30am–6pm in summer, till 5pm in winter; tel: 03-752 0796) provide information about the activities available in the area. There are some 110 km (68 miles) of walking tracks through a sanctuary of varied native forest and birdlife, all dominated by the lofty peaks of Cook, Tasman and La

Map on page 234

The first European to explore Franz Josef Glacier was the Austrian Julius von Haast, in 1865, who named it after the then Austrian emperor.

BELOW:
ice walkers on
Franz Josef Glacier.

WALKING ON ICE

You can't come all the way here and not walk on the glaciers. Guided walks range from a half- to full-day, while a more expensive option is a heli-hike, which takes you on a helicopter flight to three icefalls before landing on a remote spot high up on the glacier for a guided walk. More adventurous travellers can try their hand at ice climbing – scaling pinnacles and vertical crevasse walls. You will be outfitted with a helmet and harness, ice crampons (metal spikes to be fastened onto boots), an axe and a rope. Needless to say, a high degree of fitness is necessary.

Less fit mortals are better off on the half-day glacier walk, which itself can be a strenuous affair if you've never walked on ice before. Dress warmly in layers, although you will be provided with boots, socks and gloves, crampons, a Gore-Tex rain coat and a trekking pole.

For walks on Fox Glacier, contact **Fox Glacier Guiding** (tel: 03-751 0825; www.foxguides.co.nz). For Franz Josef, contact **Franz Josef Glacier Guides** (tel: 03-752 0763; www.franzjosefglacier.com).

If the idea of walking on ice – even if it's not thin – doesn't appeal, hop onto a helicopter or light plane instead. There are a range of options with the more expensive trips featuring a brief snow landing on either of the glaciers.

Perouse. This trio of mountains is stunningly mirrored in **Lake Matheson**, one of the park's three calm lakes formed by the glacial dramas of 10,000 years ago. Just 10 minutes north of Franz Josef Village on SH6 is **Lake Mapourika**, the largest and arguably the most stunning of South Westland's glacial lakes.

New Zealand author Keri Hulme's Booker Prize-winning novel "Bone People" is set in the township of Okarito. The novel examines the lives of three troubled individuals caught between Maori and European traditions.

Coastal highlights

A short detour 19 km (12 miles) west of Fox Glacier township is **Gillespie's Beach**, noted for its miners' cemetery and seal colony. Some 60 km (37 miles) further north on the main road, another detour leads to **Okarito Lagoon ㉚**, New Zealand's largest natural wetland, which covers 3,240 hectares (8,006 acres). It is famous as the only breeding ground of the rare white heron. A sorry census taken just 12 years after the birds' discovery there in 1865 showed only six breeding pairs had escaped the plume hunters. Today, an exhilarating 20-minute jet-boat ride takes nature lovers to a riverside hideaway within the sanctuary to view the 250-strong colony. The Maori called them *kotuku*, the "bird of a single flight", to be seen perhaps once in a lifetime. Okarito once boomed with 31 hotels; now only a few holiday cottages remain. For the more adventurous, guided kayak trips organised by **Okarito Nature Tours** (tel: 03-573 4014; www.okarito.co.nz) are an excellent means of exploring the lagoon and the white heron colony.

Northwards, the main highway of 95 km (59 miles) to **Ross** passes the idyllic forest-enclosed **Lake Ianthe**. Ross was once a flourishing goldfield, producing the largest nugget (2,970 grammes/99 ounces) – the "Honourable Roddy" – recorded in New Zealand. Relics of its once proud history and a replica of the aforementioned nugget can be seen at the **Ross Goldfields Information and Heritage Centre** at 4 Aylmer Street (daily 9am–3pm winter; till 5pm in summer; tel: 03-755 4077; www.ross.org.nz).

BELOW: huhu grubs served at Hokitika's Wild Food Festival are not for the squeamish.

About 30 km (19 miles) north of Ross is **Hokitika ㉛**, formerly the "Wonder City of the Southern Hemisphere" with "streets of gold" and a thriving seaport. It is much quieter these days, but it again exudes a thriving air. It is served by the West Coast's main airfield, and its many tourist attractions include an historical museum, greenstone factories, a gold mine, gold panning and a glowworm dell. The country's best kiwi viewing facility is here at the **National Kiwi Centre** (daily 9am–5pm; entrance fee; tel: 03-755 5251) at 64 Tancred Street. You can view kiwis in a recreated habitat, giant eels (best at feeding times 10am, noon and 3pm), tuataras and various aquatics.

A celebration of the Coast's bush tucker is held every mid-March at the **Hokitika Wild Foods Festival** (www.wildfoods.co.nz). The gala one-day tourism event gives visitors the chance to sample wild boar, venison, huge roasted larvae called huhu grubs and gourmet "westcargot" snails, not to mention whitebait patties. At the other end of the culinary scale, the town's **Café de Paris** (tel: 03-755 8933) on Tancred Street, serves authentic French cuisine and has won a national best restaurant award.

Both **Lake Kaniere** at 18 km (11 miles), and the **Hokitika Gorge**, 35 km (22 miles) away from Hokitika respectively, are worthwhile side trips. If not, 23 km (14 miles) north of the town, at Kumara Junction, the highway is intersected by the dramatic **Arthur's Pass Highway**, another of the three mountain passes providing access to the Coast, linking it to Canterbury. A few kilometres east of the junction this intersecting road enters the old gold-mining town of **Kumara**, from where a scenic detour to **Lake Brunner**, the largest lake on the West Coast, winds its way through dense native forest.

From Shantytown to Greymouth

Towards Greymouth, about 10 km (6 miles) north of Kumara Junction, is **Shantytown**, (daily 8.30am–5pm; entrance fee; tel: 03-762 6634, 0800-742 689; www.shantytown.co.nz) a replica of a late 19th-century goldfield town offering gold-panning and a bush steam locomotive ride to the gold-panning area. Thirty historic buildings include a local saloon, gift shop, bank, jail, church, hospital and school. You are welcome to try your hand at panning for gold but if that does not appeal to you, down a Monteith's beer instead at its Golden Nugget Hotel.

At nearby **Wood's Creek**, take the 1-km (½-mile) walking track around the New River diggings dating back to 1865. Diggers smeared their bodies with rotten mutton fat to ward off sandflies, risking their lives working in the river and tributaries where water levels could rise in a matter of minutes after rain. Take a torch so you can investigate the tunnels.

Greymouth ㉜, 41 km (25 miles) north of Hokitika, can be reached by road on SH6 or, if travelling to the Coast from Christchurch, as the ultimate destination of the TranzAlpine train *(see margin note page 263)*. The largest town on the West Coast (population 13,900), Greymouth owes its commanding position to its seaport and its proximity to timber mills and coal mines. Nowadays it is reinventing itself as the Coast's adventure capital. The pioneering spirit

Map on page 234

TIP

The entrance fee to Shantytown includes a ride on one of its three vintage steam trains: the 1877 L-Class, 1896 improved F-Class Kaitangata or 1913 Climax. The ride will take you through rainforest along a line which follows the original 1800s sawmill tram track.

BELOW: Shantytown's 1913 Climax steam train.

still drives tourist ventures that cajole visitors to try their hand at gold mining, four-wheel-drive bike safaris, dolphin watching and cave rafting. Greymouth is a good base with enough diversions for a short stay. Inquire at the **i-SITE Visitor Centre** at 112 Mackay Street (tel: 03-768 5101; www.greydistrict.co.nz).

The **Jade Boulder Gallery** (daily 8.30am–9pm in summer, till 5pm in winter; free; tel: 03-768 0700) in Guinness Street showcases the greenstone with innovative displays, while **History House** (daily 10am–4pm, closed winter weekends; entrance fee; tel: 03-768 4149; www.history-house.co.nz) features a collection of photographs and memorabilia of the district dating back to the 1850s.

Another of Greymouth's attractions are tours of **Monteith's Brewery Company** (booking essential; entrance fee; tel: 03-768 4149; www.monteiths. co.nz) at the corner of Turumaha and Herbert streets. You can see beer being brewed in open fermenters by coal-fired boilers, learn about each beer's origin and taste profile, and the best part (hic) down a couple at the end of the tour.

A 20-minute drive inland from Greymouth is **Blackball** (pop. 400). This former coal-mining town is enjoying a bit of a nostalgic renaissance. A room at the **Formerly Blackball Hilton Hotel** (tel: 03-732 4705; www.blackballhilton.co.nz) comes with a candlewick bedspread and hot water bottle. Spend the day wandering around the old coal workings or explore the start of the **Croesus Track** to Barrytown. Evenings are best huddled around a fire, sipping Monteiths beer.

Pancakes at Punakaiki

Beyond Greymouth, the spectacular Coast Road to Westport hugs the coastline which, 43 km (27 miles) north at **Punakaiki**, takes on the extraordinary appearance of a pile of petrified pancakes. The **Pancake Rocks** ❸ and their blowholes

A handcarved greenstone pendant. It is also known as jade or nephrite or in Maori "pounamu".

BELOW:
multilayered
Pancake Rocks
at Punakaiki.

comprise layers of stratified limestone. Reached by a short, scenic walk from the main road, the rocks are best visited when there is an incoming tide, when the brisk westerly wind causes the tempestuous sea to surge explosively and dramatically through the chasms, spouting spray through skylight-type holes around you.

Nearby coastal tracks allow you to take in native wood pigeons (kereru) and tui feeding on the abundant kowhai trees. **Paraparoa Nature Tours** (tel: 03-322 7898) organise tours to see the Westland petrels that nest along this sculptured shoreline. Punakaiki is in fact on the edge of the **Paparoa National Park**, where the peculiarities of the limestone landscape continue inland. Here, rainwater has created deep gorges, fluted rocks and cave networks, many still unexplored.

Thirty-two km (20 miles) north is **Charleston**, the once-booming centre of the Buller district, with old gold workings nearby. At a junction 21 km (13 miles) farther to the north, the coastal road becomes SH67, leading to nearby **Westport** ❸, a useful launching pad for side trips to attractions in the area.

Just south of Westport, at **Cape Foulwind**, a popular walkway follows the coast for 4 km (2 miles). The highlight is a view of a breeding colony of New Zealand fur seals. About 14 km (9 miles) north of Westport, along the Karamea Highway, is the deserted coal-mining town of **Denniston**, once the largest producer of coal in New Zealand. The **Denniston Walkway** climbs the high plateau to the old coal town and provides views of the once breathtaking, steep tramway called the **Denniston Incline**.

The West Coast's northernmost town, 97 km (60 miles) north of Westport, is **Karamea** ❸, gateway to the vast 452,000-hectare (1 million-acre) **Kahurangi National Park** (*see page 242*) with its famous Heaphy Track. A visit to Karamea is not complete without a trip to the **Oparara Basin**; an area of majestic limestone arches and caves just north of the town. Westport shop owner Phil Wood and three caving mates discovered the entrance to **Honeycomb Cave**, just 1 km (½ mile) further up from the **Oparara Arch**, in 1980. So far, the bones of 27 extinct species of birds – giant moa and eagles, even a goose that no one knew existed – have been found in its 17 km (11 miles) of passages. Honeycomb Cave, with its delicate straw stalactites, pedestal "elephant feet" and cascades of rougher flowstone, is open to guided tours.

Five km (3 miles) south of Westport, SH6 turns inland (becoming the Buller Gorge Highway) to follow one of the South Island's most beautiful rivers, the Buller, through its lower and upper gorges for 84 km (52 miles) to Murchison. At this point the West Coast is left behind and the road continues to Nelson and Blenheim. The West Coast section of this road, however, extends two branches southward: SH69 and SH65 connect with the Lewis Pass Highway, the last major route across the South Island.

SH69, which turns off at the Inangahua Junction, traverses one of the most mineralised districts of New Zealand. About 34 km (21 miles) south, it enters **Reefton** ❸, named after its famous quartz reefs. This region was once abundant with gold and coal. The other route (SH65) to the Lewis Pass from Murchison joins up with the main Lewis Pass Highway at Springs Junction, 72 km (45 miles) south. ❑

Map on page 234

TIP

If you like seafood, and you're in the West Coast in spring, make sure you sample that scrumptious New Zealand speciality, whitebait fritters. Small but nutritious worm-like fish, bound in a light batter or just with egg, they're irresistible.

BELOW: fur seal on the rocks at Cape Foulwind.

QUEENSTOWN AND OTAGO

Located in an area of spectacular natural beauty, it's easy to understand why Queenstown is unashamedly a tourist town, with a huge range of leisure activities on offer, and great shopping

Map on page 284

A t the hub of Central Otago is the jewel in New Zealand's tourism crown. It has become such a popular destination for overseas visitors that some New Zealanders complain that they can't get a look in. In less than 30 years, **Queenstown ❶** has grown from a sleepy lakeside town into a sophisticated all-year tourist resort, a sort of Antipodean Saint Moritz. Queenstown has been nurtured on tourism and while other towns have struggled to survive in a sluggish economy, it has flourished. Within a radius of only a few kilometres, the ingenuity and mechanical wizardry of New Zealanders have combined with the stunning landscape to provide an unrivalled range of adventure activities.

Central Otago possesses a regional personality quite distinct from other parts of the country. Some of the Southern Alps' most impressive peaks dominate its western flank, towering over deep glacier-gouged lakes. Yet its enduring impact lies with more subtlety in the strange landscape chiselled and shaved from Central Otago's plateau of mica schist rock. In the dry continental climate of the inland plateau, the pure atmosphere aids the play of light, evoking nuances few other landscapes permit. The overwhelming impression is of a stark, simple landscape burnished in glowing browns tinged with white, gold, ochre and sienna. The effect has attracted generations of landscape painters to the area.

Yet scenery alone is not enough to lure people into staking out a patch of earth in what in the past has been an arid and often inhospitable region. Over nine centuries of sketchy human habitation, Central Otago's bait has been successively moa, jade, grazing land, gold, hydro-electric power and now tourism.

Hunters of moa and greenstone

The first humans to set foot in the region were Maori moa-hunters who pushed inland around the 12th century. Central Otago could not offer lasting refuge to the magnificent endangered moa. As fire ravaged native bush and forest, the moa and other birds disappeared forever. Some of New Zealand's best moa remains have been found in the banks of the Clutha River as it winds through the plateau on its 320-km (200-mile) journey to the Pacific.

Towards the end of the 15th century, the moa-hunters were conquered by the Ngati-Mamoe tribe, moving down from the north. This group, defeated in turn two centuries later by another invading Maori tribe, supposedly fled into the forest of Fiordland and thereafter disappeared into the mists of legend.

The victors, the Ngati-Tahu, then took control of the supply of the Maori's most precious stone – the New Zealand jade known variously as *pounamu*, nephrite or greenstone. Hard, durable and workable, it was in demand for adzes, chisels and weapons. So

PRECEDING PAGES: spectacular Central Otago. **LEFT:** jet boating on the Shotover River. **BELOW:** Lake Wakatipu framed by mountains.

desirable was the jade, in fact, that the Maori made epic expeditions through Central Otago and the alpine divide to bring it out from the West Coast, the only place it was found, via the head of Lake Wakatipu to the east coast. It was then "processed" and exported to northern tribes. Today, the same jade is a major feature in jewellery and souvenir industries.

Despite the lucrative trade route, the Maori population of Central Otago was never large. The extremes of temperature (the severest in New Zealand) were too harsh for the descendants of Polynesian voyagers from the tropical Pacific. In 1836, the last few remaining Maori settlements disappeared entirely when they were raided by a war party from the North Island.

Gold in them hills

For about 10 years trespassing man was absent and Central Otago was left to nature, as if gathering strength for the sudden stampede of people and merino sheep that would soon disturb the deep peace. The European era began in 1847 when a surveyor blazed a trail for pioneers in quest of land to establish large sheep runs. By 1861 the new settlers were squatting on most of the potential grazing land, battling ravages wrought by winter snows, spring floods, summer droughts, fires, wild dogs, rats, rabbits and kea.

These pioneers, predominantly of Scottish origin, were just settling in when, in 1861, the first major discovery of gold was made in a gully along the Tuapeka River by Gabriel Read, a prospector with experience of the California gold rush of 1849. Central Otago's gold boom had begun. In just four months, 3,000 men were swarming over the 5-km (3-mile) valley, probing and sifting each centimetre for glowing alluvial gold. A year on, the population of the Tuapeka gold-

In the early days Central Otago was the great divide that the Maori had to cross in order to access the greenstone, or "pounamu", from the mountains of the West Coast. The stone was often used to make "tiki", Polynesian amulets in the shape of a human figure, believed to be endowed with "mana" or power.

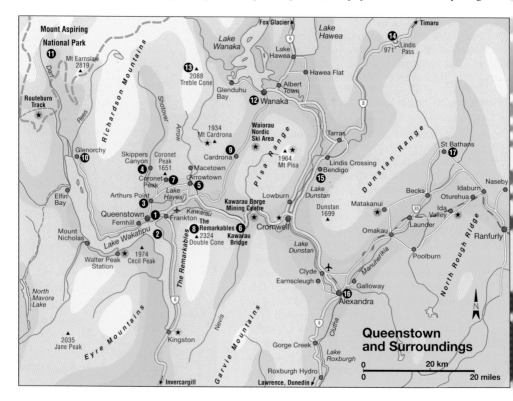

field was 11,500, double that of the fast-emptying provisional capital, Dunedin. Otago's income trebled in 12 months, while the number of ship arrivals quadrupled, many of the 200 vessels bringing miners from Australia's goldfields.

As prospectors moved inland to the then inhospitable hinterland of Central Otago, new fields were discovered in quick succession in other valleys – the Clutha at the foot of the Dunstan Range, the Cardrona, Shotover, Arrow and Kawarau. In 1862 the Shotover, then yielding as much as 155 grammes (5 ounces) of gold by the shovelful, was known as the richest river in the world. In one afternoon two Maori men going to the rescue of their near-drowned dog recovered no less than 11 kg (388 ounces) of gold.

Map on page 284

Adventurers' Arcadia

One of the best introductions to Queenstown is to admire the magnificent views of the town and surroundings from **Bob's Peak** by taking an exciting gondola ride with **Skyline Gondolas** (daily 9am till late; entrance fee; tel: 03-441 0101; www. skyline.co.nz) on Brecon Street. After the 790-metre (2,592-ft) climb, take the chairlift higher up the peak and ride the thrilling downhill luge on the way down.

At the top of Brecon Street is **Kiwi and Birdlife Park** (daily 9am–6pm; entrance fee; tel: 03-442 8059; www.kiwibird.co.nz). Easy walks through native bush leads to aviaries where you will see not just tui, bellbird, fantail and the shy kiwi but also rare and endangered birds such as the black stilt and banded rail.

Queenstown has a wide variety of accommodation, restaurants, entertainment and shops displaying handcrafted New Zealand products such as suede and leather goods, sheepskin and woollen products, and attractive greenstone jewellery. But for most people, these are mere distractions from the town's great outdoors. The **i-SITE**

Riding the luge down the twisting track on Bob's Peak is heaps of fun. But try the beginners' "scenic" route before progressing to the more winding advanced route.

BELOW: Bob's Peak with views over Lake Wakatipu.

Visitor Centre at the corner of Shotover and Camp streets (daily 7am–6pm, till 7pm summer; tel: 03-442 4100, 0800-668 888; www.queenstown-vacation.com) has all the details you need on how to spend your time in Queenstown.

Commercial water adventures on Queenstown's lakes and rivers include canoeing, yachting, windsurfing, parasailing, water-skiing, canyoning, rafting and hobie-cat sailing. Queenstown is also synonymous with bungy-jumping and you don't even have to leave town to get your first bungy under your belt. A short but spectacular jump called **The Ledge Bungy** is found at the top of the Skyline gondola; here too you'll find the **Ledge Sky Swing** (tel: 03-442 4007; www.ajhackett.com).

Some of the world's finest scenic flights, on both helicopter and light plane, operate from Queenstown, over lakes, alps and fiords, many providing access to spectacular scenery and locations which cannot easily be reached in any other way. For those with enough derring-do to dispense with machines, there is also para-gliding, hang-gliding and sky-diving, strapped to your guide of course (the Visitor Centre has all the details). Another unusual air-borne activity is **Fly By Wire** (tel: 03-442 2116; www.flybywire-queenstown.co.nz) where a high-speed miniature plane is piloted along a wire strung between two hills.

More sedate pastimes

But more sedate activities are available around the town too – trout fishing in rivers and streams, or an excursion in the steamship TSS *Earnslaw* (daily 10am–4pm; tel: 03-249 7416; www.realjourneys. co.nz), a grand old coal-fuelled lady who has graced the waters of **Lake Wakatipu ②** since 1912 when it was first used to carry goods to remote settlements. What's inside is almost as fascinating as the views beyond, and passengers are encouraged to view the vessel's engine

room and historic displays. An optional extra is a visit to a working farm in a magnificent location, the **Walter Peak High Country Farm**, where you can have lunch or tea and the chance to see a part of New Zealand's economic backbone first-hand. In summer you can also opt for a wine heritage tour (daily 4pm).

Passenger launches on Lake Wakatipu also take visitors trout fishing. In the fishing season (1 Oct–31 July), jet boat, helicopter and four-wheel-drive excursions are available to remote pristine waters. Perhaps the most haunting body of water in Central Otago, Lake Wakatipu has captured man's imagination with its strange serpentine shape, rhythmic "breathing" and constant coldness. According to Maori legend, the lake is the "Hollow of the Giant" (Whakatipua), formed when an evil sleeping giant was set on fire by a brave youth, thus melting the snow and ice of the surrounding mountains to fill the 80-km (50-mile) long double-dog-legged hollow.

In fact, the major lakes of Wakatipu, Wanaka and Hawea were all gouged by glaciers, and the peculiar rise and fall of Wakatipu every five minutes is not the effect of a giant's heartbeat, as legend dictates, but of a natural oscillation caused by variations in atmospheric pressure. These lakes are indisputably handsome. "I do not know that lake scenery can be finer than this," enthused Trollope in 1872.

Equally fine are the **Queenstown Gardens**, directly

across the lake from the steamer wharf, a tranquil, fir-surrounded expanse of broad lawns and rosegardens that also afford excellent views of Walter Peak, Ben Lomond and The Remarkables. If you prefer a more structured horticultural experience, **Queenstown Garden Tours** (tel: 03-442 3799; www.queenstowngardentours.co.nz) depart from Queenstown's visitor centre, and take in three splendid local residential gardens in the spring and summer months with Devonshire tea.

Outside Queenstown

But for most of the activities for which Queenstown is renowned you will have to venture a little distance from the town itself. One way to combine a little adventure with a dash of history is to take a round trip to **Arrowtown**, 21 km (13 miles) to the northeast. Following the **Gorge Road** north out of town will bring you to **The Rungway** (tel: 03-409 2508; www.rungway.co.nz). A first in the southern hemisphere, this series of iron rungs, ladders and wires attached to a mountainside enables the inexperienced to duplicate the experience of rock climbing. Abseiling and rock climbing options cater for both first-timers and experts.

River thrills

Swift-flowing rivers near Queenstown also set the scene for white-water rafting and jet boating adventures. The latter is New Zealand's home-grown style of running rivers, upstream as well as down. Propellerless powerboats speed over rapid shallows barely ankle-deep. These nifty craft are thrust along by their jet-stream as water, drawn in through an intake in the bottom of the hull, is pumped out at high pressure through a nozzle at the rear. The typical jet boat can skim over shallows no more than 10 cm (4 inches) deep, and can execute sudden 180-degree turns

Map on page 284

TIP

If visiting wineries is more your scene, book a tour with Queenstown Wine Trail, which takes you to premier wineries in Central Otago – like Gibbston Valley, Peregrine, Waitiri Creek and Chard Farm. Tel: 03-442 3799; www.queenstownwinetrail.co.nz.

BELOW: TSS *Earnslaw* (left) on Lake Wakatipu.

within a single boat length. The best-known of the dozen or so commercial options, **Shotover Jet** (daily dawn till dusk; tel: 03-442 8570; www.shotoverjet.com) takes passengers from **Arthur's Point ❸**, 5 km (3 miles) north of Queenstown, on a thrilling ride, swerving up and down the **Shotover River** only a hair's breadth away from jagged cliffs. It is without a doubt one of the more accessible adventure experiences in Queenstown. Free shuttle service from Queenstown is available.

For those who want to be more involved in the action, a 14-km (9-mile) stretch of the Shotover River with Grade 3–5 rapids, depending on the time of the year, is more challenging than the **Kawarau River** to the east which has a 7-km (4-mile) run that is more suitable for inexperienced rafters. Several companies – like **Queenstown Rafting**, tel: 03-442 9792; www.rafting.co.nz – offer trips with bus transfers to the launch point, wetsuits and a brief lesson before you take off.

North of Arthur's Point is **Skippers Canyon ❹**, the very centre of the region's gold mining activity from the 1860s till recently. Also known as Skippers Grand Canyon, this 8-hectare (20-acre) area encompasses a number of attractions. The dramatic **Skippers Road**, hand-hewn from solid rock, is an adventure in itself. Self-driving is not recommended; a sign advises that car insurance is invalid here. **Nomad Safaris** (tel: 03-442 6699; www.nomadsafaris.co.nz) offers daily four-wheel-drive tours into the canyon to the old settlement with a restored school house, cemetery and the **Skippers Canyon Suspension Bridge**, which spans the swift waters of Shotover River 102 metres (335 feet) below.

Gold towns

Just past Arthur's Point the road forks west to Coronet Peak and right to tiny **Arrowtown ❺**. This is the most picturesque and best preserved gold-mining

TIP

Almost no one visits Queenstown without taking a ride on the Shotover Jet. Be sure to dress warmly and get a firm grip on the bar in front of you when the driver announces that he is going to do the 360-degree spin!

BELOW: negotiating the river on the Shotover Jet.

settlement in Central Otago and arguably the prettiest small town in New Zealand, never more so than in autumn.

Arrowtown is home to New Zealand's quirkiest movie house – **Dorothy Brown's Cinema, Bar and Bookshop** on Buckingham Street, which shows art-house films and boasts unusually comfortable seating, an open fire and a bar.

At the end of Buckingham Street, heading towards the river, lie the evocative remains of the **Chinese Settlement**. At the peak of the gold rush in the 1880s, this sad collection of tiny stone buildings was home to some 60 Chinese miners. Their story is told in the **Lakes District Museum** (daily 8.30am–5pm; entrance fee) further along Buckingham Street. This is a mine of information with gold and mineral specimens, miners' tools, relics of the Chinese miners, plus colonial-era memorabilia, a collection of horse-drawn vehicles, a recreated streetscape and a Victorian school room.

Ghost towns are scattered throughout this region, shadows of the calico, sod and corrugated-iron settlements that seemed "ugly" to visiting English novelist Anthony Trollope in 1872. One such place, **Macetown**, haunts the hills 15 km (9 miles) northwest of Arrowtown and is a worthwhile detour. This is not self-drive country but best visited with a reputable tour company such as **Nomad Safaris** (*see page 288*). The town is now a handful of buildings in various states of ruin, yet has an almost park-like quality, partly thanks to remnants of past gardens which have gone their own way. Macetown began life last century as a collection of tents for miners who hunted first for gold then quartz. When the resources were exhausted, the town declined. The last mine closed in 1914, and after World War II its sole inhabitants were two old men.

Leaving Arrowtown, take the Arrowtown/Lake Hayes Road back to Queen-

Map on page 284

Bungy jump off the Kawarau Bridge into Kawarau River.

LEFT: autumn colours in Arrowtown. **BELOW:** Arrowtown's old-world post office.

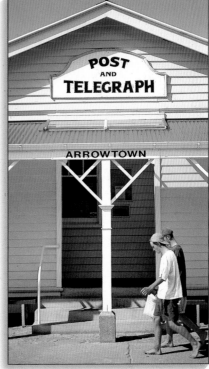

stown. For most of this section of the trip you will be driving alongside the much-photographed mirror-like **Lake Hayes** and bypassing the luxury **Millbrook Resort**, with its Bob Charles-designed golf course. New Zealand's own distinctive architectural styles are visible in the thoughtfully designed farmlet dwellings where craftspeople, artists, and retired folk enjoy a gentle way of life.

At the junction of State Highway (SH) 6 turn left and you will soon be at the world's first commercial bungy site, the historic **Kawarau Bridge ❻**, 6 km (4 miles) south of Arrowtown, opened in 1988 by A.J. Hackett. For those who don't fancy the real deal, there is the behind-the-scenes **Secrets of Bungy Tour** (tel: 03-442 4007, 0800-286 498) at the adjacent **Kawarau Bungy Centre**. This includes a look at bungy-cord making and exclusive access to viewing decks. After taking the plunge or just watching the expressions of those who do, you may feel in need of a little something at the centre's **Freefall Wine Bar** or at the **Winehouse & Kitchen** (open daily; tel: 03-442 7310; www.winehouse.co.nz), a farm-style restaurant specialising in wine tasting. From here, return to Queenstown via SH 6.

Skiing and tramping

The largest ski fields in the South Island are Coronet Peak, The Remarkables, Treble Cone and Cardrona. **Coronet Peak ❼** is Queenstown's backyard ski-field, located only about 18 km (11 miles) by sealed road north. Coronet Peak's ski season extends from July to September (sometimes into October) and is noted for the variety of its terrain and innovations such as night skiing under floodlights. In the summer, sightseers can take chairlifts to the summit (1,645 metres/5,397 ft) for a spectacular view, while thrill-seekers can enjoy a rapid descent in a Cresta Run toboggan.

A.J. Hackett also run one of the highest bungy-jumps in the world, the mind-blowing 134-metre (440-ft) Nevis Highwire Bungy, on the Nevis River (a tributary of the Kawarau) 32 km (20 miles) from Queenstown. The site can only be accessed by four-wheel drive.

BELOW: ski action at Queenstown's Coronet Peak.

The second major ski field is **The Remarkables ❽**, 20 km (12 miles) east, the rugged range that forms the famous spectacular backdrop to Queenstown. Its ski runs are popular with beginner and intermediate skiers but there are also more challenging runs for advanced skiers. The third ski area is **Cardrona ❾**, 57 km (35 miles) from Queenstown, on the way to Wanaka via the Crown Range Road. The highest road in New Zealand, it offers stunning views.

Some 42 km (26 miles) northwest of the town lies **Glenorchy ❿**, an area of exceptional beauty in a region where exceptional beauty seems to be the norm. For much of the distance from Queenstown, the road follows the shores of Lake Wakatipu's western arm. Some 25 km (16 miles) from town you will reach the top of a hill which provides a spectacular view of Lake Wakatipu with its three islands – Tree Island, Pig Island and Pigeon Island.

Despite its pristine landscape, Glenorchy is a hot bed of activity. Kayaking, jet boating, horse riding, fishing, canoeing and canyoning are all popular pursuits here. **Dart River Safaris** (tel: 03-442 9992, 0800-327 853; www.dartriver.co.nz), leads groups on many of these activities, including an exciting 80 km (50 miles) safari by jet boat along **Dart River** between mountains and glaciers, through the landscape of Tolkien's "Middle Earth", before turning round at Sandy Bluff at the edge of **Mount Aspiring National Park ⓫**. The latter is a World Heritage Site and is a 160-km (100-mile) long alpine reserve dominated by New Zealand's Matterhorn, **Mount Aspiring**, at 3,030 metres (9,941 ft). The park and the lonely valleys extending into Lake Wanaka *(see next page)* present unrivalled opportunities for hiking, tramping and fishing in unspoilt wilderness.

Of all the many tracks in the Wakatipu Basin, the most rewarding is certainly the **Routeburn Track**, which commences at Glenorchy. Trailing through splen-

The highlight of the ski season in Queenstown is the week-long Queenstown Winter Carnival in the third week of July. One of the best websites for skiing in this region is www.nzski.com. Also worth checking out is www.cardrona.com and www.treblecone.co.nz.

didly isolated country at the head of Lake Wakatipu to the Upper Hollyford Valley, this four-day trek is one of New Zealand's best, but requires a greater degree of experience and fitness than the famed Milford Track in neighbouring Fiordland. High points of the walk include a variety of flora – and some fauna – waterfalls and rapidly changing landscapes.

Wanaka and its environs

At the zany Puzzling World, your senses will be challenged in more ways than one .

Wanaka ⑫, 34 km (21 miles) from Cardrona, though it dislikes being described so, is a sort of mini-Queenstown, relatively devoid of the bigger centre's in-your-face commercialism and masses of people, but with its own lake, ski fields and everything else that's required of a southern playground – with a good range of accommodation and restaurants. Wanaka's **i-SITE Visitor Centre** (tel: 03-443 1233; www.lakewanaka.co.nz) has all the details you need to plan a stay here.

One of the more unusual attractions is Stuart Landsborough's **Puzzling World** (daily 8.30am–6pm, till 5.30pm in winter; entrance fee; tel: 03-443 7489; www. puzzlingworld.co.nz), about 2 km (1 mile) south from Wanaka. Its main features are the tilted buildings that make up the complex and a challenging 1½-km (¾-mile) maze. Inside are numerous fascinating "how-does-that-work?" optical illusions, holograms as well as the unique Hall of Following Faces, in which faces of famous people seem to float and follow you everywhere.

Treble Cone ⑬ (tel: 03-443 7443; www.treblecone.co.nz) is 19 km (12 miles) northwest of Wanaka. Proud of its powder and the number of international awards it has won, it styles itself as the ski field where the locals go to ski and boasts the longest vertical rise in the district.

BELOW: Wanaka's pristine lake.

Follow SH6 east of Wanaka and head north on SH8 to encounter one of New

Zealand's best-kept secrets. The **Lindis Pass** links northern Central Otago with Mount Cook and the Mackenzie Country and winds through some of the most evocative hill country in New Zealand.

Former gold-rush towns

Bendigo , near the Clutha River 40 km (25 miles) southeast of Wanaka (off SH8), is a dream ghost town, especially when the wind whistles through the tumbledown stone cottages at the bleak crossroads. The southern extension of SH8 is the main artery to the heart of Central Otago. It runs parallel with the Clutha River, past the former gold towns of Roxburgh, Alexandra, Clyde and Cromwell. These prospering towns are still vital today through their connection with Otago's lifeblood: that same mighty Clutha. The river that once surrendered gold has since, through irrigation, transformed parched land into fertile country famous for its stone fruit. Now it is a major generator of electricity.

The road south of Bendigo runs for 15 km (9 miles) to **Cromwell**. This is wine- and fruit-growing country but Cromwell's greatest asset is **Lake Dunstan**, the body of water on which the town sits. The lake is used extensively for watersports and has an abundance of birdlife. In 1993 a dam was built close to where the Clutha River leaves the Cromwell Gorge near **Clyde**, 20 km (12 miles) southeast of Cromwell. The water behind expanded through the gorge, drowning the old town of Cromwell and much of the lower Clutha Valley. **Alexandra** ⑯, 31 km (19 miles) southeast of Clyde, distinguishes itself yearly by its colourful, blossom-parade tribute to spring. In winter, ice-skating and curling take place on natural ice on the Manorburn Dam.

Heading south from Alexandra, there are tiny gold-rush towns, with substance as well as atmosphere, that have refused to die. The original gold-rush settlement – which was then known as Tuapeka, now **Lawrence** – still survives with a strongly Victorian flavour. Pockets of old gold towns are stitched into the ranges, gullies, gorges and valleys elsewhere in Central Otago.

SH85 leads northeast of Alexandra back to the coast through the Manuherikia Valley, offering a worthwhile side trip to historic **St Bathans** ⑰, one of the best-preserved sites in the Otago Goldfields. Among its 19th-century wood, stone and mud brick buildings is the celebrated **Vulcan Hotel**, built in 1882, whose resident ghost is a not-infrequent visitor – after you have downed too many beers. The town stands on the edge of disused goldworkings, which date back to the 1860s gold rush. Contained therein is the **Blue Lake**, whose intense colour is caused by minerals. Ice skating and curling are popular sports here in winter. Another worthwhile destination via SH85 is **Naseby**, a quaint hillside hamlet with period buildings, craft shops, a village green, and the Cottage Garden Café.

Central Otago is an intense experience, whatever the time of year. The area enjoys greater variety between seasons than many other parts of New Zealand. In autumn, poplars planted by the settlers glow gold. In winter, nature transforms power lines into glistening lace-like threads of white across a frosty fairyland. ❏

Map on page 284

TIP

Forty-six kilometres (29 miles) south of Queenstown on SH6 is Kingston, the base for a vintage steam train, the *Kingston Flyer*. This operates between October and May. The return trip to Fairlight costs NZ$40. For more information check out www.kingstonflyer.co.nz; tel: 0800-435 937. *(See also page 315)*

BELOW: foxgloves in bloom.

DUNEDIN

Behind the solid, sombre façade of a city built by Scots and leavened in gold rush wealth lies a lively university town splendidly placed to take advantage of surroundings rich in natural treasures

Map on page 296

Dunedin reclines, all-embracing, at the head of a bay, a green-belted city of slate and tin-roofed houses, of spires, chimneys and churches, of glorious Victorian and Edwardian buildings, of culture, of learning. In the opinion of its 120,000 friendly citizens, 20,000 of whom are students, this is as it should be, for here is a way of life, a peace and a tranquillity that few cities can match.

The best first view is from the haven of Otago Harbour, the 20-km (12-mile) long, shallow-bottomed fiord where container ships and coastal traders now ply in place of Maori war canoes, whaling ships and three-masters. Around the road-fringed harbourside sprout green hills; among them are the 300-metre (984-ft) dead volcano of Harbour Cone on the steep and skinny Otago Peninsula, and the perpetually cloud-carpeted cap of 680-metre (2,230-ft) Mount Cargill.

A proud history

While Dunedin is still a very proud city, it was once also the richest and most populous in all New Zealand. In the 1860s, with the discovery of gold in the Otago hinterland and a rush that rivalled California's, Dunedin rapidly became the financial centre of the country. Immigrants flocked from around the world, head offices of national companies sprang up, industry and civic enterprise flourished. Here was the country's first university, medical school, finest educational institutions, first electric trams, the first cable-car system in the world outside the United States, the country's first daily newspaper.

Even centuries before that, the coast of Otago was more densely settled than any part of the North Island. The moa-hunters lived here, often nomadic Maori groups who thrived on fish, waterfowl and the moa, the giant flightless bird. When Captain Cook sailed past Otago in 1770, he missed the harbour entrance, while noting the long white beaches now called St Kilda and St Clair. "A land green and woody but without any sign of inhabitants," he logged. There were Maori there, of course; small numbers of nomadic communities.

Fewer than 30 years later, sealers and whalers gathered in the Otago region. Soon, Europeans were a familiar sight along the coastline, if not always popular with the locals. In 1813, four sailors were killed and eaten by Maori; in 1817, at what is still called Murdering Beach, just north of the harbour entrance, three sealers offended natives and were killed.

Religious fervour on the other side of the world led to Dunedin's European colonisation. Disruption in the Presbyterian Church of Scotland gave birth to the idea of a new settlement in the colony of New Zealand where "piety, rectitude and industry" could flourish. Free Kirk advocates Captain William Cargill, a veteran of the Peninsula War, and the Rev. Thomas

LEFT: Moeraki Boulders are found north of Dunedin. **BELOW:** Dunedin's Scottish heritage is very evident.

*Early Dunedin poet
Thomas Bracken was
so inspired by the
city that he wrote:
Go, trav'ler, unto
others boast of
Venice and of Rome,
Of saintly Mark's
majestic pile, and
Peter's lofty dome.
Of Naples and her
trellised bowers, of
Rhineland far away.
These may be grand,
but give to me
Dunedin from
the Bay.*

BELOW: poet Robert
Burns immortalised
at the Octagon with
"his back to the
kirk and his face to
the pub".

Burns, nephew of poet Robbie, were the leaders. The ships *John Wickliffe* and *Philip Laing* landed 300 Scots in March and April 1848 to a site already chosen by the London-based New Zealand Company and purchased – for £2,400 – from the local Maori. Its first name was New Edinburgh; soon it became Dunedin (Edin on the Hill).

Once gold was discovered inland, there was no holding Dunedin back. In two years, the population of Otago rocketed from 12,000 to 60,000 – 35,000 of them immigrant gold-seekers. Dunedin was the arrival point for the miners, the service centre for the goldfields and the bank for the gold. With all this new prosperity came saloons, gambling dens, brothels and dubious dance halls. Pubs there were aplenty, breweries too. Dunedin to this day has retained a high reputation for its well-patronised licensed premises.

For a quarter of a century, Dunedin boomed. And where Dunedin went, the rest of New Zealand followed, until the gold ran out. Gradually, commercial and climatic attractions in the north led to the decline of the southern cities and provinces. For the past few decades, Dunedin has fought the inevitable drift north. Its greatly expanded university – now with more than 17,000 students – together with the College of Education for training schoolteachers and the Otago Polytechnic, pour over 20,000 youngsters into the Dunedin community, consolidating Dunedin's place as a leading city of learning in New Zealand.

Tartan town

Dunedin is known as New Zealand's Scottish city and its Victorian city. A giant statue of Scottish poet Robbie Burns sits in the town centre, fittingly with the bard's back to the Anglican St Paul's Cathedral, and facing what was formerly

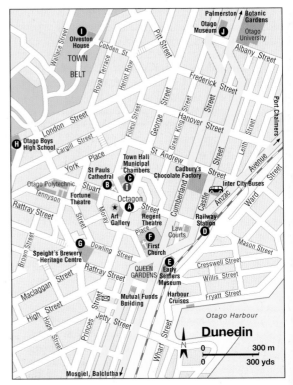

a corner pub. Here too are the country's only kilt manufacturer, lots of highland pipe bands and regularly celebrated Burns' Nights.

But Dunedin folk are a little weary of continual references to the "Edinburgh of the South" and "Victorian City"; there are equally fine examples of Edwardian and later-style buildings that qualify the city as the most architecturally interesting and diverse in the country. The range is delightful, from full-fashioned ornate Victoriana through Edwardian splendour to impressive art deco and modern concrete-and-glass structures that have won national awards.

Map on page 296

Around the Octagon

To explore Dunedin, start in the **Octagon Ⓐ**, which links Princes and George streets in the centre. Tall, leafy trees and grass plots bordered by historic buildings make this a popular lunch spot. Immediately west is the **Dunedin Public Art Gallery** (daily 10am–5pm; tel: 03-477 4000; www.dunedin.art.museum), the oldest in New Zealand. It houses one of the country's finest collections with works by Van der Velden, Frances Hodgkins, Constable, Gainsborough, Monet, Pissaro and Reynolds.

Just north of the gallery is **St Paul's Anglican Cathedral Ⓑ** (tel: 03-477 4931), its Gothic Revival pillars rising 40 metres (130 ft) to support the only stone-vaulted nave roof in New Zealand. Built between 1915 and 1919, it is constructed entirely of stone quarried from nearby Oamaru.

Next door to St Paul's are the century-old **Municipal Chambers Ⓒ**, which were designed by the noted colonial architect Robert Lawson, and behind it the 2,280-seat **Town Hall**, which was once the largest in the country. The Chambers, also built from Oamaru stone, have been replaced by the adjacent **Civic Centre**

Close-up of the Oamaru stone used in the consruction of St Paul's Cathedral.

BELOW: the Municipal Chambers with St Paul's Cathedral on the left.

Stained-glass window detail from the landmark Dunedin Railway Station.

BELOW: Dunedin Railway Station.

as local government offices, although the modern, stepped design of the latter has drawn criticism for its contrast with the Victorian-era Municipal Chambers. The city's **i-SITE Visitor Centre** (tel: 03-474 3300; www.cityofdunedin. com), as well as conference facilities, are housed in the Municipal Chambers, whose imposing clock tower and spire were re-erected in 1989 amid an overall spring-cleaning of the city centre. Moving east, down Lower Stuart Street, look out for classic old buildings such as the Allied Press newspaper offices, the law courts and the police station, which are excellent examples of art in stone.

Near the junction of Castle Street and Anzac Avenue is the **Dunedin Railway Station ➌**, perhaps the finest stone structure in the country. It earned designer George Troup a knighthood and the nickname "Gingerbread George". Built between 1904 and 1906 in the Flemish Renaissance style, it has a 37-metre (121-ft) high square tower, three huge clock faces and a covered carriageway projecting from the arched colonnade. In the main foyer is a mosaic-tiled floor with nine central panels showing a small English "Puffing Billy". The original floor consisted of 725,760 half-inch Royal Doulton porcelain squares. Other ornamentation in the station is in original Doulton china and stained glass. From here, trains to the spectacular Taieri River Gorge *(see page 303)* and beyond depart daily.

On the first floor of the station is the **New Zealand Sports Hall of Fame** (daily 10am–4pm; entrance fee; tel: 03-477 7775; www.nzhalloffame.co.nz), the national sports museum that pays tribute to that great New Zealand obsession with a dizzying array of memorabilia and exhibits – such as the arm guard All Blacks rugby player Colin Meads wore when he played a test match with a broken arm.

Maybe it's not surprising that Dunedin has such a remarkable railway station, as the city has a fascination with trains. *Josephine*, one of the country's first

steam engines (a double-boiler, double-facing Fairlie) is protected in a glass case on display beside the **Otago Settlers Museum** (daily 10am–5pm; entrance fee; tel: 03-477 5052; www.settlers.museum) at 31 Queens Gardens. Also on show is *JA1274*, the last Dunedin-made steam locomotive to haul the main trunk-line trains.

Other city highlights

The country's first skyscraper, the **Mutual Funds Building** (1910), stands near the station, close to the original centre of Dunedin, the Stock Exchange area. Land reclamation has since pushed back the harbour edge with a proliferation of fine old office buildings, but movement of the city centre north has forced many into use as storage areas and some into demolition. A gargoyled "bride's-cake" monument in here pays homage to founder Captain Cargill. It sat atop men's underground toilets until public opprobrium led to the conveniences being closed.

First Church , in Moray Place, is another Robert Lawson design and arguably his best work. Actually the third church to be built on this site, it has a magnificent spire rising 54 metres (180 ft) heavenwards. Inside, the wooden gabled ceiling and rose window above the pulpit are worthy of inspection.

Two blocks west at 200 Rattray Street lies **Speight's Brewery Heritage Centre** (guided tours daily 10am, noon and 2pm, plus Fri–Sun 4pm and Mon–Thur 7pm; entrance fee; tel: 03-477 7697; www.speights.co.nz). You can tour the brewery where the beer in which southerners take so much pride is brewed, and there is, of course, a tasting session at the tour's conclusion.

Some of the banks and other churches in the central city area inspire praise, as does the Lawson-designed **Otago Boys High School** tower block, domi-

Map on page 296

TIP

You don't need to be a child to enjoy a tour of Cadbury World on Cumberland Street. It's a slightly unreal atmosphere of tumbling chocolate eggs and giant bunnies, with all the chocolate you can eat. Bookings essential: tel: 03-467 7967, 0800-223 287; www.cadburyworld.co.nz.

BELOW: Speight's Brewery.

nant above the city. It is situated just below the **Town Belt**, a 200-hectare (490-acre) and 8-km (5-mile) long green swath that separates the city from its suburbs.

A walk through the Town Belt offers some of the best views of the city and its harbour. Hear the tui and the bellbird; observe, too, the many wooded reserves and sports fields, fine golf courses, cotula-turfed bowling greens, huge heated swimming pools and fine swimming and surfing beaches.

Within the Town Belt area also lies "the jewel in Dunedin's crown", **Olveston ❶** (booking essential; guided tours only; entrance fee; tel: 03-477 3320; www.olveston.co.nz). Built between 1904 and 1906 to the design of celebrated English architect Sir Ernest George for a local businessman, David Theomin, it was bequeathed to the city in 1966. The 35-room house of double brick and oak is rated the best example of a grand Edwardian-style manor found in New Zealand.

North of the Octagon

In the north of the city are the (almost) combined campuses of the University of Otago, Otago Polytechnic and Dunedin College of Education. Dominating the Gothic rockpiles of the university, beside the grass-banked water of the Leith, is the main clock tower. Just west is the fascinating **Otago Museum ❷** (daily 10am–5pm; free; tel: 03-474 7474; www.otagomuseum.govt.nz) on Great King Street, with Pacific Island and Maori artefacts, maritime relics and colonial-era collections. If you have time for only one museum visit in Dunedin, this has to be it. **Discovery World** (entrance fee) on level one will appeal especially to children.

Also in the north on the slopes of Signal Hill is the **Botanic Gardens** (open daily daylight hours; free). New Zealand's oldest, it covers 65 hectares (160 acres) and is world renowned for its rhododendron dell and its great variety of gardens.

Baldwin Street, north of the city centre, is believed to be the world's steepest residential street. At 38 degrees, it's indisputably a remarkable sight, arduous climb and magnet for innovative thrill-seekers who attempt to devise ever more ingenious ways of propelling themselves down it.

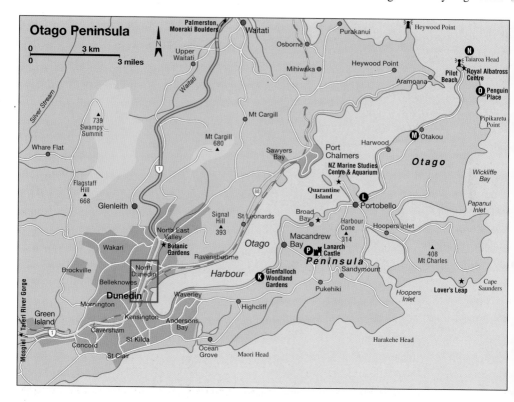

Otago Peninsula drive

To fully appreciate the **Otago Peninsula** and its views of the city, take the "low road" and return via the "high". The following 64-km (40-mile) round trip can take anything from 90 minutes to a full day. The narrow, winding road calls for careful driving as part of it was built by convict labour for horse and buggy traffic. (The prisoners were housed in an old hulk that was dragged slowly along the seafront.) The first sight you will see along the curving western coastline is **Glenfalloch Woodland Garden** (open during daylight hours; free; tel: 03-476 1006), 12 hectares (30 acres) of lovely rambling gardens encircling a 1871 homestead.

The winding Portobello Road runs along the peninsula coast to **Portobello**, 8 km (5 miles) from Glenfalloch. In Portobello village, you can visit Guy Garey, a traditional blacksmith who forges iron in the time-honoured manner at **Chestnut Tree Forge** (Sun–Thur 1.30–4.30pm; free; tel: 03-478 1133; www.chestnut treeforge.co.nz) on Hatchery Road. Visit also the **Otago Peninsula Museum Historical Society** (Sun 1.30–4.30pm; or by appointment; free; tel: 03-478 0255).

Continue along Hatchery Road to the **New Zealand Marine Studies Centre and Aquarium** (open at 10.30am for a 60-minute guided tour and noon–4.30pm for self-guided tours; entrance fee; tel: 03-479 5826; www.marine.ac.nz). Operated by the University of Otago as a marine laboratory, the centre has a life-size model of a colossal squid that is based on the only specimen of the largest squid ever fished. Aquariums are filled with everything marine from seahorses to octopuses. The touch pool allows a tactile experience with the smaller sea creatures.

At **Otakou**, about 4 km (2 miles) further north, is a Maori church and meeting house which appear to be carved, but are actually cast in concrete. In

Maps: Town 296 Area 300

The Otago Peninsula Museum has a collection of stuffed kakapo from the early colonial era, with interesting clippings explaining how they came to be stuffed, throwing light on the bird's current near-extinction.

BELOW: Maori church and meeting house in Otakou.

the cemetery behind are buried three great Maori chiefs of the 19th century – the warlike Taiaroa, Ngatata (a northern chief said to have welcomed the Pakeha to Cook Strait) and Karetai, induced by the missionaries to abandon cannibalism and take up the Bible. The *marae* here is sacred to local Maori and is still the most historic Maori site in Otago. (The name "Otago", in fact, is a European corruption of "Otakou".) There's a Maori **museum** here, but to assure that it is open, call in advance (tel: 03-478-0352).

Just north lie remains of the whaling industry founded in Otago Harbour in 1831, 17 years before European settlement. The old factory is clearly visible and marked by a plaque. Another plaque across the road commemorates the first Christian service held in Otago Harbour, by Bishop Pompalier, in 1840.

Wildlife and a castle

As you crest the hill past Otakou and look towards lofty **Taiaroa Head** , the tip of the peninsula, glance up. Those huge seabirds resting lazily on the wind are the world's largest birds of flight, rare royal albatrosses. Incredibly graceful, they swoop, turn and soar with barely a flick of their 3-metre (10-ft) wings. They mate for life, and up to 30 pairs from this tiny colony circle the globe, at speeds of up to 110 kph (68 mph), before returning here to mate and produce a chick every two years.

The **Westpac Royal Albatross Centre** (daily 9am–5pm, daily 9am–9pm summer; entrance fee; tel: 03-478 0499; www.albatross.org.nz) has viewing galleries and display areas. Escorted groups observe the breeding cycle and the pre-flight peregrinations of the fledgelings. While here, take in (for free) the antics of a southern fur seal colony at nearby **Pilot Beach**, and visit also **Fort Taiaroa**, where the unusual **Armstrong Disappearing Gun**, transported here in 1886 on the per-

TIP

If you're making a special effort to see the albatrosses at Taiaroa Head, do check to see if they're going to be at home. Sept: adults arrive; Oct: courting and mating; Nov: eggs are laid; Feb: chicks hatch; Sept: chicks fly the nest.

BELOW: fur seal on Pilot Beach.

ceived threat of an attack by Tsarist Russia, is found. The 15-cm (6-inch) cannon is hidden in the bowels of the earth, rising to fire, then sinking again for reloading.

Two km (1 mile) to the east, along a farm road, is **Penguin Place ⓞ** (daily 10.15am–90 minutes before sunset summer, 3.15– 4.30pm winter; entrance fee; tel: 03-478 0286; www.penguinplace.co.nz). Here, rare Chaplinesque yellow-eyed penguins strut in the surf and can be observed at close proximity through a unique system of hides and tunnels.

The *MV Monarch* provides a regular service from Dunedin down Otago Harbour to Taiaroa Head, but for a very different view of the peninsula and its wildlife, contact **Wild Earth Adventures** (tel: 03-473 6535; www.wildearth. co.nz), which leads kayak tours, visiting the royal albatross and fur seal colonies by sea and taking in a great variety of other wildlife on the way.

One has to return along the Taiaroa Head access road to Portobello to gain the "high road" back to the city. Up there is **Larnach Castle ⓟ** (daily 9am–5pm; entrance fee; tel: 03-476 1616; www.larnachcastle.co.nz), a century-old baronial manor that is New Zealand's only castle. It took 14 years to build (from 1871) as the home of the Hon. William J.M. Larnach, financier and later Minister of the Crown. An English workman, along with two Italian craftsmen, spent 12 years carving the ceilings. The castle fell into disrepair but has now been fully restored and most of its 43 rooms, including accommodation, are open to the public. The "high road" that leads back to suburbia has commanding views of the harbour.

Further afield

Dunedin visitors should not restrict themselves to the city. Beyond the outskirts lie fascinating sights of natural and historic beauty. Eighty km (50 miles) north are the bizarre **Moeraki Boulders ❶** *(see map page 308)*, huge round stones that lie "like devil's marbles" on the seashore. Said to be the food baskets of a wrecked canoe according to Maori legend, they were actually formed by the gradual erosion of the mudstone cliffs just behind the beach. Over a period of 60 million years, lime salts accumulated around the eroded pieces, forming the boulders you see today, some up to 4 metres (13 ft) in circumference and weighing several tonnes.

Both north and south of Dunedin are areas of immense natural beauty, peopled by relatively few and as yet undiscovered by the tourist hordes. At the **Taieri River Gorge ❷**, northwest of Dunedin, jet-boat and whitewater raft tours tumble adventurous tourists between virgin bush-edged cliffs.

Special excursion trains run north and sometimes south on the main trunk line from the Dunedin Railway Station *(see page 298)*. On the **Taieri Gorge Railway** (tel: 03-477 4449; www.taieri.co.nz), both vintage 1920s wooden carriages renovated by the Otago Excursion Train Trust and modern air-conditioned steel carriages enter Otago's hinterland through the rugged and spectacularly bridged Taieri River Gorge. You can make a return journey to **Pukerangi**, 58 km (36 miles) away or continue another 19 km (12 miles) to the terminus at **Middlemarch** in Central Otago where coach connections can take tourists onward to Queenstown. ❑

Maps:
Otago 300
Area 308

Yellow-eyed penguins abound at Penguin Place.

BELOW:
Larnach Castle.

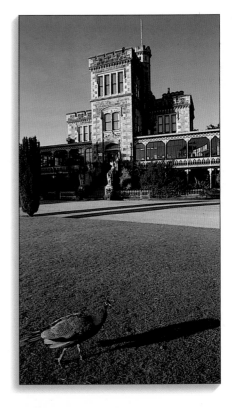

SOUTHLAND

Stepping into Southland's staggeringly beautiful but otherworld landscape, you could be excused for feeling like you were at the ends of the earth

Map on page 308

t's the expansiveness of the place that first takes you – wide open spaces with a distinctive quality of bold light which so impressed the early European landscape painters. The land here was settled by a determined breed of Scottish settlers who demanded provincial government in 1861. Nine years of heady development followed – in towns, country, rail and roads – to such extent that the provincial government went bankrupt and their province was legally and administratively fixed to their neighbour, Otago, in 1870.

The 100,000 people who proudly call themselves Southlanders today have scant regard for the historical purist's arguments about their legitimacy. They live in New Zealand's southernmost land district – Murihiku, the last joint of the tail, as the Maori called it. This "province" takes in about 28,000 sq km (some 11,000 sq miles), its boundary starting just above the breathtaking hills and valleys of Milford Sound on the West Coast, skirting the southern shores of Lake Wakatipu bordering Central Otago, and meandering its way through some of the lushest, most productive farmland in New Zealand to join the southeast coast near an unspoiled area called the Catlins.

Signs of Maori settlement go back as far as the 12th century around the southern coast, and since the days of rapid development in the 1860s, Southlanders have developed a land of unlimited potential for agricultural purposes and regained the conservative reputation for which their largely Scottish forebears were known. Yet there is a grittiness in the Southland character. It manifests itself in an agrarian excellence – the region is responsible for a quarter of New Zealand's export receipts – that would not have been achieved had conservatism dominated.

Contrasts abound in the land itself. On the West Coast, deep fiords lap against towering mountains and snow-capped peaks reach skywards amidst a myriad of vast bush-clad valleys in an area that is called, not surprisingly, Fiordland. Inland stretch the two massive plains, on which the province's prosperity has grown to depend, surrounding the commercial heart of the city of Invercargill, and eventually reaching the southern and southeastern coasts.

PRECEDING PAGES: Milford Sound reflecting Mitre Peak in its waters. **LEFT:** sunset at Milford Sound. **BELOW:** Fiordland's ancient forest.

Scottish Invercargill

The 49,480 people who live in **Invercargill ❸** – located some 217 km (135 miles) southwest of Dunedin, or 283 km (176 miles) south of Queenstown – reside close to an estuary once plied by steamers and sailing ships. The city's Scottish heritage is well-reflected in its street names, many elegant buildings, neat gardens and tree-lined parks. The original town planners were generous in the amount of space devoted to main thoroughfares and public spaces. Today, **Queens Park**, the central

Southern South Island

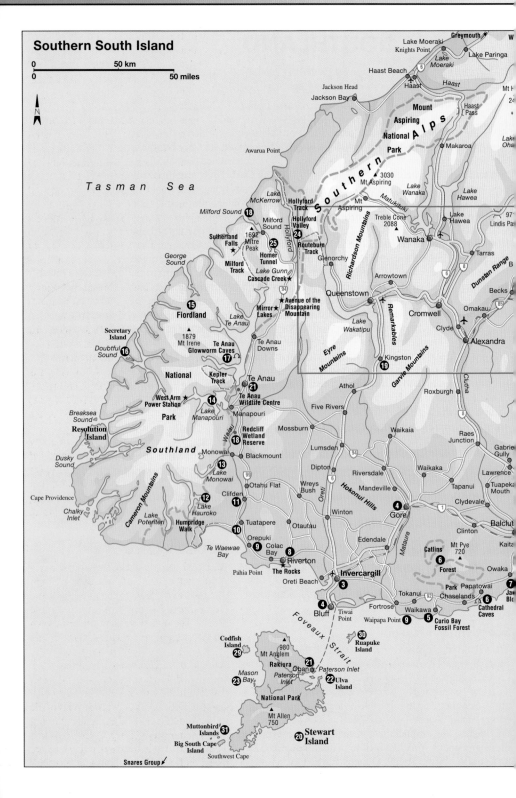

0   50 km
0   50 miles

N

Tasman Sea

Greymouth
Lake Moeraki
Knights Point
Lake Paringa
Lake Moeraki
Haast Beach
Haast
Haast
Mt H
24
Jackson Head
Jackson Bay

Awarua Point

Mount
Aspiring
National
Park

Southern Alps

Haast
Pass

Lake
Oha

Makaroa

▲ 3030
Mt Aspiring
Lake
Wanaka
Lake
Hawea

Lake
McKerrow
Hollyford
Track

Mt
Aspiring

Richardson Mountains

Matukituki

Lake
Hawea

97
Lindis Pas

Milford Sound   **18**
Milford
Sound

Hollyford
Valley   **24**
Hollyford

Treble Cone
2088 ▲

Wanaka

Sutherland
Falls ★   ▲ 1692
Mitre
Peak   **25**
Homer
Tunnel

Routeburn
Track

Glenorchy

Tarras

Dunstan Range

George
Sound

Milford
Track

Lake Gunn ★
Cascade Creek ★

Arrowtown

Becks

Omakau
85

★ Avenue of the
Disappearing
Mountain

Queenstown

Cromwell

Clyde

Alexandra

15
Fiordland

Lake
Te Anau

Mirror ★
Lakes

Lake
Wakatipu

Remarkables

Secretary
Island
Doubtful
Sound   **16**

▲ 1879
Mt Irene   Te Anau
Glowworm Caves   **17**

Te Anau
Downs

Eyre
Mountains

Garvie Mountains

Kingston   **19**

Cluthа

National
Kepler
Track

Te Anau

Athol

Roxburgh

West Arm
Power Station ★   **14**
Lake
Manapouri   **21**
Te Anau
Wildlife Centre

Five Rivers

Breaksea
Sound
Resolution
Island

Park

Manapouri

Redcliff
Wetland   **18**
Reserve

Mossburn

Waikaia

Raes
Junction

Gabrie
Gully

Dusky
Sound

Southland   Monowai ★

Blackmount

Lumsden

Waikaka

Lawrence

Tuapeka
Mouth

Cape Providence

13
Lake
Monowai
Otahu Flat

Dipton

Riversdale

Mandeville

Tapanui

Clydevale

Chalky
Inlet

12
Lake
Hauroko
11
Clifden

Wreys
Bush

Winton

Hokonui Hills

4
Gore

Clinton

Balclut

Lake
Poteriteri

Cameron Mountains

Humpridge
Walk

Tuatapere

10
Orepuki

Otautau

Edendale

Mataura

Mt Pye
720

Catlins

Kaita

Te Waewae
Bay

9
Colac
Bay   **8**
Riverton

The Rocks

Pahia Point

Oreti Beach

Invercargill   **3**

Tokanui   92

Bluff   **4**
Tiwai
Point

Fortrose
Waikawa   **9**

Waipapa Point

Curio Bay   **5**
Fossil Forest

Catlins
Forest   **6**

Owaka

Papatowai   **7**
Ja
Bl
Chaselands   **6**
Cathedral
Caves

Foveaux Strait

Ruapuke   **30**
Island

Codfish
Island   **29**

▲ 980
Mt Anglem

Rakiura   **21**
Oban
Paterson Inlet

Mason
Bay   **23**
Paterson
Inlet   **22** Ulva
Island

National Park

▲ Mt Allen
750

Muttonbird
Islands   **31**

Big South Cape
Island   Southwest Cape

Snares Group

20 **Stewart**
Island

W

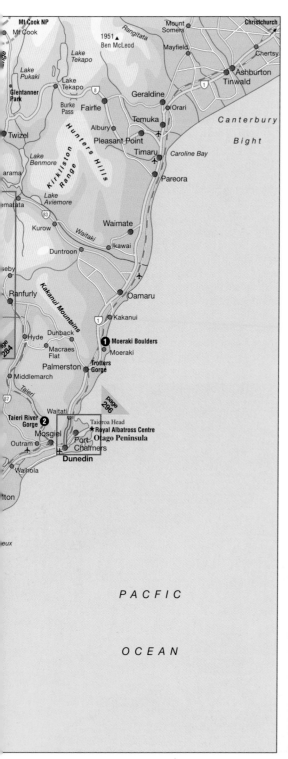

focus of the city, provides a wide range of recreational pursuits for the visitor, from sunken rose gardens and statuary created by Sir Charles Wheeler to a golf course and swimming pool.

Invercargill's biggest attraction is the **Southland Museum and Art Gallery** (Mon–Fri 9am–5pm, Sat–Sun 10am–5pm; donation fee; tel: 03-218 9753; www.southlandmuseum.com) at the Gala Street entrance of Queens Park. There are galleries devoted to the Maori, history and art but the displays on the Sub-Antarctic region, the cluster of islands between New Zealand and the Antarctic, alone are worth the visit. The audio-visual film *Beyond the Roaring Forties* will add immeasurably to your understanding of this windswept and isolated region. Another highlight of the pyramid-shaped museum is a "tuatarium" where visitors can observe ancient reptiles called tuatara, last survivors of the dinosaur era, roaming at leisure in a large, natural sanctuary.

At the ground level of the museum is Invercargill's **i-SITE Visitor Centre** (tel: 03-214 6243; www.invercargill.org.nz) where you can get more information on the rest of the attractions in the city.

Just 10 km (6 miles) south of the city centre is **Oreti Beach**, a long stretch of sand popular amongst the hardy locals for swimming, yachting and water-skiing. The beach is also famous for the succulent toheroa, a rare shellfish that grows up to 15 cm (6 inches) in length.

Bluff's highlights

About 27 km (17 miles) south of Invercargill is the land's end port of **Bluff** ❹. The next stop after here is Stewart Island *(see page 316)* and the sub-Antarctic waters. The road leading to this port town emphasises Southland's agricultural development. A massive fertiliser works processing phosphate rock imported from Pacific and Asian lands underpins the fact that Southland's soils need constant nourishment. Deer farms along both sides of the road are evidence of the fast-developing pastoral industry. Thirty years ago, deer were found only in the bush; today they are raised on farms by the thousands and their velvet, in particular, is keenly sought, mainly for use in Asian traditional medicines.

There is no mistaking Bluff's importance as a port. Large vessels tie up at a massive man-made island within the inland harbour and workers toil around the clock. Snake-like conveyor machines, their tails buried in a large building and their heads in ships' holds, load hundreds of thousands of frozen carcasses of lamb and mutton for worldwide markets.

Across the harbour, look out for three buildings, each 600 metres (2,000 ft) long, surrounded by other massive structures and dominated by a huge chimney stack 137 metres (450 ft) high. These make up the **Tiwai Point aluminium smelter**, which produces 334,000 tonnes of aluminium a year. Tucked away on the lonely Tiwai Peninsula where almost non-stop winds disperse smoke-laden effluent, the smelter is the major industrial employer in the south. Free tours of the smelter can be arranged; call 03-218 5999 for details.

Bluff is famous, above all, for its plump oysters from the Foveaux Strait, the 35-km (22-mile) stretch of water that separates Stewart Island from the mainland. In the early 1980s, the oyster beds were stricken with *Bonamia,* a protozoan disease, but careful management has ensured their recovery and a quota system prevents over-harvesting. Unique to New Zealand, this shellfish is not exported as the local market takes the full quota. The Bluff oyster season runs from March to August with the highlight being the hugely popular annual **Bluff Oyster and Southland Seafood Festival** (www.bluffoysterfest.co.nz) in April.

If you're interested in the local maritime history, the small **Bluff Maritime Museum** (Mon–Fri 10am–4.30pm and Sat–Sun 1–5pm; entrance fee; tel: 03-212 7534), at 241 Foreshore Road, is worth a visit. Here you can climb aboard and explore the workings of the oyster boat *Monica II*.

A Bluff local, Jim Burke, is the world-record holder for opening the most oysters – 1,719 – in an hour. That's opening 28 oysters a minute for a solid hour.

BELOW:
hoisting a dredge full of oysters from the waters of Foveaux Strait.

East to the Catlins Coast

Head southeast of Invercargill for 80 km (50 miles) towards the small fishing port of **Waikawa**, reached by a comfortable road through rolling countryside which not long ago was bush-covered. Waikawa is on the Southern Scenic Route, a major tourism highlight which stretches from Balclutha in South Otago, along the southern coast, past Waikawa, and eventually ends in Te Anau. Heading northeast from Waikawa the route takes in much of the **Catlins**, an area whose diverse natural beauty is supplemented by the many opportunities it affords to see such wildlife as fur seals, sea lions, the occasional, awe-inspiring elephant seal and rare yellow-eyed penguins.

At the end of the road from Invercargill, 5 km (3 miles) before Waikawa, are the remains of a petrified forest buried millions of years ago at a place called **Curio Bay ❺**. This freeze-frame of time has caught every grain of timber in the fossilised stumps; boulders which have been broken open by some unknown force show patterns of leaves and twigs. Adjacent is **Porpoise Bay**, a pleasant swimming beach as long as you are willing to share the waters with the rare, small Hector's dolpins with their distinctive black and white markings, which frequent the bay.

Some 34 km (21 miles) north of Porpoise Bay is the vast **Waipati Beach**, where there is a walkway to the spectacular 30-metre (98-ft) high **Cathedral Caves ❻**. The caves can only be entered two hours either side of low tide. A torch is essential lest you tread on a sleeping seal or sealion. Travel another 10 km (6 miles) north to **Papatowai**, which is home to a few essential stores but, more importantly, the starting point for numerous magnificent beach and forest walks.

Follow the Southern Scenic Route another 24 km (15 miles) north to **Owaka**, a thriving township, albeit one of New Zealand's most remote, stopping off at the

Map on page 308

TIP

Nearly 500 km (311 miles) of fishing waters stretch along Southland's three main fishing rivers – the Mataura, the Oreti and the Aparima – which cut the province in three. The brown trout fishing here is among the best in the world.

BELOW: petrified tree stumps at Curio Bay.

stunning **Purakaunui Falls** along the way. The three-tiered falls are located off the main road but are well worth the trek. At Owaka, there are restaurants and accommodation and you might choose to stay here as a base to explore bush walks and waterfalls, or indulge in some birdwatching. The **Catlins Visitor Centre** here (tel: 03-415 8371; www.catlins-nz.com) can supply you with all the details you need. Some 6 km (4 miles) northeast of Owaka is **Jack's Blowhole** ➐, a 55-metre (180-ft) deep hole of surging seas located some 200 metres (656 ft) from the beach.

From here you can continue 30 km (19 miles) north on the Southern Scenic Route to **Balclutha**, and turn northeast to Dunedin, or retrace your steps to Invercargill and head into isolated Fiordland.

West of Invercargill

Invercargill may be flat, but its residents cannot help but raise their eyes westward to the distant mountains that border Fiordland. For those in a hurry, this vast natural area can be reached in less than two hours, travelling northwest across the central Southland plains via Winton and Dipton, over the Josephville Hill and through Lumsden, until rolling tussock country indicates that you are in land of an altogether tougher nature. This journey, through prime country carrying several million head of stock, aptly shows how Southland has grown on agricultural production.

Continuing west, the historic town of **Riverton** ➑ nestles by the sea, 38 km (24 miles) from Invercargill. Sealers and whalers made this their home in 1836 and Southland's first European settlement still bears signs of those times. Preservation is a way of life here. In 2002 the New Zealand Historic Places Trust offered a whaler's cottage for sale for the sum of just NZ$1, so long as the owner promised to preserve it according to the trust's specifications. Further 10 km (6 miles) west is **Colac Bay**. Once a Maori settlement, it grew into a town with a population of 6,000 during the gold-rush days of the 1890s, and – now is a popular holiday spot for Southlanders. Further west is **Orepuki** ➒ town, where history merges with the present: an old courthouse is now a sheep-shearing shed. Along the shore, look out for macrocarpa trees turned inwards by strong southerly winds.

Travellers have a fine view of thundering surf between Orepuki and **Tuatapere** ➓, 20 km (12 miles) away. Across **Te Waewae Bay**, where Hector's dolphins and southern right whales can sometimes be spied, bush-clad mountains loom, the first signs of what is to come. New Zealand's newest walk, the **Tuatapere Hump Ridge Track** (www.humpridgetrack.co.nz), a 53-km (33-mile), 3-day circuit, starts and finishes at the western end of the bay. From the timber town of Tuatapere, where fishing and deer-hunting stories are as common as logs from the town's mills, the road heads north 12 km (8 miles) to **Clifden** ⓫, notable for the nearby **Clifden Suspension Bridge** (built in 1899) and the spooky **Clifden Caves**. The caves can be explored without a guide but make sure you have at least two torches and follow the signposted instructions. From Clifden, a 30-km (19-mile) unsealed road leads to New Zealand's deepest lake, **Lake Hauroko** ⓬, set among dense bush and steep slopes. Its name means "sounding wind" after the exposure it has to winds from both north and south.

Macrocarpa trees near the shore at Orepuki, bent from years of beating by fierce winds.

BELOW:
Purakaunui Falls near Owaka.

Continuing north from Clifden the road leads through Blackmount and then to the **Redcliff Wetland Reserve**, where lucky birdwatchers might sight the predatory bush falcon in action. The town of Monowai is 6 km (4 miles) northwest of Blackmount, a base for the recreational mecca of **Lake Monowai ⓭** – renowned for its excellent fishing and hunting.

Fiordland National Park

Beyond the wetlands is **Lake Manapouri ⓮**, 28 km (17 miles) north of Monowai. It has been described as a soft feminine lake, with a scattering of wooded islands, banks dense with bush and a horizon bounded by the **Kepler Mountains**. It is indeed in a magnificent setting, and rising majestically ahead the mountains and lakes of Fiordland. With an area of 1.2 million hectares (3 million acres), **Fiordland National Park ⓯** is New Zealand's largest and part of the South West New Zealand World Heritage Area. That first glimpse across Lake Manapouri, to sheer mountains and remote deep valleys on the other side of the lake, gives the observer some understanding of why ancient Maori legends never lose their romantic hold in this wild region.

To experience the glorious nature, you can take a launch across Lake Manapouri to its **West Arm**. Ponder man's folly of trying to raise this lake by 27 metres (89 ft) for hydro-electric purposes. Conservation interests eventually prevailed, although the massive **Manapouri Underground Power Station** was built at West Arm to supply power to the Tiwai Point aluminium smelter (*see page 310*). Guided tours to the vast machine hall located 200 metres (660 ft) underground are operated by **Real Journeys** (tel: 03-249 7416, 0800-656 501; www.realjourneys.co.nz) as part of their Doubtful Sound day excursion.

Map on page 308

TIP

Bring your waterproof coats and wellingtons if visiting Milford Sound or walking the Milford Track – in this area the rainfall is measured in metres. Insect repellent is a must – to keep the voracious sandflies away.

BELOW: trampers at the Milford Track, Fiordland National Park.

A necessary part of the construction was the building of a road from West Arm, at the westernmost point of Lake Manapouri, across the Wilmot Pass, to the southernmost point of **Doubtful Sound** ⓰, the deepest of Fiordland's sounds, in an area known as Deep Cove. This is virgin country where bottlenose and dusky dolphins frolicking in the deep blue waters. Divers can view black coral, which grows at an unusually shallow depth due to the darker fresh water that pours into the cove from the power station and surrounding hills.

The hub of this vast wilderness is the tourist town of **Te Anau**, 22 km (14 miles) north of Manapouri, with its many hotels, motels and lodges. The valley floors behind the town are the scene of perhaps the biggest land projects in New Zealand, with scores of new farms being developed. A highlight of this area is the **Te Anau Glowworm Caves** ⓱ on the western shores of **Lake Te Anau** at the base of the Murchison Mountains. The caves, believed to have been known to early Maori explorers, were only rediscovered in 1948. A trip to the caves takes 2½ hours and can be booked at **Real Journeys** (*see page 313*) in Te Anau. A walkway and two short punt rides take people to the heart of the cave system, which also features whirlpools, magical waterfalls and a glowworm grotto. The Department of Conservation runs the **Te Anau Wildlife Centre** (daily 24 hours; tel: 03-2497921; www.doc.govt.nz), just outside the town on the road to Manapouri. It is one of the very few places where you can see the rare takahe, among other bird species.

Mighty Milford Sound

The second, more spectacular way to the sea through Fiordland is the 120-km (75-mile) long road to **Milford Sound** ⓲ from Te Anau, world-renowned and

The takahe, one of New Zealand's rarest birds can be seen at the Te Anau Wildlife Centre. Once thought to be extinct, it was rediscovered in 1948 in the Murchison Mountains.

BELOW: majestic Milford Sound.

described by Rudyard Kipling as "the eighth wonder of the world". Authors and artists have struggled to put into words the beauty that unfolds as the road, following Lake Te Anau for the first 30 km (19 miles), enters dense forests then passes serenely beautiful features such as the **Mirror Lakes**, 58 km (36 miles) from Te Anau, and the **Avenue of the Disappearing Mountain** where the eyes are not to be believed as the mountain appears to shrink while driving towards it. Forests, river flats and small lakes pass by, until the road drops towards the forested upper **Hollyford Valley** at Marian Camp.

From there, the road splits in two directions. One arm ventures into the no-exit **Hollyford Valley** with its **Gunns Rest**, a well-established motor camp run by one of Fiordland's most interesting characters. At the end of this road is the start of the **Hollyford Track**. The other fork proceeds west, steeply up the mountain towards the eastern portal of the **Homer Tunnel**. This 1,240-metre (4,118-ft) unlined tunnel, hewn from solid rock, was begun in 1935 as an employment project for five men who lived in tents and used only picks, shovels and wheelbarrows. It was completed in 1954, but not before avalanches claimed the lives of three men. Homer can be Fiordland at its roughest.

From the Milford side, the road drops 690 metres (2,264 ft) in 10 km (6 miles) between sheer mountain faces to emerge in the **Cleddau Valley** with its awe-inspiring **Chasm Walk**, where you can stroll to a series of steep falls formed by the plunging Cleddau River. Back on the road, it's another 10 km (6 miles) to the head of Milford Sound, where a small clutch of hotels await.

Boats from the southernmost end of Milford Sound regularly carry visitors on excursions to the open sea. They are very popular and should be booked well in advance. **Red Boat Cruises** (tel: 03-441 1137, 0800-264 536; www.redboats.co.nz) operates short boat trips that take in most highlights while **Real Journeys** *(see page 313)* has both short scenic cruises as well as overnight trips on the *Milford Wanderer* and *Milford Mariner*. Milford Sound is dominated by the unforgettable **Mitre Peak** – a 1,692-metre (5,551-ft) pinnacle of rock – and several landmarks, notably the **Lady Bowen Falls** (162 metres/532 ft).

If you have more time and energy you may consider a sea-kayak trip. Milford tends to buzz with day-trippers, but remains remarkably empty at either end of the day. It also buzzes with sandflies, so insect repellent should be liberally applied.

Milford Sound is also accessible on foot. A launch takes walkers from Te Anau to Glade House at the head of the lake. From there, through some of the most majestic scenery nature can devise, walkers take three days to reach the Sound via the famous **Milford Track**, *(see page 243)* described as one of the finest walks in the world. Fiordland boasts other famous treks, including the **Routeburn Track** and the spectacular **Kepler Track** which meanders along mountain tops and through valleys across the lake from Te Anau.

From Southland, you can travel north towards Queenstown via **Kingston ⓳**, where a vintage steam train, the *Kingston Flyer* (www.kingstonflyer.co.nz) chugs to and fro between Fairlight and Kingston from October to May. Alternatively, motorists can proceed northeast toward Dunedin via the Mataura Valley. ❑

Map on page 308

TIP

The road trip from Queenstown to Milford Sound is a tiring 4–5 hours each way so book a coach and boat trip with Great Sights (tel: 03-442 5252; www.thestation.co.nz) instead. Better still, take the flight option back to Queenstown.

BELOW:
Mirror Lake takes its name from the uncanny reflections its surface creates.

Map
on page
308

Auckland
North Island

Wellington

Christchurch

South Island

STEWART ISLAND

*Little known, even to New Zealanders, the country's
"third island" is a wildlife paradise and
ecotourist's dream come true*

The Maori called it Te Punga o te Waka a Maui – "Anchorstone of Maui's Canoe" – the weight that held the other islands of New Zealand together. The most commonly used and known Maori name is, however, Rakiura, meaning "glowing skies". One William Stewart, first officer on a sealing expedition in 1809 began charting the island's coasts and lent it the name by which it is now known. Today, **Stewart Island** ⓴ metaphorically serves as one of the great foundation stones of the New Zealand environment, acting as a safe haven for many kinds of wildlife which otherwise would struggle to survive. It helps that it has just 28 km (17 miles) of sealed roads and 350 inhabitants.

Stewart Island can be reached by plane from Invercargill Airport, which takes just over 20 minutes, or by express catamaran ferry from Bluff, which takes an hour. If you take the ferry from Bluff to Oban, across Foveaux Strait, particularly in the winter months, be prepared for a fairly rough trip, as the Strait has a well-earned reputation as one of the roughest stretches of water in New Zealand. They ain't called the "roaring forties" for nothing. On the bright side, the larger seabirds, such as albatrosses and mollymawks, need strong winds to remain aloft, so the rougher the weather, the more you are likely to see.

From the air, Stewart Island looks deceptively small, and on fine days you can

BELOW:
stunning sunset
at Paterson Inlet.

take in the entire island at a glance. It is roughly triangular in shape, with the west coast stretching almost 60 km (37 miles) from Black Rock Point in the north, and south to Southwest Cape. Although there are two large bays, Dough-boy and Mason, there are no all-weather anchorages and rollers constantly thunder onto the shore from the Tasman. The southeast coast is also fairly exposed. However, there are several good anchorages at Port Pegasus, Port Adventure, Lord's River and in Paterson Inlet, which just about cleaves the island in two.

Oban and neighbouring Ulva Island

Most destinations on the island radiate out from **Oban** ㉑. Centred around Half Moon Bay and Horseshoe Bay, with its charming cottages nestled almost hidden among the trees, Oban is one of the most delightful settlements in New Zealand. Some of the houses date back to the days when the Norwegians had a whaling base at nearby **Paterson Inlet** and some were built by the descendants of whalers and sealers. Not far east of Oban on the way to Acker's Point is **Acker's Cottage**, New Zealand's oldest surviving dwelling. A few years ago it was rather unsympathetically restored, but it is still worth a visit. It was built by an American whaler, Lewis Acker and his wife, Mary Pi, around 1835.

Oban now boasts a wide range of accommodation, from hostels for backpackers to some expensive homestays. Prices on Stewart Island tend to be a bit steeper than those on the mainland, as just about everything, bar fish, needs to be imported. There is also accommodation available at the local watering hole, the **South Seas Hotel** (tel: 03-219 1059; www.stewart-island.co.nz) at the shore end of Main Road, which claims to be the most southerly hotel in the world – which it isn't, unless there really are no hotels in Patagonia.

Rakiura Museum (Mon–Sat 10am–noon, Sun noon–2pm; entrance fee) in Ayr Street in Oban holds many items relating to the island's maritime history and pre-European days, and is a good place to learn about the local fauna before encountering them in the wild.

Around Oban are many delightful shore walks for a wide range of fitness levels. There are some fine stands of trees, and the native fuchsia is particularly prolific. Native birds can be readily seen and, as they are seldom harassed, they will allow you to approach quite near. Kakariki, bellbirds, fantails, tui and tomtits are among the species commonly encountered, and also the native pigeon, the kereru. The raucous cries of one of the native parrots, the kaka, flying overhead, can often be heard around Oban; there are now sadly very few other settled areas in New Zealand where this occurs.

Well worth a visit is **Ulva Island** ㉒, about 3 km (2 miles) offshore in Paterson Inlet, accessible by water taxi, or, for the more adventurous, a kayak. Ulva has been cleared of predators in recent years and a number of bird species have been introduced. The most conspicuous of these is the South Island saddleback, but there are also the engaging Stewart Island robin, riflemen and yellowheads. Also on Ulva is a flourishing population of Stewart Island weka. Signs discourage you from feeding them, but weka are nothing if not optimists, and are certainly not above helping themselves to an unattended lunch.

Map on page 308

TIP

South Seas Hotel is a good place to meet up with the locals, mostly fishermen or workers from the local salmon farm. If the urge takes you, visits to the salmon farm (tel: 03-219 1282) can be arranged and you can also visit the local abalone farm.

BELOW: a hardy Stewart islander.

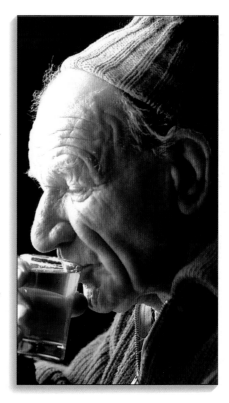

Ulva has never been milled, so there are fine stands of mature trees. Rimu, totara, miro and kamahi are all here in good numbers, and also smaller plants such as ferns and orchids. There are also kiwi on Ulva and because they sometimes forage during the day due to the short nights of mid-summer, there is a better chance of seeing kiwi here than in any other part of New Zealand. **Mason Bay ㉓**, on the west coast, is a kiwi stronghold and they are often to be seen in the late afternoon foraging among the flax and tussock grasses and even searching for sandhoppers along the beach.

A haven for birdwatchers

The native kaka parrot, seldom seen elsewhere in New Zealand, can be spotted on Stewart Island.

Another good place for viewing birds is at the relatively exposed **Acker's Point**, 3 km (2 miles) to the east of Oban. Larger seabirds such as albatrosses and mollymawks tend to stay out of the sheltered bays as the winds there are generally not strong enough to keep them aloft. If you walk out to Acker's Point in the evening, you'll hear blue penguins calling to each other as they float in rafts just offshore, waiting until it is dark enough to venture ashore to their burrows. During the summer breeding season, you'll also hear the calls of the homecoming sooty shearwater, or titi, which nest in burrows under and around the beacon.

Sooty shearwaters generally go by the rather unflattering name of muttonbirds, and if you get tired of looking at them, the South Seas Hotel in Oban sometimes features them on its menu. They taste either like fish-flavoured mutton or mutton-flavoured fish. In any event, it is a rather unhappy gastronomic combination, and muttonbirds are definitely at their best, feathered and flying.

BELOW:

green fern fronds at Ulva Island.

The waters around Stewart Island offer some of the best opportunities in the world for viewing seabirds. Over half the world's known albatrosses and mol-

GIANT SEABIRDS

Probably the best area of all for spotting seabirds lies to the south of Stewart Island towards the **Snares Group**. Although the public are not permitted to land on the Snares, you are allowed to sail just offshore, and in the evenings, the cacophony of homecoming shearwaters and penguins is impossible to miss.

At last count there were an estimated 8 million sooty shearwaters nesting on this island each summer. For the dedicated birder wanting to add magnificent albatrosses and mollymawks to their lifelist, there is no other way of seeing them, and you had better see them while you can. With the craven attitude taken by the New Zealand government on enforcing the regulations on long-line fishing in the southern waters, the numbers of these birds are fast plummeting. Thousands are drowned each year when they get hooked on the fishing lines of boats from Asia and Russia.

For safety reasons, the only way of getting to the Snares is with **Talisker Charters** (tel: 03-219 1151; www.sailsashore.co.nz), whose experienced skipper knows his birds – a lot of the other locals point towards a bird, mutter something, and hope that you are too seasick to notice.

Map on page 308

lymawks frequent the waters around Stewart Island, along with a plethora of other seabirds, including petrels, shearwaters, skuas, prions and penguins. Also commonly encountered are cape pigeons, known somewhat irreverently by the locals as "Jesus Christ birds", because of their habit of pattering across the water. There is also a plethora of seabirds found near the **Snares Group**, 125 km (78 miles) from the southernmost tip of Stewart Island (*see box on opposite page*).

Rakiura National Park

However, if you choose to keep your feet on dry land, there is plenty to keep you occupied on Stewart Island itself, as there are about 245 km (152 miles) of walking tracks. A particularly good tramp is the 29-km (18-mile) long **Rakiura Track**, which starts and ends at Oban and takes three days to complete. Huts along the way provide decent overnight stays. The tracks in the north take you through stands of totara, rimu and rata, while those in the south run up from beautiful forested bays out into shrublands and sub-alpine vegetation. These southern areas, around the Tin Range, were until fairly recently home to New Zealand's rarest bird, the kakapo. In the 1970s they were moved to the safety of offshore islands like **Codfish**, which lies not far off Stewart Island's west coast.

With 85 percent of the island gazetted as the **Rakiura National Park**, there is a multitude of areas to visit, and things to do. And even if you are not the tramping sort, there are few other places where it is as pleasant just to sit and take in some of nature at its very best. The fern groves, particularly those around **Dynamite Point**, are very luxuriant, especially now that the introduced white-tail deer are being kept under control, and there is a particularly good collection of plants in the gardens at the **Motarau Moana Reserve**, on the road to Horseshoe Bay. ❑

Stewart Island's Maori name Rakiura, meaning "glowing skies", was inspired by the stunning sunsets or the Aurora Australis (or Southern Lights) that is a feature of the sky this far south.

BELOW: Stewart Island's huge albatrosses are a sight to behold.

INSIGHT GUIDES
TRAVEL TIPS

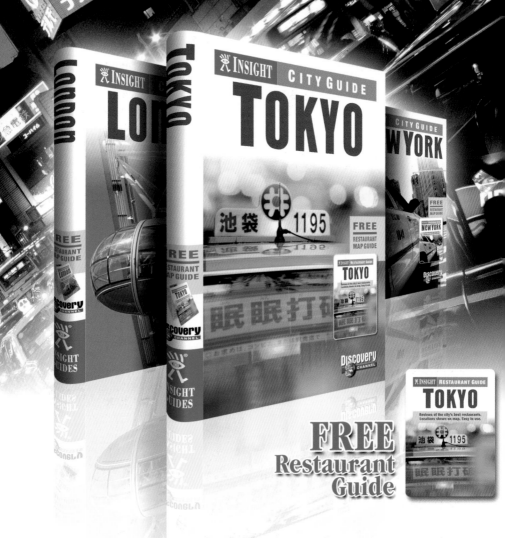

CONTENTS

Getting Acquainted

The Place 324
Geography 324
Climate 324
Economy 324
Government 325

Planning the Trip

What to Bring 325
Visas & Passports........326
Customs.......................326
Health & Safety 326
Currency 326
Credit Cards 326
Goods & Services Tax..326
Public Holidays............326
Overseas Tourism
    Offices 327
Overseas Missions 327
Getting There 327

Practical Tips

Business Hours 328
Tipping........................328
Media..........................328
Postal Services............328
Communications 328
Local Tourism Offices ..329
Local Missions 329
Disabled Travellers 329
Gay Travellers..............329
Travelling with
    Children 329
Personal Security 329
Medical Services 329
Health & Beauty 329
Photography................330
Language....................330
Useful Websites 330

Getting Around

By Air 330
By Sea 330
By Rail 331
By Bus 331
By Car 331

Where to Stay

Accommodation 332

What to Eat

General 333
What to Drink 333
Where to Eat 333

Culture

General 334
Maori Culture 334

Festivals

Diary of Events........335–7

Shopping

What to Buy 338

Outdoor Activities

General 339
Land Sports 339
Water Sports 340
Winter Sports 341

Further Reading

History & Biography 342
Literature/Fiction 342

Regional Listings: North Island

Auckland 343
Auckland's
    Surroundings 346
Northland 350
Waikato 353
Coromandel &
    Bay of Plenty 356
Rotorua &
    Volcanic Plateau 358
Poverty Bay &
    Hawke's Bay............362
Taranaki, Wanganui &
    Manawatu 365
Wellington &
    Surroundings 367

Regional Listings: South Island

Nelson & Marlborough 369
Christchurch &
    Surroundings 372
Canterbury 375
The West Coast 377
Queenstown & Otago ..380
Dunedin &
    Surroundings 384
Southland....................386
Stewart Island 388

Getting Acquainted

The Place

Situation: Located in the Southern Hemisphere in the middle of the Pacific Ocean, New Zealand is 1,900 km (1,200 miles) east of Australia.

Area: 268,680 sq. km (103,788 sq. miles)

Capital: Wellington (pop. 451,600) is the political, cultural and financial centre of New Zealand.

Population: 4.1 million

Language: English/Maori

Religion: Predominantly Christian (81 percent)

Currency: New Zealand dollar

Weights & measures: Metric

Telephone Code: International dialling code: 64

Electricity: New Zealand's AC electricity supply operates at 230/240 volts, 50 hertz, which is the same as Australia's. Most hotels and motels provide 110-volt, 20-watt AC sockets for electric razors only. A transformer is necessary to operate all other electrical equipment. Power outlets only accept flat 3- or 2-pin plugs,

Early Start of the Day

Travellers from the western hemisphere moving west into New Zealand lose a full day crossing the International Dateline, and regain a full day returning eastwards. Because the country is so advanced in time, given its proximity to the International Date Line, it is one of the very first nations to welcome each day, preceded only by Fiji, Kiribati and some of the other small Pacific islands.

depending on whether an earth connection is fitted.

Time Zone: There is only one time zone throughout most of the country – 12 hours ahead of Greenwich Mean Time (GMT).

From early October until late March, time is advanced by one hour to give extended daytime throughout summer. Time in the remote Chatham Islands, 800 km (500 miles) east of Christchurch, is 45 minutes ahead of that in the rest of the country.

Geography

New Zealand has three main islands – the North Island, the South Island and Stewart Island – running roughly from north to south over 1,600 km (994 miles), between 34°S and 47°S. The two main islands, the North and South Islands, are separated by a 22 km- (14 mile-) wide body of water called Cook Strait.

New Zealand's spectacular landscape comprises vast mountain chains, steaming volcanoes, sweeping coastlines, indented fiords and lush rainforests.

In the South Island, the Southern Alps run from north to south, and in the southwest meet the sea in the deeply indented coast of Fiordland. The highest point is Mount Cook, now standing at 3,754 metres (12,316 ft) – a major rock slide reduced the height of the mountain by 10 metres (33 ft) in December 1991. The Canterbury Plains lie to the east of the mountains.

The North Island is mainly hilly with isolated mountains, including volcanoes, three of which are active. Lowlands on the North Island are largely restricted to coastal areas and the Waikato Valley.

The principal rivers are the Waikato, Clutha, Waihou, Rangitikei, Mokau, Whanganui and Manawatu.

Climate

New Zealand's climate is the reverse of that of the Northern Hemisphere. This means New Zealanders enjoy a warm Christmas in the sun, while June and July are

Sizing it Up

New Zealand's combined total land area of 268,680 sq. km (103,788 sq. miles) is approximately 36 times smaller than the US. It is similar in size to Colorado and somewhere in between the size of Japan and the United Kingdom.

among the coldest months.

The north of New Zealand enjoys a mainly subtropical climate. The climate in the south is generally temperate, with rainfall spread fairly evenly throughout the year, although the weather is very changeable.

The summer and autumn seasons from December to May are the most settled and the best for a visit. New Zealanders traditionally take their main family holiday break at Christmas and into January, so visitors are advised to make advance bookings for accommodation and domestic transport over this period – when pressure on travel and tourist facilities is greatest.

Winds can be strong at any time on the Cook Strait, which separates the two main islands, but summer days are generally warm and pleasant in most of the regions. Winters can be cold in the central and southern North Island and coastal districts of the South Island, and can be severe in the central regions of the South Island.

The NZ weather service's website, www.metservice.co.nz, has details on weather conditions.

Economy

New Zealand's export earnings mainly come from tourism and agriculture – in particular from meat, wool and dairy products, forest products and food processing – plus iron and steel production.

National Symbols

The national plant of New Zealand is the pohutukawa and the national bird is the flightless kiwi.

Temperature Ranges

Winter (June–August) and summer (December–February/March) temperature ranges are as follows:

Auckland: 8–15°C (48–59°F) in winter; 14–23°C (57–74°F) in summer.

Wellington: 6–13°C (43–55°F) in winter; 12–20°C (53–69°F) in summer.

Christchurch: 2–11°C (33–52°F) in winter; 10–22°C (50–73°F) in summer.

Queenstown: -1–10°C (30–50°F) in winter; 19–22°C (66–73°F) in summer.

Dunedin: 4–12°C (39–53°F) in winter; 9–19°C (48–66°F) in summer.

Forestry is now an expanding business and supports an important pulp and paper industry. Apart from coal, lignite, natural gas and gold, the country has few natural resources, although its considerable hydro-electric power potential has been exploited to produce plentiful electricity – an important basis of New Zealand's manufacturing industry. Natural gas – from the Kapuni Field in the North Island and the Maui Field off the Taranaki coast – is converted to liquid fuel for both domestic and foreign markets.

New Zealand is increasingly stronger in food processing, technology, telecommunications, textiles, plantation forest products, electronics, climbing equipment and apparel. In recent years, there has also been a great interest in the production of specialised lifestyle products such as yachts. Major trading partners are Japan, Australia and the USA.

Despite the country's small domestic market and its remote location, far from the world's major industrial powers, New Zealanders enjoy a high standard of living.

Government

New Zealand has a centralised democracy with a Western-style economy. Suffrage is extended to everyone 18 years and above, women having gained the vote in 1893. The 120-member House of Representatives is elected by means of a system called Mixed Member Proportional (MMP) representation for a period of three years. There are four constituencies specifically for those Maori who choose to vote on a separate roll. Half of the remainder of the house is decided according to the proportion of each party's support in a special "party" vote on election day. The rest of the members of parliament represent constituencies.

The Governor General – the representative of the British Queen, who is also sovereign of New Zealand – appoints the Prime Minister. He also has the power to dismiss the Prime Minister and dissolve parliament. The Prime Minister, who commands a majority in the House, in turn appoints a Cabinet, which is responsible to the House.

New Zealand is divided into 16 regions, which form the highest level of local government. It is also divided into 74 territorial authorities, of which 16 are cities, and 57, in the more rural areas, are districts, each governed by a council directly elected by the residents. The Chatham Islands, a separate district, are not included in any region. Tokelau is an autonomous island territory, which is legally part of the Dominion of New Zealand.

Thanks to the introduction of the Mixed Member Proportional system in 1996, New Zealand has a strong multi-party system with eight parties currently represented in parliament. Of these, the two largest and also the oldest, the Labour Party (centre-left progressive) and the National Party (centre-right conservative), have dominated New Zealand politics since the 1930s. The others, comparative newcomers, include New Zealand First (nationalist), United Future (family values), ACT (Association of Consumers and Taxpayers), the Greens (environmentalist left-wing), the Progressives and the Maori Party.

Planning the Trip

What to Bring

Travel as lightly as possible because there are plenty of bargains to be found in New Zealand – you can pretty much buy anything you need, from spectacles and prescription medicines to clothing and shoes. Remember to stock up on plenty of sunscreen and insect repellent during summer.

CLOTHING

New Zealanders are regarded as fairly casual dressers, although you will need to bring something dressy if you plan to go to any arts events and fancy restaurants. For clubbing, you'll need to wear something smart and fashionable, too. Some nightclubs and bars do not allow shorts or trainers.

For summer visits, you are advised to bring sweaters or wind-breakers for the cooler evenings or brisk days, especially if you are planning to travel to regions in the South Island.

Medium-thick clothing, plus a raincoat or umbrella, is adequate for most regions most of the year, but in midwinter in Rotorua, Taupo and Queenstown, sturdy winter clothing and footwear are essential. The South Island is generally considerably colder than the North.

Note: New Zealand is noted for its high level of ultraviolet radiation and the brilliance of its light. This means you may develop severe sunburn even on days when the temperature may seem deceptively low. It is important to wear sunscreen lotions, a hat, sunglasses and protective clothing.

Visas & Passports

All visitors to New Zealand require passports, which must be valid for at least three months beyond the date you intend leaving the country.

Visa requirements differ, depending on nationality, purpose of visit and length of stay. Visitors must produce an onward or return ticket and sufficient funds to support themselves during their stay. Check with the New Zealand diplomatic or consular office in your country of residence *(see page 327)* or on www.immigration.govt.nz.

Customs

New Zealand has three levels of control at all points of entry into the country: immigration, customs and agriculture. On arrival, you must complete an arrival card. Present this to an immigration official with your passport, and, if required, a valid visa.

The following classes of people are prohibited by law from entering, either as tourists or immigrants, regardless of country of origin:
• Those suffering from tuberculosis, syphilis, leprosy, or any mental disorders.
• Those convicted of an offence which drew a sentence of imprisonment of over one year.
• Those who have previously been deported from New Zealand.

A visitor, over the age of 17, may import 200 cigarettes or 200 grams of tobacco; 50 cigars or a mixture of all three not exceeding 250g; 4.5 litres of wine or beer and one 1,125 ml bottle of spirits. Excess quantities are subject to customs charges.

Strict laws prevent the entry of drugs, weapons, illicit material, wildlife products, firearms and quarantine items.

FARM REGULATIONS

Because New Zealand relies heavily on agricultural and horticultural trade with the rest of the world, it has stringent regulations governing the import of animals, as well as vegetable and animal matter. Visitors planning to bring in any material of this sort should make inquiries at the New Zealand Government offices overseas before proceeding. Live animals legally brought into the country must undergo strict quarantine periods.

Health & Safety

Only limited medical treatment is available free to visitors, so health insurance is recommended. Visitors are covered by the government-run Accident Compensation Scheme (ACC) for personal injury resulting by accident, regardless of fault. To be eligible for the same health care benefits as New Zealand residents, you must have been or intend to remain in New Zealand for two years or more. There are two types of hospitals: public and private. In most cases, you pay for private or public hospital care.

Most tap water in New Zealand is safe to drink. Never drink untreated water from lakes and streams.

Smoking in all public buildings, restaurants and pubs is prohibited by law.

There are no snakes or dangerous wild animals in New Zealand, although a bite from the red-backed katipo spider and white-tail spider requires medical treatment. Sandflies and mosquitos are prevalent in some areas – bring insect repellent.

Currency

The New Zealand dollar (NZ$), divided into 100 cents, is the unit of currency. Currency exchange facilities are available at Auckland, Wellington and Christchurch international airports, as well as most banks and bureaux de change in the larger cities and resorts.

There is no restriction on the amount of domestic or foreign currency (or traveller's cheques in New Zealand dollars) a visitor may bring into or take out of New Zealand. The New Zealand dollar is frequently called "the kiwi" because the dollar coin features a kiwi, the national bird, on one side.

At time of press, US$1 was roughly equivalent to NZ$1.43 while €1 gets you NZ$1.85.

Credit Cards

Credit cards, including Visa, American Express, Diners Club and MasterCard, are widely accepted throughout New Zealand. If your credit card is encoded with a PIN, you may be able to withdraw cash from automatic teller machines (ATMs), situated at banks and shopping centres throughout the country.
Amex, tel: 0800-656 660
Diners Club, tel: 0800-346 377
Mastercard, tel: 0800-449 140
Visa, tel: 0508-600 300

Goods & Services Tax

A goods and services tax (GST) of 12.5 percent is applied to the cost

Public Holidays

January New Year's Day (1st) and next working day; provincial anniversaries: Wellington (22nd), Northland and Auckland (29th)
February Waitangi Day (6th); provincial anniversaries: Nelson Day (1st)
March Provincial anniversaries: Otago (23rd), Taranaki (31st)
Good Friday and Easter Monday
April ANZAC Day (25th)
June Queen's Birthday (usually the first Monday)
October Labour Day (usually the last Monday)
November Provincial anniversaries: Marlborough and Hawke's Bay (1st)
December Provincial anniversaries: Westland (1st), Canterbury (16th); South Canterbury (16th, but observed in late September); Christmas (25th, 26th and next working day)
Note Provincial anniversaries are usually observed on the Monday closest to the actual date.

of all goods and services and is generally included in all prices. GST is not charged on duty-free goods, or where the items are posted by a retailer to an international visitor's home address. Neither is GST included in international airfares purchased in New Zealand.

Overseas Tourism Offices

The official **Tourism New Zealand** website, **www.newzealand.com**, has comprehensive information in several languages. Alternatively, contact one of the following Tourism New Zealand offices:

London: New Zealand House, Level 7, 80 Haymarket, London SW1Y 4TQ, tel: 0207-930 1662.
New York: 222 East 41 Street, Suite 2510, New York, NY 10017, tel: 212-661 7088.
Los Angeles: 501 Santa Monica Boulevard, Suite 300, Santa Monica, CA 90401, tel: 310-395 7480.
Sydney: Suite 3, Level 24, 1 Alfred Street, Sydney NSW 2000, tel: 02-8220 9000.
Singapore: 391A Orchard Road, 15–01 Ngee Ann City, Tower A, Singapore 238873, tel: 65-6738 5844.

Overseas Missions

There is a New Zealand Diplomatic Post finder at www.nzembassy.com which details all New Zealand embassies and consulates around the world. Here are a few of them:
Canberra: New Zealand High Commission, Commonwealth Avenue, Canberra, ACT 2600, Australia, tel: 02-6270 4211; e-mail: nzhccba@bigpond.net.au.
France: New Zealand Embassy, 7ter, rue Léonard de Vinci, 75116 Paris, France, tel: 01-4501 4343; e-mail: nzembassy.paris@ fr.oleane.com.
Germany: New Zealand Embassy, Friedrichstrasse 60, 10117 Berlin, Germany, tel: 030-206 210; e-mail: nzembassy.berlin@t-online.de.
London: New Zealand High Commission, New Zealand House,

80 Haymarket, London SW1Y 4TQ, United Kingdom, tel: 020-7930 8422; e-mail: aboutnz@newzealand hc.org.uk.
New York: New Zealand Consulate-General, 222 East 41st Street, Suite 2510, New York, NY 10017-6702, tel: 212-832 4038.
Singapore: New Zealand High Commission, 391A Orchard Road, #15-06/10, Ngee Ann City, Tower A, Singapore 238873, tel: 65-6235 9966; e-mail: enquiries@nz-high-com.org.sg.
Sydney: New Zealand Consulate-General, Level 10, 55 Hunter Street, Sydney, NSW 2000, Australia, tel: 02-8256 2000; e-mail: nzcgsydney@bigpond.com.
Washington DC: New Zealand Embassy, 37 Observatory Circle, Washington DC 20008, USA, tel: 202-328 4800; e-mail: info@nzemb.org.

Getting There

BY AIR

More than 99 percent of the 2 million tourists who visit New Zealand each year arrive by air.

International Airports

The main gateway is the **Auckland International Airport** (www.auckland-airport.co.nz) at Mangere, 24 km (15 miles) southwest of downtown **Auckland**. Bus, shuttle and taxi transfers into the city are available.

There is also an international airport in **Hamilton** (www.hamilton airport.co.nz), although this tends to service only New Zealand and Australian flights.

The airport at **Wellington** (www. wellington-airport.co.nz), the capital city, has restricted access for most wide-bodied aircraft types because of the runway length.

There is a good international airport at Harewood, close to the main South Island city of **Christchurch** (www.christchurch-airport.co.nz). Many international airlines run scheduled flights there.

Direct flights to and from Australia land at and take off from

Departure Tax

A tax of NZ$25 must be paid when you leave New Zealand. Please note that this tax is not included in your ticket price.

the airport at Queenstown.

New Zealand has direct air links with the Pacific Islands, all the major Australian cities, many of the Southeast Asian destinations, and cities in North America and Europe. Passengers arriving on long-haul flights should allow themselves a couple of rest days on arrival.

BY SEA

A few cruise ships visit New Zealand, but there are no regular passenger ship services to the country. Most cruises in the South Pacific originate in Sydney, Australia, so cruise operators generally fly their passengers to and from New Zealand. However, P&O Line, Royal Viking and some other cruise lines travel to New Zealand, mostly between November and April. Some cargo vessels also take small groups.

DVT Caution

To prevent deep-vein thrombosis (DVT) on long-haul flights, take note of the following guidelines:
• Be comfortable in your seat.
• Bend and straighten your legs, feet and toes every half-hour or so while seated during the flight.
• Press the balls of your feet down hard against the floor or foot-rest to help increase the blood flow.
• Do some upper body and breathing exercises to improve circulation.
• Take occasional short walks up and down the aisles.
• If the plane stops for re-fuelling, get off the plane and walk around, if this is permitted.
• Drink plenty of water.
• Don't drink too much alcohol.
• Avoid taking sleeping pills, which also cause immobility.

Practical Tips

Business Hours

Shops are open for business 8.30am– 5.30pm (Mon–Fri), and usually stay open until 9pm one night of the week. Hours on Saturday are usually from 10am until the early afternoon. Main cities and the larger tourist areas have extended opening hours, with many shops open seven days a week.

Banks are open 9.30am–4.30pm (Mon–Fri), and ATMs are plentiful.

Bars, pubs and taverns are open 11am–late (Mon–Sat). Nightclubs usually open their doors 7.30–8pm and close around 3am.

All banks, post offices, government and private offices and most shops close on public holidays. Most nightclubs and bars also close at midnight the night before each public holiday.

Tipping

Tipping is becoming more widespread in New Zealand, although it is still regarded as a foreign custom. In the major centres, tipping is encouraged but not expected. You should tip 5–10 percent of your restaurant bill if you feel the service was worthy. Service charges are not added to hotel or restaurant bills.

Media

PRINT

English is the most widely used language, followed by Maori, the indigenous language. There is a high level of literacy in New Zealand: most communities have a decent library, and sales of books, magazines and newspapers on a

per capita basis are among the highest in the world. One in four people in Auckland buys *The New Zealand Herald*, the morning daily. Most large towns have their own newspaper, and community newspapers abound.

International newspapers can be found in the larger bookshops and outlets at New Zealand's international airports.

Cuisine magazine is an excellent guide to New Zealand food and wine, with regular new restaurant reviews from around the country.

TV & RADIO

There are six public broadcasting channels. Two television channels are administered by a nominally independent government corporation: Television One and TV2. Two more channels, TV3 and Prime, are run by a Canadian-owned company. National and international news and current affairs programmes are usually carried on Television One and Prime. There are also several regional television stations. Many New Zealanders, and most hotels and motels, subscribe to the Sky satellite TV service for international sports and news, movie and music channels and a variety of other programming.

New Zealand has a selection of AM- and FM-band radio stations, satisfying a wide variety of tastes.

Postal Services

Post offices are generally open 9am–5pm (Mon–Fri). Some are also open Saturday mornings until midday. In many areas, postal services and stamps are also available from shops and other outlets. Post offices sell stamps, magazines and a range of stationery. NZ Post also offers a courier service within New Zealand.

Communications

To call New Zealand from overseas, dial its country code (64), but omit the 0 prefix on all area codes. Dial

the 0 prefix of the area code only when calling within New Zealand. To phone overseas from New Zealand, dial 00 followed by the national code of the country you are calling.

Note: Some businesses have free 0800 numbers which can only be dialled within New Zealand. 0900 numbers are charged to the caller by the minute, and are at premium rates.

Phone numbers appear in the White Pages (alphabetical listings) and the Yellow Pages (business category listings).

Public phones: Most public telephones accept cards that can be purchased from bookstalls and newsagents with a minimum value of NZ$5. Some public telephones also accept credit cards, and a few accept coins. Calls made from public telephones to the local area (free call zone) cost NZ50¢.

E-mail and Internet: There are numerous Internet cafés throughout New Zealand that provide access to Internet and e-mail. Many hotels and motels also have Internet access. You will need a RJ45 type plug to be able to connect your laptop into a computer socket in New Zealand and an adaptor with a flat two- or three-point power plug to connect to the power supply.

Mobile phones: Check with your phone company before leaving home about international mobile roam facilities in New Zealand. Mobile phones can also be hired on arrival

Telephone Area Codes

Northland: 09
Auckland: 09
Waikato: 07
Bay of Plenty: 07
Gisborne: 06
Hawke's Bay: 06
Taranaki: 06
Wairarapa: 06
Wellington: 04
Nelson: 03
West Coast and Buller: 03
Christchurch: 03
Timaru/Oamaru: 03
Otago: 03
Southland: 03

in New Zealand (outlets are available at international airports). To save on mobile phone bills, consider buying a prepaid phone card. Check with **NZ Telecom** (www.telecom.co.nz) and **Vodafone** (www.vodafone.com) shops in major towns and cities.

Local Tourism Offices

New Zealand is well served in terms of visitor information. In the city of Auckland, a team of "Ambassadors" wander the streets, waiting to answer every query. You can also find desks offering information and booking services at most airports and at over 60 prime locations around the country. A good start point is the **Tourism New Zealand**'s website www.newzealand.com. For specific contact details of local visitor information centres, see relevant regional listings on pages 343–88.

Local Missions

For information on foreign embassies in New Zealand, check the Ministry of Foreign Affairs and Trade website: www.mfat.govt.nz. Most foreign embassies are located in Wellington.
Australia: 72–76 Hobson Street, Thorndon, Wellington, tel: 04-473 6411.
France: 34–42 Manners Street, Wellington, tel: 04-384 2555.
Great Britain: 44 Hill Street, Thorndon, Wellington, tel: 04-924 2888.
United States: 29 Fitzherbert Terrace, Thorndon, Wellington, tel: 04-462 6000.

Disabled Travellers

Every new building or major reconstruction in New Zealand is required, by law, to provide "reasonable and adequate" access for people with disabilities. Most facilities have wheelchair access but it pays to check when booking.
Parking concessions are available for people with disabilities and temporary display cards can be issued for the length of the visitor's stay. For more information, check

the **Weka** website, www.weka.net.nz, New Zealand's disability information website, or call tel: 0800-171 981. Weka can direct you to any of the 23 Local Disability Resource Centres around the country.
Most transport operators can cater to people with special needs, although most urban transport buses are not equipped to cater to the disabled. A few tour operators provide custom holiday packages for individual and group travellers with disabilities. Contact:
Accessible Kiwi Tours, P.O. Box 550, Opotiki, New Zealand, tel: 07-315 6988; www.toursnz.com.
Ucan Tours New Zealand Ltd, 8 Campbell Street, Sumner, Christchurch, tel: 03-326 7881; www.ucantours.com.

Gay & Lesbian Travellers

There are plenty of facilities in New Zealand catering for the gay, lesbian and bisexual traveller. There is a range of diverse activities for this segment of travellers in the main cities. The best organisations to contact for information are:
Gay Tourism New Zealand: P.O. Box 11–462, Wellington 6015, tel: 04-917 9176; www.gaytourismnewzealand.com.
New Zealand Gay and Lesbian Tourist Association, QNZ Marketing Ltd: P.O. Box 638, Camp Street, Queenstown, tel: 21-762 796; www.gaypages.co.nz.
Other useful websites are www.gaytravel.co.nz and www.gaynz.net.nz.

Travelling with Children

New Zealand is a great place to visit with children, with a range of activities for the whole family to enjoy. Most hotels have reliable babysitters, kids' clubs and activities. For more information about planning family holidays in New Zealand, contact:
Familystophere.com: P.O. Box 12087, Wellington 6038, tel: 04-971 0646; www.familystophere.com

Personal Security

New Zealand is considered to be one of the safer countries in the world for travellers and suffers only isolated incidences of serious crime. However, petty crime is a problem. Take precautions to secure and conceal your valuables at all times, and never leave them in a car.
To report a crime, contact your nearest police station. New Zealand police generally do not carry weapons. You should find them approachable and helpful.
In an emergency dial 111 for ambulance, police or fire service. Emergency calls are free from public call boxes.

Medical Services

For non-emergencies, full instructions for obtaining assistance are printed in the front of telephone directories. Hotels and motels normally have individual arrangements with duty doctors for guests' attention, and they can also assist you in finding a dentist.
New Zealand's medical and hospital facilities, both public and private, provide a high standard of treatment and care. It is important to note that medical services are not free to visitors, except treatment for injuries in an accident.

Health and Beauty

PHARMACIES

Pharmacies, or chemists, are generally open 9am–5.30pm weekdays. Some also open on Saturday mornings and for one late night a week. Most major cities also have urgent dispensaries for emergencies, which remain open overnight and at weekends.

SPAS

Health Spas
Since the 1800s, New Zealanders have been soaking in the country's natural mineral waters, and the Maori have been doing so for a great

deal longer. But it wasn't until the latter part of the 19th century that the spa industry in New Zealand really began in earnest. Waiwera, to the north of Auckland, was the site of New Zealand's first natural spa.

Today, there are numerous natural spas and thermal resorts in New Zealand. These include the **Polynesian Spa** in Rotorua, the **Taupo Hot Springs Health Spa** in the North Island, and **Hanmer Springs Thermal Pools and Spa** in the South Island, to name a few.

Beauty Therapy and Day Spas

Beauty therapy clinics offering services such as sunbeds, day spas, manicures, pedicures, massages, body wraps, waxing, skin care and make-up can be found throughout New Zealand. Prices range from NZ$50 for a 40-minute massage to around NZ$500 for a full-day, complete beauty spa experience. Check the Yellow Pages for the nearest beauty salon or day spa.

Photography

Most New Zealanders don't mind being photographed but it's best to ask before you click. There are professional photographic labs and camera centres throughout the country. They have the most up-to-date digital and film-processing technology, and the latest camera and video gear. At some stores you can even hire equipment. You can also drop your film off at local pharmacies to be processed. There are also plenty of camera repair services throughout New Zealand. Check the Yellow Pages or the Internet for camera store locations.

Language

English is the common language of New Zealand. However, as this is a multicultural society, you may hear other languages spoken including Te Reo Maori, the other official language. The vast majority of New Zealand place names are of Maori origin. There are also television and radio programmes which broadcast entirely in the Maori language.

Useful Websites

www.newzealand.com – Tourism NZ's award-winning website.
www.holiday.co.nz – A travel guide and vacation planner with holiday options from motorcycle tours to accommodation.
www.aotearoa.co.nz – New Zealand and Pacific arts and crafts. You can order bone carvings, glass art, wood carvings and designer jewellery online.
www.nzedge.com – A comprehensive and eclectic site that explores the lives and achievements of New Zealanders living overseas and connects them on a global scale. The site contains a unique online shopping guide, news stories, a section dedicated to New Zealand "heroes", image galleries, speeches, web links and a global register.
www.nzmusic.com – The diversity of the Pacific sound is at your fingertips here. It has a catalogue of Kiwi artists, biographies, music, news, an extensive gig guide and a section dedicated to forums.
www.allblacks.com – Official site of the New Zealand Rugby Football Union and the All Blacks.
www.aa.co.nz – NZ's leading motoring organisation. Driver, accommodation and travel info.
www.nzmuseums.co.nz – An exhaustive listing of museums great and small, throughout the country.

Useful Maori Phrases

Kia ora – your good health (hello)
Kia ora tatou – hello everyone
Tena koe – greetings to you (said to one person)
Tena koutou – greetings to you all
Haere mai – welcome
Haere ra – farewell
Ka kite ano – until I see you again (good-bye)
moana – sea
puke – hill
roto – lake
tomo – cave
wai – water
whanga – bay
waitomo – water cave

Getting Around

By Air

Air New Zealand and **Qantas** are the main domestic carriers. The no-frills **Freedom Air**'s subsidiary **Freedom Air International** flies between Australia and New Zealand.

Helicopters are readily available in main cities and in the main tourist resort areas.

Although domestic flights can be expensive, there are plenty of deals around for flying in off-peak times, Internet and advance bookings or for booking ahead from overseas. Flights can be booked online, or with travel agents and accredited agents.

Air New Zealand, Sales and Reservations, tel: 0800-737 000 (reservations) or 0800-737 767 (travel centres); www.airnz.co.nz.
Qantas New Zealand, 191 Queen Street, Auckland, tel: 0800-808 767; For reservations, tel: 09-357 8900; www.qantas.co.nz.
Freedom Air, tel: 0800-600 500; www.freedomair.com.

By Sea

The North and South Islands are linked by modern ferries operated by *Interislander* and *Bluebridge*. The ferries sail between Wellington and Picton and carry passengers, vehicles and freight. There are frequent daily crossings in both directions, though it is important to book vehicle space in advance during summer. The journey time takes 3 hours (the *Interislander*).

There is a wide range of facilities and entertainment on board the *Interislander* including a bar, lounges and a café. Ferry tickets can be purchased at NZ Post outlets, travel agents and visitor information centres.

The *Interislander*, tel: 04-498 3302 or 0800-802 802; www.interislander.co.nz.
***Bluebridge*,** tel: 0800-844 844; www.bluebridge.co.nz.

By Rail

Tranz Scenic (tel: 04-495 0775, 0800-872 467; www.tranzscenic. co.nz) has two long-distance train services covering the South Island and one in the North Island. These services cut across some of the most spectacular scenery in the world. The trains are comfortably outfitted with an onboard dining car serving light meals and beverages.

Tranz Coastal: Along the coast between Picton and Christchurch. Connects with the ferries for the sea crossing over Cook Strait to Wellington in the North Island.

Tranz Alpine: Between Christchurch in the east and Greymouth on the west.

The Overlander: Between Wellington and Auckland.

A weekday-only commuter service, **Capital Connection,** links Palmerston North with Wellington.

Tickets can be purchased online, from any Tranz Scenic accredited agency, travel agents and visitor information centres. Enquire about the **Scenic Rail Pass,** which allows you to hop on and off Tranz Scenic trains (*see box on this page*).

Auckland and Wellington both have a commuter train system linking the outer suburbs to the centre of the city. Contact **Tranzmetro,** tel: 0800-801 701; www.tranzmetro.co.nz.

By Bus

City transport: Major cities all have extensive local bus services for getting you out and about economically. Check with visitor information centres in each town for details of how they operate. Have coins ready, as you usually pay on boarding. Bus passes are available from visitor centres and local convenience stores.

Inter-city coaches: There is an excellent inter-city coach network throughout the country, using modern and comfortable coaches (some with toilets). It is wise to reserve seats in advance, especially during summer months.

The major bus operators are **InterCity Coachlines** and **Newmans**. Travel and information centres throughout New Zealand can book bus tickets and multi-day passes for visitors. Services on main bus routes are frequent but slow. In addition, several smaller bus and shuttle companies operate regional and inter-city coach services. Check with local visitor information centres for contacts.

InterCity Coachlines:
www.intercitycoach.co.nz
Auckland, tel: 09-623 1503
Wellington, tel: 04-385 0520
Christchurch, tel: 03-365 1113
Dunedin, tel: 03-471 7143
Newmans Coach Lines:
www.newmanscoach.co.nz
Auckland, tel: 09-623 1504
Rotorua, tel: 07-348 0999
Wellington, tel: 04-385 0521
Christchurch, tel: 03-365 1114

Taxis

All cities and most towns have 24-hour taxicab services. Chauffeur-driven cars are also readily available.

By Car

Driving offers one of the best ways to see New Zealand's immense natural beauty.

Road conditions: Multi-lane highways are few – they generally only provide immediate access to and through major cities – and single-lane roads are the norm. While traffic is generally light by European standards, the winding and narrow nature of some stretches of roads means you can only go as fast as the slowest truck, so do not underestimate driving times. Main road surfaces are good and conditions are usually comfortable; the main problem you

Have Pass Will Travel

If you're planning to rely on public transport, consider buying a travel pass that allows a combination of bus, train, ferry and plane travel nationwide at a substantial discount. One such deal is the **New Zealand Travelpass** from InterCity Group (NZ) Ltd, tel: 09-638 5788, 0800-339 966; www. travelpass. co.nz. You can purchase this online or from any of the 400 agents nationwide. This pass can be used over 12 months.

Tranz Scenic (tel: 04-495 0775, 0800-872 467; www.tranzscenic.co.nz) has a 7-day **Scenic Rail Pass** for train travel either in the South Island or in the whole country, with an optional ferry crossing.

might encounter are wet road surfaces after heavy rains. Signposting is generally good.

Petrol: Unleaded 91- and 96-octane petrol is sold, along with diesel, at most service stations. Compressed natural gas and liquid petroleum gas are also offered.

Motoring Associations: A comprehensive range of services for motorists is available from the Automobile Association, and reciprocal membership arrangements may be available for those holding membership of foreign motoring organisations. **Automobile Association,** Head Office, 99 Albert Street, Auckland City, tel: 0800-500 543; www.aa.co.nz.

Documentation: You can legally drive in New Zealand for up to 12 months if you have a current driver's licence from your home country or an International Driving Permit (IDP).

Steep Streets

Dunedin in the South Island has the steepest street in the world. Baldwin Street has a 38 percent gradient, and motorists are advised not to try driving up it.

CAR HIRE

To hire a car, you must be 21 years of age or over and hold a current New Zealand or international driver's licence. Third-party insurance is compulsory, although most hire companies will insist on full insurance cover before hiring out their vehicles.

It is wise to book in advance. Major international hire firms such as Avis, Hertz and Budget offer good deals for pre-booking. If you have not pre-booked, tourist information desks at most airports can direct you to other operators to fit your budget.

The approximate cost per day for rental of a mid-sized car is NZ$80–$110, with competitive rates negotiable for longer periods.

Campervans are very popular in New Zealand and are both an economical and flexible means of exploring the country.

Car Hire Companies

Avis:
Auckland: tel, 09-379 2650
Wellington: tel, 04-801 8108
Christchurch, tel: 03-379 6133
Queenstown, tel: 03-442 3808
Dunedin, tel: 03-486 2780
www.avis.com

Ace Rental Cars:
Nationwide, tel: 0800-502 277
Auckland, tel: 09-303 3112
Wellington, tel: 0800-535 500
Christchurch, tel: 0800-202 029
Queenstown, tel: 0800-002 203
www.acerentalcars.co.nz

Budget:
Nationwide, tel: 0800-283 438
Auckland, tel: 09-976 2270
Wellington, tel: 04-802 4548
Christchurch, tel: 03-366 0072
www.budget.co.nz

Hertz:
Auckland, tel: 09-367 6350
Wellington, tel: 04-384 3809
Christchurch, tel: 03-366 0549
Queenstown, tel: 03-442 4106
Dunedin, tel: 03-477 7385
www.hertz.com

National Car Rentals:
Nationwide, tel: 03-366 5574 or 0800-800 115
www.nationalcar.co.nz

Where to Stay

Accommodation

HOTELS & MOTELS

International-standard hotels are found in all large cities, in many provincial cities, and in all resort areas frequented by tourists. In smaller cities and towns, more modest hotels are the norm.

Motels are generally clean and comfortable, with facilities ideal for families. Many offer full kitchens and dining tables, and some provide breakfast.

The New Zealand tourism industry uses Qualmark as a classification and grading system to help you find the best accommodation and shopping. There are five levels of grading from one star (minimum) to five stars (best available). Participation in the Qualmark system is voluntary so if a motel or hotel doesn't have a grading, its location and tariffs will usually give a reliable

Rules of the Road

- In New Zealand, you drive on the left side of the road and overtake on the right.
- Give way to traffic on the right.
- If you are turning left, you should give way to right-turning oncoming traffic.
- The wearing of seat belts – by the driver and all passengers – is compulsory.
- The legal speed limits are 100 km/h (60 mph) on open roads and 50 km/h (30 mph) in built-up areas, but watch for signposts superceding these limits.
- New Zealand's road signs follow the internationally recognised symbols.

indication of what to expect. Expect to pay surcharges for additional occupants and peak season.

Travel agents will be able to give details of concessions for children. (A guide is: children under two years of age, free; two to four, quarter of tariff; five to nine, half tariff; 10 years and over, full tariff.) Goods and Services Tax (GST) of 12.5 percent is added to most bills.

For recommendations on where to stay, see the regional listings on pages 343–88.

Hotel Price Guide

Approximate prices per night (off peak) for two people in a double room, including GST:

$	= below NZ$100
$$	= NZ$100–150
$$$	= NZ$150–200
$$$$	= NZ$200–250
$$$$$	= over NZ$250

FARMSTAYS, HOMESTAYS AND BED & BREAKFASTS (B&B)

More New Zealanders are opening their homes to visitors. There is a large number of B&B properties in cities, towns and rural locations, ranging from historic and heritage buildings to boutique inns.

Farmstays are an excellent way for visitors to see the real New Zealand, which has been dependent on farming since the colonial days. You may share the homestead with the farmer and his family, or, in many cases, may have the use of a cottage on the farm. Depending on the farm, you may get the chance to share home-cooked meals with your hosts and join in activities like sheep shearing and fruit harvesting.

If you are on a limited budget, you can try working farmstays. Over 180 farms offer free accommodation, meals and friendly hospitality in exchange for 4 hours of light work a day, doing tasks such as gardening and feeding animals. It is also possible to work flexible hours so that you have time to explore the area. Contact visitor information centres, or check the websites listed below.

New Zealand Farmstays and Homestays: 10 Locarno Street, Opawa, Christchurch, tel: 03-960 4394; www.nzhomestay.co.nz.

Rural Holidays New Zealand, P.O. Box 2155, Christchurch, tel: 03-355 6218; www.ruralholidays.co.nz.

Rural Tours NZ, P.O. Box 228, Cambridge, North Island, tel: 07-827 8055; www.ruraltourism.co.nz

Bed & Breakfast Collection, P.O. Box 31-250, Auckland, New Zealand, tel: 09-478 7149; www.bedandbreakfast.collection.co.nz.

HOSTELS

The **Youth Hostel Association of New Zealand** offers an extensive chain of hostels to members throughout New Zealand. Details of membership and hostel locations can be obtained from its National Office at Level 1, 166 Moorhouse Avenue, P.O. Box 436, Christchurch, New Zealand, tel: 03-379 9970, 0800-278 299; www.yha.org.nz.

MOTOR CAMPS

Most motor camps (caravan parks with tent sites as well) offer communal washing, cooking and toilet facilities. The camper is required to supply his own trailer or tent, but camps in larger towns and cities have cabins available.

Motor camps are licensed under the Camping Ground Regulation (1936) and are all graded by the New Zealand Automobile Association. It is a good idea to check with the AA on current standards within the camps.

In summer, do book ahead, as New Zealanders are inveterate campers. For details, contact: **Automobile Association**, Head Office, 99 Albert Street, Auckland , tel: 0800-500 543; www.aa.co.nz.

Top 10 Holiday Parks, 294 Montreal Street, Christchurch 8015, New Zealand, tel: 03-377 9900, 0800-867 836 ; www.topparks.co.nz.

Where to Eat

General

An abundance and variety of quality fresh meat, fish and garden produce fill the New Zealand larder with riches on which a world-class cuisine has been built.

New Zealand's market gardens are perhaps rivalled only by those of California in the US. Vegetables such as asparagus, globe artichokes and silver beet (swiss chard) – luxuries in some countries – are abundant here, as are pumpkins and kumara, the waxiest and most succulent of the world's sweet potatoes. Kiwifruit, apples, tamarillos, strawberries, passion-fruit, pears and boysenberries are shipped all over the globe, but while you are here, it's also well worth trying less famous fruits, such as pepinos, babacos and prince melons.

The waters surrounding New Zealand contain an abundant harvest, being the source of at least 50 commercially viable types of fish and shellfish – including crayfish, mussels, oysters, *paua* (abalone) and the tiny whitebait.

New Zealand lamb is perfection and richly deserves its world-renowned acclaim. Dishes that are particularly worthy of note are crown roast lamb and lamb spare ribs. The beef is excellent too, and game – including venison – is plentiful.

If you want to savour a national dish, you won't go far wrong with a helping of pavlova – a delicious concoction of meringue, topped with fresh fruit and whipped cream.

What to Drink

Wine: New Zealand wines win awards all over the world and are

well worth trying. The country's cool maritime climate and its summer rains produce light, elegant, fruity white wines – and, in recent years, some very fine red wines. See *Cuisine*, pages 99–103 and *Wine*, pages 107–109 for more details.

Beer: New Zealanders, with Australians, are among the biggest beer drinkers in the world: many of New Zealand's beers – Steinlager, Speights, Tui, DB Draught, Monteiths – rank with the great beers of Denmark and Germany.

Most nightspots, restaurants and cafés serve liquor, and you can buy alcohol from liquor outlets and supermarkets (beer and wine only) – if you're 18 and over.

Where To Eat

Good restaurants abound in the cities of Auckland, Wellington, Christchurch and Dunedin, and in major resort towns. Many of them specialise in international cuisines, most notably Japanese, Vietnamese, Indonesian, Chinese, Indian, Italian and Thai.

There are formal restaurants, of course, but New Zealanders tend to be more casual, and outdoor dining is popular in the summer months.

BYO means "Bring Your Own" bottle, and indicates that a restaurant is licensed for the consumption of alcohol, but not for selling it. At BYO restaurants you are likely to be charged a small "corkage" fee for supplying glasses and opening your bottle.

For recommendations on where to eat, look up the regional listings on pages 343–88.

Restaurant Price Guide

The following symbols indicate average prices per person for dinner, including service and tax:

$ = NZ$10–15
$$ = NZ$15–25
$$$ = NZ$25 and over

Culture

General

New Zealand's nightlife options can vary considerably, depending on the size of the place you are visiting. In small towns, you will find little more than a humble pub. Pubs are a great New Zealand social institution and you will seldom find yourself short of conversation or an opinion. In recent years, many city pubs have become more sophisticated, with "boutique" beer brewed on the premises, brasserie-style food and more fashionable furnishings.

The main cities have a variety of cosmopolitan dance clubs with a predominantly young clientele, as well as late-night bars. In Auckland and Wellington, and to a growing extent Christchurch, activity in the bars doesn't peak until after midnight. Auckland and Wellington are busy most nights of the week, while it is a little quieter in Christchurch until Thursday, Friday and Saturday nights. Queenstown reaches a critical mass at times, such as during the winter festival, when the parties don't seem to stop.

New Zealand's culture comprises a blend of influences, including Maori and Pacific Island, European, US and Asian. New Zealand performers, film-makers, writers, designers and musicians have made their mark with their own unique style and talent.

Museums and Galleries: New Zealand has a vibrant contemporary art scene, and most towns have museums and art galleries. Keep an eye out for works by some of the country's top artists including Ralph Hotere, Colin McCahon, Michael Parekowhai and Robyn Kahukiwa. The Dunedin Public Art Gallery is the country's oldest viewing room.

Classical Music and Ballet: The country has three professional symphony orchestras, including the New Zealand Symphony Orchestra, and its own professional ballet company, the Royal New Zealand Ballet. A number of contemporary dance companies are operating throughout the country, including Black Grace Dance Company

Maori Culture

The Maori people were the first to arrive in New Zealand and are the indigenous people of this country, or the *Tangata Whenua* (people of the land). The Maori make up about 14 per cent of the population and most live in the North Island. The Maori language *(te reo)* is spoken throughout New Zealand and the vast majority of place names are of Maori origin. As Maori are a tribal Polynesian people, they have a unique protocol which should be observed on a *marae* (which, as well as being a community centre, is a religious site). There are many tourist operators in New Zealand, particularly in Rotorua and Tauranga, who can organise *marae* visits.The important things to remember when visiting a *marae* are to take off your shoes before entering a meeting house and greeting your hosts with a *hongi* – a traditional Maori welcome where you press noses to signify friendship. Visitors to *marae* are often welcomed with a *powhiri* (formal welcome) and a *wero* (challenge). Many places in New Zealand have significant historical and spiritual value and are sacred to Maori. Visitors are urged to recognise the cultural significance of these places and treat them with respect.

If you would like more information about Maori culture, visit the following website: www.maori.org.nz.

(Auckland) and Footnote Dance Company (Wellington).

Contemporary Music: The music scene varies from rappers and DJs to jazz musicians and opera singers. It has produced some world-class performers from Kiri Te Kanawa to Neil Finn (Crowded House) and Pauly Fuemana (OMC). Other Kiwi performers making a name for themselves include Pacifier, Bic Runga, Stellar, The Datsuns, D4 and Hayley Westenra.

Theatre: Theatre is a thriving industry and New Zealand boasts a number of theatre companies, including Taki Rua in Wellington and the Auckland Theatre Company. There are venues for live theatre in most towns and cities, and many fine repertory theatre companies throughout the country.

Festivals: Festivals are plentiful, and there are arts festivals in most major New Zealand towns – from Bluff in the South to the Bay of Islands in the North. (See pages 334–336 for listings.)

Film: Movies such as Peter Jackson's *Lord of the Rings*, Lee Tamahori's *Once Were Warriors* and the hit cult television series, *Xena, Warrior Princess* have established the country's film-makers as some of the best in the world.

Listings: To find local cultural events, check the entertainment pages of the local newspaper or go to: www.artscalendar.co.nz. Other useful sources of information are: the monthly magazine *Theatre News*; *NZ Musician* (modern music); *Music in New Zealand* (classical); *Rip it Up*, *Real Groove* (pop/rock) and *Pulp*, all available at major newsagents or in libraries.

Most major events can be booked through the national ticketing agency, **Ticketek**. There are more than 200 Ticketek outlets in New Zealand. Contact: **Auckland**, tel: 09-307 5000; **Wellington**, tel: 04-384 3840; **Christchurch**, tel: 03-377 8899; www.ticketek.co.nz.

For recommendations on nightlife and entertainment, look up the regional listings on pages 343–88.

Festivals

Auckland

Anniversary Regatta – Annual sailing regatta that celebrates Auckland's birthday (one-day event).
ASB Bank Classic – Leading international and national women tennis players battle it out in this annual one-week tournament.
Heineken Tennis Open – International men's ATP tennis tour that precedes the Australian Open (week-long event).
New Zealand Golf Open – New Zealand's official golf championship. An open event that features players from throughout Australasia (three-day event).

Christchurch

World Buskers Festival – The world's best street acts converge on Christchurch (10-day event).

Rotorua

Opera in the Pa – International performers thrill capacity audiences in the ancestral grounds of Ohinemutu Geothermal Village on the shores of Lake Rotorua.

Wellington

Summercity – A series of small festivals around the city supported by the local council (two-month event).

February

Auckland

Devonport Wine and Food Festival – A two-day food and wine festival that is one of the highlights of the Auckland summer calendar.
Waiheke Island Wine Festival – An event for wine lovers showcasing the island's vineyards. Located on Waiheke Island in the Hauraki Gulf (two-day event).

Blenheim

BMW Marlborough Wine and Food Festival – Gourmet cuisine, local wine, workshops and music make up this extremely popular festival (one-day event). www.bmw-wine marlborough-festival.co.nz.

Canterbury

Coast to Coast – Longest running multisport event in the world. National and international participants run, kayak and cycle 238 km (148 miles) from the West Coast to Sumner Bay (two-day event).

Christchurch

Garden City Festival of Flowers – Helps Christchurch live up to its billing as New Zealand's garden city with abundant floral displays centred on Christchurch Cathedral.

Hamilton

Hamilton Gardens Summer Festival – A celebration of opera, theatre, concerts and performing arts in a garden setting.

Napier

Art Deco Weekend – This deco jewel of a town steps back in time en masse. Many deco landmarks are open to the public on this weekend.

Waitangi

Waitangi Day – The signing of the nation's founding document is celebrated in the Treaty House grounds with much pageantry, including a spectacular display of *waka* (canoes).

Wanganui

Masters Games – The largest multisport event in New Zealand (one-week event).

Various locations

Aotearoa Maori Traditional Performing Arts Festival – Teams of Maori performers from all over the country compete in traditional Maori performing arts (*kapa haka*) in even-numbered years. For locations check its website at www.maoriperformingarts.co.nz.

March

Auckland

Auckland Cup – One of the biggest days in New Zealand for thoroughbred horse racing.
Pasifika Festival – The biggest one-day Pacific Island Festival, celebrating Pacific Island cultures with food, arts and crafts, music, theatre, comedy and arts.
Round the Bays – Its moderate distance of 8.6 km (5 miles) makes for a high level of participation in this fun-run, and the waterfront route is unbeatable.
Hokitika Wild Foods Festival – This festival celebrates such gourmet delights as possum pie, huhu grub sushi, scorpions and the ever-popular euphemism – mountain (or prairie, depending where you come from) oysters.

Ngaruawahia

Ngaruawahia Regatta – The town's location at the meeting point of two rivers makes it the natural site for highly competitive Maori *waka* (canoe) races. This is an exciting event, and is also the only time the Turangawaewae Marae is open to the public.

Taupo

Ironman New Zealand – This is the longest endurance triathlon in New Zealand. It is one of the six qualifying races for the Ironman Triathlon World Championships (one-day event).

Tauranga

National Jazz Festival – Tauranga's bars and nightclubs come alive with the sounds of jazz during this weekend festival.

Waipara

Waipara Wine and Food Festival – Described as the "biggest little best wine-and-food celebration", this festival features leading wine makers and purveyors of fine food.

Wairarapa
Golden Shears – The world's premiere shearing and woolhandling championships (four-day event) celebrates one of New Zealand's foremost rural industries.

Wellington
New Zealand Arts Festival – Even numbered years only – New Zealand's premiere arts festival featuring national and international acts (four-week event).

April

Arrowtown
Arrowtown Autumn Festival – There's no prettier town in autumn, and local heritage is celebrated with numerous performances, parades and markets.

Auckland
Auckland Wine and Food Festival – Food event of the year. A unique opportunity for Aucklanders to treat their taste buds to a feast laid on by New Zealand's premier suppliers of cheeses, antipasto, continental meats, wine and premium beer.
Royal Easter Show – Livestock competitions, arts and crafts awards, wine awards and one of the largest equestrian shows in the southern hemisphere (one-week event).
Waiheke Jazz Festival – First-rate acts in a magnificent setting, and an opportunity to hear quality New Zealand (and overseas) musicians.

Bluff
Bluff Oyster and Southland Seafood Festival – The annual celebration of Southland's most precious gourmet delight with numerous oyster-themed events.

Christchurch
Montana Christchurch International Jazz Festival – New Zealand's biggest jazz festival, an annual event featuring local and international jazz luminaries. www.jazzfestchristchurch.com.

Hamilton
Balloons Over Waikato – A five-day event during which up to 40 hot air balloons grace the skies over the Waikato landscape. Includes a mass ascension of balloons at sunrise and sunset. The Night Glow event is unforgettable.

Taihape
Gumboot Day – Find out why Taihape is the gumboot capital of the world as rural New Zealand puts on a light-hearted celebration of itself.

Wanaka
Southern Lakes Festival of Colour – Wanaka hosts some of the country's most respected names in art, music, theatre and dance during this biennial celebration. www.festivalofcolour.co.nz.

May

Auckland
Great Barrier Island Seafood Celebration – a lively celebration of the island's bountiful seafood. www.seafoodgreatbarrier.com
International Laugh Festival – Comedy festival showcasing the best local, national and international comedians (two-week event).

Christchurch
Savour New Zealand – Every two years, a mouth-watering weekend of food, wine, cooking demonstrations and wine workshops takes place.

Manawatu
Manawatu Jazz Festival – Live jazz at various venues throughout Palmerston North (one-week event).

Rotorua
International Rally of Rotorua – FIA Pacific Rally championships in Rotorua's forest roads (two-day event).
Rotorua Tagged Trout Competition – Rotorua's premier fishing competition with a NZ$50,000 trout waiting to be hooked (two-day event).

June

Queenstown
Queenstown Winter Festival – One of the southern hemisphere's biggest and brightest winter parties in downtown Queenstown. The events range from the zany and hilarious to serious winter sports competitions (two-week event).

Waikato
Festival of New Zealand Theatre – A biennial, three-week national festival of theatre held in Hamilton.
National Agricultural Field Days – One of the largest agricultural shows in the world, held at Mystery Creek (three-day event).

July

Auckland and Wellington
International Film Festival – Three weeks of movie madness and the year's best cinematic offerings.

Volcanic Plateau
Ski Fest – The Ruapehu and Turangi skiing areas of the North Island host a more sedate version of the Queenstown event (above).

Wanaka
World Heli-Challenge – The annual gathering of the world's leading snowboarders and skiers in the premier helicopter-accessed free ski and free-ride competition. The two-week event ends with the Wanaka Big Air (free-style ski and snowboard championships).

August

Christchurch
Bay of Islands Jazz and Blues Festival – Jazz and blues on the streets and in selected venues in Paihia and Russell during this three-day event that draws both international and national talent.
Christchurch Winter Carnival – The week-long winter carnival celebrates the great features of Christchurch and Canterbury with skiing and snowboarding championships, "extreme" winter games, and a celebrity charity ball and dinner.

September

Alexandra
Alexandra Blossom Festival – Central Otago celebrates the

coming of spring with a parade, sheep-shearing competitions, entertainment and garden tours.

Auckland

New Zealand Fashion Week – A showcase of some of New Zealand's best fashion designers, with catwalk shows and a trade exhibition (one-week event).

Hastings

Hastings Blossom Festival – Hawke's Bay is one of the country's leading apple exporters and Hastings is known as the fruit bowl of New Zealand, so the blossoms are outstanding this time of the year. Highlights of this celebration of spring include a huge parade, performances by celebrity artists, concerts and a big fireworks finale. www.blossomfestival.co.nz

Rotorua

Rotorua Trout Festival – Marks the annual opening of the Rotorua Lakes. Anglers, who have been kept at bay since June, are out in full force (one-day event).

Te Puke

Kiwifruit Festival – The national fruit is celebrated in style, with a festival covering all aspects of kiwifruit, in the "home town" of the furry delicacy.

Wellington

Montana World of Wearable Art Awards – A fashion extravaganza of weird and wonderful designs by national and international designers, craftspeople and artists (three-day event).
Wellington Fashion Festival – The capital kicks off spring in style with fashion shows and in-store promotions (one-week event).

October

Gisborne

Gisborne Wine and Food Festival and International Chardonnay Challenge – The festival brings together a range of Gisborne wines and the culinary expertise of top New Zealand chefs using quality Gisborne produce (one-day event). www.internationalchardonnay challenge.com

Hawke's Bay

Hawke's Bay Show – One of Hawke's Bay's biggest events, attracting 60,000 spectators each year. Plenty of attractions, competitions and entertainment, with and without an agricultural bias (two-day event). www.hawkesbayshow.co.nz

Nelson

Nelson Arts Festival – An annual two-week showcase of artists from all over New Zealand, with cabaret, music, theatre, comedy and visual art. www.nelsoncitycouncil. co.nz/artsfestival

Taranaki

Taranaki Rhododendron Festival – This regional garden festival encompasses over 60 private gardens that are open to the public during the 10-day blooming period for rhododendrons (one-week event). www.rhodo.co.nz

Tauranga

Tauranga Arts Festival – Street theatre, dance, literature and other performing arts are brought to the fore in this biennial event, which is staged throughout the region (10-day event).

Various Locations

Fiji Day celebrates the anniversary of Fiji's independence, and involves communities throughout the country. Call the Fiji High Commission, tel: 04-473 5401 for details.

Wellington

Kaikoura Seafest – A celebration of the abundance of the ocean and the region's wines and foods, with continuous live entertainment. Bookings essential. www.kaikoura.co.nz/seafest
Wellington International Jazz Festival – One of the country's largest jazz festivals representing many different kinds of music from New Orleans, swing and fusion to experimental jazz (three-week event). www.jazzfestival.co.nz

November

Auckland

Ellerslie Flower Show – This is the largest floral exhibition in the southern hemisphere (five-day event). Combines with great food and wine, live entertainment "art".
Waitakere Pacifica Living Arts Festival – Enjoy fashion shows and try creative activities in traditional craft workshops during this cultural celebration of Pacific art, music, crafts and fashion.

Christchurch

Royal New Zealand Show – The country's biggest A&P (agriculture and pastoral) show, with a programme of events for all ages (two-day event).
Cup Carnival – The strongly contested New Zealand Trotting and Galloping Cups are just a part of the celebrations that form the Christchurch A&P Show.

Martinborough

Toast Martinborough – A wine, food and music festival that promotes the top-quality wine region of Martinborough. This is a hugely popular festival so get tickets early (one-day event). www.toastmartinborough.co.nz

December

Nelson

Nelson Jazz Festival – A variety of local and national jazz bands saturate Nelson with music in a week-long festival.

Taranaki

Festival of Lights – New Plymouth's Pukekura Park is beautifully illuminated by lights each December. The festival that is held when the lights are switched on is a one-day event, but the lights stay on for several weeks.

Wellington

Summercity – Not a big bash, but a series of small festivals that take place all around the city. It is supported by the local council (two-month event).

Shopping

SHEEPSKIN

With more than 45 million sheep in New Zealand, it comes as no surprise that among the country's major shopping attractions are its sheepskin and woollen products. You are unlikely to find cheaper sheepskin clothing anywhere in the world, and the colour and variety of items make them ideal gifts or souvenirs. Many shops stock a huge range of coats and jackets made from sheepskin, possum, deerskin, leather and suede.

WOOLLENS

New Zealand is one of the world's major wool producers, and experienced manufacturers take the raw material right through to quality finished products such as the beautiful Possum-marino garments, light, soft and so warm. Handknitted, chunky sweaters from naturally dyed wool or mohair are ideal if you are heading back to a northern winter. Innovative wall hangings created from home-spun yarns make another worthwhile purchase.

WOODCARVINGS

The time-honoured skills involved in Maori carvings have been passed down from one generation to the next. Carvings usually tell stories from mythology and often represent a special relationship with the spirits of the land. Maori carvings of wood and bone can command high prices.

GREENSTONE

New Zealand jade, more commonly referred to as greenstone, is a distinctive Kiwi product. The jade, found only on the West Coast of the South Island, is worked into jewellery, figurines, ornaments and Maori *tiki*. Factories in the West Coast towns of Greymouth and Hokitika allow visitors to see the jade being worked.

JEWELLERY

Jewellery made from greenstone and the iridescent *paua* (abalone) shell and bone have been treasured by Maori for centuries. You can buy such ornaments and unique contemporary jewellery from specialised stores.

HANDICRAFTS

There has been an explosion of handicrafts in recent years – sold by local craftsmen and craftswomen and by local shops catering specifically to tourists. Pottery is perhaps the most widely available craft product, though patchwork, quilting, canework, Kauri woodware, wooden toys, glassware and leather goods are among the enormous range of crafts available at the major tourist centres.

SPORTSWEAR & OUTDOOR EQUIPMENT

New Zealanders love the great outdoors, so it should come as little surprise that they have developed a wide range of hard-wearing clothing and equipment to match tough environmental demands.

Warm and rugged farm-wear like Swanndri bush shirts and jackets are popular purchases, while mountaineering equipment, camping gear and backpacks set world standards. Some items have even become fashion success stories, such as the Canterbury range of rugby and yachting jerseys.

Most shops are open from 9am–5.30pm (Mon–Fri); and 9am–4pm on Saturday and Sunday. Late night shopping (until 9pm) usually occurs on a Thursday or Friday night in cities and major towns depending on which part of the country you are in.

For recommendations on shopping places, look up the regional listings on pages 343–88.

CONTEMPORARY ART

Quality contemporary art, from the conservative to the ground-breaking, is surprisingly affordable in New Zealand. Artist's prints in particular are well-priced and easy to transport. The larger cities have private galleries that usually keep a wide range of artwork in stock.

DESIGNER CLOTHING

New Zealand designers, such as World, Karen Walker, Trelise Cooper, Sharon Ng, Sabatini, Nom*D and Zambesi, are making their mark on the international catwalks. Boutiques in the principal cities stock these award-winning New Zealand labels, as well as a range of international designers.

FOOD AND WINE

Processed items like local jams, chutney, pâtés, smoked beef and honey do not need documentation, and make excellent gifts as they are attractively packaged.

Wines are a real New Zealand success story. The country's young wines, with their fresh and exciting flavours, are jumping up and demanding attention in the international market. White varietal wines such as sauvignon blanc and chardonnay are consistent winners in New Zealand and have received many international awards.

Outdoor Activities

General

New Zealanders love the outdoors and there are plenty of places to cycle, walk, swim, ski, climb, bungy jump, fish, play golf or go rafting. Because the country has a low population density and spectacular scenery, you are never very far from an outdoor activity, whether an organised adventure or a peaceful walk in the bush. The opportunity to participate in so many activitites at low cost in some of the world's most beautiful locations is a major tourist drawcard, and local tourism operators have risen to the challenge by meeting this demand with a high level of professionalism and, equally important, safety.

For recommendations on outdoor activities, look up the regional listings on pages 343–88.

Land Sports

ABSEILING

New Zealand provides numerous opportunities to abseil down cliffs, waterfalls, canyons and some spectacularly deep holes in the ground. In some cities, it is possible to perform the urban equivalent and rappel down the outside of skyscrapers.

BUNGY JUMPING

Developed in the 1980s by New Zealand adventurers A.J. Hackett and Henry Van Asch, this exhilarating experience of throwing oneself off a high platform with a large rubber-band attached to the ankles has become world famous.

Today, there are four official **A.J. Hackett** (www.ajhackett.com) bungy jump sites in **Queenstown**, including the world's first 43-metre (47-yd) site at Kawarau Bridge, and a site at **Auckland Bridge**.

Bungy jumps are also offered by other operators.

CLIMBING

Rock climbing has experienced a phenomenal growth in New Zealand. There are now lots of indoor climbing walls in towns and cities, rock climbing clubs and excellent terrain to discover throughout the country. New Zealand has adopted the Australian "Ewbank" numerical grading system which uses a single numerical value to indicate route difficulty. Some of the best rock climbing areas include **Wharepapa**, south of the Waikato, which has more than 700 climbs and the **Canterbury** area which has more than 800 climbs.

For more information, contact: **Climb New Zealand**; www.climb.co.nz.

CYCLING

New Zealand's windy, rainy weather can sometimes take the pleasure out of cycling, as can the hilly terrain and narrow winding roads crowded with badly driven recreational vehicles. Cycle touring nevertheless offers huge rewards, and some organised tours include a bus to carry your luggage. Mountain bikes are available for hire. Some of the best places for cycling are in the South Island, in areas such as **Wanaka**, **Glenorchy**, **Queenstown** and the **Fiordland**. Highlights include abandoned gold-diggers' villages such as Macetown, breathtaking ravines in the Nevis Valley, and the roads leading up to the ski resorts, which offer superb lakeland views. One book providing detailed route descriptions is *Classic New Zealand Mountain-Bike Rides*, which has over 400 rides researched from Cape Reinga to

Scott Base. You can order the book online: www.kennett.co.nz/books.

GOLF

There are around 400 golf courses in New Zealand, with an average green fee of around NZ$15, and equipment for hire at low cost. The finest courses are in the Bay of Islands (Waitangi), near Taupo (Wairakei International Golf Resort), in Auckland (Titirangi) and in Arrowtown (Millbrook Golf and Country Club).

HIKING

New Zealand has 14 national parks and more than 5 million hectares – a third of New Zealand – is protected in parks and reserves. There are hundreds of walking opportunities in conservation areas and other places throughout New Zealand, as well as heritage walks which explore the country's cultural and natural history.

There are nine routes, known as

Hiking Hints

With the increase in the number of visitors to New Zealand, the impact on the country's natural environment has increased. There are several things you can do to protect the environment.
• Do not damage or remove plants in the forests.
• Remove rubbish. Do not burn or bury it.
• Keep streams and lakes clean.
• Take care when building fires.
• Keep on the track when walking.
• Respect New Zealand's cultural heritage.

To find out more information about how you can protect New Zealand's environment, visit the nearest Department of Conservation office or check out the Department's website www.doc.govt.nz, and the Biosecurity New Zealand website www.biosecurity.govt.nz.

the **Great Walks**, for which you need a pass. These are obtainable from offices of the Department of Conservation (DOC), and cost NZ$7–35 per night if you sleep in a hut during high season (Oct–Apr), or NZ$5–10 for a serviced campsite (which has flush toilets, tap water, kitchen, laundry, hot showers, rubbish collection, picnic tables and some powered pitches).

If you like hot showers and other home comforts, it is best to book a guided walk. But if you don't mind "roughing it" then try independent walking, staying in basic huts and tents. For detailed maps and information on hikes and hiking passes nationwide, contact the **Department of Conservation** (DOC), Conservation Information Centre, Ferry Building, Quay Street, Auckland, tel: 09-379 6476. There are DOC offices in all the main cities or check out the DOC's website www.doc.govt.nz.

Guided walking tours amid some of the country's most impressive scenery are available. Contact: **Active Earth** (tel: 25-360 268, 0800-201 040; www.activeearth newzealand.com), which takes small groups on hiking and trekking trips off the North Island's beaten track. **Hiking New Zealand** (tel: 274-360 268, 0800-697 232; www.nzhike. com) is another company that conducts small-group hiking tours throughout the south, accompanied by knowledgeable guides.

HORSE RIDING

Seeing New Zealand on horseback is one of the best ways of experiencing the country and its people at close quarters. Operators throughout the country organise treks which range from half-day to full-day and overnight trips.

MOUNTAINEERING

Before Sir Edmund Hillary (a New Zealander) conquered Everest, he practised in the Southern Alps. But even if your ambitions are less lofty,

you'll find plenty of climbing opportunities in New Zealand. There are numerous mountaineering and climbing clubs, including the New Zealand Alpine Club, which has a strong nationwide membership. Contact: **New Zealand Alpine Club**, Unit 6, 6 Raycroft Street, Opawa, Christchurch, New Zealand, tel: 03-377 7595; www.alpineclub.org.nz.

ORIENTEERING

This is something of a specialist activity, but for those who like having to find their way across unknown terrain with just a map and a compass, New Zealand is the perfect spot. Its varied, often rugged terrain provides plenty of challenges, with the bonus, usually, of some splendid scenery along the way. There are courses available for a variety of competence levels.

PARAPENTING/HANG GLIDING

Parapenting involves unfurling a canopy that lifts you from the ground as you take off down a hill. Once airborne you gain height and drift lazily around the sky. It can be done in tandem with an experienced operator. In hang gliding, you are strapped to a giant kite (together with the pilot of course!) and literally run off a mountain.

SKYDIVING

If launching yourself into the air from a mountainside is too passé for you – try jumping from a plane. Tandem skydiving has made this thrill accessible to all. Attached to an experienced skydiver by a special harness, there is little you need to do except follow the instructions and keep control of your fear. The bonus with this thrill is the stunning views offered by the plane ride as you circle above the drop zone. Operators are found throughout the country, but especially in **Queenstown** and **Wanaka**.

Mountain Tops

Did you know that the Southern Alps (stretching more than 700 km/435 miles) are larger than the French, Austrian and Swiss Alps combined?

Water Sports

DIVING

Diving in New Zealand's clear waters is an absolute delight, and not surprisingly the country has more divers per head of population than anywhere else in the world. There are many shipwrecks to explore in the **Marlborough Sounds** and **Bay of Islands**, where you'll find the remains of the anti-nuclear Greenpeace ship, the *Rainbow Warrior*, which was bombed by French agents in 1985.

FISHING

From October to April, New Zealand's tranquil waters attract anglers from all over the world. One in four New Zealanders goes fishing, but there are plenty of fish to go around. The best places for trout fishing are **Lake Rotorua** and **Lake Tarawera**. In the **Nelson Lake District**, in the north of the South Island, a guide will help you find eels weighing 20 kilos (44 lbs) and brown trout up to 50 cm (20 in) in length.

KAYAKING

With so much water around, both along the coast and on the lakes, this sport is enjoying a veritable boom in New Zealand, particularly in **Malborough Sounds** and the **Bay of Islands**. You can hire kayaks for guided or independent tours lasting one or more days.

RAFTING/JET BOATING

Wild, untamed rivers and spectacular scenery provide the perfect backdrop for New Zealand's numerous wild-water rafting expeditions.

Jet boats, which are fast, manoeuvrable and skim the surface of the water, were invented by a New Zealand farmer. One of the best places for this activity is Queenstown's **Shotover River**. Alternatively, many of New Zealand's rivers are ideally suited to white-water rafting, and you can enjoy the thrills and spills in an inflatable with up to seven other people; some of the most exciting rivers are the **Shotover** and **Kawarau** (both in Queenstown) and the **Kaituna** (Rotorua).

Less intrepid souls can go black-water rafting through the caves of **Waitomo** in the Waikato. You'll discover a labyrinth of dark caves with waterfalls, lit by glow-worms and providing endless fun.

SAILING

The best conditions for sailing occur between October and April. You will find the widest range of sailing boats for one-day and longer trips, with or without a skipper, in the **Bay of Islands**, **Auckland** and the **Marlborough Sounds**.

Chartering a fully equipped 12-metre (40-ft) yacht costs between NZ$2,000 and NZ$3,000 a week, depending on the season. One of the most scenic trips you can make is the "coastal cruise" along the coast of Auckland into the Bay of Islands; a 10-day minimum charter fee applies. A day's sailing in a group costs around NZ$60 per person.

SURFING

New Zealand's surrounding coastline ranges from gentle sloping beaches to rocky cliffs. There are excellent surfing conditions throughout the country from **Raglan** in the North Island to **Dunedin** in the South. Water temperatures vary, and the best waves are usually found in the winter months. A wetsuit is required most of the year, although surfers can get by with a

rash shirt in the North during the summer months (Dec–Mar). You'll find clean, barreling waves on the **East Coast** and heavier sets, sometimes as big as 3 metres (10 ft), on the **West Coast**.

For daily weather and surf conditions, up-to-date access to satellite images, surf cams and photographs of some of New Zealand's top surfing spots, plus information about contests, surf travel and surf stores around the country, check out: www.surf.co.nz or call **Wavetrack Surf Report**, tel: 0900-99 777 (New Zealand only, calls are at premium rates).

WHALE/DOLPHIN WATCH

You can get close to whales at **Kaikoura**, on the east coast of the South Island. Here, huge sperm whales swim barely 1 km (½ mile) off the coast between April and June; orcas can also be seen during the summer, and humpbacks put in an appearance during June and July.

In the **Bay of Islands**, you'll encounter bottlenose dolphins, orcas and sperm whales. Some trips also allow you to get into the water to cavort with the dolphins.

WINDSURFING

New Zealand is an ideal place for windsurfing because windless days are few and far between and there are miles of coastline, harbours and lakes in which to enjoy the sport.

Wavesailing conditions similar to those of Hawaii can be found in the North Island province of Taranaki. Those who prefer lakes will find plenty of opportunities at Lake Taupo, the largest in the country, or on the alpine lakes of the South Island. Other good windsurfing destinations include **Orewa Beach** (north of Auckland), **Piha Beach** (northwest of Auckland), **New Plymouth and Makatana Island** near Tauranga, and **Gisborne**. In the South Island, the wind and waves are particularly good at **Kaikoura**, **Whites Bay** (Blenheim), **Pegasus**

and **Sumner** bays near Christchurch, and the bays around **Dunedin and Cape Foulwind** (Westport). For more information check out: www.winzurf.co.nz.

Winter Sports

SKIING AND SNOWBOARDING

With the spectacular triple peaks of the North Island and the magnificent alps which run most of the length of the South Island, New Zealand is one of the world's great skiing destinations.

In winter, the Kiwis are magically transformed into "Skiwis". Between July and October, as soon as sufficient new snow has accumulated, snow-loving New Zealanders migrate from the water to the mountains. There are 27 peaks higher than 3,000 metres (9,843 ft), and another 140 exceeding 2,000 metres (6,562 ft), and many of the ski resorts have spectacular views of green valleys and deep blue lakes far below. The snowline is usually at around 1,000 metres (3,300 ft), and all the skiing areas are above the tree-line. This means there is plenty of space for everyone, and conditions are particularly ideal for the very popular sport of snowboarding. Most skifields have impressive, long runs and a range of slopes from beginner to professional-only. Fields pride themselves on having long vertical drops.

The main ski season runs from July to September, though this is often extended using artificial snow. A day pass costs NZ$74–79 for adults. Multi-day passes and season passes are also available. Ski gear including boots, skis and poles can be hired for around NZ$40–60 a day and snowboards and boots for around NZ$40–54.

Heli-skiing is an affordable luxury in New Zealand: three to five runs a day cost between NZ$645 and NZ$945. There are also week-long private heli-skiing charters, as well as daily heli-skiing packages tailored to your ability.

Ski Centres

The major **ski centres** in the **South Island** are at:

Cardrona: www.cardrona.com
Treble Cone: www.treblecone.co.nz
Coronet Peak:
www.nzski.com/coronet
Craiaieburn: www.icraiaicburn.co.nz
The Remarkables:
www.nzski.com/remarkables
Mount Hutt: www.nzski.com/mthutt
Ohau: www.ohau.co.nz
Porter Heights:
www.skiporters.co.nz
Temple Basin:
www.templebasin.co.nz

North Island ski centres are located at Tongariro National Park and around Mount Ruapehu, specifically Whakapapa (National Park or Whakapapa Village) and Turoa (Ohakune):
www.MtRuapehu.com

For more information, look up www.nzski.com and www.snow.co.nz.

Snow Safety

Be aware that even the most glorious mountain weather can deteriorate very rapidly, so be prepared for the worst conditions.

The NZ MetService provides weather forecasts for mountain areas, daily reports on ski conditions and the latest AA highway reports.

Central North Island: tel: 0900-999 15
Nelson Lakes: tel: 0900-999 02
Canterbury: tel: 0900-999 26
Southern Lakes: tel: 0900-000 81

For up-to-date information from ski areas on snow conditions, snow-cams and operating facilities, check out www.snow.co.nz.

When you're up on a mountain, you need to protect yourself from the elements. If you become cold, don't wait until you are shivering, move to shelter and warm up; if possible, have a hot drink. Remember that children tire more easily than adults. Carry snacks and eat regularly, as skiing and snowboarding are high-energy sports, and drink plenty of fluids. Don't forget lip balm, sunblock and sunglasses or goggles to prevent snow blindness.

Further Reading

History & Biography

Dictionary of New Zealand Biography (Dept. of Internal Affairs, 1990– 1998). A three-volume anthology covering the period since 1769.
Maori: A Photographic and Social History, by Michael King (Heinemann, 1984). Comprehensive illustrated history by one of New Zealand's foremost Maori historians.
The Penguin History of New Zealand, by Michael King (Penguin, 2003). An unprecedented bestseller; the definitive New Zealand history.
The Old-Time Maori, by Makereti, (New Woman's Press, 1986). The first of its kind: this ethnographic work, written by a Maori, was first published in 1938.
The Oxford Illustrated History of New Zealand, by Keith Sinclair (ed.). 2nd edition. (Oxford University Press, 1997). A complete general history.
Two Worlds: Meetings between Maori and Europeans 1642–1772, by Anne Salmond (University of Hawaii Press/Viking, 1991). A fascinating account, which attempts to give both points of view.
Wrestling with the Angel: A Life of Janet Frame, by Michael King (Picador, Macmillan, 2001). The award-winning authorised biography of acclaimed author Janet Frame by her close friend King.

Literature/Fiction

A Good Keen Man (Reed, 1960); **Hang on a Minute Mate** (Reed, 1961) and others by Barry Crump. Popular books by Kiwi adventurer.
A House at Karamu by Beryl Fletcher (Spinifex, 2003). In this excellent autobiography, Fletcher recalls her wartime childhood, love of opera and awakening to feminism.

The Book of Fame by Lloyd Jones (Penguin, 2001). The national pre-occupation with rugby comes under the eye of a post-modern novelist.
Dogside Story by Patricia Grace (Penguin, 2001). Internationally acclaimed novel explores the strength and conflicts of the whanau (family), the power of the land, and the aroha (sustaining love) and humour of the community.
Leaves of the Banyan Tree (Lane, 1979); **Ola** (Penguin, 1991), and others by Albert Wendt. Fine Samoan novelist, poet and short-story writer.
Once Were Warriors by Alan Duff (Tandem, 1990). A first novel that has been made into an internationally acclaimed film.
Owls Do Cry (W.H. Allen, 1961), **Living in the Maniototo** (G. Braziller, 1979) and other novels and short stories by Janet Frame; also a fascinating three-volume autobiography trilogy **To The Is-Land** (G. Brazillier, 1982), **An Angel at My Table** (1984) and **The Envoy from Mirror City** (1985), which was made into the award-winning film An Angel at My Table, directed by Jane Campion.
Playing God by Glenn Colquhoun (Steele Roberts, 2002). Prize-winning verse by a poet who is also a practising doctor.
Plumb by Maurice Gee (Faber and Faber, 1978). The first volume in the critically acclaimed trilogy including **Meg** (1981) and **Sole Survivor** (1983); provides a rich and complex insight into life in New Zealand over three generations.
The Oxford Companion to New Zealand Literature, ed. Roger Robinson and Nelson Wattie (Oxford University Press, 1998) offers an easily accessible, comprehensive record of New Zealand writing, with more than 1,500 entries on writers, novels, plays, poetry, periodicals, anthologies, literary movements, and professional organisations.
Pounamu, Pounamu by Witi Ihimaera (Reed, 1972). Acclaimed short stories, and the first book by one of New Zealand's most prolific writers.
Star Waka by Robert Sullivan

(Auckland University Press, 2000). Epic verse, which combines Pakeha and Maori issues, in part through the story of Captain Cook.

The Bone People by Keri Hulme (Spiral/Hodder and Stoughton 1983). Winner of the British Booker McConnell prize for fiction.

The Oxford Book of New Zealand Short Stories, by Vincent O'Sullivan (ed.) (Oxford University Press, 1992).

The Penguin Book of New Zealand Verse, by Allen Curnow (ed.) (Penguin, 1960).

The Penguin History of New Zealand Literature, by Patrick Evans (Penguin, 1990).

The Season of the Jew by Maurice Shadbolt (Hodder and Stoughton, 1986). The best-known novel of this prolific and highly regarded contemporary writer.

The Stories of Katherine Mansfield: ed. A. Alpers (Oxford University Press Auckland, 1984). Definitve edition of stories by New Zealand's best-known literary export.

The Vintner's Luck by Elizabeth Knox (Victoria University Press, 1998) . Unusually imaginative – for New Zealand – novel about a man's love affair with an angel.

The Woman Who Never Went Home (Penguin Books, 1987); ***The Grandiflora Tree*** (Viking Penguin, 1989***); Fifteen Rubies by Candlelight*** (Vintage, 1993), and others by Shonagh Koea.

Traditional Maori Stories. Translated by Margaret Orbell. Edited by Ian Wedde and Harvey McQueen (Reed, 1992).

Bookstores

Bearing in mind that New Zealand boasts the highest per capita readership of books and periodicals anywhere in the world, it is well worth paying a visit to some of New Zealand's fine bookshops. Whitcoull's is the country's major bookstore (and stationer) and offers a good selection of quality titles. There is a wealth of reading related to New Zealand.

North Island

Auckland

Getting There

The main gateway to New Zealand is the **Auckland International Airport** at Mangere, 24 km (15 miles) southwest of the city's downtown area. Bus, shuttle and taxi transfers are available into the city. You'll find them lined up outside the main terminal. Shuttles and buses cost about NZ$13–18 (Airbus) and take about an hour to reach the city. A taxi takes about half the time, but will cost about NZ$45–50.

As New Zealand's largest city, Auckland is well connected by a network of domestic flights and inter-city coaches, as well as rail services. See also Getting Around on pages 330–2.

Visitor Information

Auckland i-SITE Visitor Centre, Atrium, Sky City, corner of Victoria and Federal streets; daily 8am–8pm; tel: 09-363 7182–5; www.aucklandnz.com.

New Zealand Visitor Centre, AMEX Princes Wharf, corner Quay and Hobson streets; Mon–Fri 9am–5pm winter, 8.30am–6pm summer, Sat–Sun 9am–5pm; tel: 09-979 2333; www.aucklandnz.com.

City Transport

There is a great inner-city bus service and plenty of taxi services to choose from. You'll find taxi stands throughout the central city. Contact **Auckland Co-operative Taxis**, tel: 09-300 3000; www. cooptaxi.co.nz. Flagfall is NZ$2 and trips are charged at NZ$2.30 per kilometre; waiting time is charged at NZ70 cents per minute.

A NZ$14 **Auckland Discovery Day Pass** (tel: 09-366 6400;

www.maxx.co.nz) gives you unlimited rides on most buses, train and ferries for a day. You can buy the pass on any Link or Stagecoach bus, or at the ferry office. The Link bus is a convenient way to travel around the inner city. It travels both clockwise and anti-clockwise in a loop travelling through Ponsonby, K Road and the City. A ride costs only NZ$1.50.

Auckland also has a commuter train system, **Connex**, linking the city to the outer suburbs.

For all public transportation enquiries, call MAXX, tel: 09-366 6400; www.maxx.co.nz.

Where to Stay

Barrycourt Suites Hotel, 10–20 Gladstone Road, Parnell, tel: 09-303 3789; www.barrycourt.co.nz. Located 2 km (1 mile) from the city, 1 km (½ mile) from the beach, this hotel offers rooms, motel units with kitchens and serviced apartments, many with grand harbour and sea views. Licensed restaurant, bar and spa. 107 units and suites. **$–$$$$$**

Heritage Auckland, 35 Hobson Street, tel: 09-379 8553; www.heritagehotels.co.nz. Located downtown near the America's Cup Village and transformed from a landmark building which used to house Auckland's most significant department store. Two distinctive wings offer full services. The Tower Wing has an indoor lap pool, sauna, spa and gym, while the Hobson Street Wing (the old department store) has a rooftop pool, spa and gym. Other facilities include an all-weather tennis court, two restaurants and a bar. 467 rooms and suites. **$$$–$$$$$**

Hilton Auckland, 147 Quay Street, Princes Wharf, tel: 09-978 2000; www.hilton.com. One of Auckland's contemporary five-star properties, this boutique hotel occupies a prime position 300 metres (328 yds) out to sea on Princes Wharf, commanding uninterrupted views of the harbour. 166 rooms and suites. **$$$$–$$$$$**

Hyatt Regency Auckland, corner of Waterloo Quadrant and Princes streets, tel: 09-355 1234; www.auckland.regency.hyatt.com. Completely refurbished in 2003, the hotel has 385 rooms, many with lovely views of the harbour, city and parks. Guests have access to a luxury health and fitness spa. **$$$$–$$$$$**

Langham Hotel Auckland, 83 Symonds Street, tel: 09-379 5132; www.langhamhotels.com. Situated in the heart of the city, the Langham offers five-star luxury in its 410 rooms. Featuring 24-hour service, butler service, an outdoor heated pool, gym and business centre with high-speed broadband. **$$$–$$$$$**

New President Hotel, 27–35 Victoria Street West, tel: 09-303 1333; www.newpresidenthotel.co. nz. Comfortable rooms and suites with kitchenettes. Ideally situated between Skycity and Queen Street. **$$–$$$$**

Parnell Village Motor Lodge, 2 St Stephens Avenue, Parnell, tel: 09-377 1463; www.parnellmotorlodge. co.nz. Choose between elegant Edwardian rooms and modern apartments near Parnell shops. Five minutes from downtown Auckland. **$–$$$**

Ranfurly Evergreen Motel, 285 Manukau Road, Epsom, tel: 09-638 9059; www.ranfurlymotel.co.nz. Spacious self-contained units, sleeping up to five, located 500 metres (547 yds) from restaurants and 1 km (½ mile) from the racecourse and showgrounds. On airport bus route. 12 units. **$$**

Rendezvous Hotel Auckland, corner of Vincent Street and Mayoral Drive, tel: 09-366 3000; www.rendezvous hotels.com/auckland. Near the waterfront and within walking distance of the main commercial and entertainment area. The Rendezvous has 24-hour room service, shops, currency exchange and some executive rooms. 452 rooms. **$$$$$**

Sky City Grand Hotel, 90 Federal Street, tel: 09-363 7000, 0800-804 111; www.skycityauckland. co.nz. Located in the heart of the city adjacent to Sky City Hotel, this is one of Auckland's newest hotels,

with 316 rooms, a spa, gym, indoor lap pool, club lounge and business centre. It also has two restaurants, most notably the highly acclaimed Dine by Peter Gordon (tel: 0800-759 2489), which serves superlative food with imagination and flair. **$$$$–$$$$$**

Sky City Hotel, Victoria Street, tel: 09-363 6000, 0800-759 2489; www.skycityauckland.co.nz. Located in the Sky City complex, this hotel has luxury and premier suites, a heated roof-top pool and gym, restaurants and bars. Among its range of nightlife options are two on-site casinos. Free parking. 344 rooms. **$$$$$**

The Ascott Metropolis, 1 Courthouse Lane, tel: 09-300 8800, 0800-202 828; www.theascottmetropolis.com. Voted New Zealand's leading hotel in the 2005 travel awards, this hotel in the heart of the city combines influences from cosmopolitan Manhattan and Chicago. Elegant one- and two-bedroom suites offer unashamed luxury, with separate living and dining areas, a designer kitchen and breathtaking views of the harbour and nearby Albert Park. **$$$$–$$$$$**

The Great Ponsonby Bed and Breakfast, 30 Ponsonby Terrace, Ponsonby, tel: 09-376 5989, 0800-766 792; www.greatpons.co.nz. Located close to all the major attractions, this small hotel in a restored 1898 villa offers a range of rooms. **$$$–$$$$$**

Where to Eat

Antoine's, 333 Parnell Road, tel: 09-379 8756; www.antoines restaurant.co.nz. Elegant, highly innovative gourmet restaurant, on a busy shopping street with many other good eateries. The menu offers New Zealand cuisine with French undertones. **$$$**

De Post Belgian Beer Café, 466 Mount Eden Road, Mount Eden, tel: 09-630 9330; www.de post.co.nz. This very popular bar has a great range of Belgian beers and some of the best mussel dishes anywhere. **$$**

Euro Restaurant and Bar, 22 Princes Wharf, tel: 09 309 9866. Fashionable restaurant that was *the* place to be during the America's Cup. The high-quality food and service is still maintained, and the focus is on fresh New Zealand produce. **$$$**

Harbourside Seafood Bar and Grill, 1st Floor, Ferry Building, 99 Quay Street, tel: 09-307 0556; www. harboursiderestaurant.co.nz. Like CinCin on the ground floor, this restaurant offers imaginative seafood cooking. Great view. **$$$**

Iguacu, 269 Parnell Road, tel: 09-358 4804; www.iguacu.co.nz. Large, busy bar and restaurant featuring Pacific Rim food. **$$**

Kermadec Ocean Fresh Restaurant, Viaduct Quay (opposite the Maritime Museum), tel: 09-309 0412; www.kermadec.co.nz. Very good fish dishes. **$$**

KK Malaysian Cuisine, 463A Manukau Road, Epsom, tel: 09-630 3555. Malaysian food doesn't come any fresher or tastier, and you're spoilt for choice in this unpretentious, inexpensive eatery set amongst Epsom's antique shops. **$**

Prego, 226 Ponsonby Road, Ponsonby, tel: 09-376 3095. Great food, Italian classic and more cooked with panache. A top restaurant. **$$$**

Rice, 10–12 Federal Street, CBD, tel: 09-359 9113; www.rice.co.nz. International cuisine, with mouth-watering recipes derived from 20 types or derivates of rice. Try the entrée platter, especially the BBQ pork and crispy vermicelli. Modern and chic, it has a stylish bar. **$$**

Rocco, 23 Ponsonby Road, Ponsonby, tel: 09-360 6262; www.rocco.co.nz. Modern and healthful cuisine is served in an intimate and cosy atmosphere, with an extensive range of wines. **$$$**

Soul Bar and Bistro, Viaduct Harbour, tel: 09-356 7249; www.soulbar.co.nz. By far the best choice at the Viaduct Harbour, with fabulous fish dishes. Enjoy some of New Zealand's most popular soul food while appreciating the harbour views. **$$–$$$**

SPQR, 150 Ponsonby Road, Ponsonby, tel: 09-360 1710; www.spqr.co.nz. One of Auckland's most famous and best-loved restaurants, with great cuisine, notably the linguini and clams. It becomes a popular nightspot once the plates are cleared away. Dark interior; pavement tables. **$$$**

The French Café, 210 Symonds Street, tel: 09-377 1911; www.thefrenchcafe.co.nz. Winner of many prestigious awards, including *Cuisine* magazine's 2006 Restaurant of the Year, the French Café serves contemporary European cuisine in a friendly and intimate environment. There's a relaxed bar for pre- and post-dinner drinks and a conservatory room that overlooks the courtyard where one can enjoy dining alfresco.

Where to Shop

Auckland's **Queen Street** is a good place to start, and at the top is **Karangahape Road**. "Karangahape" translates as "winding ridge of human activity", an apt description of one of Auckland's busiest and oldest commercial streets – and red-light district central. Small second-hand clothing and furniture shops compete for business with spacious department stores. There are also plenty of souvenir shops on Queen Street.

For mainstream international brands, head to **St Lukes** in Mount Albert. The suburbs of **Parnell**, **Ponsonby** and **Newmarket** also offer a wide choice. Check out the back streets in Newmarket where there are many interesting shops.

Modish **Vulcan Lane**, fashionable **High Street** and the **Chancery** shopping area are home to many chic boutiques and stores of New Zealand designers such as Karen Walker, World, Zambesi and Ricochet. **Pauanesia** in High Street stocks designer jewellery and ornaments from throughout the Pacific.

The Old Customhouse, corner of Customs and Albert streets near the downtown Ferry Building is the place to go for luxury labels and duty free shopping.

Make sure you pay a visit to **Victoria Park Market** (www.victoria-park-market.co.nz), with its distinctive chimney stack on Victoria Street. It's filled with stalls, shops and cafés. On Friday and Saturday the stallholders in the **Aotea Square Markets** outside the Aotea Centre, Queen Street, offer a variety of Pacific Rim arts and crafts, souvenirs and clothing – some collectable, some forgettable.

At **Elephant House**, 203 Parnell Road, over 300 craftspeople exhibit their handcrafted wares.

Entertainment

New Zealand's biggest city is home to several dance and theatre companies, its own arts festival, and 3 theatres: the Civic, Aotea Centre and Sky City Theatre. The entertainment section of the *New Zealand Herald* is the best source of performances listings. Book for major events through **Ticketek** (Aotea Centre, Aotea Square, Queen Street, tel: 09-307 5000; www.ticketek.co.nz).

Theatre/Dance

The 700-seat **Sky City Theatre**, which opened in 1997 in the Casino Complex (entrance at the corner of Hobson and Wellesley streets), tel: 09-912 6000; www.skycity.co.nz; **Maidment Theatre** (in the university, corner of Princes and Alfred streets, tel: 09-308 2383; www.maidment.auckland.ac.nz), the **Herald Theatre** and **ASB Auditorium** (Aotea Centre complex, tel: 09-309 2677; www.the-edge.co.nz) are three of the most popular venues for drama. The opulent **Civic** (tel: 09-309 2677; www.civictheatre.co.nz) is usually used for touring musicals and shows.

Details of performances at various venues by the Auckland's main theatre group, **Auckland Theatre Company**, are available at tel: 09-309 3395; www.atc.co.nz. For the **Auckland Music Theatre Company**, contact tel: 09-846 7693.

Smaller venues producing more innovative work include **Silo**, Lower Greys Avenue in central Auckland,

The main concert and opera venues are the modern **Aotea Centre** and the **Town Hall** (Aotea Square, Queen Street, tel: 09-309 2677; www.the-edge.co.nz). There's also the **Bruce Mason Theatre** on the North Shore, which is mostly used for larger productions. For bookings, tel: 09-488 2940; www.bmcentre.co.nz. Smaller, part-time venues include the old theatre complexes in the city centre, which host concerts and shows by international DJs and musicians.

Authentic Maori ceremonies and dances are performed daily at 11am, noon and 1.30pm in the **Auckland War Memorial Museum** (Domain, tel: 09-309 0443). Performances last approximately 45 minutes.

tel: 09-366 0339; www.silotheatre.co.nz, and **Depot Arts Space**, 28 Clarence Street, Devonport, over the Harbour Bridge on the North Shore, tel: 09-963 2331; www.depotartspace.co.nz.

Auckland is also home to the all-male dance company, **Black Grace**, featuring some of New Zealand's finest and most respected contemporary dancers, tel: 09 358 0552; www.blackgrace.co.nz.

Nightlife

It's hard to escape the buzz of Auckland's nightlife. Walk along Ponsonby Road, turn left into K Road, then down Queen Street and through to the viaduct and you'll hear music pulsating from every doorway. Most clubs have dress codes and you won't get in wearing shorts or gym shoes. Some clubs are discreetly hidden away up staircases or down alleyways, and only the locals know they exist, but follow the music and you're bound to find them. Some of the popular bars include:

Caluzzi, 461–463 Karangahape Road, tel: 09-357 0778; www.caluzzi.co.nz. For a unique, unforgettable night out with great food, this is the place. Plus a disco, DJs and an interactive show by award-winning drag artistes.

Fu Bar, 166 Queen Street, tel: 09-309 3079. Fu Bar is a relaxed hideaway with friendly staff, attracting drum-and-bass fans.

Hush Lounge Bar, corner of Paul Matthews Road and Omega Street, Albany, North Shore, tel: 09-414 5679. A swish watering hole in the heart of Albany. Boasts a comprehensive cocktail list, small dinner menu and has a sunny outdoor courtyard.

Khuja Lounge, 3rd Floor, 536 Queen Street, tel: 09-377 3711. An intimate Moroccan-themed bar hidden away up three flights of stairs. Great DJs, soulful jazz and excellent chocolate martinis.

Outdoor Activities

Auckland is a great centre for outdoor activities. You can do just about everything, from hurling yourself from the Sky Tower on a cable and climbing over the harbour bridge to sailing and golf.

Bridge Climb

For a bird's eye view of the city, try a ½-hour guided climb over the Auckland Harbour Bridge. A maze of catwalks and surprising twists and turns add to the thrill of this outdoor adventure. Contact: **Auckland Bridge Climb**, Curran Street, Westhaven Reserve, tel: 09-361 2000; www.ajhackett.com.

Bungy Jumping

A.J. Hackett Bungy, Curran Street, tel: 09-361 2000; www.ajhackett. com. This was the world's first harbour bridge bungy jump, run by the outfit that originally developed the sport. The latest in adventure technology is used – with a purpose-built jump pod and retrieval system for maximum safety and comfort for the jumpers.

Skyjump, Sky Tower, corner of Victoria and Federal streets, tel: 0800-759 586 or 09-368 1835; www.skyjump.co.nz. Touting itself as a world-first adventure experience, the 192-metre (630-ft) Skyjump is a cable-controlled base jump with

great views. Jumpers drop at up to 80 km/h (51 mph).

Golf

Akarana Golf Club, 1388 Dominion Road, Mount Roskill; tel: 09-620 5461; www.akaranagolf.co.nz. This course has tree-lined fairways, with bunkers protecting most greens, and panoramic views from the clubhouse.

Windsurfing

There are plenty of great wind-surfing spots in Auckland, including the popular **Point Chevalier** near the city centre, **Orewa Beach** (north of Auckland) and **Piha Beach** (northwest of Auckland). Winds are consistent, but seldom very strong. You can hire from **Point Chev Sailboards**, 5 Raymond Street, Point Chevalier, tel: 09-815 0683.

Wineries

Fine Wine Tours, 33 Truro Road, Sandringham, tel: 09-849 4519,

---

Sailing in Auckland

Auckland isn't called the City of Sails for nothing. The best conditions for sailing occur between October and April. You will find a wide range of sailing boats for 1-day and longer trips. Chartering a fully equipped 12-metre (40-ft) yacht costs between NZ$2,000 and NZ$3,000 a week, depending on the season. Or take a daily cruise on the former America's Cup New Zealand yachts, NZL 40 and NZL 41 (NZ$135 adult, NZ$110 child for 2 hours). Match racing in the yachts is also available from October to April (NZ$195 adult, NZ$175 child). Contact **Sail NZ**; tel: 0800-724 569; www.sailnz.co.nz. Another sea-going option is **Auckland Dolphin and Whale Safari**, tel: 0800-397 567; www.explorenz. co.nz. Alternatively, take a 2½ hour dinner cruise on a 15-metre (49-yards) yacht around the Auckland harbour. Price: NZ$95. **Pride of Auckland**, tel: 09-373 4557; www.prideofauckland.com.

021-626 529, 0800-023 111; www.insidertouring.co.nz. Conducts personalised wine-tasting tours for one to nine people.

Auckland's Surroundings

WAITAKERE CITY & WEST COAST BEACHES

Visitor Information

Destination Waitakere, tel: 0800-724 636; www.waitakerenz.co.nz. **Arataki Visitors Centre**, daily 9am–5pm summer; 10am–4pm winter; tel: 09-817 4941. The place to plan explorations of the Waitakere Ranges and west coast beaches.

Where to Stay

Auckland Waitakere Estate, 573 Scenic Drive, Waiatarua, tel: 09-814 9622; www.waitakereestate. co.nz. A private paradise surrounded by rainforest, perched at 244 metres (800 ft) above sea level, yet within easy reach of the city centre. $$$–$$$$

Hobson Motor Inn, 327 Hobsonville Road, Upper Harbour, tel: 09-416 9068; www.hobson.co.nz. This inn has fully self-contained units, plus swimming pool, spa, sauna and mini-golf course. 29 units. $$–$$$

Karekare Beach Lodge, 7 Karekare Road, Karekare Beach, tel: 09-817 9987; www.karekarebeachlodge. co.nz. A secluded getaway opposite one of the coast's most stunning beaches, the location for the movie *The Piano*. $$$–$$$$$

Lincoln Court Motel, 58 Lincoln Road, Henderson, tel: 09-836 0326; www.lincolncourtmotel.co.nz. Ideally located for exploring the Waitakere Ranges and west coast beaches. $–$$

Piha Lodge, 117 Piha Road, Piha, tel: 09-812 8595; www.pihalodge. co.nz. This small, award-winning facility has magnificent views of the sea and bush, plus pool, spa and games room. 2 units. $$

Vineyard Cottages, Old North Road, Waimauku, tel: 0800-846 800. Self-contained cottages set in an attractive vineyard with picturesque gardens. $$$$

Where to Eat

Beesonline Honey Centre and Café, 791 SH16, Waimauku, tel: 09-411 7953; www.beesonline.co.nz. It's not just for apiarists – this stylish licensed café serves first-class food with an emphasis on fresh organic produce, local ingredients and honey. **$–$$**

Devines, 1012 Scenic Drive, Swanson, tel: 09-832 4178. A popular haunt for the locals, with outside dining in summer. **$**

The Elevation, 473 Scenic Drive, Waiatarua, tel: 09-814 1919. Good food, wine and music in a prime location high on top of the Waitakere Ranges, with fantastic panoramic views of Auckland city. A great stopover on a day trip to Piha, serving brunch on weekends. Dinner reservations are recommended. **$$$**

The Hunting Lodge, Waikoukou Valley Road, Waimauku, tel: 09-411 8259; www.thehuntinglodge.co.nz. Fine dining; game is a speciality. **$$$**

Outdoor Activities
Walks

Arataki Park Visitor Centre, Scenic Drive, Titirangi, tel: 09-817 0077. For guided walks of varying degrees of difficulty through some of west Auckland's most impressive stands of forest. Alternatively, contact **Friends of Arataki** at 09-827 3803; www.friendsofarataki.org.nz.

Golf

Muriwai Golf Club, Muriwai Beach, tel: 09-411 8454; www.muriwai. nzgolf.net, is a links course with fantastic views over the west coast and undulating fairways over the natural landscape.

Titirangi Golf Club, Links Road, New Lynn, tel: 09-827 5749; www.titirangigolf.co.nz. One of New Zealand's top courses, with tight fairways, deep gullies and subtle bunkers set amid exotic trees, native bush and streams.

Surfing

The best surf beaches in Auckland are on the west coast, and include **Piha**, **Maori Bay**, **Muriwai** and

Bethells. Up north along the east coast are **Mangawhai** and **Whangapaoroa**. Keep an eye on serious rips and tidal changes, especially on the west coast, which is renowned for its danger spots. **Dial-a-forecast:** 0900-99 990 (premium rates apply).

Wineries

Collard Brothers, 303 Lincoln Road, Henderson, tel: 09-838 8341; e-mail: collardsnzwines@ xtra.co.nz; Mon–Sat 9am–5pm, Sun 11am–5pm. This family-owned winery, producing award-winning wines, offers tastings (Jun–Nov) by appointment.

Matua Valley Wines, Waikoukou Road, Waimauku, tel: 09-411 8301; www.matua.co.nz. Open daily 10am–5pm. In a delightful garden setting, this winery offers cellar-door sales.

Soljans Estate Winery, 366 SH16, Kumeu, tel: 09-412 5858; www.soljans.co.nz. Tours and tastings by arrangement. Offers complementary tastings and a café.

HELENSVILLE

Where to Stay

Frech Orchards Estate Bed and Breakfast, 85 Shelly Beach Road, tel: 09-420 210; www.chrissys preserves.co.nz. This quality homestay overlooking Kaipara Harbour is set in an organic avocado orchard close to an 18-hole golf course. It is also the home of **Chrissy's Preserves and Kitchen**, a purveyor of jams and chutneys made from freshly picked fruit, An exercise/sauna room is available and an outdoor swimming pool opens October to April. The upstairs guest lounge has great views. **$$**

Where to Eat

Café Regent, 14 Garfield Road, tel: 09-420 9148. Standard fare served with a flourish in a converted cinema. **$$**

Macnuts Farm Café and Shop, 914 South Head Road, Parakai, tel: 09-420 2501; www.macnut.co.nz. Book to tour the macadamia

orchard and enjoy lunch from a somewhat macadamia-dominated menu at the farm café. **$**

Riverview Restaurant and Corridor Bar, 88 Commercial Road, tel: 09-420 6040. Enjoy good food and great views from the deck overlooking the Kaipara River.

Outdoor Activities
Hiking

Beach Walks, from SH16 take the Rimmers Road turn-off for some bracing walking along lesser-known beaches of the west coast.

Swimming

Aquatic Park Parakai Springs, Parkhurst Road, Parakai, tel: 09-420 8998; www.parakaisprings. com. Enjoy a relaxing soak in the mineral pools, hire a private pool or have fun on the giant water slide. Open daily 10am–10pm.

SOUTH AUCKLAND

Visitor Information

Franklin i-SITE Visitor Centre, SH1, Mill Road, Bombay, tel: 09-236 0670; www.franklincountry.com.

Auckland Airport i-SITE Visitor Centre, International Terminal, Mangere, tel: 09-275 6467; www.aucklandnz.com.

Where to Stay

Airport Goldstar Motel, 255 Kirkbride Road, Mangere, tel: 09-275 8199; www.airportgoldstar. co.nz. Airport-handy accommodation in a quiet setting. **$–$$$**

Cedar Park Motor Lodge, 250 Great South Road, Manurewa, tel: 09-266 3266; www.cedarparkmotor lodge.co.nz. Conveniently sited for the airport and other South Auckland attractions. **$–$$**

Centra Auckland Airport, corner of Ascot and Kirkbride roads, tel: 09-275 1059, 0800-651 110; www. centra.co.nz. Set in 4 hectares (10 acres) of tranquil gardens, this is a relaxing hotel, some 4 km (2 miles) from the airport and 14 km (8½ miles) from the city. Facilities include a sauna, gym, outdoor swimming pool and play area. 242 rooms. **$$$**

Clevedon Maritime Resort, 261 North Road, Clevedon, tel: 09-292 8572; e-mail: m.e.balemi@xtra.co. nz. With its own marina, golf course and lake, and a self-contained guesthouse and double rooms. **$$$**
Jet Inn Airport Hotel, 63 Westney Road, Mangere, tel: 09-275 4100, 0800-538 466; www.jetinn.co.nz. Five minutes from the airport and 15 km (9 miles) from downtown, this 131-room hotel has four room types to accommodate different needs. Has a 24-hour complimentary courtesy shuttle. **$$–$$$$$**

Where to Eat
Broncos Steak House, 712 Great South Road, Manukau, tel: 09-262 2850. As reliable as restaurants with "steak house" as part of the name the world over. **$–$$**
Volare, 91 Charles Prevost Drive, Manurewa, tel: 09-267 6688. Famous for its convivial atmosphere and one of the most popular restaurants in south Auckland. International cuisine. **$$**

Outdoor Activities
Golf
Aviation Country Club of NZ, Tom Pearce Drive, Auckland International Airport, tel: 09-275 6265. Part of this 18-hole course at the airport runs beside the Manukau Harbour.

Wineries
Villa Maria Estate, 118 Montgomerie Road, Mangere, tel: 09-255 0660; www.villamaria. co.nz. One of New Zealand's leading, and longest-established, wineries. Cellar shop tastings, sales and winery tours.

Otara Market

New Zealand's largest street market, Otara Market (Sat 6am–noon), at Newbury in South Auckland, is not to be missed. It's where sensible tourists shop for souvenirs – not just because they are better value for money than the shops in the tourist traps, but also because of the obvious authenticity.

DEVONPORT

Visitor Information
Devonport i-SITE Visitor Centre, 3 Victoria Road, tel: 09-446 0677; www.northshore.org.nz; Mon–Fri 8am–5pm, Sat–Sun and public holidays 8.30am–5pm.

Where to Stay
Devonport Motel, 11 Buchanan Street, tel: 09-445 1010. A historic building, close to all the main attractions, provides privacy, comfort and great value. 2 units. **$$**
Earnscliff Mansion Bed and Breakfast, 44 Williamson Avenue, tel: 09-445 7557; www.earnscliff. co.nz. Bed-and-breakfast accommodation in this beautifully restored 1822 mansion with Victorian-style rooms, set in extensive gardens. **$$$$$**
Esplanade Hotel, 1 Victoria Road, tel: 09-445 1291; www.esplanade hotel.co.nz. Built in 1903, this lovingly restored luxury boutique hotel has it all – charm, ambience and friendly service. It's a 10-minute ferry ride from downtown Auckland. 17 suites. **$$$–$$$$$**

Where to Eat
Buona Sera, 99 Victoria Road, tel: 09-445 8133. Good international food; the pizzas are deservedly praised. **$$**
Manuka Restaurant, 49 Victoria Road, tel: 09-445 7732. Superior dining with a relaxed and friendly atmosphere. **$$$**
Monsoon Café Restaurant, 71 Victoria Road, tel: 09-445 4263. Specialises in Thai and Malay food, to eat in or take out. **$–$$**

OREWA

Visitor Information
The Hibiscus Coast Visitor Information Centre, 214A Hibiscus Coast Highway, Orewa, tel: 09-426 0076. Open daily 10am–4pm.

Where to Stay
Anchor Lodge Motel, 436 Hibiscus Coast Highway, Orewa, tel: 09-427 0690; www.anchorlodge.co.nz.

Devonport Shops

Art of this World, Shop 1, 1 Queens Parade, tel: 09-446 0926; www.artofthis world.co.nz. Art and sculpture by New Zealand-based artists.
Flagstaff Gallery, 25 Victoria Road, tel: 09-445 1142; www.flagstaff.co.nz. Contemporary New Zealand art.
Green Planet Enterprises Ltd, 87 Victoria Road, tel: 09-445 7404; www.greenplanet. co.nz. High-quality, New Zealand-made eco-friendly merchandise.

Next to the seafront and a safe swimming beach and close to shops and restaurants. **$–$$$**
Edgewater Motel 387 Main Road, Orewa Beach, tel: 09-426 5260; www.edgewaterorewa.co.nz. One- and two-bedroom family units, plus a luxury beachfront honeymoon suite with spa bath. **$–$$$**

Where to Eat
Kaizen Café, 350 Hibiscus Coast Highway, Orewa, tel: 09-427 5633; www.kaizencafe.co.nz. Delicious Italian-style food made with organic and free-range produce. Try the organic Italian coffee and fruit gelato. The queue for the very addictive breakfast starts at 7am.
Sahara Café and Restaurant, 336 Hibiscus Coast Highway, tel: 09-246 8828. Mediterranean-style cuisine. **$$**

WARKWORTH AREA

Visitor Information
Warkworth i-SITE Visitor Centre, 1 Baxter Street, Warkworth, tel: 09-425 9081; www.warkworth-information. co.nz. A good website for the area is www.matakanacoast.com.

Where to Stay
Bridgehouse Lodge, 16 Elizabeth Street, Warkworth, tel: 09-425 8351; www.bridgehouse.co.nz. Comfortable rooms, gaming room and the most stunningly appointed bar and restaurant. **$$**

Leigh Sawmill Café, 142 Pakiri Road, Leigh, tel: 09-442 6019; www.sawmillcafe.co.nz. Five spacious double suites with ensuites and private courtyards, plus two comfy bunkrooms. Great restaurant and microbrewery. Live music performances too – Russell Crowe played here in 2006. **$–$$**
Walton Park Motor Lodge, 2 Walton Avenue, Warkworth, tel: 09-425 8149; www.waltonpark.co.nz. Studio and family units, handy for the town centre and Kawau Island ferry. **$–$$**

Where to Eat
Café and Bar, 1 Omaha Flats Road, Matakana, tel: 09-422 7360. Hearty meals are the hallmark of this large, family-friendly country café. The complex includes a children's playground, Saturday craft market and horse-riding centre. Very popular, so reservations are recommended. **$$$**
Fallowfield Historic Homestead Café, 11 Paihia Road, Taumarere, Kawakawa, tel: 09-404 1555. New Zealand produce is featured in a vast park-like setting surrounding a Victorian villa. **$$**
Leigh Sawmill Café, 142 Pakiri Road, Leigh, tel: 09-422 6019; www.sawmillcafe.co.nz. One of the area's most esoteric cafés, specialising in fresh local fish (straight from the commercial fishery next door) and pizzas.
Millstream Bar and Grill Theatre, 15–17 Elizabeth Street, Warkworth, tel: 09-422 2292. Popular bar and restaurant serving excellent fare but pricey. **$$$**
The Meeting House Restaurant, 10 Elizabeth Street, Warkworth, tel: 09-422 2555; www.meetinghouse. co.nz. Perhaps this doesn't have great kerb appeal, but don't be put off. There's beautiful contemporary New Zealand–Maori cuisine here. Indigenous ingredients are used and seafood is especially recommended. Warm ambience and good local wines. **$$$**

Outdoor Activities
Diving
Dive Tutukaka, Marina Road, Tutukaka, tel: 09-434 3867; www.

diving.co.nz. Centred on the Poor Knights Islands, which some divers have rated among the 10 best diving spots in the world.
Goat Island Dive, 142A Pakiri Road, Leigh, tel: 09-422 6925, 0800-348 369; www.goatislanddive.co.nz. Diving operation and boat charter based at the magnificent Goat Island Marine Reserve.

Horse Riding
Pakiri Beach Horse Rides, Rahuikiri Road, Pakiri Beach, Wellsford, tel: 09-422 6275; www.horseride-nz.co.nz. Ninety minutes' drive from Auckland. Sharley and Laly Haddon cater for all riding abilities, beginners included. Daily one- and two-hour rides, half- and full-day rides and also multi-day safaris, including a 7-day Great Northern coast-to-coast ride.

Wineries
Ascension Vineyards and Café, 480 Matakana Road, Matakana, tel: 09-422 9601; www.ascension vineyard.co.nz. Open for tastings and sales daily, and excellent food is available in the café.
Heron's Flight Vineyards and Café, 49 Sharp Road, Matakana, tel: 09-422 7915; www.heronsflight.co.nz.

Warkworth Shops

Craft Co-Op @ Sheepworld, 324 SH1, Warkworth, tel: 09-425 0525. This is New Zealand's largest craft co-op, with a dazzling variety of locally produced goods made from both traditional and more innovative materials. Good café.
Honey Centre, corner SH1 and Perry Road, Warkworth, tel: 09-425 8003; www.honeycentre. co.nz. Sells all varieties of New Zealand's excellent honey.
Morris and James Pottery and Café, 48 Tongue Farm Road, Matakana, tel: 09-442 7484; www.morrisandjames.co.nz. This establishment has a devoted following among locals and tourists alike for its brightly coloured pottery.

Air New Zealand ranks this as one of the best five wineries to visit in the country. The courtyard café has a great view – and herons to spot.
Hyperion Wines, 188 Tongue Farm Road, Matakana, tel: 09-422 9375; www.hyperion-wines.co.nz. This winery produces mostly cabernet sauvignon and merlot, also pinot gris and chardonnay.

WAIHEKE ISLAND

Visitor Information
Waiheke Island i-SITE Visitor Centre, 2 Korora Road, Artworks, Oneroa, tel: 09-372 1234; www.waihekenz.com

Where to Stay
Beachside Lodge, 48 Kiwi Street, Oneroa, tel: 09-372 9884; www.beachsidelodge.co.nz. Self-contained apartments or bed and breakfast, near the beach. **$$**
Crescent Valley Ecolodge, 50 Crescent Road East, tel: 09-372 3227; www.waiheke.co.nz/ ecolodge.htm. Hidden away in native bush that's home to tuneful songbirds, yet just five minutes to popular Palm Beach. Organic meals available. **$$**
Le Chalet Waiheke Apartments, 14 Tawas Street, Little Oneroa, tel/fax: 09-372 7510; www.waiheke.co.nz/ lechalet. Self-contained luxury apartments near beaches, with private decks and sea views. **$$**

Where to Eat
Nourish Café, 3 Belgium Street, Oneroa, tel: 09-372 3557. Fresh, seasonal gourmet café fare with takeaways available. **$**
Vino Vino Restaurant, 3/153 Ocean View Road, Oneroa, tel: 09-372 9888; www.vinovino.co.nz. Casual Mediterranean platters or à la carte dining, on a deck with stunning bay views. Reservations are essential. **$**

Outdoor Activities
Wineries
Mudbrick Vineyard and Restaurant, Church Bay Road, tel: 09-372 9050; www.mudbrick.co.nz. A

popular wine-and-dine location, featuring international cuisine.
Te Whau Vineyard Restaurant, 218 Te Whau Drive, Rocky Bay, tel: 09-372 7191; www.tewhau.com. With New Zealand's longest wine list, including its own, this restaurant has a stunning sea view and serves New Zealand–Pacific cuisine.

KAWAU ISLAND

Where to Stay

The Beach House Resort, Vivienne Bay, tel: 09-422 8850; www.kawauresort.co.nz; e-mail: beachhouse@paradise.co.nz. Comfortable accommodation located on a pristine beach ideal for swimming, kayaking, snorkelling and fishing. With bush walks on the property as well. Restaurant serves international-style cuisine. **$$$$$**
Kawau Lodge, tel: 09-422 8831; www.kawaulodge.co.nz. An island homestay set amid native bush, accessible only by water. Queen rooms with ensuites, kayaks for guests' use, plus sailing and fishing options. **$$–$$$**

Where to Eat

Mansion House Café, Mansion House, tel: 09-422 8903. Open for light snacks and coffee. **$**

GREAT BARRIER ISLAND

Visitor Information

Great Barrier Island Visitor Information Centre, Claris Postal Centre, tel: 09-429 0033; www.greatbarrier.co.nz. Note: there are no banks on the island so do bring cash, although credit card and EFTPOS facilities are available at most commercial outlets.

Where to Stay

Great Barrier Lodge, Whangaparapara, RD1, tel: 09-429 0488; www.greatbarrierlodge.com. Modern studios and cottages in a water-front setting. **$–$$**
Medlands Beach Backpackers, Masons Road, tel: 09-429 0320; www.medlandsbeach.com.

Comfortable family accommodation with great views. **$**
Tipi & Bob's Waterfront Lodge, 38 Puriri Bay, Tryphena, tel: 09-429 0550; www.waterfrontlodge.co.nz. Qualmark-rated lodge with spectacular sea views, licensed restaurant and bar. **$$$**

Where to Eat

Claris Texas Café, Hector Sanderson Road, tel: 09-429 0811. Standard café fare for breakfast and lunch. Daily from 8am. **$**
Currach Irish Pub, Pah Beach, Stonewall, Tryphena, tel: 09-429 0211. Authentic Irish atmosphere, great pub food with Guinness and Kilkenny on tap. **$$**

Outdoor Activities

Kayaking
Aotea Kayaks, 6 Mulberry Grove, Tryphena, tel: 09-429 0664; e-mail:

Island Excursions

The main islands of the Hauraki Gulf – Rangitoto, Waiheke, Tiritiri Matangi and Great Barrier – are accessible by the fast ferries operated by **Fullers Cruise Centre** (Ferry Building, 99 Quay Street, Auckland, tel: 09-367 9111; www.fullers.co.nz). Don't miss the return ferry, as there is no accommodation on some islands and alternative transport to the mainland is expensive.
If you wish to bring your car to Great Barrier Island, book with **Sea Link**, 45 Jellicoe Street, Auckland Viaduct, tel: 09-300 5900; www.sealink.co.nz.
Great Barrier Island is also serviced by flights scheduled three times daily. Contact **Great Barrier Airlines**, Auckland Domestic Airport Terminal, tel: 09-2759 120, 0800-900 600; www.greatbarrierairlines.co.nz.
Kawau Island and all the islands in the Hauraki Gulf are served by **Reuben's Water Taxis and Kawau Cruises**, Sandspit Wharf, Warkworth, tel: 09-425 8006, 0800-111 616; www.watertaxi.co.nz.

aoteakayak@hotmail.com. Provides fully equipped rentals, guided kayaking and snorkelling trips.

Fishing and Diving
Tryphena Charters, tel: 09-429 5969; e-mail: tryphena.charters@xtra.co.nz. Coastal charters of up to four people. Craig McInman is a font of local knowledge and can tailor a charter to suit, be it fishing, diving and sightseeing, or a combination of all three.

Northland

Visitor Information

Far North i-SITE Visitor Centre, Jaycee Park, South Road, Kaitaia, tel: 09-408 0879; www.visitnorthland.co.nz.

Getting There

The Bay of Islands is about 250 km (155 miles) north of Auckland. **Air New Zealand** operates daily flights from Auckland to **Kerikeri** airport, Northland's main city. The flight time is around 45 minutes. There's a shuttle service from the airport.
The **Northliner** operates a daily luxury express coach service from Auckland to the Bay of Islands and to Kaitaia in the far north. Prices are NZ$49–72 one way. Contact: **Northliner Travel Centre**, Sky City Terminal, Auckland, tel: 09-307 5873; www.intercitycoach.co.nz.
The Bay of Islands is 3½ hours' drive from Auckland via the East Coast Highway or five hours if you travel past the mighty Waipoua forest (the largest kauri forest in New Zealand). See also Getting Around on pages 330–2.

City Transport

Northland is well served by buses in and out of the region, as well as inner-city bus and taxi services in most towns.

PAIHIA

Visitor Information

Bay of Islands i-SITE Visitor Centre, The Wharf, Marsden Road, tel: 09-402 7345; www.paihia.co.nz.

Where to Stay

Abel Tasman Lodge, corner of Marsden and Bayview roads, tel: 09-402 7521; www.abeltasman lodge.co.nz. Superior waterfront apartments plus family motel units. A minute's walk to Paihia wharf and town centre. 25 units. **$–$$$$**

Beachcomber Resort, 1 Seaview Road, tel: 09-402 7434, 0800-732 786; www.beachcomber-resort.co. nz. A splendid resort with a private beach for safe bathing, plus heated swimming pool, tennis courts and sauna. It also has an award-winning restaurant and bar, and is close to all town centre amenities and restaurants. 45 rooms. **$$–$$$$$**

Blue Pacific Quality Apartments, 166 Marsden Road, tel: 09-402 0011; www.bluepacific.co.nz. Just minutes from Paihia township, these high-quality one- to three-bedroom apartments, have breathtaking views of the Bay of Islands. Each has a full kitchen plus a private balcony or courtyard. 11 units and 1 studio. **$$$–$$$$$**

Paihia Beach Resort and Spa, 116 Marsden Road, tel: 09-402 0111; www.paihiabeach.co.nz. Panoramic sea views from its suites and studios, which have private patios, spa baths, and kitchen and dining facilities. Spa and heated seasonal swimming pool. **$$$$$**

Where to Eat

Bistro 40 and Only Seafood, 40 Marsden Road, tel: 09-402 7444; www.bistro40.co.nz. Right on Paihia's waterfront, Bistro 40 offers some of the best of New Zealand's cuisine and wines. **Only Seafood** (tel: 09-402 6066) upstairs is a more casual restaurant overlooking the Bay of Islands, serving fresh local seafood. **$–$$**

Pure Tastes Restaurant, Paihia Beach Resort, 116 Marsden Road, tel: 09-402 0003; www.puretastes. co.nz. Award-winning chef Paul Jobin serves superlative dishes using local produce. Reservations recommended. **$$$**

The Sugar Boat, Waitangi Bridge, tel: 09-402 7018; www.sugarboat. co.nz. Waterfront dining on a beautifully restored sugar lighter,

one of six built in 1890 by the Chelsea Sugar Company. There is an open-air cocktail bar on the top deck. The elegant dining room below deck serves Mediterranean-style fare made with fresh local ingredients. **$$$**

Tides Restaurant, Williams Road, tel: 09-402 7557. A restaurant that specialises in New Zealand cuisine, close to the Pahia wharfs. **$**

Waikokopu Café, Treaty Grounds, Waitangi, tel: 09-402 6275. Award-winning café, set in a shady garden at the entrance to Waitangi Treaty Grounds. Food ranges from breakfast and light snacks to main meals of lamb, beef and seafood. **$–$$**

Outdoor Activities

Cruising/Sailing

Fullers Bay of Islands, Maritime Building, Pahia Waterfront, tel: 09-402 7421; www.fboi.co.nz. The Bay of Islands is renowned for sailing and Fullers has luxury cruises, the 90-minute high-speed Excitor Tour to Cape Brett and through the famous Hole in the Rock, plus "swimming with dolphins" adventures.

Kings Dolphin Cruises and Tours, Maritime Building, Pahia Waterfront, tel: 09-402 8288; www.dolphin cruises.co.nz. Operates various boat trips to the Bay of Islands, including to the Hole in the Rock and Cathedral Cave. The 600hp *Mack Attack* carries 30 passengers and can travel up to speeds of 50 knots (90km/h). Also organises dolphin-watch and swimming tours and trips to Cape Reinga and Ninety Mile Beach.

Diving

Dive North, Main Wharf, tel: 09-402 7079; www.divenorth.co.nz. Takes divers to many dive locations in the Bay of Islands, including the wreck of the *Rainbow Warrior*, the Cavalli Islands and Cape Brett.

Paihia Dive, P.O. Box 210, Paihia, tel: 09-402 7551, 0800-107 551; www.divenz.com. Trips to the *Rainbow Warrior*, as well as the Three Kings diving area.

Dolphin- and Whale-Watching

Explore NZ, New Zealand Post Building, corner of Marsden and

Williams roads, tel: 0800-365 7446; www.explorenz.co.nz. Runs regular trips from Paihia and Russell to see bottlenose dolphins, orcas and sperm whales.

Golf

Waitangi Golf Club, Paihia, tel: 09-402 8207; www.waitangigolf.co.nz. One of New Zealand's finest golf courses with impressive scenery.

Kayaking

Coastal Kayakers, Te Karuwha Parade, Ti Bay, Waitangi, tel: 09-402 8105; www.coastalkayakers. co.nz. There are more than 150 scenic islands to explore by sea kayak. Coastal Kayakers conducts guided tours, from half-day to three days. NZ$55 to NZ$480 per person.

Scenic Flights

Salt Air, Paihia Waterfront, tel: 09-402 8338, 0800-472 582; www. saltair.co.nz. Operates light plane and helicopter flights to scenic spots in the Bay of Islands and to Cape Reinga. The latter combines with a four-wheel drive tour of the sand dunes at Ninety Mile Beach.

RUSSELL

Visitor Information

Russell Information Centre and Wahoo Fishing Charters, end of the Wharf, tel: 09-403 8020.

Where to Stay

Commodore's Lodge Motel, The Waterfront, tel: 09-403 7899; www. commodoreslodgemotel.co.nz. These spacious and luxurious self-contained, studios open onto a subtropical garden on the waterfront. Solar-heated pool, children's pool, spa and barbeque. 11 units. **$$–$$$$$**

The Duke of Marlborough Hotel, Waterfront, tel: 09-403 7829; www.theduke.co.nz. "The Duke" holds New Zealand's oldest liquor licence and has been a haven of hospitality for over 150 years. An elegant refurbished hotel, it offers superb dining and well-equipped ensuite rooms of various types. It is right on the waterfront, next to the ferry terminal. 25 rooms. **$$$–$$$$$**

Eagles Nest, 60 Topeka Road, tel: 09-403 8333; www.eaglesnest. co.nz. Luxury retreat with self-contained villas, a spa, sauna and 20-metre (65-ft) horizon-edge heated lap pools. The restaurant serves Pacific Rim cuisine and the extensive cellar stocks some of the best local and French wines. Beautiful native bush walks lead to private beaches. **$$$$$**

Where to Eat
The Duke of Marlborough Hotel, Waterfront, tel: 09-403 7829. The hotel has a fine restaurant, where you can't go wrong with the locally caught seafood. **$$**

Gannets Brasserie, York Street, Town Square, Russell, tel: 09-403 7990; www.gannets.co.nz. Seafood is a speciality here, and vegetarians are well catered for. **$$**

The Gables, The Strand, tel: 09-403 7618. Housed in one of New Zealand's oldest buildings, built in 1847, the Gables has retained many original features, including kauri panelling, open fires, original maps and old photographs. The menu is contemporary Mediterranean. **$$$**

Kamakura, The Strand, tel: 09-403 771. Great waterfront location for fine dining and wining. **$$$**

Strand Shopping
The Strand is Russell's premiere all-weather retail therapy centre with everything from fine food to high fashion and gifts.

Outdoor Activities
Cruises
Fullers Russell, The Strand, tel: 09-403 7866; www.fboi.co.nz. The Cape Brett Hole in the Rock cruise includes the eponymous gap, Cape Brett Lighthouse and Grand Cathedral Cave, and includes a stop ashore on Urupukapuka Island.

Fishing
Major Tom Charters, tel: 09-403 8553, 027-437 7844; www. majortom.co.nz. A serious fishing boat whose fun-loving crew hold numerous New Zealand and world records for marlin, broadbill, swordfish, tuna, kingfish, snapper and sea bass. For game fishing, plan for mid-December to mid-May; fishing for grouper, kingfish, sea bass, snapper and saltfly is available year round.

Winery
Omata Estate, Aucks Road, tel: 09-403 8007; www.omata. co.nz. Stunningly sited premium winery attached to the Omata luxury resort and two restaurants, the Mediterranean-style Omata Estate Vineyard Restaurant and the alfresco The Chef's Bench. Booking essential.

KERIKERI

Where to Stay
Kerikeri Homestead Motel, 17 Homestead Road, tel: 09-407 7063; www.kerikerihomestead motel.co.nz. In a tranquil area, with views of Kerikeri golf course, each boutique unit has cooking facilities and four have spa baths. Huge pool and outdoor spa. Close to a restaurant and bar. 12 units. **$$**

Ora Ora Resort, 28 Landing Road, tel: 09-407 3598; www.oraora resort.co.nz. This upmarket resort promises a panoply of pampering options, and its Makai Restaurant serves fine organic food, wines and beer. **$$$$$**

Pagoda Lodge, 81 Pa Road, tel: 09-407 8617; www.pagoda. co.nz. This charming 1930s lodge harmoniously blends elements of

the East and the West. Its peaceful grounds overlook a river and bush reserve. Luxury tent accommodation is also an option. **$–$$**

Where to Eat
Café Blue, 582 Kerikeri Road, tel: 09-407 5150; www.cafeblue.co. nz. Great family-friendly indoor and outdoor dining with a children's playground. Set in an orchard that provides oranges, figs, macadamias and culinary herbs. **$$$**

Fishbone Café, 88 Kerikeri Road, tel: 09-407 6065. Good, straightforward café fare and friendly atmosphere. **$–$$**

Redwoods Café, Kerikeri, at fork of SH1, north of town, tel: 09-407 6681; www.redwoodscafe.co.nz. Good, healthy food amidst the vegetable garden of a small farm. **$**

Outdoor Activities
Sailing
Woodwind Yacht Charters, Wharau Road, RD3, tel: 09-407 5532; www.woodwindyachtcharters.co.nz, offers fast, safe and comfortable sailing in a 15-metre (48-ft) ocean-going kauri-built cutter.

Winery
Marsden Estate Winery and Restaurant, Wiroa Road, tel: 09-407 9398; www.marsdenestate.co. nz. Original cuisine and wines can be enjoyed in a relaxed courtyard overlooking the lake and vines. Also wine sales, tastings and tours. **$**

DOUBTLESS BAY

Visitor Information
Doubtless Bay Information Centre, The Waterfront Beach Road, tel: 09-406 2046; www.doubtlessbay.co.nz.

Where to Stay
Acacia Lodge, Mill Bar Road, Mangonui, tel: 09-406 0417; www.acacia.co.nz. A comfortable motel on the waterfront, with all rooms facing the sea. **$$**

Taipa Bay Resort, 22 Taipa Point Road, tel: 09-406 0656; www.taipa bay.co.nz. A top-rated complex with its own beachfront café, pool and tennis court. **$$–$$$$$**

Where to Eat
Mangonui Fish Shop, Beach Road, tel: 09-406 0478. This place wins prizes for its traditional fish and chips, and its seafront location is unbeatable. **$**

Waterfront Café and Bar, Waterfront Road, tel: 09-406 0850. Reliable fare for breakfast, lunch and dinner, right on the waterfront. **$$**

WHANGAREI

Visitor Information
Whangarei i-SITE Visitor Centre, 92 Otaika Road, Tarewa Park, tel: 09-438 1079; www.whangareinz.org.nz.

Where to Stay
Central Court Motel, 54 Otaika Road, tel/fax: 09-438 4574; www.centralcourtmotel.co.nz. Close to Whangarei and next door to a restaurant. Finnish sauna and spa room available. 21 units. **$**

Pacific Rendezvous, Tutukaka, tel: 09-434 3847; www.pacific rendezvous.co.nz. A world-renowned holiday resort overlooking Tutukaka Harbour, with accommodation ranging from one-bedroom chalets to three-bedroom suites. Two private beaches, petanque and swimming pool. 30 units. **$$–$$$$**

Settlers Hotel, 61–69 Hatea Drive, tel: 09-438 2699; www.settlersho tel.co.nz. In the city centre, overlooking the Hatea River and Parahaki, this quaint hotel has ensuite rooms, a restaurant, spa pool and swimming pool. 53 rooms. **$–$$**

Where to Eat
A Deco Restaurant, 70 Kamo Road, Kensington, tel: 09-459 4957; www.a-deco.co.nz. Nationally acclaimed cuisine using Northland's best produce, in a stunning art deco setting. Open Wed–Fri for lunch and Tues–Sat for dinner. Reservations essential. **$$$**

Caffeine Espresso Café, 4 Water Street, tel: 09-438 6925; www. caffeinecafe.co.nz. Serves some

of the best coffee in the country and provides mouthwatering meals in a cosy atmosphere. Open for breakfast and lunch. **$**

Killer Prawn, 26–28 Bank Street, tel: 0800-661 555; www.killer prawn.co.nz. New Zealand and Pacific Island cuisine at its best. Try the restaurant's signature Killer Prawn bowl and other tasty seafood. Enjoy a cocktail in the main bar or soak up the sun in the garden bar. **$$$**

Reva's on the Waterfront, 31 Quay Side, Town Basin Marina, tel: 09-438 8969; www.revas.co.nz. An extensive menu of traditional and contemporary cuisine, pizzas and seafood, plus "famous original" Mexican dishes. **$$–$$$**

Outdoor Activities
Diving
Poor Knights Dive Centre, Marina Road, Tutukaka RD3, tel: 09-434 3867; www.diving.co.nz. The Poor Knights, 22 km (14 miles) off the east coast at Whangarei, is one of New Zealand's best dive sites, with large numbers of mao mao fish and steep coral walls.

Winery
Longview Estate Vineyard and Winery, SH1, Otaika, tel: 09-438 7227; www.longviewwines.co.nz. Uses traditional techniques with modern technology to produce individual, handcrafted wines with intense fruit flavours.

OTHER LOCATIONS

Where to Stay
Harbourside Bed and Breakfast – Omapere, SH12, tel: 09-405 8246; e-mail: harboursidebnb@xtra.co.nz. This beachfront house, with great views of the sandhills, is an easy walk from restaurants and close to the Waipoua Forest and west coast beaches. Two rooms, both with ensuites and private decks. **$**

Kingfish Lodge, Whangaroa Harbour, tel: 09-405 0164; www.kingfishlodge.co.nz. A premier sportfishing resort with a fine seafood restaurant, this exclusive

family-owned retreat is at the headland of Whangaroa Harbour in Kingfish Cove. Access is only by cruise up the harbour. Luxurious rooms on the water's edge. 12 rooms. **$$$$$**

Orongo Bay Homestead, Aucks Road, Orongo Bay, tel: 09-403 7527; www.thehomestead.co.nz. Built in the 1860s and known as New Zealand's first American Consulate, this is set on 7 private hectares (17 acres) on the coast. Organic wines from an underground cellar, a vintage Austrian grand piano, spacious grounds and spectacular sea views are all part of the package. Rooms have super-king beds, private bathrooms and CD collections. Gourmet meals by arrangement. **$$$$$**

Waipoua Lodge, SH12, Katui, tel: 09-439 0422; www.waipoualodge. co.nz. Perched on a ridge overlooking the Waipoua Forest, this villa was built as a private home over a century ago. Now restored, it includes three pioneer-style, self-contained cottages with super-king and queen bedrooms, ensuite bathrooms, lounge and kitchenette. Restaurant and bar on site. **$$$$**

Waikato

HAMILTON

Getting There
Hamilton, is located about 2 hours south of Auckland, with bus links to most cities and towns. **Hamilton International Airport** is 15 km (9 miles) or so south of the city, with daily links with major New Zealand cities. **Freedom Air International** flies direct from Australia's Gold Coast. This no-frills airline also has regular links to Auckland,

Palmerston North, Wellington, Christchurch and Dunedin.

Hamilton is also on the main trunk line, with rail services by the **Overlander** between Auckland and Wellington. Journey time is just over 2 hours. See also Getting Around on pages 330–2.

Visitor Information
Hamilton i-SITE Visitor Centre, Transport Centre, 373 Anglesea Street, tel: 07-839 3580; www.visithamilton.co.nz.

City Transport
Hamilton is serviced by excellent inner city bus and taxi services. There are also plenty of car hire agencies in the city.
Hamilton City Buses, tel: 07-846 1975; www.busit.co.nz.
Hamilton Taxis, tel: 07-847 7477; www.hamiltontaxis.co.nz.

Where to Stay
Anglesea Motel, 36 Liverpool Street, tel: 07-834 0010, 0800-426 453; www.angleseamotel.co.nz. A five-star hotel close to the city centre. Studio and one-bedroom units have modern facilities. Outdoor swimming pool, spa bath units and gym. **$$–$$$**
Barclay Motel, 280 Ulster Street, tel: 07-838 2475, 0800-808 090; www.barclay.co.nz. Luxury spa suites and family units and studios, 21 in all, set around a spacious courtyard dotted with colourful geraniums and potted palms. Solar-heated swimming pool, spa pool and children's playground. **$$–$$$**
Kingsgate Hotel Hamilton, 100 Garnett Avenue, tel: 07-849 0860; www.kingsgatehotels.co.nz. City-centre hotel with rooms with ensuite bathroom and 24-hour room service. 147 rooms. **$$**
Novotel Tainui Hamilton, 7 Alma Street, tel: 07-838 1366; www.accorhotels.co.nz. A four-star hotel on the banks of the Waikato River in the CBD. Luxurious rooms, restaurant and bar, plus gym, spa and sauna. 177 rooms. **$$$**
Ventura Inn and Suites Hamilton, 23 Clarence Street, tel: 07-838 0110, 0800-283 688; www.ventura

inns.co.nz. Some rooms have king-size beds and spa baths. Central location. 50 rooms. **$–$$**

Where to Eat
Balcony Restaurant, 20 Alma Street, tel: 07-838 3718; www.balcony.co.nz. This spacious eatery beside the Waikato River occupies Hamilton's old broadcasting building. Extensive wine list and great service complement top ingredients and original fare. **$$$**
Domaine Restaurant, 575 Victoria Street, tel: 07-839 2100. Voted Best Restaurant by *Waikato Times* readers in 2005, this eatery serves Mediterranean-style and Asian-inspired dishes. **$$**
Thai Village Café, The Market Place, Hood Street, tel: 07-834 9960; www.thaivillage.co.nz. Excellent Thai cuisine with a wide range of curry, rice and noodle dishes. Generous servings and cheap prices. **$**
The Narrows Landing, 431 Airport Road, tel: 07-858 4001; www.thenarrowslanding.co.nz. Gourmet cuisine with New Zealand and European influences. Its medieval style is enhanced by huge wooden doors, lots of iron, a metal mesh staircase and candlelight. **$$$**

Entertainment
Hamilton has a variety of entertainment on offer – from arts and film festivals to live theatre, music and dance. National and international touring groups visit Hamilton and play at one of the three venues – **Founders Theatre**, the **Community Theatre** and **The Meteor**, tel: 07-838 6603.

Check out **The Fuel Festival**, held in Hamilton in June. The city has an abundance of nightclubs and bars, and some of the top DJs from Auckland often perform here.

CAMBRIDGE

Visitor Information
Cambridge Information Centre, corner of Victoria and Queen streets, tel: 07-823 3456; www.cambridge.co.nz.

Where to Stay
Huntington Stables, 106 Maungakawa Road, tel: 07-823 4120; www.huntington.co.nz. Formerly an old stable complex, this has been converted into luxurious studio accommodation, within some of the area's most verdant farmland. **$$$$$**
Souter House Country Lodge, 19 Victoria Street, tel: 07-827 3610; www.souterhouse.co.nz. This historic home has been converted to provide 7 luxurious suites and an elegant, award-winning silver service restaurant. **$$–$$$**

Where to Eat
Rosso, 72 Alpha Street, tel: 07-827 6699. Discerning New Zealanders come here for the quality dining. Has a warm and welcoming open fire in winter. **$–$$**
The Lily Pad Café, 1242 Kaipaki Road, tel: 07-823 9134; www.lilypadcafe.co.nz. Open daily for breakfast and lunch, Thur–Sat for dinner (summer only). It takes a little drive to reach this countryside café, but it is well worth the trip. Set in a delightful garden filled with sculptures, the café serves wholesome seasonal fare prepared with artistic flair. With a handpicked selection of wines. **$$–$$$**

TE AROHA

Visitor Information
Te Aroha i-SITE Centre, 102 Whitaker Street, tel: 07-884 8052; www.tearoha-info.co.nz.

Horsing Around

New Zealand Horse Magic, SH1, south of Cambridge, tel: 07-827 8118; www.cambridgethoroughbredlodge.co.nz; daily 10am–3pm; entrance fee. Daily performances showcase a variety of breeds, from a Lippizaner stallion (the only one in New Zealand) to the New Zealand wild horse, the Kaimaniwa, plus Arabian, Clydesdale and Hackney specimens. Bookings essential for shows.

Where to Stay

Aroha Mountain Lodge, 5 Boundary Street, tel: 07-884 8134; www.aroha mountainlodge.co.nz. Cosy lodgings in a picturesque villa. **$–$$$$**

Palace Hotel, 167 Whitaker Street, tel: 07-884 9995, e-mail: palacehotel@xtra.co.nz. Friendly local hotel with a restaurant open Wed–Sun for lunch and Thur–Sun for dinner. Also organises weekend tours to the summit of Te Aroha (weather permitting).

Villa Dale, 13 Terminus Street, tel: 07-884 4248. Bed and breakfast in a lovely old villa set in a beautiful garden. Guided garden rambles in the district also available. **$**

Where to Eat

The Cottage Café, Te Aroha Domain, tel: 07-884 9222. Café fare daily; evening meals by arrangement. **$**

Mokena Restaurant, 6 Church Street, tel: 07-884 8038. Licensed restaurant serving homestyle cooking. **$$**

Outdoor Activities

Cycling

Te Aroha Mountain Bike Track. This 1-hour round trip through native bush and hilly terrain is one of the best cycle tracks in the country.

Hiking

Waiorongomai Valley Walk. This hike takes you through old gold-mining ruins. Another popular walk is the **Whakapipi Lookout Track**. A Department of Conservation brochure and map with full details of all walks is available from the Information Centre.

Swimming

Te Aroha Mineral Pools, tel: 07-884 8717; www.tearohapools.co.nz; daily 10am–1pm; entrance fee. Public and private pools, some in original 19th-century bath houses.

WAITOMO

Visitor Information

Waitomo i-SITE Visitor Centre, 21 Caves Road, Waitomo Caves, tel: 07-878 7640, 0800-474 839; www.waitomo-museum.co.nz.

Where to Stay

Abseil Inn, 709 Waitomo Caves Road, Waitomo Village, tel: 07-878 7815; www.absailinn.co.nz. Comfortable bed and breakfast with nice views of the countryside. **$$**

Waitomo Caves Hotel, Lemon Point Road, tel: 07-878 8204; www.wai tomocaveshotel.co.nz; Victorian-style hotel, 19 km (12 miles) from Te Kuiti and near the limestone caves. 37 rooms. **$–$$$**

Where to Eat

Roselands, 579 Fullerton Road, Waitomo Caves, tel: 07-878 7611. An award-winning restaurant amid native bush in a rural landscape. The mouth-watering menu is prepared using fresh Kiwi produce. Try the barbecue-style lunch. Open for lunch only. **$$**

Outdoor Activities

Caving/Black-water Rafting

Blackwater Rafting Company, 585 Waitomo Caves Road, tel: 07-878 6219; www.blackwaterrafting.co.nz. Well-known operator of cave tubing trips; organises underground adventures of varying difficulty. Some trips involve abseiling (rappelling) and flying fox (zip line) rides.

Waitomo Adventures, Waitomo Caves Road, tel: 07-878 7788, 0800-924 866; www.waitomo.co.nz. Offers a 2-hour black-water journey, as well as various permutations of abseiling into underground holes and down waterfalls.

OTHER LOCATIONS

Where to Stay

Bleskie Farmstay, 296 Storey Road, Te Awamutu, tel: 07-871 3301; e-mail: sophy@ihug.com.nz. A working dairy farm with a host of other animals to see. There's also a swimming pool and tennis court for energetic guests. **$$**

Brooklands Country Estate, RD1, Ngaruawahia, Waikato, tel: 07-825 4756; www.brooklands.net.nz. This country retreat has a reputation for being one of the finest 5-star lodges in New Zealand. It was originally the gracious homestead of a pioneer farming family, and retains beautiful decor, fine paintings and large open fireplaces. Award-winning food is served, and you can dine alfresco. The sumptuous rooms have French windows overlooking the garden; tennis court and swimming pool. 10 rooms. **$$$$$**

Where to Eat

Bosco Café, 57 Te Kumi Road, Te Kuiti, tel: 07-878 3633. In the heart of King Country, a great stopover for some good hearty food, decent coffee and excellent home-made cake and muffins. **$**

Out in the Styx Guesthouse, 2117 Arapuni Road, Te Awamutu, tel: 0800-461 559; www.styx.co.nz. A bed-and-breakfast retreat with a restaurant focusing on New Zealand cuisine. It offers only a three-course set menu, plus coffee. **$$–$$$**

The Olde Bank, 201 Alexandra Street, Te Awamutu, tel: 07-870 4055. This café offers a range of Asian and standard fare; a good spot to refuel. **$**

Outdoor Activities

Horse Riding

Pirongia Clydesdales, RD6, Te Awamutu, tel: 07-871 9711; www.clydesdales.co.nz, is home to several equine stars of *The Lord of the Rings* and *Xena: Warrior Princess*. Wagon rides also available.

Rock Climbing

Wharepapa is one of the best rock climbing areas in New Zealand, with over 800 routes, short easy walks to the climb, and an equipment store nearby. Wharepapa South is between Te Awamutu and Mangakino. For accommodation, equipment and information, contact the **Wharepapa Outdoor Centre**, tel: 07-872 2533; e-mail: wharerock@xtra.co.nz. Also check out www.climb.co.nz.

Surfing

Raglan Beach is a popular resort on Waikato's rugged west coast.

The point breaks Indicators and Manu are the fastest and best surfing spots in Raglan; Whale Bay tends to provide a slower ride.

Coromandel and Bay of Plenty

Getting There

About 90 minutes from Auckland and Rotorua, the Coromandel is on the Pacific Coast Highway. There are flights to Whitianga from Auckland with **Air Coromandel** (tel: 0800-900 600). There are also door-to-door shuttle services between Whitianga, Tairua, Thames and Auckland, which cost around NZ$60 (one way) and NZ$108 (return). Contact: **Go Kiwi Shuttles and Adventures**, tel: 07-866 0336; www.gokiwi.co.nz. Or drive the 2½ hour scenic, winding route up the Pacific Coast Highway from Auckland. See also Getting Around on pages 330–2.

THAMES

Visitor Information

Tourism Coromandel, 1st Floor, Goldfields Shopping Centre, 100 May Street, tel: 07-867 9073, 0800-888 222; www.thecoromandel.com.

Where to Stay

Rapaura Watergardens, 56 Tapu-Coroglen Road, tel: 07-868 4821; www.rapaurawatergardens.co.nz. The accommodation here is located at a sightseeing attraction – water gardens with gentle walks, abundant native flora, lily ponds, bridges, streams, waterfall and sculptures of *ponga* (native fern). **$$–$$$$**
Tuscany on Thames, SH25, Jellicoe Crescent, tel: 07-868 5099; www. tuscanyonthames.co.nz. Italian-style motel nestled between beautiful coast and bush-covered hills. It has modern facilities, including large ensuite bathrooms. 14 units. **$$–$$$**

Where to Eat

Ow Place, Pollen Street, tel: 07-868 5548. Serves Pacific Rim cuisine.
Sealey Café, 109 Sealey Street, tel: 07-868 8641. Set in a charming

Pan for Gold

Goldmine Experience, Main Road, SH25, Thames, tel: 07-868 8514; www.goldmine-experience.co.nz; daily 10am–4pm. In the heart of the gold-mining district, this unique attraction offers gold panning, guided tours under-ground and through the stamper battery, and a photographic museum.

1907 villa, with courtyard and verandah dining, this café has a menu of Mexican, Italian, New Zealand and Lebanese dishes. **$$**

Outdoor Activities
Bush Walks
Kauaeranga Valley DOC Visitor Centre, Kauaeranga Valley Road, tel: 07-867 9080, can provide information on more than 20 bush walks in the area.

WHITIANGA

Visitor Information

Whitianga i-SITE Visitor Centre, corner of Albert Street and Blacksmith Lane, tel: 07-866 5555; www.whitianga.co.nz.

Where to Stay

Kuaotunu Bay Lodge, SH25, Kuaotunu, tel: 07-866 4396; www.kuaotunubay.co.nz. An elegant beach house, 18 km (11 miles) north of Whitianga, with beach access and a private deck with panoramic views of the peninsula. It's a great winter getaway, with open-fire, underfloor heating and ensuite bathrooms. 3 rooms. **$$$**
Mercury Bay Beachfront Resort, 111–113 Buffalo Beach Road, tel: 07-866 5637; www.beachfrontresort.co.nz. This has one to three bedrooms, and its full range of facilities includes a heated spa pool and barbecue site. 8 units. **$$$**
Waterfront Motel, 2 Buffalo Beach Road, tel: 07-866 4498; www.waterfrontmotel.co.nz. Overlooking Buffalo Beach with magnificent sea views, the apartments and suites

are all self-contained, with private balconies and spa baths. **$$–$$$$$**

Where to Eat

Captain Cook Restaurant, Mercury Bay Club, 69 Cook Drive, tel: 07-866 4750. Seafood specialist with an extensive menu. **$$**
Eggsentric Café and Restaurant, 1047 Purangi Road, Flaxmill Bay, Cooks Beach, tel: 07-866 0307. Good food, live music nightly, films every Wednesday, art exhibitions and classes, afternoon concerts and ceramic painting.
The Fire Place, 9 The Esplanade, tel: 07-866 4828; www.thefireplace-restaurant.com. The seafood and wood-fired pizzas are particularly popular in this rustic eatery. With its lovely waterfront location, it's a treat to dine alfresco on the lovely big deck in summer. In winter, cosy up to the fireplace. **$$–$$$**

Outdoor Activities
Cruises
Cave Cruzer Adventures, Whitianga Wharf, tel: 07-866 2275; www.cavecruzer.co.nz. You can explore the Coromandel's scenic coastline in an ex-Navy inflatable rescue boat, and head into a sea cave to hear the amazing sound of dolphins and whales calling, plus Maori instrument demonstrations.

Fishing and Diving
Waters Edge Charters, Whitianga, tel: 07-866 5760; www.watersedgecharters.co.nz. Experienced skipper Craig Donovan will take you out for a spot of bottom fishing, game fishing, diving or scenic tours, tailored to suit your needs.

Golf
Mercury Bay Golf & Country Club, Golf Road, tel: 07-866 5479. An 18-hole course north of Thames. Idyllic surroundings with level walking. Visitors welcome.

HAHEI

Where to Stay
Hahei Holiday and Cathedral Cove Villas, Harsant Avenue, Hahei

Beach, tel: 07-866 3889; www. cathedralcove.co.nz. Beachfront accommodation a short walk from Cathedral Cove. Rooms have sea or garden views. 16 units. **$$$**

Hot Water Beach Bed and Breakfast, 48 Pye Place, tel: 07-866 3991; www.hotwaterbedand breakfast.co.nz. Award-winning bed and breakfast on Hot Water Beach, only 6 km (4 miles) south of Hahei. Short walk to the beach. **$–$$**

The Church Accommodation and Restaurant, 87 Hahei Beach Road, tel: 07-866 3533; www.thechurchha hei.co.nz. Eleven cosy cottages set in beautiful bush and garden. **$$**

Where to Eat

Café Luna, 59 Beach Road, tel: 07-866 3016. Good food and great coffee served by friendly staff.

The Grange Road Café, 7 Grange Road, tel: 07-866 3502. Good home-cooked comfort food and the only place in Hahei where you'll find beer on tap. Laid-back courtyard and deck dining. **$–$$$**

Outdoor Activities
Cruises

Hahei Explorer, Hahei Beach Road, tel: 07-866 3910; www.hahei explorer.co.nz. Daily adventure boat trips in the Hahei Marine Reserve, viewing Cathedral Cove, islands, reefs and sea caves. Snorkel gear also available for hire.

Kayaking

Cathedral Cove Sea Kayaking, Hahei, tel: 07-866 3877; www.sea kayaktours.co.nz, organises both half- and full-day tours to Hot Water Beach and Cathedral Cove.

WHANGAMATA

Visitor Information

Whangamata i-SITE Visitor Centre is at 616 Port Road, tel: 07 865 8340; www.whangamatainfo.co.nz.

Where to Stay

Breakers Motel, 324 Hetherington Road, tel: 07-865 8464; www. breakersmotel.co.nz. Tucked away

in a reserve bordering the estuary, this attractive motel building resembles a wave. The units all overlook a swimming pool complex with a waterfall and large barbecue area, and include a private deck with spa pool. 21 suites. **$$–$$$$**

Cabana Motel, 101-103 Beach Road, tel: 07-865 8772. The only motel on the water's edge, with fully self-contained units, close to excellent fishing, swimming and other outdoor activities. 9 units. **$–$$**

Palm Pacific Resort, 413 Port Road, tel: 07-865 9211; www.palmpacificresort.co.nz. Good accommodation for families and tour groups, close to shops, cafés and a short walk from the beach. Each unit has a fully equipped kitchen and patio area. 27 units. **$–$$**

Where to Eat

Nero's, Port Road, tel: 07-865 6300. Gourmet-style pizzas with exotic toppings. **$$**

Obsidian, 415 Port Road, tel: 07-865 8433. Steak and seafood. **$$**

The Whanga Bar and Café, 101 Winifred Avenue, tel: 07-865 6472. Café fare; open daily for breakfast and lunch, plus dinner on weekends. **$**

Outdoor Activities
Bushwalks

Kiwi Dundee Adventures, Pauanui, Tairua and Whangamata, tel: 07-865 8809; www.kiwidundee.co.nz. Two of New Zealand's foremost guides offer personalised walks, hikes and tours.

TAURANGA/MOUNT MAUNGANUI

Getting There

From the Coromandel, you can take the Pacific Coast Highway to the Bay of Plenty. The trip into Tauranga takes 1 to 2 hours. Or catch an **InterCity** bus to Tauranga from most North Island destinations. Also try **Bayline Coaches**, tel: 07-578 3113.

Visitor Information

Tauranga i-SITE Visitor Centre, 95 Willow Street, tel: 07-578 8103; www.tauranga.govt.nz; www.bayofplentynz.com.

Where to Stay

Accommodation at Te Puna, 4 Minden Road, RD6, Tauranga, tel: 07-552 5621; www.tepunalodge. co.nz. A comfortable motel with family-size units, some with spa baths. **$–$$**

Bay Palm Motel, 84 Girven Road, Mount Maunganui, tel: 07-574 5971; www.baypalmmotel.co.nz. Comfortable units with spa baths, close to shops and beach. Heated swimming pool. 16 units. **$–$$$**

Best Western Summit Motor Lodge, 213 Waihi Road, Tauranga, tel: 07-578 1181; www.summit motorlodge.co.nz. With quiet, private and spacious self-contained units, sleeping up to six. Close to the city, Mount Maunganui, the surf and shops. There's a spa pool, a games room and laundry facilities. 25 units. **$$**

Oceanside Twin Towers Resort, 1 Maunganui Road, Mount Maunganui, tel: 07-575 5371, 0800-466 868; www.oceanside.co. nz. A premier resort with motel and apartment accommodation. The motel rooms are spacious and feature ensuite bathrooms and kitchenettes. The complex also has lap and hot pools, gym and sauna and is close to shops, restaurants and the beach. The apartments,

Bay of Plenty Shops

There are several major shopping centres in the Bay, from Tauranga to Mount Maunganui's Phoenix Centre, Bayfair and Palm Beach Plaza. Walk the streets of an earlier age at the **Compass Community Village** (www. compass-foundation.co.nz) on 17th Avenue West in Tauranga and discover colonial buildings and craft shops, then rest your feet at the village café (tel: 07-571 3700). There's a farmers' market every Saturday.

with ensuite baths and full kitchens, have impressive views. Minimum two-night stay required in the apartments. **$$–$$$$$**

The Terraces, 346 Oceanbeach Road, Mount Maunganui, tel: 07-575 6494; www.terraces-ocean beach.co.nz. Spacious three-level apartments with full kitchen, laundry and balcony. **$$**

Where to Eat
Bravo Café and Restaurant, Red Square, tel: 07-578 4700; www. cafebravo.co.nz. All-day dining, good service and sunny tables. The spicy mussels, gourmet pizzas and wood-fired bread are all excellent. **$–$$**

Harbourside Brasserie and Bar, the old Yacht Club, The Strand, Tauranga, tel: 07-571 0520, 0800-721 714; www.harboursidetga.co. nz. Waterfront dining at its best – watch the boats come in as you dine on imaginative cuisine. A wide range of dishes, from lamb shanks Provençale to apple-roasted pork rack. Or try some New Zealand's finest seafoods here. **$$–$$$**

Kestrel at the Landing, Water's Edge, 120 The Strand, Tauranga, tel: 07-928 1123; www.thekestrel. co.nz. The restored Devonport ferry has been transformed into a floating restaurant attached with a purpose-built, two-level glass section on a steel pontoon. Serves great Pacific Rim cuisine and an extensive wine list. Daily 11am till late. **$$–$$$**

The Lobster Club, Harbourside, Tauranga, tel: 07-574 4147. Set on the water's edge in the Harbour Bridge Marina. Fine dining with a wide range of dishes, from light meals to fabulous platters and a huge variety of seafood. **$$$**

Entertainment
Tauranga hosts a vast range of events, including jazz festivals, arts festivals and sports marathons. It also has a vibrant nightlife scene, and most bars around the Tauranga and Mount Maunganui region are packed during the weekends. The **Baycourt Theatre** stages a number of exhibitions, festivals and events, tel: 07-577 7198.

Outdoor Activities
Fishing
Mission Charters, Tauranga Bridge Marina, Tauranga, tel: 07-549 0055; www.missioncharters.co.nz. This company organises a range of fishing trips, from single-day excursions to an extended cruise, anchoring in some idyllic bay for the evening. The crew are experienced and these trips are ideal for everyone, from novices to experts.

Kayaking
Oceanix Sea Kayaking, Mount Maunganui, tel: 07-572 2226; www.oceanix.co.nz. This outfit leads kayaking trips that will take you island-hopping on an inner-harbour expedition visiting Maori *pa* sites or along the foreshore.

Volcano Tours
White Island Tours with PeeJay, 15 The Strand East, Whakatane, tel: 07-308 9588; www.whiteisland. co.nz. Experience the awesome might of a live volcanic island.

Winery
Tasting Tours and Charters, 31 Albero Drive, Tauranga, tel 07-544 1383; www.tastingtours.co.nz. Tours to local wineries, breweries and producers of gourmet foods.

OTHER LOCATIONS

Where to Stay
Pacific Harbour Lodge, Tairua Beach, tel: 07-864 8581; www.pacificharbour.co.nz. 31 Island-style lodges, set amidst tropical vegetation with shell-covered pathways to the chalets, beach and award-winning restaurant. Spacious units. **$$**

Pauanui Pines Motor Lodge, 174 Vista Paku, Pauanui Beach, tel: 07-864 8086; www.pauanui pines.co.nz. Located next to a golf course, this award-winning motor lodge includes one- and two-bedroom units in nine colonial-style cottages. All units include a TV and kitchen, and there's a tennis court and heated swimming pool (winter only). 18 units. **$–$$$**

Where to Eat
Manaia Café and Bar, corner of Main and Manaia roads, Tairua, tel: 07-864 9050. Open 10am till late for brunch, lunch and dinner. Menus change regularly with the seasons and focus on fresh flavours. Dine alfresco in the spacious courtyard or indoors. Happy hour on Friday from 5.30pm; great music and atmosphere. **$–$$**

Shells Restaurant & Bar, 227 Main Road, Tairua, tel: 07-864 8811. One of the peninsula's most popular restaurants, situated next to Pacific Harbour Lodge. **$–$$**

Rotorua and Volcanic Plateau

ROTORUA

Getting There
Air New Zealand has flights in and out of Rotorua. The airport is about 15 minutes from the centre of Rotorua. You can also catch one of a number of inter-city coaches such as **Newmans** and **InterCity** in and out of all major New Zealand destinations. See also Getting Around on pages 330–2.

City Transport

There are plenty of shuttle services that will take you around all the volcanic "hot spots" of Rotorua, such as that run by **Waimangu Volcanic Valley** tel: 07-366 137; www.waimangu. com. There is a good public bus service; contact **Rotorua Super Shuttle**, tel: 07-345 7790, 0800-748 885. For taxis, contact **Rotorua Taxis**, tel: 07-348 1111.

Visitor Information
Rotorua i-SITE Visitor Centre, 1167 Fenton Street, tel: 07-348 5179; www.rotoruanz.com.

Where to Stay
Acapulco Motel, corner Malfroy Road and Eason Street, tel: 07-347 9569, 0800-100 069; e-mail: acapulco@xtra.co.nz. Quiet location near city centre, just a short walk

from restaurants and shops. 15 rooms. **$**

Birchwood Spa Motel, 6 Sala Street, tel: 07-347 1800, 0800-881 800; www.birchwoodspa motel.co.nz. Close to the thermal reserve and golf course, these luxury units all have a spa bath or spa pool. 17 units. **$$**

Duxton Hotel Okawa Bay, Mourea, Lake Rotoiti, tel: 07-362 4599; www.duxton.com. Award-winning resort on the shores of Lake Rotoiti, with trout fishing and hot pools trips. 44 rooms. **$$$**

Gibson Court Motel, 10 Gibson Street, tel: 07-346 2822; www.gib soncourtmotel.co.nz. A short drive from the racecourse and 1 km (½ mile) from the thermal reserve, this motel offers private, authentic mineral pools with some units. Rooms are spacious and have central heating. 10 rooms. **$–$$**

Kingsgate Hotel Rotorua, Fenton Street, tel: 07-348 0199, 0800-808 228; www.kingsgatehotels. co.nz. This hotel is adjacent to the racecourse, sports ground and golf courses. 136 rooms. **$$**

Lake Plaza Rotorua Hotel, 1000 Eruera Street, tel: 07-348 1174; www.lakeplazahotel.co.nz. Opposite the Polynesian Pools, with superb views of the lake and thermal areas, this hotel is also close to the city centre. Golf packages available. 250 rooms. **$$**

Millennium Rotorua, corner of Eruera and Hinemaru streets, tel: 07-347 1234, 0800-645 685; www.millenniumrotorua.co.nz. Ask for a room overlooking the Polynesian Pools and Lake Rotorua. You get a great view from the balcony. Friendly staff, and facilities include a gym and pool. **$$$**

Muriaroha Lodge, 411 Old Taupo Road, tel: 07-346 1220; www.muria rohalodge.co.nz. This is a charming guesthouse set in acres of landscaped grounds, 3 km (2 miles) from centre. The accommodation is luxurious, and there are private mineral pools. 6 rooms. **$$$$$**

The Princes Gate Hotel, 1057 Arawa Street, tel: 07-348 1179, 0800 500705; www.princesgate. co.nz. Built in 1897 and recently refurbished, this boutique accommodation comes complete with spas, sauna, heated pool, gym and tennis court.

Silver Fern Motor Inn, 326 Fenton Street, tel: 07-346 3849, 0800-118 808; www.silverfernmotorinn. co.nz. A touch of California in this city-centre motor inn. Executive suites have spa pools and other modern facilities. 20 suites. **$$**

Solitaire Lodge, Lake Tarawera, RD5, tel: 07-362 8208, 0800-765 482; www.solitairelodge.co.nz. Luxury accommodation in a stunning lake-edge location with superb views. Suites have timber cathedral ceilings, large beds, private deck and spacious bathroom. Open fire in the main lounge. 10 suites. **$$$$$**

Westminster Lodge, 58A Mountain Road, tel: 07-348 4273; 0800-937 864; www.westminsterlodge.co.nz. Nestled on the slopes of Mount Ngongotaha but away from the sulphur smells, yet only 5 minutes from the city centre. Friendly hosts Barry and Gill Gillette offer superb hospitality and delicious Continental breakfasts. Five bedrooms, three ensuite units, plus a two-bedroom self-catering cottage. **$**

Wylie Court Motor Lodge, 345 Fenton Street, tel: 07-347 7879, 0800-100 879; www.wyliecourt.co. nz. Resort-style complex, with private heated pools, in park-like grounds. Modern facilities include a large heated swimming pool. 36 rooms. **$$–$$$**

Where to Eat

Bistro 1284, 1284 Eruera Street, tel: 07-346 1284; www.bistro1284. co.nz. An award-winning restaurant set in a historic 1930s building in Rotorua. **$$–$$$**

Fat Dog Café and Bar, 1161 Arawa Street, tel: 07-348 8411. Delicious and reasonably priced breakfasts, lunches and coffees make this a good place to start the day, or to sit and have coffee when you are writing those postcards home. **$**

Freos Licensed Café, 1103 Tutanekai Street, tel: 07-346 0976; www.freos.co.nz. A bustling family restaurant delivering all the

Rotorua Shopping

With attractive wide streets, Rotorua provides an abundance of shops from clothing and fashion to souvenirs, food and pharmacies. Tutanekai and Hinemoa are the streets to visit, while City Focus Square is within walking distance. There are souvenir shops galore in the city, including **The Jade Factory** in Fenton Street, tel: 07-349 3968, which showcases quality jade from throughout New Zealand and elsewhere. **The Souvenir Centre**, tel: 07-348 9515, also in Fenton Street, stocks a wide range of New Zealand arts and crafts.

standard fare: soups, burgers, fish, lamb, chicken and pasta. **$–$$**

Katsubi Restaurant and Sushi Bar, 1123 Eruera Street, tel: 07-349 3494. Authentic Japanese and Korean cuisine is served at this restaurant specialising in sushi, teriyaki, tonkatsu and bento. **$**

The Landing Café, Lake Tarawera, tel: 07-362 8595; www.purerotorua. com. Nestled on the shores of Lake Tarawera, this famous café is themed around the lake's famous Pink and White Terraces, the Tarawera eruption and trout memorabilia. Features a mouthwatering menu of traditional winter fare like venison, bacon and mushroom pie and more delicate summer dishes like scallops in a boysenberry sauce. Famous for their mussel chowder. **$–$$$**

Lewishams Café and Restaurant, 1099 Tutanekai Street, tel: 07-348 1786; www.lewishamsrestaurant. co.nz. Established over 20 years ago, this serves European cuisine with Pacific Rim accents. Daily 9am till late. **$–$$$**

Restaurant Nikau, Millennium Hotel Rotorua, corner of Eruera and Hinemoa streets, tel: 07-347 1234. New Zealand and Maori ingredients are used to create innovative and delicious fare. **$–$$**

Zanelli's, 23 Amohia Street, tel: 07-348 4908. Popular Italian restaurant. Famous for mussels topped with garlic and crumb gratin, home-made gelato and tiramisu. Reservations essential. **$$$**

Nightlife
Pubs/Bars
Barbarella, 1263 Pukuatua Street, tel: 07-347 6776. Rotorua's main live-music venue and you're as likely to find the latest punk band from Auckland as a DJ keeping things happening.
Fuze Bar, 1122 Tutanekai Street, tel: 07-349 6306; www.fuzebar.co.nz. This upmarket café and bar is bright and airy and offers light gourmet meals and great coffee. In the evenings, it's one of the most popular dance clubs in town.
Henneseys Irish Bar, 1210 Tutanekai Street, tel: 07-343 7901; Mon–Sat 11am till late, Sun noon–1am. Live entertainment on Thur and Sat. Outside seating available. Full bar menu and snacks.
O'Malleys Irish Bar, 1287 Eruera Street, tel: 07-347 6410. Open daily 2pm until late. Nice atmosphere, friendly people and good music. Live entertainment every second Friday night, with happy hour from 5–7pm.
The Pheasant Plucker, Arawa Street, tel: 07-343 7071. Live music Thur–Sat nights, bar snacks and meals.
Pig and Whistle, corner of Haupapa and Tutanekai streets, tel: 07-347 3025; www.pigandwhistle.co.nz. Naturally brewed beers, a garden bar, hearty pub meals and live entertainment on Fri and Sat.

Outdoor Activities
Horse Riding
The Farm House, Sunnex Road, tel: 07-332 3771, Hire ponies and horses and ride over 245 hectares (600 acres) of bush-edged farmland. Daily 10am–3pm.

Jet Boating
Agrojet, Western Road, tel: 07-357 2929. A 450hp 4-metre (13-ft) raceboat offers a thrilling ride, accelerating up to 100km/h (62 mph) in just four seconds, with no slowing down for corners on a man-made water course.

Mountain Biking
Planet Bike, tel: 07-346 1717; www.planetbike.co.nz. Rotorua has world-class mountain biking in **Whakarewarewa Forest** close to the city centre. Choose from flat, easy rides for first-timers or fast, technical single-track action for the more experienced. Half-day or two-day adventures too. You could also try a combination of mountain biking, horse riding, rafting and kayaking. A half-day single track exploration costs about NZ$79 or you can take a 2-hour night ride for about NZ$69. Equipment, bikes, guides and refreshments are included.

Off-Road Riding
Off Road NZ, SH5, daily 9am–5pm; entrance fee; tel: 07-332 5748; www.offroadnz.co.nz. This is for those who like to go very fast and make a lot of noise, especially in self-drive four-wheel-drive vehicles.

Rafting and Kayaking
Kaituna Cascades Raft and Kayak Expeditions, Trout Pool Road, Okere Falls, tel: 07-345 4199, 0800-524 8862; www.kaituna cascades.co.nz. Offers single-day and multi-day adventures down the Kaituna, Wairoa, Rangitaiki and Motu rivers. The company has award-winning guides, custom-built rafts and first-class equipment.

Scenic Flights
Volcanic Air Safaris, Rotorua City lakefront, tel: 07-348 9984, 0800-800 848; www.volcanicair.co.nz. Floatplane and helicopter tours of the Rotorua region and central volcanic plateau, including Mount Tarawera and White Island. Costs range from NZ$60 for an 8-minute flight (minimum 4 persons) over the town area to NZ$665 for a 3-hour helicopter flight to White Island.

Mineral Baths
Polynesian Spa, Lake end of Hinemoa Street, daily 6.30am–11pm; entrance fee; tel: 07-348 1328; www.polynesianspa.co.nz. There are 31 thermal pools of varying temperatures, each with its own special mineral content.

Trout Fishing
There are plenty of trout fishing guides and companies for hire in Rotorua. **Down to Earth Trout Fishing** (9 Tumai Road, tel: 07-362 0708) offers lake-edge and boat fishing with a professional guide. Maori guide **Greg Tuuta** has plenty of local knowledge and specialises in trolling, harling and jigging. Check out his "no fish no pay" policy, tel: 07-362 7794; www.ikanuicharters.com. **Clearwater Cruises** (537 Spencer Road, tel: 07-362 8590; www.clearwater.co.nz) and **Hamill Adventures** (tel: 07-348 4186; www.hamillcharters.co.nz) both have a variety of trout-fishing excursions.

Winery
Mamaku Blue Winery, SH5, daily 10am–5pm; free entrance; tel: 07-332 5840; www.mamakublue.co.nz. This is the only place in NZ making blueberry wine. Tours of the winery and orchard are available.

TAUPO

Getting There
Taupo is about midway between Auckland (4 hours to the north) and

Maori Culture
The **Civic Theatre** is a popular venue for *kapa haka* and Maori performing arts, and there are Maori concerts and shows throughout Rotorua. The famous **Opera In The Pa** concerts are held in January at Rotowhio Marae. For more information, contact the **Rotorua i-SITE Visitor Centre**, tel: 07-348 5179; www.rotoruanz.com. At the **World of Maori Cultural Experiences** (daily in summer, winter by arrangement; entrance fee; tel: 07-348 8969, 0800-476 864; www.worldofmaori.co.nz), visitors enjoy a very traditional experience, including a concert and hangi, at the Rakeiao *marae* (meeting area), plus the opportunity to sleep over communally in the *wharenui* (meeting house).

Wellington (4 hours south), on the classic touring route – the Thermal Explorer Highway – which runs through Taupo en route from Auckland to Rotorua and Hawke's Bay. There are direct **Air New Zealand** flights daily from Auckland and Wellington to Taupo Airport with connections to the South Island.

Visitor Information
Taupo i-SITE Visitor Centre, 30 Tongariro Street, tel: 07-376 0027; www.laketauponz.com.

Where to Stay
Bayview Wairakei Resort, SH1, tel: 07-374 8021, 0800-737 678; www.wairakei.co.nz. In the heart of the Wairakei Thermal Valley, this resort is just 9 km (6 miles) north of central Taupo. There is a sauna, gym, six large spa pools and two swimming pools. More than 180 rooms and villas. **$$–$$$$**
Baywater Motor Inn, 126 Lake Terrace, tel: 07-378 9933, 0800-926 822; www.baywater.co.nz. There are magnificent lake and mountain views from this motor inn 1 km (½ mile) from the town centre. The self-contained units have a large in-room spa bath and balcony or patio. 12 units. **$$**
Boulevard Waters Motor Lodge, 215 Lake Terrace, tel: 07-377 3395; www.boulevardwaters.co.nz. Lake-edge motel with luxury features, such as in-room spas, king-size beds, underfloor heating and thermal pool. 10 suites. **$$–$$$**
The Cove, 213 Lake Terrace, tel: 07-378 7599. Luxury boutique hotel situated on the lake shore, 3 km (2 miles) from the edge of town. Lake views, restaurant with extensive menu and comprehensive wine list. **$$$–$$$$$**
Gables Motor Lodge, 130 Lake Terrace, tel: 07-378 8030; www.gablesmotorlodge.com. Opposite Taupo's main swimming pool, with lake and mountain views. 12 one-bedroom suites, each with own private spa pool. **$$**

Where to Eat
Pimentos, 17 Tamamutu Street, tel: 07-377 4549. A popular

evening eatery with an eclectic menu. Open Wed–Mon. **$$**
The Bach, 2 Pataka Road, tel: 07-378 7856; www.thebach.co.nz. The award-winning menu here is prepared by an impressive line-up of international and local chefs, and there's a superb selection of wines. One of New Zealand's most popular restaurants, favourite dishes are lamb rump and confit of duck. **$$$**
The Bantry Restaurant, 45 Rifle Range Road, tel: 07-738 0484. The flavoursome fare ensures the popularity of this fine-dining restaurant housed in a renovated 1950s bungalow. Tues–Sat from 6pm. **$$$**
Villino, 47 Horomatangi Street, tel: 07-377 4478; www.villino.co.nz. A European-style restaurant in the Taupo CBD, with a menu that focuses on fresh seasonal fare, gluten-free and vegetarian options. **$$$**
Walnut Keep, 77 Spa Road, tel: 07-378 0777. Delicious New Zealand cuisine is complemented by an extensive wine list. **$$**
Zest Café, 65 Rifle Range Road, tel: 07-378 5397. Owner-chef Greg Heffernan of Huka Lodge fame applies his considerable skills to this small café serving great food. Takeout is also available. Mon–Fri 8.45am–4pm, Sat–Sun 9am–2pm.

Outdoor Activities
Bungy Jumping
Taupo Bungy, Spa Road, tel: 07-377 1135, 0800-888 408; www.taupobungy.co.nz. Solo and tandem jumps from above the Waikato River.

Golf
Wairakei International Golf Course, SH1, P.O. Box 377, Taupo, tel: 07-374 8152; www.wairakeigolfcourse.co.nz. Voted one of the top 20 golf courses outside the USA by *Golf Digest*, the Wairakei International Golf Course has magnificent fairways and large greens with 101 bunkers.

Fishing
Albion Lodge Fishing Guides, 378 Lake Terrace, Two Mile Bay, Taupo, tel: 07-378 7788; www.albionfishing.co.nz. Famous for trout fishing,

Taupo has numerous rivers and streams that are superb for fly fishing. Rainbow trout in Lake Taupo average 2 kg (4 lb) while brown trout average 3 kg (6 lb).

WHAKAPAPA VILLAGE/ NATIONAL PARK

Getting There
To get to the Whakapapa Village-National Park area and Ohakune – from where the North Island's ski slopes are easily accessible – take the **Overlander** train from Auckland, or the **InterCity** bus that connects with Ohakune from Auckland and Wellington. See also Getting Around, pages 330–2.

Visitor Information
Whakapapa Visitors Centre, Whakapapa Village, tel: 07-892 3729; e-mail: whakapapa@doc.govt.nz. Open 8am–6pm (Oct–Mar), 8am–5pm (Apr–Sep).

Where to Stay
Whakapapa Village
Château Tongariro, Whakapapa Village, Tongariro National Park, tel: 07-892 3809; www.chateau.co.nz. Completed in 1929, this is one of NZ's few hotels located in the middle of a World Heritage park. Known as "the grand old lady of the mountain", it is renowned for its grandeur, and offers a range of rooms, from executive to economy. **$$$–$$$$**
Skotel Alpine Resort, Whakapapa Village, Tongariro National Park, tel: 07-892 3719; www.skotel.co.nz.

Taupo Nightlife

For a town of its size, Taupo has quite a number of bars to while away the evening hours. **Holy Cow!** (tel: 07-378 0040) at 11 Tongariro Street is one of the most popular nightspots. **Finn MacCuhal's** (tel: 07 378 6165; www.finns.co.nz), an Irish bar at the corner of Tuwharetoa and Tongariro streets, is another lively place to down a pint of Guinness.

Located at the edge of the village, this resort has accommodation ranging from deluxe rooms to simple cabins and chalets. **$–$$$**

National Park
Adventure Lodge & Motel, Carroll Street, National Park Village, tel: 07-892 2991; www.adventure nationalpark.co.nz. Studio motel units, standard lodge rooms and budget bunk beds. Transport to the ski slopes can be arranged. **$–$$**
Ski Haus, Carroll Street, National Park Village, tel: 07-892 2854; www.skihaus.co.nz. Basic double, bunk and family rooms, and campervan sites. Bar and spa pool. **$**

Skiing and Tramping

The primary activity in the Central Plateau is skiing at Whakapapa or Turoa in winter and tramping – the one-day Tongariro Crossing or multi-day Tongariro Northern Circuit or Round the Mountain Track – in summer. For information on the Tongariro Crossing, contact Taupo-based **Alpine Scenic Tours**, tel: 07 378 7412; www.alpine scenictours.co.nz. Whakapapa's Grand Château (see listings below) also has packages which include the Tongariro Crossing.

Whakapapa ski area is located on the northwestern slopes of Mount Ruapehu and, on a clear day, has spectacular views across central North Island. Skiers either base themselves at Whakapapa Village, a 6-km (4-mile) drive via Bruce Road to the foot of the slopes, or at the National Park area, 15 km (9 miles) to the west.

Turoa ski area is located on the southwestern slopes of Ruapehu and has spectacular views out towards Mount Taranaki. A 17km drive up the Mountain Road above Ohakune village (which has a wide range of accommodations, cafés and restaurants) will take you to the base of the slopes.

Check www.MtRuapehu.com for more information on skiing in these areas.

OHAKUNE

Visitor Information
Ruapehu Visitor Centre, 54 Clyde Street, tel: 06-385 8427, 0800-782 734; www.ruapehu.tourism.co.nz.

Where to Stay
Alpine Motel & Sassi's Bistro, 7 Miro Street, tel: 06-385 8758; www.alpinemotel.co.nz. Situated in the town centre, this motel offers quality studios, family units and spacious chalets, most with cooking facilities. Casual dining at its Sassi's Bistro. **$**
Hobbit Motor Lodge and Restaurant, corner of Goldfinch and Wye streets, tel: 06-385 8248, 0800-843 462; www.the-hobbit.co.nz. Completely refurbished in 2006. Beds are normal size, despite the lodge's name, and accommodation includes family units and studio apartments. Also has a licensed restaurant and bar open every evening except Sun. **$–$$**
Powderhorn Château, bottom of Mountain Road, tel: 06-385 8888; www.powderhorn.co.nz. The Château, 20 minutes' drive from Turoa Ski area, combines the ambience of a traditional European ski chalet with the luxury of a hotel. Rooms include the Mansion, a luxury apartment which can sleep up to eight adults. Dine at the downstairs restaurant, soak in the hot pool, or enjoy a drink around the log fire in the main bar, the Powder-keg. The Powderhorn ski and board shop is next door. 30 rooms. **$$$**
Tussock Grove, 3 Karo Street, tel: 06-3858 7771; www.tussock grove.co.nz. Boutique hotel in park-like setting with a restaurant and a bar. Lounge with log fire, sauna, spa, drying room and adjacent tennis court. **$–$$$**

Poverty Bay and Hawke's Bay

GISBORNE

Getting There
Gisborne is a 6-hour car ride south on the Pacific Coast Highway from

Dining Options

The best and widest range of restaurants and cafés are found in Ohakune. Of note is **Fat Pigeon Café** (2 Tyne Street, tel: 06-385 9423). At Whakapapa Village and National Park, the pickings are slim and mainly limited to the hotel, motel or lodge that you will be staying at.

Auckland. Regular flights connect major North and South island centres to Gisborne airport. Coaches also operate regular schedules from around the country. See also Getting Around on pages 330–2.

Visitor Information
Gisborne i-SITE Visitor Centre, 209 Grey Street, tel: 06-868 6139; www.gisbornenz.com.

Where to Stay
Alfresco Motor Lodge, 784 Gladstone Road, tel: 06-863 2464, 0800-222 550; www.alfrescolodge. co.nz. Located close to the airport and golf courses. Comfortable ground-floor units, some with spa baths, all have cooking facilities. 14 units. **$–$$**
Champers Motor Lodge, 811 Gladstone Road, tel: 06-863 1515, 0800-702 000; www.champers. co.nz. Modern complex, close to the city centre and airport, with luxurious ground-floor units and studios, some with double spa baths. Heated outdoor pool in landscaped grounds. 14 units. **$–$$**
Ocean Beach Motor Lodge and Sandbar Restaurant, Wainui Beach, tel: 06-868 6186, 0800-250 800; www.oceanbeach.co.nz. Mediterranean-style luxury motor lodge, located at Wainui Beach. One- and two-bedroom apartments with spacious private courtyards and designer kitchens. **$$–$$$**
Opou Country House, tel: 06-862 8732; www.opoucountryhouse. co.nz. Near the small village of Manutuke, 10 km (6 miles) from Gisborne, this historic 120-year-old mansion is set in 12 hectares (30

acres) of park-like grounds surrounded by farmland. Luxury lodge accommodation with outstanding food and wine. Each room is individually styled with fine European and antique Asian furniture and objets d'art. **$$$$$**
The Quarters, Te Au Farm, Nuhaka, Mahia, tel: 06-837 5751; www. quarters.co.nz. Modern and stylish holiday cottage with stunning ocean views. Complimentary home-made bread and cheese on arrival, scenic walks, bush tramping, swimming, hunting, surfing or just relaxing. Sleeps six to eight people. **$$**

Where to Eat
Café Villagio, 57 Balance Street, tel: 06-868 1611; www.cafevillagio. co.nz. A popular institution serving flavoursome fare, great Italian-style pizzas and fabulous desserts. **$$**
Gordon Gecko Restaurant and Bar, 1 Wharf Shed, 60 The Esplanade, tel: 06-868 3257; www.gordon gecko.co.nz. Quality food using fresh local produce, generous servings; great atmosphere, excellent wine list and a harbourfront location. **$$–$$$**
The Colosseum Café and Wine Bar, 4 River Point Road, Matawhero, tel: 06-867 4733. Country café cuisine in a vineyard setting. **$$**
The Fettucine Brothers, 12 Peel Street, tel: 06-868 5700. A highly regarded pasta restaurant, in the heart of the city. **$$**
Trudy's Restaurant, Gisborne Hotel, corner of Huxley and Tyndall roads, tel: 06-868 4109. Good, wholesome local produce is used for a menu that specialises in lamb, beef and seafood. **$**
Ussco Bar and Bistro, 16 Childers Road, tel: 06-868 3246; www. ussco.co.nz. Located in the old Union Steam Ship Company Building – hence the name. Its menu caters to all, from kids to those who want to enjoy a platter with a glass of wine, to others who want substantial meals. The Szechuan squid is a must.
Wharf Café Bar and Restaurant, on the Waterfront, tel: 06-868 4876; www.wharfbar.co.nz. Seafood and game specialities are the main

attraction here. Features one of the best wine lists in the country. Bookings essential. **$**

Outdoor Activities
Horse Riding
Waimoana Horse Treks, Waimoana Station, Lysnar Street, Wainui, tel: 06-868 8218. Organises riding through farmland and native bush, with ocean and high-country views.

Hunting
New Zealand Safari Adventures, Tangihau Station, Rere, tel: 06-867 0872; www.nzsafari.co.nz. Experienced guides take you hunting for trophy red stags. Bush hut and homestay cottages available.

Walking
The East Coast has a selection of excellent walking tracks to explore, including beach walks, privately owned walkways and old piers. You can also enjoy a leisurely historic walk through Gisborne city or take an early morning Alpine climb to the top of Mount Hikurangi, which, at 1,752 metres (5,748 ft), is the first point on mainland New Zealand to see the sunrise. For details, contact the Department of Conservation office (DOC) or Visitor information Centre.

Fishing
Charter or take a cruise on Poverty Bay with an experienced skipper on a 10-metre (33-ft) Bruce Farr-designed sloop. Contact **Sail-A-Bay Yacht Charters and Cruises**, Harbour Marina, Gisborne, tel: 06-868 4406; mobile tel: 025-239 3335; e-mail: sailabay@clear.net.nz.

TE UREWERA NATIONAL PARK

Visitor Information
Aniwaniwa Visitor Centre, SH38, Aniwaniwa, Wairoa, tel: 06-837 3803; e-mail: urewerainfo@doc. govt.nz. Daily 8am–5pm.

Where to Stay
As well as the motor camp beside Lake Waikaremoana, there

are numerous DOC huts dotted around the park. For bookings, contact the Aniwaniwa Visitor Centre *(see above)*.

Outdoor Activities
Boating
DOC hires dinghies for the strong of shoulder to explore the glories of the lake. Tel: 06-837 3803.

Walking
Some of the finest and least-known walks in the country are here. The DOC Visitor Information Centre at Aniwaniwa can advise, or you can buy maps online at www.cpp.co.nz.

NAPIER

Getting There
Napier is 3 hours' drive from Gisborne. Regular flights connect major North and South island centres to Hawke's Bay Airports. Coaches also operate regular schedules from around the country. See also Getting Around, pages 330–2.

Visitor Information
Napier i-SITE Visitor Centre, 100 Marine Parade, tel: 06-834 1911, 0800-429 537; www.napiervic.co.nz.

Where to Stay
Bella Tuscany On Kennedy, 371–373 Kennedy Road, tel: 06-843 9129; www.bellatuscany.co.nz. Architecturally-stunning, the Tuscany offers Mediterranean-style accommodation, with spa bath suites, private courtyards and tasteful furnishings. **$–$$$**
The County Hotel, 12 Browning Street, tel: 06-835 7800; www.coun tyhotel.co.nz. Luxurious Edwardian

Art Deco Napier

Art Deco Trust Napier, Desco Centre, 163 Tennyson Street, Napier, tel: 06-835 0022; www. artdeconapier.com. Your one stop for information on all things art deco in Napier, with walking maps, guided tours and a shop.

art deco building in a central location. Its restaurant, Chambers, serves award-winning international cuisine. Extensive wine list. **$$$$**
Deco City Motor Lodge, 308 Kennedy Road, tel: 06-843 4342; www.decocity.co.nz. Provides mid-range accommodation in lovely art deco style buildings. **$$–$$$**
McHardy House, 11 Bracken Street, tel: 06-835 0605; www.mchardyhouse.com. With fabulous food, this is possibly the only former maternity home providing visitor accommodation in the country. **$$$$$**

Where to Eat
Pacifica Restaurant, 209 Marine Parade, tel: 06-833 6335. A contemporary seafood restaurant with a strong Pacific ambience. **$$**
Ujazi, 28 Tennyson Street, tel: 06-835 1490. Cosy café that is particularly interesting for its exhibitions by local artists. **$**
Westshore Fish Café, 112A Charles Street, Westshore, tel: 06-834 0227. Slightly outside the centre of town, but worth the journey for the excellent and inexpensive fish. **$$**

Outdoor Activities
Wineries
Church Road Winery, 150 Church Road, Taradale, tel: 06-845 9137; www.churchroad.co.nz. This winery is one of New Zealand's leading producers and among its oldest, having been founded in 1897.
Mission Estate, 198 Church Road, Taradale, tel: 06-845 9350; www.missionestate.co.nz. New Zealand's oldest winery, established in 1851 and, housed in a graceful building that is in itself worth a visit.
Royalty Wine Tours, 12 Browning Street, tel: 06-835 7800; www.countyhotel.co.nz. Named because both Queen Elizabeth II and Princess Diana enjoyed this jaunt. Operated by The County Hotel.

HASTINGS

Getting There
Hastings is just over 3 hours' drive from Gisborne. Regular flights

connect major centres to Hawke's Bay airports. Coaches also operate regular schedules from around the country. See also Getting Around, pages 330–2.

Visitor Information
Hastings i-SITE Visitor Centre, corner of Russell and Heretaunga streets, tel: 06-873 5526, 0800-429 537; www.hastings.co.nz.

Where to Stay
Aladdin Lodge Motel, 120 Maddison Street, tel: 06-876 6322; www.aladdins.co.nz. Ground-floor fully self-contained units close to city centre. Swimming pool and spa pools. 11 units. **$**
Omahu Motor Lodge, 357 Omahu Road, tel: 06-870 7061, 0800-166 248; www.omahumotorlodge.co.nz. Quality air-conditioned units opposite Hawke's Bay Hospital. **$$–$$$**

Where to Eat
Rush Munro's Ice Cream Gardens, 704 Heretaunga Street, tel: 06-878 9634; www.rushmunro.co.nz. This all-natural hand-churned ice cream has to be tasted to be believed, a testament to the extraordinary quality of New Zealand dairy products. **$**
Terroir, 253 Waimarama Road, Havelock North, tel: 06-873-0143; www.craggyrange.com. The restaurant attached to Craggy Bay winery has an impeccable pedigree and sophisticated, original fare, including notable desserts. **$$$**
Thorps Coffee House, 40 Hastings Street, tel: 06-835 6699. An art deco coffee house, ideal for either an inexpensive lunchtime snack or something more substantial. **$**

Outdoor Activities
Ballooning
Early Morning Balloons, 71 Rosser Road, tel: 06-879 4229; www.early-am-balloons.co.nz. You'll spend an hour drifting peacefully above Hawke's Bay, with the traditional balloon picnic onboard.

Fishing
Jack Trout Fishing Guides, 27 Tainui Drive, Havelock North, tel:

06-877 7642; www.jacktrout.co.nz. Professional guides provide one-on-one fishing opportunities for all levels, reaching the best spots by helicopter and raft.

Nature Tours
Gannet Safaris Overland, Summerlee Station, 396 Clifton Road, Te Awanga, Hastings, tel: 06-875 0888, 0800-427 232; www.gannetsafaris.com. On these excursions, you ride in style and comfort in four-wheel-drive vehicles, for the unique experience of visiting the largest mainland colony of gannets in the world on the rugged Cape Kidnappers Coast.

Lavender Farms
Casa Lavanda, 176 Mangatahi Road, tel: 06-874 9300, 0800-460 922; www.casalavanda.co.nz. Extensive lavender fields plus a small café and barn selling lavender products and art.
Whitebay World of Lavender, 527 SH5 Esk Valley, tel: 06-836 6553; www.whitebay.co.nz. Stunning lavender gardens; you can purchase lavender health care products here.

Water Parks
Splash Planet, Grove Road, Hastings, daily 10am–6pm, summer; entrance fee; tel: 06-873 8033, 0508-775 274; www.splashplanet.co.nz. This is a fun, family-oriented park, with such amusements as a life-size pirate ship, a castle and thrilling water slides and many more escapes from reality.

Wineries
Vidal Estate, 913 St Aubyn Street East, tel: 06-876 8105; www.vidal.co.nz. Vidal Estates have many of their award-winning bottles on the wine list at their restaurant, which

was the first winery restaurant in the country.

On Yer Bike Wine Tours, 129 Rosser Road, Hastings, tel: 06-879 8735; www.onyerbikehb.co.nz. Tour seven wineries on a bicycle, along reasonably level roads through the vineyards, orchards, ostrich farms and olive groves of Hawkes Bay. A unique one-day cycling experience.

Taranaki, Wanganui and Manawatu

NEW PLYMOUTH

Getting There

This region has its own airport, which is serviced by **Air New Zealand**. Inter-city coaches also run services. **New Plymouth**, a little off the beaten track, is about a 5-hour drive from Auckland along SH43. See also Getting Around, pages 330–2.

Visitor Information

New Plymouth i-SITE Visitor Centre Puke Ariki, 1 Ariki Street, tel: 06-759 6060; www.pukeariki.com; daily 9am–6pm, until 9pm Wed and 5pm weekends; free. Town-centre museum, public library and visitor centre in one.

Where to Stay

93 By the Sea, 93 Buller Street, tel: 06-758 6555; www.93bythe sea.co.nz. A cosy bed and breakfast on the coastal walkway, near ocean and rivers. $$–$$$

Airlie House, 161 Powderham Street, tel: 06-757 8899; www.airliehouse.co.nz. This 110-year-old house provides two large ensuite bedrooms plus a self-contained studio apartment. All rooms have broadband Internet access and Sky digital TV. The seafront, shops, restaurants and other local attractions are an easy 5-minute walk away. $$

Brougham Heights Motel, 54 Brougham Street, tel: 06-757 9954, 0800-107 008. Executive and spa-bath units, plus business lounge and conference facilities. 34 suites. $$

Copthorne Hotel Grand Central New Plymouth, 42 Powderham Street, tel: 06-758 7495; www.copthornenewplymouth.co.nz. Central hotel, with premier to executive rooms, most with spa bath, and a first-class café. 60 rooms and suites. $$–$$$

Issey Manor, 32 Carrington Street, tel: 06-758 2375; www.isseymanor.co.nz. Intimate boutique accommodation with a high standard of service. $–$$

Nice Hotel and Restaurant, 71 Brougham Street, tel: 06-758 6423; www.nicehotel.co.nz. Formerly a small hospital, this hotel has individually styled bedrooms with contemporary art and designer bathrooms with double spa baths. Award-winning Table Restaurant. 7 luxury suites. $–$$$$

Where to Eat

André L'Escargot Restaurant and Bar, 37–41 Brougham Street, tel: 06-758 4812; www.andres.co.nz. Run by Frenchman Andre Teissonniere, L'Escargot has a definite French feel, including the namesake dish – baked Burgundy snails – and the music playing in the bar. $$$

Arborio, Puke Ariki Museum, St Aubyn Street, tel: 07-759 1241; www.macfarlanes.co.nz. Lively café in the museum overlooking the foreshore walkway. Enjoy authentic Italian risottos, home-made pizzas and pasta dishes indoors or alfresco. Daily 9am till late. $$–$$$

Laughing Buddha, corner of Devon and Currie streets, tel: 06-759 2065. It's a bit of a climb to reach this Chinese eatery but well worth it. The food is authentic and choices range from dim sum to whole snapper. Tues–Sun 6pm till late. $$

Portofino, 14 Gill Street, tel: 06-757 8686; www.portofino.co.nz/new_plymouth. This Italian restaurant is a great favourite with locals for its quality food and noisy, friendly atmosphere. $$

Table Restaurant, Nice Hotel, 71 Brougham Street, tel: 06-758 6423; www.nicehotel.co.nz. This award-winning restaurant in the gorgeous Nice Hotel serves cuisine with a Mediterranean slant and offers a huge selection of wines plus superb service. Also has an outdoor deck surrounded by a lush tropical garden. $$

Outdoor Activities

Canoeing

Canoe and Kayak, 631 Devon Road, Ball Block, tel: 06-769 5506. This company runs guided tours and courses, and have kayaks for hire, plus a large range of kayaks and accessories for sale.

Cycling

Cycle Inn, 133 Devon Street East, tel: 06-758 7418. Bicycle hire.

Diving

New Plymouth Underwater, 16 Hobson Street, tel: 06-758 3348; www.newplymouthunderwater.co.nz. Operates dive charters and a shop.

Fishing

Whanganui, Manawatu and Taranaki offer great fishing and boating. Both regions have lakes with excellent trout and perch fishing. Licences must be purchased for sport fishing, contact: **Taranaki Fish and Game Council**, 1H Taupo Quay, Wanganui, tel: 06-345 4908.

Four-Wheel-Drive Tours

4WD Waka, Ngatoto Road, tel: 06-755 2068; www.4wdwaka.com, organises both four-wheel-drive and quad bike trips, as well as canoe trips on board a replica Maori *waka* – a beautifully carved 12-metre (40-ft) boat – to various historical sites.

Horse Riding

Gumboot Gully, Piko Road, Okoki. Rides and overnight excursions with this company range from half-day to week-long treks, including river crossings, old stock routes, native bush tracks, pine forests and high ridge tops with spectacular views and quiet misty gullies. Overnight treks between November and May, and year round for day rides.

Walking/Tramping/Climbing

There are fabulous walks both in the **Egmont** and **Whanganui** National Parks. It's best to check the weather before you embark on any walk or hike, but especially if you intend to climb **Mount Taranaki**. The nearest Department of Conservation office will be able to advise about weather and hiking conditions. Professional guiding services are available in Taranaki. There are also many fabulous river and coastal walks to be found throughout both regions.

For details, contact **North Egmont Visitor Centre** at Egmont Village, Egmont Road, tel: 06-756 0991. Alternatively, call **MacAlpine Guides**, tel: 06-765 6234; www.macalpineguides.com.

Wineries

Cottage Wines, 81 Branch Road, tel: 06-758 6910; www.cottage wines.co.nz. Visitors are always welcome for complimentary tastings of the delicious range of fruit wines produced here. Winery tours by prior arrangement. Daily 9am–6pm.
White Cliffs Brewing Company Ltd, SH3, tel: 06-752 3676; www. organicbeer.co.nz. You can visit this fully organic working brewery to buy and sample Mike's Mild Ale, an award-winning handcrafted, English-style mild ale, and Mountain Lager, a full-strength German-style lager, both produced using only natural ingredients using traditional methods. Daily 10am–6pm.

WANGANUI

Getting There

Wanganui has its own airport serviced daily by **Air New Zealand**. Inter-city coaches also run services to the region. It is a 3-hour drive from Wellington, New Plymouth, Napier or Taupo. You can also reach Wanganui from Auckland – a 6-hour drive – via Taranaki or along SH4. See also Getting Around, pages 330–2.

Visitor Information

Wanganui i-SITE Visitor Centre, 101 Guyton Street, tel: 06-349 0509; www.wanganuinz.com.

Where to Stay

Arlesford House, 202 SH3, RD4 Westmere, tel: 06-347 7751;

www.arlesfordhouse.co.nz. An elegant country home-stay, with spacious rooms and private bathrooms set in 2.4 hectares (6 acres), with a swimming pool and floodlit tennis court. **$$$–$$$$**
Kings Court Motel, 60 Plymouth Street, tel: 0800 221 222; www.kingscourtmotel.co.nz. Clean and tidy accommodation in a convenient central location. **$**
Kingsgate Hotel The Avenue Wanganui, 379 Victoria Avenue, tel: 06-349 0044; www.theavenue wanganui.com. Offers an extensive range of accommodation, international cuisine at its award-winning 379 The Avenue Restaurant, and a swimming pool. Located a 10-minute walk from the central business area, arts and cultural centres and sports venues. **$–$$**
Rutland Arms Inn, 48–52 Ridgway Street, Wanganui, tel: 0800-788 526; www.rutland-arms.co.nz. Modern facilities are combined with sophisticated old-world surroundings, and a top-quality restaurant. **$$–$$$**

Where to Eat

Legends Café and Restaurant, 25 Somme Parade, tel: 06-348 7606. Set on the western banks of the Whanganui River, this restaurant is noted for its generous meals and extensive menu which includes game and seafood dishes. Closed Wed in winter. **$–$$**
Redeye Café, 96 Guyton Street, tel: 06-345 5646. Organic produce, a fast-growing New Zealand trend, is an attraction of this popular café. **$**
Victoria's Restaurant, 13 Victoria

Windsurfing/surfing

Windsurfing and surfing conditions similar to those in Hawaii, can be found in Taranaki. There are numerous spots to choose from up and down the coast, from Awakino in the North to Wanganui in the south. The best place to find out about them is the local surf shops. There is also plenty of accommodation suitable for surfers and wind-surfers along the Taranaki coast.

Avenue, tel: 06-347 7007. This award-winning restaurant offers an à la carte menu, comprising mostly traditional Kiwi fare, and a café menu that's more European with fettucine, spaghetti and sandwiches. **$$**

Outdoor Activities

Jet Boating

Bridge to Nowhere Jet Boat Tours, tel: 0800-480 308; www.bridgetono wheretours. Escorted jet boat tours of the magnificent Whanganui River with an option to stay overnight at the Bridge to Nowhere Lodge.

Canoeing

Blazing Paddles, Piriaka (10 km south of Taumarunui on SH4), tel: 0800-252 946; www.blazing paddles.co.nz. Self-guided canoe trips on the river from 1 hour to 5 days, with various canoe options to choose from.

Mountain Biking

Some of the region's best biking trails are within minutes of Wanganui. Contact **Rayonier NZ**, Hylton Park and Whanganui River Road, tel: 06-347 1774.

PALMERSTON NORTH

Getting There

Palmerston North, the heart of the Manawatu, is about 1 hour's drive south of Wanganui. It is serviced by **Air New Zealand**. Inter-city coaches also run to the region. The town is also on the main Auckland to Wellington trunk line with rail services on the **Overlander**. See also Getting Around, pages 330–2.

Visitor Information

Palmerston North i-SITE Visitor Centre, 52 The Square, tel: 06-350 1922; www.manawatunz.co.nz.

Where to Stay

Ann Keith's Bed and Breakfast, 123 Grey Street, tel: 06-358 6928; www.grandmas-place.com. Comfortable accommodation in a 1920s villa, complete with period furniture and modern ensuite facilities. Hearty breakfast

inclusive. Children and pets welcome. Hosts Don and Liz also run the nearby motel units and Grandma's Place. **$–$$**
Chancellor Motor Lodge, 131 Fitzherbert Avenue, tel: 06-354 5903; www.chancellormotel.co.nz. Close to the city centre, this motel has comfortable units, with fully equipped kitchens and spa baths. 18 units. **$$**
Rose City Motel, 120–122 Fitzherbert Avenue, tel: 06-356 5388; www.rosecitymotel.co.nz. Offers studio and mezzanine units, and one- to two-bedroom suites. Sauna, spa pool and squash court. Convenient location. **$$**
Rydges Coachman Palmerston North, 134–140 Fitzherbert Avenue, tel: 06-356 5065; www.rydges.com. Colonial-style boutique hotel with gym and pool, handy to all the town's amenities and attractions. **$$**

Where to Eat
Spostato, 213 Cuba Street, tel: 06-952 3400. A real wee gem, hidden up a narrow staircase. Offers fine evening dining in a cosy, old-fashioned setup with eclectic décor. Open daily from 6pm. **$$$**
The Bathhouse Restaurant and Bar, 161 Broadway Avenue, tel: 06-952 5570; www.thebathhouse.co.nz. Marbled walls, an earthen fireplace and the menu provide a Mediterranean atmosphere, and there's an all-weather courtyard for year-round alfresco dining. **$$**
The Herb Farm Café, Grove Road, Ashhurst, tel: 06-326 7479; www.herbfarm.co.nz. A short drive from Palmerston North, this is Manawatu's most popular destination café, in a tranquil rural setting. It serves beautifully presented, garden-fresh meals. Also offers a range of herbal tours and workshops, and a well-stocked studio with herbal products, many of which are manufactured on site. **$–$$**

Outdoor Activities
Rafting
River Valley, Mangahoata Road, Pukeokahu, tel: 06-388 1444; www.rivervalley.co.nz. This location

in the Rangitikei River canyon offers New Zealand's premier Grade 5 rafting trip through great rapids such as Fulcrum and Max's Drop. Daily trips year round. Family and scenic trips are available on gentler sections. Hill country horse treks are another option. Accommodation in lodges and cabins.

Horse Riding
Timeless Horse Treks, Gorge Road, Ballance, Pahiatua, tel: 06-376 6157; www.timelesshorsetreks.co.nz. Rides include gentle river trails and challenging hill country.

Wellington and Surroundings
WELLINGTON

Getting There
Wellington International Airport has services from Australia and some South Pacific islands, as well as having good regional and national links. It's about half an hour's drive from the city centre – taxis cost about NZ$25–35 and a shuttle, which takes a little longer, costs about NZ$10–12. The **Stagecoach Flyer** runs from the airport to the city, Lower Hutt and Upper Hutt, taking 15 minutes to 1¼ hours.
Wellington is also well served by inter-city coaches and can be reached from Auckland by train.
Ferry services link Wellington with Picton in the South Island. See also Getting Around, pages 330–2.

Visitor Information
Wellington i-SITE Visitor Centre, corner of Wakefield Street and Civic Square, tel: 04-802 4860; www.wellingtonnz.com.

City Transport
The Wellington public transport system **Metlink** (tel: 0800-801 700; www.metlink.org.nz) runs regular bus, commuter train and ferry services throughout the city and outer regions, including the **Stagecoach Flyer** (tel: 04-801 7000) and the **City Circular** (NZ$5 day pass) that loops the inner city every 15 minutes. There are plenty of taxi stands

around the inner city. However Wellington is compact enough that it's easy to walk from one end of Lambton Quay to Courtenay Place.
You can visit historic Somes Island or Eastbourne on the **Dominion Post Ferry** (tel: 04-499 0282; www.eastbywest.co.nz) or catch the unique **Cable Car** (tel: 04-472 2199) from Cable Car Lane off Lambton Quay, to the suburb of Kelburn and the top of the Botanic Gardens. Wellington also has a commuter train system, the **Tranzmetro** (tel: 0800-801 700), linking the city to the outer suburbs as far as Upper Hutt.

Where to Stay
Apollo Lodge Motel, 49 Majoribanks Street, tel: 04-385 1849; www.apollo-lodge.co.nz. Motel units, executive suites and apartments for up to five people, close to the shopping centre and 5 minutes from Oriental Bay. 50 units. **$$**
Duxton Hotel Wellington, 170 Wakefield Street, tel: 04-473 3900; www.duxton.com. In a good mid-town location, near Michael Fowler Centre and the waterfront, this hotel is favoured by business travellers. Burbury's restaurant on the top floor offers fine dining. **$$$–$$$$$**
InterContinental Wellington, corner of Grey and Featherston streets, tel: 04-472 2722; www.wellington.intercontinental.com. In an excellent waterfront location, this hotel is good for both business and leisure guests. It has a restaurant, bars and room service, plus a good fitness centre with a heated pool. 232 rooms and suites. **$$$$–$$$$$**
James Cook Hotel Grand Chancellor, 147 The Terrace, tel: 04-499 9500; www.grandhotelsinternational.com. Well-managed landmark hotel in a central location close to the shops. It was one of the first grand hotels in Wellington, but has kept up with the times. Joseph Banks restaurant and wine bar is popular. **$$$–$$$$$**
Kingsgate Hotel Oriental Bay, 73 Roxburgh Street, Mount Victoria, tel: 04-385 0279; www.kingsgate

orientalbay.co.nz. Fine modern hotel overlooking the harbour and close to city centre. 117 rooms. **$$–$$$**
Mercure Hotel Willis Street, 355 Willis Street, Te Aro, tel: 04-803 1000; www.accorhotels.co.nz. Modern hotel with indoor swimming pool, fitness suite, restaurant and bar. 84 rooms. **$$–$$$**
Novotel Capital Wellington, 133–137 The Terrace, tel: 04-918 1900; www.novotel.co.nz. Modern hotel in the centre of the CBD, near Lambton Quay, with swimming pool. **$$–$$$$$**
Tinakori Lodge Bed and Breakfast, 182 Tinakori Street, Thorndon, tel: 04-939 3478; www.tinakorilodge.

Theatre and Ballet

Bats Theatre, 1 Kent Terrace, tel: 04-802 4175. This small and cosy venue has the courage to experiment with lesser-known works, which means you can often book tickets at short notice.
Circa Theatre, 1 Taranaki Street, tel: 04-801 7992; www.circa.co. nz. This theatre, managed by the actors themselves, offers stimulating drama in a waterside location, by Te Papa Museum.
Downstage Theatre, 2 Courtenay Place, tel: 04-801 6946; www. downstage.co.nz. Located in the restaurant and café district, this theatre stages a comprehensive variety of plays – from modern authors to Shakespeare – plus performances by the leading Maori theatre company, Taki Rua.
Royal New Zealand Ballet, 77–87 Courtenay Place, tel: 04-381 9000; www.nzballet.org.nz. The country's principal ballet company was formed in 1953, and is based at the St James Theatre. Tickets from Ticketek, tel: 04-384 3840.
St James Theatre, 77–87 Courtenay Place, tel: 04-802 4060; www.stjames.co.nz. The finest lyric theatre in New Zealand. This restored heritage building is *the* Wellington venue for opera, ballet and major musical shows. Also the site of the Ticketek box office agency.

co.nz. Hosts Julene and Richard see to your every need in the comfort of their historic guesthouse situated close to Wellington's inner city. Quality facilities and restful atmosphere with a conservatory lounge overlooking native bush-clad hills. Within easy walking distance of Wellington's main attractions. **$–$$**
Victoria Court Motor Lodge, 201 Victoria Street, tel: 04-472 4297; www.victoriacourt.co.nz. Located near the city centre, the pleasant units and off-street parking make it a good option. From here it is only a short stroll to the eateries of Cuba Street and the shopping facilities of Manners Mall. **$$–$$$**

Where to Eat

Arbitrageur, 125 Featherstone Street, tel: 04-499 5530. Described by *Cuisine* magazine as "a serious temple of gustatory pleasure", this serves exquisite food in an elegant 1930s European ambience. It has a wine list of 600 bottles, 60 of which are available by the glass. **$$$**
Café Bastille, 16 Majorbanks Street, Mount Victoria, tel: 04-382 9559; www.bastille.co.nz. Traditional French bistro serving good old-fashioned French food and some very good French and New Zealand wines, served by the glass. Reservation recommended. **$$$**
Café L'Affare, 27 College Street, tel: 04-385 9748; www.laffare. co.nz. This place serves excellent breakfasts and roasts its own coffee. It's very popular, so you'll need to arrive early to avoid disappointment. **$**
Citron 270, Willis Street, tel: 04-801 6263. Set in a tiny two-storey colonial house, Citron is the showcase of Rex Morgan, an inventive chef who delights with wonderful flavour combinations and impeccable presentation. **$$$**
Mac's Brewery Bar and Restaurant, Cable Street, tel: 04-381 2282. Located on the waterfront in a restored wharf building. Watch your favourite beer being brewed before your eyes.
Martin Bosley's Yacht Club Restaurant, Royal Port Nicholson Yacht Club, 103 Oriental Parade,

tel: 04-385 6963; www.martin-bosley.com. Location doesn't come any better, and with Bosley's flamboyant dishes to match, the combination is perfect. **$$$$**
Monsoon Poon, 12 Blair Street, Courtney Place, tel: 04-803 3555; www.monsoonpoon.co.nz. A melting-pot of the cuisines of the Far East, this richly decorated eatery resembles an Eastern trading house. Diners can feast their eyes directly on the large open kitchen where it all happens.
One Red Dog, Steamship Building, North Queens Wharf, tel: 04-918 4723. Wellington's leading gourmet pizza restaurant, with a bubbly atmosphere, more than 50 wines by the glass and award-winning, naturally brewed beers on tap. **$$**
Shed 5 Restaurant and Bar, Queens Wharf, tel: 04-499 9069; www.shed5.co.nz. This restaurant occupies a converted warehouse opposite the Maritime Museum. **$$$**
Taste, 2 Ganges Road, Khandallah, tel: 04-479 8449. Taste is a good example of the type of relaxed restaurant that features dishes reflecting New Zealand's diverse cultural influences. **$$**
Zibibbo, 25–29 Taranaki Street, tel: 04-385 6650; www.zibibbo.co.nz. Contemporary cuisine in a stylish restaurant upstairs. Cocktail and lounge bar downstairs. Resident DJ on Friday and Saturday nights. **$$**

Where to Shop

Wellington City is divided into several distinct shopping precincts – **Cuba Quarter** is where you'll find the more alternative, funky stores and second-hand shops. **Lambton Quarter** is home to five shopping centres, including the famous Kirkcaldie & Stains – the oldest classic department store in New Zealand – while **Willis Quarter** has local designer stores, sports shops and cafés. For antiques shops, head to the character-filled streets of Wellington's historical district, **Thorndon**. Otherwise, nip over to the **Wairarapa** where you'll discover amazing wineries and antiques and craft shops among the beautiful historic houses and buildings.

Entertainment

Wellington has three repertory theatres, a wide range of musical events, and numerous music, art and theatre festivals. It's also home to the Royal New Zealand Ballet, New Zealand Symphony Orchestra, New Zealand String Quartet, Chamber Music New Zealand, Wellington Sinfonia and NBR New Zealand Opera. At the end of the year, there are performances by the New Zealand School of Dance and the New Zealand Drama School, Toi Whakaari.

For ticketing details, contact Wellington's **Ticketek** office at tel: 04-384 3840; www.ticketek.co.nz.

Film

Wellington has more screens per capita than anywhere else in the country, which show mainstream and arthouse, international and local films. There is a highly regarded film festival every year. The **Embassy Theatre** (tel: 04-384 7657), at the end of Courtenay Place, is Wellington's grandest cinema.

Nightlife

Bodega, 101 Ghuznee Street, tel: 04-384 8212; www.bodega.co.nz. Bodega specialises in New Zealand ale, including the local Tuatara beer, and serves the city's only hand-drawn ales plus 17 different tap beers. Also famous as a venue for live, original New Zealand music. **Hummingbird**, 22 Courtenay Place, tel: 04-801 6336. This is a stylish café and bar in a great location, and it attracts a more mature crowd than some of the other establishments along Courtenay Place. **Monkey Bar**, 25 Taranaki Street, tel: 04-802 5090. If you're looking for a quiet evening, this sophisticated lounge bar makes a good choice. It takes great pride in its extensive wine and cocktail lists. **Welsh Dragon Bar and Scorpio's Restaurant**, Middle of the Road, Cambridge Terrace, tel: 04-385 6566. This has been compared to the best pubs in Ireland for atmosphere, yet it is Welsh – complete with Welsh beer and

owners. Live music three nights a week; there's a piano for impromptu performances. Closed Mondays.

Outdoor Activities
Mountain Biking

There are scores of exhilarating mountain bike tracks around the city, meaning that you don't have to travel far to enjoy the outdoors. Classic rides include the town belt on **Mount Victoria**, the **Rollercoaster** from the Wellington wind turbine to Highbury, the **Te Kopahau Reserve** and the **Makara Peak Mountain Track**.

Nature Encounters

Karori Wildlife Sanctuary, Waiapu Road, tel: 04-920 9213; www.sanctuary.org.nz. Daily 10am–5pm, last entry 4pm; entrance fee. This wildlife oasis has 35 km (21 miles) of tracks within the 252 hectares (622 acres) of regenerating forest. There's also a 19th-century goldmine on the site.

Seal Watching

Seal Coast Safari, departing i-SITE Visitor Centre, corner of Victoria and Wakefield streets, tel: 04-139 7839; 0800-732 5277; www.sealcoast.com. These boat trips get you up close to Wellington's resident seal colony.

Walking

There are plenty of parks, reserves, rivers and forests to walk on the outskirts of Wellington. You can head to **Makara Beach**, 35 minutes west of Wellington city, for a 3- or 4-hour stroll along the coast, or take a 2-hour coastal walk to **Red Rocks** and visit its colony of New Zealand fur seals (May–Oct). There are also plenty of city heritage walks that trace Wellington's history.

Wineries

Wairarapa Gourmet Wine Escape, run by Tranzit Coachlines, 316–318 Queen Street, Masterton, tel: 06-377 1227, 0800-471 227; www.tranzit.co.nz. Takes visitors on a lip-smacking tour of four Martinborough wineries, and finishes at the Martinborough Wine Centre.

South Island

Nelson & Marlborough

PICTON AND THE SOUNDS

Getting There

Ferry services between Wellington and Picton are frequent. The **Interislander** and **Bluebridge** ferries take 3 hours to get you across Cook Strait. See also Getting Around, pages 330–2.

Visitor Information

Picton i-SITE Visitor Centre, Foreshore, Picton, tel: 03-520 3113; www.destinationmarlborough.com.

Where to Stay

Bay of Many Coves Resort, Queen Charlotte Sound, tel: 03-579 9771, 0800-579 9771; www.bayofmanycovesresort.co.nz. In the heart of the Marlborough Sounds, this is a quiet and attractive holiday retreat. 11 self contained apartments and great food. **$$$$–$$$$$**
Furneaux Lodge, Endeavour Inlet, tel: 03-579 8259; www.furneaux.co.nz. This exclusive bush retreat and eco-resort in the heart of the Marlborough Sounds offers luxury suites, self-catering cabins and backpacker hostels. Facilities include a seafood restaurant–bar and a marine centre. All scuba diving requirements are supplied. Good fishing off the wharf. From here you can embark on the Queen Charlotte hike. **$–$$$$**
Harbour View Motel, 30 Waikawa Road, Picton, tel: 03-573 6259; www.harbourviewpicton.co.nz. Twelve tastefully furnished studios with great harbour views. **$$**
Portage Resort, Kenepuru Sound, tel: 03-573 4309; www.portage.co.

nz. A famous resort in the beautiful Marlborough Sounds. Facilities include swimming pool, spa, leisure activities and the superb Portage Restaurant. Hillside and garden rooms, bunk rooms, and lodges available. **$$–$$$$**
Punga Cove Resort, Endeavour Inlet, tel: 03-579 8561; www.pungacove.co.nz. Chalets are nestled in the bush, with superb views of the surrounding bay. Each has an ensuite bathroom, modern facilities, a sun deck and barbecue (on request). The Punga Lodge sleeps 10 people while the studio chalets can accommodate two to three. It has a private beach, with good swimming and excellent fishing. **$$–$$$**
Raetihi Lodge, Kenepuru Sound, tel: 03-573 4300; www.raetihi.co. nz. Luxury lodge with 14 theme rooms, all with ensuites and elegant furnishings. Large guest lounge, licensed bar, restaurant, games room and plenty of outdoor activities. **$$–$$$$**

Where to Eat
Le Café, 14–26 London Quay, Picton, tel: 03-573 5588; www. lecafepicton.co.nz. Great location on the waterfront, with an excellent menu featuring seasonal local produce, and, wherever possible, organic fare. Over 50 wines, beers and a selection of cigars. **$$**
The Barn Café, Restaurant and Bar, High Street, Picton, tel: 03-573 7440. Traditional steak, chicken and seafood dishes cater to mainstream tastes. **$$**

Outdoor Activities
Kayaking
Marlborough Sounds Adventure Company, The Waterfront, Picton, tel: 03-573 6078 or 0800-283 283; www.marlboroughsounds. co.nz. This company organises kayaking, and also conducts walks and bike trials around the 1500 km (930 miles) of bays in the area.

Sailing
Compass Charters, Unit 1, Commercial Building, Waikawa Marina, tel: 03-573 8332;

www.compass-charters.co.nz. Explore the magical Marlborough Sounds on a yacht, runabout or launch.

Skydiving
SkyDive the Sounds, tel: 03-573 9101, 0800-373 264; www.skydive thesounds.com. Tandem skydiving, either from Marlborough with views across Cook Strait and deep into the North and South islands, or from Wellington Airport and across Cook Strait into the South Island.

BLENHEIM

Getting There
Air New Zealand flies to Blenheim, which is on SH1 36 km (22 miles) south of Picton. See also Getting Around, pages 330–2.

Visitor Information
Blenheim i-SITE Visitor Centre, Railway Station, SH1, tel: 03-577 8080; www.destinationmarlborough.com.

Where to Stay
Criterion Hotel, 2 Market Street, tel: 03-578 3299. Handy to the centre of town with a good restaurant and comfortable bars. **$**
Marlborough Hotel, 20 Nelson Street, tel: 03-577 7333; www.marlboroughhotel.co.nz. Classy, contemporary hotel with a very good restaurant. **$$–$$$**
Swansdown Cottage, Riverina Riverlands, RD4, tel: 03-578 9824; www.swansdown.co.nz. Experience New Zealand farm life in the seclusion and tranquility of your own private self-contained bed and breakfast accommodation. **$$**

Where to Eat
Bellafico Restaurant and Wine Bar, 17 Maxwell Road, tel: 03-577 6072; www.bellafico.co.nz. Modern New Zealand cuisine, imaginatively prepared seafood and the area's great wines. **$$**
Hotel d'Urville Restaurant, 52 Queen Street, tel: 03-577 9945; www.durville.com. A world-acclaimed restaurant with

accommodation, set in a historic building. It also includes an international cooking school. 11 rooms. **$$$$**
Rocco's Italian Restaurant, 5 Dobson Street, tel/fax: 03-578 6940. Run by the Rocco brothers from Northern Italy, this place specialises in home-made fresh pasta and prosciutto, as well as New Zealand seafood, lamb and chicken cooked in the traditional Italian way. Extensive menu and wine list. **$$**

Outdoor Activities
Walking
Southern Wilderness and Wilderness Guides, tel: 03-578 4531; www.southernwilderness. com. Guided walks and sea kayaking. Gourmet food and wine on the way.

Wineries
Cloudy Bay, Jacksons Road, tel: 03-520 9140; www.cloudybay.co.nz. Cloudy Bay produces some of New Zealand's best wines. Offers tastings and sales of the vineyard's current releases, including limited-release wines.
Montana Brancott Winery, SH1, Riverlands, tel: 03-578 2099; www.pernod-ricard-nz.com. Wine tours and tastings, children's playground and restaurant.
Villa Maria Estate, corner Paynters and New Renwick roads, Fairhall, tel: 03-577 9530; www.villamaria. co.nz. A modern winery in an impressive location, specialising in pinot noir and sauvignon blanc.
Wairau River Winery, 264 Rapaura Road, tel: 03-572 9800; www. wairauriverwines.com. Good food crafted from Marlborough's local produce at the Wairau River Restaurant, and award-winning wines at cellar-door prices.

KAIKOURA

Getting There
Kaikoura, the world's whale-watching capital, is midway between Blenheim and Christchurch. It can be reached by road or rail. The

journey down the east coast to Kaikoura is picturesque and magnificent. See also Getting Around on pages 330–2.

Visitor Information

Kaikoura i-SITE Visitor Centre, West End, tel: 03-319 5641; www.kaikoura.co.nz.

Where to Stay

Admiral Court Motel, 16 Avoca Street, tel: 03-319 5525; www.kaikouramotel.co.nz. In a quiet location with mountain and sea views, this motel has units equipped with kitchens. There's off-road parking, courtesy car to bus or rail stations, and a spa pool. **$$–$$$**

Donegal House, School House Road, tel: 03-319 5083, 0800-346 873; www.donegalhouse.co.nz. Located 3 km (2 miles) north of Kaikoura, this award-winning Irish pub has 28 bed-and-breakfast ensuite rooms furnished with an Irish theme. Outdoor spas, three huge open fires, tranquil gardens and lake. There's also an excellent restaurant and an Irish bar serving over 100 Irish and Scottish whiskeys as well as Guinness and Kilkenny on tap. **$$**

Panorama Motel, 266 Esplanade, tel: 03-319 5053; www.panoramamotel.co.nz. Beachfront location, with sea and mountain views from all units. Plenty of off-street parking for boats and cars. 22 units. **$–$$**

The Old Convent Bed and Breakfast, Mount Fyffe Road, tel: 03-319 6603; www.theoldconvent.co.nz. Set in a beautifully renovated 1911 convent, with the majestic Kaikoura Mountains as the backdrop, the Old Convent has an atmosphere of French charm. Its restaurant is fully licensed and offers superb local produce. There are family-size, double and twin rooms. Murder mystery weekends; petanque also available. **$–$$**

Where to Eat

The Craypot Café and Bar, 70 West End Road, tel 03-319 6027; www.craypot.co.nz. Centrally located, this restaurant has an open fire, and the varied menu includes mulled wine, fresh crayfish and vegetarian options. All-day dining till late. **$$$**

Donegal House, School House Road, tel: 03-319 5083, 0800-346 873; www.donegalhouse.co.nz. Located 3 km (2 miles) north of Kaikoura, this acclaimed Irish pub has an excellent restaurant serving fresh local seafood, Kaikoura crayfish and the local ribeye steak are specialities. Good local wine selection, and, of course, Guinness on tap. **$$**

Outdoor Activities

Seal Watching

Topspot Sealswims, 22 Deal Street, Kaikoura, tel: 03-319 5540. Slip into a wetsuit and get up close to New Zealand fur seals.

Whale- and Dolphin-Watching

Kaikoura is world famous for its whale and dolphin population. Huge sperm whales swim barely a kilometre off the coast between April and June; orcas can also be seen during the summer, and humpbacks put in an appearance during June and July.

The following companies organise trips to see both whales and dolphins; you should book a few days in advance:

Whale Watch Kaikoura, Railway Station Road, tel: 03-319 6767, 0800-655 121; www.whalewatch.co.nz.

Dolphin Encounter, 96 The Esplanade, tel: 03-319 6777, 0800-733 365; www.dolphin.co.nz.

Wings Over Whales, Kaikoura Airfield, tel: 03-319 6580, 0800-226 629; www.whales.co.nz. Spectacular 30-minute whale-watching flights.

NELSON

Getting There

Nelson Regional Airport has regular airlinks with Auckland, Wellington and Christchurch, as well as a range of provincial centres. See also Getting Around, pages 330–2.

Plenty of coach services link Nelson with Motueka and the southern entrance of the Abel Tasman Park. Contact: **Abel Tasman Coachlines**, tel: 03-548 0285; www.abeltasmantravel.co.nz. You can also hire a car or motorhome and drive to most surrounding towns in less than 2 hours. Contact the nearest Visitor Centre for more details.

Visitor Information

Nelson i-SITE Visitor Centre, Millers Acres Centre, 77 Trafalgar Street, tel: 03-548 2304; www.i-SITENelsonNZ.com.

Where to Stay

Beachside Villas Hotel, 71 Golf Road, tel: 03-548 5041; www.beachsidevillas.co.nz. A Mediterranean-style boutique motel in a beautiful garden setting, offering luxurious self-contained apartments where the cast and crew of The Lord of the Rings stayed while filming in the Nelson region. 6 units. **$$–$$$**

Bella Vista Motel, 178 Tahunanui Drive, tel: 03-548 6948. A bit of a walk from the city centre (30 minutes), but close to a beautiful beach and the harbour entrance. Good cafés and shops nearby. One unit has a spa bath, while two rooms are wheelchair accessible. 18 units. **$–$$**

DeLorenzo's Motel and Studio Apartments, 43–55 Trafalgar Street, tel: 03-548 9774; www.delorenzos.co.nz. These luxury apartments, close to business and shopping areas, are furnished in a modern style and have super-king beds, ensuite bathrooms, spa baths and Sky TV. Business facilities and room service available. **$$–$$$$**

Kimi Ora Spa Resort, Kaiteriteri, tel: 0508-546 4672; www.kimiora.com. Swiss-style chalet apartments with sea views. The resort has a health complex with an extensive range of spa treatments, heated indoor and outdoor pool with swim channel, sauna, steam room, spa pool, tennis courts and fully licensed restaurant with panoramic ocean views. 20 units. **$$–$$$$$**

Tuscany Gardens Motor Lodge, 80 Tahunanui Drive, tel: 03-548 5522. Studio one- and two-bedroom family units have full kitchens, but it's only a 5-minute walk to local eateries (and the beach). 12 units. **$$–$$$**
Wairepo House, 22 Weka Road, Mariri, tel: 03-526 6865; www.wairepohouse.co.nz. A three-storey colonial homestead with rich native timbers, chapel ceilings and sunny decks, set in an apple and pear orchard. **$$$$$**

Where to Eat
Boat Shed Café, 350 Wakefield Quay, tel: 03-546 9783; www.boatshedcafe.co.nz. A very pleasant and popular restaurant, with views across the water and imaginative seafood dishes. Booking essential. **$$–$$$**
The Cut Restaurant and Bar, 94 Collingwood Street, tel: 03-548 9874. Modern Mediterranean cuisine in a classic setting. **$$**
The Honest Lawyer, 1 Point Road, Monaco, tel: 03-547 8150; www.honestlawyer.co.nz. An old-style country pub in a historic building just outside Nelson, with a large beer garden and accom-modation. Delicious New Zealand and British cuisine plus a wide-ranging wine list and selection of beers on tap. **$$**
The Oyster Bar, 15 Hardy Street, tel: 03-545 8955. Lovers of sushi,

Craft Crawl

There are more than 350 full-time artists and craftspeople in the Nelson region, so expect to see plenty of craft shops in the centre of town. The Saturday morning market in Montgomery Square is popular, and there are stalls with everything from arts and crafts to regional produce and gourmet foods. There are also weekend markets in Motueka and Golden Bay. At the Motueka Information Centre you can get a copy of *Creative Pathways*, a guide to the studios of more than 30 local artists and craftspeople.

sashimi and oysters will enjoy this New York-style bar.
The Smokehouse Café, Shed Three, Mapua Wharf, Mapua, tel: 03-540 2280; www.smokehouse.co.nz. A unique smokehouse and café using the freshest local seafood. The menu is based on fish, mussels and vegetables, delicately hot-smoked on site using a traditional brick kiln and manuka shavings. **$$$**

Outdoor Activities
Skywire
Happy Valley Adventures, 194 Cable Bay Road, tel: 03-545 0304; www.happyvalleyadventures.co.nz. Fifteen minutes north of Nelson, this offers the world's first Skywire ride that is also New Zealand's longest flying fox. Strapped in a four-seat carriage suspended by a

Coastal Kayaking

Abel Tasman National Park, located some 60 km (37 miles) from Nelson, has emerald bays and a granite-fringed coastline, and is best savoured by walking the Coastal Track *(see page 243)*. The full walk takes 3–4 days. If you prefer to take to the water, kayak trips around the bays, both guided and unguided, have exploded in popularity in recent years. The following operators are recommended.
Abel Tasman Kayaks, RD2 Marahau, Motueka, tel: 03-527 8022; www.abeltasmankayaks. co.nz. Half-day to multi-day guided sea kayaking trips with camping and boat-stay options.
Ocean River Sea Kayaking, Marahau Beach, Marahau, tel: 03-527 8266; www.oceanriver. co.nz. Freedom rentals at the entrance to the park. Ocean River offers a fully equipped base, parking and luggage storage.
Abel Tasman Wilson's Experiences, 265 High Street, Motueka, tel: 03-528 7801; www. abeltasmannz.co.nz. One- or multi-day trips, including boat cruise, walking and sea kayaking options.

cable high over native forest, you are flown over 3 km (2 miles) at speeds of up to 100 km/h (62 mph). Also popular are the four-wheel bike rides through farmland and native forest, Maori cultural tours, plus high-speed river crossings in the amphibious argo.

Christchurch & Surroundings

CHRISTCHURCH

Getting There
Christchurch is served by a busy international airport, and has comprehensive road and rail links and a thriving deep-water port. There's a public bus service from the airport to the city, which will cost about NZ$4 per person and take 30–40 minutes; the shuttle will take around 20–30 minutes at a cost of NZ$12–18 per person. The more expensive option of a taxi will cost NZ$25–30, but it will get you there much faster – about 12–20 minutes.
If travelling from Greymouth, on the west coast, you should try to take the scenic **TranzAlpine** train (tel: 0800-277 482; www.tranz scenic.co.nz), which cuts through some spectacular scenery. Christchurch is also well-served by inter-city coaches from other New Zealand destinations. See also Getting Around, pages 330–2.

Visitor Information
Christchurch & Canterbury i-SITE Visitor Centre, Cathedral Square, tel: 03-379 9629; www.christchurchnz.net.

City Transport
There are plenty of inner-city bus and taxi services, but to experience a taste of old world charm, take one of Christchurch's historic trams. The trams do a circuit from Worcester Street, past the Arts Centre, museum and Christ's College, and you can hop off and on at any of the stops along the way, making this ideal for sightseeing (tel: 03-366 7511; www.tram.co.nz).

There is a dedicated shuttle service to Hanmer Springs, which leaves the Christchurch Information Service at 9am every day and arrives in Hanmer Springs 2 hours later. Contact: **Hanmer Connection**, tel: 0800-377 378, **Blue Star Taxis**, tel: 03-3799 799 or **Gold Band Taxis**, tel: 03-379 5795.

Where to Stay

Admiral Motel, 168 Bealey Avenue, tel: 03-379 3554; www.admiral motel.co.nz. Near Cathedral Square and the town hall, this motel has units sleeping up to six people. 9 units. **$–$$**

Airport Gateway Motor Lodge, 45 Roydvale Avenue, Burnside, tel: 03-358 7093; www.airportgateway.co. nz. Free stretch-limo airport transfers. Larger units sleep up to six people per unit. It's close to the airport, and has a restaurant and conference facilities. 40 studios. **$$–$$$**

Ashleigh Court Motel, 47 Matai Street West, Lower Riccarton, tel: 03-348 1888; www.ashleighcourt motel.co.nz. A short walk from the museum, shopping centre and gardens, units have kitchen facilities and ensuite bathrooms. **$–$$$**

Belmont Motor Inn, 172 Bealey Avenue, tel: 03-379 4037; www.belmontmotorinn.co.nz. This conveniently located motor inn is only 10 minutes from the city centre and has one- and two-bedroom units. **$$**

Christchurch YMCA, 12 Hereford Street, tel: 03-365 0502; www.ymcachch.org.nz. Quality accommodation for all budgets, located next to the Arts Centre and just opposite the Botanic Gardens and Museum. **$–$$$**

Country Glen Lodge, 107 Bealey Avenue, tel: 03-365 9980, 0800-229 980; www.glenlodge.com. Luxurious apartments close to the city centre. Extensive facilities including luxury spa bath units. **$$–$$$**

Crowne Plaza Hotel Christchurch, corner of Kilmore and Durham streets, tel: 03-365 7799; www.christchurch.crowneplaza.com. Magnificent location on Victoria

Square in the city centre, connected to town hall and convention centre. Immaculate rooms, spacious corridors and top-class amenities. 298 rooms. **$$$$**

Gothic Heights Motel, 430 Hagley Avenue, tel: 03-366 0838. Opposite Hagley Park, within walking distance of the museum, the Arts Centre, restaurants and botanical gardens. 15 studio and family units. **$$**

Holiday Inn City Centre, corner of Cashel and High streets, tel: 03-365 8888; www.holidayinn.co.nz. In a central location, close to retail and business districts, this hotel has its own restaurant and bar. 146 rooms and 3 apartments. **$$–$$$$$**

Hotel Grand Chancellor, 161 Cashel Street, tel: 03-379 2999; www.ghihotels.com. Excellent location in central Christchurch, only a short walk from Cathedral Square. Comfortable rooms and prompt service. **$$$**

Latimer Hotel and Apartments, 30 Latimer Square, tel: 03-379 6760; www.latimerhotel.co.nz. Low-rise travellers' lodge near the city centre, with good-value rooms and off-street parking. **$$–$$$**

Millennium Hotel Christchurch, 14 Cathedral Square, tel: 03-365 1111, 0800-645 536; www.millen niumchristchurch.co.nz. Modern, city-centre hotel with restaurant, bar, gymnasium, sauna and business centre. 179 rooms. **$$$–$$$$$**

Scenic Circle Cotswold Hotel, 88 Papanui Road, tel: 03-355 3535; www.scenic-circle.co.nz. Modern comforts are combined with old-world charm and authentic period furnishings at this hotel, just 5 minutes from the city. Nearby restaurant offers Continental cuisine. 99 rooms and suites. **$$–$$$$**

The Charlotte Jane, 110 Papanui Road, tel: 03-355 1028; www.char lotte-jane.co.nz. Located near Merivale Village, this charming boutique property is only a 20-minute walk to the city. Converted from an old Victorian school for girls and named after one of the first four ships that brought Christ-

church's founding fathers to its shores, its 12 spacious ensuite rooms are tastefully furnished and come with a gourmet breakfast each morning and a glass of sherry or wine in the evenings. **$$$$$**

The George Hotel, 50 Park Terrace, tel: 03-379 4560; www.thegeorge. com. A low-rise luxury hotel on a great site across the road from the Avon River and Hagley Park. Nice willow-shaded rooms with balconies. Ten-minute walk to the city centre. Top-rated fine dining restaurant. **$$$$**

Windsor Hotel Bed and Breakfast, 52 Armagh Street, tel: 03-366 1503; www.windsorhotel.co.nz. Family-run traditional bed and breakfast in a centrally located, attractive colonial-style accommodation. **$$**

Where to Eat

Asian Food Court, 266 High Street, tel: 03-365 0168. The only truly Asian food court in the South Island. A veritable melting pot of Asian cuisines: India, Thai, Indonesian, Malay, Chinese and Vietnamese. **$**

Cook 'N' With Gas, 23 Worcester Boulevard, tel: 03-377 9166; www.cooknwithgas.co.nz. The atmosphere is casual but the food is seriously good in this converted villa opposite the Arts Centre. Canterbury ingredients and New Zealand heritage foods feature on the menu. There's also a good selection of boutique beers. This was Canterbury's Restaurant of the Year in 2006. Mon–Sat from 6pm. **$$$**

Cup, corner of Hackthorne and Dyers Pass roads, tel: 03-332 1270. The food is good and the view is probably the best in Christchurch, taking in the whole city. **$$**

Dux de Lux, The Arts Centre, corner of Montreal and Hereford streets, tel: 03-366 6919; www.thedux. co.nz. Laid-back dining in a buzzing restaurant-bar complex. The menu is extensive, and includes a large number of seafood and vegetarian options. Try the brewed-on-the-premises beer. There's a great

outdoor garden bar which can be used in all seasons. **$$$**
Ginko, 153–157 Hereford Street, tel: 03-374 2523. This restaurant prides itself on serving the spicy specialities of Szechuan from original recipes without Western adaptations. Here, it's the real deal. **$–$$**
Honeypot Café, 114 Lichfield Street, tel: 03-366 5853. Casual eatery serving full meals as well as sandwiches. The pizzas include innovative toppings such as tandoori chicken, and Cajun with sour cream. Great desserts and coffee too. **$**
Indochine, 209 Cambridge Terrace, tel: 03-365 7323; www.indochine. co.nz. The food is an eclectic mix of Asian-inspired fare. The atmosphere, cocktails and desserts are a blend of the exotic and seductive. **$$–$$$**
Lone Star Café and Elvis Bar, 26 Manchester Street, tel: 03-365 7086. Be prepared for giant servings of tender cuts of meat in a noisy, friendly atmosphere. **$$**
Pedro's, 143 Worcester Street, tel: 03-379 7668; www.pedros restaurant.co.nz. Pedro comes from the Basque country, and is a popular local figure. Superb Basque cuisine served in a relaxed atmosphere. **$–$$$**
Raj Mahal, corner of Worcester and Manchester streets, tel: 03-366 0521; www.rajmahal.co.nz. The wide-ranging menu features Punjabi, northern and southern India, Mughlai, Goan and Gujarati dishes. There's also a good array of vegetarian dishes and breads. Takeaway service available. Tues–Sun 4.30–10pm. **$–$$**
Tiffany's Restaurant, corner of Oxford Terrace and Lichfield Street, tel: 03-379 1350; www.tiffanys. co.nz. Fine wines, first-rate regional cuisine and top-class service are on offer here. Tiffany's has a picturesque riverside location, but is still close to the centre of town. Their alfresco lunches are recommended. **$$$**
The Blue Note, 20 New Regent Street, tel: 03-379 9674; www.bluenote.co.nz. Offers great

food with a Mediterranean influence accompanied by live jazz. The ambience is warm and welcoming, and the setting on a pedestrian-only street is superb. **$$–$$$**
The Seafood Kitchen, 819 Colombo Street, tel: 03-365 6543. This restaurant has a changing menu dedicated to seafood, featuring whatever is fresh on the day, carefully cooked and simply presented. Also has a small selection of delicious desserts. Tues–Sat from 6pm. **$$$**

Entertainment
Christchurch is a fairly laid-back city, many artists and craftspeople. The theatre and concert scene is varied, and events are listed in the Christchurch and Canterbury Visitors' Guide. *The Press* newspaper also has details of current arts events. Christchurch is also home to the yearly Arts Festival, the Festival of Romance and the Winter Carnival.

Theatre
Court Theatre, 20 Worcester Boulevard, tel: 0800-333 100; www.courttheatre.org.nz. This is regarded as New Zealand's leading theatre, with a small, high-quality ensemble and guest actors from Britain playing middle-of-the-road modern drama. It's also home to the Southern Ballet and Dance Theatre.
Isaac Theatre Royal, 145 Gloucester Street, tel: 03-366 6326; www.theatreroyal.co.nz. Built in 1908, this Edwardian-style lyric theatre seats about 1,300 people and hosts concerts, comedy and a whole range of other events and arts performances.

Concerts
Convention Centre, **Town Hall**, and **Westpac Centre**, 95 Kilmore Street, tel: 03-366 8899; www.convention.co.nz. This modern building near the casino plays host to major musical events. It is also the headquarters of a leading nationwide theatre and concert ticket agency – and New Zealand's largest indoor sports stadium.

Nightlife
On Fridays and Saturdays, nearly all pubs have live bands performing. The **Christchurch Casino** (tel: 03-365 9999) in Victoria Street is also a hive of activity.
Work your way through the various establishments such as **Viaduct** (tel: 03-377 9968) on **The Strip** along **Oxford Terrace**. Cafés by day, they become bars by night.
The Dux de Lux, 299 Montreal Street, tel: 03-366 6919; www.thedux.co.nz. Trendy but laid-back crowd. Brews its own beers, and you can drink in one of three bars in or outside. Live music, often folk and blues.
The Loaded Hog, corner of Cashel and Manchester streets, tel: 03-366 6674; www.loadedhog.co.nz. The premier bar on a busy corner. Like its Auckland counterpart, it is big,

Christchurch Shopping

Christchurch offers excellent prospects for shopping, and you will find a selection of designer stores, nationwide chain stores, souvenir shops and shopping malls throughout the city.
The **Arts Centre** in Worcester Boulevard has more than 40 craft studios, galleries and shops, all offering unique New Zealand-made souvenirs.
Canterbury Museum specialises in *paua* shell jewellery and souvenirs, New Zealand-designed pottery, glass, stone and wood pieces. It also features a great selection of Maori carvings.
For New Zealand-made products with a wintery theme, check out the **Antarctic Shops** at the International Antarctic Centre and Christchurch International Airport.
On Colombo Street you will find **Ballantynes**, on the corner of the City Mall, a pedestrian precinct. Ballantynes is the city's foremost department store, considered as Christchurch's Harrods or Marshall Field's. The assistants dress in black and are notoriously helpful.

bold and a popular place to be seen. **The Ministry**, 90 Lichfield Street, tel: 03-379 2910; www.ministry. co.nz. Plays the latest sounds from around the world to a frequently gay crowd. Big dance floor and great sound system adds to the frenetic atmosphere late at night.

Outdoor Activities
Skiing
Mount Hutt, **Methven** and **Porter Heights** are a 90-minute drive away from Christchurch. Contact: **Mount Hutt Ski Area**, tel: 03-308 5074; www.nzski.com/mthutt or **Porters Ski Area**, tel: 03-318 4002; www.skiporters.co.nz.

Skydiving
Skydiving NZ.Com, Wigram Aerodrome, tel: 03-343 5542, 0800-697 593; www.skydivingnz. com. Experience the adrenaline rush from free-falling at speeds of up to 200 km/h (124 mph).

Exploring Antarctica

Not a journey to be undertaken lightly, a visit to one of the world's most remarkable places can be made from Christchurch through a few specialist local companies. **The Adventure Travel Company**, 60 Oxford Terrace, Christchurch, tel: 03-364 3409; www.adventuretravel.co.nz. Sails on month-long cruises from New Zealand through the ice packs of the Ross Sea in the footsteps of Shackleton and Scott. You'll visit explorers' huts and encounter the remarkable southern wildlife. **Heritage Expeditions**, 53B Montreal Street, Christchurch, tel: 03-365 3500; www.heritage-expeditions.com. Cruises to Antarctica and the sub-Antarctic Islands – the "Galapagos of Antarctica" and among the last remaining unspoiled environments in the world. Groups number less than 50, and the emphasis is on getting you on shore as often and for as long as possible.

Swimming
Queen Elizabeth II Park, 171 Travis Road, tel: 03-941 6849; www.qeii park.org.nz; Mon–Fri 6am–9pm, Sat–Sun and public holidays 7am–8pm; entrance fee. Stadium and sports complex built for the 1974 Commonwealth Games, but substantially upgraded with many special aquatic features.

Windsurfing/Surfing
Pegasus and Sumner bays near Christchurch offer the best windsurfing and surfing conditions, but the water is freezing so it is advisable to wear a wetsuit.

AKAROA

Visitor Information
Akaroa Information Centre, 80 Rue Lavaud, tel/fax: 03-304 8600; www.akaroa.com.

Where to Stay
Akaroa Critereon Motel, 75 Rue Jolie, tel: 03-304 7775, 0800-252 762; www.holidayakaroa.co.nz. Twelve luxury studio units with harbour views. **$–$$$**
Driftwood Wai-Iti Motel, 56–64 Rue Jolie, tel: 03-304 7292; www.driftwood.co.nz. Family-size accommodation on the seafront; within walking distance of shops and restaurants. **$–$$$**
Maison des Fleurs, 6 Church Street, tel: 03-304 7804; www.maisondesfleurs.co.nz. Luxury boutique cottage with sunny balcony and secluded courtyard. **$$$$$**

Where to Eat
C'est La Vie Bistro/Café, 33 Rue Lavaud, Akaroa, tel: 03-304 7314, specialising in French cuisine and seafood dishes. **$$$**
French Farm Winery and Restaurant, Valley Road, tel: 03-304 5784; www.frenchfarm.co.nz. One of the highlights of dining here is the glorious scenery around the outdoor dining patio. The menu emphasises fresh local ingredients, including Akaroa salmon and vegetables. Daily 10am–4pm for lunch, dinner by arrangement. Next

to it is La Pizzeria serving traditional European-style pizzas. **$$**
Harbour 71, 71 Beach Street, tel: 03-304 7656. Located in a century-old former store overlooking Akaroa Harbour, this award-winning restaurant serves gourmet pizzas for lunch and afternoon snacks. A more substantial menu is served in the evening. The fresh grouper and salmon are not to be missed. **$$–$$$**
Little River Café and Store, Main Road, Little River, Banks Peninsula, tel: 03-325 1933. This unpretentious café and general store is a popular halfway stopover on the road to Akaroa. Enjoy scrumptious country food, made on the premises, and good coffee in a private sculpture garden. **$**
Ma Maison Restaurant and Bar, 6 Rue Balguerie, tel: 03-304 7668. Waterfront location with quality food and a good wine list. **$$**

Outdoor Activities
Dolphin Experience, 61 Beach Road, tel: 03-304 7726; www.dolphins akaroa.co.nz. Two-hour cruises observing fur seals, blue penguins and the rare Hector's dolphin. On the swimming tour, you can dive in and swim with the dolphins.

Kayaking
Akaroa Boat Hire and Akaroa Sea Kayaks, Foreshore, Beach Road, Akaroa, tel: 03-304 8758. Paddle boats, kayaks, sea kayaks, motor boats, double canoes and rowing boats available.

Canterbury

HANMER SPRINGS

Visitor Information
Hurunui i-SITE Visitor Centre, 42 Amuri Avenue, tel: 03-315 7128; www.hurunui.com.

Where to Stay
Alpine Lodge, corner Amuri Drive and Harrogate Street, tel: 03-315 7311, 0800-993 377; www.alpine lodgemotel.co.nz. Accommodation, close to shops and pool complex, ranges from traditional chalets to

luxurious tower suites. Facilities vary in each suite. 23 units. **$$–$$$$**

Greenacres Chalets and Apartments, 84 Conical Hill Road, tel: 03-315 7125, 0800-822 262; www.greenacresmotel.co.nz. Separate units in park-like setting overlooking the Hanmer Basin. Chalets and delux townhouse units apartments have decks, balconies and full kitchen facilities. Close to Hanmer Township and thermal pools. **$–$$**

Hanmer Resort Motel, 7 Cheltenham Street, tel: 03-315 7362, 0800-777 666; www.han merresortmotel.co.nz. Motel units here accommodate up to six people. It's located adjacent to hot mineral pools. 15 rooms. **$–$$$**

Hanmer Springs Larchwood Motel, 18 Bath Street, tel: 03-315 7281, www.larchwoodmotel.co.nz. Spacious rooms, which can sleep up to six, handy to squash courts, hot pools and forest walks. 16 rooms. **$–$$$**

Where to Eat

Hot Springs Hotel, 2 Fraser Close, tel: 03-315 7799; www.hotsprings. co.nz. This is a friendly pub with a bistro menu. **$**

Malabar Restaurant and Cocktail Bar, 5 Conical Hill Road, tel: 03-315 7745. The finest Asian and Indian cuisine with an excellent selection of local wines. Reservations are essential.

The Dining Room, Heritage Hanmer Springs, 1 Conical Hill Road, tel: 03-315 7804; www.motorlodge. co.nz. Pacific Rim flavours meet French cuisine in this elegant dining room. **$$$**

The Old Post Office, 2 Jacks Pass Road, tel: 03-315 7461. The old Post Office has been transformed into a delightful award-winning restaurant serving flavoursome fare. **$$$**

Outdoor Activities

Golf

Hanmer Springs Golf Club, 133 Argelins Road, tel: 03-315 7110; www.hanmersprings.nzgolf.net. A challenging 18-hole course, amid breathtaking mountain scenery.

Thrillseekers Canyon Adventure Centre, Hanmer Springs, tel: 03-315 7046; www.thrillseekers canyon.co.nz. Located 8 minutes from Hanmer, this one-stop action adventure land has it all – bungy, jet boating, go-kart safaris, argo trips, river rafting and paintball.

Horse Riding

Hurunui Horse Treks, Ribbonwood, Hawarden (between Hammer Springs and Christchurch), tel/fax: 03-314 4204; www.hurunui.co.nz. This company conducts horse-back tours through the farmland of North Canterbury.

Hot Springs

Hanmer Springs Thermal Pools and Spa, Amuri Avenue, daily 10am–9pm; entrance fee; tel: 03-315 7511, 0800-442 663; www.hotfun.co.nz. These hot mineral pools are set in a garden of giant conifers. Few experiences are more pleasurable than relaxing in the warmth of these open-air pools on a winter's night, watching the snowflakes dissolve silently in the steam.

METHVEN

Visitor Information

Methven i-SITE Visitor Centre, 121 Main Street, tel: 03-302 8955, 0800-764 444; www.methveninfo.co.nz.

Where to Stay

Canterbury Hotel (Brown Pub), Mount Hutt Village, tel: 03-302 8045; www.nzpub.com. This historic hotel has been a haven for travellers for more than 120 years. Basic but comfortable facilities. Good family restaurant. **$**

Mount Hutt Motels, 205 Main Street, tel: 03-302 8382; www.mounthuttmotels.com. This is the closest motel to Mount Hutt. Spacious, self-contained studio units and apartments set in park-like surroundings with spa and lawn tennis courts. 10 units. **$**

Powderhouse Country Lodge, 3 Cameron Street, Mount Hutt,

tel: 03-302 9105; www.powder house.co.nz. A beautifully restored Edwardian villa. Luxurious bedrooms have private ensuites. Eight-person spa available. 3 rooms. **$$$**

Where to Eat

Abisko Lodge, 74 Main Street, Mount Hutt Village, Main Road, tel: 03-302 8875; www.abisko.co.nz. Specialists in feeding hungry skiers. **$–$$**

Café 131, 131 Main Street, tel: 03-302 9131. Hearty breakfasts, lunches and snacks, all reasonably priced. Closed for dinner. **$–$$**

Outdoor Activities

Ballooning

Aoraki Balloon Safaris, 20 Barkers Road, tel: 03-302 8172, 0800-256 837; www.nzballooning.com. Soar aloft for views of Mount Cook and the National Park Mountains, plus a full panorama of the entire Canterbury Plains.

Heliskiing

Methven Heliskiing, Main Street, tel: 03-302 8108; www.heliskiing. co.nz. This company flies skiers by helicopter, deep into the heartland where there are long ski runs through unbeatable scenery.

LAKE TEKAPO

Visitor Information

Lake Tekapo Information Centre, Main Highway next to Lake Tekapo, Senic Resort, tel: 03-680 6686; www.laketekapountouched.co.nz.

Where to Stay

Lake Tekapo Grandview, 32 Hamilton Drive, tel: 03-680 6910; www.laketekapograndview.co.nz. Living up to its name, this luxury bed and breakfast accommodation has stunning views of the alps and lake from every room. **$$$–$$$$**

Lake Tekapo Scenic Resort, Main Highway, tel: 03-680 6808; www.laketekapo.com. Centrally located accommodation with good views. Budget accommodation available. **$$–$$$$**

Where to Eat

Reflections Café and Restaurant, at the Lake Tekapo Scenic Resort, Main Highway, tel: 03-680 6234. Fresh local produce including salmon and venison are on the menu here, accompanied by spectacular mountain and lake views. **$$**

Outdoor Activities

Horse Trekking

MacKenzie Alpine Trekking Company, Godley Peaks Road, tel: 0800-628 269; matc.thelakestroll. co.nz. Horseback treks through the tussock grasslands, glacial lakes and forests of the Mackenzie High Country at Lake Tekapo, with the option for the "Lake Stroll", a 6–7 day adventure hike over three famous sheep stations to enjoy stunning views of Aoraki Mount Cook. All levels catered for with treks from 1 hour to overnight.

Mountaineering

Alpine Recreation Canterbury, Murray Place, tel: 03-680 6736; www.alpinerecreation.com. Climbing courses and guided ascents of major peaks and glaciers.

Star Gazing

Tekapo Tours Star Watching, Main Road, tel: 03-680 6007; www.stargazing.co.nz. Take advantage of the unusually clear skies in this region to go on one of these spectacular, if chilly, night-time adventures.

AORAKI MOUNT COOK NATIONAL PARK

Visitor Information

Aoraki Mount Cook Visitor Centre, Bowen Drive, Mount Cook, tel: 03-435 1186; www.doc.govt.nz.

Where to Stay

Aoraki Mount Cook Alpine Lodge, Aoraki Mount Cook Village, tel: 03-435 1860; www.aorakialpinelodge. co.nz. Located in the heart of Aoraki Mount Cook National Park. Quality, self-catering accommodation for the budget-conscious traveller, with superb panoramic views of Mount

Cook and the Southern Alps. 16 ensuite rooms. **$–$$$**

Mount Cook Youth Hostel, corner of Kitchener and Bowen Drives, Mount Cook, tel: 03-435-1820; www.yha.co.nz. A modern complex with a wide range of facilities. Single sex and mixed dormitories, double and twin rooms. Shop, TV room, central heating showers, toilets, free sauna, coin-op laundry. Newmans and Great Sights buses arrive and depart from outside the hostel daily. **$**

The Hermitage Hotel, Terrace Road, Mount Cook, tel: 03-435 1809; www.mount-cook.com. Luxurious accommodation and amazing scenery at the foot of New Zealand's tallest mountain in the Aoraki Mount Cook National Park. Sauna, clothing outlet, coffee shop, two restaurants and a bar. 250 rooms. **$$$$–$$$$$**

The Hermitage Mount Cook Chalets and Motels, Terrace Road, Mount Cook, tel: 03-435 1809; www.mount-cook.com. Nestled deep in the Aoraki Mount Cook National Park, this alpine resort comprises the Hermitage Hotel and self-contained family-size motels and chalets. With a range of restaurants and bars. The views are great. **$$$–$$$$$**

Where to Eat

The Old Mountaineers Café Bar and Restaurant, Aoraki Mount Cook Village, next to the DOC Visitor

Mountaineering

Alpine Guides Aoraki, the only resident guide company in Aoraki/Mount Cook National Park, offers alpine touring, mountaineering courses, private instruction, mountain expeditions and guiding programmes through the Southern Alps. The cost for a seven-day expedition up Mount Cook (3,754 metres/12,348 ft) is NZ$4,850. Aircraft access is included in the price. Contact: **Alpine Guides Trekking**, Bowen Drive, Mount Cook, tel: 03-435 1834; www.alpineguides.co.nz.

Centre, tel: 03-435 1890. Sir Edmund Hillary is one of the mountaineers this café is named after. The extensive menu covers just about everything, from towering mountain burgers and steaks to chicken and apple crumble. Of note are the house speciality pork sausages named after Sir Edmund. **$–$$$**

Outdoor Activities

Boat Tour

Glacier Explorers, The Hermitage, Mount Cook, tel: 03-435 1077; www.glacierexplorers.com; Oct–May. Cruise the glacial lake formed by the melting face of New Zealand's' largest glacier, touch and taste 500-year-old ice. Guides give an informative commentary.

Scenic Flights

Aoraki Mount Cook Skiplanes, Mount Cook Airport, SH80, near Aoraki Mount Cook Village, tel: 03-435 1026, 0800-800 702; www.skiplanes.co.nz. Offers scenic flights to view the glaciers up close and the only fixed-wing snow landing in the Southern Alps.

Cloud 9 Heli Hiking, tel: 03-435 1077. Fly directly up to Mount Dark and amble in the silent wonderland. Heli-flights tailor-made to suit all time frames, ages and needs.

Skiing

Alpine Guides Aoraki, Bowen Drive, Mount Cook, tel: 03-435 1834; www.heliskiing.co.nz. Tasman Glacier can be skiied from July to September but access to its magnificent slopes is only via fixed winged skiplanes. Be warned that skiing the Tasman can be an expensive affair, although heliskiing in New Zealand is cheaper compared to the US and Europe.

The West Coast

Getting There

If you drive, access is either through the Buller Gorge from Nelson, through the Lewis Pass via historic Reefton, over the high Alpine Arthur's Pass from

Christchurch or via Haast Pass from Queenstown. Driving time is about 3–5 hours.

There are airports at Hokitika and Westport, with regular scheduled services. Or take the **TranzAlpine** train through the Southern Alps from Christchurch to Greymouth (or vice versa). The West Coast is also well served by **InterCity Coachlines**. See also Getting Around, pages 330–2.

HAAST

Visitor Information

Haast Visitor Centre, Department of Conservation, Haast Junction, tel: 03-750 0809; e-mail: haastvc@doc.govt.nz.

Where to Stay

Wilderness Lodge, Lake Moeraki SH6, tel: 03-750 0881; www.wildernesslodge.co.nz. A stunning setting, with fantastic bush and coastal walks and abundant wildlife. **$$$$$**

Where to Eat

Fantail Café, SH6, tel: 03-750 0055, 0800-681 682. Dine in or get takeaway at this conveniently located café. Serves standard café fare such as fish and chips, pies, vegetarian food and sandwiches. Menu features blue cod when available. Daily 7.30am–5pm. **Haast World Heritage Hotel**, SH6, tel: 03-750 0828, 0800-502 444; www.world-heritage-hotel.com. Wild West Coast food, such as lamb, blue cod, venison, salmon and whitebait, are on the menu here. **$–$$$** **McGuires Lodge Café Restaurant and Bar**, SH6, tel: 03-750 0020, 0800-624 847; www.mcguires lodge.co.nz. One of the best eateries around the area. Its menu draws on local ingredients from crayfish to Hereford steak to blue cod. Part of the McGuires Lodge with 19 rooms.

Outdoor Activities

Jet boating

Waiatoto River Jet Boat Safaris, The Red Barn, SH6, Haast Junction, tel: 03-750 0780, 0800-538 723. The world's only sea-to-mountain river eco-jet boat safari explores a remote part of the South West World Heritage Area.

FOX GLACIER

Visitor Information

Fox Glacier Visitor Centre, Department of Conservation, SH6, tel: 03-751 0807; www.west-coast.co.nz; www.glaciercountry.co.nz.

Where to Stay

Fox Glacier Lodge, Sullivan Road, Fox Glacier, tel/fax: 03-751 0888, 0800-369 800; www.foxglacier lodge.co.nz. This is in the heart of Fox Glacier and on the edge of the glowworm forest. Modern units with ensuites, some with double spa baths, cooking facilities and mountain views. Montain bike hire available. **$–$$$** **Fox Glacier Resort Hotel**, corner of Cook Flat Road and SH6, tel: 03-751 0839; www.resorts.co. nz. Built in 1928, the hotel has been refurbished to retain its charm and atmosphere. Restaurant, lounge bar, guest lounge and Internet services. 80 rooms. **$–$$** **Scenic Circle Glacier Country Hotel**, Fox Glacier, tel: 03-751 0847; www. scenic-circle.co.nz. In Westland's World Heritage Park in the Fox Glacier township, this hotel includes a guest laundry, room service and restaurant. 51 rooms. **$$$**

Where to Eat

Café Neve, Main Road, tel: 03-751 0110. Award-winning café in the heart of Fox Glacier township offering indoor and alfresco (summer only) dining. The menu features fresh seafood, lamb, beef, vegetarian meals and a selection of pasta dishes and salads. **$$–$$$** **High Peaks Bar and Restaurant**, 163 Cook Flat Road, tel: 03-751 0131. The place to sample authentic West Coast cuisine: the venison hot pot is one of its most popular dishes. The restaurant has an extensive wine list; the café has a good selection of bistro meals. Great views from every table. **$$**

Outdoor Activities

Ice Walking

Fox Glacier Guiding, Main Road, SH6, Franz Josef Glacier, tel: 03-751 0825, 0800-111 6000; www.foxguides.co.nz. Glacier walks, ice climbing and even "heli-hikes".

FRANZ JOSEF GLACIER

Visitor Information

Franz Josef Glacier Visitor Centre, Department of Conservation, SH6, tel: 03-752 0796; www.glaciercountry.co.nz.

Where to Stay

Alpine Glacier Motel, Condon Street, tel: 03-752 0226, 0800-757 111; www.alpineglaciermotel .com. Warm, spacious studio and family units close to restaurants, 5 km (3 miles) to the glacier. **$–$$$$** **Glacier Gateway Motor Lodge**, Main Road, tel: 03-752 0776; www.franzjosefhotels.co.nz. Among the closest accommodation to any glacier in New Zealand, with glacier access by road. Basic facilities, but two rooms have baths, and there's a spa and sauna. Close to shops and restaurants. 23 units. **$–$$** **Karamea Bridge Farm Motels**, Bridge Street, Karamea, 1RD, Westport, tel: 03-782 6955, 0800-527 263; www.karameamotels. co.nz; One- and two-bedroom suites on a private farm, with views across the wilderness of Kahurangi National Park and beyond. Each suite has a large private lounge. Only 400 metres (437 yds) from the centre of Karamea. 8 units. **$–$$** **Scenic Circle Franz Josef Glacier Hotel**, SH6, tel: 03-752 0729; www.scenic-circle.co.nz. Comprising two distinctive properties 1 km (1 mile) apart, the hotel has three wings surrounded by lush native bush and superb alpine views. 177 luxury rooms. **$$$$$**

Where to Eat

Beeches Restaurant, SH6, Franz Josef Glacier, tel: 03-752 0721.

Specialising in authentic West Coast cuisine, including venison and beef, it also offers light meals and has an extensive wine list. **$$**
Blue Ice Café, SH6, tel: 03-752 0707. The eclectic menu ranges from Italian and Indian dishes to New Zealand cuisine, but pizzas are the speciality. Extensive wine list. Upstairs bar with pool table. **$$**

Outdoor Activities
Ice Walking
Franz Josef Glacier Guides, Main Road, tel: 03-752 0763, 0800-484 337; www.franzjosefglacier.com. Thanks to novel equipment, even novices can venture into glacier terrain that's normally only accessible to the experienced.

Birdwatching
Okarito Nature Tours, Franz Josef, Whataroa, tel: 03-753 4014; www.okarito.co.nz. Kayak deep into the heart of the forest for awesome alpine views or to spot some of the 70 bird species in the area, notably the *kotuku* (white heron).
White Heron Sanctuary and Accommodation, SH6, Whataroa, tel: 03-763 4120, 0800-523 456; www.whiteherontours.co.nz. Visit New Zealand's only white heron nesting colony from late September to March. Jet boating and sight-seeing tours available all year round. Accommodation includes cabins, motel and studio units. **$–$$**

ARTHUR'S PASS

Visitor Information
Arthur's Pass Visitor Information Centre, tel: 03-318 9211; www.apinfo.co.nz.

Where to Stay
Trans Alpine Lodge, Main Road, Arthur's Pass, tel: 03-318 9236; www.arthurspass.co.nz. Great Alpine scenery and chalet-style accommodation in the Southern Alps. For a unique experience, try treatments in the outdoor spa. Restaurant specialises in lamb, salmon, venison and beef. 14 rooms. **$–$$**

HOKITIKA

Visitor Information
Westland i-SITE Visitor Centre, Carnegie Building, Hamilton Street, tel: 03-755 6166; www.west-coast.co.nz.

Where to Stay
Best Western Shining Star Beachfront Chalets, 11 Richards Drive, tel: 03-755 8921. Centrally located, these fully self-contained timber chalets have their own decks and direct beach access. Near glowworm cave. **$–$$**
Fitzherbert Court Motel, 191 Fitzherbert Street, tel: 03-755 5342; www.fitzherbert court.co.nz. Luxury units with self-contained kitchens, some with spa baths. The motel is located close to town, airport and beach. **$–$$**
Kapitea Ridge & Cottage, Chesterfield Road, SH6, Kapitea Creek, RD2, tel: 03-755 6805; www.kapitea.co.nz. Luxury lodge accommodation with sea views. **$$$**

Where to Eat
Café de Paris, 19–21 Tancred Street, tel: 03-755 8933. Genuine French cooking, including mouthwatering desserts in a place that's about as far from Paris as you can get. **$$**
Stumpers Bar And Café, 2 Weld Street, tel: 03-755 6154; www.stumpers.co.nz. This warm and cosy café offers a menu featuring lamb shanks, fresh pasta, locally caught whitebait (in season) and venison, to name a few. Check out the copper artwork by local artists that adorns the walls. **$$**

West Coast Walks
Experience the beauty and history of the west coast on the numerous great walks and hiking trails within the region. These include the Heaphy Track, the Wangapeka Track and the Charming Creek Walkway. Check with the local information office or Department of Conservation for track conditions.

Trappers Restaurant and Bar, 131–137 Revell Street, tel: 03-755 6859. Aptly named, this restaurant specialises in wild and exotic food and seafood. Budget accommodation also available. **$$**

Outdoor Activities
Bonz and Stonz, 16 Hamilton Street, tel: 03-755 6504, 0800-214 949; www.bonz-n-stonz.co.nz. Offers a full-day workshop where you can design and carve your own pendants in jade, bone, *paua* and mother-of-pearl shells. Advance bookings essential.
Paddle Boat Cruises, Main South Road, 5 km (3 miles) south of Hokitika, tel: 03-755 7239; www.paddleboatcruises.com. This 90-minute return trip takes you through magnificent scenery, including virgin rainforest, sighting rare birds. With an informative commentary. Seats up to 20, children free.

GREYMOUTH

Visitor Information
Greymouth i-SITE Visitor Centre, corner of Mackay and Herbert streets, tel: 03-768 5101, 0800-767 080; www.westcoast bookings.co.nz.
Greymouth Travel Centre, Railway Station, 164 MacKay Street, tel: 03-768 7080; www.westcoast travel.co.nz.

Where to Stay
Aachen Place Motel, 50 High Street, tel: 03-768 6901; www.aachenmotel.co.nz. Award-winning studio apartments and

West Coast Crafts
For genuine handcrafted South Island *pounamu* (greenstone), check out **Te Waipounamu Jade**, 27 Sewell Street, Hokitika. The **Gray Fur Trading Co Ltd**, 20 Sewell Street, specialises in making items from possum fur and sheep skins, tel: 03-756 8090; www.possum-nz.com.

units with great views of the sea and mountains. Centrally located and self-contained. Supermarket nearby. **$–$$**
Gables Motor Lodge, 84 High Street, tel: 03-768 9991; e-mail: gables@xtra.co.nz. Luxury units with large beds and fully-equipped kitchens, Some have spa baths, while others have showers. Close to supermarket and shops. **$–$$$**

Where to Eat
Café 124 On Mackay, 124 Mackay Street, tel: 03-768 7503. Situated in newly built premises. Great food and coffee. Indoor and outdoor dining. **$–$$**
The Bay House Café, Tauranga Bay (near Westport), tel: 03-789 7133; www.thebayhouse.co.nz. Good food in an oceanside location, tucked away under the shelter of Cape Foulwind, well worth going out of your way for. The seasonal menu features West Coast specialities, fish in particular. Don't miss the chowder. Wash it down with a glass or two of Good Bastards, Green Fern or Monteiths local beer.
The Smelting House Café, 102 MacKay Street, tel: 03-768 0012. Set in a converted historic West Coast bank building and run by a registered dietician. Specialising in home-style food. Open Mon–Sat 8am–5pm. **$–$$**

Outdoor Activities
Wild West Adventure Company, 8 Whall Street, tel: 03-768 6649; www.fun-nz.com. Various activities including black-water and white-water rafting (eight rivers to choose from for the latter) as well as glowworm-cave rafting. rainforest cruises, gold and gemstone prospecting, guided walks and multi-day adventure tours.

Queenstown and Otago

QUEENSTOWN

Getting There
Air New Zealand has regular flights to Queenstown, and you can reach it direct from main centres such as Wellington, Christchurch and Auckland. Daily flights also operate to and from Sydney, Australia and Brisbane. There are daily coach and shuttle services to and from Christchurch, Mount Cook, Dunedin, Te Anau, Wanaka, Franz Josef and Milford Sound.

Visitor Information
Queenstown i-SITE Visitor Centre, Clock Tower Building, corner of Shotover and Camp streets, tel: 03-442 4100, 0800-668 888; www.queenstown-nz.co.nz.

City Transport
In Queenstown, you can reach most places by walking or taking a short taxi ride. You'll need to hire a car to really get out and see the country-side, and there are plenty of car-hire companies in Queenstown. Getting to and from Arrowtown is also easy, with a regular coach service.

Where to Stay
Alpine Sun Motel, 18 Hallenstein Street, tel: 03-442 8482; www.alpinesun.co.nz. In central Queenstown, with self-contained studio and family units. Facilities include a guest laundry and activities desk. 10 units. **$$**
Azur, 28 McKinnon Terrace, tel: 03-409 0588; www.azur.co.nz. This nine-villa luxury lodge is in the Sunshine Bay area, 5 minutes from Queenstown. Each villa boasts sensational panoramic views, a lounge area with a fireplace and an outside deck. Rates include breakfast, afternoon tea and pre-dinner drinks, plus all transfers. **$$$$$**
Copthorne Lakefront Resort and Hotel, corner of Adelaide Street and Frankton Road, tel: 03-442 8123; www.copthornelakefront.co.nz. Four-star accommodation with 241 cosy rooms, many with views of the lake and mountains. Not in the centre of Queenstown but within walking distance of the main shopping area. Shuttle service available. **$$$–$$$$$**
Kingsgate Hotel Terraces, 88 Frankton Road, tel: 03-442 7950; www.kingsgatehotels.co.nz. Ten minutes' walk from the town centre. The rooms all have magnificent views of the lake and mountains, and some rooms also have cooking facilities. Complimentary private spa pool. 85 rooms. **$$$**
Mercure Resort, Sainsbury Road, tel: 03-442 6600; www.accorhotels.co.nz. Overlooking the Remarkables mountain range, with expansive lake views, just 5 minutes from the town. Facilities include 24-hour room service, spa, tennis courts, gym, saunas and an observation deck. **$$–$$$$$**
Millennium Queenstown, corner Frankton Road and Stanley Street, tel: 03-441 8888; www.millennium hotels.com. A top-class hotel with tasteful rooms, a restaurant, bar, parking, gym and spa. 220 rooms. **$$$–$$$$$**
Novotel Gardens, corner of Marine Parade and Earl Street, tel: 03-442 7750; www.accorhotels.co.nz. A modern hotel on the lakefront. The spacious and welcoming foyer gives a hint of the quality of the rooms. Management and staff provide top-class and unobtrusive service. **$$–$$$$**
Nugget Point Boutique Hotel, Arthur's Point, tel: 03-441 0288; www.nuggetpoint.co.nz. Award-winning boutique hotel with a fine restaurant, only 10 minutes drive from Queenstown. The suites are impeccably furnished and the more expensive ones have stunning views of the Shotover River and Coronet Peak. Competent staff provide first-class service. **$$$$$**
The Heritage Queenstown, 91 Fernhill Road, tel: 03-442 4988; www.heritagehotels.co.nz. A European-style lodge, with forest and waterfall rooms and lakeside suites, crafted from centuries-old schist and cedar. Facilities include comprehensive day spa, sauna, gym and swimming pool. **$$$**

Where to Eat
Boardwalk Seafood Restaurant and Bar, Steamer Wharf Village, tel: 03-442 5630; www.boardwalk.net.nz. Popular with tourists – and Bill Clinton once dined here – this

restaurant serves both meat and seafood dishes with a modicum of flair. **$$$**

Lone Star Café and Bar, 14 Brecon Street, tel: 03-442 9995; www.lonestar.co.nz. As the name implies, a Western-style restaurant where the portions are huge, and the food is good. **$$**

Minami Jujisei, 45 Beach Street, tel: 03-442 9854. Award-winning traditional Japanese cuisine, mixed with modern influences; particularly good for those who have never tried Japanese food before. **$$**

Roaring Megs Restaurant, 53 Shotover Street, tel: 03-442 9676; www.roaringmegs.co.nz. Set in a gold-miner's cottage dating back to the late 1800s, this restaurant has won awards for its European/Pacific Rim style of cuisine. Candle-lit dining in a relaxed, cosy atmosphere. **$$**

Solera Vino, 25 Beach Street, tel: 03-442 6082. An attractive place serving French Mediterranean cuisine and a good range of wines. **$$–$$$**

The Bathhouse, 28 Marine Parade, tel: 03-442 5625; www.bathhouse. co.nz. An old bathhouse, built in 1911, right on the beach with amazing lake and mountain views. It offers nostalgic indoor and awe-inspiring outdoor dining from an award-winning menu. **$$–$$$**

The Birches, Nugget Point Resort, tel: 03-442 7273; www.nuggetpoint. co.nz. This complex is 10-minutes from downtown Queenstown, not a great inconvenience to sample the creative and innovative dishes, which use the freshest New Zealand produce. The rack of lamb is to die for. **$$$**

Entertainment/Nightlife

The **Queenstown Winter Festival** in July is an unmissable event. Highlights include the festival parade, opening party, jazz nights, celebrity ski race and Queenstown Mardi Gras. More information tel: 03-442 2453; www.winterfestival.co.nz.

Queenstown has plenty of superb bars and nightclubs that are often packed with international travellers and backpackers as well as local skiers and adventurers.

Bardeaux, Eureka Arcade, off The Mall, tel: 03-442 8284. Sumptuous surroundings, extensive wine and cocktails list, plus a huge open fire place make this a very popular spot for locals and tourists alike.

Pog Mahone's, 14 Rees Street, tel: 03-442 5328; www.pogmahones.com. As Irish as they come in Queenstown. The Guinness flows smoothly, and it packs out when live bands are playing (usually Wed and Sun). Food available.

The World Bar, Restaurants and Nightclub, 27 Shotover Street, tel: 03-4426 757. Often filled with backpackers and young adventurers, this is a lively and often very noisy venue renowned for happy hours that go on till late.

Surreal, 7 Rees Street, tel: 03-441 8492. It's a restaurant in the early evening, but as the night comes on, techno music takes hold and this venue transforms into one of the cooler nightspots in town. Great food and service.

Outdoor Activities
Bird Encounters

Kiwi and Birdlife Park, Brecon Street, tel: 03-442 8059; www.kiwibird.co.nz; daily 9am–6pm; entrance fee. Easy walking through native bush to aviaries where you will see not just tui, bellbirds, fantails and kiwi, but also rare and endangered birds and the rare tuatara. Conservation shows daily at 11am, 1 and 3pm. The 3pm show includes a Maori cultural show. In the evenings (7–10pm), you may opt to have a four-course feast of kiwi kai and enjoy Maori cultural entertainment, plus a special visit to the kiwi house at feeding time. Booking essential.

Bungy Jumping

Queenstown is the home of bungy jumping, the place where it all began in 1988. The world's first bungy site, the Kawarau Bridge, has evolved into the **Kawarau Bungy Centre**, a busy hub from where A.J. Hackett (tel: 03-442 1177, 0800-286 495; www.ajhackett.com) operates the Bungy Shop, a café,

the **Freefall Wine Bar** and the newest addition, the **Secrets of Bungy Tour** (tel: 0800-286 498), a behind-the-scenes insight into the bungy phenomenon for those who don't fancy the real deal. This tour leaves hourly and includes the Bungy Theatre and Interactive Zone where you can get a first-hand look at bungy-cord making as well as exclusive access to viewing decks where you observe alongside the jump crews. At the end of the car park is another new addition, **The Winehouse & Kitchen** (tel: 03-442 7310; www.winehouse.co.nz), a farm-style restaurant with a special wine-tasting experience.

In addition to the Kawarau Bridge Bungy (adults NZ$150 child 10–15 years NZ$100), A.J. Hackett operates two other bungy sites around Queenstown, **The Ledge Bungy** (NZ$150 with gondola, NZ$135 without gondola), and the **Nevis Highwire Bungy** (NZ$210), billed as the wildest. Their Thrillogy package gives the option of all three for NZ$350.

Garden Tours

Queenstown Garden Tours, tel: 03-442 3799; www.queenstown gardentours.co.nz; daily 8.30am–noon, Oct–March. Tours include at least three splendid local residential gardens, chosen according to season, providing a delightful opportunity to see New Zealand domestic gardening at its best. Devonshire tea included. The Garden Tour can be combined with a Wine Tour – check details on www.queenstown winetrail.co.nz.

Golf

Millbrook Resort, Malaghans Road, Arrowtown, tel: 03-441 7010; www.millbrook.co.nz. Play a round of golf at the Millbrook Resort's spectacular par 72 championship golf course, which was designed by New Zealand's renowned master golfer, Sir Bob Charles.

Jet Boating

Shotover Jet, Shotover Jet Beach, Arthurs Point, Queenstown, tel: 03-

442 8570; www.shotoverjet.com.
One of the best places for jet
boating in Queenstown – and all of
New Zealand – is the Shotover
River. Courtesy shuttle from
Queenstown.
Dart River Safaris, Mull Street,
Glenorchy and also 27 Shotover
Street, tel: 03-442 9992;
www.dartriver.co.nz. This company
takes you on a 80 km (50 miles)
safari by jetboat between
mountains and glaciers through the
landscape of "Middle Earth" into
Mount Aspiring National Park, a
World Heritage Area.

White-water Rafting
Challenge Rafting, The Station,
corner of Shotover and Camp
streets, tel: 03-442 7318; www.
raft.co.nz. Enjoy the thrills and spills
of white-water rafting in an inflatable
with up to seven other people; some
of the most exciting rivers are the
Shotover and Kawarau.

Cable Car/Luge
Skyline Gondolas, Brecon Street,
tel: 03-441 0101;
www.skyline.co.nz; daily 9am till
late; entrance fee. After the 790-
metre (2,600-ft) climb by cable car,
take a ride on the thrilling downhill
luge. Minimum age is 3.

Paragliding
**Coronet Peak Tandem Paragliding
and Hang Gliding**, tel: 0800-467
325; www.tandemparagliding.com.
Take off from 700 metres (1,100 ft)
above the Wakatipu Basin while
harnessed to an instructor. In
winter you take off from Coronet
peak, a great way to descend after
a day's skiing.

Hang Gliding
Queenstown Hang Gliding, tel: 03-
442 5747, 0800-878 4373;
www.hangglide.co.nz. Fly in tandem
with the world's most experienced
pilot–instructors. You are literally
run off the scenic Coronet Peak,
the highest launch in town at 1,160
metres (3,800 ft). Prices from
NZ$185. Allow 2–2½ hours for the
activity. Departs 9am, noon, 3pm,
6pm or on demand.

Skydiving
NZONE The Ultimate Jump, tel: 03-
442 5867; www.nzone.biz. The
tandem jumps are priced variably,
depending on whether you jump at
2,743 metres (9,000ft), 3,658
metres (12,000 ft) or the ultimate
4,572 metres (15,000 ft).

Flying
Fly By Wire, 37 Shotover Street,
tel: 0800-359 299; www.flybywire-
queenstown.co.nz. Experience
exhilarating speeds, total
weightlessness and a huge
adrenaline rush during this 5-
minute, self-controlled flight in a
tethered rocket-plane before gliding
gently to a stop. Minimum age 12,
$129; $20 for a spectator.
Queenstown Paraflights,
Queenstown Main Pier, tel: 03-441
2242; www.paraflights.co.nz.
Take off from a boat on Lake
Wakatipu and feel yourself lift gently
into the air, to rise up to 200
metres (656 ft). Land back on the
boat. Minimum age is 3.

4-Wheel-Drive Tours
Nomad Safaris, Lord of the Rings
Shop, 19 Shotover Street, tel: 03-
442 6699, 0800-688 222;
www.nomad
safaris.co.nz. Tours depart 8.30am
and 1.30pm and last 4 hours.
Various tour options include the
spectacular off-road scenery of
Middle Earth, Skippers Canyon
and Macetown.

Rock Climbing
The Rungway, via Ferrata, tel: 03-
409 2508; www.rungway.co.nz. The
southern hemisphere's first "Iron
Way" is, simply, a series of iron
rungs, ladders and wires, attached
to a mountainside, which enables
the inexperienced to duplicate the
experience of rock climbing. Two
departures daily, 9am and 1pm.

Rope Swing
Shotover Canyon Swing,
tel: 03-442 6990, 0800-279 464;
www.canyonswing.co.nz. At 109
metres (358 ft), this is the world's
highest rope swing. You'll freefall
60 metres (197 ft) into the canyon

until the ropes pendulum you in a
giant arc (200 metres/656 ft) at
150 kph (93 mph). Minimum
age is 10.

Skiing
The best-organised ski centres in
the South Island are Cardrona,
Treble Cone, Coronet Peak and The
Remarkables, all close to
Queenstown and Wanaka. Check
the following websites for more info
or contact the visitor centres at
Queenstown and Wanaka. For
general information on skiing and
snowboarding, see also the
Activities section of Travel Tips.
Cardrona
www.cardrona.com
Treble Cone
www.treblecone.co.nz
Coronet Peak
www.nzski.com/coronet
The Remarkables
www.nzski.com/remarkables

Steamship Cruise
TSS Earnslaw, Lake Wakatipu, tel:
03-442 7500, 0800-656 503;
www.realjourneys.co.nz; daily every
two hours (10am–8pm summer;
noon–4pm winter). This grand, coal-
fuelled old lady has graced the

Heli-skiing

Harris Mountains Heli-Ski offers
a range of packages including
private heli-ski charters as well
as week-long and daily heli-skiing
packages tailored to your skiing
ability. Skiers get to explore the
vast terrains of the Southern
Alps, with its untracked powder,
massive peaks, stunning valleys
and challenging chutes. The best
time for heli-skiing is July to
September. Contact: **Harris
Mountains Heli-Ski**, The Station,
corner of Shotover and Camp
streets, Queenstown, tel: 03-442
6722 or 99 Ardmore Street,
Wanaka, tel: 03-443 7930
(winter only); www.heliski.co.nz;
e-mail: hmh@heliski.co.nz. Harris
Mountains Heli-Ski operates
in Queenstown, Wanaka and
Mount Cook.

waters of Lake Wakatipu since 1912 when she was first used to carry goods to remote settlements. You may opt to visit Walter Peak High Country farm, a working farm, for lunch and a guided horse trek.

Wineries

Chard Farm, RD1, Queenstown, tel: 03-442 6110; www.chardfarm. co.nz. On a back country byway which used to be part of the main coach link between Queenstown and Cromwell.

Gibbston Valley Wines, SH6, Gibbston, tel: 03-442 6910; www.gvwines.co.nz. Award-winning winery in stunning location. The wine tour is not to be missed. Very impressive wine cave.

Lake Hayes Amisfield Cellars, 10 Lake Hayes Road, Lake Hayes, tel: 03-442 0556; www.amisfield.co.nz. A wine-tasting experience in a stunning lakeside location 10 minutes from Queenstown. Amisfield Bistro was voted best winery restaurant in *Cuisine* magazine's Restaurant of the Year Awards 2006.

Peregrine Wines, Kawarau Gorge Road, Queenstown, tel: 03-442 4000; www.peregrinewines.co.nz. Pinot noir specialists with a vineyard in rugged mountain country.

ARROWTOWN

Getting There
Arrowtown is 18 km (11 miles) northeast of Queenstown.

Visitor Information
Arrowtown Promotion & Business Association, 49 Buckingham Street; www.arrowtown.org.nz.

The Lakes District Museum operates the local **Information Centre**, tel: 03-442 1824; www.museumqueenstown.com, www.hansonhistory.com.

Where to Stay
Millbrook Resort, Malaghans Road, tel: 03-441 7000; www.millbrook.co.nz. A world-class luxury resort where accommodation varies from country-style rooms and cottages to 2-bedroom villas.

There's a superb golf course, restaurant and health and fitness spa. **$$$$$**

Settlers Cottage Motel, 22 Hertford Street, tel: 0800-803 801; www.settlerscottage.co.nz. Pretty, cosy and quiet rooms in a converted house, a short walk from the main street. **$$**

Shades of Arrowtown, 9 Merioneth Street, tel: 03-442 1613; 03-442 1824; www.shadesofarrowtown. co.nz. Tastefully furnished studios and apartments in a garden setting on Arrowtown's tree-lined avenue. Close to shops and restaurants. **$-$$**

Where to Eat
Pesto, 18 Buckingham Street, tel: 03-442 0885; www.pesto.co.nz. Family-friendly fare, featuring pizza, pasta and other Italian staples. **$$**

Saffron, 18 Buckingham Street, tel: 03-442 0131; www.saffron restaurant.co.nz. With its classy Asian influenced menu, Saffron has been included in Conde Nast Traveller's list of the most exciting restaurants in the world. **$$$**

The Postmasters House Restaurant, 54 Buckingham Street, tel: 03-442 0991; www.post mastershouse.com. Award-winning restaurant in a meticulously restored historic house. Superb food, fine wine list and excellent service. **$$$**

Old-World Cinema

Dorothy Brown's Cinema Bar and Bookshop, 18 Buckingham Street, Arrowtown, tel: 03-442 1968. In a class of its own, this 42-seat cinema shows arthouse movies in an opulent setting (red possum fur cushions, chandeliers) and full bar.

WANAKA

Getting There
Wanaka is about an hour's drive north of Queenstown. Alternatively, you can take a shuttle service or inter-city bus. There are also scenic flights – the one from Queenstown

to Wanaka takes approximately 20 minutes.

Visitor Information
Lake Wanaka i-SITE Visitor Centre, Waterfront Log Cabin, 100 Ardmore Street, tel: 03-443 1233; www.lakewanaka.co.nz.

Where to Stay
Alpine Motel Apartments, 7 Ardmore Street, Lake Wanaka, tel: 03-443 7950; www.alpinemotels. co.nz. Centrally located and within walking distance of the town centre, lake and golf course, these basic family and studio suites are self-contained and comfortable. **$-$$**

Brook Vale Motels, 35 Brownston Street, tel: 0800-438 333; www.brookvale.co.nz. Close to the centre of town, but private, with views of the Southern Alps. All units have kitchens, and there's a spa pool outdoor pool, BBQ area and guest laundry. **$$**

Edgewater Resort, Sargood Drive, Lake Wanaka, tel: 03-443 8311, 0800-108 311; www.edgewater.co. nz. Modern luxury apartments and rooms with large bathrooms – some can be configured to provide family suites. Set on the edge of Lake Wanaka, there are excellent lake and mountain views. Award-winning Sargoods Restaurant. **$$$$–$$$$$**

Mount Aspiring Hotel, 109 Mount Aspiring Road, Lake Wanaka, tel: 03-443 8216; www.wanakanz.com. Built in natural stone and wood, this picturesque family-owned hotel has 57 studio rooms with private bath and shower facilities; some have a spa bath. The Tilikum Restaurant offers seasonal menus. **$$$**

Oak Ridge Pool and Spa Resort, corner of Studholme and Cardrona roads, tel: 03-443 7707; www. oakridge.co.nz. Stone's throw from the town centre. **$$–$$$$**

Where to Eat
Finchy's Restaurant and Bar, 2 Dunmore Street, tel: 03-443 6262. Built in rustic stone, wood and iron on the old 1880 Wanaka jail site, this spacious, upmarket but casual restaurant has an inviting

ambience. The open fireplace is a draw, as is the long menu and wine list. **$$$**

Kai Whakapai Café and Bar, Lakefront, tel: 03-443 7795; www.kaiwanaka.co.nz. Easy to find on the edge of Lake Wanaka, this café has panoramic views and prides itself on its freshly baked breads, pies, pasta and vegetarian selections. Pa Runga wine bar and lounge upstairs. **$**

Nightlife

Like Queenstown the nightlife and entertainment in Wanaka tends to centre around the après-ski crowd in winter and adventure bunnies in summer. There are plenty of bars and a few nightclubs. Check out the **Slainte Irish Bar**, tel: 03-443 6755, in Lower Helwick Street, open daily from noon. It serves Irish and Kiwi fare plus a huge variety of New Zealand and Irish beers.

Outdoor Activities

Climbing/Mountaineering

New Zealand Wild Walks, 10A Tenby Street, tel: 03-443

Otago Shopping

Queenstown

Visitors to Queenstown will find streets bristling with souvenir shops. Prices are usually fixed, but bargaining is becoming increasingly common here. To meet demand, Queenstown does not follow normal retail hours – most shops are open seven days a week for extended hours.

Arrowtown

The Gold Shop on Buckingham Street makes reasonably priced contemporary jewellery from local gold.

Wanaka

Everything you need is within walking distance in Wanaka. You'll find shops selling local arts and crafts, plenty of souvenir shops and such basic amenities as pharmacies, hardware and stationary shops.

4476; www.wildwalks.co.nz. Specialists in tramping and climbing in Mount Aspiring National Park and guiding small groups on single-day as well as overnight climbing trips up the mountain and on treks over glaciers.

Horse Riding

Backcountry Saddle Expeditions, Cardrona Valley, tel: 03-443 8151; www.ridenz.com. Organised horseback tours of the Cardrona Valley. Appaloosa horses with Western saddles.

Paragliding

Wanaka Paragliding, Wanaka, tel: 0800-359 754; www.wanaka paragliding.co.nz. Wanaka offers New Zealand's highest tandern paragliding (NZ$180). Also has door-to-door Flying Bus Transport service to Treble Cone (NZ$28).

Dunedin and Surroundings

DUNEDIN

Getting There

Dunedin has an international airport with direct flights on **Freedom Air** (www.freedomair.com) from Australia's Gold Coast, Sydney, Melbourne and Brisbane, as well as Auckland, Wellington, Christchurch and Rotorua. Airport shuttles to the city cost from NZ$25–$32 per person and taxis at NZ$60 are also available. The airport is about half an hour South of the city. You can also drive, catch a train or take a bus from anywhere around the country. Driving from Dunedin to Christchurch takes about 5 hours while the journey from Queenstown is about 4 hours.

Visitor Information

Dunedin i-SITE Visitor Centre, 48 The Octagon, tel: 03-474 3300; www.cityofdunedin.com

Local Transport

Dunedin, like Queenstown, is easily covered on foot or by taxi: **Dunedin Taxis**, tel: 03-4777 7777; www.dunedintaxis.co.nz. There are

also regular city bus services. For all shuttle, rail, coach and domestic flight bookings, go to the **Dunedin Railway Station** in Lower Stuart Street, tel: 03-477 4449.

Where to Stay

Abbey Lodge, 900 Cumberland Street, tel: 03-477 5380, 0800-505 380; www.abbeylodge. co.nz. In a central location, with accommodation ranging from simple motel rooms to luxurious suites. Facilities include indoor heated pool, sauna and spa. **$$–$$$$$**

Cargill's Hotel, 678 George Street, tel: 03-477 7983, 0800-737 378; www.cargills.co.nz. Central hotel, with its own restaurant, that's perfect for business travellers. Basic facilities, but comfortable rooms. **$$$**

Fletcher Lodge, 276 High Street, tel: 03-477 5552; www.fletcher lodge.co.nz. Offers luxurious and elegant accommodations in a former private residence. A few minutes walk from the centre of the city. Only 6 rooms. **$$$$$**

Hulmes Court Bed and Breakfast, 52 Tennyson Street, tel: 0800-448 563; www.hulmes.co.nz. A beautiful 1860s Victorian mansion in the heart of Dunedin, with plenty of off-street parking. A large marble fireplace is cosy during winter and there's a relaxing drawing room with authentic furnishings. **$$–$$$**

Hyland House, 1003–1011 George Street, tel: 03-473 1122, 0800-495 263; www.hylandhouse.co.nz. Ten luxurious, spacious rooms with all conveniences. **$$**

Larnach Lodge, 145 Camp Road, Otago Peninsula, tel: 03-476 1616; www.larnachcastle.co.nz. Bedrooms with private bathrooms are individually decorated in period style, and each has an amazing view of the ocean 305 metres (1,000 ft) below. Lodge guests may dine in the historic Larnach Castle dining room. 12 rooms. **$$$$$** Also stablestay, shared bathrooms. 6 rooms. **$$**

Mercure Leisure Lodge, Duke Street, Dunedin North, tel: 03-477

5360, 0800-334 123; www.
mercure.co.nz. Close to the
shopping centre and adjacent to
the Botanical Gardens, this lodge
occupies the original location of
McGavin's Brewery and still retains
the original stonework and brewery
theme. 76 rooms. **$$$**
**Scenic Circle Southern Dunedin
Cross Hotel**, 118 High Street,
tel: 03-477 0752, 0800-696 963;
www.scenic-circle.co.nz. In a central
location, with a spacious and
welcoming lobby, this historic
landmark hotel has plenty of
superior and premium rooms from
which to choose, but some rooms
by the road can be a bit noisy.
There's a great café attached to the
hotel, and service is excellent.
$$$$–$$$$$

Where to Eat
Bell Pepper Blues, 474 Princes
Street, tel: 03-474 0973; www.bell
pepperblues.co.nz. Pleasant, high-
quality restaurant with fireside
atmosphere and outstanding food.
Always very full. **$$$**
Bennu Café and Bar, 12 Moray
Place, tel: 03-474 5055. Brasserie
with imaginative Pacific Rim
flavours, Mediterranean gourmet
pizzas and great desserts, served
amid the stylish decor of the old
Savoy building. It's also renowned
for great coffee. Late night lounge
bar upstairs. **$$**
Bisztro, 95 Filleul Street, tel: 03-
471 9265. Tasty traditional food
with contemporary twists in a turn-
of-the-century villa. Good vegetarian
selection. **$$**
Etrusco at the Savoy, 8A Moray
Place, tel: 03-477 3737;
www.etrusco.co.nz. Located on the
first floor of the historic Savoy
Building, offering an extensive
menu of Tuscan favourites – pasta
dishes, thin crust pizzas, Italian
breads and antipasti. Strong Italian
coffee, desserts and extensive
wine list. **$–$$**
Highgate Bridge, 312 Highgate,
Roslyn, tel: 03-474 9222. This is
something of an oddity but it's
definitely worth trying. It's only
open on Fridays for takeaways, but
portions are huge – prepared by

James Byars, who worked for 10
years at London's superlative
Gavroche. **$–$$**
Ombrellos, 10 Clarendon Street,
tel: 03-477 8773; www.ombrellos.
com. This restaurant features highly
imaginative cuisine in an attractive,
wood-panelled interior. Excellent
wine list. **$$$**
Two Chefs, 428 George Street,
tel: 03-477 9117. This gourmet
restaurant serves contemporary
New Zealand cuisine. **$$$**

Entertainment/Nightlife
Behind the façades of its once
elegant buildings, Dunedin is still a
very youthful town. It is the home of
New Zealand's oldest university,
and the large numbers of students
give it a relaxed atmosphere, with
plenty of pub music and theatre on
offer. Dunedin has a vibrant live
music scene, and a number of
excellent New Zealand bands have
originated here. The **Fortune
Theatre**, 231 Stewart Street, tel:
03-477 8323; www.fortunetheatre.
co.nz, has a particularly good
reputation and hosts both local and
touring performances. Also the
Globe Theatre, 104 London Street,
tel: 03-477 3274, a Dunedin
institution dedicated to bringing the
best in classical and modern plays.
The **Dunedin Casino**, 118 High
Street, tel: 03-477 4545;
www.dunedincasino.co.nz is also
worth a visit. Minimum age is 20.

Outdoor Activities
Kayaking
Wild Earth Adventures, daily by
arrangement; tel: 03-473 6535;

Dunedin's Shops

Shopping in Dunedin is relaxed
and unhurried. The main
shopping centre is located
around the Octagon, Lower
Stuart Street, Princes Street,
George Street and St Andrews.
There are also a number of
suburban centres with good
shops at Mornington, The
Gardens, Andersons Bay Road
and Mosgiel.

www.wildearth.co.nz. This company
offers sea kayak tours ranging in
duration from a few hours to several
days, visiting the royal albatross
and fur seal colonies by sea, and
taking in a great variety of other
wildlife on the way.

Penguin Watching
Penguin Place, Harrington Point,
No. 2RD, tel: 03-478 0286;
www.penguinplace.co.nz; daily
10.15am to 90 minutes before
sunset in summer, 3.15–4.35pm
winter; entrance fee. Here, rare
Chaplinesque yellow-eyed penguins
strut in the surf and can be
observed at close proximity
utilising a unique system of
hides and tunnels.
Monarch Wildlife Cruises Ltd,
tel: 03-477 4276, 0800-666 272;
www.wildlife.co.nz. Unrivalled
viewing of albatross, seals and
penguins in their natural
environment. Explore Taiaroa
Head, Otago Harbour and the
Peninsula. One-hour cruises, half-
and full-day tours.

Surfing
For anyone who is brave enough
to venture into the freezing cold
ocean, Dunedin offers some of the
best waves in the country – and
there are 47 km (29 miles) of
beach within the city boundaries.
The popular surf spots include
St Clair, **St Kilda** and **Brighton**.
If you plan to surf in winter, make
sure you have a thick wetsuit, hat
and booties.

Southland

INVERCARGILL

Getting There
Invercargill Airport is a 5-minute
drive west of the city centre and is
serviced by **Air New Zealand**
flights. Coach services also connect
Invercargill with other points in New
Zealand.

Visitor Information
Invercargill i-SITE Visitor Centre,
108 Gala Street, tel: 03-214 6243;
www.invercargill.org.nz.

Venture Southland Tourism, 143 Spey Street, Invercargill, tel: 03-211 1429; www.southlandnz.com.

Where to Stay

Ascot Park Hotel/Motel, corner of Racecourse Road and Tay Street, tel: 03-217 6195; www.ilt.co.nz. A large complex in quiet surroundings, with indoor swimming pool, spa, sauna, gym and restaurant. **$–$$**

Birchwood Manor, 189 Tay Street tel: 03-218 8881; www. birchwoodmanor.co.nz. Award-winning motel with good family and business accommodation in spacious and affordable units and rooms. Closest motel to super-market, opposite city centre. **$$**

Victoria Railway Hotel, 3 Leven Street, tel: 03-218 1281, 0800-777 557; www.vrhotel.info. Intimate family-owned hotel in a historic building. Restaurant and lounge bar. **$$**

Where to Eat

El Tigre Café Bar, 16 Kelvin Street, tel: 03-214 6914. Upbeat café serving stylish fare ranging from tiger prawns and yellow-fin tuna to ostrich steaks. **$–$$**

Flannagans Seafood Restaurant, Bainfield Road, Queens Drive roundabout, Waikiwi, tel: 03-215 8156. Housed in a rambling old villa, this restaurant specialises in seafood but also caters amply to meat eaters. **$$**

HMS Kings Restaurant, 80 Tay Street, tel: 03-218 3443. Classic New Zealand seafood, prepared simply to do it justice: crayfish, oysters, whitebait, prawns, fish. **$$**

The Cabbage Tree, 379 Dunns Road, Otatara, RD9, tel: 03-213 1443; www.thecabbage tree.com. A European-inspired restaurant and wine bar with a warm atmosphere (four fireplaces) and delicious local seafood and produce. Choice of à la carte or set menus. **$$**

Outdoor Activities

Fishing

Riverside Guides in Gore, tel: 03-208 4922; www.browntrout.co.nz.

Guided fishing tours of quality rivers and streams. The Mataura River in Gore is one of the best brown trout rivers in the world – according to the locals.

Walking

For all walks in Southland, contact the nearest Department of Conservation office or Visitors Information Centre or check out the Department of Conservation at www.doc.govt.nz.

CATLINS COAST

Visitor Information

Catlins Informations Centre & Owaka Museum, 20 Ryley Stree, Owaka, tel: 03-415 8371; www.catlins.org.nz.

Where to Stay

Catlins Farmstay B&B, 174 Progress Valley Road, Catlins, tel: 03-246 8843; www.catlinsfarm stay.co.nz. Roomy accommodation on a working farm, midway between Cathedral Caves and Curio Bay. Breakfast available and you'll get an exceptionally warm Kiwi welcome here. **$$$–$$$$**

Nadir Outpost, Slope Point, The Catlins, tel: 03-246 8544. A range of basic accommodation, from tent sites to bed and breakfast, set amidst forest with spectacular views. Facilities include small souvenir and supplies shop. **$**

Nugget View and Kaka Point Motels, 11 Rata Street, Kaka Point, tel: 03-412 8602, 0800-525 278; www.catlins.co.nz. Economy to luxury spa units, all with sea views. **$–$$$**

Outdoor Activities

Walking

Catlins Wildlife Trackers Ecotours, Papatowai, RD2 Owaka, tel: 03-415 8613; www.catlins-ecotours.co.nz. Award-winning multi-day tours that get you to see penguins, sea lions and rare birds, with a fascinating commentary on history, from 180 million years ago to the present. Catlins Traverse is a two-day fully catered walk

through the inland beech forest to Papatowai Beach, with self-catering accommodation in special cottages.

Petrified Forest

Curio Bay in the Catlins is one of the most extensive and least disturbed examples of a petrified forest. The forest is believed to be about 180 million years old.

TE ANAU

Getting There

Te Anau is about a 2-hour drive south of Queenstown, with shuttle services and inter-city buses between the two towns. **Top Line Tours** in Te Anau (tel: 03-249 7959) travels from Te Anau to Queenstown every day, and there's a 45-minute flight from Queenstown. See also Getting Around, pages 330–2.

Visitor Information

Fiordland i-site Visitor Centre, Lakefront Drive (next to Real Journeys Office), tel: 03-249 8900, e-mail: fiordland-i-site@realjourneys.co.nz.

Where to Stay

Aden Motel, 57–59 Quintin Drive, tel: 03-249 7748; www.adenmotel.co.nz. Self-contained units with kitchen, close to lake and shops. 12 units. **$–$$**

Best Western Te Anau Downs Motor Inn, SH94 Milford Highway, tel: 03-249 7811; www.teanau-milfordsound.co.nz. On the highway to Milford Sound, in a quiet location. Twenty units with kitchens and king-size beds. Licensed restaurant. The owner runs two other accommodation in the area: **Fiordland National Bed and Breakfast Hotel** (tel: 03-249 7510) with 20 hotel rooms with ensuite bathrooms, and **Grumpy's Backpacker** (tel: 3-249 8133) with single, double/twin and multi-share rooms as well as self-catering kitchen facilities. All three accommodation are only 600 metres (less than ½ mile) to the Milford Track starting point. **$$**

Explorer Motor Lodge, 6 Cleddau Street, tel: 03-249 7156, 0800-477 877; www.explorerlodge.co.nz. Bright, spacious delexue apartments (studio, one- and two-bedroom) with fully equipped kitchens in this accommodation set amid the gorgeous scenery of Fiordland National Park. Close to the town centre. 17 units. **$$**

Kingsgate Hotel Te Anau, 20 Lakefront Drive, tel: 03-249 7421; www.millenniumhotels.com. Set on the shores of Lake Te Anau with manicured gardens and a restaurant and bar. 94 rooms. **$$**

Lakeside Motel, 36 Lakefront Drive, tel: 03-249 7435; www.lakesideteanau.com. Central motel in a garden, near restaurants and with unobstructed views of lake and mountains. Nineteen units with full kitchens and ensuite bathrooms. **$–$$**

Luxmore Hotel, Main Street, tel: 03-249 7526, 0800-589 6673; www.luxmorehotel.co.nz. Close to services and attractions, and only 100 metres (109 yds) from the lake front. 106 rooms. **$$$–$$$$$**

Te Anau Hotel and Villas, Lakefront Drive, tel: 03-249 7947, 0800-223 687; www.teanauhotel.co.nz. This hotel has 80 rooms, four deluxe suites and 28 garden villas, commanding spectacular lake and mountain views. It is only two minutes on foot to the town centre. Amenities include an outdoor pool, spa and sauna, business centre, restaurant/bar overlooking Lake Te Anau. **$$$$–$$$$$**

Where to Eat

Kepler's Restaurant, 23 Town Centre, tel: 03-249 7909. The menu consists of 50 percent seafood. Sautéed baby octopus and grilled prawns feature alongside traditional favourites (pavlova, lamb, venison, fish and chips) on the menu here. Kepler's has excellent food and good service. **$$**

La Toscana, 108 Town Centre, tel: 03-249 7756; www.latoscana.co.nz. A true taste of Tuscany in Te Anau with excellent service. Word from

the locals is that the al nonno pasta and cheesecake are divine. **$$**

Olive Tree Café, 52 Town Centre, tel: 03-249 8496. Open 8am–10pm for breakfast, lunch and dinner with good coffee. **$**

Redcliff Café and Bar, 12 Mokonui Street, tel: 03-249 7431. Big-city style fusion fare served in a delightful old cottage, with live entertainment. Evenings only. **$$**

Outdoor Activities

Bird Watching

The Te Anau Wildlife Centre, Lakefront Drive, Te Anau, tel: 03-249 7924. Focuses on native birds, including the rare takahe.

Cruises

Adventure Manapouri, 50 View Street, Manapouri, tel: 03-249 8070; www.adventurema napouri.co.nz. This company will take you to the many beautiful walking tracks around Manapouri that are only accessible by boat.

Milford Sound Red Boat Cruises, Milford Wharf, Milford Sound, tel: 03-441 1137; www.redboats.co.nz. The highlight of a New Zealand holiday for many is a visit to the majestic scenery of Milford Sound, including Mitre Peak, waterfalls and abundant flora and fauna.

Diving

Tawaki Dive, 44 Caswell Road, Te Anau, tel: 03-249 9006; www.tawakidive.co.nz. Remarkable guided diving at Milford Sound. This is the chance to see creatures that normally live at depths of 50–150 metres (160–480 ft) can be found here at 20 metres (65 ft). Non-divers are welcome.

Glowworm Caves

Real Journeys, Real Journeys Visitor Centre, Lakefront Drive, Te Anau, tel: 03-249 7416, 0800-656 501; www.realjourneys.co.nz. Enjoy a scenic cruise across Lake Te Anau, then venture underground on foot and on a small boat into the glowworm grotto for a magical sight. This tour lasts 2½ hours.

Horse Riding

High Ride Horse Treks & Quad Bike Adventures, Wilderness Road, RD2, tel: 03-249 8591; www.highride.co.nz. Scenic treks with wonderful views, animal encounters and ancient forests. A variety of horses is available to suit all levels of experience, and trained guides to provide tuition. It also offers quad bike tours that take you through Te Anau's back country, across rolling paddocks and to the summit of Danby Hill for attractive views of the lakes, farmland and mountains.

Walking in Southland

Southland is blessed with rainforest retreats, coastal tracks and unspoilt beaches, plus vast tracts of stunning national park land. The 53.5-km (33-mile) **Milford Track** is one of the most popular. Bookings for the **Milford, Kepler** and **Routeburn tracks** must be made with the Department of Conservation at **Great Walks Booking Desk**, Lakefront Drive, P.O. Box 29, Te Anau, tel: 03-249 8514; www.doc.govt.nz. For maps, further information on the walks and area, contact: **Fiordland National Park Visitor Centre** in Te Anau, tel: 03-249 7924. No booking is required for the **Hollyford Valley Track**.

Try the relatively new **Tutapere Humpridge Track** at the south-eastern end of Fiordland National Park. This track is a 3-day, 2-night, 43-km (27-mile) walk that starts and finishes at the western end of Te Wae Wae Bay. It is owned by a charitable trust and can be booked at tel: 03-226 6739, 0800 486 774; www.humpridgetrack.co.nz.

Near Bluff, the **Foveaux Walkway**, a 7-km (4-mile) walk along rugged coastline with great views of the coast and bush. The **Catlins** is an area with spectacular scenery and the chance to spot seals, sea lions and dolphins.

Stewart Island

Getting There
The **Stewart Island Express Ferry Service** (tel: 0800-000 511; www.stewartislandexperience.co.nz) operates daily ferry services between Bluff (departs from Bluff Visitor Terminal, Foreshore Road) and Stewart Island (departs from Stewart Island Visitor Terminal, Main Wharf).

The ferry company also runs a **Coach Connections** service to the ferry from Invercargill (pick-up and drop-off at the airport and i-SITE Visitor Centre, Tuatara Backpackers), Queenstown and Te Anau (pick-up and drop-off at Real Journeys Visitor Centres in both cities).

Stewart Island Flights also flies directly from Invercargill Airport to Stewart Island, tel: 03-218 9129; www.stewartislandflights.com. See also Getting Around, pages 330–2.

Visitor Information
Rakiura National Park Visitor Centre, Main Road, tel: 03-219 0002; www.doc.govt.nz is an indispensable source of information on how to make the most of this conservationists' paradise.
Stewart Island i-SITE Visitor Centre, Main Road, Halfmoon Bay, tel: 03-219 0009; www.stewartisland.co.nz.

Local Transport
Stewart Island Experience (Stewart Island Visitor Terminal, Main Wharf, Halfmoon Bay, Oban, tel: 0800-000 511; www.stewart islandexperience.co.nz) has cars, scooters and mountain bikes for hire. It also operates various tours and cruises, as does **Aurora Charters** (tel: 03-219 1126; www.auroracharters.co.nz), which has tours for fishing, sightseeing, bird-watching and nature walks.
Sails Ashore & Talisker Charters (tel: 0800-783 9278; www.sails ashore.co.nz) offers an **SUV Scenic Road Tour** that explores virtually every road on the island, all 28 km (17 miles), with a fascinating commentary covering the island's early history to present-day life.

Another good way to visit some of the major sites is by **water taxi**. Contact **Sails Ashore, Stewart Island Water Taxi & Eco-Guiding** (tel: 03-219 1394; www.portofcall.co.nz) or **Sea Buzzz** (tel: 03-219 1282; www.seabuzzz.co.nz).

Where to Stay
Greenvale Bed & Breakfast, Elgin Terrace, Oban, tel: 03-219 1357; www.greenvalestewart island.co.nz. Located less than a 5-minute walk from the centre of Oban town and just 50 metres (165 ft) from the sea with magnificent views of Foveaux Strait. There is exclusivity and privacy here, with only two individually designed rooms with king-size beds and ensuite bathrooms. **$$$$**
Pania Lodge, tel: 03-215 7733; e-mail: halstead@xtra.co.nz. Accommodation for three couples set in secluded bush, fronting Butterfield Beach. This is an ideal location from which to explore Oban town and Paterson Inlet. **$$**
Sails Ashore Luxury B&B, Halfmoon Bay, tel: 03-219 1151; www.sailsashore.co.nz. Luxury boutique bed and breakfast overlooking Halfmoon Bay and the islands of Foveaux Strait, a 4-minute stroll from the village. Offers a guided exploration of Ulva Island. **$$$$$**
South Sea Hotel, Elgin Terrace, Halfmoon Bay, tel: 03-219 1059; www.stewart-island.co.nz. A friendly country-style hotel, just a 25-minute walk from town. Restaurant serves local seafood. Also has studio units adjacent to the hotel. Great views, located close to Mill Creek. **$–$$**
Stewart Island Lodge, 14 Nichol Road, Halfmoon Bay, tel: 03-219 1085; www.stewartislandlodge.co.nz. Nestled in the natural beauty of the bush, with fantastic views of the bay, each suite has a super king-size bed, central heating and ensuite bathroom. Gourmet meals, feature fresh local seafood. **$$$**

Outdoor Activities
Charters
There are numerous local charter outfits, including adventure cruises,

diving and fishing excursions. For a real sense of adventure, head out on the 17-metre (57-ft) steel motorised ketch, *Talisker*. Contact: **Talisker Charters**, tel: 03-219 1151; www.sailsashore.co.nz. Explore the island by launch, or embark on guided nature walks to see dolphins, birds and scenery.

Kayaking
Kayaking is another great way to explore this region. Call **Stewart Island Sea Kayaks**, tel: 03-219 1080, **Rakiura Kayaks**, tel: 03-219 1160 or **Ruggedy Range**, tel: 03-219 1066.

Walking
There are many tracks to explore – some walks take as little as 15 minutes, others as long as three days. The 3-day **Rakiura Track**, the most popular, crosses forest and is suitable for anyone with moderate fitness and provides a good introduction to the island and its bird life, including the blue penguin.
Kiwi Wilderness Walks, 31 Orawia Road, Tuatapere, tel: 0800-733 549; www.nzwalk.com conducts multi-day guided walks with a chance of spotting kiwi in their natural environment.
Ulva's Guided Walks, tel: 03-219 1216; www.ulva.co.nz. Ulva Amos is a direct descendant of the indigenous people of Stewart Island, an authority on the area's flora and fauna, and leads gentle half-day walks which showcase the island's natural heritage.

ART & PHOTO CREDITS

Agrodome 187
Air New Zealand 80
A.J. Hackett 289M
Alexander Turnbull Library 14, 30, 39
Allan Seiden 228/229
Andy Radka/PhotoNewZealand.com 224
Angela Wong/APA 252
APA 101R, 107, 239M
Arno Gasteiger/PhotoNewZealand.com 100, 156, 174, 185, 189, 213, 310
Auckland Institute and Museum 22, 26, 32, 33, 34, 135
Auckland Public Library Photograph Collection 31
Axel Poignant Archive 18, 19, 23
Blaine Harrington back cover centre, 6B, 186, 190, 249
Bob Krist 313
Chris McLennan/PhotoNewZealand. com 8B, 161, 193, 194, 237, 260
Christchurch Art Gallery 86, 250
Craig Dowling front flap bottom, 54, 101L, 254, 262M
Darroch Donald/PhotoNewZealand.com 89
Darryl Torckler/PhotoNewZealand.com 114, 241
Dennis Buurman/PhotoNewZealand. com 236M
Dennis Lane 206
Destination Queenstown 289L
Dr David Skinner 259
Driving Creek Railway and Potteries 173M
Fotopress News Picture Agency 17, 63, 66, 81, 85, 88, 92, 93, 94, 96/97, 108, 112, 113, 137M, 138, 139M, 140, 144, 145, 148, 148M, 150M, 152, 157, 160, 166M, 168M, 169, 202
Francis Dorai/APA 254M, 265, 274R, 275, 285M, 288, 306
Fritz Prenzel 51, 150
G.R. Roberts 50
Gerald Cubitt 2/3, 6T, 48, 49, 52, 53, 55, 104, 167, 210R
Graham Charles/PhotoNewZealand.com 175
Govett-Brewster Art Gallery 209
Hans Klüche back cover bottom, 3B, 7B, 84, 132, 137, 143M, 175M, 212, 215, 232, 261, 273M, 284, 287, 303M
Harley Betts/PhotoNewZealand.com 195
Hawke's Bay Tourism 199, 204, 207, 207M
Ian Lloyd 317
Ian Trafford/PhotoNewZealand.com 69, 233, 240, 242, 243, 316
Jerry Dennis 9B, 44, 76, 78, 143, 149, 159M, 162, 179, 192, 203M, 211, 218, 218M, 221R, 244/245, 246, 247, 249M, 251M, 289R, 293, 298M, 302
Jocelyn Carlin/PhotoNewZealand.com 99, 177, 319

Julian Apse/PhotoNewZealand.com 268/269
Julia Thorne/PhotoNewZealand.com 318
Landsdown–Rigby 10/11, 60, 65, 173
Lodestone Press 35, 36
Manfred Gottschalk back cover right
Marcus Brooke spine, back cover left, back flap top, 58/59, 154/155, 182, 191, 253
Mark Orbell/PhotoNewZealand.com 285, 304/305, 312M
Mary Evans Picture Library 4B, 14/15, 24, 25, 29, 37
Matheson Beaumont/PhotoNew Zealand.com 301
Max Lawrence 4/5, 56/57, 62, 68, 70, 71, 72/73, 79, 87, 105, 110/111, 115, 122/123, 126/127, 133, 144M, 151, 153, 159, 162M, 163, 164, 168, 177M, 180/181, 183, 188, 192M, 205M, 219, 223M, 225, 226/227, 236, 239, 253M, 256, 263, 265M, 266, 267, 272, 274L, 277, 278, 282, 294, 295, 303, 307, 314M, 315
M Ross/PhotoNewZealand.com 264
Nathan Secker/PhotoNewZealand.com 210L
Neil Morrison/Impact 270
New Line Studios 90, 95
New Zealand Tourist Board 67, 102, 109, 116, 119, 147
NHPA/ANT front flap top
Nick Servian/PhotoNewZealand.com 8L, 106, 165, 166, 178
Paul van Reil 198
Peter Hutton Collection 20, 27
Photobank New Zealand 38, 41, 124/125, 221L, 258, 290, 291
Photosource 45, 214
Positively Wellington Tourism 7C, 217, 220, 222, 223
Ralph Talmont/PhotoNewZealand.com 225M, 286
Richard Casswell/PhotoNewZealand. com 255
Richard King/PhotoNewZealand.com 117
Rob Driessen/PhotoNewZealand.com 61, 257
Robert Wallace 136, 139, 141, 142
Rob Lile/PhotoNewZealand.com 7T, 118, 146, 190M, 251, 298
Sarah Masters/PhotoNewZealand.com 273
Simon Grosset 28
Simon Grosset/FSP back flap bottom, 9T, 103, 170, 171
Simon Grosset/Impact 128, 271, 280/281, 283, 314
Stan Daniels/PhotoNewZealand.com 262, 292
Stewart Nimmo/PhotoNewZealand.com 8R, 276

SuperStock/Powerstock cover
Terence Barrow Collection 21, 40, 64, 75, 77L
The New Zealand Herald and Weekly News 42, 43, 203
Wolfgang Bittmann 161M
Tony Stewart/PhotoNewZealand.com 98, 205, 279
Tony Stone Worldwide 320
Topham Picturepoint 1, 91
Tourism Dunedin 296, 297, 297M, 299
Tourism Rotorua 187M
Tourism West Coast 278M
Venture Southland Tourism 311, 312, 318M
VPA Images Pte Ltd 12/13, 208
Warren Bayliss/PhotoNewZealand.com 77R
Wayne Tait/PhotoNewZealand.com 176
World of Wearable Art and Classic Cars Museum 238

Picture Spreads

Pages 46/46: *Clockwise from bottom left-hand corner:* NHPA/ANT, NHPA/ANT, Wolfgang Bittmann, Wolfgang Bittmann, NHPA/ANT, NHPA/ANT, Hans Klüche, Craig Dowling.
Pages 82/83: *Clockwise from bottom left-hand corner:* Axel Poignant Archive, Axel Poignant Archive, Blaine Harrington, Blaine Harrington, Hans Klüche, Axel Poignant Archive, Axel Poignant Archive, Axel Poignant Archive.
Pages 120/121: *Clockwise from top left-hand corner:* Blaine Harrington, Simon Grosset/FSP, Simon Grosset/FSP, Simon Grosset/FSP, Simon Grosset/FSP, Hans Klüche, Simon Grosset/FSP.
Pages 196/197: *Clockwise from bottom left-hand corner:* Jerry Dennis, Wolfgang Bittmann, Blaine Harrington, Jerry Dennis, Blaine Harrington, Jerry Dennis, Blaine Harrington.

Map Production Polyglott Kartographie, Lovell Johns
© 2007 Apa Publications GmbH & Co. Verlag KG (Singapore branch)

INSIGHT GUIDE
NewZealand

Cartographic Editor Zoë Goodwin
Design Consultants
Klaus Geisler, Graham Mitchener
Picture Research Hilary Genin

Index

a

Abel Tasman National Park 118, 239, 240, 243
accommodation 317, 331–2
 listings 342–86
Acker's Point 318
Acker's Cottage 317
Adamson, Andrew 94
Adsett, Sandy 81
agriculture and farming 39–40, 54, 104–5, 161, 206, 307
Agrodome 187–8
aquaculture 237
 cattle and dairy 39, 103, 165, 199, 237
 deer farming 309
 fruit orchards 101, 165, 177, 206, 239, 256
 horse-breeding 165, 167–8, 213
 prawn farm 192
 sheep 36, 39, 42, 102, 104, 187–8, 199, 225, 231, 237, 261, 284
Agrodome and Adventure Park 187–8
Akaroa 247, 256–7, 375
 Akaroa Harbour 257
 Akaroa Museum 256
 Garden of Tane 257
 Kaik 257
 Langlois-Eteveneaux House 256
 Old French Cemetery 257
 St Patrick's Church 256–7
 St Peter's Church 257
Alexandra 109, 293
Amundsen, Roald 258
Anaura Bay 179
Antarctica 258–9, 375
Aoraki Mount Cook 46, 264–5, 267, 274
Aoraki Mount Cook National Park 267, 376–7
Aoraki Mount Cook Village 266–7
architecture 89, 215–6, 297
 art deco (Napier) 203–5
 traditional Maori 76, 81
Arrowtown 287, 288–90, 382
 Chinese Settlement 289
 Dorothy Brown's Cinema, Bar and Bookshop 289

Lakes District Museum 289–90
art and crafts 20, 85–7, 161, 240
 Creative New Zealand 85
 Driving Creek Potteries 173
 Maori art (ancient) 75–80
 Maori art (modern) 81
 Maori crafts 82–3
 Maori Treasures (Lower Hutt) 224
 metalwork 301
 murals of Katikati 175
 New Zealand Maori Arts and Crafts Institute 82, 186
 tattoo art (moko) 23, 77, 81
Arthur's Pass 263
Arthur's Pass Highway 276
Arthur's Pass National Park 263
Arthur's Point 288
arts and entertainment 91–5, 333
 Aotea Centre (Auckland) 92, 93–4, 139
 Auckland Philharmonia 91
 Bats Theatre (Wellington) 94, 218
 Centrepoint Theatre (Palmerston North) 93
 Christchurch Arts Centre (Christchurch) 251
 Circa Theatre (Wellington) 93, 218
 Civic Theatre (Auckland) 93, 139–40
 Classic Theatre (Auckland) 94
 Clinic, The (Christchurch) 94
 contemporary music 92
 Court Theatre (Christchurch) 93, 251
 Fortune Theatre (Dunedin) 93
 Maidment Theatre (Auckland) 94
 Maori music and dance 91, 142
 New Zealand Opera 92
 New Zealand Symphony Orchestra 91, 219
 Royal New Zealand Ballet 91, 92
 Silo Theatre (Auckland) 94
 Theatre Royal (Nelson) 238
Ashhurst 213
 Tatatua Wind Farm 213
Athenree Gorge 175
Athfield, Ian 89, 218

Auckland 35, 52, 64, 131, 133–44
 Acacia Cottage 144
 accommodation listings 343
 Albert Park 140
 Aotea Centre 92, 93–4, 139
 Aotea Square 139
 Auckland Anniversary Regatta 115, 133
 Auckland Art Gallery 85, 140
 Auckland Domain 141–2
 Auckland Harbour Bridge 119, 150
 Auckland Town Hall 139
 Auckland War Memorial Museum 142
 Auckland Writers Festival 88
 Auckland Zoo 144
 beaches 143
 Central City Library 140
 Civic Theatre 93, 139–40
 Classic Theatre 94
 Comedy Festival 94
 Constitution Hill 141
 eating out 139, 343–4
 Eden Garden 144
 The Edge 139
 entertainment and activities 344–5
 Ferry Building 137
 Gow Langsford Gallery 140
 High Court 141
 Karangahape ("K") Road 143
 Kelly Tarlton's Antarctic Encounter and Underwater World 143, 259
 Maidment Theatre 94
 Mataora Gallery 81
 Mount Eden 144
 Museum of Transport and Technology 144
 Newmarket 141
 New Zealand National Maritime Museum 137
 Old Arts Building 141
 Old Customhouse 138
 Old Government House 140
 One Tree Hill 44, 144
 Pacifika Festival 335
 Parnell 141
 Ponsonby 143
 public transport 147, 151
 Queen Elizabeth Square 138
 Queen Street 138–9
 Remuera 141
 shopping 139, 141
 Silo Theatre 94

Sky City Tower 89, 119, 139
Te Taumata Gallery 81
Town Hall 139
University of Auckland 140
Viaduct Harbour 138
Victoria Park Market 143
Waiheke Island Jazz Festival 92
War Memorial Museum 76
Aupori Peninsula 162
Australia-New Zealand Army Corps (ANZAC) 40
Avenue of the Disappearing Mountain 315
Avon River 231, 247, 250
Awanui 162
Ancient Kauri Kingdom 163
Awakino River 209
Awatere Valley 237

b

Balance, John 39
Balclutha 312
Banks, Joseph 27
Banks Peninsula 27, 247, 256–7
Bason Botanical Reserve 211
Baxter, James K. 88, 211
Poem in the Matukituki Valley 88
Bay of Islands 34, 107, 131, 157
boat trips 160–61
Bay of Plenty 23, 176–7
beaches 148–9, 151, 175, 179, 213, 224, 231, 309
Beaglehole, Dr J.C. 25, 28
Beckett, Bernard 88
Belich, James 88
Bendigo 293
Bennet, Mary Jane 224
Bishop, Gavin 88
Blackball 278
Black Grace 93
Black Jack Road 174
Blake, Sir Peter 113
Blenheim 235, 370
Bluff 309–10
Maritime Museum 310
Body, Jack 91
Bolger, Jim 43, 44
Boock, Paula 88
Bornholdt, Jenny 89
Bracken, Thomas 296
Braithwaite, Joanna 86
Brickell, Barry 87, 173
Brown, Rev. A.N. 176

Brown, James 89
Brunner, Thomas 272
Buck, Sir Peter 76, 209
Buller Gorge 273
Buller River 279
Bulls 212
Flock House 212
bungy jumping 290
Buried Village 190
Te Wairoa Waterfalls Track 190
Burke Pass 265
Burns, Rev. Thomas 295–6
Busby, James 33, 34, 107, 158
Bushy Park 211

c

Cable Bay 162
Cambridge 167–8, 353–4
New Zealand Horse Magic 167–8
St Andrew's Anglican Church 167
Camp, Kate 89
Campbell, Sir John Logan 144
Campion, Jane 91, 93, 94
The Piano 94, 148
Campion, Richard and Edith 93
Canterbury Association 247–8
Canterbury Plains 36, 116, 261–7
Canvastown 237
Cape Colville 173
Cape Farewell 26
Cape Foulwind 279
Cape Kidnappers 206
gannet colony 206
Cape Palliser 225
Cape Reinga 78, 161–3
Cape Runaway 178
Cardrona 291
Cargill, Captain William 295
Caro, Niki 94
Memory and Desire 94
Whale Rider 94, 179
Cathedral Cove 175
Catlins, The 307, 311, 385
Central Otago 109, 283
Central Plateau 52
Channell, Ian Brackenbury 249
Charleston 279
Chestnut Tree Forge 301
children 327
Christchurch 36, 62, 116, 131, 231, 247–56, 372
accommodation 373
Antarctica cruises 258

Armagh Street 252
Ballantynes 250
Botanic Gardens 251
Bridge of Remembrance 250
Canterbury Museum 251
Canterbury Provincial Council Buildings 252
Cathedral of the Blessed Sacrament 253
Cathedral Square 249
Chalice 86
Christchurch Art Gallery 85, 86, 89, 250–51
Christchurch Arts Centre 251
Christchurch Casino 253
Christchurch Cathedral 247, 249–50
Christchurch Gondola 254
Christchurch Normal School 252
Christ's College 252
City Mall 250
Clinic, The 94
Court Theatre 93, 251
Cranmer Square 252
eating out 373–4
entertainment 374
Fendalton 254
Ferrymead Heritage Park 255
Gethsemane Gardens 254
Hagley Park 247, 252
International Antarctic Centre 255, 259
Merivale 254
Mona Vale 248–9
New Regent Street 253
Orana Wildlife Park 255
Port Hills 247, 254
Queen Elizabeth II Park 256
Riccarton House & Dean's Bush 247
St Barnabus church 248
St Michael and All Angels Church 250
Science Alive 253
Southern Encounter Aquarium 250
Summit Road 254
Sumner 255
Town Hall 252
Victoria Square 252
Wizard of Christchurch 249
Clarence Valley 261
Clarke, Helen 45
Cleddau Valley 315
Chasm Walk 315
Clifden 312
Clifden Caves 312

Clifden Suspension Bridge
312
climate 20, 206, 215, 261,
283, 284, 322
rainfall 50, 117, 165, 263,
272
Roaring Forties 233
sunshine hours 231, 233
temperature 323
Clutha River 283, 293
Clyde 293
Coastal Track 46, 240, 243
Codfish Island 319
Colac Bay 312
Colenso, William 32
Collingwood 241
Collins, Billy 88
Colquhoun, Glenn 89
Colville 173
Conical Hill 262
Conway River 261
Cook, Captain James 21, 23,
25, 26–9, 31, 157, 174–5,
199, 233, 256, 258, 271–2,
295
Cook, W. Douglas 201
Cook Strait 26, 233
Cook's Bay 174–5
Cooper, Trelise 145
Cooper's Beach 162
Copland Track 47
Cormack, Danielle 94
Coroglen 174
Coromandel 131, 172–3
Coromandel Historical
Museum 173
Coronet Peak 114, 291
Cotton, Shane 86
Cowley, Joy 88
The Silent One 88
Craters of the Moon 192
crime and safety 327
Croesus Track 278
Cromwell 293
Crowe, Russell 91, 94
Curio Bay 53, 311
petrified forest 53, 311
Curnow, Allen 89
currency see **money matters**
customs regulations 324

d

D4, The 92
Dadson, Philip 91
Damaru 89
Dannevirke 207
Dargaville 163

Dargaville Museum 163
Dart River 292
Datsuns, The 45, 92, 167
Dawson, Neil 86
Chalice 86
Ferns 86
de Balboa, Vasco Nuñez 25
de Goldi, Kate 88
Closed, Stranger 88
Denniston 279
Denniston Incline 279
Denniston Walkway 279
Devonport 151, 346–7
Diamond Harbour 256
disabled travellers 327
Dobson, Arthur Dudley 263
Dodd, Lynley 88
Hairy McLary stories 88
dolphin watching 237
Domett, Alfred 63
Donaldson, Roger 94
Cocktail 94
Sleeping Dogs 94
Doubtful Sound 231, 314
Doubtless Bay 162, 352
Drake, Sir Francis 25
Driver, Don 86
**Driving Creek Railway and
Potteries** 173
Duder, Tessa 88
Duff, Alan 88, 149
Once Were Warriors 88, 149
du Fresne, Marion 29
Duncum, Ken 93
Dunedin 36, 63, 89, 231, 285,
295–300
accommodation 383
Botanic Gardens 300
Cadbury World 299
Civic Centre 297–8
Dunedin Public Art Gallery 85,
297
Dunedin Railway Station 298
eating out 383
First Church 299
Fortune Theatre 93
Municipal Chambers 297
Mutual Funds Building 299
New Zealand Sports Hall of
Fame 298
Octagon 297
Olveston 300
Otago Boys High School 299
Otago Settlers Museum 299
Otago Museum 300
Otago Peninsula Museum
Historical Society 301
St Paul's Anglican

Cathedral 297
Speight's Brewery Heritage
Centre 299
Town Belt 300
D'Urville, Dumont 29, 237
D'Urville Island 23, 237
Dusky Sound 28
Dutch East India Company 25

e

earthquakes 215
Eastbourne 224
East Cape 27, 131, 178, 179
eating out 41, 103, 332
Echo Point 242
ecology and conservation 54,
153, 222–3, 271, 313
economy 40, 42, 43, 44, 135,
231, 323
Egmont National Park 210
Egmont Village 210
electricity 322
Emerald Lakes 47
emergencies 328

f

Fairburn, Miles 88
Fairlie 265
Farewell Spit 241–2
Farr, Gareth 91
fashion 145
Featherstone 225
Feilding 213
stud-farm tours 213
Fell Locomotive Museum 225
festivals and events 94, 334–6
ANZAC Day 40
Art Deco Weekends (Napier)
204
Auckland Anniversary Regatta
(Auckland) 115, 133
Auckland Writers Festival
(Auckland) 88
BMW Marlborough Wine and
Food Festival 236
Bluff Oyster and Seafood
Festival 310
Comedy Festival (Auckland) 94
Ellerslie Flower Show 150
Golden Shears competition
(Masterton) 225
Hokitika Wild Foods Festival
(Hokitika) 276
hui 70, 71
International Arts Festival
(Wellington) 88

New Zealand Festival
(Wellington) 92, 94, 219
Pacifika Festival (Auckland) 62
Queenstown Winter Carnival
(Queenstown) 291
Rhododendron Festival (New
Plymouth) 210
Taranaki Arts Festival (New
Plymouth) 92
Waiheke Island Jazz Festival
(Auckland) 92
World of Wearable Art Awards
(Nelson) 94, 238–9
Wellington Jazz Festival
(Wellington) 92
Womad 92
Fiordland 51, 55, 115, 117, 231
Fiordland National Park 243,
313
Firth, Josiah Clifton 168
Fletcher Bay 173–4
Coromandel Walkway 174
flora and fauna 55
see also **wildlife**
Flying Nun Records 92
food and drink 99–103, 231,
279
see also **eating out**
beer 241, 278, 299
Maori cooking 100
mineral water (Paeroa) 175
wine 107–9
Foveaux Strait 310
Fox Glacier 47, 274–5
Fox Glacier township 275,
377–8
Fox, Sir William 184
Frame, Janet 88
Franz Josef township 275, 378
Franz Josef Glacier 47, 115,
274–5
Freud, Clement 136
French Pass 237
Freyberg, Bernard 40
Frizzell, Dick 86
Fu, Che 92
Fuchs, Sir Vivian 259
further reading 341–2

g

gay travellers 327
geography 322
geology 49–52
volcanoes 52, 135, 178, 189,
190, 191, 197
glaciers 47, 115, 274–5
Geraldine 265

getting around 147, 151, 233,
263, 329–30
getting there 325
Gillespie's Beach 276
Gisborne 179, 199, 362–3
Eastwoodhill Arboretum 201
Kaiti Hill 199, 201
Tairawhiti Museum 199, 201
Te Poho-o-Rawiri 201
Glenfalloch Woodland Garden
301
Glenorchy 291
Godley, John Robert 247
gold 36, 51, 63, 131, 171, 172,
175, 237, 241, 271, 272,
277, 284–5, 289–90, 293,
296
Golden Bay 26, 240, 241
Graham, Brett 81
Graham, Fred 81
Great Barrier Island 153, 348–9
greenstone 51, 80, 82, 271,
276, 278, 283–4, 337
Grey, Sir George 35, 153
Greymouth 277–8, 379
History House 278
Jade Boulder Gallery 278
Monteith's Brewery Company
278
Greytown 225

h

Haast 273, 377
Haast Pass 273
Haast Visitor Centre DOC 273
Hackett, A.J. 119
Hadfield, Gordon 81
Hadlee, Sir Richard 113
Hahei 175, 356
Hall, Roger 93
Hamilton 165–6, 353
Exscite Centre 166
Hamilton Gardens 166
Waikato Museum 165–6
Hamilton, Captain Fane Charles
165
Hamilton, Sir William 266
Hammond, Bill 86
Hamurana Springs 188
Hanmer Springs 261, 262,
375–6
Harrap, Neil 116
Harrison, Pakaariki 81
Harwoods Hole 241
Hastings 203, 205–6, 364
scenic drive 206
Splash Planet 206

Hauraki Gulf 133, 152–3
Havelock 237
Havelock North 206
Arataki Honey 206
Hawke's Bay 27, 109, 202
earthquake (1931) 203
Wine Trail 109
health and medical matters
324, 327–8
sandflies 315
sunburn 323
Heaphy Track 115, 242, 243,
279
Hell's Gate 189
Hurutini Pool 189
Wai Ora Spa 189
Henderson Valley 108, 147
Hibiscus Coast 157, 349
Hicks Bay 179
Hill, David 88
Hillary, Sir Edmund 46, 62, 67,
113, 121, 259, 267
history
arrival of Maori 19–23
European settlement 25–36
independence 39–41
New Zealand Wars 36, 165
Treaty of Waitangi 34–6, 44,
71, 83, 131, 158, 159
Wairau Massacre 35
Waitara Land Deal 36
World Wars I and II 40
**Hobson, Captain/Governor
William** 33–4, 35, 158
Hokianga Harbour 163
Hokitika 276, 378–9
Hokitika Wild Foods Festival
276
Jacquie Grant's Eco World
276
National Kiwi Centre 276
Hokitika Gorge 276
Hollyford Track 315
Hollyford Valley 315
Homer Tunnel 315
Hone Heke, Chief 35, 159–60,
163
Honey Hive 193
Hongi, Chief 32
Hotere, Ralph 81, 85
Hot Water Beach 175
Huka Falls 193
Hukutaia Domain 178
Hulme, Keri 87, 276
The Bone People 87, 276
Hundertwasser, Frederick 89,
157
Hunger, Felix 65

Huntly 167
Hutt River 95
Hutt Valley 223

i

Ihimaera, Witi 87, 94
  Pounamu Pounamu 87
  The Whale Rider (the novel) 87
  The Whale Rider (the movie)
    94
immigration 45, 61–7, 135,
  295
industry
  aluminium 310
  coal 167
  manufacturing 42
International Date Line 322
Invercargill 307–9, 384–5
  Queens Park 309
  Southland Museum and Art
    Gallery 309
Irishman Creek 266

j

Jack's Blowhole 312
Jackson, Anna 89
Jackson Bay 273
Jackson, Peter 91, 94, 129,
  256
  see also Lord of the Rings
  Heavenly Creatures 256
Jerusalem 211
Johnston, Andrew 89
Jones, Lloyd 88
  Here at the End of the World
    We Learn to Dance 88
  The Book of Fame 88

k

Kahukiwa, Robyn 81
Kahurangi National Park 242,
  243, 279
Kaiangaroa Forest 183
Kaikohe 163
Kaikoura 55, 236–7, 370–1
Kaitaia 163
Kaiteriteri 233
Kaiti Hill 199, 201
Kaituna River 189
Kakahi Falls 189
Kapiti Coast 224
Kapiti Island 55, 224
Karaka, Emare 81
Karamea 279

Karekare 148
Katikati 175
Kauaeranga Valley 171
Kawakawa 89, 157
Kawarau Bridge 290
Kawarau Bungy Centre 290
Kawarau River 119, 288–9
Kawau Island 153, 348
  Mansion House 153
Kendall, Thomas 32
Kepler Mountains 313
Kepler Track 95, 315
Kerikeri 161, 351
  Kemp (Mission) House 161
  Kororipa Pa 161
  Rewa's Village 161
  Stone Store 161
Killeen, Richard 86
King, Michael 88
Kingston 292, 315
  Kingston Flyer 293, 315
Kipling, Rudyard 271, 314
Knights Point 274
Knox, Elizabeth 88
  The Vintner's Luck 88
Kopu 172
Kouka, Hone 93
Kumara 276
Kumeu Valley 108, 147

l

Lady Bowen Falls 315
Lake Brunner 276
Lake Dunstan 293
Lake Grassmere 236
Lake Hauroko 312
Lake Hayes 290
Lake Ianthe 276
Lake Kaniere 276
Lake Manapouri 95, 313
Lake Matheson 47, 275
Lake Monowai 313
Lake Ohakuri 192
Lake Okataina 189
Lake Paringa 273
Lake Pukaki 266
Lake Rotoaira 194
Lake Rotoehu 189
Lake Rotoiti 183, 189
Lake Rotoiti (Nelson Lakes
  National Park) 242
Lake Rotokakahi 189
Lake Rotoma 189
Lake Rotomahana 190
Lake Rotoroa 46, 242
Lake Rotorua 183, 185–6
  boat trips 186

  Hinemoa's Pool 186
  Mokoia Island 186
Lake Tarawera 188, 189, 190–91
  Lake Tarawera Launch Cruises
    191
Lake Taupo 52, 131, 183, 188,
  193–4
Lake Te Anau 314
Lake Tekapo 265–6, 376
  Church of the Good Shepherd
    266
Lake Tikitapu 189
Lake Waikareiti 202
Lake Waikaremoana 202
Lake Wakatipu 51, 286, 307
Lake Wanaka 51
Lange, David 42–32
language 19, 21, 32, 70, 89,
  322, 328
  Kohanga Reo (language
    nests) 70
Lardelli, Derek 81
Lawrence 293
Lawson, Robert 299
Lemalu, Jonathan 92
Leonard, Robert 85
Lewis Pass 261, 263
Lilburn, Douglas 91
Limbs 92
Lindale Centre 224
Lindis Pass 293
literature 87–9
  see also individual writers
Lord of the Rings 13, 94, 95,
  129, 168, 286
Lower Hutt 223
  Maori Treasures 224
Lye, Len 85, 209–10
  Wind Wand 85, 210
Lyttelton 254–5

m

Mahy, Margaret 88
McCahon, Colin 86, 148
McDonald, Tom 207
Macetown 290
Mackenzie Country 265
Magellan 25
Mahia Peninsula 202
Mahy, Margaret 88
Major, Malvina 91
Malaspina, Don Alessandra 29
Manawai 131
Manawatu Gorge 213
Manawatu River 213
Mangapurua 211
  Bridge to Nowhere 211

Mangarakau 242
Mangere Mount 150
Manhire, Bill 89
Mansfield, Katherine 45, 87
  birthplace (Wellington) 222
Manukau City 149
  Otahuhu 149
  Otara Market 149–50
  Rainbow's End 150
Manukau Harbour 148–9
Manurewa 150
  Auckland Regional Botanic
    Gardens 150
Maori 61, 69–71, 301–2
  culture 19–23, 183, 333, 360
  land ownership 33, 36, 39,
    43–4, 105, 158, 165, 201
  legends 13, 82–3, 129, 161,
    162, 173, 177–8, 183,
    185–6, 189, 190, 194,
    196, 204, 215, 287
  Maori Cultural Experience
    (Wairakei) 192
  Maori King Movement 36, 69,
    166, 169
  New Zealand Maori Arts and
    Crafts Institute 82, 186
  Rotoiti Tours World of Maori
    189
  Tamaki Maori Village 191
Marahau 240
Marakopa Falls 169
Marlborough Sounds 51–2,
  117, 233
Marsden, the Rev. Samuel 32,
  135
Martinborough 225
  Martinborough Wine Centre
    225
Martin, Sir William 34
Martins Bay 53
Mason Bay 318
Mason, Bruce 93
Massey, William 40
Masterton 65, 225
  Golden Shears competition
    225
Matakana 107
Matamata 95, 116, 168
  Firth Tower Historical Museum
    168
  Kaimai-Mamaku Forest Park
    168
  Wairere Falls 168
Matchitt, Paratene 81
Mawson, Sir Douglas 258
Mayor Island 23
media 326

Melbourne, Hirini 91
Mercury Bay 27, 174
Methven 264, 376
Michener, James A. 40
Middlemarch 303
Milford Sound 231, 307, 314–5
  boat trips 315
Milford Track 46, 115, 231,
  243, 315
Mirror Lakes 315
Mitre Peak 231, 315
Moehau Range 173
Moeraki Boulders 303
Molesworth Station 237
money matters 324
Morere 202
Morrinsville 168
Motu River 178
Motueka 239–30
Motura 55
Motutapu Island 135, 152
Mount Aspiring National Park
  243, 292
Mount Cook *see* **Aoraki Mount
  Cook**
Mount Eden 144
Mount Egmont *see* **Mount
  Taranaki**
Mount Hutt 264
Mount Isobel 262
Mount Isobel Track 262
Mount Lees Reserve 212
Mount Maunganui 176–7
Mount Murchison 263
Mount Ngauruhoe 47, 95, 194
Mount Ngongotaha 187
Mount Paku 175
Mount Parahaki 163
Mount Rolleston 263
Mount Ruapehu 114, 194, 195
Mount Stewart 212
Mount Tapuaenuku 237
Mount Taranaki 47, 114, 209
Mount Tarawera 184, 190, 197
Mount Taupiri 167
Mount Te Aroha 168
Mount Tongariro 194
Mount Victoria 151
Mountfort, Benjamin W. 252
Muldoon, Sir Robert 42, 66
Murdering Beach 295
Muriwai 148
Murphy, Geoff 94
  Utu 94
museums and galleries
  Airforce Museum (Ohakea)
    212
  Akaroa Museum (Akaroa) 256

  Auckland Art Gallery
    (Auckland) 85, 140
  Auckland War Memorial
    Museum (Auckland) 142
  Canterbury Museum
    (Christchurch) 251
  Christchurch Art Gallery
    (Christchurch) 85, 86, 89,
    250–51
  City Gallery (Wellington) 85,
    219
  Colonial Cottage Museum
    (Wellington) 223
  Coromandel Historical
    Museum (Coromandel) 173
  Dargaville Museum
    (Dargaville) 163
  Dunedin Public Art Gallery
    (Dunedin) 297
  Ferrymead Heritage Park
    (Christchurch) 255
  Firth Tower Historical Museum
    (Matamata) 168
  Founders Historic Park
    (Nelson) 238
  Govett-Brewster Art Gallery
    (New Plymouth) 85, 209
  Gow Langsford Gallery
    (Auckland) 140
  Haast Visitor Centre DOC 273
  Hawke's Bay Museum
    (Napier) 205
  International Antarctic Centre
    (Christchurch) 255, 259
  Jade Boulder Gallery
    (Greymouth) 278
  Lakes District Museum
    (Arrowtown) 289–90
  Maritime Museum (Bluff) 310
  Mataora Gallery (Auckland) 81
  Mineralogical Museum
    (Thames) 171
  Museum of Transport and
    Technology (Auckland) 144
  Museum of Wellington City
    and Sea (Wellington) 220
  New Zealand National
    Maritime Museum
    (Auckland) 137
  New Zealand Rugby Museum
    (Palmerston North) 212–3
  New Zealand Sports Hall of
    Fame (Dunedin) 298
  Otago Settlers Museum
    (Dunedin) 299
  Otago Museum (Dunedin) 300
  Otago Peninsula Museum
    Historical Society

(Portobello) 301
Pataka Gallery (Porirua) 85
Petone Settlers' Museum
(Petone) 223
Plimmer's Ark Gallery
(Wellington) 220
Public Art Gallery (Dunedin) 85
Puhoi Bohemian Museum
(Puhoi) 152
Rakiura Museum (Oban) 317
Rotorua Museum (Rotorua)
184, 185, 197
Russell Museum (Russell)
160
Science Alive (Christchurch)
253
Silver Stream Railway
Museum (Wellington) 223
Southland Museum and Art
Gallery (Invercargill) 309
Southward Car Museum
(Kapiti Coast) 224
Suter Gallery (Nelson) 238
Tairawhiti Museum (Gisborne)
199, 201
Te Awamutu Museum (Te
Awamutu) 169
Te Papa Tongarewa – Museum
of New Zealand (Wellington)
85, 89, 217–18
Te Taumata Gallery (Auckland)
81
Tokomaru Steam Engine
Museum (Tokomaru) 213
Volcanic Activity Centre (near
Taupo) 193
Waikato Museum (Hamilton)
165–6
Waitomo Museum of Caves
(Waitomo) 169
War Memorial Museum
(Auckland) 76
Whanganui Regional Museum
(Wanganui) 211
World of Wearable Art and
Collectable Cars Museum
(Nelson) 239
Mussel Inn 241
MV Waipa Delta 166

n

Napier 89, 203–5, 363–4
Ahuriri 205
Art Deco Shop 204
Art Deco Trust 204
Art Deco Weekends 204
Bluff Hill 205

County Hotel 204
guided walks 204
Hawke's Bay Museum 205
Marineland 204
Marine Parade 204
Napier Hill 205
National Aquarium of New
Zealand 205
Statue of Pania 204
Naseby 293
**national parks and nature
reserves** 46–7
Abel Tasman National Park
118, 240, 243
Aoraki Mount Cook National
Park 267, 376–7
Arthur's Pass National Park
263
Bason Botanical Reserve 211
Egmont National Park 210
Fiordland National Park 243,
313
Kahurangi National Park 242,
243, 279
Kaimai-Mamaku Forest Park
(Matamata) 168
Kaitoke Regional Park 95
Mount Aspiring National Park
243, 292
Nelson Lakes National Park
242
Paparoa National Park 279
Pohangina Reserve 213
Poor Knights Islands Marine
Reserve 117
Rakiura National Park 319
Redcliff Wetland Reserve
312–3
Rimutaka Forest Park 224
Te Urewera National Park 131,
202, 363
Tongariro National Park 95,
115, 183, 194
Trounson Kauri Park 163
Westland National Park 50,
275
Whanganui National Park 211
Neill, Sam 67, 94
Nelson 23, 35, 109, 237–9,
371–2
beaches 238
Botanical Hill 238
Christ Church Cathedral 238
Founder's Historic Park 238
Miyazu Gardens 238
Nelson Markets 238
School of Music 238
Suter Gallery 238

Theatre Royal 238
World of Wearable Art Awards
94, 238–9
World of Wearable Art and
Classic Cars Museum 239
Nelson Lakes National Park 242
Nesian Mystik 92
Nevis River 119, 290
New Plymouth 35, 209, 364–5
Brooklands Zoo 209
Coastal Walkway 209–10
Govett-Brewster Art Gallery
85, 209
Hurworth Cottage 210
Puke Ariki 209
Pukeiti Rhododendron Trust
210
Pukekura Park 209
Rhododendron Festival 210
Richmond Cottage 209
Taranaki Arts Festival 92
St Mary's Church 209
Wind Wand 85, 210
New Zealand Antarctic Society
258–9
New Zealand Company 34, 35,
36, 62, 296
**New Zealand Marine Studies
Centre and Aquarium** 301
New Zealand Players 91, 93
Ngaruawahia 69, 166–7
Turangawaewae Marae 69,
166–7
Ngaruroro River 109
Ngata, Sir Apirana 62, 69, 76
Ngawha Hot Mineral Springs 163
Ninety Mile Beach 161, 163
Norsewood 207
North Head 151
North Shore City 151

o

Oamaru 116
Oban 317
Rakiura Museum 317
Off Road NZ 188–9
Ohakea 212
Airforce Museum 212
Royal New Zealand Air Force
Base 212
Ohakune 195, 362
Ohinemutu 76
Tama-te-Kapua 76
Ohope Beach 178
Okains Bay 256
Okarito Lagoon 276
Okere Falls 189

Okuti Valley 256
Oneroa 152
Oparara Basin 279
  Honeycomb Cave 279
  Oparara Arch 279
Opononi 163
Opotiki 178
Opua 159
Orakei Korako 192
Orepuki 312
Oreti Beach 309
Orewa 151
O'Shea, John 94
  Broken Barrier; Don't Let It
    Get You 94
Otakou 301–2
Otago Peninsula 54, 301
Otira Tunnel 263
Overseas Experience 65
overseas missions 325
Owaka 311–12

p

Paekakariki 116
Paeroa 175
Paihia 32, 131, 157–8, 349–50
  see also **Waitangi**
Pakawau 242
Palmerston North 212–13,
  366–7
  Centrepoint theatre 93
  Dugald Mackenzie Rose
    Garden 213
  International Pacific College
  Lido Aquatic Centre 213
  Massey University 213
  New Zealand Rugby Museum
    212–13
  The Square 212
  Te Manawa 212
  Victoria Esplanade 213
Pancake Rocks 278
Paparoa National Park 279
Papatowai 311
Paquin, Anna 94
Paradise Valley Springs 188
Parakai 152
Paraparaumu 224
Parekowhai, Michael 81, 85
Parker, John 87
Parmenter, Michael 92
Paterson Inlet 317
Pauanui 175
Pelorus Sound 237
Pencarrow Lighthouse 224
people 61–7
  see also **Maori**

No. 8 wire mentality 45, 64,
  67
Petone 223
  Petone Settlers' Museum 223
Petre, Francis W. 253
Pick, Seraphine 86
Picton 233, 235, 269–70
  Echo 235
  Edwin Fox Maritime Centre
    235
Piha 148
Pilot Beach 302
Pipiriki 211
Plimmer, John 220
Pohangina Reserve 213
Pohotu Geyser 186
politics 39–45, 323
  Antarctic Treaty 259
  anti-nuclear movement 42–3
  ANZUS security pact 41, 42–3
  CER pact 43
  Labour Party 40, 41, 42, 44,
    69
  Liberal Party 39
  Maori King Movement
    (Kingitanga) 36, 69, 166,
    169
  NAFTA 43
  National Party 41, 42, 44
  New Zealand First Party 44,
    proportional representation
    (MMP) 44, 45
  Reform Party 40
  social and welfare issues 39,
    40, 44, 45, 69, 149
  Waitangi Tribunal 44, 71
Poor Knights Islands 117
  Marine Reserve 117
Porirua 85
  Pataka Gallery 85
Porpoise Bay 311
Porter's Pass 264
Port Jackson 173–4
Portobello 301
  Larnach Castle 303
  Otago Peninsula Museum 301
postal services 326
Poverty Bay 27, 199
Prawn Farm 192
Preston, Gaylene 947
  Mr Wrong 94
public holidays 324
Puhoi 152
  Puhoi Bohemian Museum 152
Pukerangi 303
Puketi Forest 83
Punakaiki 278–9
  Pancake Rocks 278–9

**Pupu Springs (Waikoropupu
  Springs)** 241
  Pupu Walkway 241
Purakaunui Falls 312
Putangirua Pinnacles 225

q

Queen Charlotte Sound 27, 233
Queenstown 116, 231, 283
  accommodation 379–80
  boat trips on Lake Wakatipu
    286–7
  Bob's Peak 285
  Brecon Street 285
  eating out 379
  entertainment 380
  Gorge Road 287
  Kiwi and Birdlife Park 285
  Queenstown Bungy Rocket
    287–8
  Queenstown Gardens 286
  Queenstown Winter Carnival
    291
  The Rungway 287
  Walter Peak High Country
    Farm 286
Queenstown Wine Trail 287
Quiros 25

r

Raglan 167
  Surfing Academy 167
Rainbow's End 150
**Rainbow Spring Nature Park
  and Kiwi Encounter** 187
Rainbow Warrior 117, 163
rainforests 50, 233, 271, 274
Rai Valley 237
Rakiura National Park 319
  Dynamite Point 319
  Motarau Moana Reserve 319
Rakiura Track 319
Randerson, Jo 93
Rangihaeata 35
Rangitikei River 211
Rangitoto Island 135, 143, 152
Rapira-Davies, Shona 81
Ratana 212
Redcliff Wetland Reserve 312–3
Reefton 279
Reeves, William Pember 39
Reihana, Lisa 81
religion 295–6, 322
  Christianity 32
  of the Maori 22–3, 77–8
  Rastafarian 179

Ringatu 201–2
Remarkables, The 291
Richmond 239
Rimutaka Forest Park 224
Ring, Charles 172
Riverton 312
Riwaka River 240
Robertson, Natalie 81
Robinson, Peter 86
Ross 276
   Ross Goldfields Information
     and Heritage Centre 276
Rotoiti Tours World of Maori
  189
Rotorua 131, 183–7, 196–7,
  358–61
   see also **Lake Rotorua**
   Arikapakapa Golf Course 187
   Blue Baths 184
   boat trips 186
   Government Gardens 184, 197
   hot mineral baths 184
   New Zealand Maori Arts and
     Crafts Institute 82, 186
   Ohinemutu 185
   Pohutu geyser 186–7, 197
   Polynesian Pools 185
   Rotorua Museum 184, 185,
     197
   St Faith's Church 185
   Tamatekapua Meeting House
     185
   Te Puia 186
   Tudor Towers 197
   Whakarewarewa 186–7
   Whakarewarewa Thermal
     Village 187
Routeburn Track 46, 115, 243,
  292, 315
Ruatoria 179
Runga, Bic 92
Russell 31, 35, 131, 159–60,
  350–51
   Christ Church 159
   Pompallier 160
   Russell Museum 160
Rutherford, Sir Ernest 62

s

St Arnaud 242
St Bathans 52, 293
   Blue Lake 293
   Vulcan Hotel 293
Salmond, Anne 88
Sargeson, Frank 88
Sarkies, Duncan 93
Savage, Michael 40

Scott, John 89
Scott, Robert Falcon 258
Seddon, Richard John 39
Selwyn, Bishop George
  Augustus 161
Shackleton, Ernest 258
Shantytown 277
Shaw, George Bernard 183,
  189, 253
Sheppard, Kate 62
Ship Cove 27, 233
Ship Creek 274
Shipley, Jenny 45
shopping 147, 336–7
Shotover River 118, 288
Silver Stream Railway Museum
  223
Skipper, Rangi and Julie 81
Skippers Canyon 95, 119, 288
Skyline Skyrides 187
Smith, Briar Grace 93
Snares Group 318
Soda Springs 189
Solander, Daniel 27
Southern Alps 46, 50, 95, 114,
  231, 261, 262, 274–5, 283
Southland 231
Southward Car Museum 224
spas and thermal pools 129,
  131, 183, 231
   Hell's Gate 189
   Hot Water Beach 175
   Morere 202
   Ngawha Hot Mineral Springs
     163
   Rotorua 131, 184–7, 196–7,
     358–61
   Soda Springs 189
   Te Aroha 168, 354
   Te Puia 179
   Waingaro Hot Springs 167
   Wai-O-Tapu Thermal
     Wonderland 192, 196
   Waiwera Thermal Resort 152
Spirits Bay 162–3
Split Enz 169
sport and activities 113–21,
  337–41
   see also Travel Tips listings
   adventure sports 115–6,
     120–21, 169, 187, 188,
     193, 231, 241, 277, 286
   airborne activities 116,
     120–21, 206, 254, 264,
     267, 275, 286
   All Blacks 65, 113, 212
   America's Cup 115, 133, 137
   bungy-jumping 119, 120, 139,

     151, 176, 286, 289, 290
   caving and canyoning 118
   climbing 150–51, 263, 267,
     288
   cricket 113, 223
   fishing 114, 160, 178, 187,
     188, 193–4, 242, 273,
     286, 311, 313
   golf 114, 187
   hiking 46, 115, 121, 171,
     190, 242, 243, 273, 275
   horse riding 189, 190
   hunting 114, 225, 313
   mountainboarding 194
   netball 65, 113
   New Zealand Sports Hall of
     Fame (Dunedin) 298
   rugby union 113
   skywire 119, 371
   swimming with dolphins 178
   volleyball 113
   watersports 115, 116–8, 133,
     160–61, 167, 178, 195,
     199, 211, 235, 240, 250,
     288–9, 291–2, 303, 314
   winter sports 52, 114, 195,
     210, 263, 264, 267, 291,
     293, 361
   zorbing 121
Steaming Cliffs 191
Stevenson, Michael 85
Stewart Island 27, 55, 231,
  316–19, 386
Stewart, William 316
Stoke 239
   Broadgreen Historic House 239
Stony Bay 174
Stringer, Terry 86
Sullivan, Robert 89
Suter, Andrew 238
Sutton, W.A. (Bill) 86
Sydney, Grahame 86
Sylvester, Kate 145

t

Taiaroa Head 302
   Fort Taiaroa 302
   Penguin Place 54, 303
   Westpac Royal Albatross
     Centre 302
Taieri River Gorge 303
   Taieri Gorge Railway 303
Tairua 175
Takaka 241
Takaka Hill Road 240
Takapuna 151
Tamaki Maori Village 191

tandem skydiving 120–1, 235
Tane Mahuta 46
Tapu 172
  Rapaura Watergardens 172
  Tapu-Coroglen Road 172
Taranaki 131
Tasman, Abel Janszoon 25, 26,
  31, 240, 258, 271
Tasman Glacier 267
Taupiri 167
  Candyland 167
Taupo 116, 360–61
Tauranga 176, 356–7
  Elms Mission House 176
  Monmouth Redoubt 176
Tawharanui 152
Te Anau 95, 314, 385–6
  Te Anau Glowworm Caves 314
  Te Anau Wildlife Centre 314
Te Araroa 179
**Te Arikinui Dame Te
  Atairangikaahu** 69
Te Aroha 168, 354
  Hot Springs Domain 168–9
  Mokena Geyser 168–9
  Te Aroha Mineral Pools 169
Te Awamutu 169
  St John's Anglican Church
  169
  Te Awamutu Museum 169
Te Kaha 178
  Raukokore Church 178
Te Kanawa, Kiri 67, 91, 94
  *Broken Barrier; Don't Let It
  Get You* 94
Te Kao 162
Te Kauwhata 108
Te Kirikamu, Hene 176
Te Kooti 201–2
Te Kooti Rikirangi 169
Te Kuiti 169
Te Mata Peak 206
**Te Puea Herangi of Waikato,
  Princess** 69
Te Puia 179
Te Puke 177
  Kiwifruit 360 177
Te Rangi Hiroa *see* **Buck, Sir
  Peter**
Te Rangikaihoro Nicholas 81
Te Rauparaha, Chief 35
Te Urewera National Park 131,
  202, 363
Te Waewae Bay 312
Te Waru-Rewiri, Kura 81
telephone 322, 326–7
Temple, Philip 88
Thames 171, 355

Goldmine Experience 171
  Mineralogical Museum 171
  School of Mines 171
Three Kings Islands 163
Tikitiki 179
  St Mary's Church 179
time zone 322
tipping 326
Tiritiri Matangi Island 55, 153
Titirangi 148
Tiwai Point aluminium smelter
  310, 313
Tobbeck, Joel 94
Tokomaru 213
  Tokomaru Steam Engine
  Museum 213
Tokomaru Bay 179
Tolaga Bay 179
Tongariro Crossing 195
Tongariro National Park 95,
  115, 183, 194
Tongariro Northern Circuit 47
Tory Channel 233
Totara Reserve 213
Totaranui 240
tourism 41, 259
  eco-tourism 178, 273, 316
  overseas tourism offices 325
TranzAlpine 263
Treble Cone 292
Trollope, Anthony 290
Trounson Kauri Park 163
Tuatapere 312
  Tuatapere Hump Ridge Track
  312
Turanganui River 199
Turangi 194
Turoa 195
Tuwhare, Hone 89
Twizel 265

u

Ulva Island 55, 317–18
Upham, Charles 40
Upper Hutt 223
Urewera Range 202

v

Van Asch, Henry 119
Vancouver, George 29
van Diemen, Anthony 26
visas and passports 324
Visscher, Frans 26
Vogel, Sir Julius 39
Volcanic Activity Centre 192
Volkner, Rev. Carl 178

**von Bellinghausen, Admiral
  Fabian Gottlieb** 258
von Haast, Julius 274
von Tunzelmann, Alexander 258

w

Waihau Bay 178–9
Waiheke Island 108, 152–3, 348
Waihi 175
  Martha Hill Mine 175
  Waihi Arts Centre and
  Museum 175
Waikato 131, 165–9
Waikato, Chief 32
Waikato River 131, 165, 166,
  193
Waikawa 311
Waikoropupu Springs, *see* **Pupu
  Springs**
Waimangu Cauldron 191
Waimangu Volcanic Valley 191–2
Waimate North 161
  Te Waimate Mission 161
Waingaro Hot Springs 167
Wainuiomata 224
Wainui Beach 179
Waioeka Gorge 178
Wai-O-Tapu Thermal Wonderland
  192, 196
  Bridal Veil Falls 192
  Champagne Pool 192, 197
  Lady Knox Geyser 192, 197
Waipa River 165
Waipara 109, 261
Waipati Beach 311
  Cathedral Caves 311
Waipoua Kauri Forest 46, 163
Waipukurau 207
Wairakei 192
  Maori Cultural Village 192
  Wairakei Terraces 192
Wairarapa 109, 116, 224–5
Wairau Valley 242
Wairoa 202
Waitaki River 261
Waitakere City 147, 345–6
Waitakere Ranges 136, 147–8
Waitangi 83, 107, 158–9
  Waitangi National Trust Treaty
  Grounds 158
Waitomo 169, 354
  Waitomo Caves 169
  Waitomo Museum of Caves
  169
Waiwera Thermal Resort 152
Wakamarina River 237
Wakefield 239

St John's church 239
Wakefield, Captain Arthur 35
Wakefield, Edward Gibbon 32, 33, 34, 36, 62, 215
Wakefield, William 215
Walau Waterworks 174
Walker, Karen 145
Wanaka 116, 292, 382–3
Puzzling World 292
Wanganui 35, 131, 210–11, 365–6
Durie Hill 211
Memorial Tower 211
Putiki Church 211
Sarjeant Gallery 211
Whanganui Regional Museum 211
Ward, Vincent 94
The Navigator 94
Vigil 94
Warkworth 152, 347
Honey Centre 152
websites 328
Weir, Peter 40
Gallipoli 40
Wellington 35, 36, 131, 215–23, 322
accommodation 367
Alexander Turnbull Library 221
Basin Reserve cricket ground 223
Bats Theatre 94, 218
Beehive, The 221
Botanic Gardens 222
Carter National Observatory 222
Circa Theatre 93, 218
City Gallery 85, 219
Civic Square 89, 218–9
Colonial Cottage Museum 223
Courtenay Place 218
Downstage Theatre 93, 218
eating out 367–8
Embassy Theatre 219
entertainment 368
Ferns 86
General Assembly Library 221
International Arts Festival 88
Karori Wildlife Sanctuary 222
Katherine Mansfield's Birthplace 222
Lambton Quay 220–21
Michael Fowler Centre 219
Mount Victoria 95
Museum of Wellington City and Sea 220
National Library 221
Newtown 223

New Zealand Festival 92, 94, 219
Old Government Buildings 221
Old St Paul's Cathedral 89, 221–2
Old Town Hall 219
Parliament Buildings 221
Plimmer's Ark Gallery 220
St James 92
St Paul's Cathedral 221
Taj 219
Te Papa Tongarewa – Museum of New Zealand 85, 89, 217–8
Thorndon 222
Turnbull House 221
wharves 219–20
Wellington Cable Car 215
Wellington City Library 89, 219
Wellington Jazz Festival 92
Wellington Zoological Gardens 223
World of Wearable Art Awards 239
West Arm 313–14
Manapouri Underground Power Station 313–14
Westhaven Inlet 242
Westland National Park 50, 275
Westport 279
Whakapapa 195, 361–2
Whakatane 177–8
Whakarewarewa 186, 197
Thermal Village 187
whale watching 236–7
Whangaehu River 195
Whangamata 175, 356
Whanganui National Park 211
Whanganui River 210
Whanganui River Road 211
Whangaparaoa Peninsula 151, 179
Whangara 179
Whangarei 163, 351–2
beaches 163
Claphams Clocks – The National Clock Museum 163
Whangaroa Harbour 162
Whararariki Beach 242
Whatipu 148
Whirinaki Forest 115
White Bay World of Lavendar 202
White Island 178, 183
Whitianga 174, 355–6
Whitianga Harbour 174
Wholemeal Café 241
wildlife 46, 52–5, 311, 316
albatross and mollyhawk 302,

316, 318–9
dolphins 235, 237, 257, 277, 311, 312, 314
endangered species 55
gannet colonies 148, 206, 242
kiwi 50, 52–3, 318
moa (extinct) 20, 52–3, 54, 283
penguins 303, 311, 319
tuatara 52
whales 236–7, 242, 312
Wilkinson, Areta 81
Wilson, Arnold Manaaki 81
wine industry 41, 153, 199, 206–7, 231, 235
Ata Rangi 109
Babich 108
Black Ridge 109
BMW Marlborough Wine and Food Festival 236
Canterbury House 261
Church Road winery and wine museum 206
Cloudy Bay 109, 236
Collards 108
Eskdale 109
French Farm 257
Fromm 109
Goldwater Estate 108
Heron's Flight 107
Kumeu River 108, 147
Mamaku Blue 189
Martinborough Vineyard 109
Matua Valley 108, 147
Montana Brancott Winery 235
Neudorf 109
Nobilo 147
Pegasus Bay 261
Pernod Ricard New Zealand 235
Queenstown Wine Trail 287
Rongopai 108
Soljans 108
Stonecroft 109
Te Kairanga 109
Te Mata Estate 108–9, 106
Trinity Hill 206
Villa Maria 109
Westbrook 108
women's issues 45, 78
Wood's Creek 277
Wright, Douglas 92

y

Young, Nicholas 199
Young Nick's Head 26, 199